PENGUIN REFERENCE

MEDICINE, PATIENTS AND THE LAW

Margaret Brazier has been a Professor of Law at the University of Manchester since 1990. She has written widely on medical law and ethics. She chaired a review of laws relating to surrogacy from 1996 to 1998 and chaired the Retained Organs Commission from 2001 to 2004. She is the Editor of the *Medical Law Review*.

Dr Emma Cave is a Senior Lecturer in tort and medical law at the University of Leeds. Her research interests include ethics and legal and ethical issues in reproductive medicine and she is author of *The Mother of all Crimes*, published by Ashgate in 2004.

Medicine, Patients and the Law

Fifth Edition

Margaret Brazier and Emma Cave

PENGUIN BOOKS

PENGUIN BOOKS

Published by the Penguin Group
Penguin Books Ltd, 80 Strand, London WC2R ORL, England
Penguin Group (USA) Inc., 375 Hudson Street, New York, New York 10014, USA
Penguin Group (Canada), 90 Eglinton Avenue East, Suite 700, Toronto, Ontario, Canada M4P 2Y3
(a division of Pearson Penguin Canada Inc.)
Penguin Ireland, 25 St Stephen's Green, Dublin 2, Ireland (a division of Penguin Books Ltd)
Penguin Group (Australia), 250 Camberwell Road, Camberwell, Victoria 3124, Australia
(a division of Pearson Australia Group Pty Ltd)
Penguin Books India Pvt Ltd, 11 Community Centre, Panchsheel Park, New Delhi – 110 017, India
Penguin Group (NZ), 67 Apollo Drive, Rosedale, Auckland 0632, New Zealand
(a division of Pearson New Zealand Ltd)
Penguin Books (South Africa) (Pty) Ltd, 24 Sturdee Avenue, Rosebank, Johannesburg 2196, South Africa

Penguin Books Ltd, Registered Offices: 80 Strand, London WC2R ORL, England

www.penguin.com

First edition published 1987
Second edition published 1992
Third edition published 2003
Fourth edition published 2007
This edition published in Penguin Books 2011
1

Typeset by Jouve (UK), Milton Keynes
Printed in England by Clays Ltd, St Ives plc

ISBN: 978-0-241-95259-7

www.greenpenguin.co.uk

MIX
Paper from
responsible sources
FSC® C018179
www.fsc.org

Penguin Books is committed to a sustainable
future for our business, our readers and our
planet. This book is made from paper certified
by the Forest Stewardship Council.

Preface

The pace of change in the National Health Service (NHS), Parliament and the law courts has not slowed down at all since our last edition in 2007. We have struggled to keep up. As we sought to complete the text at the start of 2011, the Health and Social Care Bill was published, heralding the most radical changes to the NHS since its foundation in 1948. It has proved a very exciting time to be writing about medical law. In 2010, the last ruling of the House of Lords, before it moved to the new Supreme Court, changed the face of assisted suicide. A number of cases prompted new debates about the role of the criminal law in cases of 'mercy killing'. The Human Fertilisation and Embryology Act 2008 amended the 1990 Act, dealing with past problems and creating new ones. The Health and Social Care Bill has prompted a reassessment of the interface between the various regulatory regimes in medicine. The fate of the Human Fertilisation and Embryology Authority and the Human Tissue Authority lies in the balance. Lord Justice Jackson's proposals for reform of clinical negligence claims are under consideration and legal aid for such claims looks set to be abolished. Both the Clinical Trials Directive and the Data Protection Directive are under review. We can only apologise to our readers for the number of times they will encounter the phrase 'at the time of writing'. We have tried to identify sources to guide the reader through this tumultuous period of medical law reform.

The first edition of this book was published in 1987. There was much less medical law to write about then, and in 2011 it often seems as though every chapter of the book could easily grow into a book in its own right. We cannot cover every key issue in the depth that we might wish to. We continue to hope that the work remains readable to a broad audience, and offers a picture of the way that law and medicine relate to each other that will engage the interest of students, lawyers, health professionals and the general public. We are all affected by how law regulates medicine. As before, we do not attempt to cover mental health law as such. To do so would double the length of the book. We do, in chapter 6, address complex and seemingly intractable questions about vulnerable patients, mental capacity and consent to treatment. We have merged chapters 11 (Family Planning) and 12 (Pregnancy and Childbirth) into one chapter entitled Contraception, Pregnancy and Childbirth. As medical care involves women and men, as both doctors and patients, we use the pronouns she and he interchangeably. We could not be comfortable with the 'old' legal tradition of using only the male pronoun, and he/she (or s/he) seems intolerably clumsy.

We remain in debt to Professors Harry Street and Gerald Dworkin who were initially to have co-written this work with Margaret Brazier. Harry Street's untimely death, and Gerald Dworkin's many other commitments, prevented those original plans coming to fruition. We want to thank all our colleagues at Manchester, Leeds and elsewhere for their unstinting help and advice. Colleagues from the disciplines of law, bioethics and medicine have listened patiently as we tried out ideas on them, and advised us as the work progressed. We owe a particular debt over many years to Maureen Mulholland, Marie Fox, Jean McHale, Sara Fovargue, Suzanne Ost, John Harris and Charles Erin. Jean McHale and Hazel Biggs kindly advised on a number of issues relating to this new edition. We owe special thanks to Anne-Maree Farrell and Kirsty Keywood who have helped us immensely with materials and advice for chapters 6 and 8, and to Sarah Devaney, Neil Allen and Peter Gooderham who patiently read draft chapters for us. It was a great sorrow that Peter died so suddenly in February 2011. We are indebted to David Pickworth and Helen Moore for their invaluable advice on the practical implications of recent reforms. We also thank our students who often challenge our views and force us to think again on many issues. And we are especially grateful to Beverley Clough and Chantel Davies who prepared all the Tables for us. This edition could not have been written without the support and encouragement of our families, Rodney and Victoria Brazier, and Simon, Hannah and Tom Cave.

Any criticism of medical practice in this book is the result of academic endeavour and not personal experience. We are grateful for the care our families have received from general practice and NHS hospitals. We care passionately about the NHS. Were all care of the standard that we have received, this book would be shorter.

No book on this subject is ever wholly up to date. This book is (we trust) up to date to 7 February 2011.

Introduction

The law's relationship with medicine has become a highly publicised affair. Rarely a day passes without media coverage of some new controversy surrounding medical practice, or medical ethics. Cases relating to the rights and responsibilities of doctors and patients feature regularly in the Law Reports. The medical profession finds itself in the limelight. One day the doctor is hailed as a saviour. The next she is condemned as authoritarian or uncaring. Advances in medical science, extending life at one end and bringing new hope to the childless at the other, have given rise to intricate problems of law and ethics. At every level of medical practice, law plays a role. Doctors cannot escape the reach of the law. For many medical practitioners, the rise in the number of malpractice claims is their main concern. Despite legislation designed to tackle a perceived 'compensation culture', doctors still fear an epidemic of US proportions. Some refuse to risk an apology or even to explain what went wrong, lest their careers and reputations suffer should the patient choose to litigate. Patients still find the pursuit of any grievance frustrating. Despite significant reforms of the civil justice system, litigation is expensive and slow. In 2011, people also seek a greater say in their own treatment. Patients are no longer prepared to be patient. The extent to which patients have a right to determine their own treatment is a question for the law. How far patients who claim rights are also subject to responsibilities is increasingly debated.

It is not only the narrow question of our own health needs that concerns people today. Many of the recent scientific developments are themselves controversial. Research on embryos, 'saviour siblings', human cloning, organ retention – all excite controversy. Older controversy about abortion and euthanasia gets no less difficult with time. The purpose of this book, then, is to examine how medical practice is regulated, to analyse the rights and responsibilities of doctors and patients, to look at the provision of compensation for medical wrongdoing or error, and to explore the framework of legal rules governing those delicate questions of life and death when medicine, morals and the law overlap. It is easy to perceive law's relationship with medicine as one of conflict, mirroring conflict between doctors and their patients. We suggest that this is a 'false' conflict. What the medical profession, patients and the public need is for:

- the medical profession to be properly regulated;

- where possible, the rights and obligations of patients, doctors and other health professionals to be clearly defined;
- there to be an adequate, fair and rational system of compensation for patients suffering injury;
- there to be effective means of investigating medical accidents and errors;
- the law (together with professional guidelines) to offer comprehensive guidance on those areas of medical practice of moral and ethical sensitivity.

Sources of law

In contrast to most European countries, the law of England is not to be found neatly encapsulated in any Code. The task of the non-lawyer seeking to establish her rights, or ascertain his duties is far from easy. The law relating to medical practice is to be discovered from a variety of sources. Parliament has enacted a number of statutes governing medical practice. The regulation of medical practice and the disciplining of the defaulting doctor have traditionally been entrusted by Act of Parliament to the General Medical Council (GMC), by virtue of the Medical Act 1983. That Act has already been substantially amended, and further reforms altering the powers of the GMC are planned. The organisation of the health service has been governed by a series of statutes on the National Health Service, now consolidated in the National Health Service Act 2006, which will require significant amendment if the Health and Social Care Bill 2011 survives the Parliamentary process. The Medicines Act 1968 is concerned with the safety of drugs. A number of other Acts of Parliament, such as the Abortion Act 1967 and the Human Fertilisation and Embryology Act 1990 (as amended), the Human Tissue Act 2004 and the Mental Capacity Act 2005, are crucially relevant to questions about medicine, patients and the law. An Act of Parliament can create only a general framework of legal rules. Acts of Parliament, therefore, commonly empower government ministers to make subsidiary regulations known as statutory instruments. These regulations may determine crucial questions. For example, most of the duties of GPs within the NHS are dealt with by regulations and not by Acts of Parliament.

It is impossible today to understand the legal rules governing the practice of medicine without reference to European law. In matters within the jurisdiction of the Treaty of Rome and subsequent treaties, notably the Treaty of Amsterdam, the EU is empowered to make laws affecting all member states. This may be by way of regulations which immediately and directly become law in the UK, or by way of directives which oblige the UK government to introduce an appropriate Act of Parliament to give effect to the directive. In 1985, a Community directive on liability for unsafe products resulted in the Consumer Protection Act 1987 which, as we shall see in chapter 9, introduced strict liability for defective drugs. The Data Protection Directive is considered in chapter 4. The Clinical Trials Directive, promulgated in April 2001, obliged the UK to introduce reforms of the law governing medical research. This was done by way of a new set of regulations – the Medicines for Human Use (Clinical Trials) Regulations 2004. At the time of writing both the Clinical Trials

Directive and the Data Protection Directive are under review. New scientific innovations and pressure to facilitate medical research provide strong incentives for reform. Provisions of the EU treaties themselves may be invoked to make a case for greater rights for patients. This is how Diane Blood won her case to be allowed to be inseminated with her dead husband's sperm abroad.

The EU must not be confused with the European Convention on Human Rights. That Convention is a separate treaty to which the UK is a party. The Convention seeks to establish the rights of the individual and directly addresses questions such as rights to life, to privacy, and to found a family. The Human Rights Act 1998 renders rights granted by the Convention enforceable against public authorities in the United Kingdom. As we shall see, the Act has transformed areas of medical law and, as a living instrument, that potential does not diminish with time.

Conventions, statutes and statutory regulations alone, be they British or European legislation, by no means paint the whole picture of English medical law. Much of English law remains judge-made: the common law of England. Decisions (judgments handed down by the courts) form precedents for determining later disputes and define the rights and duties of doctors and patients in areas untouched by statute. The common law largely governs questions of compensation for medical accidents, the patient's right to determine her own treatment, parents' rights to control medical treatment of their children and, as we shall see, several other vital matters.

We deal with English law. The common law is not confined to England. Decisions of courts in the USA, Canada and elsewhere are mentioned from time to time. Such judgments do not bind an English court. They can be useful as examples, or warnings, showing us how the same basic principles of law have developed elsewhere. Finally, it must be remembered that for the lawyer, Scotland counts as a foreign country. Scotland maintains its own independent legal system and, post-devolution, enjoys the power to legislate independently on most issues relating to medical care. Scotland has, for example, enacted its own Human Tissue (Scotland) Act 2006. On many of the questions dealt with in this book, English and Scottish law coincides. Occasionally, the law in England and Scotland diverges. We confine ourselves to stating the law as it applies in England and Wales. The problems of law and medicine embodied in the book are common to the UK as a whole.

Part I

Part I of this book begins by seeking to examine the overall framework of medicine today. How does the law seek to ensure that patients are treated by competent, qualified doctors practising ethical medicine? Does the GMC, which for over a century and a half has regulated the medical profession, meet patients' needs? What rights do we enjoy in the context of health care and how has the Human Rights Act 1998 affected medical law? Law can, at best, only set basic standards of behaviour. So we explore some of the ethical principles and dilemmas in modern medicine. Then in the final chapter of this first Part, we examine that critical component of any doctor–patient relationship, the necessity for trust and confidence. Can we be assured that our doctors will respect our privacy so that we can feel confident enough to be wholly frank with them? In what exceptional circumstances should that duty of confidence be breached to fulfil some more pressing responsibility to others?

Part II

In this Part, we examine what remedies the law affords a patient dissatisfied with the medical care which he or she has received. A patient may feel that he has not been fully consulted or properly counselled about the nature and risks of treatment. He may have agreed to treatment and ended up worse, not better. Consequently the patient may seek compensation from the courts. Or he may simply want an investigation of what went wrong, and to ensure that his experience is not suffered by others. It is the rise in litigation that has caused so much anxiety among doctors.

The law relating to medical errors, often described as medical malpractice, operates on two basic principles. (1) The patient must agree to treatment. (2) Treatment must be carried out with proper skill and care on the part of all the members of the medical profession involved. Any doctor who operated on or injected, or even touched, an adult patient against her will might commit a battery, a trespass against the patient's person. A doctor who was shown to have exercised inadequate care of his patient, to have fallen below the required standard of competence, would be liable to compensate the patient for any harm he caused her in the tort of negligence. In short, to obtain compensation, the patient must show that the doctor was at fault. And if she sues for negligence, she must show that the doctor's 'fault' caused her injury. Three overwhelming problems are inherent in these two simple statements.

First, how do courts staffed by lawyer-judges determine when a doctor is at fault? We shall see that the judges in England used to defer largely to the views of the doctors. Recent case law suggests judges are now more ready to scrutinise medical practice. Establishing what constitutes good practice will still cause the court some difficulty. The courts remain dependent on expert evidence and a clash of eminent medical opinions is not unusual.

Second, as liability, and the patient's right to compensation, is dependent on a finding of fault, doctors naturally feel that a judgment against them is a body blow to their career and their reputation. Yet a moment's reflection will remind the reader of all the mistakes she has made in her own job. A solicitor overlooking a vital piece of advice from a conference with a client can telephone the client and put things right when he has a chance to check what he has done. A carpenter can have a second go at fixing a door or a cupboard. An overtired, overstrained doctor may commit a momentary error which is irreversible. He is still a good doctor despite one mistake.

Finally, the doctor's fault must be shown to have caused the patient harm. In general, whether a patient is treated within the NHS or privately, the doctor only undertakes to do his best. He does not guarantee a cure. The patient will have a legal remedy only if he can show that the doctor's carelessness or lack of skill caused him injury that he would not otherwise have suffered. So if you contract an infection and are prescribed antibiotics which a competent doctor should have appreciated were inappropriate for you or your condition, you can sue the doctor only if you can show either: (1) that the antibiotic pre-scribed caused you harm unrelated to your original sickness, for example, brought you out in a violent allergy; or (2) that the absence of appropriate treatment significantly delayed your recovery. And in both cases you must prove that had the doctor acted properly, the harm would have been avoided.

We shall see therefore that the law is a remedy only for more specific and seri-ous grievances against a doctor. It is in any case an expensive and unwieldy weapon. Many patients have complaints, particularly about hospitals, which do not amount to actionable negligence. They complain about being kept waiting, inadequate visiting hours, or rudeness on the part of NHS staff. We shall look in this Part at extra-legal methods of pursuing complaints against a hospital or a doctor, and we consider if the whole system for compensating medical errors should be replaced by a no-fault compensation scheme. Nor do we limit our examination to faults alleged against medical practitioners. Many medical mishaps arise from the dangers inherent in certain drugs. We consider the liability of the drug companies and attempts by government to ensure that available medicines are safe.

Finally, we should say a word about legal 'language' today. The person who initiates a legal action, for example, the patient suing a doctor for battery or negligence, used to be referred to as the plaintiff. When Lord Woolf recom-mended radical reforms of the civil justice system, some of which are discussed in chapter 8, he also proposed that old-fashioned language should be changed into plain English. So today, the patient bringing a claim against a doctor is simply called the claimant. Where we discuss cases decided before 1999, we use the old term 'plaintiff'. Defendants, thankfully, remain just that, defendants.

Part III

The first two Parts of this book focus on the relationship of doctors and patients, both the framework of that relationship and how the law deals with conflict when a patient is dissatisfied with the care that he has received. Part III looks at the dramatic questions in medical law where what is at stake is not only what an individual patient may be entitled to, but also what society should allow. The range of questions addressed is broad. Others are omitted simply on grounds of space. We consider whether parents who find themselves with an unplanned child after receipt of negligent medical advice or treatment, should receive compensation to meet the cost of raising that child. What duties are owed to an unborn child, and should pregnant women continue to enjoy legal immunity from liability to their future children? We venture into the troubled waters of the reproductive technologies, seeking to explain and analyse the law governing such matters as the creation of 'saviour siblings', human cloning, hybrid embryos. But we also attempt to address practical questions – how to define parental status, and access to information about gamete donors. Medical research, transplantation and the especial problems around the medical care of children are addressed. We end (appropriately) by examining laws relating to the end of life, and debates about euthanasia.

Law matters

Medical law has altered beyond recognition in the twenty years since the first edition of this book. No-one who reads a newspaper or watches television can be unaware of the sorts of questions which we address. On an almost weekly basis, new initiatives or new laws are proposed. Sometimes it seems as though the dizzying pace of reform reflects little thought about the whole picture. More attention is paid to policy and ethical debate than law. There is insufficient rigorous analysis of what the limits of the law's remit should be. One set of lawyers, doctors and patient groups address the adequacy (or inadequacy) of malpractice litigation. Ethicists, journalists and legal theorists join doctors and theologians in debating the grand moral dilemmas of medicine. Lay people tend not to get much of a chance to have their say until some controversy breaks, such as the scandals around poor standards of care at Mid-Staffordshire Foundation Trust. For all these reasons, this book seeks to concentrate more on law than ethics as such, and to attempt to locate our discussions of the law in a practical context. We hope that we can dispel the myth that law is 'boring'. We hope that our discussion may cast some light on what the role of the law should be in the context of modern medicine.

Contents

Part I
MEDICINE, LAW AND SOCIETY

Chapter 1
THE PRACTICE OF MEDICINE TODAY 3

Contents

Part II
MEDICAL MALPRACTICE

Contents

Chapter 8
MALPRACTICE LITIGATION

Chapter 9
COMPLAINTS AND REDRESS

Contents

Part III
MATTERS OF LIFE AND DEATH

Chapter 11
CONTRACEPTION, PREGNANCY AND CHILDBIRTH.........307

Chapter 12
ASSISTED CONCEPTION 345

Contents

Contents

Table of Cases

A

D

G

H

I

J

K

PAGE

L

M

N

O

P

Q

R

S

T

X

Decisions of the European Court of Justice are listed below numerically. These decisions are also, included in the preceding alphabetical list.

Table of Statutes

Table of Statutory Instruments

Table of European and International Material

Table of European and International Material

Part I

MEDICINE, LAW AND SOCIETY

Chapter 1

THE PRACTICE OF MEDICINE TODAY

1.1 Few professions still stand so high in public esteem as medicine.[1] Nonetheless, as the new millennium unfolded, scandal after scandal beset doctors, dealing a blow to the reputation of the medical profession in the UK. Between 2005 and 2008, high mortality rates and patient neglect at Stafford Hospital were blamed in part on strategic focus on financial targets.[2] Poor mentoring was blamed for the deaths of young cardiac patients at John Radcliffe Hospital in Oxford.[3] Surgeons carrying out cardiac operations on infants in Bristol were found to have continued to operate despite incurring higher death rates for such surgery than their peers.[4] The Bristol Inquiry[5] uncovered a 'club culture'.[6] Staff were caring and well motivated, but care was badly organised; the standard of care was poor and there was a lack of effective communication. In Bristol,[7] and in Liverpool,[8] evi-

---

[1] See R Tallis, *Hippocratic Oaths: Medicine and Its Discontents* (2004) Atlantic Books, p 102.

[2] Healthcare Commission, *Investigation into Mid Staffordshire NHS Foundation Trust* (2009), p 11.

[3] *Review of Paediatric Cardiac Surgery Services at Oxford Radcliffe Hospitals NHS Trust* (2010).

[4] But see criticism of the GMC's Professional Conduct Committee which found three doctors guilty of serious professional misconduct: P M Dunn, 'The Wiseheart Affair: Paediatric Cardiological Services in Bristol 1990–95' (1998) 317 *BMJ* 1144, complains (inter alia) that the Committee did not include anyone with experience of cardiac surgery and that, given that many of the charges against the surgeons were dropped or not proved, the finding was prompted largely by public and political pressure. And see alternative view: S N Bolsin, 'The Wiseheart Affair: Responses to Dunn' (1998) 317 *BMJ* 1579.

[5] *Learning from Bristol*, The Report of the Public Inquiry into Children's Heart Surgery at the Bristol Royal Infirmary 1984–1995, CM 5207 (1) (2001) (hereafter *The Bristol Inquiry*).

[6] *The Bristol Inquiry*, Summary, para 3.

[7] Interim Report, *Removal and Retention of Human Material* (available at www.bristol-inquiry.org.uk).

[8] Royal Liverpool Children's Inquiry Report HC 12–11 (2001) (hereafter the Redfern Report).

dence emerged of hospitals retaining children's organs without their parents being told that only parts of their children's bodies were returned to them for burial. Subsequently, it became apparent that organ retention in relation to children and adults was a widespread practice.[9] A gynaecologist was struck off the medical register after years of gross malpractice involving bungled operations, removing women's ovaries without their consent, and a record of appalling rudeness to patients.[10] A consultant urogynaecologist, who was allegedly ignored by management when he complained of feeling 'overwhelmed', was suspended in 2008 leaving upwards of 200 women seeking damages.[11] Harold Shipman was convicted of fifteen counts of murder and later found to have killed at least 215 of his patients.[12] A GP, Clifford Ayling, was convicted of indecent assault on twelve female patients.[13] Disturbing reports of degrading treatment of learning disabled people in NHS establishments surfaced in 2006.[14] These so-called 'scandals' reflect poorly on individuals, but also on the NHS which promises to ensure a safe service of the quality that patients and their families are entitled to expect.[15]

What are the implications for medical regulation? Four distinct tiers of regulation have been identified. First, personal regulation involves a doctor's individual commitment to a code of ethics, found in part in documents such as the Hippocratic Oath and the General Medical Council's *Good Medical Practice* guidance.[16] We consider the ethical responsibilities of doctors in chapter 3. Second, team-based regulation requires all healthcare professionals to take responsibility for their team's performance and conduct. Third, professional regulation, which we consider in the next section, is undertaken by statutory regulators such as the General Medical Council (GMC) and the Nursing and Midwifery Council[17] which are overseen by the Council for Healthcare Regu-

---

[9] See most recently, *The Redfern Inquiry into Human Tissue Analysis in UK Nuclear Facilities* (2010) on radiochemical analysis of organs removed at post-mortem between 1960 and 1992.

[10] Department of Health (hereafter DH), Report of the Committee of Inquiry into How the NHS Handled Allegations About the Conduct of Richard Neale, CM 6315 (2004). See **9.2** below on public inquiries.

[11] 'More than 200 Patients Sue Liverpool Women's Hospital' *BBC News* (on-line) 12 May 2010. See below at **10.8**.

[12] See http://www.the-shipman-inquiry.org.uk.

[13] DH, Committee of Inquiry – Independent Investigation into how the NHS Handled Allegations about the Conduct of Clifford Ayling, CM 6298 (2004).

[14] Healthcare Commission and the Commission for Social Care Inspection, Joint Investigation into the Provision of Services for People with Learning Disabilities at Cornwall Partnership NHS Trust (2006).

[15] See NHS Constitution, s 2(a).

[16] In essence, the doctor must seek to be a good person, a tradition dating back to the work of the nineteenth-century physician Thomas Percival; see below at **3.2**.

[17] We concentrate on the role of the GMC. Other professional regulators include the General Chiropractic, Dental, Optical, Pharmaceutical and Osteopathic Councils, the Nursing and Midwifery Council and the Health Professions Council (proposed to be renamed the Health and Care Professions Council in the Health and Social Care Bill, HC 132 (2011). The Council for Healthcare Regulatory Excellence (which,

latory Excellence (CHRE)[18] which monitors nine healthcare regulators, sets standards and enhances consistency. Finally, work-based regulation involves a system of clinical governance and performance management which we consider in the latter half of this chapter.

In recent years the medical profession has witnessed an unprecedented increase in all four types of regulation.[19] The previous administration addressed deficiencies in the NHS by asserting greater control. The GMC has been radically reformed. New work-based regulation emphasised monitoring designed to ensure good practice rather than simply react to bad practice. More recently, however, the coalition government has promised to reduce bureaucracy and cut down the number of arm's-length bodies. The aim is to give *doctors* control – to 'liberat[e] the NHS from central control and political interference'.[20] It is hoped that transparency, competition and choice will promote a rise in standards and patient safety. Critics fear that these hopes are ill founded.[21]

The various tiers of regulation do not always work in harmony. As we shall see, work-based regulation is designed not only to enhance patient safety, but also to ensure the economic accountability of NHS organisations. Job freezes and staff cuts have an impact on the level of care a hospital can provide. Economy may compromise safety and reduce the ability of the individual doctor to offer the kind of care that she might wish to.

Angels or demons?

1.2 Praised to the skies for their triumphs, few individuals attract greater public odium than the doctor or nurse who falls from her pedestal. The revulsion occasioned by Nazi atrocities in the concentration camps was nowhere as marked as in the case of Dr Mengele. That he used his skills as a doctor, taught to him that he might heal and comfort the sick, to advance torture and barbarism causes horror, more than half a century after the end of the Nazi era. The transformation of a supposed angel of mercy into the angel of death makes the blood run cold.

it is proposed, will be renamed the Professional Standards Authority for Health and Social Care) oversees them all.

18 The National Health Service Reform and Health Care Professions Act 2002, ss 25–29 established the Council for the Regulation of Health Care Professions, renamed the Council for Healthcare Regulatory Excellence in the Health and Social Care Act 2008, s 113. The CHRE is, at the time of writing, an arm's-length body but reform proposals intend to make it self-funding by 2013, widen its remit to encompass social care and change its name (ibid).

19 A Davies, 'Don't Trust Me, I'm a Doctor: Medical Regulation and the 1999 NHS Reforms' (2000) 20 *Oxford Journal of Legal Studies* 437.

20 A Lansley, Secretary of State for Health, in *Transparency in Outcomes – A Framework for the NHS* (2010), p 3.

21 See below at **1.3**.

Public passion is rightly aroused by the likes of Mengele and Shipman. Passion is never far away from everyday relationships between doctor and patient. Clients usually remain unemotional about their solicitor. If he does a good job they may appreciate him. If he is incompetent they sack him. He will rarely be loved or hated. The family doctor arouses more intense feelings. When doctors meet their patient's expectations, they are rewarded by admiration and affection. Woe betide them if they do not. One error, one moment of exasperation or insensitivity, may transform a beloved doctor into a hate figure. The hospital consultant enjoys or endures a similarly ambivalent role. Consultants were once accorded godlike status. They inspired awe visiting the ward attended by a retinue of junior doctors and nurses. Their exalted status insulated them from personal contact with patients and protected them from the sort of complaints voiced freely to nursing staff. They paid a price. Gods are expected to work miracles. They are not expected to be subject to human error. When a consultant proved to be human, when medicine could not cure, the patient found it hard to comprehend failure and rightly or wrongly, often wrongly, regarded the doctor as personally incompetent.

Medical attitudes are changing, if slowly. Family doctors are becoming a different breed. Many try hard to persuade patients to see their doctor as a partner in promoting good health. Doctors are urged to prescribe less freely and to talk more to their patients. The good GP is as interested in the prevention of ill health as its cure.[22] A new generation of consultants is taking over in the hospitals. They are (in most cases) less grand and more prepared to listen to patients and nursing staff.

One, or even several, 'bad apples' should not destroy the reputations of thousands of other medical practitioners who do their job diligently and compassionately. All professions have their miscreants. The medical profession should not be punished for Shipman's bizarre and apparently motiveless murders. The heart of the problem and the damage to the 'image' of medicine is that too little is sometimes seen to be done by the profession and its regulators to identify and remedy doctors' failings. It seems amazing that no colleague noted or acted on evidence of the number of apparent healthy patients on Shipman's list who died suddenly, in certain cases even in his surgery. The Public Interest Disclosure Act 1999 is designed to protect whistle-blowers. But whistle-blowing at Mid-Staffordshire proved inadequate,[23] and in 2010 Sharmila Chowdhury was reinstated with full salary having been sacked after revealing allegedly fraudulent activities of senior managers in 2007. Her accusations were ignored and she was counter-accused of fraud.[24] A new guide on whistle-blowing was issued in 2010,[25] and there are proposals to amend the

---

[22] And will, if reforms proposed by the government are implemented, take on an additional commercial role. See below at 1.3.

[23] P Gooderham, 'Changing the Face of Whistleblowing' (2009) 338 *BMJ* b2090.

[24] N Lakhani, 'Sacked NHS Whistleblower Vindicated' *Independent,* 11 July 2010.

[25] Social Partnership Forum & Public Concern at Work, *Speak up for a Healthy NHS:*

NHS Constitution[26] to insert an expectation that NHS staff will raise concerns about safety as early as possible and pledge to support them when they do so.[27] But it is clear that the law needs greater powers if employees are to feel safe to speak out.[28]

The responsibility for detecting and reacting to bad practice lies not only with NHS workers, but also with the regulators who oversee them. Reforms following the *Bristol Inquiry* attempted to enhance professional regulation but this did not prevent high mortality rates and patient neglect at Stafford hospital between 2005 and 2008. As we shall see, new measures were introduced when the Care Quality Commission was set up in 2009 to register and monitor providers of health and social care.

There are certain features of the profession of medicine which will render doctors more vulnerable to attack than other professionals. The doctor deals with the individual's most precious commodity: life and health. On a mundane level she may determine whether patient X is to be sanctioned to enjoy seven days off work for nervous exhaustion brought about by overwork, or classified as another malingerer.[29] At the other end of the scale, the doctor may hold in his hands the power of life and death. He is the man with the skill and experience. In his hands, as the patient sees it, rests the power to cure. As Ian Kennedy has said, the patient appears before the doctor '. . . naked both physically and emotionally'. It is hard to overstate the power vested in doctors.[30] The price of power is that those who exercise it must expect constant scrutiny from those subject to it and from the public at large. The age of deference is past. Doctors cannot be surprised when failure, incompetence or controversy attracts equal notoriety. Unfortunately, representatives of the profession sometimes react in an over-defensive manner, exacerbating the original criticism or complaint.

The NHS

1.3 How well doctors can do their job is at least in part dictated by the environment in which they work. In England, most health care is still provided within the NHS. Since 1974, the NHS has been subject to a steady stream of political reform.[31] Such constant change does not help doctors and nurses do

How to Implement and Review Whistle blowing Arrangements in Your Organisation (2010).
[26] The Health Act 2009, s 1, provides for a NHS Constitution. See below, at **2.15**.
[27] DH, *The NHS Constitution and Whistle blowing* (2010). The Consultation closed in January 2011.
[28] See below at **9.11** on draft Health Care Workers (Duty of Co-operation) Regulations 2010 seeking to impose a 'duty of cooperation' on NHS staff to share information likely to enhance patient safety.
[29] I Kennedy, *The Unmasking of Medicine* (1981) Allen & Unwin, ch 1, p 9ff.
[30] *The Unmasking of Medicine*, p 8.
[31] The numerous NHS Acts were consolidated into the National Health Service Act

their jobs. In 1991, NHS hospital trusts were first created and the NHS divided into 'purchasers' and 'providers'. In early 2010 the House of Commons Health Committee stated: 'if it does not begin to improve soon, after 20 years of costly failure, the purchaser/provider split may need to be abolished'.[32]

The Conservative government introduced the internal 'market' and GP fund-holding in 1995. The government's philosophy was that local health authorities or GP fundholders would seek out the best quality and best value hospital treatment and other secondary care for all their patients. Hospital trusts would compete to attract patients. GP fundholding was abolished by the incoming Labour government in 1997. Twenty-eight Strategic Health Authorities (SHAs) were created in 2001 to manage the performance of the NHS locally. Three hundred and three Primary Care Trusts (PCTs) were created to provide health services. Less emphasis was placed on financial management and many NHS organisations incurred deficits. New emphasis was placed on decentralisation: a patient-led NHS. Focus on patient choice led to the reinstatement of competition between trusts in 2004, and in 2006 the existing SHAs merged into 10 and the 303 PCTs merged into 152, reminiscent of the regional offices and health authorities abolished in 2001.

Commissioning is central to the NHS.[33] Primary care is the 'front line' of the NHS. The local surgery is often the patient's first point of contact. There she can see a range of healthcare professionals, such as a nurse, GP or midwife, and access a range of services. PCTs were established in 2000 to plan and commission services for the locality from NHS trusts, NHS foundation trusts, NHS or independent sector treatment centres and other independent sector providers. From April 2003, 75 per cent of the NHS budget devolved to PCTs.[34] PCTs could devolve their responsibilities to GP practices (or groups of GP practices), which were given indicative budgets and allowed to commission services ('Practice Based Commissioning'[35]). In 2010 the coalition government proposed a much bigger transfer of powers – a wholesale devolution of commissioning powers to local consortia of GP practices. If the controversial reform proposals survive parliamentary scrutiny, the reformed NHS will take on the following form:

2006, the National Health Service (Wales) Act 2006 and the National Health Service (Consequential Provisions) Act 2006. The Health and Social Care Bill 2010–11, HC 51/1, Sch 4, Pt 1 proposes amendments to implement the White Paper, *Liberating the NHS*.

[32] House of Commons Health Committee, *Commissioning* HC 268-I (2010), para 202.

[33] See, for example, section 2(a) of the NHS Constitution which states: 'You have the right to expect your local NHS to assess the health requirements of the local community and to commission and put in place the services to meet those needs as considered necessary.'

[34] DH, *Sustaining Innovation through New PMS Arrangements* (2004) ref: 2545, p 7.

[35] DH, *Commissioning a Patient-Led NHS* (2005) ref: 5312.

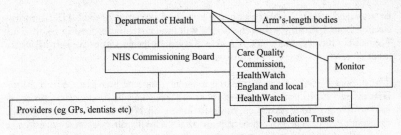

NAO, *Health Resource Allocation* (2010), p 5 (abridged)[36]

Several consultations followed the 2010 White Paper, *Equity and Excellence: Liberating the NHS*. The government made responses to three of them in December 2010,[37] outlining plans for a Health and Social Care Bill, which was published in January 2011. At the time of writing (February 2011), much remains uncertain. If the provisions are adopted, GP commissioning will be put on a statutory footing. PCTs will be phased out[38] by 2013 and replaced with GP consortia (Commissioning Consortia – CC). Every GP practice will be a member of a consortium, which will commission the majority of[39] health services required by patients. CCs are well placed to make commissioning decisions based on local need, and they will be required to seek appropriate advice when discharging their functions.[40] But they will be forced to spend considerable time and resources tendering, and an array of contracts and pathways of care will emerge.[41]

The Bill seeks to establish a new quango, the NHS Commissioning Board, which is intended to oversee the process, calculate budgets and allocate money to each consortium. In addition it will commission local primary care and specialist services. At the time of writing, it remains uncertain how both underperformance by CCs (for example, overspending or incompetence) and variation in clinical practice (which will result from individualised care and new care pathways) will

---

[36] For a more detailed diagram upon which this is based, see NAO, *Health Resource Allocation* (2010), p 5.

[37] DH, *Liberating the NHS: Legislative Framework and Next Steps* (2010).

[38] The first 'Pathfinder Consortia' were announced in December 2010. During the transition, PCT Clusters (groups of PCTs with a single management team) are (at the time of writing) being formed in an attempt to retain effective management capacity. See DH, *PCT Cluster Implementation Guidance* (January 2011).

[39] Excluding dentistry, community pharmacy, primary ophthalmic services and GP contracts and services, which will be commissioned by the NHS Commissioning Board. CC are expected to control around £80bn of the commissioning budget and the Commissioning Board around £20bn.

[40] The Royal College of Physicians argues that there should be a requirement that secondary care specialists are involved in commissioning decisions. See *RCP Response to the Health and Social Care Bill* (January 2011), accessible at http://www.rcplondon.ac.uk. And see *BMA Response to Health Select Committee Inquiry on Commissioning* (October 2010).

[41] See Royal College of Physicians, Response to Department of Health Consultation – Liberating the NHS: Greater Choice and Control (January 2011).

be managed. Sir David Nicholson, the first chief executive of the NHS Commissioning Board, promises that the Board will take a strong leadership role.[42] The Board may have 'management tiers' at a regional level to improve sensitivity to local diversity.

The previous administration created a wider range of providers. From 2006, GPs offered NHS patients needing hospital treatment or diagnosis a choice of four to five different providers, often including an NHS or independent sector treatment centre. The government plans that CC will commission services from 'any willing provider', including not-for-profit organisations, independent and autonomous providers.[43] This represents an opportunity for gradually increasing involvement from the private sector. The CC will be judged according to national standards, enhanced by specific 'Quality Standards' produced by the National Institute of Health and Clinical Excellence (NICE), which will be put on a statutory footing.[44] The national standards are intended to enable the government to monitor the overall effectiveness of the NHS and set targets for improvement.

Patients too will have greater choice. At the time of writing, patients can choose a GP practice within their catchment area. There are plans to give patients more freedom to choose a GP practice which is convenient to their needs.[45] For example, some patients might prefer to register with a practice near their place of work. If implemented, this would inevitably impact on CC's ability to plan their services and rural practices might suffer. Could GPs commit to visit their patients at home? And would more affluent patients seeking treatment that not all CCs provide travel to a CC which does, leaving poorer, less mobile patients with much more limited choices?

New freedoms in commissioning will be matched by increased autonomy for providers. Foundation trusts were established by the Health and Social Care (Community Health and Standards) Act 2003.[46] Whilst subject to NHS inspection and standards, they are independent not-for-profit public benefit corporations with unique governance arrangements. Under these terms, investment from both the public and private sectors is encouraged. They are authorised by 'Monitor', an independent regulator, and governed by people elected from and by the membership base which includes patients, the public and staff. The aim was for all NHS trusts to be given the opportunity to apply for foundation trust status by 2008. The initiative lost momentum which the coalition government seems to rekindle. Under their proposals, all trusts will attain foundation trust status by

---

[42] D West, 'Nicholson: My Commissioning Board Won't be Shy'(2011) *Health Service Journal*, 18 February.

[43] There will be new entrants to the market but will competition necessarily improve quality? See letter, 'Health Bill is a Step towards Privatisation of NHS' (2011) *The Times*, 17 January.

[44] And renamed the National Institute for Health and Care Excellence. See Health and Social Care Bill 2011, Pt 8.

[45] DH, Response to Consultation: *Your Choice of GP Practice* (October 2010).

[46] Consolidated in the National Health Service Act 2006, Ch 5 (ss 30–65).

2013, and Monitor will become the economic regulator for all providers of NHS care.[47] Though the intention is not to privatise foundation trusts, they will be given greater freedoms and employee-led control. Every procedure carries a fixed price and hospitals are paid for what they do: 'payment by results' (PbR), or, more accurately, payment by activity. PbR will be extended to hospitals from 2011 and to mental health, community services and end-of-life care from 2012.[48]

Foundation trust status was linked to quality goals which some hospitals failed to reach. At first these standards will continue to apply. Beyond the transition period, the raft of regulatory standards are likely to give way to other, less tangible quality drivers.[49] The coalition government aims to enhance patient choice[50] through 'an NHS information revolution'.[51] The Health and Social Care Bill makes provision for a new Health and Social Care Information Centre[52] with powers to require health and social care bodies to provide information, and requirements to publish certain information. Patients will choose their provider on the basis of outcome-based statistics. Convenience will continue to play a role, but so too will the hospital's safety record, cleanliness, and the testaments of other patients. They will choose providers which offer the best quality care.

Compliance with new standards will be monitored by the Care Quality Commission and the results made public via the Care Quality Commission and independent reports such as *Dr Foster's Hospital Guide*.[53] Standards will focus on outcomes rather than structures or processes.[54] It is currently envisaged that there will be five 'domains': three will promote effectiveness and one each will promote a positive patient experience and patient safety:

(1)   preventing people from dying prematurely;
(2)   enhancing quality of life for people with long-term conditions;
(3)   helping people to recover from episodes of ill health or following injury;
(4)   ensuring that people have a positive experience of care;
(5)   treating and caring for people in a safe environment and protecting them from avoidable harm.[55]

---

[47]   See Health and Social Care Bill 2011, Pt 4.
[48]   See DH, *Payment by Results – Guidance for 2010–11* (2010) ref: 13591. And see criticism in *BMA Response to Health Select Committee Inquiry on Commissioning* (October 2010): 'The current system of Payment by Results (PbR) is not fit for purpose, encourages perverse behaviours and is highly bureaucratic'.
[49]   DH, *Regulating Health Care Providers* (2010), para 1.7. And see A Lansley, 'An Open Transparent NHS is a Safer NHS' (2010) *Guardian*, 27 November.
[50]   DH, *Liberating the NHS: Greater Choice and Control* (Consultation) (2010).
[51]   *Liberating the NHS: An Information Revolution* (Consultation) (October 2010); Health and Social Care Bill 2011, Pt 9.
[52]   Replacing the Special Health Authority of the same name. See Health and Social Care Bill 2011, Pt 9, Ch 2.
[53]   See http://www.drfosterhealth.co.uk/docs/hospital-guide-2010.pdf
[54]   DH, *Transparency in Outcomes – A Framework for the NHS: Government Response to Consultation* (2010) ref: 15265.
[55]   Reiterating what was first presented in *Equity and Excellence: Liberating the NHS*, pp 18–42.

The categories are broad and there will be much freedom in determining how the framework will be delivered at a local level, within the context of the over-arching goals.[56] Defining indicators of quality, measuring outcomes and apportioning responsibility when problems emerge will be complex. There is no 'value-for-money' domain, yet this will inevitably play a central role in the NHS Commissioning Board's choices. It is proposed that Monitor and the NHS Commissioning Board set a maximum national tariff which the British Medical Association fear will result in price competition,[57] especially when combined with the proposal that providers might exceptionally offer services below the tariff price.[58] In February 2011 the government clarified that price competition does not form part of their plans.[59] Nevertheless, we fear that, in light of the £20bn savings the NHS is required to make, quality will suffer.

Successful foundation trusts will benefit from the lifting of the cap on the income they can earn. Failures will be allowed to go bankrupt. The reforms will have a significant impact on NHS workers. Commissioning power comes at the price of responsibility. The government will be distanced from failures and unpopular commissioning decisions. Competition will be fierce. Cash, as always, is tight.

Entitlement to practise

1.4 One of the crucial functions of regulation is to ensure the competence of professionals offering services to the public. So who is entitled to practise medicine? The GMC maintains a register of medical practitioners and in 2009 the licence to practise was introduced[60] as part of reforms aiming to monitor doctors in order to assess their accordance with principles of *Good Medical Practice*[61] set down by the GMC. Only registered practitioners can apply for a licence. Both registration and a licence are required to perform certain tasks, such as writing prescriptions or signing death certificates, and a criminal offence is committed when a person deliberately and falsely represents himself as being

---

[56] Which are defined in DH Business Plan 2011–2015: Consultation on the Transparency Framework (2010).

[57] Health and Social Care Bill 2011, cl 103. See BMA, *Written Evidence to the Public Bill Committee for the Health and Social Care Bill* (February 2011), para 20.

[58] See *NHS Operating Framework for 2011/12* (20 December 2010), para 5.43. And see House of Commons, *Health and Social Care Bill* Research Paper 11/11 (27 January 2011), p 35.

[59] Sir D Nicholson (letter to NHS chief executives), *Equality and Excellence: Liberating the NHS – Managing the Transition* (2011) 17 February, p 14: 'Services subject to tariff will continue to compete on quality: there is no question of introducing price competition'.

[60] The General Medical Council (Licence to Practise) Regulations Order of Council 2009, SI 2009/2739. Under powers derived from the Medicines Act 1983, Pt IIIA, s 29A(2).

[61] GMC, *Good Medical Practice* (2006).

a registered and licensed practitioner or having a medical qualification.[62] However, unregistered and unlicensed practitioners can still use the title 'doctor'. No law expressly prohibits any unregistered, unlicensed or unqualified person from practising most types of medicine or even surgery. The rationale of the criminal law is that people should be free to opt for any form of advice or treatment, however bizarre, but must be protected from rogues claiming a bogus status and from commercial exploitation of untested 'alternative' medicine.

A tradition of self-regulation – to be consigned to history?

1.5 By virtue of the Medical Act 1983, the regulation of the medical profession was entrusted to the profession itself, acting through the General Medical Council, continuing a tradition of self-regulation, endorsed by Parliament, dating back to 1858. Prior to 1858, there were in effect three separate medical professions, the physicians, the surgeons, and the apothecaries. The Royal Colleges of Physicians and Surgeons wielded great power. Those colleges, joined later by others, for example, the Royal College of Obstetricians and Gynaecologists, continued to control specialist education and specialist practice. Self-regulation has long been the hallmark of the learned professions. The Bar Council used to enjoy extensive powers to regulate barristers, and the Law Society enjoyed a similar jurisdiction over solicitors. Doctors' patients and lawyers' clients were increasingly unconvinced that the professional regulators protected public interests. The GMC came under especially vigorous attack. Its composition was seen as too biased in favour of the doctors, and its capacity to ensure that patients were treated by competent doctors truly fit to practise was doubted. Thus, although the Medical Act 1983 remains on the statute book, it has been radically amended by statutory instruments in 2002,[63] 2006,[64] 2007,[65] 2008[66] and 2010.[67]

The Medical Act 1983 (Amendment) Order 2002 sets out the central tenet of all attempts to reform the GMC. It amends section 1 of the 1983 Act so that section 1A says simply:

---

[62] Medical Act 1983, s 49; and see *Younghusband v Luftig* [1949] 2 KB 354; *Wilson v Inyang* [1951] 2 KB 799. Unregistered practitioners are expressly prohibited from certain fields of practice, eg venereal disease (Venereal Disease Act 1917). And they are barred from holding certain positions (Medical Act 1983, s 47).

[63] The Medical Act 1983 (Amendment) Order 2002, SI 2002/3135.

[64] The Medical Act 1983 (Amendment) and Miscellaneous Amendments Order 2006, SI 2006/1914.

[65] The European Qualifications (Health and Social Care Professions Regulations) 2007, SI 2007/3101.

[66] The Health Care and Associated Professions (Miscellaneous Amendments) Order 2008, SI 2008/1734; The Medical Professions (Miscellaneous Amendments) Order 2008, SI 2008/3131.

[67] The General and Specialist Medical Practice (Education, Training and Qualifications) Order 2010, SI 2010/234.

> The main objective of the General Council in exercising their functions is to protect, promote and maintain the safety of the public.

Historically, while the GMC has policed admission to the medical register, little was done to ensure a doctor continued to be competent, and up to date, in her practice. She remained 'licensed' to practise, unless disciplinary proceedings, or health or performance procedures, were invoked against her. Initial registration established that a doctor in her twenties starting out in practice satisfied set criteria for competence. Twenty years after she left medical school, was she still competent? Amendments to Part III of the 1983 Act introduce a scheme for revalidation of medical competence. The GMC issues doctors a licence to practise on first registration. Then, as we shall see, doctors will be required to renew that licence periodically, proving their continued competence through a scheme of continuing evaluation of practice. The long-awaited revalidation scheme has been delayed again by the proposed restructuring of the NHS. It is now expected to be rolled out in late 2012.[68]

If the absence of processes to monitor doctors' competence caused public concern, what were seen as feeble and apparently prejudiced disciplinary proceedings to deal with complaints against doctors aroused anger.[69] The historic concept of 'infamous conduct in a professional respect' was replaced by the notion of 'serious professional misconduct' in the Medical Act 1969. Critics still argued that the threshold of what constituted such misconduct was set too high, and when such a finding was made, penalties were too lenient. Thus, in 2002 the whole of the existing system for disciplining defaulting doctors, dealing with sick doctors, and addressing under-performing doctors was revised. The critics were far from satisfied. Dame Janet Smith's inquiry[70] into the Shipman debacle led to a review of medical regulation by the Chief Medical Officer (CMO), Sir Liam Donaldson. The CMO published a consultation document, *Good Doctors, Safer Patients*, in 2006, concluding that the GMC is 'too secretive, too tolerant of sub-standard practice and too dominated by the professional interest, rather than that of the patient'.[71] Sir Liam recommended a further shake-up of the GMC. The Health and Social Care Act 2008 provided for a new independent body, the Office of the Health Professions Adjudicator (OHPA), which the previous administration intended would take

---

[68] GMC, *Changes to Registration Requirements for UK Doctors* (2009); GMC, *Revalidation: A Statement of Intent* (2010).

[69] See D Irvine, *A Doctors' Tale* (2003) Radcliffe Medical Press, in particular sections 3 and 4. Sir Donald Irvine was the President of the GMC from 1995 to 2002.

[70] Shipman Inquiry, *Safeguarding Patients: Lessons From the Past–Proposals for the Future* 5th report (Cm 6394) (2004) (hereafter *Shipman Inquiry*).

[71] DH, *CMO's Report, Good Doctors, Safer Patients: Proposals to Strengthen the System to Assure and Improve the Performance of Doctors and to Protect the Safety of Patients* (2006) (hereafter *Good Doctors, Safer Patients*), para 60. Published simultaneously was the DH, *The Regulation of Non-Medical Health Care Professionals* (2006). Though the two reach similar conclusions, there are divergences. A consultation period ran from July–November 2006.

over the adjudication of fitness to practise cases.[72] But the government are cutting down the number of arm's-length bodies. They announced in 2010 that the case for the OHPA was neither proportional nor appropriate. Instead, the GMC's processes should be 'strengthened'.[73] The GMC, it seems, will retain its adjudicatory role, albeit in a revised form. Mark Davies argues that, whilst the GMC has responded to challenges to its powers with inventiveness, reforms, such as revalidation, are increasingly state-led.[74] A watered-down state of self-regulation endures.

Composition of the General Medical Council

1.6 Who regulators are influences how confident the public will be in the process and objectivity of the regulatory framework. In 1983, the GMC comprised 104 members. The lay element was less than 25 per cent. Doctors chosen by their peers dominated the Council. Such a large Council is on any analysis an unwieldy organisation to govern any profession, and reforms gradually whittled down the numbers to the present-day position where the Council consists of twelve lay members and twelve medical members.[75]

So what does the GMC do? The Medical Act 1983 lists four principal functions of the GMC:

(1)   to provide advice for doctors on ethics and standards of professional conduct;
(2)   to oversee medical education;
(3)   to maintain a register of qualified doctors, license doctors and, probably from 2012, to 'revalidate' them;
(4)   to investigate and (in some form) adjudicate allegations about the fitness to practise of doctors.

Let us examine each in turn.

Advisory function

1.7 First, the Council is charged with providing advice for doctors on ethics and standards of professional conduct, standards of professional performance and medical ethics.[76] Reference to this advice is made throughout this book.

---

[72] Health and Social Care Act 2008, s 98.
[73] Ministerial Statement, HC Deb, 26 July 2010 c65–6WS. Discussed below 1.11.
[74] M Davies, 'The Demise of Professional Self-Regulation? Evidence from the "Ideal Type" Professions of Medicine and Law' (2010) 26(1) *Professional Negligence* 3, at 9.
[75] GMC (Constitution) Order 2008, SI 2008/2554.
[76] See Medical Act 1983, s 35, as amended by the 2002 Order (SI 2002/3135). At the time of writing there are twenty ethical guidelines promulgated by the GMC; see http://www.gmc-uk.org/guidance/ethical_guidance.asp.

The core guidance is contained in *Good Medical Practice*, which was first produced in 1995 and was comprehensively revised in 2006. The 2006 version emphasises the importance of partnership between doctors and patients, and places new weight on equality and diversity. Most importantly, it clarifies the standard of professional conduct which underpins the GMC's fitness to practise procedures. The aim is to achieve greater certainty and consistency in both patient expectations and doctors' professional standards.

Medical education

1.8 Second, the Council sets standards and outcomes for medical education.[77] In the past the GMC was responsible for undergraduate medical training and the first year of foundation training. The Postgraduate Medical and Education Training Board (PMETB) looked after the second year of foundation training and specialty training.

Following the Tooke report,[78] a merger took place in 2010[79] and the GMC became the sole regulator of medical education throughout the different stages of training. The PMETB was abolished in April 2010 and the GMC created three boards: the Undergraduate Board; Postgraduate Board; and the Continued Practice Board.

Requirements for undergraduate training are set out in *Tomorrow's Doctors*.[80] On completion of the medical degree, section 10A of the Medical Act 1983 requires that provisionally registered, newly qualified doctors receive two years of foundation training (F1 and F2) to bridge the gap between medical school and specialist or GP training.[81] At the end of F1, full registration and a licence to practise is dependent upon demonstration of outcomes set by the GMC's Education Committee. Year F2 is the doctor's first year as a fully registered, licensed doctor.

At the end of the F2 year, doctors compete for training in their chosen speciality or GP training. The Joint Royal Colleges of Physicians Training Board (JRCPTB) set specific standards of specialist training to complement the GMC's generic standards. Trainees are required to register with the JRCPTB so that their progress can be reviewed and they can be awarded a Certificate of Completion of Training (CCT). The CCT confirms that the doctor has

---

[77] GMC, *Tomorrow's Doctors: Recommendations on Undergraduate Medical Education* (2009).

[78] Professor Sir John Tooke, Final Report of the Independent Inquiry into Modernising Medical Careers (2008).

[79] The General and Specialist Practice (Education, Training and Qualifications) Order 2010, SI 2010/234.

[80] GMC, *Tomorrow's Doctors* (2009).

[81] The Medical Act 1983 (Amendment) and Miscellaneous Amendments Order 2006, SI 2006/1914, Art 21 amends s 5 of the Medical Act 1983 accordingly.

completed his training and can be entered onto the GP Register or the Specialist Register.

Maintaining a register

1.9 Third, the General Medical Council is charged with the maintenance of the 'list of registered medical practitioners' and provides licences to practise. Doctors listed on the medical register have full, provisional, specialist or GP registration.[82] The registers are accessible on-line. The GP register is a list of GPs eligible to work in the UK. It does not include GP registrars (trainee GPs). It provides information for patients and aids pre-employment checks. The Specialist Register identifies medical practitioners by their specialties, accreditation and qualifications. Equivalent qualifications from other member states of the EU must be recognised by the Joint Royal Colleges of Physicians Training Board.

The GMC assess the language skills and clinical competence of doctors coming from outside the EU.[83] In 2010 a German doctor, Daniel Ubani, on his first shift as an out-of-hours GP, prescribed a fatal dose of morphine to a pensioner. At a fitness to practise hearing, Dr Ubani was struck from the register. The GMC called for a change in the rules to allow them to assess doctors from the EU, a recommendation echoed by the Health Select Committee in 2011.[84] We await review of the relevant European Directive in 2012.

Registration alone used to be sufficient to permit a doctor to practise medicine and hold herself out as a medical practitioner. Amendments to the Medical Act 1983[85] additionally require that doctors hold a licence to practise.[86] The licence is granted by the GMC at registration and is required of any doctor, private or NHS, part- or full-time, if they wish to work in the NHS, write prescriptions or sign death certificates.

Doctors need to show that their fitness to practise is not impaired at the point of registration and licensing with the GMC. Failure to declare relevant factors could lead to the doctor being struck from the register and losing his licence to practise. Doctors are also required to carry professional indemnity or insurance cover from the point of registration and failure to do so could amount to impaired fitness to practise. Since 2010, doctors can appeal against decisions

---

[82] Both set up under SI 2003/1250, Pt IV. Categories of doctors eligible for inclusion in the specialist register and GP registers are set out in the Postgraduate Medical Education and Training Order 2010, SI 2010/473.

[83] The English language requirements changed on 1 February 2011. See http://www.gmc-uk.org.

[84] House of Commons Health Committee, *Revalidation of Doctors* HC557 (2011).

[85] The Medical Act 1983 (Amendment) Order 2002, SI 2002/3135, Pt V, inserts a new Pt IIIA 'Licence to Practise and Revalidation' into the Medical Act 1983.

[86] The General Medical Council (Licence to Practise) Regulations Order of Council 2009, SI 2009/2739.

to withdraw or refuse registration or a licence to practise under Schedule 3A to the Medical Act 1983.[87]

Revalidation

1.10 Licensing was the first step towards 'revalidation' whereby doctors are to be appraised to ensure their general fitness to practise and compliance with *Good Practice* guidance. The previous government planned that revalidation would be introduced as early as 2005,[88] but the 5th Report of the *Shipman Inquiry* highlighted a number of serious concerns.[89] The concept of revalidation had been watered down:[90]

> [R]evaluation (on a five-yearly basis) would involve a statement from a doctor's employer, confirming the lack of any significant concerns and documentary evidence of participation in an annual process of peer-appraisal. ... Furthermore, the consequences of failing to revalidate were not made explicit: would a practitioner have to cease to practise, or would they 'limp on' in substandard practice, through to the next revalidation cycle?

Consequently, in December 2004, Lord Warner announced that the scheme would be postponed pending the outcome of the CMO's consultation on medical regulation. The CMO recommended a more rigorous scheme of revalidation[91] involving separate evaluations for re-licensing and recertification. But this complex system was dropped in favour of a single evaluation whereby doctors would be appraised against the specific standards (which build on the GMC's generic standards) adopted in their specialist area. The GMC outlined plans and ran a consultation,[92] which revealed 'that revalidation is the right way forward but that it must be straightforward and proportionate and must not place excessive burdens on doctors or employers'.[93] A 'simpler and streamlined' revalidation process will be piloted in 2011. It is thought that revalidation will form a continuous assessment based largely on local systems of annual appraisal. Doctors will keep a portfolio of supporting information. New responsible officers will be created. Their statutory role will be to appraise doctors, usually every five years. Responsible officers will be senior doctors such as medical directors and they will rely on the annual appraisals, doctors' portfolios and clinical governance when advising the GMC as to whether the doctor in question is fit to be revalidated by virtue of having demonstrated his reaching the GMC's generic and specialist standards of good practice. The scheme is expected to be put in place in late 2012. The

---

[87] Under Medical Act 1983, Sch 3A (registration) and s 29F(1) (licence). The General Medical Council (Registration Appeals Panels Procedure) Rules Order of Council 2010, SI 2010/476 sets out the procedure.
[88] The Medical Act 1983 (Amendment) Order 2002, SI 2002/3135, Pt V.
[89] *Shipman Inquiry,* ch 26 and paras 27.261–27.262.
[90] As recognised by the CMO in *Good Doctors, Safer Patients,* para 50.
[91] CMO, *Medical Revalidation – Principles and Next Steps* (2008).
[92] GMC Consultation, *Revalidation: The Way Ahead* (2010).
[93] GMC, *Revalidation: A Statement of Intent* (2010), p 2.

House of Commons has promised to enhance scrutiny of the GMC in an attempt to prevent further slippage.[94] But will the new streamlined process differ significantly from the watered-down scheme criticised by Dame Janet and the CMO?

Disciplining doctors – fitness to practise

1.11 The doctor's employer may initiate disciplinary proceedings which are regulated by Department of Health issued Circulars[95] and aided by the National Clinical Assessment Services, which are currently part of the National Patient Safety Agency. The disciplinary procedures are exceedingly complex[96] and will not be dealt with in any detail here.

In addition, complaints about doctors – whether they emanate from patients, other doctors or their organisations – can be put to the GMC which may then investigate whether or not the doctor is fit to practise.[97] Criticisms of the complaints mechanisms led to calls for GMC 'affiliates' to respond to complaints at a local level and refer relevant cases to the GMC. Two successful pilot studies were conducted in 2008 based on thirty-five affiliated pairs (one clinician and one GMC employee) covering England.[98] However, it seems that a lack of funding may thwart the scheme.[99]

Once a complaint reaches the GMC, there are two stages to the fitness to practise process – investigation and adjudication. Currently, the GMC oversees both stages. The previous administration sought to change this, in order to make the two stages independent of one another but, as we shall see, the current government proposes less radical reform.

The format of fitness to practise proceedings was reformed in 2004. The separate streams of health, performance and conduct were abandoned and complaints about doctors were analysed 'in the round'. The aim was to create a general overview of the doctor's fitness to practise. Under section 35C(2) of the Medical Act 1983, as amended, impairment can result from all or any of the following:

[94] House of Commons Health Committee, *Revalidation of Doctors* HC557 (2011).
[95] See Restriction of Practice and Exclusion from Work Directions (2003) and Maintaining High Professional Standards in the Modern NHS: A Framework for the Initial Handling of Concerns About Doctors and Dentists in the NHS, HSC 2003/012, updated 2005 to form the Directions on Disciplinary Procedures 2005.
[96] See *Mezey v South West London & St George's Mental Health NHS Trust* [2010] EWCA Civ 293. discussed in A White, 'What the Doctor Ordered' (2010) 154(19) *Sol Jol* 17.
[97] Alternatively a complaint can be made through the NHS complaints process outlined in ch 9.
[98] GMC, *GMC Affiliates Pilot Studies Launched* (website) accessible at: http://www.gmc-uk.org/GMCtoday_Affiliates_article_oct08.pdf_25397660.pdf.
[99] P Middlemiss, 'GMC affiliates "Improve Handling of Complaints"' (2010) *Healthcare Republic*, 5 February.

(a)   misconduct;
(b)   deficient professional performance;
(c)   a conviction or caution in the British Islands for a criminal offence, or a conviction elsewhere for an offence which, if committed in England and Wales, would constitute a criminal offence;
(d)   adverse physical or mental health; or
(e)   a determination by a body in the United Kingdom responsible under any enactment for the regulation of a health or social care profession to the effect that his fitness to practise as a member of that profession is impaired, or a determination by a regulatory body elsewhere to the same effect.

At the investigation stage, the case examiners (one medical and one lay) can refer the doctor to an interim orders panel where there is a clear need to protect patients or the public interest.[100] The panel has the power to impose an interim order restricting or suspending the doctor's right to practise pending the full investigation.[101] Where the public interest is not threatened, the GMC has since advised that a single test which emphasises the GMC's duty to the public is applied to determine whether a doctor should be referred to a fitness to practise panel for a full hearing:[102]

> The investigation committee or case examiner must have in mind the GMC's duty to act in the public interest, which includes the protection of patients and maintaining public confidence in the profession, in considering whether there is a realistic prospect of establishing that a doctor's fitness to practise is impaired to a degree justifying action on registration.

At this stage the GMC may issue a warning:[103] a measure introduced for cases which call for an official response, but which are not serious enough to justify restrictions on the doctor's registration, when either 'there has been a significant departure from *Good Medical Practice*' or 'a performance assessment has indicated a significant cause for concern'.

If the case proceeds to the adjudication stage, at the time of writing the GMC panellists apply the following, much-simplified single test:

> Do the findings we have made show that the doctor's fitness to practise is impaired to a degree justifying action on registration?[104]

If the answer is 'no', then, in common with the investigation stage, a warning can be issued[105] or no further action taken. If the answer is 'yes', then the panel have three options:

---

[100]   Medical Act 1983, s 35C(8).
[101]   Medical Act 1983, s 41A.
[102]   GMC, *Making Decisions on Cases at the End of the Investigation Stage: Guidance for Case Examiners and the Investigation Committee* (2006), para 14.
[103]   Medical Act 1983, s 35C(6).
[104]   Media Briefing Paper: *The GMC Reforms: Making Fitness to Practise Fit for Practice* (6 December 2004) GMC.
[105]   Medical Act 1983, s 35D(3).

(1) erasure from the medical register (except in health cases),
(2) suspension from the register for a maximum of twelve months,
(3) conditional registration based on compliance with requirements imposed by the panel.[106]

The fitness to practise panel must take care to ensure that conditions do not effectively amount to suspension. In *Udom v GMC*,[107] a consultant anaesthetist's fitness to practise was found to be impaired by reason of a combination of health issues and clinical conduct. Conditions were applied giving him an observational role which did not require registration. He successfully appealed on the basis that this effectively stopped him from practising medicine.

In some cases, the facts will be disputed. The burden of proof rests with the GMC which makes the allegations. The Health and Social Care Act 2008 amended Part 3 of the Health Act 1999 to replace the criminal standard of proof (which was thought to be inappropriate and potentially too lenient on doctors) with a civil standard.[108] Doctors are now judged on the balance of probabilities rather than establishing proof 'beyond reasonable doubt'. The civil standard is a sliding standard which can be flexibly applied.[109] The more serious the matter, the greater the degree of probability required.

There is a long history of criticism of the GMC's handling of fitness to practise cases. Public hearings are slow and stressful for both patients and doctors. In January 2011 the GMC launched a consultation[110] proposing to speed up the fitness to practise process and reduce reliance on public hearings. At the end of an investigation, where doctors consent to the imposition of sanctions or measures to protect the public, the GMC propose that a public hearing might be unnecessary. In addition the Council suggests that certain crimes (the obvious one being murder) might carry a presumption that the doctor's name be erased from the register.

A more significant problem was highlighted in 2004 when the *Shipman Inquiry* recommended that the GMC investigate the complaint, but hand over adjudication to an independent body. Allowing the GMC both to investigate and adjudicate has been likened to allowing the police to arbitrate criminal proceedings. Clearer separation of powers would enhance the confidence of both patients and doctors, whilst potentially reducing costs and speeding up the process. In line with these recommendations, as we have seen, the previous government proposed that the GMC would hand over its responsibility for adjudicating fitness to practise cases to the Office of the Health Professions Adjudicator (OHPA), an independent body created by the Health and Social

---

[106] Medical Act 1983, s 35D(2).
[107] [2009] EWHC 3242 (Admin).
[108] Health Act 1999, s 60A.
[109] *R (N) v Mental Health Review Tribunal* [2006] QB 468, CA.
[110] GMC, *Reform of the Fitness to Practise Procedures at the GMC – Changes to the Way We Deal with Cases at the End of an Investigation* (closes April 2011).

Care Act 2008. The GMC would retain its role as investigator of allegations about fitness to practise and decide whether or not to refer the individual to a hearing. It would also issue guidance on standards and sanctions which the OHPA would use when sentencing doctors.

However, the government is not convinced that the OHPA will offer sufficient benefit to justify its expense. The CHRE's 2010 audit[111] of the GMC's fitness to practise procedures pronounced them robust and effective.[112] The reforms, it seems, are having a positive effect. A consultation was launched in 2010,[113] proposing a new Doctors' Disciplinary Tribunal (DDT). The tribunal, which would be set up by the GMC, would have an independently appointed President, shorter hearings and improved case management. It would be *more* independent, but according to the OHPA it would not be independent enough. The government proposes to abolish the OHPA in its Health and Social Care Bill.[114] It seems that the GMC will retain its adjudicatory function for the time being.

Appeals to the High Court and the Council for Healthcare Regulatory Excellence[115]

1.12   A doctor whose fitness to practise is found to be impaired has a right of appeal to the High Court under s 40 of the Medical Act 1983. The doctor can apply for termination of suspension pursuant to the Medical Act, or make an application for judicial review. There is some confusion as to which route is preferable but it is clear that the court has the jurisdiction to interfere with the fitness to practise panel's decision.[116]

The court will decide if the decision of the fitness to practise panel was 'wrong'.[117] For example, the panel may have acted improperly or the sanction might be disproportionate. In the latter case, the court is entitled to prioritise the public interest – in particular public confidence and the standing of the profession.[118] The court has a range of powers. It can dismiss the appeal, quash, amend or substitute the direction, or remit the case back to the GMC fitness to practise panel.[119]

---

[111] In accordance with the Health and Social Care Act 2008, s 115.

[112] CHRE, Fitness to Practise Audit Report (2010), p 27.

[113] DH, *Fitness to Practise Adjudication for Health Professionals: Assessing Different Mechanisms for Delivery* (2010).

[114] Bill HC 132, cl 215.

[115] The Health and Social Care Bill 2011 proposes to rename the Council for Healthcare Regulatory Excellence the Professional Standards Authority for Health and Social Care and make it self-funding.

[116] *Sosanya v GMC* [2009] EWHC 2814 (Admin) per Davis J, para 2.

[117] *GMC v Meadow* [2006] EWCA Civ 1390, paras 125–128.

[118] See *Robert Allan Odes v GMC* [2010] EWHC 552 (Admin); *Cheatle v GMC* (2009) EWHC 645 (Admin).

[119] Medical Act 1983, s 40(7).

Doctors can appeal if they feel they have been dealt with harshly.[120] So too the CHRE may appeal to the High Court under a section 29 order if a decision appears unduly lenient.[121] In *Council for the Regulation of Healthcare Professionals v GMC and Ruscillo* the Court of Appeal stated:

> The test of undue leniency in this context must, we think, involve considering whether, having regard to the material facts, the decision reached has due regard for the safety of the public and the reputation of the profession.[122]

There were no court judgments on CHRE cases in 2009/10, but there were six in 2008/9 (a total of 0.36 per cent of cases referred) – of which five were settled and one appeal was dismissed.[123] In 2006 the CHRE successfully appealed the GMC's finding that locum GP Dr Biswas was not guilty of serious professional misconduct following a diagnostic error following which the patient died.[124] The case was sent back to the GMC fitness to practise panel which suspended his registration. In 2009 an appeal was dismissed when an allegation of sexual misconduct was made against a consultant, Dr Khanna, in relation to a dental student and a junior house officer. The suspension of registration was not found to be unduly lenient.[125]

Section 29 orders have caused some disquiet on the basis that the criteria for determining undue leniency include the 'maintenance of public confidence in regulation' which might potentially go beyond the merits of the case.[126] In 2004, the Court of Appeal clarified the CHRE's powers.[127] Not only may it refer cases to the High Court when it is of the view that regulators have acted too leniently in applying 'penalties', but it may also do so when the regulator acquits a healthcare professional. Thus, even if a doctor is acquitted by the GMC, the CHRE may refer him to the High Court which may impose a sanction. Mason and Laurie point out that the element of double jeopardy such doctors are subjected to has potential to offend their rights under Article 6 of the European Convention on Human Rights.[128]

---

[120] See for example *Southall v GMC* [2009] EWHC 1155 (Admin), discussed below at **8.14**.

[121] National Health Service Reform and Health Care Professions Act 2002, s 29.

[122] [2005] 1 WLR 717 at 73.

[123] CHRE, *2008/2009 S 29 Statistical Summary* accessible at http://www.chre.org.uk, para 6.

[124] *Council for the Regulation of Health Care Professionals v GMC & Anr* [2006] EWHC 464.

[125] *R (Council for the Regulation of Healthcare Professionals) v GMC* [2009] EWHC 596 (Admin).

[126] See, for example, Editorial, 'Concerns Raised About CHRE's Powers and Its Use of Spin Doctors' (2004) 273 *The Pharmaceutical Journal* 578.

[127] [2005] 1 WLR 717.

[128] J K Mason and G T Laurie, *Mason and McCall Smith's Law and Medical Ethics* (8th edn, 2010) OUP (hereafter *Mason and McCall Smith*), p 18. And see A Samanta and J Samanta, 'Referring GMC Decisions to the High Court' (2005) 330 *BMJ* 103.

Regulating the NHS

1.13 The first part of this chapter examined the regulation of individual doctors. We now turn to methods by which NHS organisations are regulated.

Supervising, managing and protecting employees

1.14 Individual doctors face sanctions when they fall short of good medical practice. But what of the employing organisation? Poor treatment often has several causes. Poor doctors are created by poor systems. In 2000, a thirty-one-year-old father was admitted to hospital for minor knee surgery. The operation was a success, but he went on to develop an infection which resulted in toxic shock syndrome from which, tragically, he died. Doctors Misra and Srivastava had failed to diagnose the infection and were convicted of gross negligence manslaughter in 2003,[129] and suspended from the medical register by the GMC in 2005. In 2006, Southampton University Hospital NHS Trust became the first NHS trust to be prosecuted under the Health and Safety at Work Act 1974 for failing to manage the two junior doctors adequately. The trust pleaded guilty to a charge of improper supervision and was fined £100,000 and ordered to pay £10,000 costs.[130]

The Corporate Manslaughter and Corporate Homicide Act 2007,[131] whilst not creating any new duties, may improve accountability of companies and organisations, including healthcare businesses,[132] for fatalities which result from system failures. Penalties include fines, publicity orders (whereby the organisation must publicise its prosecution) and remedial orders (where the organisation must take steps to ensure the mistake will not be repeated).[133]

Organisations must safeguard their patients, but also have a duty to protect their employees. Work-related stress amongst NHS staff is widespread.[134] Long working-hours exacerbated the problem. The European Working Time

---

[129] See below at **7.22**. See also O Quick, 'Medicine, Mistakes and Manslaughter: A Criminal Combination' (2010) *Cambridge Law Journal* 186.

[130] *R v Southampton University Hospital NHS Trust* [2006] EWCA Crim 2971.

[131] See below at **7.24**.

[132] C Dyer, 'New Law Puts NHS Trusts at Risk of Charges of Corporate Manslaughter' (2008) 336 *BMJ* 741; R Craig, 'Thou Shall Do No Murder – a discussion paper on the Corporate Manslaughter and Corporate Homicide Act 2007' (2009) 30 *Company Lawyer Compensation Law* 17; A Samuels, 'The Corporate Manslaughter and Corporate Homicide Act 2007: How Will it Affect the Medical World?' (2007) 75(2) *Medico-Legal Journal* 72.

[133] The first prosecution under the Act was *R v Eaton & Cotswold Geotechnical Holdings Ltd* (2011) (unreported at the time of writing). See http://www.cps.gov.uk/news/press_releases/107_11/.

[134] See BBC News, 'Work Stress Finding in NHS Survey' 6 March 2006 (available at http://news.bbc.co.uk).

Directive[135] imposed a 48-hour week, but this puts pressures on the finite resources of the NHS. More doctors are needed to fill the rotas; there are more time-consuming hand-overs to make at the end of a shift; and there is less time for training.[136] The problem was aggravated by the European Court of Justice rulings in *SiMAP*[137] and *Jaeger*.[138] On-call staff resident at work out-of-hours are considered to be 'working' whilst on duty, whether or not they are called to the bedside. In 2010 NHS Medical Education England reviewed the effects of the Directive on medical training, concluding that the problems are worst when the trainee doctor is involved in emergency care or has a significant 'out-of-hours' workload.[139] The Royal College of Surgeons has spoken out against the 'lunacies' of the Directive which, it feels, adversely affects both training and patient safety.[140]

Governance

1.15 NHS organisations are responsible for a rigorous system of clinical governance, the central aim being to ensure continuous quality improvement and consistency between organisations. A formal requirement for clinical audit in the NHS was introduced in 1989.[141] But the system was found lacking by the *Bristol Inquiry*[142] which recommended that clinical audit should be at the core of a system of local monitoring of performance.

Since that time there has been a bewildering array of reforms designed to enhance and monitor quality in the NHS. Historically, the Commission for Health Improvement issued 'star ratings' to providers from 2003. This body was replaced with the Commission for Healthcare Audit and Inspection (the 'Healthcare Commission') in 2004[143] which abandoned the star ratings in favour of an 'annual health check'. Following the White Paper *High Quality*

---

[135] 93/104/EC. Implemented in SI 1998/1833.

[136] Trainee doctors were initially excluded from the regulations, until the Working Time (Amendment) (No 2) Regulations 2009, SI 2009/2766. Extended to fifty-two hours in special circumstances until 2011: the Working Time (Amendment) Regulations 2009, SI 2009/1567.

[137] *Case C-303/98 Sindicato de Medicos de Asistencia Publica (SiMAP) v Conselleria de Sanidad y Consumo de la Generalidad Valenciana* [2000] ECR 1-7963.

[138] *Case C-151/02 Landeshauptstadt Kiel v Norbert Jaeger* [2003] ECR I-8389.

[139] Prof Sir J Temple, *Time for Training: A Review of the Impact of the European Working Time Directive on the Quality of Training* (2010).

[140] See http://www.rcseng.ac.uk/news/rcs-response-to-department-of-health-announcement-of-review-into-medical-training-under-ewtd.

[141] Secretaries of State for Social Services, Wales, Northern Ireland and Scotland, *Working for Patients* Cm. 555 (1989) HMSO.

[142] See above at **1.1**.

[143] Set up under the Health and Social Care (Community Health and Standards) Act 2003, s 41. The Healthcare Commission incorporates the Commission for Health Improvement, the Mental Health Act Commission and the National Care Standards Commission which oversaw the independent healthcare sector.

Care For All,[144] the Health and Social Care Act 2008 established the independent Care Quality Commission (CQC) which, in April 2009, took over the regulation of both health and social care, in NHS, private and voluntary organisations.[145] From April 2010 all providers of adult healthcare were required to register with the CQC. Registration is dependent upon demonstration that the provider reaches outcome-based standards.[146] The registration status of trusts is published on the CQC website. Monitoring is achieved through audit, annual quality accounts[147] and unannounced visits. Failure leads to meaningful sanctions.[148]

The CQC has a central role in the planned NHS reforms announced in the White Paper, *Equity and Excellence: Liberating the NHS*. The government seeks to reform the regulatory system in order to reduce bureaucracy and 'set providers free' to improve outcomes and respond to local needs.[149] The Health and Social Care Bill 2011 proposes decisive steps in that direction. We have seen that foundation trust status will be extended to all NHS trusts. Monitor, the independent regulator of foundation trusts, will have an expanded role covering the economic regulation of health and social care in England; setting prices and promoting competition in addition to overseeing foundation trust status. Following consultation, Monitor will set a national tariff stating which services the NHS will provide and how to determine prices. Monitor and the CQC will operate a joint licensing system for NHS providers. To obtain a license from Monitor, providers will need to demonstrate successful registration with the CQC and compliance with conditions relating to Monitor's role in setting prices and promoting competition. General licences will occasionally be supplemented with special licences whereby Monitor can set down extra conditions, to promote continuity of care, for example. If the conditions of a licence are flouted, Monitor will be able to impose fines or revoke the licence. Licensing applies only to NHS providers. Providers of other services, such as adult social care and private health care, will still require registration with the CQC.

[144] DH, *High Quality Care for All – NHS Next Stage Review Final Report*, Cm 7432 (2008).

[145] The Care Quality Commission (Additional Functions) Regulations 2009, SI 2009/410; The Care Quality Commission (Membership) Regulations 2008, SI 2008/2252.

[146] Care Quality Commission, *Making a Difference to People's Lives through Modern Health Care and Social Care Regulation* (2010). The six standards include: Information and Involvement; Personalized Care, Treatment and Support; Safeguarding and Safety; Suitability of Staffing; Quality and Management; and Suitability of Management.

[147] Health Act 2009, ss 8–10; the National Health Service (Quality Accounts) Regulations 2010, SI 2010/279.

[148] The Health and Social Care Act 2008, ss 17(1), 18(2) and 31 – sanctions include conditions, cancellation or suspension of registration. Under s 35 contraventions of the regulations is an offence punishable with a fine up to £50,000.

[149] DH, *Liberating the NHS: Regulating Healthcare Providers* (2010).

Specialist regulators

1.16 As we have seen, work-based regulation involves a system of clinical governance and performance management. Much of this sort of 'regulation' has been decentralised. To ensure common standards across the country, special 'regulators', such as Monitor and the CQC, may be created to monitor local activity. Most are independent of government, at least in theory.

Various non-departmental public bodies, created when certain kinds of medicine were deemed to pose particular risks or aroused exceptional ethical controversy, were casualties of an arm's-length bodies review conducted in 2004.[150] The Xenotransplantation Interim Regulation Authority (UKXIRA), Public Health Laboratory Service and the National Biological Standards Board, to name a few, were subsumed within other arm's-length bodies. In 2010 a second arm's-length bodies review[151] recommended even more sweeping changes (a 'bonfire of the quangos') to cut costs and reduce bureaucracy. At the time of writing, the Public Bodies Bill[152] is making its way through Parliament, amid criticism of its radical nature. If enacted, it will create the legislative framework whereby around 400 of the 900 or so existing public bodies (many of which were set up by primary legislation) could be amended, reformed or abolished through mere ministerial order.[153] Following criticisms from two House of Lords Select Committee Reports,[154] the government was defeated in a vote to amend the Bill to introduce greater restriction on ministerial powers in November 2010.

The Department of Health divides arm's-length bodies into three groups.[155] First is an executive agency, the Medicines and Healthcare Products Regulatory Agency (MHRA), which was set up in 2003 to license and regulate medicines and devices. We examine the role of the MHRA in licensing products in chapter 10 and in monitoring and regulation of clinical research in chapter 15. In the latter case, regulation by the MHRA is complemented by internal NHS research and development governance arrangements and by independent research ethics committee scrutiny. In addition, the MHRA is advised by specialist boards and a range of expert advisory groups. The MHRA will retain a central role in the reformed NHS.

Second, 'special health authorities' include (amongst others) the NHS Litigation Authority (chapter 8), which is being subjected to an industry review to

---

[150] DH, *Reconfiguring the Department of Health's Arm's Length Bodies* (2004) ref: 3552.
[151] DH, *Liberating the NHS: Report of the Arm's Length Bodies Review* (2010).
[152] HL Bill 25 of 2010–11.
[153] See also N Hawkins, 'This is No Way to Cull the Quangos' (2010) 341 *BMJ* 808.
[154] House of Lords Constitution Select Committee, *The Public Bodies Bill* (2010); House of Lords Delegated Powers and Regulatory Reform Committee, *The Public Bodies Bill* (2010).
[155] DH, *Arm's Length Bodies*, accessible at: http://www.dh.gov.uk/en/Aboutus/OrganisationsthatworkwithDH/Armslengthbodies/DH_4105577.

see if it can be run more efficiently; NICE (chapters 2 and 3), which currently produces guidance for the NHS on public health, health technologies and clinical practice; and the National Patient Safety Agency (NPSA) (chapter 15) which currently oversees the National Research Ethics Service, and monitors the safety of care through reporting and analysing 'near misses' involving NHS patients. The NPSA is expected to be abolished in 2013[156] and its activities taken over by a new research regulator, the Health Research Agency, and the NHS Commissioning Board.

Third, 'non-departmental public bodies' include four examples which have already been given: 'Monitor' regulates foundation trusts and will, in future, set tariff levels, regulate and (together with the CQC) license providers of NHS care; the CHRE regulates professional bodies such as the GMC. Whilst it will survive the reforms, it will need to become self-funding and is unlikely to remain a non-departmental public body;[157] the quality inspectorate, the CQC will continue to register, license and monitor health and adult social care providers; and the new NHS Commissioning Board will support Commissioning Consortia (CC) and hold them to account. In addition, the government proposes that NICE is re-established as a non-departmental public body and renamed the National Institute for Health and Care Excellence. It will produce (and is producing[158]) around 150 specific 'Quality Standards' which will aid the proposed NHS Commissioning Board when supporting and incentivising CC (when they replace PCTs in 2013). These bodies must account to the government for the use of their resources and publish annual accounts.

A new arm's-length body – HealthWatch England – expected to be launched nationally in 2012, will sit within the CQC. Local HealthWatch organisations (which will replace Local Involvement Networks) are intended to enhance patient involvement in commissioning decisions, and promote complaints advocacy. Anyone with concerns will be able to relate them to HealthWatch England which will be able to propose CQC investigations of providers.

Other non-departmental public bodies include the Human Tissue Authority (HTA)[159] (chapters 17 and 18) and the Human Fertilisation and Embryology Authority (HFEA),[160] (chapters 12 and 13). The 2004 review recommended that a new Regulatory Authority for Tissues and Embryos take on the combined role of both the HTA and HFEA, but this plan was later abandoned. The government now intend to abolish both Authorities and divide their functions between a new research regulator, (which the Academy of Medical

---

[156] Health and Social Care Bill 2011, Pt 10.

[157] As we have seen, it is proposed in the Health and Social Care Bill 2011 that the CHRE is renamed the Professional Standards Authority for Health and Social Care.

[158] D Cohen, 'NICE Issues the First of 150 Quality Standards for the NHS' (2010) 341 *BMJ* 3536.

[159] See Human Tissue Act 2004, ss 13–15 and Sch 2.

[160] Created by the Human Fertilisation and Embryology Act 1990, s 5.

Science suggests be named the Health Research Agency[161]) and other arm's-length bodies, notably the CQC. This may well dilute both the necessary specialist advice in relation to controversial areas of medicine and suppress the lay voice now prominent in bodies such as the HFEA.

Whither the NHS?

1.17   The NHS does not stand still, nor should it. It is an organisation for the people and must evolve to take account of changing needs. But the scale and pace of reform, according to an article in *The Times*, based on a letter from six unions, including the BMA and Royal College of Nursing, 'run the risk of disaster'.[162] We have briefly examined systems of regulation at local, organisational, and national levels. Regulation serves a variety of purposes which do not always coincide. Economic accountability may result in a health service that represents value for money; resource allocation decisions and their local variations will inevitably result in injustice to some. Aggrieved patients may look to the law for redress, both if they are denied treatment, or if they are harmed by sub-standard treatment. There remains much to do to ensure confidence in both the 'new' systems for regulating medical professions, and the NHS itself.

---

[161] See Academy of Medical Sciences, *A New Pathway for the Regulation and Governance of Health Research* (January 2011), chaired by Sir Michael Rawlins, discussed in chs 12 and 15.

[162] R Watson, S Lister, 'Reforms to the NHS "Run the Risk of Disaster"' (2011) *The Times*, 17 January.

Chapter 2

DOCTORS' RESPONSIBILITIES: PATIENTS' RIGHTS

2.1 When we are ill we want to be treated by competent doctors – that is why debates about regulation of the medical profession are so crucial. However, we may also wish to assert our own rights, especially in the context of decision-making. Patients are no longer content to be passive recipients even of 'good' care. They want a say in what 'good' care comprises. The pace of medical developments is such that, particularly in the context of reproductive medicine and genetics, new questions surface daily around the implications of certain kinds of treatment. These may concern entitlement to treatment, or how far choices about treatment belong to individual patients alone. Or they may focus on the role of the state. Or the interests of commerce may be involved. How does the law begin to address patient rights in 2011? What relevance does the Human Rights Act 1998 have to medicine?

Medical law, Ian Kennedy and Andrew Grubb declared,[1] is essentially '. . . a sub-set of human rights law'. The fundamental nature of the relationship between doctors and patients amply proves their point. At stake within the realm of medical law is our right to make our own decisions about how we live our lives and how we die. Our interests in privacy and in family life, in having or not having children, are central to our dealings with health professionals. So the Human Rights Act 1998 might be expected to transform healthcare law radically.

However, the European Convention on Human Rights (the Convention to which the 1998 Act gives domestic effect) addresses only a limited range of rights. There is no *positive* right to health care; there is no equivalent to Article 25 in the Universal Declaration of Human Rights. In a number of instances, what the Convention confers are *negative* rights – ie prohibitions against certain kinds of infringement of basic freedoms, although the jurisprudence of the Convention is moving to a greater recognition of *positive* rights. The Human Rights Act does not (whatever the media says) incorporate the Convention

---

[1] I Kennedy and A Grubb, *Medical Law* (3rd edn, 2000) OUP, p 3.

into English law. It renders the Convention enforceable against *public authorities*. The Act is relevant to disputes about enforced treatment or arguments that the government is violating patients' privacy. Where what is at stake is a failure by the NHS to provide certain sorts of care, or concerns about allowing, for example, insurers to demand medical details about you, the utility of the Act will need to be tested. The European Court of Human Rights is an international court which sits in Strasbourg and hears applications from individuals and member states on potential breaches of the Convention. The Court is divided into various Chambers, which can make a judgment or, in very important or controversial cases, relinquish the case to the Grand Chamber. Following a Chamber judgment, parties have three months to request referral to the Grand Chamber before the decision is considered final. The Grand Chamber can reconsider the case, but referrals are accepted only on an exceptional basis.

Even when a patient can bring her claim squarely within the ambit of a Convention right, she may find that the violation of her right is found to be justified. Many Convention rights are qualified. A good example is Article 8(1) – the right to respect for private and family life. In certain circumstances, Article 8(2) provides that infringement of the right may be justifiable; a violation of a patient's privacy could be held justified on grounds of public health, or for the protection of health or morals, as long as that infringement is proportionate. That means that interference with the individual's right must be shown to be 'necessary in a democratic society'. Moreover, Articles of the Convention may 'contradict' each other in certain circumstances: for example, Article 2 (life) and Article 8 (privacy). Finally, the jurisprudence of the European Court of Human Rights expressly endorses a doctrine oddly entitled the 'margin of appreciation'. That is, national jurisdictions will be allowed a degree of freedom in defining their own criteria of public policy (morality).[2] English courts will still enjoy some degree of discretion to determine English views of ethical dilemmas in medicine.

Nor should you expect the European Court of Human Rights itself to be startlingly radical in relation to health care. Many European countries adopt a conservative approach to healthcare rights. For example, in relation to fertility treatment and embryology, France restricts access to heterosexual couples where the woman is of normal childbearing age, and Italy enacted legislation radically curtailing options for fertility treatment and effectively giving the force of law to Roman Catholic doctrine.[3] Be wary of arguments that English law violates the Convention where a consequence would be that other European countries are also in breach. Remember that as the supreme arbiter of the Convention, the European Court of Human Rights is an international court with judges representing several jurisdictions.

---

[2]   See *A B and C v Ireland* [2010] ECHR 25579/05, discussed below at **2.10**.
[3]   See R Fenton, 'Catholic Doctrine Versus Women's Rights: The New Italian Law on Assisted Reproduction' (2006) 14 *Medical Law Review* 73.

It should be also noted that, in practice, English courts referred to, and deferred to, the Human Rights Convention for several years prior to 1998, in developing the common law. The Human Rights Act 1998 does not replace or eliminate existing common law principles. Albeit the common law relating to health care has developed piecemeal, with an apparent emphasis on wrongs rather than rights, in many instances the existing law may suffice to vindicate rights endorsed in the Convention. Decisions of the English courts so far that address the Human Rights Act tend not to declare new rights, but review whether the existing common law 'rights' are sufficient in the light of the Convention.

How the Human Rights Act 1998 works[4]

2.2   Understanding how the Human Rights Act works is crucially important to assess how the Act may affect healthcare law. As we have noted, the Act does not directly incorporate the Human Rights Convention. In a claim against a private litigant, the claimant cannot sue for violation of Convention rights. The Act, first, requires that primary and subordinate legislation be interpreted where possible in a way which is compatible with Convention rights[5] and renders it 'unlawful for a public authority to act in a way which is incompatible with a Convention right'.[6]

'Convention rights' are the fundamental rights and freedoms[7] set out in Articles 2 to 12 and 14 of the Convention, Articles 1 to 3 of the First Protocol (concerning rights to property, education and free elections) and Articles 1 and 2 of the Sixth Protocol (abolishing the death penalty). Section 11 of the Act makes it crystal clear that Convention rights are in addition to, not in substitution for, rights and freedoms already endorsed at common law. It may seem odd that no express provision of the Act requires that judges develop the common law in a manner consistent with Convention rights. However, as noted above, English judges already, wherever possible, seek to ensure that the common law is consistent with such rights. More importantly, section 6 of the Act, which makes it unlawful for any public authority to act in a way incompatible with Convention rights, provides that courts are classified as public authorities. A judge hearing a patient's claim must, by virtue of section 6, consider compatibility with Convention rights and ensure consistency between common law and Convention rights.

However, the domestic rules on precedent are unaffected. If a decision of the Court of Appeal contradicts a decision of the European Court of Human Rights, the Court of Appeal in subsequent cases is bound by its previous decision. Only a higher court – the Supreme Court in this example – could hold that

---

[4]   An excellent introductory text to the Act is: J Wadham and H Mountfield, C Gallagher, E Prochaska, *Blackstone's Guide to the Human Rights Act 1998* (5th edn, 2009) OUP.

[5]   Human Rights Act 1998, s 3.

[6]   Human Rights Act 1998, ss 6–8.

[7]   Human Rights Act 1998, s 7.

the Court of Appeal case was wrongly decided on the basis that it conflicts with a decision in the European Court of Human Rights.[8] For example, when Debbie Purdy argued that a lack of guidance on assisted suicide breached her rights under Article 8, the Court of Appeal[9] held that they were bound by the House of Lords decision in *Pretty*[10] where it had been found that Article 8(1) was not engaged under these circumstances. This is despite the fact that, subsequently, the European Court of Human Rights found that Diane Pretty's Article 8(1) rights *were* engaged.[11] It was for the House of Lords (in their final decision before the Supreme Court was established) to 'release the knot'. In a landmark ruling, the Law Lords allowed Debbie Purdy's appeal, so aligning domestic law and the Strasbourg jurisprudence.[12]

Not only do the rules of precedent delay the application of Strasbourg rulings in domestic cases, but section 2(1) of the Human Rights Act requires that domestic courts must '*take into account*' European Court of Human Rights jurisprudence, not follow it slavishly. The court can provide reasons why a Strasbourg decision should not be followed where aspects of the domestic law were not fully appreciated.[13]

Similarly, where a claim alleging violation of a Convention Right involves legislation, section 3 of the Act requires any court or tribunal to seek to interpret that rule in a way which is compatible with the relevant Convention right. However, if such an interpretation is not possible, the courts are not granted powers to strike down legislation. The judicial role remains limited by doctrines of Parliamentary sovereignty.[14] Section 4(2) provides that:

> If the court is satisfied that the provision is incompatible with a Convention right, it may make a declaration of that incompatibility.

The government should then act to amend legislation to 'cure' the relevant incompatibility. Section 10 enables them to do so by secondary legislation making a 'remedial order'. Failure to act to remove the stated incompatibility would give rise to a claim against the UK before the European Court of Human Rights at Strasbourg. The dissatisfied patient could bring another claim suing the government itself.

This can be illustrated by considering a controversial provision of the Human Fertilisation and Embryology Act 1990 which was the subject of a declaration

---

8   *Kay v Lambeth London Borough Council, Price v Leeds City Council* [2006] UKHL 10. Applied in *Johnson v Havering London Borough Council and Secretary of State Affairs* [2007] EWCA Civ 26.

9   *R (on the application of Purdy) v DPP* [2009] EWCA Civ 92.

10 *R (Pretty) v DPP* [2002] 1 AC 800, HL.

11 *Pretty v UK* (Application No 2346/02) (2002) 35 EHRR 1.

12 *R (on the application of Purdy) v DPP* [2009] UKHL 44.

13 *R v Horncastle* [2009] UKSC 14.

14 For an introductory account of how the Act works, see H Fenwick, G Phillipson, R Masterman, *Judicial Reasoning Under the Human Rights Act* (2011) CUP.

of incompatibility. Section 28(6)(b) of the Act, prior to its amendment by the Human Fertilisation and Embryology Act 2008, provided that if the sperm of any man was used after his death, he was not to be treated as the father of the child. Diane Blood[15] fought a long battle to be able to undergo insemination with her deceased husband's sperm. She ultimately gave birth to two sons after fertility treatment abroad. Section 28(6)(b) meant that the boys' birth certificates recorded the father as 'unknown'. Mrs Blood and her sons succeeded in their contention that the Act violated their rights to respect for private and family life endorsed by Article 8 and, in response, Parliament enacted the Human Fertilisation and Embryology (Deceased Fathers) Act 2003.[16] The 2003 Act is now repealed but the 1990 Act has been amended to the same effect.[17]

For the healthcare professional, the most crucial element of the Act is the provision that 'Convention rights' are directly enforceable against public authorities, and that an individual who considers that her rights have been violated by a public authority can sue for damages. Where an individual considers that a public authority has acted in breach of Convention rights, a number of rather different outcomes must be considered. First, in many cases, the self-same rights conferred by the Convention are already recognised by the law of torts. For example, Article 5 provides for a right to liberty and security and protects the citizen against arbitrary detention. The ancient tort of false imprisonment protects that same fundamental interest. A patient alleging unlawful detention in hospital may not need to resort to claiming a breach of Article 5. He can sue in false imprisonment. In determining whether his detention was lawful, the court will be mindful of the provisions of Article 5 and the jurisprudence of the European Court of Human Rights.

The position is more complex when a Convention right is not so well established in domestic law. Privacy was not, though the common law is developing rapidly. The claimant might then choose to bring his claim directly under the Act alleging breach of Article 8 which requires respect for private and family life. If he elects for a Convention remedy alone, he can sue under the Act only if the defendant is a public authority. Were we to discover that the Department of Health was bugging our offices, suing a government department would be straightforward. What if a tabloid newspaper splashed our medical history all over its front page? There is an argument that the newspaper, too, might be classified as a public authority, for section 6(3)(b) classifies as a public authority 'any person certain of whose functions are functions of a public nature'.[18]

---

[15] *R v Human Fertilisation and Embryology Authority, ex p Blood* [1999] Fam 151. Mrs Blood brought an application for judicial review of s 28(6)(b) and the incompatibility of that provision with Convention rights was conceded; see J K Mason and G T Laurie, *Mason and McCall Smith's Law and Medical Ethics* (8th edn, 2010) OUP (hereafter *Mason and McCall Smith*), p 58, and see below at **12.13**.

[16] And see the similar case of *L v Human Fertilisation and Embryology Authority* [2008] EWHC 2149 (Fam), discussed at **12.13**.

[17] See now Human Fertilisation and Embryology Act 1990, ss 28(5)A–I.

[18] See below at **2.3**.

2.3 Doctors' Responsibilities: Patients' Rights

Suppose, however, a private individual, a colleague, for example, invades our privacy by steaming open our private correspondence and finds letters from our doctors revealing an embarrassing medical complaint. What then? In practical terms, often some common law remedy may be found within which to frame a cause of action. The 'snooper' who peers through windows or opens our mail could be liable for harassment, or trespass to goods. If no common law remedy can be identified so that the defendant appears to be immune from liability, Article 6 of the Convention comes into play. Article 6 grants a right that, in determination of his civil rights and obligations, everyone is entitled to a fair trial. It grants a right of access to justice. If no remedy for violation of Article 8 (right to privacy) appears to exist, the court must in effect develop a remedy,[19] or the court acts unlawfully in failing to implement Article 8. And the government is in breach of the Convention in failing to provide a legal remedy, violating the citizen's right to access to justice.

Article 6 will affect the development of the English law in two ways. Relatively rarely, Article 6 will come into play because the common law offers *no* remedy for violation of a Convention right. More commonly, the Article will be invoked in order to overcome some restriction on the claimant's common law right. For example, in one case, the High Court ruled that there was a breach of Article 6(1) when a fourteen-year-old witness was called upon at short notice and without legal representation to consent to the disclosure of her medical records as evidence in a sexual abuse case.[20] The High Court held that the child's right to privacy under Article 8(1) had been breached.

Who can be sued?

2.3   As we have seen, the Act does not define public authority. Section 6(3) provides that public authority includes: (a) a court or tribunal; and (b) any person certain of whose functions are of a public nature. What does this mean for the NHS? National Health Service trusts, including PCTs (and in future GP consortia), are public authorities. So are bodies such as NHS Research Ethics Committees. 'Quangos' such as the Care Quality Commission are equally clearly public authorities, as are regulatory bodies such as the General Medical Council. Individual health professionals, doctors and nurses working within the NHS, are performing functions of a public nature and face potential claims under the Act (although normally such claims would be brought against their employer). GPs and other non-employed NHS personnel might be more directly in the firing line. Professionals in private practice and private hospitals raise tricky questions. Whilst a doctor is a public authority in relation to their NHS functions, the same does not apply to doctors in private practice. So if

---

[19] *Campbell v Mirror Group Newspapers* [2004] UKHL 22. But see *Wainwright v Home Office* [2003] UKHL 53 where the Court deferred any responsibility for the creation of a tort of privacy to Parliament.

[20] *R (on the Application of TB) v CPS and South Staffordshire Healthcare NHS Trust* [2006] EWHC 1645 (Admin). See below at **4.9**.

patient A contracts with Dr B to carry out surgery at Clinic C, paying out of his own pocket, or via private health insurers, the relationship is entirely private. However, if patient A later sues Dr B or Clinic C, in determining the nature of his redress, the court must seek to develop the common law consistently with the Convention on Human Rights. If this is not possible, patient A may have redress against the government under Article 6 for violating his right to a fair trial to determine his civil rights and obligations.

Do private clinics treating NHS patients perform functions of a public nature? They will not be regarded as 'core' public authorities under section 6, but might they be viewed as 'hybrid bodies' under section 6(3)(b)? As we have seen, under section 6(3)(b) a public authority includes 'any person certain of whose functions are functions of a public nature'. However, section 6(5) provides that: 'In relation to a particular act, a person is not a public authority ... if the nature of the act is private.' The test therefore, relates to the particular act of which complaint is made.[21] The European Court of Human Rights has held, for example, that by delegating responsibilities to private schools, the UK government cannot escape liability under the Convention.[22] The question is whether the act is a private act, or the discharge of a public function?[23]

It was held in *R (Heather) v Leonard Cheshire Foundation (Cheshire)*[24] that a charity responsible for providing a home and care for a number of disabled people paid for by the local authority was neither a 'core' nor a 'hybrid' public authority for the purposes of the Human Rights Act. It was created by private individuals. It was not obliged to accept publicly funded residents, nor was it closely regulated by the state. In *Aston Cantlow* PCC *v Wallbank*[25] the House of Lords held that a Parish church council was not a public authority, but Lord Nicholls urged a 'generously wide scope to the expression "public function" in section 6(3)(b)'.[26] Does this throw doubt on the Court of Appeal decision in *Cheshire*? In 2007, the House of Lords held that a private care home was not performing functions of a public nature even though the care of the patient had been arranged by the local authority. Lord Bingham and Baroness Hale dissented.[27] The decision was much criticised[28] but the matter was resolved when section 145 of the Health and Social Care Act 2008 provided that private care homes fall within section 6 of the Human Rights Act. Section 145 relates to certain social care; private treatment falls outside its ambit.

---

[21] See for example *London and Quadrant Housing Trust v R (on the application of Weaver) and Equality and Human Rights Commission* [2009] EWCA Civ 587.

[22] See *Costello-Roberts v UK* (1993) 19 EHRR 112, para 27.

[23] See *Aston Cantlow Parish Church Council v Wallbank* [2003] UKHL 37, per Lord Nicholls at para 16.

[24] [2001] EWHC Admin 429.

[25] [2003] UKHL 37.

[26] [2003] UKHL 37, para 11.

[27] *YL v Birmingham City Council* [2007] UKHL 27.

[28] See L Williams, 'Contracting Out and "Functions of a Public Nature"' (2008) 4 *European Human Rights Law Review* 524; and B Hale, 'Dignity' (2009) 31(2) *Journal of Social Welfare and Family Law* 101.

Who can sue?

2.4 Only a person who is a 'victim' of the alleged violation of the Convention can bring a claim under the 1998 Act. The concept of victim derives from the Convention and jurisprudence of the European Court of Human Rights. A victim must be actually and directly affected by the act or omission which is the subject of the complaint. There is no direct provision for interest groups to sue to vindicate Convention rights.

What does this mean in practice? Obviously a claimant who is detained in hospital against her will can ground a claim on Article 5 (although a claim in false imprisonment will usually suffice).[29] A person who alleges that he has been experimented on without consent may have a claim under Article 3 (prohibiting inhuman or degrading treatment) or Article 8.[30] However, it may be difficult for individuals to fund claims about important principles. Interest groups will want to use the Convention to challenge and change existing law (for example, the ban on voluntary euthanasia). Will they be able to do so, given interest groups cannot sue as groups? It is not necessary to show that a claimant has actually already suffered from the consequences of an alleged violation. 'Victims' need only show a real risk of being directly affected by a breach. Gay men in Northern Ireland were allowed to challenge laws criminalising all homosexual conduct.[31] Abortion centre counsellors acting with women wishing to receive advice successfully challenged Irish laws prohibiting dissemination of any information about abortion.[32] Representative interest groups involving groups of victims are able to gain standing under the Act.

Convention rights

2.5 Reference will be made to relevant Convention rights throughout the chapters which follow. All that we do now is give a brief overview of those Convention rights which are likely to have the most significant impact in the rights and obligations of doctors and patients in England.[33]

Article 2

2.6 Article 2 provides that 'Everyone's right to life shall be protected by law.' This might be invoked to challenge a number of entrenched principles of

---

[29] But see *HL v UK* (2005) 40 EHRR 32, discussed below at **2.8**.
[30] For a discussion of the application of Arts 3 and 8 in this context see *R (on the application of B) v S* [2005] EWHC 1936 (Admin), where a patient contested a decision by doctors that he lacked capacity to decide and could therefore be forced to undergo treatment in his best interests.
[31] *Dudgeon v UK* (1982) 4 EHRR 149.
[32] *Open Door and Dublin Well Women v Ireland* (1992) 15 ECHR 244.
[33] See T Murphy, *Health and Human Rights* (2011) Hart; E Wicks, *Human Rights and Healthcare* (2007) Hart.

English law. Consider the following questions. Could a patient whose life (health) is endangered by refusal of treatment (eg denied expensive chemotherapy) use Article 2 to obtain a court order demanding that he be given priority in treatment?[34] Article 2 imposes on the state a positive obligation to intervene to protect people whose lives are at real and immediate risk.[35] In the case of *Savage*,[36] the House of Lords made a preliminary ruling concerning a mentally ill patient who absconded from a hospital where he was compulsorily detained.[37] It was held that actual or constructive knowledge of a patient's risk of self-harm could breach Article 2 if the trust failed to do all that could reasonably be expected to avoid the risk. In the subsequent High Court ruling[38] it was held that the trust had breached its positive obligation under Article 2 when the patient went on to commit suicide. Thus, Article 2 is likely to be engaged in cases where death has or may have been caused by a lack of adequate systems to protect the lives of patients, and the patient is detained.[39] In other cases, as we shall see in chapter 7, patients or their relatives may sue in negligence.

But what limits may or must be placed on the right to life? When does such a right crystallise? Is it an absolute right entitling the patient to any possible treatment? How are competing rights of other patients to be addressed? Remember that such a right would necessarily impose an obligation to provide publicly funded care. The European Court of Human Rights has made it clear that where protection from disease requires use of state resources, individual countries are left considerable freedom to assess their own aims and priorities.[40]

Article 2 will also affect legal issues surrounding allowing patients to die. It was suggested that Article 2 might render decisions that it is lawful to withhold/withdraw treatment in certain circumstances unlawful, in particular that Article 2 might alter the law on withdrawing artificial nutrition and hydration

---

[34] This argument was raised in *R v Swindon NHS PC Trust* [2006] EWCA Civ 392 (see below at **2.19**) but the court found that the policy of the PCT to refuse to fund the appellant with the breast-cancer drug, Herceptin, was irrational and therefore unlawful. Therefore it did not need to go on to consider whether the PCT breached Art 2 or Art 14 of the European Convention on Human Rights: at para 83 per Sir Anthony Clarke MR.

[35] See *Osman v UK* (1998) 29 EHRR 245.

[36] *Savage v South Essex Partnership NHS Foundation Trust* [2008] UKHL 74.

[37] Compare with *Rabone v Pennine Care NHS Trust* [2009] EWHC 1827 (QB) where it was held that no operational obligation could arise under Art 2 in respect of mental patients who were treated on a voluntary basis.

[38] *Savage v South Essex Partnership NHS Foundation Trust* [2010] EWHC 285.

[39] Though there must be an additional element of risk (to the real and immediate risk of death) before state authorities came under an 'operational obligation' under Art2: *Rabone v Pennine Care NHS Trust* [2010] EWCA Civ 698; *Savage* [2010] EWHC 285 approved. In *Rabone,* C's daughter was a voluntary patient at a psychiatric hospital who committed suicide when allowed home. C's daughter was not detained and therefore there was no operational obligation.

[40] *Osman v UK* (1998) 29 EHRR 245.

from patients in persistent vegetative state.[41] However, in *NHS Trust A v M; NHS Trust B v H*,[42] the then President of the Family Division (Elizabeth Butler Sloss P) ruled that Article 2 does not impose an obligation to prolong life in such cases.

Finally, could Article 2 affect laws permitting abortion or case law denying foetuses any legal personality? Could the judgment in *St George's NHS Trust Hospital v S*[43] be subjected to a foetal life challenge? Refusing to strike down national abortion laws, the European Commission has not applied Article 2 to foetuses in the first trimester of pregnancy.[44] And in *Vo v France*[45] the European Court of Human Rights confirmed that the question of when a right of life accrued fell within the margin of appreciation allowed to contracting states.

Article 3

2.7   Article 3 provides that 'No one shall be subjected to torture or to inhuman or degrading treatment or punishment'. It has been suggested that this could be used to challenge failure to provide treatment or poor quality treatment. Does being left on a trolley constitute degrading treatment? It seems unlikely.[46] More disturbing cases, such as the appalling standards of care and resulting morbidity and mortality at Mid Staffordshire NHS Trust, might.[47]

Are laws prohibiting voluntary euthanasia contrary to Article 3? An argument might run linking Article 3 and 8. The case could be put, for example, that a patient dying of some terrible degenerative disease or suffering acute pain from terminal cancer was, by being denied the option of active euthanasia, subjected to inhuman and degrading treatment, contrary to Article 3. Moreover, if her doctor, or some other third party, was willing to help her die, preventing them from doing so might violate her privacy, contrary to Article 8. We shall see that when Dianne Pretty,[48] a woman dying of motor neurone disease, sought to invoke Articles 3 and 8 to support her claim that her husband should be granted immunity from prosecution if he helped her to commit suicide, her claim failed. The House of Lords refused to interpret Article 3 to

---

[41]   *Airedale NHS Trust v Bland* [1993] 1 All ER 821, HL.

[42]   [2001] 1 All ER 801. And see *NHS v D* [2000] 2 FCR 577.

[43]   [1998] 3 All ER 673; see below at **11.22**.

[44]   See *Bruggeman and Scheuten v Federal Republic of Germany* [1977] EHRR 24; *Paton v BPAS* [1981] 2 EHRR 408; see below *at* **13.16**.

[45]   [2004] ECHR 326; see below at **13.17**.

[46]   See *R v North West Lancashire Health Authority, ex p A, D & G* [2000] 1 WLR 977, CA.

[47]   In *Z v UK* (2001) 34 EHRR 97, neglect and abuse of four children and failure of the state to protect them was deemed capable of violating Art 3. And see D Campbell, 'Stafford Hospital Care So Bad it Denied Human Rights' (2010) *Guardian*, 10 November.

[48]   See *R (on the application of Pretty) v DPP* [2001] UKHL 61 (discussed below at **19.6**); and see *Rodriguez v British Columbia A-G* (1993) 82 BCLP (2d) 273.

affirm a right to die with dignity. Her further appeal to the Strasbourg Court also failed.[49] Nor can Article 3 be relied upon to compel doctors to continue futile or inappropriate treatment. Leslie Burke, who suffered from a degenerative neurological condition, cerebellar ataxia, fought for the right to artificial nutrition and hydration in the event that he was unable to voice his wishes. He unsuccessfully sought to invoke Articles, 2, 3, 8 and 14 to challenge guidance from the General Medical Council which stated that where a patient's disease is severe and the prognosis poor, artificial nutrition and hydration will not always be appropriate, even if death is not imminent.[50] The Court of Appeal and the European Court of Human Rights turned his claim down.[51] Doctors cannot be forced to administer treatment which they believe to be clinically unnecessary, futile or inappropriate.

Article 3 will raise other questions about our existing common law. Might certain forms of non-consensual treatment fall foul of Article 3?[52] Consider cases relating to feeding anorexic patients. What effect might Article 3 have on principles relating to consent to clinical research and research involving patients incapable of giving consent?

Article 5

2.8 The relevant parts of Article 5(1) provide:

> Everyone has the right to liberty and security of person. No one shall be deprived of his liberty save in the following cases and in accordance with a procedure prescribed by law . . .
>
> (e) the lawful detention of persons for the prevention of the spreading of infectious diseases, of persons of unsound mind, alcoholics or drug addicts or vagrants.

We have seen that the common law tort of false imprisonment already gives protection to the liberty and security of persons. However, a lacuna in mental health law came to light in *R v Bournewood Community and Mental Health Trust, ex p L*.[53] L was a forty-nine-year-old man who had autism and lacked capacity. He was an in-patient at Bournewood Hospital but was not detained under the provisions of the Mental Health Act 1983. Instead he was detained in his best

---

[49] *Pretty v UK* [2002] 2 FLR 45.

[50] GMC, *Withholding and Withdrawing Life-Prolonging Treatments: Good Practice in Decision-Making* (2002). Paragraph 16 provides: '. . . Doctors must take account of patients' preferences when providing treatment. However, where a patient wishes to have a treatment that – in the doctor's considered view – is not clinically indicated, there is no ethical or legal obligation on the doctor to provide it . . .' The guidance has since been updated. See below at **19.13**.

[51] *R (on the application of Burke) v GMC* [2005] EWCA Civ 1003; *Burke v UK* [2006] App 19807/06.

[52] See *Herczegfalvy v Austria* (1992) 18 BMLR 48. See *R (N) v M* [2003] 1 WLR 562, CA.

[53] [1998] 3 All ER 299, HL.

interests, under the common law doctrine of necessity.[54] The High Court held that L's detention was lawful and proper. But the case was successfully challenged in the European Court of Human Rights in *HL* v *UK*.[55] Detention under the common law was arbitrary and lacked sufficient safeguards. It was therefore incompatible with Article 5. A change to the Mental Capacity Act 2005 was introduced in the Mental Health Act 2007, closing the 'Bournewood gap' and introducing (in 2009) Deprivation of Liberty Safeguards (see chapter 6).[56]

Article 6

2.9   Article 6 provides that:

> In the determination of his civil rights and obligations or of any criminal charge against him, everyone is entitled to a fair and public hearing within a reasonable time by an independent and impartial tribunal established by law.

It has been held that doctors undergoing disciplinary hearings do not necessarily have a right under Article 6 against their employers,[57] unless there are 'exceptional circumstances'. This was the case in *Kulkarni*,[58] where Smith LJ said (obiter) that Article 6 was engaged when a doctor faced disciplinary proceedings equivalent to a criminal charge. The doctor was therefore entitled to legal representation.

Could Article 6 impede attempts to reduce litigation, for example by excluding any right to sue within a no-fault scheme?[59] In 2004, Article 6 was successfully invoked by an ophthalmic optician when the General Optical Council found her guilty of serious professional misconduct.[60] The committee had a duty under Article 6 to give reasons for its decision within a reasonable time.

Article 8

2.10   Article 8 will have far-reaching effects. Article 8(1) provides: 'Everyone has the right to respect for his private and family life, his home and his correspondence'. Note the wording, the right is a right to *respect*. Does that connote an absolute claim to privacy? As with Article 2, the question arises of what kind of

---

[54]   *F v West Berkshire Health Authority* [1989] 2 A11 ER 545.

[55]   (2004) App No 45508/99.

[56]   And see *G v E, A Local Authority and F* [2010] EWCA Civ 822, on the respective requirements under Art 5 under the Mental Health Act 1983 and the Mental Capacity Act 2005.

[57]   *Hameed v Central Manchester University Hospitals NHS Foundation Trust* [2010] EWHC 2009 (QB).

[58]   *Kulkarni v Milton Keynes Hospital NHS Trust* [2009] EWCA Civ 789.

[59]   See *Osman v UK* (1998) 29 EHRR 245.

[60]   *Threlfall v General Optical Council* [2004] EWHC 2683 (Admin). But in *Abu-Romia v GMC* [2003] EWHC 2515 (Admin) the High Court found that the GMC had sufficient evidence to reach its conclusion. See paras 55, 57 per Wall J.

obligations Article 8 creates. Does it impose positive obligations on the state to act to promote a right to privacy or simply a duty not to interfere with privacy?[61] It is clear that some sort of positive obligation is imposed by Article 8. Then we have to consider how to define parameters of private and family life. Prohibition of contraception, for example, obviously constitutes an interference with that right – interfering with intimate relationships. However, does regulation of third parties involved in assisted conception fall into the same category? In some cases, one person's right to private life may conflict with another's right to family life. Imagine A tests positively for an inherited form of bowel cancer. A's children have a one in four chance of inheriting the condition also, but A refuses to inform her estranged daughter of this possibility. Does respecting A's privacy violate her daughter's right to family life or her right to life under Article 2?

What is clear is that Article 8 is strongly influencing the development of medical law, as was recognised by Coleridge J in 2003:[62]

> The advent of the Human Rights Act 1998 has enhanced the responsibility of the court to positively protect the welfare of these patients and, in particular, to protect the patient's right to respect for her private and family life under Art 8 (1) of the European Convention . . .

Thus in *Glass v UK*,[63] the Strasbourg Court held that a child's rights under Article 8 were breached when he was given diamorphine against the wishes of his mother. Doctors believed the twelve-year-old boy was dying and sought to administer the drug as a palliative measure. His mother disagreed and argued that diamorphine would diminish his chances of recovery. Doctors administered it nonetheless. They did not seek a court order, though they had ample time to do so. In these circumstances, their failure to secure a declaration from the court that such treatment was lawful contravened Article 8(1).[64]

Article 8(1) was also instrumental in a notable victory for Debbie Purdy, who sought clarification of the Director for Public Prosecution's guidance on prosecution in cases of assisted suicide. Not only were Debbie Purdy's rights under Article 8(1) engaged, but the breach could not be justified under Article 8(2).[65] The DPP issued new guidelines in 2010.[66]

We will see in chapter 4 that the common law duty of confidentiality is changing in terminology, if not in substance, to the extent that, in 2004, Lord Nicholls recommended that the tort should be renamed the 'misuse of private

---

[61] See *R v North West Lancashire Health Authority, ex p A, D & G* [2000] 1 WLR 977, CA.

[62] *D v NHS Trust (Medical Treatment: Consent: Termination)* [2003] EWHC (Fam) 2793, para 31.

[63] (2004) 1 FLR 1019.

[64] And see *Re OT (A Baby)* [2009] EWHC 635 (Fam), discussed below at **14.11**.

[65] *R (on the application of Purdy) v DPP* [2009] UKHL 45.

[66] DPP, *Policy for Prosecutors in respect of Cases of Encouraging or Assisting Suicide* (2010).

information'.[67] Could Article 8 be used to prevent certain information ever being sought from individuals? The government conceded that insurers could require applicants for insurance to give results of certain genetic tests including tests for Huntington's Chorea. Does such a policy violate Article 8? Could it be justified under Article 8(2)? Article 8(2) graphically illustrates the qualified nature of certain Convention rights. It provides:

> There shall be no interference by a public authority with the exercise of this right except such as is in accordance with the law and is necessary in a democratic society in the interests of national security, public safety or the economic well-being of the country, for the prevention of disorder or crime, for the protection of health or morals, or for the protection of the rights and freedoms of others.

Note the width of potential exceptions to Article 8(1).[68] The jurisprudence of the European court illustrates both the complexity of Article 8 and judicial conservatism on its part of the ECHR.[69] In *Evans v UK*[70] the Grand Chamber held that the UK had not exceeded its margin of appreciation under Article 8(1) in relation to the requirement under the Human Fertilisation and Embryology Act 1990 that Evans's partner's consent be required to implant their embryo in her uterus. Natalie Evans and her partner stored the embryos after cancer treatment, but sadly their relationship ended.

Breach of Article 8(1) must be proportionate. Consider *Szuluk v UK*.[71] A prisoner with a severe neurological condition complained that confidentiality with regard to his medical correspondence had not been respected. A prison officer was able to read all his letters in order to ensure that he was not planning criminal activity. The European Court of Human Rights held that the breach of his rights was not justified under Article 8(2). Mr Szuluk should be allowed uninhibited contact with his medical practitioner. There was no danger that the letters would lead to criminal activity.

In 2010 three women alleged that Irish abortion laws breached their rights under Article 8. The law provides that abortion is unlawful except where the mother's life is at risk.[72] The women sought to exercise their rights according to this law. Two of the women's cases failed on the basis that their health rather than their lives were at risk. The third woman feared that her pregnancy posed a risk of a rare cancer returning. She complained that there was no effective legal procedure by which she could establish her right to abortion. The Court ruled in her favour.[73] Ireland is obliged to comply with the ruling.

---

[67] *Campbell v MGN* [2004] UKHL 22 at para 14. And see *R (on the application of Axon) v Secretary of State for Health* (2006) EWHC 37.

[68] *Z v Finland* (1997) 25 EHRR 371; *M S v Sweden* (1997) 45 BMLR 133; *Brown v UK* [1997] 24 EHRR 39.

[69] *Rees v UK* [1986] 9 EHRR 56; *Cossey v UK* [1990] 13 EHRR 622; *B v France* (1992) 16 EHRR.

[70] (6339/05), May 2 2007, ECtHR (Grand Chamber).

[71] [2009] ECHR 36936/05. See **4.4** below.

[72] The Irish Constitution, s 40.3.3.

[73] *A, B and C v Ireland* [2010] ECHR 25579/05.

Article 9

2.11 Article 9 protects religious freedom providing:

> Everyone has the right to freedom of thought, conscience and religion; this right includes freedom to change his religion or belief and freedom, either alone or in community with others and in public or private, to manifest his religion or belief, in worship, teaching, practice and observance.
>
> Freedom to manifest one's religion or beliefs shall be subject only to such limitation as are prescribed by law and are necessary in a democratic society in the interests of public safety, for the protection of public order, health or morals, or for the protection of the rights and freedoms of others.

This has a bearing on medical-treatment decisions in a number of ways.[74] In *Re J*,[75] for example, the rights and freedoms of a non-practising Christian mother and the welfare of the child were balanced against a Muslim father's wish to manifest his religion by having his son circumcised. The Court of Appeal held that a failure to sanction the operation did not offend his rights under Article 9.

As we shall see, English courts have on a number of occasions overruled parental objections to treatment of their children contrary to their faith.[76] The classic example is where a court orders that a blood transfusion is given to a child of Jehovah's Witness parents. The parents might argue that requiring that their child undergo a transfusion violates the family's religious freedom and their right to respect for their family life (Article 8). Do the rights of the child, especially her right to life under Article 2, trump the parents' claims?

Article 10

2.12 Nor must Article 10 be overlooked. Article 10 guarantees freedom of expression, a right embracing freedom of the press. All too often Articles 8 and 10 conflict and the courts must embark on a delicate balancing exercise.[77]

---

[74] See J McHale, 'Health and Health Care Law, Faith(s) and Beliefs: New Perspectives and Dilemmas' 9(4) (2009) *Medical Law International* 279; M Fox, M Thomson, 'Older Minors and Circumcision: Questioning the Limits of Religious Actions' 9(4) (2009) *Medical Law International* 283; J McHale, 'Health Care Choices, Faith and Belief in the Light of the Human Rights Act 1998: New Hope or Missed Opportunity' (2009) 9(4) *Medical Law International* 331.

[75] *Re J (Child's Religious Upbringing and Circumcision)* [2000] 1 FLR 571 per Thorpe LJ at para 12. And see *Re S (Specific Issue Order: Religion: Circumcision)* [2004] EWHC 1282 (Fam). Female circumcision was prohibited in the UK under the Prohibition of Female Circumcision Act 1985, replaced by the Female Genital Mutilation Act 2003. See generally, A R Gatrad, A Sheikh, H Jacks, 'Religious Circumcision and the Human Rights Act' (2002) 86 *Archives of Childhood Diseases* 76.

[76] See *Re S (A Minor) (Medical Treatment)* [1993] 1 FLR 376; discussed below at **14.9**.

[77] Graphically illustrated in *Campbell v Mirror Group Newspapers* [2004] UKHL 22.

Article 12

2.13 Finally, Article 12 might be thought to guarantee a right to reproduce as it states that:

> Men and women of marriageable age have the right to marry and found a family, according to the national laws governing the exercise of that right.

Could Article 12 be used to challenge limitations on access to fertility treatment? It has been held by the Court of Appeal and the Strasbourg Court that Articles 8 and 12 were not infringed when a prisoner was refused the right to services which would enable the artificial insemination of his wife.[78]

Convention on Human Rights and Biomedicine

2.14 It will be apparent that patients' rights are not centre-stage in the European Convention on Human Rights. To raise a question about patients' rights, the relevant dispute must somehow be fitted into the pigeonhole of general rights. A further European convention, the European Convention on Human Rights and Biomedicine,[79] (the Bioethics Convention) directly addresses doctor/patient relationships. This Convention (agreed in 1997) by states party to the main Human Rights Convention has not been signed or ratified by the UK. We are not yet a party to that treaty. Even if and when the UK does ratify this Convention, it will not have direct force. A patient will not be able to sue for violation of a right granted by the Convention. Nor is there any right of individual petition to the European Court of Human Rights at Strasbourg. Nonetheless, Articles of the Human Rights Convention may be interpreted with reference to the much fuller explanations and definitions of human rights offered in the Bioethics Convention.

NHS constitution

2.15 Section 1 of the Health Act 2009 made provision for the NHS Constitution,[80] which emanated from the *NHS Next Stage Review* led by Lord Darzi. Published in 2009,[81] various health bodies are required to have regard

---

[78] *R (on the application of Mellor) v Secretary of State for the Home Department* [2001] EWCA Civ 472; *Dickson v Premier Prison Service Ltd* [2004] EWCA Civ 1477; and *Dickson v UK* (2006) App No 00044362/04. And see H Codd, 'Regulating Reproduction: Prisoners' Families, Artificial Insemination and Human Rights' (2006) 1 *European Human Rights Law Review* 39.

[79] See H D C Roscam Abbing, E H Hondius, J H Hubben (eds), *Health Law, Human Rights and the Biomedicine Convention* (2005) Martinus Nijhoff Publishers.

[80] See S Farg, A Chapman, 'Who Cares Wins' (2010) 160 (7417) *New Law Journal* 671.

[81] See also NHS, *The Handbook to the NHS Constitution* (2009), revised (March 2010).

to the Constitution. Much of it sets out existing rights and obligations, but it also contains a number of 'pledges' – commitments to enhance the protection of patient interests. The coalition government has stated that it remains committed to the Constitution which covers:

- quality of care and environment;
- respect, consent and confidentiality;
- informed choice;
- involvement in your health care and in the NHS;
- complaints and redress;
- access to health services;
- nationally approved treatments, drugs and programmes.

These key areas will be explored throughout this book, but we will turn to the last two in the next sections.

Access to health care[82]

2.16 Provided a decision is made fairly and rationally, the European Court of Human Rights is reluctant to interfere with the rationing decisions of member states.[83] Article 3 might be invoked if the refusal of treatment constitutes 'inhuman or degrading treatment'[84] and Article 14 if the decision discriminates on the ground of disability or age. It has been held that Article 8 does not impose a positive obligation to provide treatment.[85] If the European Convention on Human Rights fails to endorse a direct unequivocal right to health care, can we construct such a right from other sources? First, let us briefly consider how rationing decisions are made in the NHS. This task is complicated by virtue of the fact that we stand on the cusp of radical change and, at the time of writing, the government's plans are not wholly formed.

NICE

2.17 The National Institute for Health and Clinical Excellence (NICE) was established as a special health authority.[86] One of its existing roles is to advise PCTs about whether to fund new medicines or other treatments, having regard to 'the promotion of clinical excellence and the effective use of available

---

[82] See C Newdick, *Who Should We Treat? Rights, Rationing and Resources in the NHS* (2nd edn, 2005) OUP, hereafter, 'Newdick'.

[83] See E Jackson, *Medical Law: Texts and Materials* (2nd edn, 2010) OUP, pp 87–89. See for example *Scialacqua v Italy* (1998) 26 EHRR CD164.

[84] Note that in *Price v UK* (2001) 34 EHRR 1285, the prison authorities breached Art 3 in their deficient care of a prisoner who was a thalidomide victim.

[85] *R v North West Lancashire Health Authority, ex p A, D and G* [2000] 1 WLR 977, CA.

[86] See the National Institute for Clinical Excellence (Establishment and Constitution) Order 1999, SI 1999/220 as amended by SI 2005/497.

resources in the health service'.[87] NICE currently makes these 'technology appraisals' on the basis of the cost per quality-adjusted life year (QALY),[88] and adopts a cost per QALY of about £30,000.[89] Though application is not rigid, there must be substantial evidence to support the drug's approval if it goes beyond this threshold.[90] This made costly treatment of patients with a short life expectancy a relatively low priority. NICE issued new advice in 2009, allowing a more flexible appraisal of such treatments,[91] but Jackson suggests that the guidelines are so tightly framed as to make little practical difference to patients.[92] Patient Access Schemes,[93] offering the NHS discounts on drugs where it is mutually beneficial to the Department of Health and the pharmaceutical companies to do so, have perhaps proved more effective.

Since 2002, NHS organisations are required, normally within three months, to fund treatments recommended by NICE in its technology guidance.[94] NICE's decisions are subject to judicial review.[95] For example, in *Eisai Ltd v National Institute for Health and Clinical Excellence*[96] it was held that NICE acted unfairly in failing to make a full version of their economic model available during the appraisal process of Alzheimer's drugs.[97] NICE also produces clinical guidance, which is not mandatory, though it does provide a benchmark for the management of clinical conditions by local healthcare organisations. Will the guidelines define the standard of care in negligence cases?[98] At the very least, a clinician defending a negligence claim is likely to be called upon to justify divergence with the guidance.[99]

[87] See Newdick, p 205.
[88] See NICE website, http://www.nice.org.uk/newsroom/features/measuringeffective nessandcosteffectivenesstheqaly.jsp. See below at **3.6**.
[89] NICE website. And see J Raftery, 'Should NICE's Threshold Range for Cost per QALY be Raised? No' 228 (2009) *BMJ* 185; A Towse, 'Should NICE's Threshold Range for Cost per QALY be Raised? Yes' 338 (2009) *BMJ* 181.
[90] J Wise, 'NICE Recommended Four in Five Drugs it Evaluated in Past Decade' (2010) 341 *BMJ* 3935.
[91] NICE, *Appraising Life-Extending, End of Life Treatments* (2009).
[92] E Jackson, *Medical Law: Text, Cases and Materials* (2nd edn, 2010) OUP, p 68.
[93] See the DH, *Pharmaceutical Price Regulation Scheme 2009* (2008). Patient Access Schemes will no longer be necessary if, as proposed, value-based pricing is introduced in 2014.
[94] See section 2(a) of the NHS Constitution.
[95] An example of successful judicial review of a NICE decision is *Servier Laboratories v NICE* [2010] EWCA Civ 346.
[96] [2008] EWCA Civ 438. See C Brasted, H Dedman, 'A Model Consultation' (2009) 159 (7373) *New Law Journal* 850.
[97] But see R *(in the application of Bristol-Myers Squibb Pharmaceuticals Ltd) v NICE* [2009] EWHC 2722 (Admin).
[98] See A Samanta, J Samanta, M Gunn, 'Legal Considerations of Clinical Guidelines: Will NICE Make a Difference?' (2003) 96 *Journal of the Royal Society of Medicine* 133.
[99] See *Mason and McCall Smith*, p 385.

A significant limitation is NICE's inability to negotiate with pharmaceutical companies on the pricing of medicines. A new pricing system is proposed.[100] The government's intention is to introduce a 'value-based' pricing system in 2014.[101] The price the NHS is willing to pay will be linked to the value of the treatment. The central aims are to cut high payments for drugs of limited efficacy, promote innovation and free up resources to pay for expensive but highly effective treatment. The government will 'set a range of thresholds or maximum prices reflecting the different values that medicines offer'.[102] A White Paper is expected in 2011. Who will determine value and how will that determination relate to prices?[103] The QALY is likely to have a role, though the government is consulting on alternatives. Value is unlikely to be determined purely by NICE.

Part 8 of the Health and Social Care Bill proposes significant changes to the role of NICE, which will be renamed the National Institute for Health and Care Excellence. On one hand, as we saw in chapter 1, its role producing clinical 'Quality Standards' will be strengthened. But the government plans (in its Health and Social Care Bill) to end central control of health provision has implications for NICE. Part of its role is likely to be devolved to GP consortia, potentially exacerbating regional variation, or what has become known as 'the postcode lottery'. There may still be a role for technology appraisals of new medicines, but it will be more limited and they are likely to carry less force. In broad terms, it is likely that NICE's appraisals, coupled with other 'value indicators', will result in a reimbursement price for new medicines. GP consortia will then make commissioning decisions based on NICE's clinical guidelines, local needs, and, let us not forget, the outcome-based measures through which the Commissioning Board will hold GP consortia to account.

A right to health care?[104]

2.18 Before looking at the case law, let us reflect for a moment on what a right to health care might involve. Article 25 of the Universal Declaration of Human Rights provides:

> Everyone has the right to a standard of living adequate for the health and well-being of himself and his family, including food, clothing, housing and medical care ...

---

[100] DH, *Liberating the NHS* (2010), at 3.23.

[101] And a Cancer Drug Fund from 2011. See DH, *A New Value-Based Approach to the Pricing of Branded Medicines – A Consultation*, ref 15205 (2010).

[102] *A New Value-Based Approach to the Pricing of Branded Medicines – A Consultation*, para 4.5.

[103] A Maynard, K Bloor, 'The Future Role of NICE' (2010) 341 *BMJ* c6286.

[104] The previous Administration issued a Green Paper, *Rights and Responsibilities: Developing our Constitutional Framework*, Cm 7577 (2009), suggesting that the right to healthcare (amongst other rights) might be enshrined in a Bill of Rights and Responsibilities. It did not aim to create new rights and has not been taken forward by the new government.

Other rights within Article 25 can be easily defined and quantified. Basic needs for food and clothing alter little from one person to another. Desires may vary widely, but no one would argue that they have a fundamental human right to caviar and champagne every day. Basic needs for medical care vary widely. A baby born prematurely at twenty-four weeks may consume as much health-care resource in his first week of life as others do in a lifetime. What constitutes need is hotly debated. Treatment for pneumonia falls comfortably into a definition of need. Where would you place breast augmentation as part of gender reassignment?[105] Note the World Health Organization definition of health as '. . . a state of complete physical mental and social well-being and not just the absence of disease or infirmity'. What would a right to health so defined involve and whose duty is it to ensure that we enjoy such health?

Ultimate responsibility for the health of the NHS lies with the Secretary of State for Health. The National Health Service Act 2006 now provides in section 1:[106]

> The Secretary of State must continue the promotion in England of a comprehensive health service designed to secure improvement –
>
> (a)   in the physical and mental health of the people of England, and
> (b)   in the prevention, diagnosis and treatment of illness.

Section 3 of the Act imposes on the Secretary of State a further duty to provide, to such extent as he considers necessary to meet all reasonable requirements, services including hospital accommodation, medical, dental, nursing and ambulance services and such other services as are required for the diagnosis and treatment of illness. High-sounding sentiments and expressions of political will these may be, but is there any legal significance in this 'duty' imposed on the Health Minister? Do patients have a right to health care? Judges were once wary of involving the courts in disputes about allocation of resources, or priorities for treatment. Two developments signal change. First, there are signs of greater judicial activity in relation to access to health care. Second, the European Court of Justice has established a limited right to access to other national health systems if your own cannot provide the care you need without undue delay.

Challenging NHS resource-allocation decisions[107]

2.19   In the domestic courts, early attempts to challenge decisions about access to health care met with little success. In 1979, four patients who had spent long periods vainly awaiting hip-replacement surgery went to court alleging that the Minister had failed in his duty (then imposed by the National Health

---

[105]   *A C v Berkshire West PCT & Equality and Human Rights Commission* [2010] EWHC 1162 (Admin). A PCT's decision to define this as a 'non-core' procedure (and therefore not necessarily funded by the NHS) was upheld.

[106]   Previously the National Health Service Act 1977, s 1.

[107]   For a comparative perspective, see K J Syrett, *Law, Legitimacy and the Rationing of Healthcare: A Contextual and Comparative Perspective* (2007), CUP.

Service Act 1977) to promote a comprehensive health service and to provide hospital accommodation and facilities for orthopaedic surgery. The patients alleged: (1) that their period on the waiting list was longer than was medically advisable, and (2) that their wait resulted from a shortage of facilities, caused in part by a decision not to build a new hospital block on the grounds of cost. The patients asked for an order compelling the Minister to act, and for compensation for their pain and suffering. The Court of Appeal[108] held that:

(a) the financial constraints to which the Minister was subject had to be considered in assessing what amounts to reasonable requirements for hospital and medical services;

(b) the decision as to what was required was for the Minister, and the court could intervene only where a Minister acted utterly unreasonably so as to frustrate the policy of the Act. An individual patient could not claim damages from the Minister for pain and suffering.

The patients lost the immediate legal battle. They gained valuable publicity. And the courts did not entirely abdicate control over the Minister. A public-spirited patient resigned to getting no damages himself, could (by way of an application for judicial review) still challenge a minister whom he alleges had totally subverted the health service (for example, a minister using his position and powers exclusively to benefit private medicine at the expense of the NHS).[109]

The Court of Appeal rejected any legally enforceable right to health care actionable by a patient for his own benefit. Did any such right exist against local health providers? In 1987, the parents of two sick babies who needed cardiac surgery sought to enforce such a right on their sons' behalf. They applied to the Divisional Court for a court order that their sons be operated on. The health authority explained that lack of resources and lack of trained nurses meant that each baby kept missing out on his operation to other more urgent cases. The court refused to make an order that the operation be carried out immediately.[110] The parents had no right to demand immediate treatment for their sons. The health authority could do only what was reasonable within their limited resources, human and financial. It is difficult to see what else the court could have done in these cases. The court could not provide the resources needed to operate on all sick babies. In effect, the judges were being asked to decide that baby X needed surgery more urgently than baby Y, and judges are not qualified to make clinical judgments.

---

[108] *R v Secretary of State for Social Services, ex p Hincks* (1980) 1 BMLR 93, CA. And see *R v N and E Devon Health Authority, ex p Coughlan* [1999] Lloyd's Rep Med 306, CA.

[109] Chances of success are not high, and the government of the day could always change the law, but they can be made to do it openly and not be permitted to pay lip-service to a duty to a public health service which may have been abandoned.

[110] *R v Central Birmingham Health Authority, ex p Walker* (1998) *Times*, 26 November; *R v Central Birmingham Health Authority, ex p Collier* (1988) *Times*, 6 January, CA. See the highly critical analysis of *Collier* by Newdick, at 98–100.

In *R v Cambridge District Health Authority, ex p B*,[111] the Court of Appeal again demonstrated reluctance to become involved in questions of allocation of resources. B was a ten-year-old girl suffering from non-Hodgkin's lymphoma. In 1994, she received a bone marrow transplant from her sister. In 1995, she became ill again. The doctors treating her considered no further treatment should be given to prolong B's life. B's father obtained advice that there was a possible course of treatment. With further intensive chemotherapy, B stood a 10–20 per cent chance of remission sufficient to allow a second bone marrow transplant to succeed. The transplant itself stood a 10–20 per cent chance of success, offering B at best a 4 per cent chance of 'recovery'. The treatment package would cost about £75,000. The health authority refused to fund B's treatment. They argued (1) that such 'experimental' treatment was not in B's best interests and (2) that given the minimal prospects of successful treatment the cost could not be justified. Other demands on the limited budget took priority.

The trial judge, Laws J, was not convinced by the authority's case. He issued an order requiring the authority to reconsider the evidence in support of their decision not to treat B. They must do more than 'merely toll the bell of tight resources'.[112] The authority appealed. The Court of Appeal backed them unequivocally, rejecting Laws J's attempt to require greater transparency in decisions about allocating resources. The appeal court rested their decision largely on clinical grounds, on evidence from the doctors that the aggressive treatment proposed was not in B's interests, despite the contrary view of B's father and the child herself. Sir Thomas Bingham MR summed up judicial attitudes to problems in allocation of healthcare resources when he commented:

> Difficult and agonising judgments have to be made as to how a limited budget is best allocated to the maximum advantage of the maximum of patients. That is not a judgment which the court can make. In my judgment, it is not something that a health authority can be fairly criticised for not advancing before the court.[113]

So when will the courts intervene to question decisions about whom to treat, or what treatment patients may be entitled to? Judges do assert the power to assess the reasonableness of decision-making by NHS authorities, just as they will hold other public bodies to account for the reasonableness of their decision-making processes. In *R v St Mary's Hospital Ethical Committee, ex p Harriott*,[114] Mrs Harriott had been refused treatment by the IVF unit. The unit's informal ethical advisory committee had supported the doctors' decision not to treat Mrs Harriott because she had been rejected by the local social services department as a potential adoptive or foster mother and because she had convictions for prostitution offences. She challenged their decision. The judge held that the grounds for refusing her treatment were lawful. But he said refusal of treatment on *non-medical* grounds could be reviewed by a court. It

---

[111] [1995] 2 All ER 129, CA.
[112] (1995) 25 BMLR 16 at 17.
[113] [1995] 2 All ER 129 at 137.
[114] *R v St Mary's Ethical Committee, ex p Harriott* [1988] 1 FLR 512.

would be unlawful to reject a patient because of her race or religion or other irrelevant grounds. A patient denied renal dialysis or surgery because the consultant in charge refuses to treat divorced people, or Labour Party members, might well have a remedy. However, judges, it must be remembered, tend to be conservative. In *R v Sheffield Health Authority, ex p Seale*,[115] the judge refused to interfere with the health authority's decision to refuse fertility treatment to older women, defined as any woman over 35.

Successful challenges to decisions about provision of health care often depend on the patient identifying some obvious flaw in the decision-making process.[116] In *R v North Derbyshire Health Authority, ex p Fisher*,[117] the health authority refused to fund the costly drug Beta-interferon for any patient with multiple sclerosis. They operated a blanket ban on provision of the drug, failed to make any assessment of individual patients' needs and ignored a circular from the Department of Health advising that serious consideration be given to providing Beta-interferon to certain categories of patients with multiple sclerosis. The judge held that the authority failed to take a reasoned decision after consideration of all the relevant factors.

In *Booker*[118] it was held that an insurance payout following a road traffic accident, which enabled the claimant to purchase private care, did not absolve the NHS of its responsibility for providing a tetraplegic patient with nursing care. The decision was unlawful and irrational – the NHS Constitution provides that care is provided on the basis of clinical need. If the NHS wishes to recoup the costs of caring for a patient who is the victim of a tort, legislation is required.

A notable 'victory' for patients denied access to treatment is found in *R v North West Lancashire Health Authority, ex p A, D & G*.[119] The defendant health authority refused to pay for gender-reassignment surgery for the applicants. Such surgery was classified by the authority as a low priority along with cosmetic procedures such as face-lifts or hair transplants. Transsexuals should be provided with psychiatric and psychological services, but the authority would not 'commission drug treatment or surgery that is intended to give patients the physical characteristics of the opposite gender'. Statements in the policy document about exceptional cases based on overwhelming clinical need made it abundantly clear that in reality such a case would never be conceded. No-one would be a sufficiently *exceptional* case to qualify. The Court of Appeal quashed the decision to refuse treatment to the applicant as 'irrational'. The authority had failed to evaluate the medical evidence relating to transsexuality. They paid lip-service to the notion that the applicant's condition

[115] (1994) 25 BMLR 1.
[116] See Newdick, ch 5.
[117] [1997] 8 Med LR 327.
[118] *R (on the application of Booker) v NHS Oldham and Direct Line Insurance plc* [2010] EWHC 2593 (Admin).
[119] [2000] 1 WLR 977, CA.

constituted illness, but dismissed forms of effective treatment without proper consideration. The authority did not[120]

> ... in truth treat transsexualism as an illness, but as an attitude or state of mind which does not warrant medical treatment ... [T]he ostensible provision that it makes for exceptions in individual cases and its manner of considering them amount effectively to the operation of a 'blanket policy' against funding treatment because it does not believe in such treatment.

Another patient victory, this time in relation to unlicensed drugs, occurred in *R (Rogers) v Swindon NHS Primary Care Trust*.[121] The Court of Appeal, overturning the High Court decision, held that Swindon PCT's funding policy for the (as yet) unlicensed drug, Herceptin, was irrational and unlawful. Herceptin was licensed for late-stage HE-II, an aggressive form of breast cancer. Ann Marie Rogers (the applicant) was in the early stage of the disease. Some trusts provided Herceptin in such cases, despite the fact that it was neither licensed nor approved by NICE. The Health Secretary, Patricia Hewitt, had previously announced that Herceptin, which costs £26,000 a course, should not be refused purely on grounds of cost. Trusts would still be able to refuse treatment where cost is a factor, but in this case, Swindon PCT had declared that cost was irrelevant to its decision. The court held that there was therefore no rational basis for refusing to treat Mrs Rogers. What then would provide a rational basis for refusal of unlicensed treatment? Resource availability, combined with clinical need and individual circumstances.

One option open to the court in cases where an irrational policy has led to treatment being refused is to remit the case back to the commissioning body. The correctly applied procedure will not necessarily result in the patient being provided the treatment he seeks.[122] In other cases, the *application* of a lawful, rational policy is irrational. *R (Otley) v Barking and Dagenham NHS PCT*[123] concerns one such example. Victoria Otley had purchased cancer treatment privately, because the drug was not licensed here. The drug proved effective and she tolerated it well. She sought a further five cycles of the expensive drug, funded by her PCT. The policy was that the NHS body can refuse to fund treatment (taking into account financial restraints and the patient's circumstances) unless the circumstances are exceptional. The PCT decided that Victoria Otley's case should not be viewed as 'exceptional'. This policy was approved as fair and rational. However, it was applied irrationally. The court held that, because there were no other treatment options, her case was indeed exceptional.

A similar finding was made in *R (Ross) v West Sussex PCT*[124] where the refusal of a trust to fund potentially life-saving cancer treatment was one which 'no

---

[120] [2000] 1 WLR 977, CA, per Auld LJ.

[121] [2006] EWCA Civ 392. See J King, 'The Justiciability of Resource Allocation' (2007) 70(2) *Modern Law Review* 197; C Newdick, 'Judicial Review: Low Priority Treatment and Exceptional Case Review' (2007) 15(2) *Medical Law Review* 236.

[122] As in *R (on the application of Murphy) v Salford PCT* [2008] EWHC 1908 (Admin).

[123] [2007] EWHC 1927 (Admin).

[124] [2008] EWHC 2252 (Admin).

reasonable Trust could have made'. What constitutes 'exceptional' circumstances must necessarily be considered on a case-by-case basis. The courts have shown themselves prepared to scrutinise the process by which healthcare providers make decisions about what kinds of treatment they will provide and who will have access to such treatment. However, if the healthcare provider can demonstrate that it has fully considered the case made to it, and addressed all the relevant considerations, but ultimately determined that other treatments and other claims must be given priority, courts remain unlikely to intervene. Nor is going to court likely to advance your treatment to the head of the waiting list.

The NHS Commissioning Board will take on responsibility for ensuring equality in access to and outcomes of health care, but proposed decentralisation of budgets and commissioning freedom may lead to regional inconsistencies and ensuing dissatisfaction.[125] There will inevitably be further recourse to the courts.

Top-up treatment

2.20 What if patients want to buy treatment to 'top-up' their NHS treatment? Will NHS treatment be withdrawn if the patient opts for parallel private treatment? Until recently this was the case. The issue came to the fore when cancer patients were refused drugs considered too expensive by the NHS and sought to obtain the drugs privately. Some patients could just about afford the extra drugs but not pay for all their care privately. In 2008 the Richards Report[126] made recommendations which were implemented in NHS guidance.[127] Top-up payments were endorsed: 'The NHS should continue to provide free of charge all care that the patient would have been entitled to had he or she not chosen to have additional private care'.[128] In addition to this, patients can purchase private treatment which must be delivered separately to the NHS care.

The policy has been criticised. Whilst the guidance stipulates that patients should not be charged for NHS care and private care should never be subsidised by NHS care, it will be difficult in practice to keep the two separate. Jackson warns that it may constitute a step towards the NHS being regarded as a core, basic service.[129] The media questioned whether it might signal the

[125] See above at **1.3**.

[126] DH, *Improving Access to Medicines for NHS Patients: A Report for the Secretary of State for Health by Professor Mike Richards* (2008).

[127] DH, *Guidance on NHS Patients Who Wish to Pay for Additional Private Care* (2009).

[128] DH, *Guidance on NHS Patients Who Wish to Pay for Additional Private Care* (2009), p 5.

[129] E Jackson, 'Top-up Payments for Expensive Cancer Drugs: Rationing, Fairness and the NHS' (2010) 73(3) *Modern Law Review* 399.

end of the NHS.[130] In practice, doctors will find it difficult to judge precisely when to raise the possibility of privately funded treatment, especially if they practise private medicine and stand to profit if the patient pays for his top-up treatment.

Treatment abroad[131]

2.21 In 2002, the NHS began to fund treatment in Europe.[132] A patient requiring a knee-replacement might be sent to Belgium or Germany rather than waiting in pain for months in the UK. But first he had to receive authorisation from the PCT.

Much publicity was given to the decision of the European Court of Justice[133] that if a patient living in one member state of the EU faced *undue delay* in receiving treatment in his home country, his state insurance system must be prepared to pay for him to have treatment in another member state where treatment is available more speedily. A patient forced to wait years for a hip-replacement in England might demand to be sent to Germany where such surgery could be performed within weeks. Do we now enjoy a 'European' right to health care?

There are two routes to receiving care in another member state. The first is the E112 route.[134] A PCT (and in future a GP consortium) can issue an E112 form where treatment cannot be provided within an acceptable timescale. Each PCT establishes its own procedures. In *R (Watts) v Bedford PCT and the Department of Health*,[135] a seventy-four-year-old woman was informed by Bedford PCT that she would have to wait a year for a bi-lateral hip replacement. She applied to have the operation in France under the E112 scheme, but the PCT refused, and reduced her wait to four months. Mrs Watts, who was wheelchair-bound and in constant pain, went ahead with the operation in France, without the PCT's authorisation. The PCT refused to reimburse her

---

130 S Crompton, 'Do Medication Top-Up Fees Mean the End of the NHS?' (2008) *The Times,* 8 November.

131 See T Hervey and J McHale, *Health Law and the European Union* (2004) CUP; and see *Mason and McCall Smith*, ch 3 (by M Aziz).

132 A right now ensconced in section 2(a) of the NHS Constitution: 'You have the right, in certain circumstances, to go to other European Economic Area countries or Switzerland for treatment which would be available to you through your NHS commissioner'.

133 *BGM Geraets-Smits v Stichting Ziekenfonds VGZ and HTM* Case C-157/99. See European Community Regulation 1408/71 (EC) establishing the E112 form which enabled pre-authorised cross-border care and, from 1 May 2010, Regulation 883/2004 (EC).

134 See European Community Regulation 1408/71 (EC) establishing the E112 form which enabled pre-authorised cross-border care and, from 1 May 2010, Regulation 883/2004 (EC).

135 [2004] EWCA Civ 166, CA.

because four months was the 'normal' waiting time for a hip replacement. Did the 'normal' four-month wait constitute 'undue delay'?

The Court of Appeal referred the matter to the European Court of Justice,[136] which held that when determining whether a proposed waiting time is acceptable, member states must apply 'an objective medical assessment of the clinical needs of the person concerned in the light of all of the factors characterising his medical condition'.[137] If patients wait longer than doctors advise, regardless of NHS targets, the NHS must refund the costs where patients pay for treatment elsewhere in Europe.[138]

Post-*Watts,* cross-border health care may be authorised at the discretion of the Secretary of State for Health if treatment cannot be given without 'undue delay', which was left undefined, and will depend on the particular circumstances of the case. A draft Directive on Patients' Rights to Cross-Border Healthcare[139] was agreed in June 2010[140] and Euro MPs will vote on the second reading in January 2011. The costs will be debated along with requirements for prepayment and prior authorisation.

The second route to cross-border care is under Article 56 of the Treaty on the Functioning of the European Union. Patients can receive cross-border health care (including private care) which they would have been entitled to in their own country, and seek reimbursement. The Department of Health requires prior authorisation in some cases. Regulations[141] in 2010 pre-empt the proposed Directive and insert new sections in the NHS Act 2006. The new section 6A sets conditions for reimbursement of expenses – the patient may have to pay the costs up front. Section 6B sets out precisely when pre-authorisation from the Secretary of State is required. Some services, such as scans, that would once have been carried out in hospitals are now carried out in non-hospital settings. As a result, the Regulations require prior authorisation not merely for hospital treatment, but for 'special services' which include hospital stays,

[136] *R (Watts) v Bedford PCT and The Secretary of State for Health* [2006] Case C-372/04. See JV McHale, 'Rights to Medical Treatment in EU Law' (Commentary) 15(1) (2007) *Medical Law Review* 99.

[137] [2006] Case C-372/04 at para 79.

[138] [2006] Case C-372/04 at paras 113–114.

[139] Directive of the European Parliament and the Council on the Application of Patients' Rights in Cross-Border Healthcare 2008/0142. For analysis see H Legido-Quigley *et al,* 'Cross-Border Healthcare in the European Union: Clarifying Patients' Rights' (2011) 342 *BMJ* d296.

[140] Council of the EU, Council Agrees on New Rules for Patients' Rights in Cross-Border Healthcare (2010).

[141] The National Health Service (Reimbursement of the Cost of EEA Treatment) Regulations 2010, SI 2010/915. The Department of Health issued accompanying guidance: DH, *Cross Border Healthcare and Patient Mobility: Revised Advice on Handling Requests from Patients for Treatment in Countries of the European Economic Area: Guidance for the NHS* (2010).

procedures involving the use of anaesthesia or sedation and other specialist treatment.[142] Authorisation will be given provided:

(a)   that the requested service is necessary to treat or diagnose a medical condition of the patient;

(b)   that the requested service is the same as or equivalent to a service that the Secretary of State [the Board[143]] or a responsible authority would make available to the patient in the circumstances of the patient's case; and

(c)   that the Secretary of State [the Board] or a responsible authority cannot provide to the patient a service that is the same as or equivalent to the requested service within a period of time that is acceptable on the basis of medical evidence as to the patient's clinical needs, taking into account the patient's state of health at the time the decision under this section is made and the probable course of the medical condition to which the service relates.[144]

The ECJ ruling in *Watts* concerned freedom to provide services under EU law. The NHS is not obliged to authorise or pay for hospital treatment provided by UK private hospitals on this basis. The Health Act 1999 moved responsibility for arranging NHS care to PCTs.[145] Section 18 of the 1999 Act imposes a duty of quality:[146]

It is the duty of each health authority, PCT and NHS trust to put and keep in place arrangements for the purpose of monitoring and improving the quality of health care which it provides to individuals.

Failure to address provision of timely treatment on the part of a PCT is an obvious breach of section 18. Legislation will be required to move this responsibility to the new GP consortia and proposals are now published in the Health and Social Care Bill 2011. It proposes that a new section 1A be inserted into the National Health Service Act 2006 imposing a duty incumbent on the Secretary of State to secure continuous improvement in outcomes,[147] and a new section 13D imposing similar duties on the NHS Commissioning Board. The Board will hold GP consortia to account for the quality of services they provide. Good care is timely care. Will the courts offer a remedy to patients aggrieved by the failure of their consortium to provide timely treatment, or to

---

[142] See *European Commission v French Republic* Case C-512/08 (2010) upholding the French requirement that prior authorisation was required for treatment involving certain equipment which might not be located in hospitals.

[143] The Health and Social Care Bill 2011 proposes minor amendments to paras (b) and (c), inserting 'the [NHS Commissioning] Board' after 'the Secretary of State'.

[144] NHS Act 2006, s 6B(5), as amended.

[145] The Health Act 1999 amended the NHS Act 1977, ss 16A and 16B, now consolidated in the NHS Act 2006, ss 18, 19 and Sch 3.

[146] Words in s 18(1) inserted by National Health Service Reform and Health Care Professions Act 2002, s 37(1).

[147] On the relevance of 'outcomes' see above at 1.3.

provide the treatment of their choice? The remedy many patients may seek is compensation. Imagine that a patient is told that she will have to wait another twelve months for her hip replacement, in contravention of Department of Health guidelines. She borrows money from the bank and pays £8,000 to have her operation privately. If she is to recover that sum, the courts will have to overrule *ex p Hincks* and allow a claim for breach of statutory duty against the NHS.[148] Once again, money to compensate patients will deplete funds to treat patients. If the patient cannot raise the costs of private treatment herself, will the court grant an order requiring the consortium to arrange her operation immediately, if need be in the private sector, but paid for by the NHS? Perhaps they may. A court will at least require from a consortium a cogent explanation for delay. This scenario does not involve a judge saying, treat this patient and not some other patient in greater need. It entails a court requiring the consortium, a public body, to establish that in *not* using the powers they have to arrange this patient's care, they acted *reasonably*. Budgets remain relevant factors. A right to treatment 'on demand' is unlikely to emerge. What we may see develop in the next few years is a legal right to an equitable process of decision-making about NHS treatment. In the other contexts, one positive impact of the Human Rights Act 1998 has been to encourage the judges to scrutinise public authorities' decisions more vigorously, particularly where life may be at stake.[149]

---

[148] But consider the possibility of damages for breach of the Human Rights Act; see Newdick, pp 125–126.

[149] *R v Lord Saville of Newdigate, ex p A* [1998] 4 All ER 860, HL. And see Newdick, pp 121–125.

Chapter 3

MEDICINE, MORAL DILEMMAS AND THE LAW

3.1 Medical and bio ethics make news, but are far from new. From the formulation of the Hippocratic Oath in Ancient Greece to the present day, doctors have debated among themselves the codes of conduct which should govern the art of healing. These days philosophers, theologians, lawyers and journalists insist on joining the debate. Outside interest, or interference as doctors sometimes see it, is not new either. Hippocrates was a philosopher. The Christian churches through the centuries have asserted the right to pronounce on medical matters of spiritual import, such as abortion and euthanasia, and to uphold the sanctity of life. All other major religions across the world similarly pronounce on matters of medical ethics.[1] In the UK today, in considering the impact of faith on medical ethics and practice greater attention needs to be paid to traditions other than the Christian faith.

The Hippocratic Oath makes interesting reading. Its first premise is that the doctor owes loyalty to his teachers and his brethren. Obligations to exercise skill for the benefit of patients' health come second. Abortion, direct euthanasia and abetting suicide are prohibited. Improper sexual relations with patients are banned. Confidentiality in all dealings with patients is imposed. In 2,500 years these basic precepts of medical practice changed little. Dramatic changes in the kinds of moral and ethical problems confronting the doctor came only in the last fifty years or so. The art of the Greek philosopher physician became a science for many practitioners. Science has given the doctor tools to work marvels undreamed of by earlier generations. In vitro fertilisation and gamete donation to assist infertile couples to have children are no longer seen as extraordinary. The technology to create artificial gametes is on the horizon. So a man who produces no natural sperm might be able to father a child via sperm 'constructed' from other cells in his body. Ectogenesis may become a reality so that the foetus could be gestated in an artificial womb. A family with a child dying of certain genetic diseases can be helped to create a 'saviour sibling'. Tests will ensure that the new baby does not suffer from her

---

[1]   See, for example, D E Guinn, *Handbook of Bioethics and Religion* (2006) OUP.

sibling's disease, and is an exact tissue match for her. Then stem cells taken from the newborn infant's umbilical cord may constitute a 'cure' for the elder child.

Creating a human clone looks technically feasible now mammalian cloning has proved possible. Reproductive cloning attracts much media attention and disapproval. It is the potential for therapeutic cloning, better described as stem cell therapy, which excites doctors and scientists. The possible uses of embryonic stem cells hold out the hope of being able to replace damaged cells in patients with diseases such as Parkinson's disease. Further in the future, some suggest that stem cells can be used to grow new organs to replace diseased kidneys or livers.

Babies born at ever earlier stages in gestation, or born with severe abnormalities, can be offered a chance of survival by amazing developments in neonatal intensive care. Some forms of foetal handicap are correctable by surgery carried out while the baby is still in the womb. Ventilators keep alive accident victims whose heart and lungs have given up. Dialysis and transplant surgery save kidney, liver and heart patients from certain death. The list of technological 'miracles' is endless. They have placed in the hands of the doctors powers which humanity once ascribed to God alone.

Technological progress has been matched by social change. People are less willing to accept without question the decisions of those who exercise power, be they judges, politicians or doctors. Paternalism is out of fashion. Lawyers and philosophers, not to mention parents, wonder why the doctor is best qualified to judge whether a baby's quality of life is such as to make life-saving surgery desirable. The power of the doctor to end life, whether by switching off a ventilator, or by deciding not to put a patient on the active transplant list, disturbs us all. These moral dilemmas are just as acutely felt by doctors. Their difficulties are accentuated by the fact that the new technology cannot be made available to all those in need. There is just not enough money or resources in the NHS.[2] Above all, the medical profession in 2011 faces a society more deeply divided on virtually every moral question than ever before. The public demands a say in medical decision-making on sensitive ethical issues. Yet from the hot potato of whether doctors should help couples to have a 'saviour sibling' to help their dying child, through the debates on abortion, to euthanasia, the doctor who seeks guidance from public opinion will discover division, bitterness and confusion.

Questions of medical ethics arise throughout the whole field of medical practice. Most medical students receive education in ethics as an integral part of their studies.[3] Several texts address medical ethics in detail.[4] Increasingly, those schol-

---

[2] The Health Committee led an inquiry into public expenditure which closed September 2010. Available at: http://www.parliament.uk/business/committees/committees-a-z/commons-select/health-committee/inquiries/public-expenditure/.

[3] See G Stirrat, 'Teaching and Learning Medical Ethics and Law in UK Medical Schools' (2010) 5 *Clinical Ethics* 156.

[4] Excellent texts on medical ethics include: T L Beauchamp and J F Childress, *Prin-*

ars who address the ethics of medicine speak of bioethics rather than *medical* ethics. The change of terminology is not merely semantic. The most difficult dilemmas begin in the laboratory, not at the bedside. Consider xenotransplantation, whereby animals might be genetically engineered to produce organs compatible for transplant into humans with organ failure. The essential question is whether science should continue to pursue the research that may transform such possibilities into reality. Scientists need education in ethics as much as doctors. Equally importantly, the term bioethics is seen as less doctor-centred than medical ethics. All health professionals confront ethical dilemmas. This book focuses on doctors. Much of what we say is relevant to other health professionals too, but each health profession faces its own particular variant of ethical debate.[5] The ethics of the doctor–patient relationship are touched on throughout this book. It is not and does not purport to be a book about medical ethics, or bioethics. Miola challenges the commonly held assumption that law and ethics form a cohesive unit.[6] They may clash or create a 'regulatory vacuum' where the law hands over the responsibility for decision-making to medical ethics, and professional guidance leaves matters to the conscience of the doctor. We focus primarily on the role of the law. Two fundamental issues of ethics do need to be introduced at this juncture. Are ethics more than etiquette? How does society today understand and implement concepts of the sanctity of human life?

Ethics not etiquette

3.2 Were you to peruse the ethical guidance provided for doctors in the nineteenth and early twentieth century, what you might find would have scant relationship to what most of us today think of as medical ethics. Two sorts of advice predominated. First, the physician was envisaged as an English gentleman.[7] As long as he behaved in a gentlemanly and benevolent fashion, his own conscience and integrity would guide him towards ethical solutions in dilemmas surrounding how to treat a patient.[8] Formal advice from professional bodies, notably the General Medical Council (GMC), offered somewhat more concrete advice. Doctors were prohibited from sexual relationships

---

ciples of *Biomedical Ethics* (6th edn, 2008) OUP; J Jackson, *Ethics in Medicine* (2005) Polity Press; R Gillon, *Philosophical Medical Ethics* (1986) John Wiley; J M Harris, *The Value of Life* (1985) Routledge; and see generally, H Kuhse and P Singer (eds), *A Companion to Bioethics* (2nd edn, 2009) Wiley-Blackwell; and B Steinbock, *The Oxford Handbook of Bioethics* (2009) OUP. For a succinct introduction to bioethics in the context of medical law, see E Jackson, *Medical Law: Text, Cases and Materials* (2nd edn, 2010) OUP, ch 1.

[5] See, for example, S D Edwards, *Nursing Ethics* (2nd edn, 2009) Palgrave Macmillan; RPSGB *Medicines, Ethics and Practice* (34th edn, 2010) Pharmaceutical Press; P Lamden (ed), *Dental Law and Ethics* (2002) Radcliffe Medical Press.

[6] J Miola, *Medical Ethics and Medical Law: A Symbiotic Relationship* (2007) Hart.

[7] This model of 'ethics' was initiated by the Manchester physician Thomas Percival, in his book on *Medical Ethics,* first published in 1808; see C D Leake (ed), *Percival's Medical Ethics* (1927) Williams & Wilkins.

[8] See Gillon, *Philosophical Medical Ethics* (1986) John Wiley, ch 5.

with their patients or their patients' wives. They should not take advantage of their privileged access to patients' homes. They must avoid misuse of alcohol or drugs. They were not to tout for custom, nor must they disparage other doctors. They must refrain from any sort of collaboration with unqualified practitioners.[9] Advice centred on gentlemanly behaviour and without doubt some of the injunctions issued in earlier days had beneficial effects on patient care. However, what was styled ethics had at its core a code of etiquette. Doctors should conduct themselves in a particular way; they should show professional solidarity, and practise benevolent paternalism.

The scale of grossly unethical abuse of medicine revealed in the wake of the Second World War destroyed any complacent culture of paternalist medicine. A series of codes of medical ethics were promulgated internationally. Moral philosophers began to subject medicine to a much more rigorous critical analysis. 'Critical' medical ethics emerged, offering a framework within which ethical dilemmas could be the subject of debate and reflection. Beauchamp and Childress's seminal book *Principles of Biomedical Ethics* proved especially influential.[10]

Beauchamp and Childress formulated four basic principles, autonomy, beneficence, non-maleficence and justice, as a framework for ethical conduct. The four principles are a fashionable subject for attack.[11] They do not, and never sought to, provide easy answers to particular questions or to offer a comprehensive ethical analysis. They do, as Gillon says, '. . . help us bring more order, consistency and understanding to our medico-moral judgments'.[12] The influence of the four principles, and their delicate relationship with legal principles, make it important that in any study of the law relating to health care a brief account is given of the four principles.

Respect for autonomy – self-determination

3.3 Autonomy literally means self-rule, as opposed to heteronomy – rule by others. We should respect autonomous choices made by other people. Crude paternalism is the antithesis of respect for autonomy. Non-consensual treatment of a patient, even for her own good, violates her autonomy. Gradually, as we shall see in chapters 5 and 6, English law, via principles governing consent to treatment, clothed the moral principle of autonomy in legal reality.

Respect for autonomy does not demand unthinking deference to any choice made by another human being. To demand respect, a choice must be a maxi-

---

[9] See, for example, GMC 'Bluebook', *Professional Conduct: Fitness to Practise* (1985).

[10] See also H T Engelhard, *The Foundation of Bioethics* (2nd edn, 1996) OUP.

[11] For example, K Clouser and B Gert, 'A Critique of Principlism' (1996) 15 *Journal of Medicine and Philosophy* 219. And see J Savelescu *et al*, 'Festschrift Edition of the Journal of Medical Ethics in Honour of Raanan Gillon' (2003) 29 *Journal of Medical Ethics* 265.

[12] See Gillon, *Philosophical Medical Ethics* (1986) John Wiley, p viii.

mally autonomous choice – an informed and free choice made by someone with the capacity to make such a choice. A very young child will 'choose' not to go to the dentist and 'choose' not to be injected with antibiotics. His choice will be dictated by the nastiness of the procedure involved. He is not able to weigh the benefits of good dental care, or antibiotics to cure his streptococcal infection, against the immediate unpleasantness. An older person with severe mental disabilities may be similarly disabled from making any real choice. A paranoid schizophrenic may be constrained by his 'voices' to refuse treatment because he knows that the doctor is Satan. The preferences expressed in such cases are not autonomous choices.

In setting boundaries of mental capacity, the law struggles with the concept of what constitutes an autonomous choice. The temptation to regard a choice you disagree with as non-autonomous is strong. The outcome of the choice should be irrelevant. A woman who rejects surgery for breast cancer where the prospects of complete recovery were good but she could not tolerate any mutilation of her breast makes a decision that we see as bizarre. The Jehovah's Witness rejecting blood transfusion does so on the basis of an interpretation of the Bible which not all of us share. Their choices remain autonomous choices, made by people able to reason and on the basis of adequate information.

Beneficence – do good

3.4 An injunction to act beneficently requires doctors to frame their actions to benefit their patients. The needs of the patient should be the professional's pre-eminent concern. Patients should never be means to an end. What does such a pious hope mean in practice? The ethics of clinical research have attracted much philosophical attention. The failure of doctors to act beneficently and treatment of human subjects as little more than research tools explains that emphasis on research ethics. Ethical professionals should put the individual's welfare first, even if to do so conflicts with their own interests, for example, their research objectives.

Another problem with beneficence might be that it could be seen as just another name for paternalism. The beneficent doctor does what he thinks is best for the patient. If natural childbirth is dangerous for the patient and the child she carries, must the beneficent doctor perform a Caesarean section whether she likes it or not? The answer is no, because beneficence demands respect for autonomy. The professional should offer his judgment on what is good for the patient, but doing good for her requires that ultimately he accepts *her* decisions on what is good for her.

Translating the ethical imperative of beneficence into legal principle is tricky. The law imposes a duty of care owed by doctor to patients. That duty, however, generally involves not doing me any harm. English law does not impose any duty to be a Good Samaritan. Once a patient is admitted to hospital, staff must provide him with adequate and competent care. A doctor or nurse who witnesses a road accident but passes by on the other side commits no legal wrong. Yet if she fails to help when she could easily do so, she fails to act beneficently.[13]

Beneficence illustrates an important point about law and ethics. Ethics demands a higher standard of behaviour than the law requires. A competent surgeon who removes a patient's gallstones without mishap fulfils her legal duty of care. If she dismisses the patient's complaints of pain with scorn, makes him feel like a child, and treats him as just another patient number, is she acting ethically?

Non-maleficence – do no harm

3.5 Raanan Gillon[14] says of non-maleficence: 'Among the shibboleths of traditional medical ethics is the injunction *Primum non nocere* – first (or above all) do no harm'. Gillon does not challenge the principle of non-maleficence as such. Its importance is self-evident, what he rightly points out is that principle cannot be absolute. Medicine often involves doing harm. Removing an inflamed appendix inevitably involves a degree of risk of harm, pain and scarring. The benefits obviously outweigh the harm in that case. Practices which avoid all risk have ultimately done more harm than good. Sometimes agonising dilemmas arise, as was the case in relation to the conjoined twins, Jodie and Mary, separated by surgeons in Manchester in 2000.[15] Without surgery, both girls would die. Separating Mary from her sister would and did result in her death. Do no harm to Mary meant not doing good for Jodie.

Justice[16]

3.6 '[T]he idea that justice is a moral issue that doctors can properly ignore is clearly mistaken.'[17] Few would dissent from a proposition that doctors should treat patients justly. Justice in this context might be interpreted as meaning that patients are entitled to be treated fairly and equally by their doctors. The Queen should be treated no differently from a homeless person brought into Casualty after he is found unconscious in a doorway. Health professionals should not show preference for patients who enjoy a particular status, or provide sub-standard care for patients of whom they disapprove.

---

[13] Though she may face disciplinary proceedings, as GMC guidance requires that in an emergency a doctor must provide to anyone at risk the assistance she could reasonably be asked to provide. GMC, *Good Medical Practice* (2006), para 11.

[14] See Gillon, *Philosophical Medical Ethics* (1996) John Wiley, p 80.

[15] See *Re A (Minors) (Conjoined Twins: Separation)* [2000] Lloyd's Rep Med 425, CA. Discussed below at **14.5**.

[16] See generally, C Newdick, *Who Should We Treat? Law, Patients and Resources in the NHS* (2nd edn, 2005) OUP.

[17] See Gillon, *Philosophical Medical Ethics* (1986) John Wiley, p 87.

Alas justice is much more complex. Within the NHS resources are limited. Not every treatment can be offered to every patient who may derive clinical benefit from such treatment. Imagine that the Queen and the homeless person both needed a liver transplant. The demand for donor livers far exceeds supply. How should a just decision be made about whether either of them should receive a transplant? The Queen is eighty-five, but in good health. The homeless person is thirty-five, but an alcoholic. His general health is poor. Other contenders compete for livers, a number of them younger than the Queen and in better health than the homeless person.

We might agree then the Queen should not get a transplant just because she is the Queen.[18] We might agree that the homeless person should not be refused a transplant just because he is homeless. Is it relevant that if he continues to drink after surgery, the transplant is likely to fail? Even if he overcame his addiction his lifestyle may militate against success. Poor diet and no settled home will make it difficult for him to comply with the postoperative regime necessary to avoid rejection of the donor liver. There is a lively debate about how far lifestyle and/or 'fault' should affect access to NHS resources.[19]

The complexity of notions of distributive justice in health care, coupled with scarcity of resources, has resulted in health economists entering the debate. They have advanced the merits of an exercise based on 'quality adjusted life years' (QALYs) which measure health as years of life after treatment weighted by the patient's quality of life. QALYs embody an attempt to provide an objective framework to assess how society should determine priorities for treatment.

Both the Queen and the homeless person may do badly on a QALY test. Life post transplant is unlikely to generate for anyone years of full health. Let us award the Queen ten years[20] of 0.75 health and the homeless person twenty years at 0.25 health, the cost being the same for both 'patients'. The Queen scores 7.5; the homeless person scores 5; both will almost certainly lose out to younger, fitter patients. QALYs trigger another question. Should anyone get a liver transplant? Compare liver transplants with hip replacements. A woman of fifty having a hip replacement for arthritis may generate fifteen–twenty QALYs at lower cost. Yet arthritis is not life-threatening. It is perhaps not surprising then, as we shall see, that the English courts have been reluctant to engage in questions of health resources.

---

[18]   She can of course simply opt for private care. Is it unjust that those who can pay can obtain whatever treatment they desire?

[19]   K Sharkey, L Gillam, 'Should Patients with Self-Inflicted Illness Receive Lower Priority in Access to Healthcare Resources? Mapping out the Debate' (2010) 36 *Journal of Medical Ethics* 661.

[20]   Given her mother's longevity, this does not seem an unreasonable assumption.

NICE[21] has had no such option. The National Institute for Clinical Excellence was set up as a special health authority in 1999 to produce clinical practice guidance and promote transparency of research allocation decisions. It became the National Institute for Health and Clinical Excellence in 2005. Andrew Dillon, the Chief executive of NICE is reported to have said:

> QALYs are not perfect, and they do have limitations . . . However, they are practical, as the calculations can be carried out in a reasonable time frame, and they are a good way to make comparisons between treatments.[22]

Recent figures indicate NICE approves four out of five of the drugs it evaluates,[23] but the media react sharply to the one in five which is not approved.[24] As we saw in chapter 2, NICE's decision relating to an Alzheimer's drug was successfully challenged in *Eisai Ltd v National Institute for Health and Clinical Excellence*.[25] We also saw that the role of NICE is set to change. In the Health and Social Care Bill published in January 2011, the coalition government propose a move from national to local commissioning. GP consortia (groups of GP practices) will replace PCTs by 2013. A new NHS Commissioning Board will provide each consortium with a budget which (individually, or in groups) they will decide how to spend. The consortia will be guided and judged according to outcome frameworks produced by NICE. But GPs rather than NICE will have to make the often unpopular decisions about which treatments to fund. The QALY will probably form part of their rationale, but it will be complemented by an assessment of local clinical needs.

Autonomy and patients' responsibilities

3.7   Of Beauchamp and Childress's four principles, autonomy became *de facto* the dominant principle, especially in legal debate. So dominant did that one principle become that Daniel Callaghan declared:[26]

> Nothing has exasperated me so much as the deference given in bioethics to the principle of autonomy.

The emphasis on autonomy has meant, as Draper and Sorrell explain:[27]

---

[21]   See above **2.17**. The government propose to re-establish NICE as a non-departmental public body and rename it the National Institute for Health and Care Excellence.

[22]   J Wise, 'NICE Recommended Four in Five Drugs it Evaluated in Past Decade' (2010) 341 *BMJ* 3935.

[23]   (2010) 341 *BMJ* 3935.

[24]   See, for example, Z Cooper, 'What we Missed in the Avastin Debate' (2010) *Guardian*, 25 August, on NICE's decision not to fund the bowel cancer drug Avastin which offers approximately a six-week extension of life.

[25]   [2008] EWCA Civ 438. See C Brasted, H Dedman, 'A Model Consultation' (2009) 159 (7373) *New Law Journal* 850.

[26]   D Callaghan, 'Can the Moral Commons Survive Autonomy?' (1996) *Hastings Centre Report* 41.

[27]   H Draper, T Sorrell, 'Patients' Responsibilities in Medical Ethics' (2002) 16 *Bioethics* 335.

Medical Ethics is one-sided. It dwells on the ethical obligations of doctors to the exclusion of those of patients.

And in *R v Collins and Ashworth Health Authority, ex p Brady*,[28] Kay J commented:

... it would seem to me a matter of deep regret if the law has developed to a point in this area where the rights of the patient count for everything and other ethical values and institutional integrity count for nothing.

The problem is that the notion of autonomy has become distorted. Autonomy is wrongly understood as simply a right to what 'I want'. The doctor becomes little more than a technician delivering what the consumer-patient demands.[29] As Onora O'Neill[30] has eloquently pointed out, such an interpretation of autonomy is mistaken. Autonomy involves:[31]

... privacy, voluntariness, self-mastery, choosing freely, choosing one's moral position and accepting responsibility for one's choices.

O'Neill adds to that list 'self-control' and 'self-determination'.[32] Expressing a non-reflective preference is not a manifestation of autonomy. Responsibility requires reflection on how our choices affect others. Making a case that patients owe ethical duties to others, including their doctors, is relatively easy. Clothing such ethical responsibilities with legal force is a harder task.[33] Reflecting, however, on patients' responsibilities forces us to consider the growing support for a view of communitarian ethics.[34] In judging the ethics of a particular course of action, the impact on the community, not just the individual, must be evaluated.

Virtue ethics and the ethics of care

3.8 Virtue ethicists counter the dominance of autonomy in medical ethics by stressing the benefit of doing the right or virtuous thing in a given situation.[35] If

---

[28] [2000] Lloyd's Rep Med 355 at 367.

[29] See M Brazier, N Glover, 'Does Medical Law Have a Future?' in D Hayton (ed), *Law's Future(s)* (2000) Hart Publishing, p 371.

[30] See O O'Neill, *Autonomy and Trust in Bioethics* (2002) CUP; O O'Neill, *A Question of Trust* (2002) Reith Lectures.

[31] See R Faden, T Beauchamp (in collaboration with N M P King), *A History and Theory of Informed Consent* (1986) CUP, p 7.

[32] See O O'Neill, *Autonomy and Trust in Bioethics* (2002) CUP, p 22.

[33] See M Brazier, 'Do No Harm – Do Patients Have Responsibilities Too?' (2006) 65 *Cambridge Law Journal* 397.

[34] Note that J K Mason and G T Laurie declare their 'partial adherence to community ethics'. See J K Mason and G T Laurie, *Mason and McCall Smith's Law and Medical Ethics* (8th edn, 2010) OUP (hereafter *Mason and McCall Smith*), p 8. And see D Callaghan, 'Principalism and Communitarianism' (2003) 29 *Journal of Medical Ethics* 287; A Etzioni, 'Authoritarian versus Responsive Communitarian Bioethics' (2010) *Journal of Medical Ethics* (online advanced access).

[35] See, generally, R Hursthouse, *On Virtue Ethics* (1999), OUP.

your friend asks you for money with which he might travel to Switzerland to engage the services of the assisted-suicide clinic because he is suffering intolerably from a terminal condition, you may agree to help him because you respect his right to make his own choices, or alternatively, from a virtue ethics standpoint, you might help simply because benevolence, kindness and generosity requires it. Principalists revere autonomy, but it has less relevance to a virtue ethicist who might argue that decisions about death or abortion should be based on compassion.[36]

Feminists, too, find conventional theory lacking on the basis that it fails to take account of gender-specific disparities. Attention is directed to areas where women's interests have traditionally been neglected, such as birth control and pregnancy. But the resulting theories have significance far beyond reproductive issues. Harvard psychologist Carol Gilligan's 'Ethic of Care'[37] emphasises the importance to women of relationships. Instead of basing ethical theory on abstract principles, such as autonomy, the ethic of care addresses issues at a personal level. Health must be contextualised; physical and emotional needs must be taken into account.

To whom (or what) do we owe ethical obligations?[38]

3.9   Principles of medical ethics often conflict. If an obstetrician performs a Caesarean section without the woman's consent, he violates her autonomy. If he does not intervene and the child dies or is born severely disabled, he has done harm to the child. Withdrawing treatment from a patient in a permanent vegetative state may be seen to harm him. Yet continuing to keep him alive can equally be classified as harming him. Money spent on sustaining such a patient over several years, deprives others of treatment in a cash-strapped NHS. Keeping X alive may be an injustice to Y. The trump card invoked to demand that the foetus and the patient in PVS be accorded priority centres around beliefs in sanctity of life. What we mean by sanctity of life, whether it is a trump card, is hotly debated.

The sanctity of life: Judaeo-Christian tradition[39]

3.10   For the devout Roman Catholic, sanctity of life is straightforward. Human life is a gift from God and is literally sacred. Any act which deliberately ends a life is wrong. Life begins at conception and therefore abortion, and research on, or disposal of, an artificially created embryo, a test-tube embryo, is never permissible. Life ends when God ends it. No degree of suffering or disability justifies a premature release effected by us.

---

[36]   See, for example, L Van Zyl, *Death and Compassion: A Virtue-based Approach to Euthanasia* (2000) Ashgate; R Hursthouse, 'Virtue Ethics and Abortion' (1991) 20 *Philosophy and Public Affairs* 223.

[37]   C Gilligan, *In a Different Voice* (1982) Harvard University Press.

[38]   See Gillon, *Philosophical Medical Ethics* (1996) John Wiley chs 7 and 8.

[39]   See J Finnis, *Natural Law and Natural Rights* (1980) OUP; O O'Donovan, *Begotten or Made* (1984) OUP.

Yet even so there remain grey areas in the application of belief that life is sacred. Abortion is banned because the only intent of that operation is to kill the child. The Roman Catholic Church forbids abortion even when pregnancy threatens the woman's life. However, a pregnant woman with cancer of the womb may be allowed a hysterectomy, albeit that the child will then die. This is called the doctrine of double effect. The operation for cancer incidentally destroys the child but that was not its primary purpose.

At the other end of life, the Church, while condemning euthanasia, does not demand that extraordinary means be taken to prolong life. Where is the line drawn? Should a severely disabled baby be subjected to painful surgery with a low success rate? Must antibiotics be administered to the terminal cancer patient stricken with pneumonia? The doctrine of double effect, and the application of a distinction between ordinary and extraordinary means to preserve life have generated substantial literature and debate.[40] Even accepting that areas of doubt exist, the orthodox Roman Catholic remains fortunate in the security of her beliefs on the sanctity of life, beliefs shared by many fundamentalist Christians of the Protestant tradition.

Other practising Christians, who subscribe in essence to the doctrine of the sanctity of life, see further problems once they seek to apply their faith. Contraception is morally acceptable to the majority, and to many Roman Catholics now, although still officially prohibited by the Church. The exact point when life begins and becomes sacred becomes of the utmost importance to determine the morality of certain contraceptive methods. Abortion to save the mother's life is accepted by many Christians, as it always has been in the Jewish and Muslim faiths. The child's life deserves protection but not at the expense of his mother's. This step taken, the extent to which the child's life may be sacrificed to his mother's has to be ascertained. Is a threat to the mother's mental stability sufficient? What about the women who suffer rape? What is the status of the early embryo created in the test-tube? These and many other issues have caused dissent within the Church of England and the other Christian traditions. For example, a number of eminent Anglican theologians[41] argued that research on the early embryo is acceptable and raised no conflict within Christian doctrine. Other Anglicans remained adamantly opposed to any form of destructive research on embryos. Nonetheless the adherent of any religious faith enjoys a framework of belief. The sanctity of life has meaning for them because that life was given by God.

The sanctity of life in a secular society

3.11 Many still subscribe to some form of belief in a divinity or higher power. Churches are popular for weddings and funerals and thriving communities of

---

[40] See, for example, the debate between J Finnis and J Harris in J Keown (ed), *Euthanasia Examined: Ethical, Clinical and Legal Perspectives* (1995) CUP.

[41] See, for example, K Ward, 'An Irresolvable Debate', in A Dyson and J Harris (eds), *Experiments on Embryos* (1989) Routledge, ch 7.

Jews and Muslims remain committed to their traditions. Britain today is an overwhelmingly secular society where the majority of the population is uncommitted to any religious creed and those people practising any religious faith are a minority.[42] How many people retain a general belief in God as the Creator is open to question. For those who do not, what meaning has the sanctity of life? If life is not bestowed by God, on what grounds is it sacred?

There can be no doubt that belief in the sanctity of life does survive the absence of religious belief. Taking life is as reprehensible to many agnostics and atheists as it is to the Christian or the Jew. Many non-believers have been more consistent in fighting for the sanctity of life than have certain warmongering Christian priests, or those 'Christians' who in the USA gather around the jails to celebrate the death penalty's return. What in a secular society is the basis of the sanctity of human life? To most people who are not philosophers the answer is simple. There is a deep and embedded instinct that taking human life is wrong. Life is a most precious possession.[43] All other possessions, all potential joys, depend upon its continued existence. An attack on one individual's right to life which goes unchecked threatens us all. Our autonomy is undermined. Our security becomes precarious. The move away from a concept of life as God-given, however, has certain consequences. If at the basis of belief in the sanctity of life is a perception of the freedom of the individual, of the joy that life can bring, then the quality of life comes into account. The right of the foetus to come into possession of his own life, his own freedom, must be balanced against his mother's rights over her own life and body. When pain and disability cause an individual to cease to wish to live, then he may be free to end that life. It is his to do with as he wishes. Individual choice becomes central to applying the concept of the sanctity of life. No one must interfere with an adult's choices on continued life. Whether any other adult can be compelled to assist a fellow to end his life raises more difficult questions. The concept of freedom of choice offers little guidance where an individual is incapable of choice. Nevertheless this uncertain position commands a fair degree of generous support. People have an intrinsic right to life. Life is sacred, but not 'inviolable'.

Sanctity of life: a different perspective[44]

3.12 A number of philosophers attack the very notion that 'taking human life is intrinsically wrong'. Life is seen as having no inherent value. Life has value only if it is worth living. Taking life is wrong because 'it is wrong to destroy a life

---

[42] On the secularisation of bioethics, see E Jackson, *Medical Law: Text, Cases and Materials* (2nd edn, 2010) OUP, pp 9–23.

[43] See R Dworkin, *Life's Dominion: An Argument About Abortion and Euthanasia* (1993) Harper and Collins.

[44] See, in particular, two persuasive and lively works: J Glover, *Causing Death and Saving Lives* (1977) Penguin; J M Harris, *The Value of Life* (1985) Routledge & Kegan Paul. And see H Kuhse (ed), *Unsanctifying Human Life: Essays on Ethics* (2001) Blackwells.

which is worth living'.[45] Side by side with a move to concentrate attention on the quality of life alone comes a redefinition of human life deserving of protection. It is *persons*,[46] not all human animals, whose lives have value. Unless there is capacity for self-awareness, for the individual to recognise himself as a functioning human person able to relate to other persons, he has no life of the quality and kind which must be preserved. Certain consequences follow. A person who can reason must be allowed to judge for himself whether continued life is worth it. A human who cannot reason for himself, who is not a person, may have that judgment made for him by others. Providing painless release for a person who considers his life not worth living, or an individual whose capacity for self-awareness has gone, so that he has ceased to be a person, becomes a moral action. The unborn are not persons. They have no rights against their mothers who are persons. Abortion is moral and it may even be considered immoral not to abort a seriously damaged foetus. Research on embryos to benefit existing persons, whether by improving treatment for infertility or seeking a cure for congenital disease, is not only morally permissible, but almost a moral imperative. Euthanasia of the hopelessly brain-damaged with no hope of recovery is entirely acceptable and may, in strictly controlled circumstances, be non-voluntary.

Sanctity of life and the medical profession

3.13 No doubt the disparity of views among the general population is reflected in the personal views of many doctors. Doctors, however, have to take decisions on matters others merely debate. How far and in what fashion is the sanctity of life a central medical ethic? The Declaration of Geneva[47] included the following undertaking:

> I will maintain the utmost respect for human life from time of conception; even under threat, I will not use my medical knowledge contrary to the laws of humanity.

When the Declaration was first formulated in 1947, 'the utmost respect for human life' no doubt imported to most doctors a prohibition on abortion, at any rate where the mother's life was not in danger, and a complete ban on any form of euthanasia. The Declaration was amended and updated in Sydney in 1968. By 1968, abortion on grounds other than immediate danger to the mother had been legalised in Britain and parts of the USA. Within a decade debate was to flourish within respected medical circles as to whether keeping alive all disabled babies was right, and whether prolonging the life of the sick and elderly had not been taken to extremes by modern medicine. The Declaration was amended again in 1984, 1994, 2005 and 2006. The most recent version contains an undertaking which simply reads:

> A physician shall always bear in mind the obligation to respect human life.

---

[45] Glover, *Causing Death and Saving Lives* (1977) Penguin, ch 3.
[46] Harris, *The Value of Life* (1985) Routledge, ch 1.
[47] For the Hippocratic Oath, Declaration of Geneva and other codes of medical ethics, see *Mason and McCall Smith*, Appendices A–D, pp 665–673.

What then does the obligation to respect human life entail? What it does not entail, and what has never existed in any code of medical ethics, is an injunction to preserve life at any price. The prevention of suffering is as much the doctor's task as the prolongation of life. Alas, the two cannot always be complementary. The doctor struggling to interpret and apply his obligation to respect life faces a number of quandaries.

The beginning and end of life

3.14   An admonition to respect human life would be easier to adhere to if there was agreement as to when life begins and ends. Few biologists see the fertilisation of the woman's egg as the beginning of a new life. They argue that egg and sperm are living organisms and point out that many fertilised eggs fail to implant. The fertilised egg may split into two, and in rare cases grow not into a baby but a hydatidiform mole. Fertilisation is just one step in a continuing process. At what stage then does life begin and attract respect? We have noted the argument that the foetus has no status because it is not a person. A growing view appears to be that the foetus as potential life attracts increased status as it grows to full human likeness.[48] This gradualist perception of the embryo resulted in the support for embryo research from most doctors' organisations in 1990, helping to ensure that members of Parliament eventually voted to permit research for a period of up to fourteen days in the Human Fertilisation and Embryology Act 1990.

The influence of the medical profession is discernible too in the more recent debates on human cloning. Nuclear substitution is a technique in which a nucleus with its complete complement of DNA is removed from a cell taken from the organism to be cloned. The nucleus is inserted in an egg cell that has had its own nucleus removed. The egg cell, now carrying the DNA from the first organism, is encouraged to divide and develop into an embryo that is genetically identical to the donor of the DNA. Experiments on mammals, such as those who produced Dolly, the most famous sheep in the world, suggest that it will be possible to produce human clones using this process. It need not be taken as far as reproductive cloning producing a new person. It is also possible to collect stem cells, undifferentiated cells with the potential to divide indefinitely and give rise to more specialised tissue cells, from the cloned embryo. As we have noted, such therapeutic cloning, stem cell therapy, could be used to provide tissue grafts, or ultimately transplant organs, to treat the donor of the DNA. Doctors and scientists mostly oppose reproductive cloning, but back therapeutic cloning. Their views carried the day with the British government.[49]

---

[48]   See, for example, T Martin, *Interests in Abortion: A New Perspective on Foetal Potential and the Abortion Debate* (2000) Avebury.

[49]   The Human Reproductive Cloning Act 2001 prohibited the placing in a woman of an embryo created otherwise than by fertilisation. This legislation became obsolete when the Human Fertilisation and Embryology Act 2008 amended the Human Fertilisation and Embryology Act 1990 to prohibit reproductive cloning (see s 3(6)).

The end of life too has no definite marker any more. It can no longer be equated with the cessation of breathing and heartbeat.[50] The development of life-support machines to replace heart and lung functions during surgery or after traumatic injury demonstrate that life can go on although the heart has stopped. When then does death occur? A definition of death as the irreversible cessation of all activity in the brain stem[51] is generally accepted within the medical profession, although some doctors still occasionally express public doubts. For the lay public the decision to agree to switch off the life-support machine of a relative causes individual anguish, and anxiety occasionally surfaces that a desire for organs for transplantation might prompt too swift a pronouncement of death.[52] The moral dilemma relating to dying arises a stage before brain-stem death. A person may suffer irreversible brain damage, be irreversibly comatose and yet still show signs of some activity in the brain stem. He is not dead according to the current definition of death. Some argue that this definition should be extended to include the irreversibly comatose. For those who regard human life as of value only where the individual can recognise himself as a person, loss of consciousness is equated with physical death.[53] If a patient is in PVS, having lost all cortical function, should we regard him as dead? Was Tony Bland alive in any real sense?[54] Is such a move really euthanasia by the back door? The question of continuing to keep alive the unkindly named 'human vegetable' will not go away. It must be faced, not by a surreptitious moving back of the moment of death but by addressing ourselves to the question of whether the doctor may ever kill.[55]

Killing and letting die

3.15 Caring for a patient as he dies in peace and dignity may be the last service his doctor can perform for him. Doctors and nurses tending the terminally ill in hospices are accorded the highest respect. The doctor's obligation to relieve suffering may on occasion cause him to refrain from prolonging life. Asked whether a doctor should invariably invoke every weapon of medical progress to prevent death, people of every shade of opinion would answer, no. For the Roman Catholic, the test would be whether 'extraordinary means' must be resorted to in order to prolong that life. Extensive surgery on a dying cancer patient offering him only weeks more life would be ruled out. Antibiotics to cure a sudden, unrelated infection pose a more difficult moral dilemma.

---

50 Note that Britain's Chief Rabbi, Jonathan Sacks, argues that death occurs upon irreversible cessation of the heartbeat. This has connotations for organ transplantation. See J Sacks, 'Organ Donor Cards are Not Incompatible with Jewish Law' (2011) *Guardian,* 14 January.

51 *Re A* [1992] 3 Med LR 3033.

52 See ch 16.

53 Glover, *Causing Death and Saving Lives* (1977) Penguin, pp 43–45.

54 See *Airedale* NHS *Trust v Bland* [1993] AC 789 HL; discussed below at **19.1.**

55 See ch 19.

Nevertheless for most of us, religious or irreligious, this satirical rhyme sums up our attitude:

> Thou shalt not kill; but needst not strive
> Officiously to keep alive.

Scratch the surface of this popular attitude and problems emerge. What amounts to 'officiously' keeping alive? Is the doctor alone to judge when a life is worth living? Lawyers and philosophers often enjoy the argument such issues generate, doctors on the whole do not. They have to provide answers. Where a patient is sane, conscious and an adult, the dilemma has today a relatively easy answer, albeit no less painful. The patient decides whether treatment continues. The doctor, if he has been frank with the patient, has little choice but to leave it to the patient. He cannot lawfully give treatment without the patient's consent.[56] Once a patient has decided to reject further treatment, the doctor must normally desist. Suicide, if refusing treatment can be so classified, is no longer a crime. The freedom of the individual to make his own moral choices, where he is able to, is largely unquestioned. A more acute dilemma arises where the patient cannot make his own decision. Here the distinction between killing and letting die takes a central role. Asked if a doctor, or anyone else, should be allowed to smother a brain-damaged patient, the average person may recoil in horror. When a parent at the end of his tether does the same to his dying and profoundly disabled child he may attract public sympathy and understanding, though public attitudes to 'mercy killing' are not consistent.[57]

Not surprisingly then, the distinction between killing and letting die has not been allowed to go unchallenged. It is subject to a three-pronged attack:

(1) Technology makes the distinction between letting die and killing difficult if not impossible to put into practice.

(2) It is argued that there is no valid moral distinction between killing and letting die.

(3) Some writers have maintained that directly and painlessly killing a patient is a morally superior decision to leaving him to a slow undignified death.[58]

The problems posed for the doctor by the technology at his disposal cannot be sidestepped. An accident victim rushed into hospital is put on a life-support machine. All that can be done is done for him. He proves to be irreversibly brain-damaged but not brain-dead. Failing to put him on a machine would have meant allowing him to die. Is disconnecting the machine killing him[59] (though comatose patients disconnected from life-support machines have lived

---

[56] See *B v NHS Hospital Trust* [2002] 2 All ER 449.
[57] See **19.2**.
[58] And see Lord Browne-Wilkinson in *Airedale NHS Trust v Bland* [1993] AC 789 at 885.
[59] *B v NHS Hospital Trust* [2002] 2 All ER 449.

on for several years in some cases)?[60] Into which category, killing or letting die, does not feeding the patient fall? A newborn baby with severe disabilities may never demand food, may be unable to feed naturally from breast or bottle. Is omitting to tube-feed that baby killing or letting die? What about failing to operate to remove a stomach obstruction? Into which category does failure to perform delicate and painful surgery to relieve hydrocephalus (water on the brain) fall? The difficulties of applying the distinction in practice can be enumerated endlessly.

So, why not abandon the distinction altogether? Several apparently persuasive arguments can be made in favour of such a change of direction.[61] The concept of the value of human life as dependent on self-awareness and the quality of life renders it moral to end a life once self-awareness has gone, or, as in the case of a newborn baby, where it has never developed. A patient still able to reason but living in pain, distress and disability retains the right to make his own judgment on his quality of life. If he is unable to reason, the decision may be taken from him. Once quality of life, not life itself, is the determining factor, it follows that directly killing the patient may be a moral imperative. For if the patient's quality of life is such that life has no instrumental value, is it not kinder to end that life painlessly than let him drag on for more days, weeks or months in undignified 'sub-human' misery? If one accepts the basic premise that the value of human life is solely dependent on life being objectively 'worth living', then logically progress to acceptance that a doctor may sometimes kill his patient must follow.

Pure logic does not, however, govern most human reactions. *Involuntary*[62] euthanasia, ending a patient's life without any direction from him or a proxy acting on his behalf and without reference to his interests, is universally excoriated. *Non-voluntary* euthanasia, ending a life on the invitation of a proxy speaking for the patient and on the basis of a considered judgment of his best interests receives some support,[63] often invoking the justification of beneficence. *Voluntary* euthanasia, assisting a competent patient who desires to die, has a growing number of committed advocates. Nonetheless, any form of active euthanasia causes some disquiet and fears of a slippery slope that modest legalisation of voluntary euthanasia in limited circumstances may rapidly metamorphose into a ready acceptance of less than voluntary euthanasia.[64] The arguments against are dismissed with some scorn by the philosophers

---

[60] See I Kennedy, 'The Karen Quinlan Case: Problems and Proposals' (1976) 2 *Journal of Medical Ethics* 3.

[61] J Coggon, 'On Acts, Omissions and Responsibility' (2008) 34 *Journal of Medical Ethics* 576.

[62] On the problems of terminology, see below at **19.1**; and see *Mason and McCall Smith*, ch 18.

[63] See L Doyal, 'Dignity in Dying Should Include the Legalisation of Non-Voluntary Euthanasia' (2006) 2 *Clinical Ethics* 65.

[64] See J Keown, *Euthanasia, Ethics and Public Policy: An Argument Against Legalisation* (2002) CUP, ch 1.

proposing a change of attitude. Suggestions that doctors are 'playing God' ought to cut little ice unless you believe in God. Fear that powers to kill may be misused could be alleviated by proper controls. Instinctive revulsion is seen as an uninformed response.

The distinction between killing and letting die is unlikely to go away. First, the conception of life as in some sense 'sacred' in itself has a greater hold on the population as a whole than its detractors appreciate. Few may now subscribe to belief in the God of the Bible, the Talmud and the Koran. Belief in a Creator of sorts is more widespread. Belief that humanity must set limits on what humanity may do is deeply ingrained. Killing those who cannot speak for themselves remains taboo. Second, the vision of the slippery slope to euthanasia (real or illusory)[65] for the unfortunate and the dissenter operates to deter acceptance of non-voluntary euthanasia. Today the hopelessly brain damaged, tomorrow the mentally disabled, the day after opponents of the government, is the fear of many. Finally, and practically most importantly, even if the exercise of judging objectively quality of life is carried out in all good faith, how can it be achieved? Who will sit in judgment?

Sanctity of life and the law[66]

3.16 Legislating on moral and ethical issues created fewer problems for the Victorian parliamentarian. Applying the common law posed no dilemma for the judge. He knew what was right and what was wrong. The Victorian was unperturbed by doubt, unconcerned by any feeling that his decision should mirror the moral attitudes of society as a whole. Divisions in moral attitudes, although they did exist, were not as deep as those pertaining today. Nor were the problems of medicine as complex. Death remained then an independent agent largely beyond the doctor's skill to combat.

Yet despite the plethora of ethical problems created daily by modern medicine and the changed moral climate, the law changes slowly. No statute expressly addresses the fate of the newborn infant with multiple disabilities who in an earlier age would have died whatever had been done for her.[67] Every attempt to legislate on euthanasia has stalled in its progress through Parliament. The first test-tube baby, Louise Brown, was born in July 1978. It was not until twelve years later that Parliament finally enacted the Human Fertilisation and Embryology Act 1990 regulating IVF. Before that Act, the Abortion Act 1967 stood alone as a legislative attempt specifically designed to tackle developments in medicine and altered moral outlooks. And the Abortion Act was

---

[65] See S Smith, 'Evidence for the Practical Slippery Slope in the Debate on Physician-Assisted Suicide and Euthanasia' (2005) 13 *Medical Law Review* 17.

[66] See G Williams, *The Sanctity of Life and the Criminal Law* (1958) Faber & Faber; P D G Skegg, *Law, Ethics and Medicine* (1984) Clarendon Press.

[67] See Nuffield Council on Bioethics, *Critical Care Decisions in Fetal and Neonatal Medicine* (2006).

piloted through Parliament not by the government of the day, but by David Steel MP by means of a Private Member's Bill. The troubled history of that Act, a compromise which pleases few, perhaps explains why governments of all political colours shy away from entering the battlefields on sanctity of human life. Attempts to amend the Human Fertilisation and Embryology Act which originally sought to reduce the time limit for abortion[68] unleashed a bitterness and outburst of vitriolic abuse unknown in even the most hard-fought party political battle. During the passage of the Human Fertilisation and Embryology Act 2008 (which updates and amends the 1990 Act), there were calls to reduce the time limit on abortion to twelve, sixteen, twenty and twenty-two weeks, but MPs voted to retain the twenty-four-week limit.

Political disinclination to engage in debate on the sanctity of life means that to a large extent the regulation of the medical profession on issues of life and death has been left to the common law. In drawing up and applying codes of practice on the treatment of the critically ill newborn, the brain-damaged and the dying, the medical profession acts within the constraints of the criminal law of murder and manslaughter. The doctor's exposure to the law can be brutal. The law holds his hand by laying down the code of practice within which he works. Struggling to decide on whether treatment should continue, he acts within guidelines agreed inside his own profession, but lacking any statutory force. Ninety-nine times out of a hundred he can comfort himself with the thought that no one will question his decision in these grey areas between living and dying. On the hundredth occasion he may face the spectre of prosecution for murder or attempted murder. The distinction between killing and letting die does not operate in the criminal law to debar a charge of murder. Allowing a patient to die, when it was the doctor's duty to treat him, when the doctor knew that and intended that death would ensue, is as much murder as stabbing the patient to death.

The crucial issue once more is what is the content of the doctor's duty? When is it his obligation to prolong life? Left to decide that issue according to conscience and professional opinion most of the time, doctors not unnaturally are resentful that intervention when it comes may take the form of criminal prosecution for murder. Doctors do not see themselves as murderers. Even the most vehement and passionate member of Life, believing as he will that medical decisions as to the care of the newborn are frequently wrong, and err too often on the side of withholding treatment, would not place the doctor on the same moral plane as the man murdering in the course of robbery.

The reaction of the medical profession has often been that the law should keep out of medical ethics. Proposals to replace the existing and hazy common law with detailed legislative rules attract little enthusiasm.[69] Procedural rules

---

[68]   But ultimately resulted in a 'liberalisation' of the law on late abortions: see s 37 of the 1990 Act (and see below at **13.12**).

[69]   J Havard, 'Legislation is Likely to Create More Difficulty than it Resolves' (1983) 9 *Journal of Medical Ethics* 18. And see below at **14.3**.

about consultation, reference to codes of practice and the keeping of records of decision-making appear more acceptable. What doctors might welcome is such legislation which additionally promises immunity from prosecution to the doctor following the correct process. Such legislation would check the maverick. It would ensure that no one doctor whose standards deviate markedly from his fellows could pursue a course of treatment or non-treatment of patients unacceptable to the majority. However, it would enshrine in the law a principle that such decisions are for the doctors alone. The rest of us would be excluded from any right to a say on these matters of life and death.

The ultimate decisions about life and death are not simply medical decisions.

This was the view expressed in an editorial in the *British Medical Journal* over twenty-five years ago.[70] We concur wholeheartedly. The meaning and application of the sanctity of life is not a matter to be left for the doctors to decide and for the philosophers to argue over. The law's involvement to ensure that society's expectations are met is inevitable. The law is far from perfect in its operation. Reform in a society divided in its moral judgments is hard to formulate. Detailed legislation is probably undesirable even if such legislation were to be agreed on. The variation in the circumstances confronting the doctor is too great. Rules cannot be invented that would meet every possible dilemma the doctor may face. The doctor's judgment cannot and should not be excluded. What can be done, if there is a will to do so, is to stimulate greater debate on the codes of practice under which the doctor works. Greater legal and lay involvement in their development should be encouraged. The gap between lawyer and doctor needs to be bridged. Doctors complain that lay people do not understand the full implications of the problems presented by the disabled and the dying and do not appreciate the complexity of modern medical technology. Only greater openness and a greater willingness to involve those outside the medical profession in decision-making will bring about better understanding. Only better understanding of the problems of medicine will bring about better law-making.

However much any government might prefer to remain aloof from debates on medicine and morals, the developments in the uses of human tissue, genetics, embryology and assisted conception have forced the British, and other European and Commonwealth governments, to legislate.

(1) Legislation may be designed to protect patients from possible abuses, to prevent what is perceived as an undesirable practice creating risks of exploitation.

(2) Legislation may be needed because gaps in the existing law place people in a legal limbo. For example, if A donates an egg which is fertilised and implanted in B, who carries and gives birth to the child, who in the law is the child's mother? If two men in a civil partnership enter into a contract to have a child with a surrogate mother who hands the child over as agreed, how can the 'fathers' acquire parental responsibility? Such

[70] [1981] BMJ 569.

questions of family law and status may be complex and sometimes controversial. Clear statutory answers are essential to safeguard the interests of the child.

(3) Developments in genetics and biotechnology may create, or exacerbate, several legal problems. Who owns genetic information, and how should access to that information be controlled? What property rights accrue from body products? If cells from a patient's body are used to develop a remedy to some disease, can she claim the ensuing profit made by a drug company? If a healthy gene taken from a patient's embryo is used and inserted to replace a defective gene from his sister's embryo, to whom does the gene belong? Can human genes be patented? All these questions require a legal answer and, if legislation does not provide the answer, expensive litigation will proliferate.

(4) Inadequate unclear laws generate distrust and anger. The fuzzy, toothless provisions of the Human Tissue Act 1961[71] contributed immensely to the outrage and agony occasioned by revelations of organ retention practices.[72]

(5) Finally, the most difficult of all aspects of legislation in this area is to decide what kinds of procedures are acceptable in our society. Are there medical possibilities whose implications are such that, though possible, they should be prohibited by law? The UK sanctions strictly controlled stem cell therapies, ie therapeutic cloning. Most of Europe outlaws cloning altogether.

Legislating on what is permissible is fraught with difficulty. Emotions run high. In 1990 anti-abortion campaigners flooded Parliament with model foetuses. Pro-embryo research lobbies played to the cameras with touching and well-timed stories of the joy brought to previously infertile women by their 'test-tube' babies. The scientific possibilities are hard to grasp and science fiction scenarios abound. Test-tube-baby technology creates fears of Aldous Huxley's *Brave New World*. But above all, each side in the moral debate is convinced they are right and the other is irretrievably wrong. What tends to be overlooked is this. In many ethical debates today there is no answer that will be accepted as unchallengeably right. The question for legislators is not to find a right answer, to achieve a moral consensus, but to determine how in a liberal, democratic society legislation can be formulated in the absence of such consensus. To evade that task is to leave the scientists free rein to do as they see fit. To criticise them with hindsight is unfair and unproductive. Theologians, ethicists, lawyers and indeed all citizens must be prepared to grapple with these awkward moral dilemmas and, probably, be ready to compromise.

---

[71] Now repealed, see below at **18.4–18.6**.
[72] The Royal Liverpool Children's Inquiry Report (2001) HC 12-11; see below at **18.2**.

Chapter 4

A RELATIONSHIP OF TRUST AND CONFIDENCE

Whatever, in connection with my professional practice, or not in connection with it, I see or hear in the life of men, which ought not to be spoken of abroad, I will not divulge, as reckoning that all such should be kept secret.

The Hippocratic Oath

I will respect the secrets which are confided in me, even after the patient has died.

Declaration of Geneva (as amended 2006)

4.1 Doctors, like priests and lawyers, must be able to keep secrets. For medical care to be effective, for patients to trust their doctor, they must have confidence that they can talk frankly to her. In its latest guidance to doctors, the General Medical Council (GMC) puts it this way:[1]

Confidentiality is central to trust between doctors and patients. Without assurances about confidentiality, patients may be reluctant to give doctors the information they need in order to provide good care.

An obligation of confidence to patients lies at the heart of all codes of ethics, but a comparison of the quotations above shows that the obligation is not necessarily absolute. The Ancient Greek physician undertook not to divulge that which 'ought not to be spoken of abroad'. He judged what fell into that category. The Declaration of Geneva is more stringent. Must *any* information given by a patient in confidence be kept secret for ever? A moment's reflection reveals the problems inherent in both absolute and relative obligations of confidence. An absolute obligation leaves the doctor powerless to do anything but try to persuade his patient to allow him to take action if, for example, a patient tells him he is HIV positive but is still having unprotected sex with his wife who knows nothing of his condition, or when a depressed mother confesses her violent impulses towards her baby. On the other hand, a relative obligation, which leaves the doctor free to breach confidence when she judges that some higher duty to another person or to society applies, may deter patients from seeking necessary treatment. This may damage not only the patient but also those very people vulnerable when the doctor treats and does not 'tell'. The wife whose husband receives no advice about 'safe sex' and HIV, and the baby whose mother seeks no counsel may be more vulnerable if fears of breach of confidence prevent the husband and the mother getting any help at all because they are afraid to confide in a doctor.

---

[1] GMC, *Confidentiality* (2009), accessible at www.GMC.uk.org/confidentiality.

4.2 *A Relationship of Trust and Confidence*

In this chapter we look at the law on confidentiality as it affects doctors and adult patients, and examine the role of the medical profession in enforcing the ethical obligation of confidence. The special problems affecting confidentiality and parents and children are considered in chapter 14. The complexity of the law may surprise some. The number of occasions when the law allows or compels the doctor to breach confidence may shock many. The chapter also explores what the patient is entitled to be told. From the patient's viewpoint, the doctor's obligation of confidence exists to prevent the doctor passing on information about the patient to third parties. A relationship of trust requires that this should not happen. Trust also requires that the doctor be frank with the patient. Information about the patient should generally not be withheld from him. It is 'his' information not the doctor's, and so we also ask how far the patient is entitled to frankness from his doctor?

Breach of confidence: medical privacy

4.2 English law on breach of confidence[2] developed haphazardly.[3] The core obligation requiring doctors to respect patient confidences derives from the common law. Judges have shown themselves willing to act to prevent the disclosure of confidential information in a wide variety of circumstances. A duty to preserve confidences has been imposed in settings as diverse as trade or research secrets confided to employees,[4] marital intimacies,[5] intimate disclosures to close friends[6] and Cabinet discussion.[7] Often the obligation of confidence arises as an implied term of a contract, as is the case with the employee bound by his contract of employment to keep his employer's business to himself. But the obligation of confidence can equally arise where no contract exists, or has ever existed, between the parties.

Confidentiality is not only a strong private interest, there is a public interest in keeping certain types of information private, and this is particularly true of medical information. In a very early case, action was taken to prevent publication of a diary kept by a physician to George III.[8] Much later, in 1974, a judge put the doctor's duty thus:[9]

> . . . in common with other professional men, for instance a priest and there are of course others, the doctor is under a duty not to disclose, [voluntarily] without the

---

2   See generally, R Pattenden, *The Law of Professional–Client Confidentiality: Regulating the Disclosure of Confidential Personal Information* (2003) OUP.
3   See Law Commission Report No 110, *Breach of Confidence*, Cmnd 8388, para 3.1.
4   F Gurry, *Breach of Confidence* (1984) Clarendon Press, chs 8 and 9.
5   *Argyll v Argyll* [1967] 1 Ch 302.
6   *Stephens v Avery* [1988] 2 All ER 477.
7   *A-G v Jonathan Cape Ltd* [1976] 1 QB 752.
8   *Wyatt v Wilson* (1820), unreported but referred to in *Prince Albert v Strange* (1849) 41 ER 1171 at 1179.
9   *Hunter v Mann* [1974] 1 QB 767 at 772.

consent of his patient, information which he, the doctor, has gained in his professional capacity, save . . . in very exceptional circumstances.

Today, any attempt to understand the law governing medical confidentiality must take account of a bewildering array of sources. In addition to the case law, it is necessary to take account of Articles 8 (right to privacy) and 10 (freedom of expression) of the European Convention on Human Rights, the Data Protection Act 1998, and voluminous guidance from the GMC and the NHS.

Article 8(1) states that: 'Everyone has the right to respect for his private and family life, his home and his correspondence'. The European Court of Human Rights has consistently upheld the right to privacy in relation to medical records. But it is not an unqualified right. The Court has upheld seizure of medical records in criminal proceedings[10] and use of records in connection with social security benefits.[11] In *Z v Finland*[12] the Court said:

> Respecting the confidentiality of health data is a vital principle in the legal systems of all the Contracting Parties to the Convention. It is crucial not only to respect the sense of privacy of a patient but also to preserve his or her confidence in the medical profession and in the health services in general.

In England, the Human Rights Act 1998 renders the Convention Articles enforceable against public authorities. So can we now assert a right to medical privacy? In the USA, and many civil law jurisdictions, an all-inclusive cause of action for invasion of privacy is recognised. No right of privacy as such is even now recognised in English domestic law,[13] but the various aspects of English law which protect privacy, including the common law action for breach of confidence, have developed to take account of Article 8. The terminology has changed, leading Lord Nicholls to call for the renaming of the tort:[14]

> The continuing use of the phrase 'duty of confidence' and the description of the information as 'confidential' is not altogether comfortable. Information about an individual's private life would not, in ordinary usage, be called 'confidential'. The more natural description today is that such information is private. The essence of the tort is better encapsulated now as misuse of private information.

And in *Ash v Mckennitt*[15] Buxton LJ said:

> [T]here is no English domestic tort of invasion of privacy . . . [As a result] the English courts have to proceed through a tort of breach of confidence into which the jurisprudence of arts 8 and 10 has to be 'shoehorned'.

The common law principles developed incrementally by the judiciary long before the Human Rights Act remain important to an understanding of medical

---

[10] *Z v Finland* [1997] 25 EHRR 371.
[11] *MS v Sweden* [1997] 45 BMLR 133.
[12] [1997] 25 EHRR 371 at para 95.
[13] *Wainwright v Home Office* [2003] 3 WLR 1137.
[14] *Campbell v Mirror Group Newspapers* [2004] UKHL 22, para 14.
[15] [2006] EWCA 1714, para 8.

confidentiality, but now have to be applied with due regard for Convention rights. So in *Campbell v Mirror Group Newspapers*,[16] to which we shall return, the House of Lords balanced human rights, Article 8 versus Article 10, rather than the traditional concepts of private and public interests, but Lord Hope commented that: 'It seems to me that the balancing exercise to which that guidance is directed is essentially the same exercise, although it is plainly now more carefully focused and more penetrating.'[17]

Article 8 of the Convention strengthens the principles long contained in the common law action for breach of confidence in which the basic general principles are these:

(1)   The courts will intervene to restrain disclosure of information where the information is confidential in nature and not a matter of public knowledge, or trivial in nature.

(2)   Where information is found to be private and confidential, any non-consensual disclosure requires justification in the public interest.[18]

(3)   Once an obligation of confidence is created it binds not only the original recipient of the information but also any other person to whom disclosure is made by the recipient when that other person knows of the confidential status of the information.[19] As well as acting in advance to prevent the disclosure of confidential information, the courts may where appropriate award compensation after information has been improperly disclosed.[20]

In *A-G v Guardian Newspapers (No 2)*,[21] Lord Goff broadened the scope of breach of confidence stating that when information is entrusted to another person in *circumstances* imposing an obligation not to use or disclose that information without the consent of the giver of the information an initial confidential relationship is not required.[22] In *Campbell v MGN*[23] (which did not involve a doctor–patient relationship), the Law Lords ruled that the *circumstances* in which the information was obtained were irrelevant. The *nature* of the information was of paramount importance. The 'old' test of a confidential relationship covered the relationship of doctor and patient. Applying the new terminology, it remains the case that a 'reasonable expectation of privacy'[24] can be established when a patient divulges information about her health to her doctor, and may extend to a broader class of health information.

---

[16]   [2004] UKHL 22, para 157.

[17]   [2004] UKHL 22, para 86.

[18]   *W v Egdell* [1990] 1 All ER 835 at 846, CA; *Campbell v Mirror Group Newspapers* [2004] UKHL 22.

[19]   *Campbell v Mirror Group Newspapers* [2004] UKHL 22.

[20]   *Cornelius v De Taranto* (2001) 68 BMLR 62.

[21]   [1990] 1 AC 109.

[22]   [1990] 1 AC 109 at 281. See also *Douglas v Hello Ltd* [2001] 2 All ER 289.

[23]   *Campbell v Mirror Group Newspapers* [2004] UKHL 22.

[24]   *Campbell v Mirror Group Newspapers* [2004] UKHL 22 per Lord Nicholls, para 21.

Disclosure after death

4.3 Does death terminate any obligation of confidence to a deceased patient? You might ask why this should matter but consider just two examples. A senior cabinet Minister dies and within weeks her GP publishes a best-selling book highlighting her multiple medical problems in graphic and prurient detail. A noted and married actor dies and his doctor tells the tabloid press all about his battle with HIV and bisexuality. Should the first doctor be allowed to make profit from the abuse of his professional relationship? Do the widow and children of the actor have a claim to consideration? For many years the GMC has instructed doctors that 'Your duty of confidentiality continues after a patient has died'.[25] It was less clear whether the law imposed such an obligation surviving the patient until in *Lewis v Secretary of State for Health*[26] Foskett J took the view that the 'obligation of confidence is capable of surviving the death of the patient'.[27] Such, he said, were the expectations of the public and the profession. The legal obligation is not necessarily permanent and the period of survival will depend on the sensitivity of the information at issue and the prospect of any harm done to surviving relatives.

Justifying disclosure

4.4 The challenging questions about medical confidentiality do not, however, lie in establishing a *general* duty of confidence, or expectation of privacy, but in determining what amounts to 'very exceptional circumstances' justifying breach of that duty.

First, disclosure will always be justified legally when the doctor is *compelled* by law to give confidential information to a third party. This may be by way of an order of the court to disclose records in the course of some civil proceedings. Doctors, unlike lawyers, enjoy no professional privilege entitling them to refuse to give evidence in court. Or it may be under some statutory provision, such as those Acts of Parliament requiring that specified diseases be notified to the health authorities.[28]

Second, it is clear that the doctor may *voluntarily elect* to disclose information in certain circumstances. Where there is a public interest in disclosure of confidential and private information, the court will consider whether harm (to either physical or moral integrity) may be caused to someone as a result.[29] The

---

[25] GMC, *Confidentiality* (2009), paras 71–72.
[26] [2008] EWHC 2196.
[27] *Lewis v Secretary of State* [2008] EWHC 2196 at para 24; and see *Bluck v The Information Commissioner and Epsom and St Helier University NHS Trust* (2007) 98 BMLR 1; and T Pitt-Payne, 'Mother, I Sue Dead People' (2007) 157 NLJ 1532.
[28] Public Health (Control of Diseases) Act 1984 (as amended); see below at **6.22**.
[29] *R v Department of Health, ex p Source Informatics Ltd* [2000] 1 All ER 786; *Campbell v Mirror Group Newspapers* [2004] UKHL 22.

public interest in disclosure must be balanced with the public and private interests in maintaining confidentiality. Thus, disclosure of private information requires justification.

In early judgments, the public interest 'defence' tended to concern disclosure of crime: 'there is no confidence in the disclosure of iniquity'.[30] Gradually it has been accepted that that defence is not limited to crime, or even misconduct. In *Lion Laboratories Ltd v Evans* (which considered the disclosure of confidential information suggesting that a breathalyser device, the Intoximeter, was unreliable), Griffiths LJ said:

> I can see no sensible reason why this defence should be limited to cases where there has been wrongdoing on the part of the plaintiffs ... it is not difficult to think of instances where, although there has been no wrongdoing on the part of the plaintiff, it may be vital in the public interest to publish a part of his confidential information.[31]

Two major cases remain central to an understanding of when public interests will justify a breach of medical confidentiality. In *X v Y*[32] a tabloid newspaper acquired, in breach of confidence from a health authority employee, information identifying two GPs who were continuing to practise after having been diagnosed as HIV-positive. The authority sought an injunction prohibiting publication of their patients' (the doctors') names. The newspaper argued that the general public, and the doctors' patients in particular, had an interest in knowing that the doctors were HIV-positive. Rose J reviewed the evidence about transmission of HIV from doctor to patient where the doctor had received proper counselling about safe practice. He found that the risk to patients was negligible. Far greater risks arose from the possibility that if they could not rely on confidential treatment, people with AIDS, or who feared they might have AIDS, would not seek medical help. The judge, granting the injunction, said:

> In the long run, preservation of confidentiality is the only way of securing public health; otherwise doctors will be discredited as a source of education, for future individual patients will not come forward if doctors are going to squeal on them. Consequently, confidentiality is vital to secure public as well as private health, for unless those infected come forward they cannot be counselled and self-treatment does not provide the best care ...[33]

By contrast in *W v Egdell*,[34] the Court of Appeal sanctioned a breach of confidence by a psychiatrist. W had been convicted of the manslaughter of five people and of wounding two others. He was ordered to be detained indefinitely in a secure hospital. He could be released only by order of the Home Secretary if he were found to be no longer a danger to public safety. As a step

---

[30] *Gartside v Outram* (1856) 26 LJ Ch 113 at 114.
[31] *Lion Laboratories Ltd v Evans* [1984] 2 All ER 417 at 433.
[32] [1988] 2 All ER 648.
[33] *X v Y* [1988] 2 All ER 648 at 653.
[34] [1990] 1 All ER 835; applied in *R v Crozier* [1991] *Criminal Law Review* 138, CA.

towards eventual release he sought to transfer to a regional secure unit. The transfer was not approved by the Home Secretary and W then applied to a mental health review tribunal for a conditional discharge. In support of his application his solicitors arranged for an independent psychiatric report from Dr Egdell. Dr Egdell's report was not favourable. He judged that W was still a dangerous man with a psychopathic personality, no real insight into his condition and a morbid interest in explosives. Unsurprisingly, W's solicitors withdrew their application for his discharge but they did not pass on the report to the tribunal or the hospital where W was detained. Dr Egdell was concerned by the fact that his report was not passed on. He ultimately sent his report to the medical director of W's hospital and agreed that a copy of that report should be forwarded to the Home Secretary. W sued Dr Egdell for breach of confidence.

The Court of Appeal made it crystal clear that Dr Egdell did owe W a duty of confidence. Had he sold his story to the press or discussed the case in his memoirs, Dr Egdell would have been in breach of confidence. But the duty of confidentiality is not absolute. The public interest in medical confidentiality must be balanced against the public interest in public safety. If Dr Egdell's diagnosis was right, W remained a source of danger to others and he was entitled to communicate his findings to the director of the hospital now detaining W, and to the Home Secretary, who would have the final say on if and when W should be released into the community.

X v Y and *W v Egdell* did not mean that a doctor may *never* disclose that a patient is HIV positive, or that he may always disclose his concerns about a patient's mental health. In each case the powerful interest in maintaining confidentiality must be balanced against the danger ensuing if confidentiality is not breached. Only where there is a clear and significant risk of the patient causing harm to others, which cannot be abated by any other means, may confidence be breached.

As we have noted, more recently judicial assessment of public and private interests has involved the careful balancing of Convention rights. *Campbell v Mirror Group Newspapers Ltd*[35] involved the disclosure of information concerning the health of a famous fashion model. Although the information was disclosed by the *Mirror* newspaper, rather than a medical practitioner, there are clear implications for medical privacy. At first instance, Naomi Campbell was awarded £3,500 in damages, but the Court of Appeal reversed the decision, holding that disclosure was in the public interest. The House of Lords balanced Campbell's right to privacy under Article 8, protected by the common law duty of confidentiality, with the freedom of the press, protected under Article 10. Both are qualified rights and neither has pre-eminence over the other. Campbell had previously falsely stated that she was not a drug addict. She was powerless to object, therefore, when the *Mirror* newspaper published information to the contrary. However, she did object to the publication of

[35] [2004] UKHL 22.

furtively taken photographs and articles proving that she was attending Narcotics Anonymous. This, she maintained, was a breach of confidence for which she was entitled to compensation under the Data Protection Act 1998. By a majority, the House of Lords found in her favour, overturning the decision of the Court of Appeal. The special nature of medical information was recognised by Baroness Hale who stated:[36]

> It has always been accepted that information about a person's health and treatment for ill health is both private and confidential. This stems not only from the confidentiality of the doctor–patient relationship but from the nature of the information itself.

Baroness Hale made the following points:

(1)   The information about Campbell's attendance at Narcotics Anonymous was private and confidential 'because it related to an important aspect of Miss Campbell's physical and mental health and the treatment she was receiving for it. It had also been received from an insider in breach of confidence . . .'

(2)   Because it was private, its publication required specific justification.

(3)   'Some [types of speech] are more deserving of protection in a democratic society than others.' Where disclosure carries little risk of harm to a person's physical or moral integrity, where for example 'a public figure has a cold or a broken leg', it might be justifiable. Note, however, that Baroness Hale was balancing Article 8 and Article 10 rights. Her words do not necessarily imply that less protection will be given to the breach of confidence relating to 'trivial' health matters where there is no competing public interest in their disclosure.

(4)   The breach of confidence had potential to cause Miss Campbell harm. Her Article 8 privacy rights took priority over the public interest in freedom of the press under Article 10.

Article 8, like the common law, imposes only a relative obligation of confidence.[37] Article 8(2) provides:

> There shall be no interference by a public authority with the exercise of this right except such as is in accordance with the law and is necessary in a democratic society in the interests of national security, public safety or the economic well-being of the country, for the prevention of disorder or crime, for the protection of health or morals, or for the protection of the rights and freedoms of others.

In *Szuluk v UK*,[38] the European Court of Human Rights has emphasised that states invoking Article 8(2) to justify a violation of medical privacy must demonstrate a necessity corresponding to a pressing social need and one proportionate to the aim pursued. While in prison, first on remand and then serving a fourteen-year sentence, Mr Szuluk had to undergo major neurosurgery twice

---

[36]   [2004] UKHL 22, para 145.
[37]   See also *R (on the Application of TB) v CPS and South Staffordshire Healthcare NHS Trust* [2006] EWHC 1645 (Admin), discussed below at **4.9**.
[38]   [2009] ECHR 36936/05.

and needed regular monitoring. He wished to be able to correspond with his consultant confidentially and sought assurances from the prison governor that his correspondence would not be opened and read by prison staff. Prison rules provided that normally all letters to and from prisoners may be opened and read. The governor's initial decision to accede to Mr Szuluk's request was overruled and arrangements made for the prison medical officer to read this correspondence. After the Court of Appeal ruled in favour of the prison authorities, Mr Szuluk took his case to the ECtHR and won. While Article 8(2) allowed for interferences with privacy for the prevention of crime and the protection of the rights and freedoms of others, and so would justify some degree of interference with prisoners' correspondence to prevent escapes or complicity in crimes, the state must show that interference with medical correspondence with a named doctor of impeccable character was truly necessary to avoid the risk of criminal activity or breaches of security. Mr Szuluk was not a Category A prisoner and the court stressed that 'uninhibited' medical correspondence with his doctors on the part of a prisoner suffering from a life-threatening condition should be afforded no lesser protection than prisoners' correspondence with their lawyers or MPs.

The General Medical Council (GMC)[39]

4.5 A doctor facing a practical dilemma about whether she can lawfully disclose information in the public interest will want more specific guidance than that available from the judgments of the courts. A primary source of such advice is the GMC, whose latest Guidance *Confidentiality* issued in 2009 runs to fifty-six pages with seven sets of supplementary guidelines. The GMC plays two crucial roles in enforcing confidentiality. First, the courts will give due regard to the profession's own view of the ethical obligations owed by its members in formulating consequential legal obligations.[40] That does not mean GMC guidelines are in any sense law or that the courts will slavishly follow the profession's view. But the guidance may be a good indicator of how the courts will resolve dilemmas as they come before them.

Second, aggrieved patients may prefer to complain to the GMC rather than take legal action in the courts. The doctor in breach of confidentiality could face a finding of impaired fitness to practise and removal from the register. The civil action for breach of confidence is an excellent weapon for restraining threatened breaches of confidence. It may be less effective in offering redress to the victim of a breach of confidence, except in a commercial setting. If a trade secret is revealed by an employee and the employer loses profits, his loss can be measured by the courts and appropriate compensation ordered. The defendant may be obliged to hand over all his illegal profits. A breach of medical

---

[39] And see British Medical Association, *Confidentiality and Disclosure of Health Information Toolkit* (2009).

[40] *Lewis v Secretary of State for Health* [2008] EWHC 2196 (QB) at para 19; *W v Egdell* [1990] 1 All ER 835 at 843 and 850.

confidence rarely results in monetary loss, but will give rise to indignity and distress for the patient. It used to be unclear if mental distress could give rise to damages for breach of confidence. In *Cornelius v De Taranto*[41] the judge at first instance awarded the claimant £3,000 in damages for mental distress caused by 'unauthorised disclosure of the confidential information' and subsequent cases have followed suit. However, legal action may be expensive and the damages low.[42] The legal claim itself may attract unwelcome publicity and complaining to the GMC may well remain a preferred option for many victims of breach of medical confidence.

The GMC makes it clear that patients have a right to expect that information about them will be held in confidence by their doctors.[43] We consider first information where the identity of the patient is disclosed: what the GMC describes as personal information. The doctor's duty is to maintain confidentiality strictly. The Guidance warns doctors to be vigilant in protecting confidential information. It rightly notes that '[M]any improper disclosures of information are unintentional'.[44] Notes should not be left lying around. Consultations with patients should not take place where they can be overheard by other patients or by staff not involved in the care of the patient. Doctors responsible for the management of records must make sure that all staff understand their responsibilities to secure patient confidentiality.

The greater part of the GMC Guidance addresses when a doctor may lawfully disclose confidential information and in the sections that follow we address both the GMC Guidance and the case law.

Disclosure with consent

4.6   Disclosure is self-evidently lawful if the patient expressly consents to disclosure. The doctor must ensure that the patient understands what is to be disclosed, the reasons for disclosure and the consequences thereof. The patient must be told to whom information will be given and how much information will be disclosed. But in a number of instances consent may be implied rather than explicit. Health care in the NHS is usually provided by a team of professionals, and sharing information within that healthcare team will normally be lawful on the basis that patients are likely to understand that a number of different health professionals will play a role in their care. The GMC makes it clear that every effort must be made to ensure that the patient is aware that

---

[41]   (2001) 68 BMLR 62. In 1981, the Law Commission had recommended the award of damages for distress. And see the Scottish decisions *AB v CD* (1851) 14 D 177; *AB v CD* (1904) 7 F 72; see J K Mason and G T Laurie, *Mason and McCall Smith's Law and Medical Ethics* (8th edn, 2010) OUP (hereafter *Mason and McCall Smith*), p 204.

[42]   Though, see *Mosley v News Group Newspapers* [2008] EWHC 1777.

[43]   GMC, *Good Medical Practice* (2006), para 37.

[44]   GMC *Confidentiality* (2009), para 12.

information about him may be disclosed to other health professionals working with his doctor and that, if a patient does not want certain information about him revealed to others, his wishes must be respected. Doctors must make sure that everyone within the team to whom information is disclosed understands that they are bound by a legal obligation of confidence. Moreover, the sharing of confidential information should be restricted to staff who are directly involved in personal care[45] but surveys have suggested that in practice a growing number of non-medical staff have access to confidential records.[46]

All doctors in clinical practice should participate in clinical audit. Provided it is undertaken by the team providing the care, or their support staff, personal information may be disclosed if the patient is aware that personal information may be disclosed for audit purposes, has been informed and has not objected. If the patient objects, it is necessary to make an assessment as to whether safe care can be provided without it. Where audit is undertaken by an external organisation, express consent should be obtained unless the data can be anonymised.[47]

Disclosure where the patient lacks capacity

4.7 What about the patient who lacks capacity to authorise disclosure of information, be she unconscious in a Casualty department or suffering from some long-term intellectual impairment. A key question will be how much information doctors can share with family or carers. Under the Mental Capacity Act 2005 there is a presumption of capacity. A person will only be shown to lack capacity in relation to a specific decision where she is unable to make a decision for herself[48] by virtue of the fact that she cannot understand, retain, weigh or use the information relevant to the decision.[49] Under section 5, those providing care for someone who lacks capacity will not incur legal liability provided they have properly assessed her capacity, and act in her best interests. The Act provides a checklist for determining best interests.[50] So the question becomes whether the disclosure of information is in the incapacitated patient's interests. And in many cases it will be.[51]

Under section 4(7) of the Mental Capacity Act 2005 the doctor has a duty, where practicable, to consult appropriate persons about her treatment. Discussing the condition of an unconscious patient in Casualty and seeking advice on her treatment with colleagues and family members is proper and lawful.[52]

---

[45] *I v Finland* (2008) 48 EHRR 740.
[46] 'NHS Breaching Citizens' Human Rights over Levels of Access' (2010) 10 *Privacy and Data Protection* 5 (1) (1).
[47] GMC *Confidentiality* (2009), paras 30–32.
[48] Mental Capacity Act 2005, s 2(1). On the 2005 Act generally, see below ch 6.
[49] Mental Capacity Act 2005, s 3.
[50] Mental Capacity Act 2005, s 4.
[51] GMC, *Confidentiality* (2009), paras 57–62.
[52] See *R (on the application of S) v Plymouth City Council* [2002] EWCA Civ 388.

However, where a patient is conscious and objects to disclosure, doctors should be wary of releasing information to the family in her 'medical interests'. Under section 4, best interests include, but are not limited to, medical interests. The patient's beliefs, values, and past and present wishes must also be taken into account. Only information that it is essential to share should be disclosed and in general there will be no need or justification to give details of past health care.[53] So if a young female patient is unconscious, having suffered serious head and abdominal injuries, it may be lawful to discuss with her family her current condition, prognosis and options but not to disclose that examinations show that some years before she had terminated a pregnancy.

Disclosure to protect the patient

4.8   Doctors may sometimes wish to disclose information to protect their patient and the GMC guidance is clear that if a patient who lacks capacity may be at risk of neglect or abuse the doctor *must* inform[54] an appropriate person or authority promptly. She must act to protect her patient. What if a patient is vulnerable or very ill, but retains capacity? Consider the dying patient. Not long ago, it was considered acceptable to ignore a patient's plea to keep knowledge of her illness from her family, or even to 'spare the patient pain' by telling her family, but not her, how close she is to death. Earlier GMC guidance expressly allowed doctors, albeit 'rarely', to bypass the patient and entrust information which might be upsetting to her to her family. Information could even be withheld from the patient. The GMC today is clear that where the patient retains capacity, information may only be shared with the family with her consent.[55] There is no legal basis for compassionate paternalism. But what if death or serious injury may result to the patient, for example, the doctor becomes aware that his patient is the victim of escalating domestic abuse but the patient refuses to allow him to contact the police or social services? Can disclosure to protect the patient be made in such circumstances? Paragraph 51 of the GMC Guidance advises:

> It may be appropriate to encourage patients to consent to disclosures you consider necessary for their protection and to warn them of the risk of refusing to consent, *but you should usually abide by a competent adult's refusal to consent to disclosure, even if their decision leaves them, but nobody else, at risk of serious harm* (our emphasis).

Note the word 'usually' may be seen as allowing for a truly exceptional case? A competent patient is free to refuse advice in his own interests as he is free to refuse treatments even when his life is at risk. Only if the threat to the patient poses risk to others can a competent refusal to disclose information be overruled. So if the doctor reasonably concludes that the husband who has battered his wife repeatedly also poses a risk to the children in the family, he may

---

[53]   GMC, *Confidentiality* (2009), para 61.
[54]   GMC *Confidentiality* (2009), para 63.
[55]   GMC *Confidentiality* (2009), paras 64–66.

contact the police in 'the public interest', but if the evidence suggests he remains a loving father whose violence is directed only towards his wife, the doctor cannot act against the woman's wishes. However, recent Department of Heath guidance[56] on safeguarding vulnerable adults appears to suggest that health professionals not only may, but should, disclose information to the police or social services if they suspect that a vulnerable patient is suffering abuse or neglect regardless of whether or not she retains mental capacity. Any adult in receipt of health care is defined as vulnerable. The guidance illustrates the inevitable tension between a desire to protect patients at risk and respect for autonomy.

Compulsory disclosure

4.9 When a disclosure of confidential information or production of medical records is required by law, the doctor has no choice but to comply, and compulsory disclosure is mandated in a variety of circumstances.

First, a doctor must give any information required by a court of law. Privilege, in the sense of being free to refuse to give evidence relating to professional dealings with clients, is something usually enjoyed by lawyers alone and not shared by any other professional colleagues.[57] A doctor can be subpoenaed to give evidence about his patient's health and may be forced to reveal intimate information. He cannot withhold information from the court and he may be ordered to produce the patient's records. He does not have to volunteer his views or expertise, but whatever questions he is asked he must answer. The protection for medical confidentiality in the courtroom lies in the judge's discretion. Judges will try to ensure that confidence is breached only to the extent necessary for the conduct of the trial. The doctor may be unhappy at having to break trust with his patient. He can be reassured that he is at no legal risk. Any breach of confidence made as a witness in court is absolutely privileged.

In exercising their powers to order disclosure of evidence or documents, courts strive to balance justice and confidentiality, in recent cases giving due regard to Article 8 of the Convention. In *D v NSPCC*[58] the plaintiff sought to compel the NSPCC to disclose who had mistakenly accused her of child abuse. The court refused to make the order. The public interest in people feeling free to approach appropriate authorities to protect young children outweighed the plaintiff's private interest in unearthing her accuser. Thus there will be some cases where the courts may refuse to help a party seeking to discover who gave damaging information about him to the police or some other authority. The courts may find that the public interest outweighs the private rights of the affected party.

---

[56] DH, *Clinical Governance and Adult Safeguarding–An Integrated Process* (2009). And see the Safeguarding Vulnerable Adults Act 2006.
[57] See J V McHale, *Medical Confidentiality and Legal Privilege* (1993) Routledge.
[58] [1977] 1 All ER 589.

Particularly sensitive information may be allowed to be withheld from the court in the public interest. So in *AB v Glasgow and West of Scotland Blood Transfusion Service*,[59] a Scottish court refused to order disclosure of the identity of a blood donor who had allegedly supplied infected blood. In *R (on the Application of TB) v CPS and South Staffordshire Healthcare NHS Trust*[60] the High Court held that the Crown Court had breached TB's right to privacy contrary to Article 6(1). TB was a fourteen-year-old witness in a criminal case against a man alleged to have sexually abused her. The Crown Court ordered disclosure of her medical records relating to psychiatric counselling she had received. In accordance with the Criminal Procedure Rules 2005 (which were under review, leading May LJ to confine his decision to the facts), the application was served on the NHS trust, but not on TB. The trust was concerned that releasing the records without giving TB a chance to make oral representations would breach their duty of confidence. In response the Crown Court judge called TB at short notice, whereupon, unrepresented, she reluctantly agreed to the disclosure. TB sought judicial review of the Crown Court decision to order disclosure. The High Court held that TB's right to privacy under Article 8(1) had been breached. Neither was the interference justified within the terms of Article 8(2).

Next, the doctor may be compelled to hand over information to the police or other authorities before any trial commences. Several statutes demand that the doctor answers questions if the police come and ask him. If a statute imposes a duty on 'any person' to answer police questions, any person includes a doctor.[61] His profession confers no exemption or privilege upon him. Where no specific statutory power aids the police in their investigation of a crime, the question becomes whether, if they believe a doctor holds records or other material constituting evidence of a crime on the part of a patient, they can search the doctor's premises and seize the relevant material. The Police and Criminal Evidence Act 1984 grants police access to medical records, but imposes certain safeguards. A search warrant to enter and search a surgery, hospital or clinic for medical records or human tissue or fluids taken for the purposes of medical treatment may be granted only by a circuit judge[62] and not, as is usually the case, by lay magistrates. The judge is directed to weigh the public interest in disclosure of the material against the general public interest in maintaining confidentiality.

Beyond the scope of the criminal law, several further examples of compulsory disclosure must be noted. Provision is made for compulsory notification of certain highly infectious diseases and of venereal disease.[63] Section 45A of the Public Health (Control of Disease) Act 1984 (as amended) makes expansive

---

[59] 1993 SLT 36.
[60] [2006] EWHC 1645 (Admin).
[61] *Hunter v Mann* [1974] 1 QB 767.
[62] Police and Criminal Evidence Act 1984, ss 8–14 and Sch 1.
[63] The National Health Service (Venereal Diseases) Regulations 1974 make provision for the tracing of sexual contacts, but also seek to ensure that the identity of patients and contacts remains confidential.

provision for compulsory notification of certain specific diseases such as cholera or typhoid and also provides that doctors should notify the appropriate authorities of any infection or contamination that 'presents or could present significant harm to human health'.[64] Successive governments resisted pressure to make HIV/AIDS a notifiable disease.[65] Again the question is one of balancing the competing public interests, the interest in patients seeking advice and treatment for disease, and the interest in protecting the health of those at risk from infection. HIV is not in the same league as diseases such as cholera. The cholera carrier immediately places his casual contacts at risk; if he is untreated, he can do little to minimise that risk. Cholera spreads like wildfire. HIV is much less infectious, and by acting responsibly, the patient can reduce the risk to others. To act responsibly he needs professional help and should not be deterred from seeking help by fear that his doctor will be forced to 'squeal' to the authorities.

Abortions must be reported. Details of drug addicts are required under the Misuse of Drugs Act 1971. Births and deaths have to be notified by doctors as well as registered by families.

Finally, a number of organisations concerned with health administration may require information in the course of performing their functions. These include the NHS Ombudsman, the Department of Health and other NHS authorities.[66] Examining the individual items on the long list of circumstances when a doctor can be forced to hand over information concerning his patients, many can be justified on grounds of public interest. The trouble is that the list grows haphazardly.

Sections 251–252 of the National Health Service Act 2006 grant the Secretary of State further powers to dilute patient confidentiality providing that:[67]

> The Secretary of State may by regulation make such provision for and in connection with requiring or regulating the processing of prescribed patient information for medical purposes as he considers necessary or expedient –
>
> in the interest of improving patient care, or
> in the public interest

As the Health and Social Care Bill 2001 progressed through Parliament, fears were voiced that Ministers would use this power to drive a coach and horses

---

[64] And see the Health Protection (Notification) Regulations 2010, SI 2010/659; and see below at **6.22**.

[65] Though provisions for detention in the Public Health (Control of Disease) Act (as amended) do extend to people with AIDS; see below at **6.22**.

[66] But powers must be used with proper regard for the patient's right to privacy under Art 8 of the Human Rights Convention; see *A Health Authority v X* [2001] EWCA Civ 2014.

[67] Originally Health and Social Care Act 2001, s 60. See P Case, 'Confidence Matters: The Rise and Fall of Informational Autonomy in Medical Law' (2003) 11 *Medical Law Review* 208.

through the common law protection of medical privacy. In a concession to opponents of the move, a Patient Information Advisory Group (PIAG) was established with whom the Minister must consult on any regulations to be made under section 60. In 2009, the PIAG was replaced by the Ethics and Confidentiality Committee (ECC) of the National Information Governance Board for Health and Social Care (NIGB).[68]

Disclosure in the public interest

4.10   As we have seen, the case law makes it clear that the public interest can justify disclosure of confidential information without consent.[69] Article 8(2) sets out a list of exceptions to the right to respect for privacy, a list that, at first sight, looks broad enough to encompass a host of exceptions to the rule. So we need to examine carefully just when a competing public interest is sufficient to outweigh the public interest in medical confidentiality. The GMC explains the public interest in disclosure as designed 'to protect the individual or society from risks of serious harm, such as serious communicable diseases or serious crime or to enable medical research, education or other secondary uses of information that will benefit society over time'.[70] We deal with the use of information for research and other secondary purposes in chapter 15. Our focus here is on disclosure to protect individuals and society from harm. The doctor is faced with a balancing exercise, weighing the harm done to the patient and the public trust by breaching confidence against the harm posed to others by the patient if he fails to act. A simple example will illustrate the point. A patient whose sight is failing and who had had several mini-strokes insists on continuing to drive. She refuses to accept that she is medically unfit to drive or to contact the Driver and Vehicle Licensing Agency (DVLA). She poses a risk of death or injury to other road-users whenever she is out on the road. The GMC advises doctors that in such a case they not only may, but should, contact the DVLA.

Serious crime

4.11   An obvious example of a public interest justifying breach of confidence is the prevention of crime. But does this include any suspicion of a criminal offence that a doctor may learn of in the course of caring for his patients? When may, or must, doctors inform the police about criminal conduct on the part of a patient? If fifteen years after the event, and plagued by guilt, a depressed patient confesses to non-violent crimes committed in her youth, is her doctor obliged to inform on her? Contrary to popular myth, a doctor is

---

[68]   See E Jackson, *Medical Law: Text, Cases and Materials* (2nd edn, 2010) OUP, pp 384–387.

[69]   See in particular *X v Y* [1988] 2 All ER 648 and *W v Egdell* [1990] 1 All ER 835, CA.

[70]   GMC, *Confidentiality* (2009), para 36.

under no general obligation to contact the police. Unless a statute specifically so provides, a doctor does not commit any offence by failing to tell the police of any evidence he may have come across professionally which suggests that a patient may have committed, or is contemplating some crime.[71] A criminal offence is committed only when a doctor or anyone else accepts money to conceal evidence of crime.[72] Section 19 of the Terrorism Act 2000 imposes a duty on everyone, including doctors, to inform the police if they believe or suspect certain offences concerning funding of terrorist activity have been committed. There are several Acts of Parliament (eg Road Traffic Acts) that require doctors to disclose information if asked to do so by police,[73] but they are not compelled to volunteer that information. In many cases, a doctor will nonetheless judge that he should do so where others are at risk and in its latest Guidance the GMC sometimes imposes a professional obligation to contact the police.

If a doctor has reason to believe that the patient or a third party may commit a serious crime, placing others at risk, then, as with Dr Egdell, the doctor may lawfully contact the police or other appropriate authorities. So if a doctor makes a judgment that a new mother with acute postnatal depression is likely to harm her baby and he cannot persuade her to seek help, he acts lawfully in contacting social services and even in extreme cases the police and/or her family to protect the child. Many disclosures to prevent crime will, however, entail a breach of confidence with someone other than the 'criminal'. A rape victim refuses to go to the police but the evidence of the brutal attack on her indicates that other women may be at risk. In such cases, disclosure may be justifiable and the GMC advises doctors that if others are at risk from offenders using weapons or from domestic violence then the patient's refusal to involve the police may be overridden.[74] In relation to gunshot and knife wounds, the GMC goes further and requires doctors to contact the police swiftly and make a judgment whether they also need to disclose personal details about their patient (the victim), including his identity.[75] In practice there would seem to be little the police could act on without such personal information and the GMC is virtually mandating disclosure in such cases.

What of cases where the public interest is not so much in the prevention of crime, but in the detection or prosecution of crime? In many cases, the choice remains the doctor's. The criminal law will not penalise him for not informing the police. Will he be in breach of confidence if he elects to do so? The judges early last century were divided on the issue of whether a doctor was justified in going to the police after attending a woman who had undergone a criminal

---

[71] Criminal Law Act 1967, s 5(5).
[72] Criminal Law Act 1967, s 5(1).
[73] For example, s 172 of the Road Traffic Act 1988 (information identifying the driver of a car involved in a road accident).
[74] GMC, *Confidentiality* (2009), paras 54–56.
[75] GMC, *Supplementary Guidance, Confidentiality; Reporting Gunshot and Knife Wounds* (2009).

abortion. Hawkins J condemned such a course as a 'monstrous cruelty' and doubted whether such a breach of confidence could ever be justified,[76] whereas Avory J saw the doctor's duty to assist in the investigation of serious crime as always outweighing his duty to his patient.[77]

In the context of confidential relationships outside the medical field, some case law would suggest that the public interest justifies disclosure of *any* crime or misdeed committed or contemplated.[78] Within the doctor – patient relationship, should freedom to disclose in the public interest be more limited in scope? Unless commission of any crime disentitles the patient from normal standards of medical care, disclosure should be strictly limited. Doctors who suspect that another person is at risk of physical injury at their patient's hands must be free to act to protect that person. Preventing harm to others outweighs the private and public interests in confidentiality. Volunteering evidence of less serious crimes, or crimes committed long ago, to the police may be seen as less straight-forward. The GMC advises that disclosure is defensible in relation to serious crime,[79] 'especially crimes against the person'. What the doctor should not do is hand over to the police information on each and every patient who transgresses the law. Parliament has legislated in numerous cases to compel breach of medical confidence. The courts should not be zealous to add to that list.

The flaw in this argument is whether a doctor found to be in breach of confidence for disclosing a crime could be condemned by a court for taking steps to combat crime, performing a moral duty cast on every citizen. The doctor is distinguished from other citizens by the presence of a positive legal duty to his patient. Enforcing his duty to his patient benefits the public as well as the patient. The Court of Appeal has robustly recognised a public interest in the maintenance of medical confidentiality.[80] Medical confidentiality is at the root of good health care. Should the courts, however, find that as upholders of the law they cannot condemn those who help bring lawbreakers to justice, the alternative solution is to fall back on the professional standard set by the GMC, and hold that breach of confidence is justified only in case of serious crime. The doctor may not break the law if he discloses details of petty crimes. He may be held accountable for professional misconduct. The legal and ethical standards do not need to be exactly the same.

Serious communicable diseases

4.12 The Public Health (Control of Disease) Act 1984 (as amended) requires doctors to notify the proper authorities about certain infectious diseases, but can doctors go further and warn those individuals who might be at risk from

---

[76] *Kitson v Playfair* (1896) *Times*, 28 March.
[77] *Birmingham Assizes* (1914) 78 JP 604.
[78] *Initial Services Ltd v Putterill* [1968] 1 QB 396 at 405.
[79] GMC, *Confidentiality* (2009), para 54.
[80] *W v Egdell* [1990] 1 All ER 845 at 849, CA.

a patient with a serious communicable disease? May a GP alert a wife to the fact that her husband is HIV-positive, or warn his employers if the patient is a surgeon continuing to operate without disclosing his HIV status? As we have seen in *X v Y*, the judge granted an injunction banning an account in the media of two GPs diagnosed as HIV-positive on the basis that the risk to patients in that case was negligible. There was no public interest in disclosure founded on the protection of others. That does not mean that it is never in the public interest to disclose information relating to patients who have a serious communicable disease and pose a risk of transmission to others. It is not uncommon for surgeons to cut themselves in the course of surgery so that there is blood-to-blood contact between surgeon and patient. Certain forms of surgery, now styled exposure-prone procedures, carry a risk of cross-infection. Such a risk is not limited to HIV. Hepatitis B,[81] for instance, is much more infectious than HIV but transmitted in the same manner. Other diseases with different modes of transmission may endanger patients, for example a health worker with untreated TB places all her patients at risk. The GMC gives very specific guidance[82] to doctors treating fellow health workers whose own ill health may endanger their patients either because they suffer from disease that they might pass on to patients or because their judgment or performance may be impaired, eg by the onset of a neuro-degenerative disease. First, the affected worker has an obligation to seek and follow advice to protect his patients, but if he fails to do so the doctor treating him *should* inform the health worker's employers or contracting body, or, where appropriate, the relevant regulator.[83] When there is a real risk of transmission of disease or a health professional's illness renders him unsafe to practise, the public interest in patient safety prevails, and the doctor acts lawfully in bringing the risk to the attention of those authorities charged to protect patient welfare.[84]

Can this *public* interest in disclosure justify disclosure, not only to a public body or official, but also to an individual at risk? If an HIV-positive surgeon refuses to refrain from unprotected intercourse or to tell his wife of his condition, can she be warned of the danger she faces? The GMC advises that doctors *may* (not must) disclose such information to known sexual contacts.[85] Doctors are urged to do all they can to persuade the infected person to inform sexual partners. If persuasion fails, then the doctor should consider whether he should inform any sexual partner at risk of infection. Would the law support a doctor who did so? In defamation, a defence of qualified privilege protects any communication which the maker has a duty to impart and the recipient a

---

[81] M Brazier and J Harris, 'Public Health and Private Lives' (1996) 4 *Medical Law Review* 171.

[82] GMC, *Supplementary Guidance, Confidentiality: Disclosing Information about Serious Communicable Diseases* (2009).

[83] See GMC, *Good Medical Practice* (2006), paras 78–79.

[84] GMC, *Supplementary Guidance, Confidentiality: Disclosing Information about Serious Communicable Diseases* (2009), paras 4–6.

[85] GMC, *Supplementary Guidance, Confidentiality: Disclosing Information about Serious Communicable Diseases* (2009), at para 10.

legitimate interest in receiving. No defence of qualified privilege as such exists in breach of confidence.[86] The defence is that the public interest demands disclosure. Private interests alone are not usually enough. However, where a genuine risk of physical danger, of injury or disease is posed to any third party, the public interest in individual security is sufficient to justify disclosure to that person so that she can protect herself appropriately. When the doctor reasonably foresees that non-disclosure poses a real risk of physical harm to a third party, he ought to be free to warn that person, especially if that person too is his patient. Courts should not be over-zealous to prove him wrong. Similarly, in such cases, if the doctor thinks it more appropriate to contact the third party's GP, he should not be condemned. Nonetheless, risk of harm must be established. A simple belief that someone else, spouse or relative, is entitled to information is insufficient, even if they have an interest, and not merely a prurient interest, in the matters at stake.[87] That is not enough. The balance of public interest in favour of preserving confidentiality should be displaced only by a significant danger of physical harm.

Freedom of the press

4.13 We have seen that, exceptionally, doctors may disclose information about patients with serious communicable diseases to protect others. The common law and Article 8(2) prioritise the protection of those others. What effect, however, does Article 10 of the European Convention on Human Rights have in such cases? Can the media rely on the right to freedom of expression in making public debates about HIV or other burning issues that could compromise patient confidentiality? Openly identifying an individual healthcare worker who is HIV-positive is highly unlikely to be lawful. A more difficult question arose in *H (A Healthcare Worker) v Associated Newspapers Ltd and N (A Health Authority)*.[88] H tested positive for HIV while working as a healthcare professional for a health authority, identified in court proceedings only as N. The health authority proposed to carry out a 'look back' exercise to notify patients treated by H and invite them to undergo HIV testing if they so chose. H sought an injunction to prevent N from notifying his patients and carrying out the 'look back' study. He provided details of at least some of his NHS patients with the utmost reluctance, and refused to supply any information about his private patients. H argued that, in his particular case, the risk to patients of HIV was so low that it did not justify breach of his, or his patients' clinical confidentiality.

Before H's case against the health authority could be heard, the *Mail on Sunday* heard about the case. The newspaper planned to publish a story about

---

[86] Law Commission Report No 110, *Breach of Confidence* Cmnd 8388, paras 6-94–6-96.
[87] For example, that a parent might want to know if an adult daughter was HIV-positive in order to offer her support, but that interest, however caring it might be, will not suffice.
[88] [2002] Lloyd's Rep Med 210, CA.

H's condition and his dispute with the health authority. He sought a second injunction to prevent publication of any details identifying him personally, or identifying either the health authority that employed him or his medical speciality. A temporary injunction was granted to him in the terms he sought. The newspaper retaliated with the headline 'Judge's Gag over AIDS Threat to Patients'.

Gross J upheld the ban on publishing details of H's identity, but would have allowed publication of the health authority's identity and H's speciality. H appealed. He argued that if the nature of his speciality and the name of his employing authority were in the public domain, he himself would be readily identifiable by a significant number of people, including some of his patients. The Court of Appeal acknowledged that H's case involved a difficult balancing exercise. They concluded that a ban on identifying the health authority should be imposed. Disclosing N's (the health authority's) identity would be likely to '. . . set in train a course of events' that could result in disclosure of H's identity and compromise his first action against the health authority to prevent it conducting the 'look back' study. Patients might also be harmed by discovering the risk to themselves without immediate access to proper advice and counselling. The appeal court, however, was not convinced that a ban on identifying H's speciality was necessary. Such a restraint would inhibit legitimate debate on a matter of public interest. The Court of Appeal in *H* granted more legitimacy to the interest in freedom of expression and public debate about the risks of HIV transmission and infected health workers than Rose J did in *X v Y*. The influence of Article 10 of the European Convention on Human Rights (guaranteeing freedom of expression) is plainly seen.[89]

Genetic information and confidentiality[90]

4.14 Especially difficult questions touching on confidentiality arise in relation to genetic screening and genetic counselling. This is a complex subject to which we can give only cursory attention here.[91] Tests which reveal that the individual patient suffers from, or is a carrier of, a genetic disease often indicate that other family members are at risk of the same disease.[92] Consider a simple example. Jenny, a medical student, having completed her initial course

---

[89] See also *Independent News and Media Ltd v A* [2009] EWHC 2858, where Hedley J had to rule if the media might attend a hearing before the Court of Protection relating to the management of the affairs of a highly gifted but severely disabled musician whose work and attainments had already been the subject of much public attention.

[90] See generally, G T Laurie, *Genetic Privacy: A Challenge to Medico-Legal Norms* (2002) CUP.

[91] See E Jackson, *Medical Law: Text Cases and Materials* (2nd edn, 2010) OUP, ch 8.

[92] Fully and eloquently discussed in *Mason and McCall Smith*, pp 219–228. And see Nuffield Council on Bioethics, *Genetic Screening: The Ethical Issues* (1993); and *Genetic Screening: Ethical Issues* (2006) Supplement (www.nuffieldbioethics.org); and R Gilbar, *The Status of the Family in Law and Bioethics: The Genetic Context* (2005) Ashgate.

in genetics, becomes concerned about her family history. There appears to be a pattern of paternal relatives succumbing to dementia and premature death. After counselling she consents to a test for Huntington's Chorea. The test proves positive. Huntington's is an autosomal dominant genetic disease which means that if a parent has the affected gene, any child has a 50 per cent chance of inheriting Huntington's. The disease does not manifest itself until early middle age when the affected person succumbs over several years to progressive dementia and early death. Jenny's diagnosis necessarily means that one of her parents must also have the affected gene, and that each of her siblings is at 50/50 risk, as will be any child whom Jenny may bear. If Jenny refuses to consent to genetic counsellors contacting her family, would the interests of those family members justify a breach of confidence? If Jenny's elder brother had just married and he and his wife were hoping to start a family, would the potential harm to the child justify disclosure?[93] The 2009 GMC Guidance[94] suggests that in rare cases the doctor may overrule the patient's refusal to share information with relatives at risk '[F]or example where family relationships have broken down or natural children have been adopted'. Breach of confidence might be justified by a duty to protect the at-risk relative from serious harm. Some thought needs to be given to what constitutes harm. Telling Jenny's parents that one of them has Huntington's may itself cause harm. They may prefer to remain in ignorance and as there is no cure for Huntington's their knowledge will not assist them to avoid or minimise the impact of the disease.[95] Contrast this scenario with another. If one sister tests positive for the BRCA 1 gene there is a 50 per cent chance that any sister of hers will also carry the gene and women with the gene are at 80–85 per cent risk of developing breast cancer. Regular screening and even an elective mastectomy can reduce the risk substantially. In this example it seems more likely that informing the sister at risk is justifiable to avoid serious harm as her health and life are at stake.[96]

Genetic privacy

4.15 Genetic information also helps us note the limits of confidentiality and that it falls short of a guarantee of privacy. An obligation of confidentiality binds the recipient of the confidence to keep private information secret. Imagine this scenario. X undergoes genetic tests to establish whether she has a gene rendering her susceptible to breast cancer. The test proves positive. A potential employer or insurer seeks to ascertain if she has undergone such a test and to find out the results. Doctors breach confidence if they release test results without the patient's consent. So the employer or insurer will simply

---

[93] See D Bell and B Bennett, 'Genetic Secrets and the Family' (2001) 9 *Medical Law Review* 130; L Skene, 'Genetic Secrets and the Family: A Response to Bell and Bennett' (2001) 9 *Medical Law Review* 162.

[94] GMC, *Confidentiality* (2009), paras 67–69.

[95] See Laurie, *Genetic Privacy: A Challenge to Medico-Legal Norms* (CUP) 2002.

[96] See K O'Donovan, R Gilbar, 'The Loved Ones: Families, Intimates and Patient Autonomy' (2003) *Legal Studies* 353.

demand that information from the patient herself. She is free to refuse to divulge her test results. The consequence will be that she is turned down for the job, or refused insurance. Her 'right' to privacy means little. Genetic information is becoming more and more important in everyday life as understanding of the role genetics play in disease increases. Knowledge will enable individuals to lower their risk by adapting their lifestyle. It is already possible for a person to have the whole of her genome decoded.

Could Article 8 establish a right to keep personal information secret and make it unlawful to ask X questions about genetic test results? Alas, an employee or insurer may seek to invoke one of the justifications for violating privacy set out in Article 8(2). In X's case, where what is established by tests is a susceptibility to breast cancer, a 'defence' based on the protection of the health or freedom of others invoked by an employer is unlikely to succeed. Were she a potential airline pilot with a genetic susceptibility to heart failure, the balance of argument might be different. Another argument that might be advanced in X's particular case might be on protection of 'economic well-being'. Can employers or insurers be forced to take on poor risks? Note, though, that Article 8(2) speaks of the economic well-being of the country, not of individual businesses. A further twist to the tale is this. Does X's daughter have any right to information about X? Could she argue that her right to life (Article 2) and 'family life' (Article 8(1)) impose an obligation on X to disclose information to her, to inform her decisions about whether to seek genetic testing?[97] Defining the scope of a right to medical privacy will prove more difficult than establishing that such a right exists.

Being able to control access to genetic information is important and if employers and insurers have unrestricted access to genetic information, the risk arises of the creation of a genetic underclass who struggle to find work and cannot for example gain the life insurance that any sensible person wants before taking on a mortgage. The Human Genetics Commission (HGC)[98] was established to develop policy and advise the government on the regulation of genetics and to provide practical solutions to the complex problems posed by developments in genetics. The HGC is now one of many arm's-length authorities that may be abolished. The HGC conducted a careful review of whether individuals applying for insurance policies[99] have a right to genetic privacy and what such a right might entail. In 2001, UK insurance companies agreed a voluntary five-year moratorium on seeking access to genetic test results in relation to life insurance policies worth less than £500,000, income protection

---

[97] See R Gilbar, *The Status of the Family in Law and Bioethics: The Genetic Context* (Ashgate, 2005); R Gilbar, 'Medical Confidentiality Within the Family: The Doctor's Duty Reconsidered' (2004) 18 *International Journal of Law and Policy and the Family* 195.

[98] See HGC, 'Inside Information: Balancing Interests in the Use of Personal Genetic Data' (2002) accessible at http://www.hgc.gov.uk.

[99] See T Sorell, 'The Insurance Market and Discriminatory Practices' in J Burley and J Harris (eds) *Companion to Genetics* (2002) Blackwell, ch 29.

policies worth less than £30,000 a year and other insurance policies worth less that £300,000.[100] In relation to policies above the higher thresholds, information may be sought in relation to tests approved by the Genetics and Insurance Advisory Committee (GAIC). At the time of writing, the only GAIC approved test is that for Huntington's for a life insurance policy worth more than £500,000. The voluntary moratorium has now been extended until 2015.[101] Should we have laws to protect genetic privacy? Section 45 of the Human Tissue Act 2004 already outlaws the taking and analysis of DNA samples without consent? Or would it make sense to legislate more generally to safeguard medical privacy? Questions about sexually transmitted infections may be as intrusive and damaging as questions about genetic tests.

Liability for failure to disclose

4.16 There are clearly circumstances when the doctor's duty of confidence to his patient may be overridden by his duty to safeguard a third party from serious harm. If he mistakenly decides the question of this conflict of duty in the patient's favour, and the risk of harm to someone else materialises, is the doctor at risk of a lawsuit by the injured party? In a highly publicised case in the USA, the student medical centre at the University of California was held liable for failing to warn a young woman of the risk posed to her by one of their patients.[102] The girl's rejected lover sought psychiatric help at the centre. He told staff there of his violent intentions towards the girl and that he had a gun. The staff warned the campus police, who decided to take no action. The medical centre said nothing to the girl. She was murdered by their patient soon afterwards. Her family sued the University for negligence. The medical centre was found liable for failing to breach their patient's confidence and warn the girl of the threat to her life.

On similar facts, we suggest that an English court would be less likely to find a doctor negligent. First the court would have to determine whether, given the value attached to medical confidentiality, a duty to breach confidence could be countenanced; the conflict of duty facing the doctor is stark.[103] Remember, however, that the GMC has in a number of instances made it clear that the doctor not only may, but should, act to disclose information to protect others at risk from the patient. So if a GP, knowing that his patient is an HIV-positive surgeon carrying out exposure-prone procedures, fails to act to protect the patients at risk and some contract HIV, could those infected patients sue? Might they argue that the failure to protect them was itself a breach of their

---

[100] S Mayor, 'UK Insurers Agree Five Year Ban on Using Genetic Tests' (2001) 323 *BMJ* 1021.

[101] Association of British Insurers, *Code of Practice for Genetic Tests* (2008), accessible at www.abi.org.uk.

[102] *Tarasoff v Regents of University of California* (1976) 551 P 2d 334; see *Mason and McCall Smith*, pp 187–188, 445–446.

[103] *Palmer v Tees Health Authority* [1999] Lloyd's Rep Med 351, CA.

Article 8 rights?[104] It must be noted that the courts in England are reluctant to make any defendant liable for a wrong committed by an adult and independent third party, unless he either had a special responsibility to exercise control over that third party or a special relationship with the claimant to safeguard him from harm at the hands of that third party.[105]

Data Protection Act 1998

4.17   The Data Protection Act 1998 was enacted to implement the Data Protection Directive,[106] which will be reviewed in late 2011.[107] The reforms will modernise and update the Directive, strengthening rights and improving clarity and coherence.

The Act offers additional statutory protection to control the use and processing of all forms of 'personal data'.[108] This includes all medical and health records whether the records are manual or computerised. The individual about whom information is held is designated the 'data subject', and the person or organisation responsible for holding that information is styled the 'data controller'. The 1998 Act applies to all kinds of information held about us, not just health records. We are, however, concerned here only with its application to health records. 'Health records' are defined as:[109]

> any record which consists of information relating to the physical or mental health or condition of an individual, and has been made by or on behalf of a health professional in connection with the care of an individual.

'Health professional'[110] is broadly defined to include doctors, dentists and nurses. The Act is lengthy, complex and not compelling reading. The fundamental points to emphasise are now discussed. Any processing[111] of data, including alteration of health records, retrieval of or use of records, *disclosure* or erasure of records, must be done in conformity with the Act. Any 'personal data' from a health record that is information relating to a living and identifiable patient is subject to stringent controls. Whenever such data is processed,

---

[104] See *Colak v Germany* [2009] ECHR 77144/01.
[105] See *Smith v Littlewoods Organisation Ltd* [1987] 1 All ER 710, HL; *Mitchell v Glasgow County Council* [2009] UKHL 11, HL.
[106] Directive 95/46/EC on the Protection of Individuals with Regard to the Processing of Personal Data and on the Free Movement of Such Data.
[107] See Rand Europe, *Review of the European Data Protection Directive* (May 2009); Ministry of Justice, *Call for Evidence on the Data Protection Legislative Framework* (closed 6 October 2010); and see http://ec.europa.eu/justice/policies/privacy/review/index_en.htm.
[108] Defined in *Durant v Financial Services Authority* [2003] EWCA Civ 1746 (which did not concern health records) as information focusing on the individual rather than a third party, incident or event in which the individual participated.
[109] Data Protection Act 1998, s 68(2).
[110] Data Protection Act 1998, s 69.
[111] See *Johnson v Medical Defence Union* (2007) 96 BMLR 99.

one at least of the conditions of Schedule 2 of the Act must be met. These include that the patient gave consent to processing, or that processing is necessary to protect the 'vital interests' of the patient, or necessary in the administration of justice, or for the purpose of legitimate interests of the data controller. Consent need not be explicit. Notices in GP surgeries and clinics about possible uses of information may suffice. A broader range of justifications for disclosure than the common law allows is sanctioned by Schedule 2.

However, health records fall within the category of 'sensitive personal data' granted additional protection by the Act. 'Sensitive personal data' is defined to include any information about a person's physical or mental health or condition. 'Sensitive personal data' may only be processed, and therefore only disclosed, either with the *explicit* consent of the patient or in the following circumstances. (Specific provision is made in relation to research and we address this later in chapter 15.) What follows is not an exhaustive list:

(1)   to protect the vital interests of a patient who cannot consent on his own behalf, or where the data controller cannot reasonably be expected to obtain consent, or to protect the vital interests of another person where the patient has unreasonably withheld consent to disclosure;
(2)   in connection with the administration of justice, or disclosure is required by law;
(3)   for medical purposes by a health professional which involves only disclosure to another person bound by a similar duty of confidentiality.

The Secretary of State is empowered to add further conditions allowing the lawful processing of 'sensitive personal data'. He has done so inter alia to allow the disclosure of health records in professional disciplinary proceedings involving health professionals, and to allow various NHS authorities to investigate mismanagement or malpractice. A wide, all-embracing provision allows processing without consent where it is in the substantial public interest and necessary for the discharge of any function designed to protect the public against dishonesty, malpractice or service failure and must necessarily be carried out without the explicit consent of the patient 'so as not to prejudice the discharge of that function'.

The range of exceptions to the duty of non-disclosure under the Data Protection Act mean that its scope is little greater than the obligation of confidentiality imposed by common law. The force of the 1998 Act lies in its remedies. A patient suspecting misuse of his health records can apply to the data controller to cease processing records when what is being done is or is likely to cause him substantial and unwarranted damage or distress.[112] A person who has suffered damage or distress as a consequence of violation of the Act has a right to compensation. He does not need to prove financial loss. However, the data controller may, in defence of such a claim, establish that he had taken all reasonable care to comply with the Act.[113] Most crucially, section 14 of the Act allows

---

[112] Data Protection Act 1998, s 10.
[113] Data Protection Act 1998, s 13.

a patient to apply to the court to correct inaccurate health records. He can act to ensure that misinformation about his health is not perpetuated for all time.

Anonymised data

4.18   Most of what has been said so far relates to information from which the identity of the patient can be ascertained. For many purposes, however, anonymised data about patients and their diseases is needed or wanted by diverse organisations. Anonymised information may be necessary to carry out clinical audits, or to compile statistics about health needs, or the epidemiological purposes. Many of us might applaud such purposes. Commercial organisations such as drug companies may also seek access to such information to help them with marketing or product development. The GMC gives extensive advice on anonymising data and its disclosure.[114] It urges doctors to explain to their patients how such data is used and what benefits flow from exchange of information. Does the confidentiality apply to anonymised information?

In *R v Department of Health, ex p Source Informatics Ltd*[115] the applicants were a data collection company. They persuaded GPs and pharmacists to supply them with anonymised information about prescribing habits. They then sold this information to drug companies. The Department of Health issued a document ruling that to disclose such information without patient consent constituted a breach of confidence. The company challenged the ruling. The trial judge found that anonymisation did not remove the obligation of confidence. Transfer of anonymised data might in certain cases be justifiable, for example, to ensure clinical audit, but information about patients was in all cases confidential, whether the patient was identifiable or not. The Court of Appeal disagreed. Disclosure of anonymised information, the appeal court ruled, did not violate the interests which obligations of confidentiality protect. The patient's privacy is not violated. He is not vulnerable to any harm. Patients have no property in information about them. Ethical safeguards now surround anonymised data. The law restricts itself to controlling information about us only where we can be identified. GPs, pharmacists and drug companies may still profit from information derived from us.

Patients' access to records[116]

4.19   We turn now to the opposite side of the coin. Patients expect their doctors to keep their secrets. Can doctors have secrets from their patients? The law relating to confidentiality prevents doctors from improperly disclosing

---

[114] See GMC, *Confidentiality* (2009).

[115] [2000] 1 All ER 786, CA.

[116] See generally on the implications of record keeping for medical confidentiality, *Report on the Review of Patient-Identifiable Information* (1997) HMSO (*The Caldicott Report*).

information from or about their patients. What if the patient seeks information about herself? When can a patient demand to see her records?

An attempt to assert a common law right of access to all health records failed in 1995.[117] Until 1998 the statutory picture was confusing. Access is now governed by the Data Protection Act 1998.[118] Section 7 of the 1998 Act establishes a right for data subjects to have access to all personal data relating to them held by the data controller. For our purposes, this means that patients have a prima facie right to access of all their health records whether manual or computerised. However, the 1998 Act, like its predecessors, allows the Secretary of State to exempt or modify rights of patient access to health records.[119]

Access is not unlimited. Certain sorts of information held for research, historical or statistical purposes are exempted from access. Special rules are laid down where information about a patient also discloses information about some third party. A host of other exemptions and limitations apply. Most crucially, access to health records may be refused where release of information would be likely to cause serious harm to the physical or mental health or condition of the patient[120] or any other person.[121] In deciding whether to refuse access, NHS authorities are required to consult the health professionals currently responsible for the patient's care.[122]

On the face of it, such exclusions from rights of access seem reasonable. A patient whose mental health is fragile and who may be devastated by a full account of his diagnosis and prognosis may be thought to be 'better off' not knowing the true state of affairs. Of course, when he is refused access he may imagine an even worse scenario. The crux of the problem, though, is the way in which relevant NHS authorities, and doctors in particular, will use the exclusions. Suppose a patient is diagnosed as having terminal cancer. His doctor decides not to tell him, and advises the health authority to refuse access to records because *he* judges that the patient could not cope with the truth. What can the patient do? Section 7 of the Data Protection Act allows him to apply to the court, so a judge can decide if access has been improperly refused.

Finally, the access provisions of the Data Protection Act 1998 apply only to living patients. Consequently a small part of the Access to Health Records Act 1990[123] is preserved to enable executors of a deceased person's estate or members of his family to gain access to his records in an appropriate case.

---

[117] *R v Mid-Glamorgan Family Health Services, ex p Martin* [1995] 1 WLR 110.
[118] Note that the Data Protection Act 1998, rather than the Freedom of Information Act 2000, governs access to personal data.
[119] See Data Protection Act 1998, s 30(1).
[120] See *Clive Roberts v Nottinghamshire Healthcare NHS Trust* [2008] EWHC 1934.
[121] Data Protection (Subject Access Modification) (Health) Order 2000, SI 2000/413, art 5(1).
[122] Data Protection Act 1998, s 7.
[123] Access to Health Records Act 1990, s 3(1)(f).

NHS practice

4.20   It is important to note that within the NHS crucial decisions on patient confidentiality and access to records may be made not by health professionals but by health service administrators. A manager, not a doctor or nurse, may decide, for example, to allow police access to patient records.[124] We have already examined the role of the GMC in enforcing the ethic of confidentiality. Their jurisdiction is limited to medical practitioners. The Nursing and Midwifery Council (NMC) enforces similar stringent ethical rules for nurses. Doctors as well as patients have expressed concern that a patient's notes are seen by an unnecessary number of persons. They complain that decisions as to when to disclose records are taken too often by administrators, and that administrators are not subject to the control of the GMC or the NMC. Doctors fear they may be less concerned about confidentiality.

Such fears should be misguided. All NHS staff are subject to the law on confidence. Information confided by the patient to her doctor remains legally confidential when passed by the doctor to NHS clerks for filing and preserving in NHS files. The NHS Code of Practice 2003[125] makes it clear that confidentiality binds everyone working within the NHS. Disclosure within the service is justified only if required in the context of the patient's health care. Disclosure to third parties outside the service is permissible only with the patient's consent, save in exceptional cases. The exceptions, for example, where disclosure is required by law or in case of serious crime, correspond closely to the exceptions sanctioned by the GMC. Generally decisions on disclosure should always be taken by a medically qualified person and where possible it should be the doctor caring for the patient. Guidelines are enforced by the sanction of disciplinary action, or even dismissal, against staff members who break them.

---

[124] See D F Pheby, 'Changing Practice on Confidentiality: A Cause for Concern' (1982) 8 *Journal of Medical Ethics* 12.
[125] DH, *Confidentiality: NHS Code of Practice* (2003).

Part II

MEDICAL MALPRACTICE

Chapter 5

AGREEING TO TREATMENT

5.1 There would be little support today, even from the most paternalistic doctor,[1] for the proposition that a sick adult should be compelled to accept whatever treatment his doctor thought best. No one suggests that adults who stay away from dentists out of childlike fear, and to the detriment of their dental and general health, should be rounded up and marched to the nearest dental surgery for forcible treatment. Few would deny the right of the adult Jehovah's Witness to refuse a blood transfusion, even if in doing so she forfeits her life. Medical treatment normally requires the agreement of the patient. The right of the patient, who is sufficiently rational and mature to understand what is entailed in treatment, to decide for herself whether to agree to that treatment is a basic human right. The right to autonomy, to self-rule rather than rule by others, is endorsed by ethicists as a right to patient autonomy. Two of their Lordships in *Chester v Afshar*[2] signalled that a patient's right to autonomy and dignity should today be accorded the highest priority by English law. Lord Steyn declared that in '... modern law, paternalism no longer rules'.[3] We shall have to consider just how far such theory translates into practice.[4]

This chapter considers only the relatively easy case of mentally competent adults. Such an adult has a right to determine what is done to his or her body. Later, in chapters 6 and 14, we look at the law in relation to patients lacking capacity and to children, and also address circumstances where legislation may endorse compulsory medical treatment. A person who intentionally touches another against that other's will commits a trespass to that person just as much as coming uninvited on to the person's land is a trespass to his land. The tort of battery is committed. Where a person consents to a contact no battery is committed. So a boxer entering the ring cannot complain of battery

---

[1]   And certainly not from the General Medical Council (GMC). See their guidance to doctors: GMC, *Consent; Patients and Doctors Making Decisions Together* (2008).

[2]   [2004] UKHL 4, paras 17 and 24.

[3]   [2004] UKHL 4, para 16.

[4]   For an elegant analysis of the relationship between autonomy and consent, see A Maclean, *Autonomy, Informed Consent and Medical Law* (2009) CUP.

when he is hit on the chin by his opponent. Battery is any non-consensual contact. Conduct which constitutes the crime of battery may also amount to the crime of assault. We should also note that contacts resulting in serious bodily harm may still constitute a *criminal* assault, even when such contacts are wholly consensual. English law does not allow you to consent to, for example, sado-masochistic practices that cause actual injury to you.[5] Any such 'injury' must be justified by some good purpose. Medical treatment and surgery are acknowledged to be such purposes.[6] So, more controversially, are 'manly sports', thus justifying the boxers' mutual exchange of blows.[7] There remains a question of whether any kind of maverick or extreme 'surgery' might be beyond the privilege usually accorded to medicine and surgery.[8]

How do the rules relate to doctors? Any doctor examining a patient, or injecting or operating on a patient makes contact with that patient's body. Normally he commits no wrong because he does so with the patient's agreement. Should he fail to obtain a patient's agreement at all, should a doctor force himself on a patient, he commits the tort of battery, and the crime of assault. Not only does he infringe on his patient's autonomy, he also violates her bodily integrity.[9] That crude scenario is unlikely. What of the surgeon who correctly decides to treat cancer of the bone in the right leg by amputating that leg, but by error amputates the wrong leg, the left leg? Once the error is discovered, the poor patient has to endure a further operation to remove the right leg. Or a patient's notes are mixed up and a woman who was scheduled for and consented to an appendectomy is given a hysterectomy. Both unfortunate victims can sue the surgeon in battery. They did not consent to the operation performed. In a Canadian case, a woman who expressed her wish to be injected in her right arm was injected by the doctor in her left. She sued in battery and succeeded.[10]

In all the above examples, the surgeon or some other member of the hospital staff has been careless. So the patient could normally sue in negligence too. However, there are differences between the two torts. In battery, a patient need not establish any tangible injury. The actionable injury is the uninvited invasion of his body. This is important. A doctor may, on medically unchallengeable grounds, decide that an operation is in the patient's best interests. He goes ahead. The patient's health improves. Yet if the operation was done without consent, a battery has still been committed. A doctor who discovered that his patient's womb was ruptured while performing minor gynaecological surgery was held liable to

---

[5]   *R v Brown* [1993] 2 A11 ER 75, HL.

[6]   See *A-G's Reference (No. 6 of 1980)* [1981] 2 All ER 1057; Law Commission Consultation Paper No 139, *Consent in the Criminal Law* (1995) HMSO.

[7]   See *R v Coney* (1882) 8 QBD 534.

[8]   For example, extreme 'cosmetic' surgery involving amputation or gross facial disfigurement.

[9]   And so breaches Art 8 of the Human Rights Convention: see *Glass v UK* [2004] 1 FLR 1019, ECtHR; *Juhnke v Turkey* (2009) 49 EHRR 24, ECtHR.

[10] *Allan v New Mount Sinai Hospital* (1980) 109 DLR (3d) 536.

her for going ahead and sterilising her there and then. She had not agreed to sterilisation.[11] A woman whose ovaries were removed without her express consent similarly recovered for battery.[12] The essence of the wrong of battery is the unpermitted contact. There is no requirement that the patient prove that if he had been asked to consent to the relevant treatment he would have refused.

Two further points should be noted. Battery may be alleged by a patient who *says* he did not consent. First, on whom does the onus of proof lie? It has been held in England that the onus of proof lies on the patient. He must establish that he did not agree.[13] Second, for what will the patient be compensated? In negligence, we shall see that a defendant is only liable for the kind of damage which he reasonably ought to foresee. In battery, the test may be more stringent. The defendant may be liable for all the damage which can factually be shown to flow from his wrongdoing. A doctor who injected a patient in the 'wrong' arm would be liable in battery *and* negligence for any unwanted stiffness in that arm, and for any adverse reaction which he ought to have contemplated in view of the patient's history. He would not be liable in negligence for a 'freak' reaction. In battery he might be so liable. Nonetheless judges in England have sought to limit the scope of battery when it overlaps with negligence. They strive to avoid subjecting a surgeon to liability in battery.

A significant disadvantage with the tort of battery as a means of vindicating patients' rights is that for a claim to lie in battery traditionally there had to be direct *physical* contact between doctor and patient. A patient who agreed to take a drug orally, having been totally misled as to the nature of the drug, could not sue in battery. Had the doctor injected him with that self-same drug, a claim in battery would lie. Recently the courts have developed the criminal law to allow prosecution for causing grievous bodily harm where no direct physical contact took place.[14] So it is possible that if a doctor deceived a patient into taking a dangerous drug that made her seriously ill, the doctor could face criminal charges.

A right to say no?

5.2 Will the law ever set limits to a competent person's right to refuse treatment? Are we free to reject life-saving treatment which others might consider it 'wicked folly'[15] to refuse? The theory is clear. In *Re T (Adult: Refusal of Medical*

---

[11] *Devi v West Midlands AHA* [1980] 7 CL 44. And see *Williamson v East London and City Health Authority* [1998] Lloyd's Rep Med 6 (woman consented to removal of breast implants but not to a mastectomy).

[12] *Bartley v Studd* (1995) 2 Medical Law Monitor, 15 July 1997 (the surgeon was disciplined by the GMC).

[13] *Freeman v Home Office* [1984] 2 WLR 130.

[14] *R v Ireland and Burstow* [1998] AC 147, HL; *R v Dica* [2004] 3 A11 ER 593, CA.

[15] See, for example, the judgment of Lord Alverstone in *Leigh v Gladstone* (1909) 26 TLR 139 authorising forcible feeding of a suffragette prisoner.

Treatment),[16] Lord Donaldson declared that an adult patient '. . . has an absolute right to choose whether to consent to medical treatment, to refuse it or to choose one rather than another of the treatments being offered'.[17] Such an absolute right to autonomy '. . . exists notwithstanding that the reasons for making the choice are rational, or irrational, unknown or even non-existent'. In *Re T*, a young woman of twenty had suffered serious injuries in a road accident. She was thirty-four weeks pregnant and consented to a Caesarean section on the following day. Later that evening she was visited by her mother, a devout Jehovah's Witness. T was not herself a baptised Witness. After her mother's visit, T told doctors that she would not agree to any blood transfusion before or during surgery. She first enquired whether alternatives to whole blood were available, and was assured that such alternatives exist. She was given a form to sign evidencing her refusal of transfusion and absolving the hospital from liability for failing to administer blood should she haemorrhage. After delivery of a stillborn child, T lapsed into a coma and suffered life-threatening internal bleeding. The hospital argued that they could not lawfully give her a blood transfusion. Her boyfriend and father sought a court order authorising a life-saving transfusion. Notwithstanding his ringing endorsement of patient autonomy, Lord Donaldson and his brethren in the Court of Appeal granted that order.

The Court of Appeal held that on the facts of the case T's refusal of treatment was not an autonomous judgment. Her decision was 'flawed':

(1) The combination of the effect of her injuries and the medication she was taking impaired her mental capacity to decide whether or not to agree to blood transfusions.

(2) T lacked sufficient information to make a decision to refuse transfusion. While she was told there were alternatives to whole blood, she was not advised about their limited utility or warned that there were circumstances where, without transfusion, her life would be at risk. Lord Donaldson[18] criticised the doctors, whom he suggested were more anxious to disclaim any possible legal liability than to ensure that T was given comprehensible and comprehensive information.

(3) Pressure from T's mother may have constituted undue influence rendering her purported refusal of blood transfusion less than independent and voluntary.

These factors, that were felt to cloud the nature of T's decision, caused the Court of Appeal to conclude that T's rejection of blood could be disregarded. The right of the individual to decide whether to accept medical treatment was paramount but in '. . . cases of doubt, that doubt falls to be resolved in favour of preservation of life, for if the individual is to override the public interest, he must do so in clear terms'.

---

[16] [1992] 4 All ER 645, CA.
[17] [1992] 4 All ER 649 at 652–653, CA.
[18] [1992] 4 All ER 649 at 663, CA.

It may be tempting to regard *Re T* as judges saying one thing (upholding the rhetoric of autonomy) and doing another (rejecting an unusual belief which caused a young woman to risk sacrificing her life). *Re T* requires careful scrutiny. Do the facts in *Re T* support judicial doubts as to whether T ever made a truly voluntary and sufficiently informed choice to reject life-saving treatment?[19] In the next chapter we explore further whether some vulnerable patients who may not clearly fail the test for mental capacity may nonetheless, like T, be unable to make a real choice because of their circumstances or pressure from those close to them.[20]

Subsequent judgments have upheld the principle of autonomy articulated in *Re T*.[21] In *Airedale NHS Trust v Bland*,[22] Lord Goff reiterated that the

> ... principle of self-determination requires that respect must be given to the wishes of the patient, so that if an adult of sound mind refuses, however unreasonably, to consent to treatment or care by which his life would or might be prolonged, the doctors responsible for his care must give effect to his wishes, even though they do not consider it to be in his best interests to do so.

In *B v An NHS Trust*,[23] Butler-Sloss P ruled that it was unlawful for doctors to refuse to switch off a ventilator keeping Ms B alive. Ms B suffered a haemorrhage in her spinal cord which left her paralysed from the neck down and wholly dependent on a ventilator to breathe. She asked her doctors to switch the ventilator off. She considered that death was preferable to survival in such a state. Her doctors disagreed. They thought that she could enjoy a reasonable quality of life living in a spinal rehabilitation unit. They expressed strong conscientious objections to 'killing' Ms B. When she first indicated her wish to have the ventilator switched off, psychiatrists questioned Ms B's mental capacity. However, she was ultimately adjudged competent to make her own decisions. The judge ruled that continuing to ventilate Ms B against her will constituted an assault on her and awarded her nominal damages of £100. She ordered that arrangements be made to transfer Ms B to a unit where doctors would be prepared to comply with her request. Butler-Sloss P unequivocally endorsed the value of patient autonomy. The crux of the matter will always turn on the capacity of the individual to make a valid choice – a subject explored further in the next chapter.

In *Re T*, Lord Donaldson's recognition of an unqualified right to refuse treatment as long as the adult patient was competent to make that decision was subject to a controversial caveat. He contended that an exception to that right might exist in '... a case in which the choice may lead to the death of a viable

---

[19] It may always be especially difficult to judge competence retrospectively: see *NHS Trust v T* [2005] 1 All ER 387.

[20] See *Local Authority v A* [2010] EWHC 1549 (Fam) and see below at **6.4**.

[21] See *Secretary of State for the Home Department v Robb* [1995] 1 All ER (forcible feeding of a mentally competent prisoner is unlawful); *Re C (Adult: Refusal of Medical Treatment)* [1994] 1 All ER (patient entitled to order prohibiting amputation of leg even if the leg became gangrenous).

[22] [1993] 1 All ER 821 at 866; and see Lord Mustill at 889.

[23] [2002] EWHC 429 (Fam); discussed further at **6.3**.

foetus'.[24] Pregnant women, and women in labour, might be excluded from the normal right to self-determination. A series of controversial cases followed *Re T* in which judges ordered women to submit to Caesarean sections. In *Re S*,[25] Sir Stephen Brown P invoked Lord Donaldson's dictum to authorise Caesarean surgery to save the life of the woman's unborn child. Other judgments[26] tended to rely more heavily on the judge's ruling that at the time she refused 'necessary' surgery, the woman's capacity to make decisions was impaired. Ultimately the Court of Appeal clarified the law. A pregnant woman 'of sound mind' retains exactly the same right to accept or refuse treatment as any other adult. The unborn child enjoyed no legal personality entitling the court to force its mother to submit to any form of intervention she elects to decline.[27] The mother's right to autonomy is not diminished or reduced merely because her decision may '... appear morally repugnant'.[28] Adults can say no to treatment as long as their mental capacity is unimpaired. Identifying when a person lacks capacity may be tricky, and judges may be naturally reluctant to stand by and watch a pregnant woman and her child both die.[29]

What is meant by consent?

5.3 Consent is mandatory but what is meant by consent? It need not usually be written.[30] Consent may be implied from the circumstances. If a patient visits his general practitioner complaining of a sore throat and opens his mouth so that the doctor can examine his throat, he cannot complain that he never expressly said to the doctor: 'You may put a spatula on my tongue and look down my throat'. A patient visiting Casualty with a bleeding wound implicitly agrees to doctors or nurses cleaning and bandaging the wound. In an American case, an immigrant to the USA complained that he had not consented to vaccination. It was found that he had bared his arm and held it out to the doctor. His action precluded the need for any verbal consent.[31]

A patient for whom surgery or any form of invasive investigation is proposed will normally be asked to sign a consent form. The Department of Health issues guidance[32] on consent to treatment advising that it 'is good practice to

---

[24] [1992] 4 All ER 645 at 653, CA.

[25] [1992] 4 All ER 671.

[26] For example, *Rochdale Healthcare (NHS) Trust v C* [1997] 1 FCR 274.

[27] *Re MB (Caesarean Section)* [1997] 8 Med LR 217, CA; *St George's Healthcare NHS Trust v S* [1998] 3 All ER 673, CA.

[28] *St George's Healthcare NHS Trust v S* [1998] 3 All ER 673 at 692.

[29] See, for example, *Bolton Hospitals NHS Trust v O* [2003] 1 FLR 824. The rights of pregnant women are dealt with more fully later at **11.21**.

[30] Sometimes legislation such as the Human Fertilisation and Embryology Act 1990 requires written consent; see *R v Human Fertilisation and Embryology Authority, ex p Blood* [1997] 2 All ER 687, CA, discussed below at **12.13**. And see ss 2(5) and 3(5) of the Human Tissue Act 2004.

[31] *O'Brien v Cunard SS Co* (Mass 1891) 28 NC 266.

[32] DH, *Reference Guide to Consent for Examination or Treatment* (2nd edn, 2009).

obtain written consent for any significant procedure'. The 2009 Guidance does not contain model consent forms. The Department is consulting on the use and format of model forms and advises NHS trusts that they may choose how to develop their own documentation based, if they wish, on amended versions of the 'old' model forms. The Department's aim is to ensure that healthcare professionals appreciate the need to give patients the information to which they are entitled.

Consent forms should ensure that patients appreciate that they are entitled to ask questions and to demand explanations about what is to be done to them. They should cover anaesthetic procedures as well as surgery. Patients are not passive recipients of what the doctor thinks best. However, a form is no more than some evidence of what the patient has agreed to. What is important is the substance of what the patient is entitled to be told and has been told, and what is then done to him. Clearly any action expressly prohibited by the patient, that is, additional procedures which on the form he states '*I do not wish to be carried out without further discussion*' would constitute a battery if imposed on the patient.

In many cases, supplementary procedures will require additional consent. However, the consent form might provide for additional procedures necessary to save life or serious injury. What sort of authority does this confer on the doctor? This would not affect liability in the cases discussed earlier of the doctor who sterilised a patient in the course of minor gynaecological surgery, or the surgeon who removed a woman's ovaries without her consent (see **5.1**). Neither measure was immediately necessary to preserve the woman's health. The doctor is only authorised to carry out further surgery without which the patient's life or health is immediately at risk. A surgeon discovering advanced cancer of the womb while performing a curettage may be justified in performing an immediate hysterectomy. Delay might threaten the woman's life. A doctor discovering some malformation, or other non-life-threatening condition, must delay further surgery until his patient has the opportunity to offer her opinion. A current issue is whether patients should be asked to give an express advance consent to any blood transfusions that may be thought likely to be needed.[33]

Some patients opt 'not to know' information, perhaps because they fear the psychological consequences. The Department of Health advises doctors to always provide basic information and, whilst respecting the patient's wishes, to stress the importance of knowing and understanding the available options, and check periodically that the patient has not changed her mind.[34] What would be the effect of a form within which a patient consented to any procedure that the surgeon saw fit to embark on? In the absence of the clearest evidence that the patient fully understood the 'blank cheque' which he handed

[33] See SaBTO Consultation, *Patient Consent for Blood Transfusion* (March 2010); and A M Farrell and M Brazier, 'Consent for Blood Transfusion' (2010) 341 *BMJ* 4336.
[34] DH, *Reference Guide to Consent for Examination or Treatment* (2nd edn, 2009), para 21.

to his doctor, such a form will be virtually irrelevant.[35] If the patient can show that despite the form he did not give any real consent to the procedure carried out, the surgeon will be liable in battery.

How much must the doctor tell the patient: real consent?

5.4 We have seen that for consent to be real the patient must be told what operation is to be performed and why it is to be done. The doctor certifies on the consent form that he has explained the proposed operation, investigation or treatment to the patient. What exactly must the doctor explain? All surgery under general anaesthetic entails some risk. Many forms of surgery and medical treatment carry further risk of harm, even if they are carried out with the greatest skill and competence. Patients have unsuccessfully sought to argue that if an operation entails an inherent risk then they cannot be said to have given a real consent to that operation if they were not told of the risk. They had inadequate information on which to make a proper decision. They could not give an 'informed consent' and therefore a claim in battery should lie. Alternatively they have contended with some greater success that if a claim in battery does not lie, they ought to be able to sue for negligence. The doctor's duty of care encompasses giving adequate information and advice. If he has given the patient inadequate information and the patient agreed to a risky procedure from which injury did ensue, the doctor, it is argued, is responsible for that damage.

Let us look first at the argument that if risks or side-effects inherent in an operation are not disclosed, then the patient has not really consented at all, and the surgeon is liable for battery. In *Chatterton v Gerson*,[36] Miss Chatterton pursued such a claim. She suffered excruciating pain in a post-operative scar. Dr Gerson proposed an operation. The operation failed to relieve her symptoms. A second operation was carried out. Miss Chatterton was no better and subsequently lost all sensation in her right leg and foot with a consequent loss of mobility. She claimed that while Dr Gerson was in no way negligent in his conduct of the surgery, he failed to tell her enough for her to give her 'informed consent'. Her claim in battery failed. The judge said that a consent to surgery was valid providing that the patient was 'informed in broad terms of the nature of the procedure which is intended'. Any claim in relation to inadequacy of information about the risks or side-effects of treatment, or availability of alternative treatment, should be brought in negligence.

By contrast, a patient who agreed to an injection which she understood to be a routine post-natal vaccination, but which was in fact the controversial long-

---

[35] See *Chatterton v Gerson* [1981] 1 All ER 257.
[36] [1981] 1 All ER 457. The nature and purpose test for battery is cogently criticised by T K Feng, 'Failure of Medical Advice: Trespass or Negligence' [1987] 7 *Legal Studies* 149. And see A Maclean, 'The Doctrine of Informed Consent: Does it Exist and Has it Crossed the Atlantic?' (2004) 24 *Legal Studies* 386 at 398–401; and A Maclean, *Autonomy, Informed Consent and Medical Law* (2009) CUP, pp 191–196.

acting contraceptive Depo-Provera, succeeded in battery. Her doctor failed the test set in *Chatterton v Gerson*. He obtained her agreement to the injection, leaving her totally unaware and indeed misleading her, albeit in good faith, as to the nature of what was being done to her.[37] A dentist who deliberately misled patients to persuade them to agree to unnecessary dental treatment was also held liable in battery. His fraud vitiated the apparent consent given him by his unfortunate patients.[38] A bogus doctor, who persuaded several women to allow him to examine their breasts, claiming that he was conducting research into breast cancer, was convicted of indecent assault.[39] The women's 'consent' depended on their belief that he had medical qualifications and that the contact to which they agreed had a proper medical purpose.

Other attempts to claim in battery, where the nature of what was to be done was honestly explained but the risks of the procedure were not, have failed just as Miss Chatterton's claim failed.[40] In *Sidaway v Royal Bethlem Hospital* in the Court of Appeal, Lord Donaldson said:

> It is only if the consent is obtained by fraud or misrepresentation of the *nature* [emphasis added] of what is to be done that it can be said that an apparent consent is not a true consent.[41]

The House of Lords unanimously endorsed his views.[42] Lord Scarman, giving the most patient-oriented opinion, nonetheless declared:[43]

> ... it would be deplorable to base the law in medical cases of this kind on the torts of assault and battery.

The Canadian courts also view battery as an inappropriate remedy for inadequate counselling. The Canadian Chief Justice has said:[44]

> I do not understand how it can be said that the consent was vitiated by failure of disclosure of risks as to make the surgery or other treatment an unprivileged, unconsented to and intentional invasion of the patient's bodily integrity ... unless there has been misrepresentation or fraud to secure consent to the treatment, a failure to disclose the attendant risks, however serious, should go to negligence rather than battery.

It is easy to understand why courts shy away from finding doctors liable in battery. The word itself is emotive. Doctors resent being accused of 'battering'

---

[37] See *Potts v North West Regional Health Authority* (1983) *Guardian*, 23 July.

[38] *Appleton v Garrett* [1996] PIQR P1. Contrast with *R v Richardson (Diana)* (1998) 43 BMLR 21, CA (dentist acquitted of criminal assault even though she failed to inform her patients that she had been struck off the dental register).

[39] *R v Tabassum* [2000] Lloyd's Rep Med 404, CA.

[40] *Hills v Potter (note)* [1984] 1 WLR 641 at 653.

[41] [1984] 1 All ER 1018 at 1026 and *Freeman v Home Office* [1984] 1 All ER 1036.

[42] *Sidaway v Board of Governors of the Bethlem Royal and the Maudsley Hospital* [1985] 1 All ER 643.

[43] [1985] 1 All ER 643 at 650.

[44] *Reibl v Hughes* (1980) 114 DLR (3d) 1.

their patients, being equated with '. . . the mugger who assaults his victim'.[45] However, distinguishing between battery and no battery on the *Chatterton v Gerson* test is not easy. Consider the example of a patient tested for HIV without his consent.[46] He agrees to a blood test preparatory to surgery. He is never told that among the tests to be carried out on his blood is a test for HIV. Did he understand the nature and purpose of the test? He understood what would be done to him and that several tests would be carried out on his blood. Opinion about whether such a practice constitutes battery is divided.[47] Normally, express and detailed information about exactly what tests are proposed when blood is given is rarely sought or offered. Patients agree to tests so that doctors can find out what problems they may encounter and treat them safely. It is difficult to say that such patients, including the patient tested for HIV, do not understand in broad terms what is going on. Were some ruse employed to obtain consent the picture might be different. Imagine that a doctor suspects a patient is HIV-positive and wants a test for that sole purpose. Fearing that the patient would refuse consent if asked outright, the doctor uses a pretext, for example, a suspicion of anaemia. Would you argue that the patient falls within the *Chatterton v Gerson* test, that his consent was obtained by fraud or misrepresentation? The difficulty is that what constitutes fraud is complex.

In the context of criminal law, the courts have tended to say that the fraud must deceive the victim about the very nature of what is being done to her.[48] The patient agreeing to the blood test, albeit believing the test is designed to check his red blood count, still understands what is being done. It may be that civil and criminal law adopts different tests of fraud. In a case where a dentist was prosecuted for assault because, unbeknown to her patients, she continued to practise when suspended from the dental register, the Court of Appeal quashed her conviction for criminal assault.[49] The patients were not misled about what was being done to them, or as to the identity of the accused. Nonetheless, Otton LJ condemned the accused's conduct as reprehensible and suggested that a civil claim for damages might well succeed.

Negligence and a duty to inform

5.5 Where no question of misrepresentation arises, a claim based on failure to give a patient adequate information about proposed treatment lies in negligence. The doctor's duty of care to his patient undoubtedly includes a duty to give him careful advice and sufficient information upon which to reach a

---

[45] See Maclean (2004) 24 *Legal Studies,* at 399.

[46] See J K Mason and G T Laurie, *Mason and McCall Smith's Law and Medical Ethics* (8th edn, 2010) OUP, at 99–104.

[47] Discussed elegantly in J Keown, 'The Ashes of AIDS and the Phoenix of Informed Consent' (1989) 52 *Modern Law Review* 790.

[48] *R v Clarence* (1888) 22 QBD 23.

[49] *R v Richardson (Diana)* (1998) 43 BMLR 21, CA.

rational decision whether to accept or reject treatment. Lord Steyn[50] has emphasised that '. . . a patient's right to an appropriate warning from a surgeon when faced with surgery ought normatively to be regarded as an important right which must be given effective protection whenever possible'. The problem is, when is the doctor in breach of his duty to warn? It is important to understand some of the history relating to information disclosure and English law, but we should be clear from the start that in 2011 doctors are required to give full explanation of the risks and benefits of proposed treatment, and to make the patient aware of possible alternative treatments. The General Medical Council (GMC) emphasises partnership between doctors and patients and states simply that, doctors must 'share with patients the information they [the patients] want or need in order to make decisions'.[51]

Much has changed in the last half century. In 1957, in the famous (or infamous) case of *Bolam v Friern Hospital Management Committee*,[52] Mr Bolam agreed to electro-convulsive therapy to help improve his depression. He suffered fractures in the course of the treatment. The risk was known to his doctor. He did not tell Mr Bolam. Mr Bolam alleged that the failure to warn him of the risk was negligent. The judge found that the amount of information given to Mr Bolam accorded with accepted medical practice in such cases and dismissed his claim. He added that even if Mr Bolam had proved that the doctor's advice was inadequate, he would only have succeeded if he could have further proved that, had he been given that information, he would have refused consent to the treatment. The test of negligence was the test of responsible medical opinion. Other early cases were even more favourable to the doctors. Lord Denning held it to be entirely for the individual doctor to decide what to tell his patient, even if the doctor went so far as to resort to what his Lordship termed 'a therapeutic lie'.[53]

The underlying trend in the English courts, until recently, was that 'doctor knew best'. Across the Atlantic, however, matters had taken a startlingly different turn. The doctrine of 'informed consent' was born. In *Canterbury v Spence*,[54] a US court said that the 'prudent patient' test should prevail. Doctors must disclose to their patients any material risk inherent in a proposed line of treatment:

> A risk is material when a reasonable person, in what the physician knows or should know to be the patient's position, would be likely to attach significance to the risk or cluster of risks in deciding whether or not to forgo the proposed therapy.

The Canadian Supreme Court also rejected the 'professional medical standard' for determining how much the doctor must disclose. Emphasis was laid upon

---

[50] *Chester v Afshar* [2004] UKHL 41, para 17.
[51] GMC, *Consent: Patients and Doctors Making Decisions Together* (2008), para 2(c).
[52] [1957] 2 All ER 118.
[53] *Hatcher v Black* (1954) *Times*, 2 July; and see *O'Malley-Williams v Board of Governors of the National Hospital for Nervous Diseases* [1975] BMJ 635.
[54] (1972) 464 f 2D 772 at 780.

'the patient's right to know what risks are involved in undergoing or forgoing surgery or other treatment'.[55] The Canadian Court did allow that a particular patient might waive his right to know, might put himself entirely in the hands of the doctors. And they said that cases might arise where '. . . a particular patient may, because of emotional factors, be unable to cope with facts relevant to the recommended surgery or treatment and the doctor may, in such a case, be justified in withholding or generalising information as to which he would otherwise be required to be more specific'. The doctor could rely on a defence of therapeutic privilege. The High Court of Australia followed Canada in rejecting the *Bolam* test of professional opinion. In *Rogers v Whittaker*,[56] failure to disclose a 1:14,000 chance of blindness in both eyes inherent in surgery was held negligent. The patient had made clear her concerns about the risks of losing her sight altogether.[57]

In England, invoking the transatlantic doctrine of informed consent, lawyers tried to breach the walls of medical silence. Miss Chatterton who, as we saw, lost in battery, also failed in negligence. The doctor, the judge said, did owe her a duty to counsel her as to any real risks inherent in the surgery proposed. He did not have to canvass every risk and in deciding what to tell the patient he could take into account '. . . the personality of the patient, the likelihood of misfortune and what in the way of warning is for the particular patient's welfare'. This standard Dr Gerson had met.

Sidaway

5.6   So what amounts to a 'real risk of misfortune inherent in the procedure'? The decision of the Law Lords in *Sidaway* remains a key part of the story. For several years, following an accident at work, Mrs Sidaway had endured persistent pain in her right arm and shoulder. Later the pain spread to her left arm. In 1960 she became the patient of Mr Falconer, an eminent neuro-surgeon at the Maudsley Hospital. An operation relieved the pain for a while. By 1973, Mrs Sidaway was again in pain. She was admitted to the Maudsley Hospital and Mr Falconer diagnosed pressure on a nerve root as the cause of her pain. He decided to operate to relieve the pressure. Mrs Sidaway gave her consent to surgery. As a result of that operation Mrs Sidaway became severely disabled by partial paralysis.

Mrs Sidaway sued both Mr Falconer and the Maudsley Hospital. She did not suggest that the operation had been performed otherwise than skilfully and carefully. Her complaint was this. The operation to which she agreed involved

---

[55]   *Reibl v Hughes* (1980) 114 DLR (3d) 1.
[56]   [1993] 4 Med LR 79: discussed in D Chalmers and R Schwartz, 'A Fair Dinkum Duty of Disclosure' (1993) 1 *Medical Law Review* 189.
[57]   For an insightful comparative analysis of the different legal responses to information disclosure in the UK and the Antipodes, see J Miola, 'On the Materiality of Risk: Paper Tigers and Panaceas' (2009) 17 *Medical Law Review* 76–108.

two specific risks over and above the risk inherent in any surgery under general anaesthesia. These were: (1) damage to a nerve root, assessed as about a 2 per cent risk; and (2) damage to the spinal cord, assessed as less than a 1 per cent risk. Alas for Mrs Sidaway, that second risk materialised and she suffered partial paralysis. She maintained that Mr Falconer never warned her of the risk of injury to the spinal cord. Throughout the long and expensive litigation, Mrs Sidaway's greatest handicap was that Mr Falconer died before the action came to trial. The courts were deprived of vital evidence as to exactly what the patient was told by her surgeon and what reasons, if any, he had for withholding information from her. The case had to proceed from the inference drawn by the trial judge that Mr Falconer would have followed his customary practice, that is, he would have warned Mrs Sidaway in general terms of the possibility of injury to a nerve root, but would have said nothing about any risk of damage to the spinal cord.

Ten years after the operation which left Mrs Sidaway paralysed, and seven years after Mr Falconer's death, the case reached the House of Lords.[58] The paucity of evidence about what actually happened when Mrs Sidaway and Mr Falconer discussed the proposed surgery rendered the case, as Lord Diplock put it, 'a naked question of legal principle'. What principle governed the doctor's obligation to advise patients and to warn of any risks inherent in surgery or treatment recommended by the doctor? The majority of their Lordships largely endorsed the traditional test enunciated in the case of Mr Bolam nearly thirty years before. The doctor's obligation to advise and warn his patient was part and parcel of his general duty of care owed to each individual patient. Prima facie, providing he conformed to a responsible body of medical opinion in deciding what to tell and what not to tell his patient, he discharged his duty properly. There being evidence that, while some neuro-surgeons might warn some patients of the risk to the spinal cord, many chose not to, Mrs Sidaway's case was lost.

The *Sidaway* judgment, some of their Lordships said, should not be seen as endorsing the view that providing a doctor follows current medical practice in deciding what information to give his patients, he will be immune from legal attack. The courts retain ultimate control of the scope of the doctor's obligation. First, for Lord Bridge and Lord Templeman, a crucial issue in Mrs Sidaway's case was that the risk of which she was not advised was a less than 1 per cent risk, and all the medical expert witnesses were agreed that it was a risk of which many responsible neuro-surgeons elected not to warn patients. Had the risk been of greater statistical significance, their Lordships *might* have held in Mrs Sidaway's favour, even if expert medical witnesses supported non-disclosure. Lord Bridge gave as an example '. . . an operation involving a substantial risk of grave adverse consequences, for example [a] 10 per cent risk of a stroke from the operation'.[59] He went on to acknowledge that there might be cases

[58] *Sidaway v Board of Governors of the Bethlem Royal and the Maudsley Hospital* [1985] 1 All ER 643; in the High Court, Mrs Sidaway also sued for battery. Both claims were dismissed and she appealed on the issue of negligence alone.

[59] [1985] 1 All ER 643 at 663.

where '... disclosure of a particular risk was so obviously necessary to an informed choice on the part of the patient that no reasonably prudent medical man would fail to make it'. Second, for Lord Diplock and Lord Templeman a vital question in the case was that Mrs Sidaway had not expressly inquired of Mr Falconer what risks the surgery entailed. For Lord Diplock, the case concerned solely what information the doctor must volunteer. Lord Templeman said that Mr Falconer could not be faulted for failing to give Mrs Sidaway information for which she did not ask.

What four out of five of the Law Lords in *Sidaway* agreed on was the rejection of the transatlantic test that what the patient should be told should be judged by what the reasonable patient would want to know; they demonstrated little enthusiasm for 'informed consent'.[60] Lord Scarman alone rejected current medical practice as the test of what a patient needed to be told. He dissented, and in a powerful judgment asserted the patient's right to know. The patient's right of self-determination, his right to choose what happened to his body, was the factor which to Lord Scarman made the issue of advice given to the patient distinct from other aspects of medical care. The doctor should be liable '... where the risk is such that in the court's view a prudent person in the patient's situation would have regarded it as significant'.[61] But, albeit the patient's right of self-determination distinguishes advice given from other stages in medical care, advice before treatment cannot be totally separated from the doctor's general duty to offer proper professional and competent service. Doctors, in Lord Scarman's view, should be to a certain extent protected by 'therapeutic privilege'. This would permit a doctor to withhold information if it could be shown that 'a reasonable medical assessment of the patient would have indicated to the doctor that disclosure would have posed a serious threat of psychological detriment to the patient'.[62] Lord Scarman recognised the right of a patient of sound understanding to be warned of material risks save in exceptional circumstances, yet he too found against Mrs Sidaway on the facts of the case. He held that she failed to establish on the evidence put forward by her counsel that the less than 1 per cent risk was such that a prudent patient would have considered it significant.

After *Sidaway*

5.7 The decision in *Sidaway* has never been formally overruled. Paradoxically, Lord Scarman's dissent comes closer to expressing the principles that now govern information disclosure today than the speeches of the majority. Two judgments of the Court of Appeal[63] shortly after *Sidaway* appeared to entrench the *Bolam* test and endorse the professional standard as the touchstone for

---

[60] In the Court of Appeal, Dunn LJ declared that, 'The concept of informed consent forms no part of English law'; *Sidaway v Board of Governors of the Royal Bethlem and Maudsley Hospital* [1984] 1 A11 ER 1018 at 1030.

[61] [1985] 1 All ER 643 at 654.

[62] [1985] 1 All ER 643 at 654.

[63] *Blyth v Bloomsbury Health Authority* [1993] 4 Med LR 151; *Gold v Haringey*

information disclosure. Patients were to be told what doctors thought they should know.[64] For nearly two decades, informed consent seemed to have no place in English law.[65] *Chester v Afshar*[66] signals that, in theory at least, the judiciary has belatedly acknowledged informed consent. Lord Steyn says simply:[67]

> Surgery performed without the informed consent of the patient is unlawful. The court is the final arbiter of what constitutes informed consent.

The trigger for change towards a more patient-oriented test came initially from the doctors themselves. Professional practice changed markedly. Doctors now endorse more open disclosure of risks. Guidance from the GMC[68] gives detailed instructions about the information that patients should be offered covering risks, benefits and burdens, uncertainties and other options. Advice should be tailored to the needs, wishes and priorities of the patient, focusing on the 'individual situation and the risk to them'. The GMC standard may, in a number of cases, in theory demand that professionals provide patients with the information not simply that a prudent patient might want, but that the particular patients might want.[69]

From about 1994 the courts incrementally became more ready to require a fuller disclosure of information about treatment risks and options for patients. In *Smith v Tunbridge Wells Health Authority*[70] a claim was brought by a twenty-eight-year-old man who was not warned of the risk of impotence inherent in rectal surgery. His claim succeeded despite expert evidence that a body of surgeons did not warn patients of that risk. The judge, citing Lord Bridge in *Sidaway,* found that failure to warn such a patient of a risk of such importance to him was 'neither reasonable nor responsible'. Mere evidence of a medical practice did not counter allegations of negligence. That practice must be reasonable in the context of providing patients with an informed choice. As we shall see in chapter 7, in *Bolitho v City & Hackney Health Authority*[71] the

---

Health Authority [1987] 2 All ER 884, CA. And see *Moyes v Lothian Health Board* [1990] 1 Med LR 471.

[64] Whether or not they asked questions (see *Blyth v Bloomsbury Health Authority* [1993] 4 Med LR 151) and whether or not the medical intervention was therapeutic or non-therapeutic (see *Gold v Haringey Health Authority* [1987] 2 All ER 888, CA).

[65] See M A Jones, 'Informed Consent and Other Fairy Stories' (1999) 7 *Medical Law Review* 103.

[66] [2004] UKHL 41.

[67] [2004] UKHL 41, para 14.

[68] GMC, *Consent: Patients and Doctors Making Decisions Together* (2008).

[69] Commenting on the GMC 's earlier Guidance from 1999, Maclean (2004) *Legal Studies* 386 took a more sceptical view; one shared by E Jackson, 'Informed Consent to Medical Treatment and the Impotence of Tort' in S A M McLean (ed), *First Do No Harm* (2006) Ashgate, p 273.

[70] [1994] 5 Med LR 334; and see *McAllister v Lewisham and North Southwark Health Authority* [1994] 5 Med LR 343; *Newall and Newall v Goldenberg* [1995] 6 Med LR 371; *Williamson v East London & City Health Authority* (1997) 41 BMLR 85; *Lybert v Warrington Health Authority* [1996] 7 Med LR 71, CA.

[71] [1998] AC 232.

House of Lords stressed that, in relation to all claims of negligence against doctors, expert evidence advanced to support the defendant's case that he acted without negligence must be shown to be responsible. To rebut negligence, a practice must have a 'logical and defensible' basis. In *Bolitho*, Lord Browne-Wilkinson seemed at one stage to suggest that in his clarification of the *Bolam* test he was not concerned with cases about informed consent.[72] That statement was not designed to exempt consent claims from judicial scrutiny, but simply to acknowledge that case law stretching back to Lord Bridge in *Sidaway* already allowed scrutiny of information disclosure practice.[73]

That the *Bolitho* approach is applicable to informed consent claims is confirmed in *Pearce v United Bristol Healthcare NHS Trust*.[74] Mrs Pearce, who was expecting her sixth child, was two weeks past her due date of delivery. She discussed the possibility of induction with her obstetrician who warned her of the risks of induction and Caesarean surgery, but did not tell her that there was a 0.1–0.2 per cent risk of stillbirth associated with non-intervention. Mrs Pearce's child was stillborn and she alleged that failure to warn her of the risk of stillbirth was negligent. The Court of Appeal held that she had not established negligence. The very slight risk of stillbirth arising from non-intervention, compared to the risks of intervention, was not a risk which the defendants were negligent in failing to disclose, especially in the light of Mrs Pearce's distressed condition at the time of the consultation. What is of interest in *Pearce* is that at first sight Lord Woolf's judgment in the doctors' favour departs radically from a simple test of whether the information offered Mrs Pearce conformed to a reasonable body of expert opinion. Relying on both Lord Bridge in *Sidaway* and Lord Browne-Wilkinson in *Bolitho*, Lord Woolf declares that '... if there is a *significant risk which would affect the judgement of a reasonable patient*, then in the normal course it is the responsibility of a doctor to inform the patient of that significant risk, if the information is needed so that the patient can determine for him or herself as to what course she should adopt' (our emphasis). Lord Woolf suggests that the reasonable doctor must tell the patient what the reasonable patient would want to know.[75]

There are critics who view Lord Woolf's judgment in *Pearce* differently. The view stated above might be one '... seeing the judgment through rose-tinted spectacles'.[76] Does Lord Woolf use 'politically correct' language to conceal continuing deference to medical opinion? In future cases, how will significant risk be defined? And ultimately, Mrs Pearce's claim failed as have so many

---

[72] [1998] AC 232 at 243.
[73] See M Brazier and J Miola, 'Bye-Bye Bolam: A Medical Litigation Revolution?' (2000) 8 *Medical Law Review* 85 at 107–110.
[74] [1998] 48 BMLR 118, CA. And see *AB v Leeds Teaching Hospital NHS Trust* [2004] EWHC 644 (QB).
[75] Brazier and Miola (2000) 8 *Medical Law Review* 85 at 110. And see *Wyatt v Curtis* [2003] EWCA Civ 1779.
[76] See Maclean (2004) *Legal Studies* 386 at 408–409.

others. *Pearce* might usefully be contrasted with *Jones v North West Strategic Health Authority*.[77] Mrs Jones was not warned of the 1–2 per cent risk of shoulder dystocia if she consented to a vaginal birth, a risk exacerbated in her case by obesity and a similar problem with an earlier delivery. The judge ruled that while some doctors would not have discussed the option of a Caesarean section, and to recommend a vaginal birth was not in itself negligent, it was a breach of duty not to discuss the surgical option with the claimant.[78]

The impact of *Pearce*

5.8 Maclean notes that the 'practical impact of *Pearce* remains to be seen'.[79] In particular, the extent to which *Pearce* moves English law to require an assessment of the patient's perception of risks will have to be watched. Lord Woolf's formulation of a patient-focused test has been endorsed by both the Court of Appeal[80] and the House of Lords.[81] And in *Birch v University College London Hospital NHS Foundation Trust*[82] Cranston J took a further step toward a more expansive duty of disclosure. Mrs Birch agreed to a cerebral catheter angiogram to test for a possible aneurysm in her brain. She suffered a stroke caused by the procedure and she had been fully warned of the risk of a stroke caused by the angiogram. She had not been informed that there was an alternate and non-invasive procedure–magnetic resonance imaging (MRI). Her counsel argued that information about other options and their comparative risks was essential to discharge the doctors' duty to give Mrs Birch adequate advice on which to found her decision about whether or not to consent to the angiogram. The judge agreed. Albeit the issue of comparative risk was not addressed by Lord Woolf in *Pearce,* Cranston J held that:

> . . . the duty to inform a patient of the significant risks will not be discharged unless she is made aware that fewer, or no, risks are associated with another procedure. In other words, unless the patient is informed of the comparative risks of different procedures she will not be in a position to give her fully informed consent to one procedure rather than another.[83]

What about understanding?

5.9 Imparting information does not of itself assist the recipient to make an informed decision. If a patient is simply deluged with complex technical details and an array of statistics, she may be in no better position to make the choice right for her than if she had simply accepted the recommendation of her

[77] [2010] EWHC 178 Civ.
[78] But note that Mrs Jones failed in her claim on causation.
[79] Maclean, *Autonomy, Informed Consent and Medical Law* (2009), at 176.
[80] *Wyatt v Curtis* [2003] EWCA Civ 1779 at para 16.
[81] *Chester v Afshar* [2004] UKHL 41 at para 15 per Lord Steyn.
[82] [2008] EWHC 2237
[83] [2008] EWHC 2237 at para 74.

doctors. The GMC emphasises the importance of sharing information in a way that the patient can understand, seeking to check that he has understood and making available additional time and support where needed. The courts have held that poor communication of risks by the medical team that led to the claimant being understandably confused did amount to breach of the duty to inform.[84] But as yet there seems to be no legal duty to seek to ensure that the patient does understand information properly communicated. In *Al Hamwi v Johnson*[85] the claimant misunderstood what she had been told of the risks of amniocentesis and radically overestimated the risk of miscarriage, believing it to be 75 per cent and not less than 2 per cent. On the basis of this misapprehension she refused amniocentesis and went on to give birth to a disabled baby. The judge held that Mrs Al Hamwi had been presented with factually accurate information and the doctor had acted correctly in giving all the relevant information. The doctor should and did take steps to satisfy herself that the patient understood the information but this 'obligation does not extend to ensuring that the patient has understood'.[86]

Causation

5.10   Proving that the doctor failed to give the patient a sufficient warning of some possible adverse risk of side-effects is not of itself enough to ensure that a claim in negligence succeeds. The patient must also establish that, had she received such a warning, she would not have consented to the treatment in question.[87] She must show that the doctor's negligent failure caused the injury of which she complains. Despite the grand statements about principles of informed consent, it was a narrow question of causation that directly concerned the Law Lords in *Chester v Afshar*.[88]

Miss Chester, a former journalist, had suffered from lower back pain for many years. She was referred to Mr Afshar, a consultant neuro-surgeon, who recommended surgery. Miss Chester, a private patient, consented to the operation. Unfortunately, the operation resulted in cauda equina syndrome. Miss Chester suffered significant nerve damage, and became partially paralysed. Miss Chester's claim that Mr Afshar had not warned her of the 1–2 per cent risk of cauda equina syndrome was accepted by this trial judge. He held that the defendant was negligent in failing to give Miss Chester such a warning.[89] The question

---

[84]   *Cooper v Royal United Hospital Bath NHS Trust* [2005] EWHC 3381.

[85]   [2005] EWHC 206; and see J Miola, 'Autonomy rued OK?' (2006) 14 *Medical Law Review* 108. And note *Nathanson v Barnet and Chase Hospitals NHS Trust* [2008] EWHC 460.

[86]   [2005] EWHC 206 at para 69.

[87]   So in *Jones v North West Strategic Health Authority* [2010] EWHC 178 (see above at 5.7) Mrs Jones's claim failed because, as she was a Jehovah's Witness, the judge ruled that she would have been unlikely to have consented to a Caesarean section with its increased risk of the need for a blood transfusion.

[88]   [2004] UKHL 41, HL.

[89]   The Court of Appeal refused leave to challenge the trial judge's findings of fact.

before the House of Lords was did Mr Afshar's negligence cause Miss Chester's paralysis? Miss Chester did not argue that, had she received such a warning, she would probably never have gone ahead with the operation. She did not say that a risk of paralysis was just too great and she would put up with the pain. Nor did she try to claim that she would have sought out a different surgeon, or a different form of operation.[90] She said only that, had she been properly warned, she would not have gone ahead with surgery on that day. She would have taken time to reflect, to seek a second opinion and consult her friends. The House of Lords found in her favour by a majority of 3:2.

The dissenting judges, Lord Bingham and Lord Hoffmann, applied the conventional principles of causation. Miss Chester had failed to show that, properly warned, she would have been likely to have refused to have surgery. She would most likely have had the operation, albeit some time later. She would have been subject to just the same risk. Her '. . . injury would have been as liable to occur whenever the surgery was performed and whoever performed it'.[91] The majority considered that the patient's right to autonomy and dignity, the right to make an informed choice, justified '. . . a narrow and modest departure from traditional causation principles'.[92] Should Miss Chester lose her claim, in conformity with the normal rules on causation, Lord Hope argued that the duty on doctors to warn patients of the risks of surgery would be rendered '. . . useless in the cases where it may be needed most'.[93] Lord Hope stressed that many patients might find a decision about whether to go ahead with risky treatment difficult. They could not with hindsight say definitively 'I would have said yes or no'. Many people might share Miss Chester's ambivalence. Patients who would find such a decision difficult should not be deprived of a remedy. Hence he agreed with the majority to modify the rules of causation, as he saw it 'modestly'. Lord Bingham saw any departure from those usual rules as 'substantial and unjustified'.[94]

What is informed consent and does it really matter?

5.11 Doctors' fears of litigation[95] surrounding 'consent' are understandable. The sheer difficulty of recalling, reviewing and interpreting conversations which took place years ago in a context a million miles from a courtroom should not be underestimated. None of these factors should be allowed to

---

90 See *Chappel v Hart* [1999] 2 LRC 341.
91 [2004] UKHL 41, HL at para 8.
92 [2004] UKHL 41, HL at para 24, per Lord Steyn.
93 [2004] UKHL 41, HL at para 86 per Lord Hope.
94 [2004] UKHL 41, HL at para 9; and see S Green, 'Coherence of Medical Negligence Cases: A Game of Doctors and Purses' (2006) 14 *Medical Law Review* 1.
95 It has been argued that informed consent claims are the thin end of the wedge, opening the door for no fault liability; see A Meisel, 'The Expansion of Liability for Medical Accidents: From Negligence to Strict Liability by Way of Informed Consent' (1977) 56 *Nebraska Law Review* 51.

override the importance of providing patients with comprehensible and comprehensive information. Information is a prerequisite of meaningful choice. The term 'informed consent' informs popular culture as much as law and medical practice. But what does it mean – has it become something of a slogan?[96] In legal debates, the term tends to be used to signal how much information must be offered to a patient, yet the two words of themselves do nothing to guide the reader to discern how much is enough. The Human Fertilisation and Embryology Act 1990 opts for the term 'effective consent'. The Human Tissue Act 2004 prefers 'appropriate consent'. Neither phrase helps us – 'effective' for what or 'appropriate' for what? Perhaps the courts can do no more than set broad parameters to indicate to doctors that they must seek to ensure that their patients know enough about any treatment proposed to be able to choose. Professional practice will kick-start that process. What is the collective experience in relation to what patients want to know and need to be told? But professional practice is only the first stage in a process. The doctor must reflect on how she might regard the proposed treatment if she were the patient. A risk of 1 per cent is statistically small. If that risk is of paralysis, many people would want to know, so that they, not their doctors, make the crucial risk: benefit assessment. Then, the particular circumstances of the patient must be considered. A less than 1 per cent risk of acquiring a hoarse voice after throat surgery might not concern many of us, particularly if the surgery were to relieve a great deal of pain. An aspiring opera singer might take a different view.

Difficulties in defining informed consent may also have played their role in the long delay in its incorporation into English law. But definition was not the only obstacle to progress. Lord Diplock in *Sidaway*,[97] suggested information might be counterproductive:

(1) Patients, he contended, do not want more information.
(2) Patients could not understand that information if they were offered it.
(3) More information would lead to patients 'irrationally' refusing much-needed treatment.

None of these reasons are sound.[98] Surveys show that most patients do want more information. A right to more information does not mean information must be forced on the unwilling patient. If a patient says, 'Doctor, it's up to you. I don't want to know any more about this operation', a prudent patient

---

[96] For an impressive analysis of the question, see Maclean (2004) 24 *Legal Studies* 169.

[97] [1985] 1 All ER 643 at 658–659. See M Brazier, 'Patient Autonomy and Consent to Treatment: The Role of the Law?' (1987) 7 *Legal Studies* 169.

[98] See, in particular, the President's Commission for the study of ethical problems in medicine: *Making Health Care Decisions* (1982) US Govt Printing Office, and '*What Are My Chances Doctor?*': *A Review of Clinical Risks* (1986) Office of Health Economics. And for harder evidence about risk-disclosure, see R Heywood, 'Informed Consent in Hospital Practice: Health Professionals' Perspectives and Legal Reflections' (2010) 18 *Medical Law Review* 152; R Heywood, 'Medical Disclosure of Alternative Treatments' (2009) 68 *Cambridge Law Journal* 30.

test does not require that he be held down and forced to listen. Patients do have difficulties understanding medical details. The remedy is to teach doctors how to communicate more effectively. As for 'irrational' treatment refusals, there is no evidence to support the contention that more information leads to more patients refusing treatment. And how is 'irrationality' to be judged? A woman is told that radical mastectomy will maximise her prospects of recovery from breast cancer. She knows that if she loses a breast her husband will leave her and that psychologically she is unable to cope with the necessary mutilation. Who can say she is 'irrational' if she opts for the statistically less 'safe' option of lumpectomy?

Undue emphasis on statistical risk bedevils debate on how much and what sort of information patients should be given about proposed treatment. The likelihood of a risk materialising is just one factor in a decision about what treatment to undergo if you are ill. The impact of the risk on the way that an individual lives her life is equally significant. It might be thought that an elderly man facing rectal surgery of the same sort as the operation involved in *Smith v Tunbridge Wells Health Authority* would contemplate a small risk of impotence with greater equanimity than the 28-year-old Mr Smith. Who but the gentleman in question can judge that risk to his own remaining hopes in life? Too ready assumptions about patients could undermine the attempts at shared decision-making so lauded by the GMC.

Therapeutic privilege

5.12 We have argued that the standard determining how much patients should be told about treatment needs to be patient-centred. As English law moves towards a more patient-centred test, we must also ask whether doctors may be able to rely on a defence of therapeutic privilege. Might a defendant surgeon be able to say this, in relation to a very elderly patient whom she failed to warn of a small risk of impotence: 'The patient is highly nervous and exaggerates risks. If he does not have the surgery he will be doubly incontinent and have to go into a home. I just don't think he could cope with the information'? It is clear that any such defence must be based on cogent reasons relating to the welfare of that particular patient. In *AB v Leeds Teaching Hospital NHS Trust*,[99] it was argued that giving families information about the retention of organs from their dead children would cause unnecessary distress, and might result in psychiatric harm. Gage J rejected a blanket plea of therapeutic privilege, saying of the defence:

> In so far as it involved the exercise of a therapeutic privilege it was one that does not appear to have been exercised on a case by case basis.

It does not follow that therapeutic privilege should never be endorsed. The doctor might be justified in withholding information where it would cause

[99] [2004] EWHC 644.

serious harm to the patient. In such a case, the GMC advises that the reasons are recorded in the patient's notes and discussed with the medical team.[100] Furthermore, a patient's state of mind may be such that certain information would cloud not clarify his judgment, especially if he is on the borderline of incapacity. Maclean warns of its ambiguity and the lack of research into its use and effect.[101]

Fiduciary obligations

5.13 The tort of negligence remains a clumsy mechanism for vindicating a patient's right to information. Battery is inappropriate both because of its emotive language and because it may exclude oral drug therapies. In Canada,[102] courts have sought to reclassify doctor–patient relationships by adapting the legal concept of the fiduciary relationship to embrace the doctor and her patient.[103] Within such a relationship of trust the doctor's duty would be to make available to the patient that information which it seems likely that individual patients would need to make an informed choice on treatment. Such a change is desirable not just to endorse patient's rights but also to enhance patient care.[104] Full participation in treatment by the patient, an alliance between patient and doctor, improves the quality of health care.[105] Interestingly, growing numbers of doctors are moving towards this view. So far English courts have found little to recommend a departure from established torts to a more innovative fiduciary approach.[106]

Does it matter who operates?

5.14 As important to many patients as what the operation entails may be the question of who operates. If a patient agrees to surgery, believing eminent consultant X will operate on him, is his consent invalidated if registrar Y operates?

---

[100] GMC, *Consent: Patient and Doctors Making Decisions Together* (2008).

[101] Maclean, *Autonomy, Informed Consent and Medical Law* (2009) CUP at 205–208. And see below on vulnerable patients and the inherent jurisdiction at **6.21**.

[102] *McInerney v MacDonald* (1992) 92 DLR (4th) 415; *Norberg v Wynrib* (1992) 92 DLR (4th) 449.

[103] Alas, such a proposition was rejected by both the Court of Appeal and the Law Lords in *Sidaway* and by the Australian High Court in *Breen v Williams* (1996) 70 AJLC 772. See M Brazier (1987) 7 *Legal Studies* 169 at 189–191.

[104] See A Grubb, 'The Doctor as Fiduciary' [1994] *Current Legal Problems* 112; P Bartlett, 'Doctors as Fiduciaries' [1997] 5 *Medical Law Review* 193; M Brazier, M Lobjoit, 'Fiduciary Relationship: An Ethical Approach and a Legal Concept' in R Bennett, C Erin (eds) *HIV and AIDS Testing, Screening and Confidentiality* (1999) OUP p 170.

[105] See H Teff, 'Consent to Medical Procedures, Paternalism, Self-Determination or Therapeutic Alliance' (1985) 101 *Law Quarterly Review* 432.

[106] *Sidaway v Royal Bethlem Hospital* [1985] 1 All ER 643 at 650–651; *R v Mid-Glamorgan FHSA, ex p Martin* [1995] 1 All ER 356, CA.

Where a private patient contracts with consultant X that he will operate, the consultant is in breach of contract if he substitutes someone else.

Within the NHS the patient would have to show that his consent was conditional on X operating. He would not have agreed to the surgery if anyone else proposed it. In practice, consent forms used within the NHS expressly provide that no assurance is given that any particular doctor will operate. A patient cannot complain if the registrar operates. If the registrar lacked the experience to perform a particular operation, he will be able to sue him and the consultant if harm ensues. He can sue the registrar for his lack of competence. He can sue the consultant for failure to provide proper supervision and for allowing an inadequately qualified member of the team to operate.

In 1984, it was reported that a vet was allowed by a surgeon friend to remove a patient's gall bladder. A patient operated on by a vet will have a claim in battery against the vet, however competent he may have proved to be. He agreed to a qualified doctor operating on him.[107] He no more agreed to surgery by a vet than to surgery by the authors of this book. An operation performed by a medical student will give rise to a claim in negligence if the student is not competent. A claim in battery may also lie if the patient was not expressly informed about the proposal to allow a student to operate. He consented to an operation and accepted, if he signed the standard form, that no particular practitioner undertook to operate. He consented to surgery performed by a practitioner, not an 'apprentice'. Teaching hospitals play a vital role. The public interest requires that medical students train on real people. Nevertheless, any contact with a patient on the part of a medical student requires the patient's consent.

Increasingly, patients are concerned about the record and experience of whoever operates on them, even lofty consultants. How does their surgeon's record of success compare to his peers? Do his mortality rates exceed the norm? Has he been fully trained in this procedure? Evidence that surgeons began to practise laparoscopic procedures ('keyhole surgery') without adequate training was depressingly common. Should the law oblige each doctor to provide information about his own background and experience? Patients are entitled to competent care. The medical profession has an obligation to monitor the standards attained by doctors launching into, or continuing to perform, procedures that they are not able to carry out with competence. 'Informed consent' is unlikely to be a fruitful means of attaining these ends. If Dr X has a 4 per cent failure rate in relation to procedure A, and Dr Y a 5 per cent rate, those who are able to make choices will opt for X. The less articulate patient in a weaker bargaining position will be treated by X. Nor is Y necessarily the poorer doctor. If Y works in a deprived area, a 1 per cent difference in outcome may be more than explained by the poorer state of health of his patients before they enter hospital. More and more league tables are now published which will include each surgeon's mortality rate.

[107] See *R v Tabassum* [2000] Lloyd's Rep Med 404, CA, discussed above at **5.4**.

Emergencies

5.15   So far in this chapter, we have discussed the patient in a fit state to give consent himself. When the patient is unconscious, treatment may have to be given immediately, before the patient can be revived and consulted. She may have been wheeled into Casualty after an accident. He may have agreed to operation X, in the course of which the surgeon discovers a rampaging tumour needing immediate excision. Where there is no available evidence of the patient's own wishes in such circumstances, section 5 of the Mental Capacity Act 2005 grants to doctors a general authority to act in the best interests of the patient and do whatever is immediately necessary to preserve the life and prevent any deterioration in her health.[108] The doctor can invoke the defence of necessity. Such a defence is not exclusive to doctors. The bystanders who rush to the aid of the unconscious accident victim and administer first aid, the ambulance crew who bring him into Casualty, are equally protected from any claim in battery. This is the case even if the patient has attempted suicide, provided there is doubt as to his intentions or capacity.[109]

Once the immediate threat to a patient's life has passed, other decisions may have to be taken before he regains consciousness. In practice, when a patient is unconscious or otherwise incapable of consenting to treatment himself, the response of the hospital staff is to consult, when possible, with the patient's relatives or friends. What legal validity has a consent given by the relatives of an adult? The answer is none. Consulting relatives is courteous, but is legally significant solely in that as a matter of evidence it establishes that the doctor's consideration of the patient's best interests has been adequately informed as required by the Mental Capacity Act 2005.[110]

One difficult problem arises when some (but inconclusive) evidence is forthcoming about the unconscious patient's own wishes. A patient is wheeled into hospital unconscious and needs an immediate blood transfusion. His wife says, truthfully, that he is a Jehovah's Witness and would refuse a transfusion. Can the doctor lawfully give a transfusion? The procedure is necessary, but the doctor knows the patient would be likely to refuse it. In *Malette v Shulman*,[111] a Canadian case, a young woman was brought unconscious into Casualty. She carried with her a card clearly stating that she was a Jehovah's Witness and that she would in no circumstances consent to a blood transfusion even if her life was in danger. The Canadian court held that the doctor who administered a transfusion committed a battery. There was in that case no room for doubt that the patient had taken pains to ensure that no doctor should be in doubt of her refusal of blood in any contingency. Attempts to argue that a refusal of treatment must be 'informed' by knowledge of the actual circumstances of

---

[108] See below in ch 6.
[109] DH, *Reference Guide to Consent for Examination or Treatment* (2009), para 53.
[110] See Mental Capacity Act 2005, s 4(7).
[111] (1988) 63 OR (2d) 243 (Ontario High Court).

treatment were rejected.[112] As we have seen in *Re T*,[113] the English Court of Appeal overruled an apparent objection by T to transfusion. The facts of the cases are markedly different. The evidence T truly and independently objected to transfusion was shaky. Mrs Malette's convictions were beyond doubt.

The validity of such advance directives is now governed by sections 24 and 25 of the Mental Capacity Act 2005. As we shall see at **6.14**, the statute may not be much help if the essence of the question is, 'did the patient voluntarily and with full capacity makes the initial advance decision?'. One matter is clarified. To be effective to refuse life-sustaining treatment, any advance decision must be both in writing and witnessed.[114]

Too much 'informed consent'?

5.16   Just as the English courts begin to move towards endorsement of a patient-centred approach to consent, a number of philosophers begin to express doubts about the dominance of 'informed consent'.[115] Doubts are cast on how far legal rules truly represent the ethical value of autonomy.[116] It is argued that an unduly libertarian view of autonomy has prevented an adequate emphasis on responsibility and that obtaining informed consent has become a mechanistic process detrimental to good communication.[117] O'Neill argues that the goal of full or complete understanding is illusory. Therefore the focus of informed consent should be on preventing coercion and allowing patients to control the amount and form of information they receive.[118] Perhaps the very fact that this debate takes place indicates how far we have come since patients could be told 'therapeutic lies'.

---

[112] Discussed in (1990) 5 *Professional Negligence* 118.
[113] [1992] 4 All ER 649, CA.
[114] Mental Capacity Act 2005, s 2(5) and (6).
[115] A Maclean, *Autonomy, Informed Consent and Medical Law* (2009), CUP, ch 7.
[116] See, in particular, K Veitch, *The Jurisdiction of Medical Law* (2007) Ashgate.
[117] See N Manson and O O'Neill, *Rethinking Informed Consent in Bioethics* (2007) CUP.
[118] O O'Neill, 'Some Limits of Informed Consent' (2003) 29 *Journal of Medical Ethics* 4.

Chapter 6

COMPETENCE, CONSENT AND COMPULSION

6.1 In chapter 5, the principles relating to consent to treatment by competent adults were examined. This chapter looks at two other dimensions of consent to medical treatment. When an adult is incapable of deciding for herself whether or not to agree to treatment, how can treatment be lawfully authorised on her behalf? If an adult refuses to agree to treatment, can that refusal ever be overruled, either on the grounds that the patient 'irrationally' refused treatment which was in her interests, or because, untreated, her physical or mental condition threatens the safety of other people?

The law relating to decision-making on behalf of people who lack mental capacity is now to be found in the Mental Capacity Act 2005. This Act endured a lengthy period of gestation. In 1995, the Law Commission made proposals to reform the existing law.[1] They recommended a new statute to provide a 'code' addressing the many complex questions raised by the care of people who cannot care for themselves. This 'code' should encompass all the different needs of patients, not just healthcare needs. If an elderly person develops dementia, decisions have to be made about where he should live, does he need to move to a nursing home, what happens to his own house, just as much as what medical treatment he receives. Social care and medical care cannot be divorced from each other. Eleven years later,[2] after further consultation,[3] the Mental Capacity Act 2005 finally became law in a far from wholly satisfactory state.

---

[1] Law Commission Report No 231, *Mental Incapacity* (1995) HMSO is extensively reviewed in a dedicated edition of the *Medical Law Review*: see (1994) 2 *Medical Law Review* 1–91.

[2] The Scottish Parliament acted more speedily; see the Adults with Incapacity (Scotland) Act 2000; J K Mason and G T Laurie, *Mason and McCall Smith's Law and Medical Ethics* (8th edn, 2010) OUP (hereafter *Mason and McCall Smith*), pp 83–84, 86.

[3] See Lord Chancellor's Department, *Who Decides? Making Decisions on Behalf of Mentally Incapacitated Adults* Cm 3803 (1997); and the government's response, *Making Decisions* Cm 3803 (1999).

6.1 Competence, Consent and Compulsion

Doctors and nurses caring for a patient who lacks capacity to consent to treatment on her own behalf confront an awkward dilemma. What does the law allow and require them to do when a patient is chronologically thirty, but has such severe learning disabilities that she is unable to make decisions about her medical care? Once a person reaches eighteen, the age of majority, no one else, be he next-of-kin or a professional carer such as a social worker, can consent to treatment on his behalf. The doctor is faced with a patient who cannot himself give the consent required to make treatment lawful, and so not a battery, and there may be no one else who can lawfully act as the patient's proxy. Not to treat the patient at all would be inhumane and a breach of the duty of care owed to every patient. If a patient's physical condition threatens her life, or grave injury to her health, necessary treatment is justified under section 5 of the Mental Capacity Act 2005,[4] just as it is when an otherwise competent patient is wheeled unconscious into Casualty. What if there is no grave emergency? An elderly lady with dementia suffers from cataracts. A middle-aged patient with severe learning disabilities has a hernia. A nineteen-year-old girl with severe learning disabilities is found to be pregnant. None of these cases are life-threatening emergencies, yet the patients' families and their doctors may agree that the patients would be 'better off' for treatment. It is these kinds of questions that the Mental Capacity Act now addresses. Much of the controversy surrounding the Act arose from misplaced fears that the Act could be used to deny vulnerable patients life-sustaining treatment; that it introduced euthanasia 'by the back door'.[5] As we shall see, in most instances, the Act is concerned with decisions about how incapacitated and vulnerable people can live as well as possible and its major importance is in providing a framework for making decisions on behalf of those who cannot determine their own medical and social care.

In considering how English law should address the dilemmas posed by those who are unable to make their own decisions about health care, proper account must be taken of human rights law. However well intentioned, non-consensual treatment is in a sense still compulsory treatment. In order to treat a patient, especially if she is actively objecting to treatment, some element of restraint or detention may also be necessary.[6] Could such treatment violate Article 3 of the Human Rights Convention? The European Court of Human Rights set out some ground rules in *Herczegfalvy v Austria*.[7] The Court emphasised the vulnerability and powerlessness of patients lacking mental capacity. Treatment could lawfully be imposed on a patient where he is entirely incapable of deciding for himself and where such treatment was a 'therapeutic necessity'. Where therapeutic necessity was conclusively established, the 'compulsory' treatment should not be regarded as inhuman or degrading.

---

[4] Formerly under the doctrine of necessity: See *F v West Berkshire Health Authority* [1989] 2 All ER 545, HL, discussed at **6.6** below.

[5] D Mason, 'Euthanasia by the Back Door?' (2004) 154 *New Law Journal* 321.

[6] Extending in some instances to the use of 'reasonable force'; see *Norfolk and Norwich NHS Trust v W* [1996] 2 FLR 613.

[7] (1993) 15 EHRR 437 (ECtHR).

Article 5 of the Convention protects the right to liberty. While Article 5(1)(e) allows for the detention of 'persons of unsound mind', we shall see that English law was found wanting in the legal protection offered to patients lacking mental capacity who are hospitalised without either their own consent or any appropriate independent authorisation.[8] This meant that the Mental Capacity Act 2005 had to be amended by section 50 of the Mental Health Act 2007 which inserted new provisions into the 2005 Act establishing the Deprivation of Liberty Safeguards (DoLS).

The Mental Capacity Act 2005 needs to be distinguished from the Mental Health Acts of 1983 and 2007.[9] The Mental Health Acts regulate treatment for mental illness, allowing (inter alia) for compulsory treatment and detention. Many people who may be mentally ill do not lack mental capacity. Few of those who lack mental capacity are eligible for compulsory treatment under the Mental Health Act. There is, however, increasing overlap between the two statutes.[10] Nor, it seems, are the statutes alone enough to meet the legal questions arising from society's obligation to meet the needs of its more vulnerable members. The inherent jurisdiction of the High Court endures and a series of cases suggest that in exceptional cases when someone is classified as a 'vulnerable adult'[11] the courts can intervene to protect that person from neglect or abuse.[12]

Not just about health care

6.2 It is important to recognise that the Mental Capacity Act 2005 addresses the whole range of decisions that need to be made once there is doubt that the individual can make her own choices about how she lives her life. The Act has generated an avalanche of case law coming close to overwhelming the new Court of Protection set up to 'preside' over the Act.[13] Many of the cases arising from the Act in the past four years are not directly about healthcare decisions. They address questions as diverse as marriage, where a person should reside, and if family members should remain in contact with him. Nonetheless such cases may have relevance to us in three senses. First, the case may clarify how we should apply the mental capacity test or understand the concept of best interests. Second, health is about much more than decisions about medical treatment. A safe and comfortable home may do more to advance the person's

---

[8] See *HL v UK* (2004) 40 EHRR 761, discussed below at **6.11**.

[9] See P Bartlett and R Sandland, *Mental Health Law: Policy and Practice* (3rd edn, 2007) OUP; *Mason and McCall Smith*, ch 13: E Jackson, *Medical Law: Text, Cases and Materials* (2nd edn, 2010) OUP, ch 6.

[10] See Special Edition, 'A Model Law Fusing Incapacity and Mental Health Legislation – Is It Viable; Is it Advisable?' (2010) *Journal of Mental Health Law*.

[11] See, for example, *Re SA (Vulnerable Adult with Capacity: Marriage)* [2005] EWHC 2942.

[12] See J Herring, 'Protecting Vulnerable Adults: A Critical Review of Current Case Law' [2009] *Child and Family Law Quarterly* 498.

[13] *G v E and others* [2010] EWHC 621 (Fam), para 4.

well-being than pills or potions. Finally, a number of cases address a mix of issues such as both where and with whom the person should live and, for example, what treatment he should receive for his epilepsy.[14] The diligent reader will thus wish to explore the whole range of judicial decisions applying the 2005 Act and the courts' inherent jurisdiction. This chapter does not attempt such comprehensive coverage and simply introduces the basic principles of English law in this area.

Not altogether new

6.3 Before looking in more detail at the provisions of the 2005 Act, we should note that in many respects the statute codifies existing case law. There are few radical changes in legal principle. The test of mental capacity remains much the same. 'Best interests' continues to be the benchmark against which lawful treatment of a patient lacking capacity is normally to be judged. Thus earlier case law remains relevant to illustrate how the Act will work. There are important changes in practice. A person can now, via a lasting power of attorney, appoint a proxy to make medical and personal decisions for him should he lose mental capacity. A court can exceptionally appoint a deputy (a kind of guardian) to act for a patient. A new Court of Protection oversees the framework of the Act. Above all, what the Act should do is offer a uniform and comprehensive framework to help decision-making on behalf of people lacking mental capacity in all the aspects of their lives. Further guidance on the interpretation and application of the Act is found in an extensive Code of Practice.[15] The Code does not add any new legal requirements, but provides guidance on the Act. Some, including (amongst others) court-appointed deputies, donees of a lasting power of attorney, and people working in a professional capacity, such as doctors and social workers, come under a legal duty to have regard to its provisions.[16] Failure to comply with the Code is taken into account in any relevant legal proceedings.

The threshold of capacity

6.4 The first question that needs to be addressed is how the law decides whether or not a person has the mental capacity to make his own decisions about medical treatment. Three different sorts of test could be used. A status test could assess intelligence, and determine that all who fell below the requisite 'score' were incapable, and all above capable. A status test would thus designate a person as competent or incompetent for all legal purposes. An outcome test would judge the capacity of the decision-maker by the rationality or wisdom of the decision made. Neither test has ever found favour with English

---

[14]   *Re P (Adult Patient: Consent to Medical Treatment)* [2008] EWHC 1403 (Fam).

[15]   Department of Constitutional Affairs, *Mental Capacity Act: Code of Practice* (updated April 2007).

[16]   See the Mental Capacity Act 2005, ss 42(4) and (5).

law, which prefers a functional test. The functional test, endorsed in case law, is retained in the Mental Capacity Act 2005. The relevant question becomes whether X enjoys the necessary understanding to embark on the particular enterprise in question, be it entering a contract, making a will, getting married, or consenting to medical treatment. Consider the illuminating case of *In the Estate of Park*.[17] Mr Park, an elderly man who had previously suffered a severe stroke, married his second wife one morning and that afternoon he executed a new will. He died soon afterwards. His family challenged the validity of the marriage. His widow challenged the will. He was found to be mentally competent to marry, but to lack the necessary mental capacity to make a will. His impaired understanding and reasoning power remained sufficient for him to grasp what was entailed in marriage, but his confusion and loss of memory disabled him from having the necessary recollection of his properties and his obligations to make a will.

The application of the functional test to consent to medical treatment was well illustrated in *Re C*.[18] C was detained in a special hospital. He had been diagnosed as suffering from chronic paranoid schizophrenia. In 1993, he developed severe problems with a grossly infected leg. Doctors judged his life might be at risk if they did not amputate the leg below the knee. Conservative treatment had no better than a 15 per cent prospect of success. C refused to consent to surgery. He sought an injunction preventing doctors from amputating the leg without his express consent. There was no doubt C was mentally ill. He suffered from a number of delusions, including a fixed belief that he himself had had a glittering career in medicine. Nonetheless, Thorpe J found that C was competent to make his own decision on the surgery in question, and granted the injunction C sought. The test set out by Thorpe J for mental capacity in medical treatment involved three stages:

(1)   Can the patient take in and retain treatment information?
(2)   Does he believe it?
(3)   Can he weigh that information and *make* a decision?

Despite his delusions, C remained capable of understanding what he was told about the proposed treatment and, in particular, he comprehended the risk of death consequent on refusing surgery.

Re C indicates that bizarre beliefs or behaviour should not necessarily result in a finding that a person lacks capacity. However, what others perceive as irrational delusions may influence a judge. Contrast *NHS Trust v T (Adult Patient: Refusal of Medical Treatment)*.[19] T suffered from borderline personality disorder and frequently self-harmed. She tended to become severely anaemic. T

---

[17]   [1954] P 112.
[18]   [1994] 1 All ER 819. Compare the decision of Thorpe J that C retained capacity with that of Kay J in *R v Collins and Ashworth Hospital Authority, ex p Brady* [2000] Lloyd's Rep Med 355.
[19]   [2004] EWHC 1279.

sought to execute an advance directive prohibiting the administration of blood transfusions. She spoke of her blood as evil, contaminating any new blood transfused into her. The judge said that irrational decisions should not be equated with lack of capacity. Nonetheless he found that Miss T's view of blood as evil constituted such a 'misconception of reality' as to indicate incapacity.

The *Re C* test forms the basis of the test of capacity within the 2005 Act. Section 1 provides that a person must be assumed to have capacity unless proven otherwise.[20] No one is to be treated as unable to make a decision unless all practical steps have been attempted to help him to do so. A person is not to be treated as lacking capacity because he makes an unwise decision.[21] Inability to make a decision must relate to an impairment of, or a disturbance in the functioning of, the mind or brain, which may be permanent or temporary.[22] Inability to make a decision depends on establishing that the person is unable:[23]

(a) to understand the information relevant to the decision;
(b) to retain that information;
(c) to use or weigh that information as part of the process of making the decision; [24] or
(d) to communicate his decision (whether by talking, using sign language, or any other means).[25]

The Act directs that what must be assessed is essentially the patient's capacity to understand what is at stake and act on that information.[26] The rationality of the decision itself should not determine the capacity of the decision-maker. However, when doctors profoundly disagree with a patient's decision, they may be tempted to suggest that the patient lacks capacity. Butler-Sloss P warned against the dangers of succumbing to such temptation in *B v An NHS Trust*.[27] Ms B was a tetraplegic patient who sought to have the ventilator keeping her alive switched off. Her doctors challenged her capacity to make such a

[20] In *Re F* (case No 11649371) (2009, unreported) it was held that a reasonable belief that the patient *may* lack capacity is sufficient to ground an application to the court to enable a full examination of the issue of capacity to be made without delay.
[21] See s 1(4).
[22] See s 2(1).
[23] See s 3.
[24] And this includes a requirement to believe that information: *Local Authority X v MM* [2007] EWHC 2003 (Fam).
[25] See *Re AK (Adult Patient) (Medical Treatment: Consent)* [2001] 1 FLR 129, CA. AK was in the terminal stages of motor neurone disease. He could communicate only by barely blinking an eye to answer yes or no to questions. He indicated that he wished doctors to switch off the ventilator keeping him alive. The court granted a declaration that it was lawful to act on his instructions. AK retained mental capacity and extraordinary means made communication possible.
[26] See *Re LT (Vulnerable Adult) (Decision Making: Capacity)* [2010] EWHC 1910 (Fam).
[27] [2002] 2 All ER 449; see also above at **5.2**.

decision, citing alleged ambivalence in her views, her lack of understanding of other options proposed to her, and supposed depression. Butler-Sloss P found that Ms B retained full mental capacity despite her desperate plight. She warned that:[28]

> It is most important that those considering the issue should not confuse the question of mental capacity with the nature of the decision made by the patient, however grave the consequences. The view of the patient may reflect a difference in values rather than an absence of competence.

It would be foolish to suggest that outcome plays no role in determining mental capacity. Capacity is unlikely to be disputed unless others disagree with the outcome. Perhaps we should be more concerned about patients of borderline mental capacity who simply acquiesce in the wishes of their doctors or relatives? And the judges themselves do not wholly ignore outcomes. Butler-Sloss P herself said in another case, *Re MB (An Adult: Refusal of Medical Treatment):*[29]

> The graver the consequences of a decision, the commensurately greater the level of competence is required to take the decision.

The importance of effective communication between patients and professionals cannot be underestimated. When a patient is known to be affected by some degree of learning disability or dementia, it may be too easy to assume a lack of capacity. Consider this example. An elderly patient with moderate dementia needs dental treatment for an abscessed tooth. He has little concept of time, sometimes does not recognise his wife, and engages in bizarre behaviour. Is he incompetent to consent to dental treatment? What does he need to be told and to understand? His tooth hurts. The tooth can be removed so the hurt will be 'cured'. Despite his dementia, does he enjoy capacity to authorise that simple procedure and so meet the test in section 3 of the Mental Capacity Act 2005?

In a number of recent cases, judges have struggled with the problem of how far an ability to appreciate the consequences of refusing treatment may be seen as impairing capacity under the Act. In *A Local Authority v A*[30] Mrs A suffered from significant learning disabilities, atypical autism, communication difficulties and problems with empathy. On two occasions her children had been removed from her at birth. For a time she acceded to contraceptive treatment by depot injection but when she married Mr A, he was fiercely opposed to her continuing contraceptive treatment and antagonistic to social and health workers' interference. Experts disagreed about Mrs A's capacity to make a decision. The first question was, did she understand the issue at stake. Experts agreed that she showed understanding of the medical aspects of contraception and the advantages and disadvantages of different types of contraception,[31] but that she did not appreciate the implication of having and rearing a child or

---

[28] [2002] 2 All ER 449 at para 100.
[29] [1997] 8 Med L R 217 at 224, CA.
[30] [2010] EWHC 1549 (Fam).
[31] And see *Sheffield City Council v E* [2005] 2 WLR 953.

that any future child might well be removed from her care. The court held that appreciation of such consequences did not mean that she lacked the understanding required by section 3(1)(a) of the Act. But more is needed and section 3(1)(c) requires the ability to weigh the information offered and make a decision. The court found that Mr A was domineering and Mrs A was scared of him. There was a 'completely unequal dynamic in the relationship' and given Mrs A's disability and vulnerability a decision to reject contraception was not the 'product of her own free will'.[32]

Note that section 3(2) of the Act indicates that lack of capacity may be due to temporary as much as permanent factors affecting the patient's mind or brain.[33] What of the patient whose understanding and reasoning powers fluctuate? At some times he comprehends what is asked of him and can act on information given to him. Days or even hours later his competence deserts him, albeit to return at some later point. Fluctuating competence may be a result of psychotic disorder, or commonly, a consequence of dementia. Prior to the 2005 Act, the courts tended to find that patients with fluctuating capacity lacked capacity.[34] The Act continues to require an ability to understand and retain information, but section 3(2) states:

> The fact that a person is able to retain the information relevant to a decision for a short period only does not prevent him from being regarded as able to make the decision.

In theory, the functional test of capacity endorsed in the 2005 Act enables many patients with some degree of learning disability to retain capacity to authorise their own treatment. It also entails the risk that, although the patient understands enough to authorise their own treatment, he may refuse to do so. The elderly patient with toothache may allow fear of the dentist to overrule his desire to be rid of the toothache. That outcome will be seen by others as undesirable. Those others will be tempted to say the patients are unable to make a decision. Care should be taken before rushing to enforce treatment in the patient's best interests. Several thousand indubitably competent people damage their dental health by staying away from the dentist. Just because a patient is labelled demented or mentally disabled, should we enforce his visit to the dentist?

Treating adults who lack mental capacity

6.5 When an adult patient does lack capacity to consent to treatment on her own behalf, two closely related questions have to be answered next. On what

---

[32] [2010] EWHC 1549 (Fam) at para 73; and see *A Local Authority v MA, NA and SA* [2005] EWHC 2942 (Fam).

[33] See discussion of *Re MB (An Adult: Refusal of Medical Treatment)* [1997] 8 Med L R 217 at 224, CA (below at **11.21**).

[34] See *Re R (A Minor) (Wardship: Medical Treatment)* [1991] 4 All ER 177 at 187; *Re D (Medical Treatment: Mentally Disabled Person)* [1998] 2 FLR 22 at 24.

basis is proposed treatment lawful, and, who authorises such treatment? Two principal tests are canvassed: 'best interests'; and 'substituted judgment'. A 'best-interests' test requires that decision-makers consider what the overall welfare of the patient demands. It is, in theory at least, an objective test. 'Substituted judgment' demands an attempt to discern what the patient would want were she able to decide for herself. It is illustrated in a famous US case, *In re Quinlan*.[35] Karen Quinlan was a young woman who succumbed to sudden illness and lay in a coma supported on a ventilator. Her father applied to the court to be appointed her guardian and sought court approval to switch off the ventilator. The court authorised his decision on the basis of evidence that this was what Karen would have wished. The US court (1) endorsed a test of substituted judgment and (2) granted Karen's father, her next of kin, powers to act on her behalf. In many civil law jurisdictions, as well as in some states in the USA, the law allows next-of-kin to make decisions on behalf of adults who lack mental capacity,[36] just as English law empowers parents to consent to treatment on behalf of their young children. Both in case law and in the Mental Capacity Act, we shall see that English law leans towards a modified version of a best-interests test and refuses to endorse any notion that next-of-kin should automatically enjoy proxy powers of consent.

Prior to the 2005 Act, the law left patients lacking mental capacity and their doctors in something of a legal limbo.[37] No one had legal authority to act as proxy and consent on behalf of the patient. Even if a patient was compulsorily detained under the Mental Health Act 1983, section 63 of that Act allowing doctors to dispense with the patient's consent applied only to treatment for mental disorder.[38] And, as we noted earlier, most patients who lack mental capacity are not detained under the Mental Health Act.[39] Nor could an adult lacking mental capacity be made a ward of court so that the court could

---

[35] *In re Quinlan* 355 A 2d 664 (NJ, 1976). Discussed below at **19.9**.

[36] A test controversially employed in extensive litigation in the USA surrounding the proposed withdrawal of artificial hydration and nutrition from Terri Schiavo. The application was supported by her husband and opposed by her parents. See *Respondent Michael Schiavo's Opposition to Application for Injunction* Case No: 04A-825, 24 March 2005 (Supreme Court, USA). See below at **19.9**.

[37] See *T v T* [1988] 1 A11 ER 613; and see the 3rd edition of this work, pp 115–117.

[38] So under the 1983 Act, doctors may require a detained patient to accept medication for schizophrenia but have no power to authorise surgery for a hernia. But it should be noted that judges tend to give mental disorder a wide meaning. Forcible feeding of anorexic patients was found to constitute treatment for mental disorder: see *B v Croydon Health Authority* [1995] 1 A11 ER 683; *Riverside Mental NHS Trust v Fox* [1994] 1 FLR 614. In *Tameside and Glossop Acute Services Trust v CH (a Patient)* [1996] 1 FLR 762 a Caesarean section was held to be treatment necessary to alleviate a detained woman's schizophrenia. In *R v Collins and Ashworth Health Authority, ex p Brady* [2000] Lloyd's Rep Med 355, forcible feeding to prevent Ian Brady starving himself to death was held to constitute treatment for his mental disorder.

[39] Or are eligible to be so detained. Patients with severe learning disabilities who are treated in hospital are usually voluntary (or informal) patients.

authorise treatment.[40] One of the extraordinary features of the history of this area of law is that not until 1987 did this question trouble the courts.[41] In earlier times, perhaps no-one gave much thought to the legality of treating patients lacking mental capacity? Doctors and families simply went ahead on the basis that 'doctor knows best'? The rise in medical litigation and increased concern for patients' rights began to worry doctors. Health professionals feared litigation if they went ahead with treatment without consent. They also feared litigation if a patient suffered harm because they did nothing.

F v West Berkshire Health Authority

6.6   The trigger for judicial action to clarify the legality of treatment of mentally disabled patients came about in the context of the sterilisation of women with learning disability over eighteen. If the girl was under eighteen, she could be made a ward of court, and the court, if sterilisation was in her best interests, could authorise that radical surgery.[42] In the first fully reported case relating to an adult, T was nineteen years old. Despite her mother's care, she became pregnant. She was described as having a 'mental age' of two and a half, she could barely communicate and she was doubly incontinent. Her mother and her doctors applied to Wood J for a declaration that to terminate T's pregnancy and then sterilise her would not be unlawful. He granted that declaration, finding that where a patient was suffering from such mental abnormality as *never* to be able to consent to proposed treatment, a doctor was justified in 'taking such steps as good medical practice demands'.[43]

In 1989, a similar case, *F v West Berkshire Health Authority*, reached the House of Lords. F was a thirty-six-year-old woman, said to have a mental age of five to six. She was a voluntary patient in a mental hospital and had entered into a sexual relationship with a male fellow patient. The House of Lords granted a declaration stating that F might lawfully be sterilised. Lord Brandon declared:[44]

> . . . a doctor can lawfully operate on, or give other treatment to, adult patients who are incapable, for one reason or another, of consenting to his doing so, provided that the operation or other treatment concerned is in the best interests of the patient.

Their Lordships made it clear that mentally disabled adults could lawfully receive medical care and treatment. The elderly confused lady with cataracts can

[40]   See B M Hoggett, 'The Royal Prerogative in Relation to the Mentally Disordered: Resuscitation, Resuscitation or Rejection' in M D A Freeman (ed), *Medicine, Ethics and the Law* (1988) Stevens, London.

[41]   See *Re T* (14 May 1987, unreported); *Re V* (1987) *Times*, 4 June; *T v T* [1988] 1 All ER 613.

[42]   See *Re B (A Minor) (Wardship: Sterilisation)* [1987] 2 All ER 206, HL, discussed further in chs 11 and 14.

[43]   *T v T* [1988] 1 All ER 613 at 625.

[44]   [1989] 2 A11 ER 545 at 551.

have those cataracts removed. But *F* empowered doctors to decide on what treatment a patient received with no formal restrictions imposed on the exercise of that power. Operating on an old lady with cataracts is one thing, sterilising a mentally disabled woman is an intervention of a different order of magnitude.[45] Disquiet about the decision in *F v West Berkshire Health Authority* arose from a suspicion that the judgment benefited doctors rather more than patients. A declaration from a High Court judge protected him from subsequent litigation.[46] Particularly if there is some dispute between the patient's relatives, or relatives and carers, the doctor benefited from the court's intervention.

Defining best interests

6.7   The most fundamental problem lay in the way their Lordships defined best interests ruling that courts should apply the *Bolam* test. Treatment would be lawful if it conformed with a reasonable and competent body of professional opinion, albeit there might be another reasonable and competent body of professional opinion which would take a contrary view.[47] The Law Commission criticised the use of *Bolam* in this context. Their Report recommended that it[48] '. . . should be made clear beyond any shadow of a doubt that acting in a person's best interests amounts to more than not treating a person in a negligent manner'. They proposed that a 'best-interests' test should be retained to assess the lawfulness of treatment of mentally disabled people, but verifiable criteria to determine that person's best interests needed to be spelled out.

After a decade of rubber stamping medical opinion, the courts adopted a much more proactive approach to best interests, well before the enactment of the 2005 Act. Refusing to authorise a vasectomy on a mentally disabled man, Thorpe LJ[49] emphasised that the decision about the patient's interests was one which the judge must make. It encompasses 'medical, emotional and other issues'.[50] In assessing the pros and cons of treatment, the judge should embark on a balancing exercise. Before authorising major invasive and irreversible procedures, the judge must be satisfied that the case for such treatment will be significantly in credit. *In Re S (Adult Patient: Sterilisation)*[51] concerned an application to carry out a hysterectomy on a twenty-nine-year-old woman with

---

[45]   Lord Griffiths dissented. He argued that a grave decision such as sterilisation with all its implications should not be left to doctors alone. He believed that it was open to the House of Lords to develop a common law rule that prior judicial approval was required before an operation as radical as sterilisation could be performed (pp 561–562).

[46]   See J Bridgeman, 'Declared Innocent?' (1995) 3 *Medical Law Review* 117.

[47]   *Bolam v Friern Hospital Management Committee* [1957] 1 WLR 582 discussed fully in ch 7 and see M A Jones, 'Justifying Medical Treatment Without Consent' (1989) 5 *Professional Negligence* 178.

[48]   Law Commission Report No 231 *Mental Incapacity,* para 3.27.

[49]   See in *Re A (Medical Treatment: Male Sterilisation)* [2000] 1 FCR 193, CA.

[50]   [2001] 1 FCR 193 at 200.

[51]   [2000] 3 WLR 1288.

severe learning difficulties. Doctors and her mother were concerned about the risk of pregnancy and the woman also suffered from severe menstrual problems. She had a phobia about hospitals. Overturning the trial judge's decision that hysterectomy would be lawful, the Court of Appeal held that other less invasive alternatives should be tried first. Butler-Sloss P said this:[52]

> The *Bolam* test [is] irrelevant to the judicial decision, once the judge [is] satisfied that the range of options was within the range of acceptable opinion among competent and reasonable practitioners.

Thorpe LJ emphasised that what the medical expert witnesses offered was expert advice on the options for treatment. The court then must exercise the choice the patient was unable to make. The patient's welfare in its broadest sense must be the paramount consideration.[53] In *R (on the application of N) v Doctor M*[54] there was a body of expert opinion testifying that a particular treatment was *not* in the patient's best interests. It was held that expert opinion was relevant, but not conclusive. The courts have made it clear that best interests embrace a great deal more than narrowly clinical interests.

'Best interests' survives: the Mental Capacity Act 2005

6.8 The Mental Capacity Act retains but reforms the best-interests test to determine how a patient lacking capacity should be treated. Section 5 provides a statutory basis, the general authority, for any act done in relation to the care or treatment of a person lacking mental capacity. It provides that:

(1) If a person ('D') does an act in connection with the care of treatment of another person ('P'), the act is one to which this section applies if –
  (a) before doing the act, D takes reasonable steps to establish whether P lacks capacity in relation to the matter in question, and
  (b) when doing the act, D reasonable believes –
    (i) that P lacks capacity in relation to the matter, and
    (ii) *that it will be in P's best interests for the act to be done.* [Emphasis added].
(2) D does not incur any liability in relation to the act that he would not have incurred if P –
  (a) had had capacity to consent in relation to the matter, and
  (b) had consented to D's doing the act.

Section 5 has a broad application extending beyond medical treatment. Anyone who intervenes to assist a person lacking mental capacity is protected from liability in battery if he acts in that person's best interests. The passer-by who pulls a distressed elderly person with dementia out of the way of oncom-

---

[52] [2000] 3 WLR 1288 at 1299.
[53] See also *Simms v Simms* [2003] 1 A11 ER 669; *A v A Health Authority* [2002] 1 FCR 481.
[54] [2003] 1 FLR 667.

ing traffic falls within section 5. The paramedics who lift her into an ambulance, and all the doctors and nurses who tend her in hospital, act lawfully by virtue of section 5. The carers who feed and wash her when she returns to a nursing home act lawfully. Note, however, that section 5 grants immunity only from battery. Should the patient's care be negligent, she retains her rights to redress.

Should Parliament have seized the opportunity to junk the best-interests test? Would 'substituted judgment' be a preferable test? The Law Commission rejected a simplistic substitution of 'substituted judgment' for best interests. The difficulty is this. Where a patient once enjoyed mental capacity, his known preferences, and even idiosyncrasies, the views which he has expressed to family and friends of what he would hope for were he ever to lack mental capacity, are useful and crucial factors on which to base treatment decisions. In the majority of cases where a patient has lacked mental capacity all his life, 'substituted judgment' is a myth. The unfortunate young woman in *T v T* was never capable of communicating her preferences and choices to others – she was never able to make autonomous choices at all. Nonetheless, the Law Commission strove to give force where appropriate to the prior preferences of someone who now lacks mental capacity.

(1) They recommended giving statutory force to advance directives.[55] 'Living wills', whereby a person gives directions about treatment which he should, and should not receive, if he becomes unable to decide such matters for himself, should be enforced. Thus we could today set out our decisions about continuing treatment in circumstances where for us death would become preferable to life.

(2) The Law Commission recommended that people should be empowered to nominate their own chosen proxy (attorney) to act for them should they lose capacity to act for themselves.

We shall see that both their recommendations are implemented in the Mental Capacity Act. The 2005 Act provides for advance refusals of treatment, hedged about with multiple restrictions. Section 9 allows the appointment of a lasting power of attorney. However, both advance refusals and lasting powers of attorney will work to reflect the wishes of the individual herself only in limited circumstances. First, the patient must at some point in her life have enjoyed the necessary mental capacity to execute such an instrument. Second, she must actually have done so, contemplated a future loss of capacity and acted to attempt to extend her autonomous choices beyond that sad event. The numbers of patients making advance refusals, or creating lasting powers of attorney may well be small.

(3) Most importantly, in their proposed definition of best interests, the Law Commission sought to ensure that any evaluation of best interests took into account any available evidence of what the patient herself might want were she able to articulate her own views. Section 4 of the Mental Capacity Act 2005 adopts (with some additions) the Law Commission's

---

[55] Law Commission, Report No 231, *Mental Incapacity,* Part V.

notion of a modified best-interests test, a test incorporating at least some element of substituted judgment.

Modified best interests

6.9 In determining best interests, decision-makers are first instructed that in making their decision they should not act merely on the basis of:[56]

(a)   the person's age or appearance, or
(b)   a condition of his, or an aspect of his behaviour, which might lead others to make unjustified assumptions about what might be in his best interests.

Simply because a patient is ninety-four does not justify assuming that she would be better off dead in some life-threatening emergency.

Next, when considering best interests, the decision-maker must consider if the patient is ever likely to recover the capacity to make her own decisions, and if so, when this may be.[57] Wherever possible, the patient must be allowed and assisted to participate in decisions as far as she is able.[58] So if X has suffered serious brain injuries in a road accident, only immediately necessary decisions should be taken by others while there remains the possibility that X will recover at least some of his reasoning powers. As X slowly recovers, where feasible, he should at least be consulted. In determining best interests, a decision-maker must consider as far as reasonably possible:[59]

- the person's past and present wishes and feelings (and in particular any relevant written statement made by him when he had capacity);
- the beliefs and values that would be likely to influence his decision if he had capacity;
- the other factors he would be likely to consider if he were able to do so.

In considering these matters, the Act further requires that a decision-maker seek the views of those people who may be best placed both to offer the views of the patient herself and judge her welfare. So where possible the decision-maker must consult:[60]

(a)   anyone named by the person as someone to be consulted on the matter in question or on a matter of that kind;
(b)   anyone engaged in caring for the person or interested in his welfare;
(c)   any donee of a lasting power of attorney granted by the person; and
(d)   any deputy appointed for the person by the court.

---

[56] See s 4(1).
[57] See s 4(3).
[58] See s 4(4).
[59] S 4(6). See *Ashan v University Hospitals Leicester NHS Trust* [2006] EWHC 2624 (importance of religious faith).
[60] S 4(7).

This modified best-interests test requires decision-makers to focus on the individual patient and make a judgment to promote her welfare, a judgment which takes proper account of any prior views that she may have expressed and involves the people most likely to know about her views. Substituted judgment becomes an integral part of best interests where such judgment can practically be discerned. The dignity of every patient, including those who never enjoyed mental capacity, is given due regard. The patient in *T v T* (discussed above) never had the capacity to make judgments. Nonetheless she would have preferences and feelings. Perhaps she may have displayed particular aversions, or especial pleasures. Treatment which transgressed those aversions or removed those pleasures could only be in her interests if strong evidence supported its continuation, despite the distress occasioned to T.

But the requirement to take into account the patient's own views and feelings, what Mary Donnelly[61] has called the consultative model, is not without problems in practice. The patient may be unable to communicate save via his family or be heavily dependent on them to the extent that it becomes hard to discern which are the real views of the patient and which are the wishes of the family member.[62]

A statutory best-interests test no longer conflates best interests with nonnegligent care. Prior to the 2005 Act, as we have seen, the courts had already rejected such a conflation and emphasised that doctors and courts assessing best interests must consider the question holistically, looking at all the effects of a decision to adopt a particular treatment. However, that does not mean that there will not be occasions when a court rightly concludes that there is no alternative to treatment that the patient or family seeks to reject. In one recent case, a patient with learning disabilities and cancer of the womb initially agreed to a hysterectomy, but failed to (and then refused to) keep further appointments. The Court of Protection agreed that surgery was in her best interests and that doctors could take any measures needed to detain her in hospital and sedate her.[63]

More difficult problems arise when family members who care for, or are close to the patient, vehemently reject treatment that a court would conclude is in the patient's medical interests. The patient may need to be removed from his family to residential care if the family will not comply with recommended treatment and that will itself harm the patient. The courts are charged with the task of weighing competing harms.[64]

---

[61] M Donnelly, 'Best Interests, Patient Participation and the Mental Capacity Act' (2009) 17 *Medical Law Review* 1.

[62] See *Re P (Adult patient: Consent to Medical Treatment)* [2008] EWHC 1403 (Fam) at para 19.

[63] *DH NHS Foundation Trust v PS (by her Litigation Friend the Official Solicitor)* [2010] EWHC 1217 (Fam).

[64] See *Re P (Adult Patient: Consent to Medical Treatment)* [2008] EWHC 1403 (Fam).

Serious medical treatment

6.10 Within the constraints of the modified best-interests test, doctors remain proxy decision-makers for their patients. The Law Commission's initial proposals called for further safeguards against paternalist decision-making. The general authority to make decisions in a patient's best interests should be subject to restrictions.[65] Certain controversial radical and/or irreversible treatments would normally demand authorisation by a court. These would include sterilisation, organ or bone marrow donation. Other debatable treatments, including hysterectomy for menstrual management and abortion, would require a certificate from an independent doctor who would review the best-interests criteria in each case.

The government rejected such restrictions on the general authority,[66] but the 2005 Act contains some more limited safeguards. Sections 30–34 of the Act set out special rules relating to the inclusion of people lacking mental capacity in medical research.[67] Section 37 obliges NHS authorities to seek advice from an independent mental capacity advocate (IMCA):

(1) if it is proposed to provide serious medical treatment for a patient lacking mental capacity; and

(2) if there is no-one (other than professional carers or advisers) who can be consulted about the patient's best interests.

Serious medical treatment is defined as:[68]

> . . . treatment which involves providing, withdrawing or withholding treatment in circumstances where –
>
>> in a case where a single treatment is being proposed, there is a fine balance between its benefits to the patient and the burdens and risks it is likely to entail for him,
>>
>> in a case where there is choice of treatments, a decision as to which one to use is finely balanced, or
>>
>> what is proposed would be likely to involve serious consequences for the patient.

Are the interests of the patient given sufficient weight? Envisage a woman of thirty-three who lacks capacity as a result of a cerebral haemorrhage, and is a voluntary patient in hospital. Her only adult relative is her husband, now living with a new partner. He readily agrees to a proposal to sterilise her and carry out a hysterectomy. The Code of Practice[69] seeks to fill any lacuna in the law. The Code strongly advises that any proposal to withdraw artificial nutri-

---

[65] See Law Commission Report No 231, *Mental Incapacity*, Part VI.

[66] *Making Decisions* (1999) Cm 3803, para 12.

[67] See below at **15.9**.

[68] The Mental Capacity Act 2005 (Independent Mental Capacity Advocate) (General) Regulations 2006, SI 2006/1832, reg 4.

[69] Department of Constitutional Affairs, *Mental Capacity Act 2005 Code of Practice* (updated April 2007), paras 8.18–8.23.

tion or hydration, or to use a person lacking mental capacity as an organ or tissue donor, or to carry out a non-therapeutic sterilisation, should be brought before a court. So should some cases involving termination of pregnancy and 'other cases where there is a doubt or dispute about whether a particular treatment will be in a patient's best interests'.

There is one further protection to be found in the statutory regime to define best interests. Section 4(5) provides:

> Where the determination relates to life-sustaining treatment [the decision-maker] must not in considering whether the treatment is in the best interests of the person concerned, be motivated by a desire to bring about his death.

We discuss this further when we consider end-of-life decisions in chapter 19.

Use of restraint and detention[70]

6.11 Many patients who lack mental capacity will simply acquiesce in treatment. What of the patient who forcefully objects – the dentist moves towards him and the patient jumps out of the chair? Section 6 of the 2005 Act authorises the use of force and restraint, if such measures are necessary, and a proportional response to: (1) the likelihood of the patient suffering harm if he is not treated; and (2) the seriousness of that harm. Sometimes, continuing treatment may require more than brief restraint. An elderly patient with dementia may need to be confined in her care home. An anorexic patient who is to be fed forcibly will also need to be detained in hospital. Prior to the 2005 Act, judges were prepared to use common law powers to authorise detention in the patient's best interests.[71] In effect the common law allowed certain patients to be deprived of their liberty without any of the safeguards that would apply to detention under the Mental Health Acts.

The inadequacy of the common law was dramatically highlighted in *R v Bournewood Community and Mental Health Trust, ex p L*.[72] The House of Lords ruled that the common law powers derived from *F* could be invoked to authorise the *detention* of patients lacking mental capacity. L was forty-eight years old, autistic and severely mentally disabled. He could not speak and had very limited understanding. L was incapable of making any of his own decisions about his health or personal care. From 1994, after nearly thirty years in mental hospitals, L lived with paid carers. One day, in 1997, he became extremely agitated at his day centre. His carers could not be contacted. L was taken by ambulance to Bournewood Hospital and ultimately admitted as a 'voluntary' informal patient. He was not formally detained under the Mental Health Act 1983. He remained in hospital for several months despite his

---

[70] For fuller advice, see para 6.44 of the Code of Practice.
[71] See *Re C (Detention: Medical Treatment)* [1997] 2 FLR 180.
[72] [1998] 3 All ER 299, HL.

carers' wish for him to return to their home. An action was brought on L's behalf, accusing the hospital of false imprisonment. The essence of the case was whether or not L had been unlawfully detained. The Court of Appeal ruled in L's favour. He had been detained against his will and no lawful grounds for his detention justified his treatment. The Law Lords by a bare majority held that L was not imprisoned in the hospital. He was kept in an unlocked ward and not actually restrained from leaving. The majority considered that evidence that had he attempted to leave he would have been restrained, did not establish that he was detained against his will. All their Lordships agreed, however, that L was 'imprisoned' in the ambulance, but his detention was in any event lawful. Given his inability to consent to admission to hospital himself, any necessary removal and detention in hospital, plus whatever consequent treatment was called for, was lawful in his best interests.

L's carers took his case to the European Court of Human Rights and won. L's detention violated Article 5[73] of the Human Rights Convention:

> Everyone has the right to liberty and security of person. No one shall be deprived of his liberty, save in the following cases and in accordance with a procedure prescribed by law.

Article 5(1)(e) permits the lawful detention of 'persons of unsound mind', but Article 5(4) requires that anyone so deprived of his liberty must have the lawfulness of his detention decided speedily by a court. In *HL v UK*,[74] the European Court of Human Rights ruled that L had been deprived of his freedom solely on the basis of clinical judgments. Moreover, he was denied the opportunity for a speedy judicial review of his detention, contravening his rights under Article 5. The lack of procedural safeguards breached the Convention. The government were thus obliged to legislate to close the 'Bournewood gap', a gap that the unamended Mental Capacity Act 2005 failed to close.

Deprivation of Liberty Safeguards (DoLS)[75]

6.12   Thus the Mental Heath Act 2007 was used to amend the Mental Capacity Act 2005 by inserting into that Act a new section 4A and Schedules A1 and 1A and so introducing the Deprivation of Liberty Safeguards (DoLS). We should note that DoLS do not apply to every instance of restraint imposed to ensure that a patient lacking mental capacity receives proper care and/or medical treatment.[76] DoLS apply to people being treated or cared for in hospitals

---

[73] See *Winterwerp v Netherlands* (1979) 2 EHRR 387; *Herczegfalvy v Austria* (1992) 15 EHRR 437.

[74] (2004) 40 EHRR 761.

[75] For a useful practice pointer, see W J Cutter *et al*, 'Identifying and Managing Deprivation of Liberty in Adults in England and Wales' (2011) 342 *BMJ* c7323.

[76] See *JE v DE* [2006] EWHC 3459 (Fam).

or care homes[77] who are not detained under the Mental Health Act 1983 but have or might in future be deprived of their liberty in order to protect their best interests. Schedule A1 runs to 188 paragraphs and is generating enough case law[78] for a book of its own. Section 4A provides that the 2005 Act does not 'authorise any person (D) to deprive any other person (P) of his liberty' except under the authorisation of a court, or an authorisation granted under Schedule A1 to the Act. The first issue is to determine whether P lacks the capacity to give a valid consent to his detention. The second is to establish whether there has been or is likely to be a deprivation of liberty. The Code does not offer an explicit definition. In some cases it is obvious – P, supported by her family, repeatedly asks to leave and the care home refuse their requests. In others it is a matter of degree. A temporarily locked door is unlikely to amount to a deprivation of liberty. Simply placing P in a care home, for example, will not deprive her of liberty unless the circumstances are such that she cannot leave should she choose and/or staff control her daily life and limit those to whom she can have access.

The rules governing DoLS are exceedingly complex. Deprivation of liberty under Schedule A1 is lawful only if (inter alia) the patient is eighteen or over,[79] is suffering from a mental disorder within the meaning of the Mental Health Act 1983, lacks capacity, has no advance decision, LPA or deputy refusing the accommodation, and the deprivation of liberty is in his best interests, and necessary to protect him from harm. The deprivation of liberty must be authorised by a 'supervisory body' (at the time of writing usually the PCT where the patient is in hospital, or the local authority where the person is in a care home[80]). In defining mental disorder for the purposes of DoLS, the provisions of the Mental Health Act excluding learning disability from the definition of mental disorder should be disregarded. The rules differ according to whether the person is in a care home or a hospital. In the former, DoLS can be used for physical and or psychiatric treatment, even if the patient objects. In the latter, DoLS can be used for physical treatment (whether or not the patient objects) or for psychiatric treatment (if the patient is compliant). The Codes of Practice assume that DoLS are less restrictive than the Mental Health Act 1983 and should be used in preference, except where an objecting patient is admitted to hospital under sections 2 or 3 of the Mental Health Act. Cairns *et al* question

---

[77] The Court of Protection must authorise any deprivation of liberty elsewhere (eg in the person's own home).

[78] For a good example of the application of the complex rules, see *G v E and Others* [2010] EWHC 621 (Fam), [2010] EWCA Civ 822 and see T Elliott, 'Deprivation of Liberty and the Mental Capacity Act 2005' (2011) *Medical Law Review* (forthcoming).

[79] Children of sixteen or seventeen years old can be detained on the authority of the court under the Children Act 1989 or the Mental Health Act 1983 (as amended).

[80] The Health and Social Care Bill 2011, Sch 5 proposes to amend Sch A1 to the Mental Capacity Act 2005 so that local authorities would constitute the supervisory body for all persons resident in England if /when PCTs are abolished.

whether the overlap and unclear interface between the Acts might lead to arbitrary decisions and claims of discrimination.[81]

An application to the Court of Protection can be made before a DoLS application, for example if the patient or his representative wishes to challenge an assessment of capacity or best interests. Alternatively the authorisation itself can be challenged in the Court of Protection. The Court can then uphold, vary or terminate the authorisation. If a decision is being sought from the Court, anything immediately necessary to preserve the patient's life, or prevent a serious deterioration in his condition may be done pending an order of the Court.[82] There is no automatic reference to the Court of Protection. Do the DoLS satisfy Article 5(4)?[83]

Let families decide?

6.13 Why not remove decision-making about patients lacking mental capacity from doctors altogether? Should decisions be entrusted to an appropriate 'guardian', often a family member?[84] Intuitively, many people may feel that if a person cannot make decisions for himself, his family are the best substitute decision-makers. The Law Commission and the government rejected both granting automatic proxy powers to families and a system whereby people lacking mental capacity are routinely subjected to guardianship.

Laws granting automatic decision-making powers to 'next-of-kin' would be fraught with difficulty and danger. Identifying *who* the decision-maker should be is not straightforward. Imagine X, a retired school teacher who is suffering from dementia at eighty-four, has lived for twenty years with Y, a longstanding friend. Y is better placed to act as X's 'guardian' than X's only niece Z who may in the strict sense be her next-of-kin. Envisage A who is a widow with three children. The 'next-of-kin' do not agree how their mother should be treated. Perhaps A has just one son, but he has visited her no more than once or twice a year in the past five decades. He will not be the ideal 'guardian' of his mother's interests. Her interests and his may conflict. He stands to inherit a substantial sum of money if she dies. If she recovers and enters a nursing home his inheritance may wither away.

---

[81] R Cairns *et al*, 'Deprivation of Liberty: Mental Capacity Act Safeguards versus the Mental Health Act' (2010) 34 *The Psychiatrist* 246.

[82] See Mental Capacity Act 2005, s 4B and *A County Council v MB* [2010] EWHC 2508.

[83] See *G v E* [2010] EWCA Civ 822 at para 58 arguing that the DoLS fill the 'Bournewood gap', discussed in T Elliott (2011) *Medical Law Review* (forthcoming). And see N Allen, 'The Bournewood Gap (As Amended?)' (2010) 18 *Medical Law Review* 78–85.

[84] See A Grubb, 'Treatment Decisions, Keeping it in the Family' in A Grubb (ed), *Choices and Decisions in Health Care* (1993) Wiley.

Such difficulties might be overcome if laws allowed the express appointment of a guardian. In the case of X, Y (her friend) could be appointed her guardian. Wholesale appointment of guardians for every person unable to make decisions for themselves is simply impracticable. The courts would sink under a flood of applications. Nor is guardianship necessarily beneficial to patients. It imposes a child-like status on an adult. Given that English law endorses a 'functional' test of capacity, the law's aim is that the person herself should take as many decisions as she is capable of making.

Advance directives[85]

6.14 An advance directive enables a person to set out his own instructions about any future treatment which he should, or should not, receive, were he to lose mental capacity to make such decisions for himself. Such decisions need not be restricted to instructions about the continuation of life-sustaining treatment. A woman might, for example, want to give instructions about the management of her pregnancy in advance. A person in the early stages of a neuro-degenerative disease might wish to set out his own care plan. Prior to the 2005 Act, the courts had made it clear that advance refusals of treatment were legally binding as long as there was unequivocal evidence that the patient's decision was voluntary, competent, and directly relevant to the factual circumstances in question.[86] So, as we have seen, the instructions given by Ms T not to administer blood transfusions were found to be defective. The threshold for finding an advance refusal to be binding was set high.

Advance requests (or demands) were not legally binding. The Court of Appeal in *R (on the application of Burke) v GMC*[87] made it crystal clear that any advance demand (or request) for treatment has no legal force:

> . . . a patient cannot demand that a doctor administer a treatment which the doctor considers is adverse to his clinical needs.

So at common law, advance refusals were binding in theory, but exceptionally difficult to execute in practice in order to ensure that the individual's wishes prevailed.[88] The 2005 Act makes the exercise no easier. 'Advance decisions'[89] operate only to prohibit specified treatment being carried out. Only advance

---

[85] Discussed further below at **19.9** and see A Maclean, 'Advance Directives, Future Selves and Decision Making' [2006] 14 *Medical Law Review* 291.

[86] See *Re T (Adult: Refusal of Medical Treatment)* [1992] 4 A11 ER 649, CA.

[87] [2005] EWCA Civ 1003 CA at para 35.

[88] See, for example, T Thompson, R Barbour, L Schwartz, 'Adherence to Advance Directives in Critical Care Decision Making: Vignette Study' (2003) 327 *BMJ* 1011, demonstrating the divergent attitudes of healthcare professionals when faced with a patient's mock advance directive.

[89] See ss 24–26 of the Mental Capacity Act 2005.

refusals have legal force.[90] An advance refusal of life-sustaining treatment must meet stringent conditions. Such a refusal must (inter alia):[91]

- be verified by a statement to the effect that it is to apply to treatment even if life is at risk;
- be in writing;
- be signed by the patient or another in his presence and acting on his direction; and
- the signature be witnessed.

In other circumstances, there is no formal requirement that the advance decision be in writing, or witnessed. Evidence that such a decision was made when the patient had capacity to make such a decision, and has not been withdrawn, must still be forthcoming.[92] If there is no written document this may be hard to establish; anecdotal evidence from family and friends may not suffice.[93] And the decision will not have effect if:[94]

- the treatment in question 'is not the treatment specified in the advance decision'; or
- 'any circumstances specified in the advance decision are absent'; or
- 'there are reasonable grounds for believing that circumstances exist which [the patient] did not anticipate at the time of his advance decision and which would have affected his decision had he anticipated them'.

These stringent conditions set by the 2005 Act illustrate the difficulty of transforming theory into practice. The conditions make the task of executing a fire-proof advance decision nigh on impossible. Imagine this scenario. A is successfully treated for a brain tumour, but warned that there is a 20 per cent risk of recurrence and poor prospects of long-term survival if the cancer recurs. Should the tumour return, it will gradually rob her of her reasoning powers, memory and capacity for independent life. So she sets out an advance decision that, should the cancer recur, and she is unable to articulate her own wishes, she should not be resuscitated if she suffers a cardiac arrest, and should not be given antibiotics if she develops an infection. The cancer recurs and advances rapidly. A suffers a cerebral haemorrhage. Her advance decision does not cover the treatment in question and so has no force. Or, the cancer does not recur, but A suffers traumatic brain injuries in a road accident. Her advance decision does not apply because it does not relate to the circumstances that materialise. In an attempt to tackle this dilemma, section 24(2) does provide

---

[90] Under s 26(1), if P has made an advance decision which is (a) valid and (b) applicable to a treatment, the decision has effect as if he had made it, and had had capacity to make it, at the time when the question arises whether the treatment should be carried out or continued.

[91] See s 25(6).

[92] See s 25(1).

[93] Well illustrated in a pre-2005 Act case; see *W Health Care Trust v H* [2004] EWCA 1324.

[94] See s 25(4).

that the 'decision may be regarded as specifying a treatment or circumstance even though expressed in layman's terms'. Perhaps then, the best advice is to express any advance decision in as general terms as possible? But then you may fall foul of section 25(3) because of failure to anticipate circumstances that might have affected your decision. Yet section 25(3) in itself is an important safeguard for patients. Consider A again. She executes her advance decision in 2011, refusing all treatment should her cancer recur. It recurs in 2015 by which time a new highly effective treatment has been developed.

Next we must consider withdrawal of any advance decision. People must be free to change their minds. What seemed intolerable at forty may be acceptable at seventy. Changes in personal circumstances will alter one's perspective of quality of life. Section 24(4) provides that a withdrawal (or partial withdrawal) need not be in writing. *HE v NHS Trust*[95] (decided prior to the Mental Capacity Act 2005) demonstrates the difficulty of establishing informed withdrawal of an advance directive. When HE was a practising Jehovah's Witness, she executed (in writing) an advance directive prohibiting any blood transfusion. Later she renounced the Witness faith and reverted back to her original Muslim faith, becoming engaged to a fellow Muslim. Her advance directive stated that it could only be revoked in writing. She had taken no formal steps to revoke her original directive. Nonetheless, Munby J found that her conduct offered sufficient evidence that her directive no longer represented her wishes. It was implicitly revoked. He went on to say that '. . . once there is some real reason for doubt, then it is for those who assert the continuing validity and applicability of the advance directive to prove that it is still operative'. In effect, the facts of each case must be assessed. As Munby J goes on to say: '. . . the longer the time which has elapsed since an advance directive was made, and the greater the apparent change in circumstance since then, the more doubt there is likely to be as to its continuing validity and applicability'.

Lasting powers of attorney

6.15 An inevitable difficulty in any form of advance directive is defining in exactly what sorts of circumstances one might lose capacity, and what sorts of disease lie in wait. Appointing a chosen proxy to act for you may be an option welcome to many people. Before the 2005 Act, it was possible to execute an enduring power of attorney[96] and thus appoint a proxy to take decisions in relation to property and financial affairs. An elderly person, who feared that his mental faculties were declining, could appoint a relative or friend to act as his agent in managing his property and finance. If he subsequently lost mental capacity, the agent could continue to act on his behalf. It was not possible to execute such a power appointing a proxy decision-maker for health care, or personal welfare decisions.

---

[95] [2003] 2 FLR 408.
[96] See the Enduring Powers of Attorney Act 1985.

Section 9 of the Mental Capacity Act introduces a significant reform of the law. A person can now execute a lasting power of attorney (LPA) whereby he nominates the chosen donee (or donees) of the power to make decisions for him, both in relation to personal welfare (including decisions about medical treatment) and in relation to his property and financial affairs. One person can be selected to manage your affairs for you. An elderly parent can now authorise a daughter to make any necessary decisions about her intimate welfare and medical care, as much as about her property. The proxy (the donee) may only make decisions about life-sustaining treatment if the donor of the power expressly authorised her to do so. In making any decision on behalf of the donor, the proxy must act in the best interests of the donor and conform fully to the principles underlying the 2005 Act. The proxy's powers are limited by any advance decision made earlier by the donor. A number of formalities are prescribed.[97]

Some people may choose to grant an LPA to a professional adviser. More may prefer to choose a close friend or relative. So is there a risk of conflict of interest again? We think not. LPAs overcome many of the difficulties inherent in automatically entrusting decisions about health care to 'next-of-kin'. The patient actively chooses her preferred 'agent'. If, in thirty (or fifty) years, we are estranged from our daughters, we will not grant them power of attorney. If we suspect that they are over-anxious to receive their inheritance, we will not give them power over our life and death. As long as the requisite rules about the execution and registration of LPAs ensure that the grant of a LPA is a free and informed decision of the patient, LPAs are an attractive option to people who want to entrust their decisions about future health to relatives, friends or professional advisers chosen by them.

Deputies

6.16 Although guardianship of adults is generally eschewed in the 2005 Act, sections 15–21 make provision for exceptional cases when the new Court of Protection may see fit to appoint a deputy authorised to make personal welfare decisions on behalf of the patient. Such an appointment must be shown to be in the patient's best interests and the court has a wide discretion to determine the scope of the powers conferred on the deputy. Where serious questions arise about the continuing treatment and welfare of a patient lacking mental capacity, a deputy may be appointed who will be authorised within strict limits, and for as short a time as possible, to act on the patient's behalf generally. Their powers would not be limited to medical care, but extend to all questions of personal welfare, health care, property and finance.

---

[97] See the Office of the Public Guardian, which lists recent cases in a regular newsletter 'OPG In Touch'; accessible at http://www.publicguardian.gov.uk.

The need for a deputy can be illustrated by the highly exceptional case of *Re P (Vulnerable Adult) (Capacity: Appointment of Deputies)*.[98] P was thirty years old. He is blind and suffers from severe autism and yet he is a musical genius and noted performer. Lacking mental capacity to make his own decisions, he needs one-to-one care. In addition to making decisions about his care, his finances have to be dealt with and travel arranged. The Court of Protection agreed to appoint his parents and sister as joint deputies. Concerns were raised that as family members they lacked independence. But Hedley J was satisfied that the appointed deputies would manage P's affairs skilfully and in his interests and suggested that where trustworthy and capable family members were available and the need for a deputy was proven, those family members would be strong candidates for appointment. But family members do not always make ideal deputies, as was made clear by Baker J in *G v E and others*:

> If Hedley J's comments in ... *Re P* were intended to indicate that family members should as a matter of course be appointed deputies irrespective of the circumstances, I would respectfully disagree ... a person who lacks capacity should wherever possible be cared for by members of his natural family, provided that such a course is in his best interests and assuming that they are able and willing to take on what is often an enormous and challenging task. That does not, however, justify the appointment of family members as deputies simply because they are able and willing to serve in that capacity. The words of section 16(4) are clear.[99]

Court of Protection[100]

6.17   Central to the Act is the new expanded Court of Protection which enjoys a wide-ranging jurisdiction to oversee the care of adults lacking mental capacity, in both health care and welfare matters. It adjudicates on disputes about what form such care should take, and can issue declarations about the legality of proposed treatment. The court can appoint deputies where appropriate and register and supervise LPAs. But, as we have noted, resort to the court to oversee especially controversial or problematic medical procedures is not mandatory. Does this matter? Can we not trust the good sense of doctors and families to seek judicial oversight of what they propose to do in cases when, and only when, such oversight is truly needed? Doctors and carers are guided by the Code of Practice, which as we have seen, requires that certain cases are brought before the court. A failure on the part of a health professional to comply with this guidance will be taken into account in any relevant proceedings in any court or tribunal. It would, for example, be relevant to an assessment of a doctor's fitness to practise before the General Medical Council. One difficulty remains. When doctors and families disagree either with each other or among themselves, an application to court is likely to be made. Where there is either consensus among the several people involved with the

---

[98]   [2010] EWHC 1592 (Fam). The case aroused great media interest; on which see *Independent News and Media v A* [2010] EWCA Civ 343.

[99]   [2010] EWHC 2512 at para 60–61, per Baker J.

[100]   See ss 45–61.

patient, or perhaps an absence of involved family or friends, resort to court is less likely. The patient, lacking an advocate, is deprived of any voice to speak on his behalf. Two limited safeguards operate. First, we have seen that under section 37, an independent mental capacity advocate (IMCA) should be appointed where doctors propose serious medical treatment of a patient who lacks capacity and does not have a family member or friend to advise as to his best interests. Second, the jurisdiction of the Court of Protection does extend to claims arising from alleged breach of the Human Rights Act 1998 and can award damages accordingly.[101]

Mental health legislation[102]

6.18 This book does not attempt to deal in any detail with the provisions of the Mental Health Acts. Some reference needs to be made here to the Mental Health Acts 1983 and 2007. The 2007 Act makes significant amendments to the earlier statute. For the purposes of this chapter, one of the most crucial provisions of the mental health legislation is that section 63 of the 1983 Act grants statutory authority to dispense with detained patients' consent to certain treatment. As we shall see, the courts have interpreted section 63 to sanction treatments that might primarily be seen as treatment for physical illness. A patient's refusal of treatment can thus be overridden, even if he meets the test of mental capacity under the 2005 Act.

Part II of the 1983 Act (as amended) makes provision for the detention in hospital of certain mentally disordered patients. Only a minority of patients with mental disorder are in fact detained in hospital under the Act. Application for admission for assessment (observation and tests) must be based on the written recommendations of two medical practitioners who testify that the patient: (1) is suffering from mental disorder of a nature or degree which warrants his detention in hospital for assessment, or assessment followed by medical treatment for at least a limited period; and (2) he ought to be so detained in the interests of his own health or safety, or to protect others.[103] Admission for the assessment authorises the patient's detention for up to twenty-eight days. If he is to be detained longer, an application for admission for treatment must be made.[104] Such an application made under section 3 of the Act must be founded on grounds that the patient:

---

[101] *YA (F) v A Local Authority* [2010] EWHC 2770.

[102] See *Mason and McCall Smith*, ch 13; E Jackson, *Medical Law: Text, Cases and Materials* (2nd edn, 2010) OUP, ch 6; Bartlett and Sandland, *Mental Health Law; Policy and Practice* (2010) OUP; P Fennell, *Treatment Without Consent* (1996) Routledge.

[103] See Mental Health Act 1983, s 2. An emergency application founded on the recommendation of one doctor may be made under s 4 and authorises detention for up to seventy-two hours.

[104] A successful application for admission for treatment authorises detention for an initial period of six months.

(a) . . . is suffering from mental disorder of a nature or degree which makes it appropriate for him to receive treatment in a mental hospital; *and*

(b) . . . ;

(c) it is necessary for the health and safety of the patient or for the protection of other persons that he should receive such treatment and it cannot be provided unless he is detained under this section; and

(d) appropriate medical treatment is available for him.

The crucial question becomes, how is mental disorder defined? Section 1(2) of the 1983 Act (as amended) adopts a very broad definition; mental disorder means 'any disorder or disability of the mind'. 'Learning disability'[105] will not, however, as such be said to constitute mental disorder. A person with learning disability will be able to be detained under section 3 of the 1983 Act only if his 'disability is associated with abnormally aggressive or seriously irresponsible conduct'.[106]

Note, too, the condition that there should be appropriate medical treatment available for any patient who is to be detained for treatment. Some mental disorders, notably personality disorders, rarely respond to drug therapy as disorders such as schizophrenia may. But section 145 of the Mental Health Act 1983 now defines treatability broadly as 'medical treatment the purpose of which is to alleviate or prevent a worsening of the disorder or one or more of its symptoms or manifestation'.

The effect of sections 2 and 3 of the 1983 Act means that the number of people lacking capacity liable to be detained under the 1983 Act is thus small:

(1) The many patients who lack capacity as a result of learning disability can be detained only if they become aggressive or seriously irresponsible.

(2) In many cases their disability will not meet the 'treatability' condition. Being shut up in hospital will not do them any good.[107]

(3) A person lacking mental capacity can usually be protected from herself by means other than detention, so condition (b) may not be met.

(4) Government policy for several years was to promote care in the community, and numerous long-stay mental hospitals were closed down.

(5) Psychiatrists maintain that there are insufficient beds in mental hospitals even for patients who indubitably meet the criteria set out in the 1983 Act. Only the most dangerously disordered or profoundly disabled patients are detained in hospital under the 1983 Act. When it is deemed necessary to confine a patient lacking capacity with learning or other

---

[105] Defined as a 'state of arrested or incomplete development of the mind which includes significant impairment of intelligence and social functioning'; see s 1(4).

[106] S 1(2A), but he could be admitted for assessment under s 2 without establishing such an association.

[107] Even though the Court of Appeal has developed a fairly broad definition of treatment to include group therapy and nursing care in a structured environment: see *R v Canon Park Mental Review Tribunal, ex p A* [1994] 2 All ER 659, CA; *R v Mental Health Review Tribunal, ex p Macdonald* (1998) Crown Office Digest 205.

disabilities for his own safety, the usual route now will be to resort to the Deprivation of Liberty Safeguards introduced into the Mental Capacity Act 2005,[108] though we must reiterate that the two systems for care and detention have in practice significant overlap.[109]

Compulsory treatment under the Mental Health Act 1983

6.19   Part IV of the Mental Health Act provides for the compulsory treatment of that minority of patients detained under the Act. Section 63 provides that:

> The consent of a patient shall not be required for any medical treatment given to him for the mental disorder from which he is suffering, not being treatment given within section 57, 58 or 58A [of the Act].

Section 63 applies to detained patients only. It cannot be used on voluntary patients, or on an out-patient basis. But that poses a dilemma. A patient may recover in hospital on appropriate medication and be fit to return home if he continues to comply with treatment, but the risk is that when he is out of hospital, he will stop taking his medicine. So at one hospital doctors admitted patients under section 3, gave them long-term medication, then released them on licence until their next dose of medication was due. That practice was found to be unlawful.[110] Section 63 could be used to dispense with a patient's consent to treatment only where that patient actually needed to be detained, the conditions laid down in section 3 for admission for treatment were not met, and the use of section 3 to enforce treatment was an unlawful fiction. The Court of Appeal, however, later held that as long as some element of hospital treatment was required, 'extended leave' could be used to 'enforce' medicating in the community.[111] Amendments inserting section 17A–G into the 1983 Act now provide for community treatment orders enabling doctors to ensure treatment in the community via the sanction of recall to hospital.

Section 63 of the 1983 Act on its face authorises psychiatric treatment, not treatment for physical illness. It has been interpreted by judges to extend to allow the forcible feeding of anorexic patients and to justify non-consensual Caesarean surgery on a detained patient. The first example is perhaps the less curious. In *B v Croydon District Health Authority*[112] the Court of Appeal authorised the naso-gastric feeding of a woman of twenty-four. She suffered from a borderline personality disorder, including among its symptoms a com-

---

[108] See above at **6.12**.
[109] See G Richardson, 'Mental Capacity at the Margin. The Interface Between Two Acts' (2010) 18 *Medical Law Review* 56.
[110] *R v Hallstrom, ex p W (No 2)* [1986] QB 824.
[111] *B v Barking, Havering and Brentwood Community NHS Trust* [1999] 1 FLR 106.
[112] [1995] 1 All ER 683, CA; *Re KB (Adult) (Mental Patient: Medical Treatment)* [1994] 2 FLR 1051. And see *R v Collins and Ashworth Hospital Authority, ex p Brady* [2000] Lloyd's Rep Med 355.

pulsion to self-harm. She was dangerously anorexic and was detained in hospital under the 1983 Act. The appeal court held that feeding constituted treatment for her mental disorder because such treatment included treatment to alleviate the symptoms of her disorder. Refusing food was such a symptom. Forcible feeding thus constituted a 'cure'.[113] *Tameside and Glossop Acute Services Trust v CH*[114] requires an even more imaginative approach to section 63. CH suffered from paranoid schizophrenia and was detained in a mental hospital. On admission to hospital she was discovered to be pregnant. At thirty-seven weeks, the retarded growth of the foetus caused doctors to suspect placental failure and they wanted to deliver the child swiftly by Caesarean section. Wall J held that such surgery was justified under section 63 as treatment for CH's mental disorder. CH maintained a belief that medical staff were malicious and out to harm her child. She could not be given the medication most appropriate to treat her mental illness while still pregnant. The judge ruled '... a successful outcome of her pregnancy is a necessary part of the overall treatment of her mental disorder'. Whether B or CH should have been compelled to submit to treatment is something reasonable people might disagree on. The extended use of section 63 as a device to compel them to do so is disturbing.

Whatever reservations judicial interpretation of section 63 of the Mental Health Act may provoke, other aspects of the 1983 Act offer safeguards for patients absent from the 2005 Act. Within its original and intended context, section 63 empowers doctors to determine what routine psychiatric treatment detained patients should receive. Sections 57, 58 and 58A provide important safeguards both for patients' welfare and autonomy.

Section 57 is unusual in that it applies to *all* patients and not just those detained in hospital. Any form of psychosurgery,[115] such as lobotomy, and any surgical implantation of hormones to reduce male sexual drive, will be unlawful[116] unless: (1) the patient consents; *and* (2) a specially appointed and independent doctor certifies that (a) the patient is capable of understanding the nature and purpose of the treatment proposed and its likely effects, and (b) the treatment is likely to benefit the patient.

Sections 58 and 58A apply to detained patients only. Any long-term medication (administered for longer than three months[117]) is authorised only if either: (a) the patient consents and a doctor certifies that he is competent to do so; or

---

[113] See K Keywood, 'Rethinking the Anorexic Body; How English Law and Psychiatry "Think"' (2003) 26 *International Journal of Law and Psychiatry* 599; P Lewis, 'Feeding Anorexic Patients Who Refuse Food' (1999) 7 *Medical Law Review* 21.

[114] [1996] 1 FCR 753.

[115] See s 57(1).

[116] See s 57(2); and the Mental Health (Hospital Guardianship and Consent in Treatment) Regulations 1983, SI 1983/ 893, reg 16(2). S 57(2) empowers the Secretary of State to bring other treatments within the ambit of s 57(2).

[117] See s 58(2).

(b) an independent doctor certifies that the patient is incapable of giving consent or has refused to do so but that none the less '. . . it is appropriate for the treatment to be given'. Section 58 used to include electro-convulsive therapy (ECT) too, but section 58A now provides that ECT cannot be given without consent (except in emergencies covered by section 62) unless the patient lacks capacity and has not refused ECT via an advance directive.

Compulsory treatment: beyond the Mental Health Acts

6.20 Should compulsory treatment of a competent patient ever be legally justifiable, outwith any Mental Health Act? Can an elderly, confused, yet still arguably competent, patient be required to submit to dental treatment in his own 'interests'? Should a patient who refuses to bathe, yet retains mental capacity, be compelled to do so in the interests of those who share a ward with him? What of the elderly widow with bed sores and severe arthritis whose overbearing daughter is determined that her mother should not move to a nursing home as she does not want to see her inheritance evaporate?

Vulnerable patients: the inherent jurisdiction[118]

6.21 Before the Mental Capacity Act 2005 came into force, the courts began to invoke the inherent jurisdiction to protect adults whose health and circumstances made them vulnerable but who may not lack mental capacity. Munby J defined such a vulnerable adult as a person who 'even if not incapacitated, is either under constraint, or subject to coercion or undue influence, or for some other reason deprived of the capacity to make free choice, or disabled from making a free choice, or incapacitated or disabled from giving or expressing a real and genuine consent'.[119] The courts would then intervene for example to protect the individual from abuse by carers or family members. An injunction could order the 'abusive' relative to cease interfering in the vulnerable person's affairs and even to ban contact altogether. Consider the third example above of a person whose daughter is actively blocking attempts to obtain proper care for her mother. An order restraining her from so behaving might seem acceptable. And such an order could enhance not diminish the patient's autonomy. The other two examples are harder. Both patients actively object to the measures proposed, the visit to the dentist and the bath. If they retain mental capacity, invoking the inherent jurisdiction to protect them from themselves seems to undermine the safeguards put in place by the Mental Capacity Act and DoLS. Nor is the third example problem free. What if the mother says to social services that she is well aware that her daughter is bullying her and is after her money, but she accepts that as she loves her daughter and does not

---

[118] See J Herring, 'Protecting Vulnerable Adults: A Critical Review of Recent Case Law' [2009] *Child and Family Law Quarterly* 498.

[119] *A Local Authority v MA, NA and SA* [2005] EWHC 2942 (Fam) at para 77.

want any intervention?[120] So far the majority of cases involving such vulnerable adults have involved social care rather than medical treatments. One example that did touch on medical care was *A Local Authority v A.*[121] A local authority feared that a husband was pressuring his wife, who has learning difficulties, to stop contraceptive treatment. The court in the end concluded that for the present no order was needed.

Protecting the public

6.22   In the UK, unlike the USA,[122] legislation has never enforced sterilisation on those seen as mentally or physically unfit to reproduce. In England, unlike in many countries in Europe, childhood vaccination has never been compulsory. Compulsory treatment has focused on the control of infectious disease, but now extends to broader risks of contamination and threats to the health of the community. The Public Health (Control of Disease) Act 1984 has been heavily amended by Part 3 of the Health and Social Care Act 2008 which inserts a new Part 2A in the Public Health (Control of Disease) Act. The Act now seeks to implement extensive measures to protect the public from the spread of infection or contamination which poses or could pose a significant harm to human health. Sections 45B–D confer extensive powers on Ministers to make regulations to protect public health from infection or contamination. The scope of such powers is extensive and coercive, enabling government to restrain people, seize property and impose quarantines.

The Health Protection (Notification) Regulations 2010[123] require doctors to notify the proper authority if they have reasonable grounds to suspect that the patient has a 'notifiable disease', or has some other infection that could present a significant harm to human health, or is contaminated.[124] The list of notifiable diseases includes most major communicable diseases such as tuberculosis, cholera, food poisoning, whooping cough and rubella. But note the doctor must also notify authorities of any other potentially dangerous infection such as a virulent new strain of flu. Such patients lose not only their right to confidential treatment, but may also lose their liberty. Magistrates may order such a patient to submit to testing, be subject to restriction on their movements, and in an extreme case be detained in hospital.[125] However, there is no power to compel the patient to submit to medical treatment.[126]

---

[120] For an analogous scenario, see *Local Authority v DL (Vulnerable Patient: Non-Molestation Injunction)* [2010] EWHC 2675 (Fam).

[121] [2010] EWHC 1549 (Fam): see above at **6.4**.

[122] For discussion of compulsory sterilisation laws in the USA, see M D A Freeman, 'Sterilising the Mentally Handicapped', in M D A Freeman (ed), *Medicine, Ethics and Law* (1988) Stevens.

[123] SI 2010/659.

[124] SI 2010/659, reg 2.

[125] See s 45G of the Public Health (Control of Disease) Act 1984.

[126] See s 45E.

HIV is not expressly listed as a notifiable disease, but a person with HIV may still be subject to the powers of a magistrate under section 45G of the Act should she pose a threat to others. Under the previous Public Health (Infectious Diseases) Regulations 1985, similar powers were to the best of our knowledge invoked only once in the case of a patient with AIDS.

Draconian powers to address infectious diseases, allowing the detention of the infected person, have a long history and many of the original notifiable diseases, such as plague or cholera, carried a high risk of potentially deadly infection to others with little possibility of the patient herself, whatever she did, of protecting others from infection. Diseases such as HIV, Hepatitis B (and even tuberculosis) do not fit into that pattern. A person may be seropositive for HIV or Hepatitis B, but not ill, and certainly not suffering from any mental impairment or confusion. If he amends his lifestyle in conformity with medical advice, the risk he poses to others is minimal. Using public health powers to force his compliance with 'safe living' necessarily involves an invasion of his liberty. For how long could society justifiably detain a person with Hepatitis B? She may never cease to be a carrier of that disease.

The legality of the powers to detain people to prevent the spread of infectious diseases was tested in the European Court of Human Rights in 2005. In *Enhorn v Sweden*,[127] a HIV-positive man who had unknowingly infected a nineteen-year-old girl, was required under Sweden's Infectious Diseases Act 1988 to attend regular medical appointments. When he failed to do so, he was compulsorily isolated in hospital. Over a period of six years, he spent around eighteen months in compulsory isolation. Did the Swedish courts unlawfully deprive Mr Enhorn of his liberty, protected by Article 5, or was the deprivation justified under Article 5(1)(e) for 'the lawful detention of persons for the prevention of spreading of infectious diseases, of persons of unsound mind, alcoholics or drug addicts, or vagrants'? The Court held that the isolation was a disproportionate response to the threat to the public. Mr Enhorn's Article 5 right to liberty had been breached.[128] Compulsory isolation must be used only as a last resort.

Criminal liability

6.23 Does a 'patient' who fails to protect other people from herself and recklessly disregards the welfare of others, commit a criminal offence?[129] A midwife knows that she is infected by Hepatitis B, conceals her condition and infects several patients; is her conduct significantly different from the train driver

---

127 [2005] ECHR 34.
128 See A Mowbray, 'Compulsory Detention to Prevent the Spreading of Infectious Diseases' (2005) 5 *Human Rights Review* 387.
129 See S H Bronitt, 'Spreading Disease and the Criminal Law' [1994] *Criminal Law Review* 21; K M Smith, 'Sexual Etiquette, Public Interest and the Criminal Law' (1991) 42 *Northern Ireland Legal Quarterly* 309.

who, knowing that he is over the alcohol limit, still takes the controls and endangers his passengers? Identifying a pigeonhole in which to fit criminal liability for spreading diseases used to be tricky. If our hypothetical midwife's patients have consented to her ministrations, their consent is unlikely to be vitiated by lack of information about her infection, so no assault is committed.[130] In one case, a surgeon continued to operate, fraudulently concealing that he had Hepatitis B. Several of his patients contracted hepatitis. The surgeon was ultimately convicted of the antiquated common law offence of causing a public nuisance.[131]

In *R v Dica*,[132] the Court of Appeal held that reckless transmission of serious disease constituted a criminal offence in English law.[133] Dica was convicted on two counts of inflicting grievous bodily harm, contrary to section 20 of the Offences Against the Person Act 1861, on lovers whom he had infected with HIV. The trial judge ruled (inter alia) that any consent on the part of the victims to the risk of contracting HIV, thus their knowledge or otherwise of the accused's seropositive status, was irrelevant and provided no defence because the women had no capacity to consent to such serious harm.[134] Following the judge's ruling, the accused chose not to give evidence and the question of whether his lovers knew of his HIV-positive condition was not left to the jury. The Court of Appeal quashed the conviction and ordered a retrial. Consensual acts of sexual intercourse do not become unlawful '. . . merely because there may be a known risk to the health of one or other participant'.[135] As Judge LJ said[136] '. . . interference of this kind with personal autonomy, and its level and extent, may only be made by Parliament'. The key question was, had the victims consented to the risk of contracting HIV? To consent they must first be aware of the accused's condition, though knowledge alone would not normally establish consent. Absence of consent to such a risk did not vitiate consent to intercourse. Dica was not guilty of rape. Inflicting serious bodily harm is no longer an offence parasitic on assault.[137] No assault need to be

---

[130] *R v Clarence* (1888) 22 QBD 23; *Hegarty v Shine* (1878) 14 Cox CC 124. But note prosecution for causing grievous bodily harm of a doctor who allegedly infected his lover with herpes; see (2002) *Times*, 12 January.

[131] *R v Gaud* (unreported); analysed in M Mulholland, 'Public Nuisance – A New Use for an Old Tool' (1995) 42 *Professional Negligence* 70.

[132] [2004] 3 A11 ER 593; see M Brazier, 'Do No Harm – Do Patients Have Responsibilities Too?' (2006) 65(2) *Cambridge Law Journal* 397.

[133] In *HM Advocate v Kelly* (2001) High Court of Judiciary, Glasgow, a Scottish court convicted a man who infected his lover with HIV of culpably and recklessly endangering her health; see J Chalmers, 'The Criminalisation of HIV Transmission' (2002) 28 *Journal of Medical Ethics* 160. And see *R v Konzani* (2005) 2 Cr App R 13; discussed in M Weait, 'Knowledge, Autonomy and Consent: *R v Konzani*' [2005] *Criminal Law Review* 673.

[134] Relying on *R v Brown* [1994] 1 AC 212, HL.

[135] [2004] 3 All ER 593 at 605.

[136] [2004] 3 All ER 593 at 606.

[137] See *R v Ireland, R v Burstow* [1998] AC 147, HL.

proven, simply the imposition on the victim of serious harm to which she has not consented.

The decision in *Dica* goes beyond the proposal in the Draft Offences Against the Person Bill to criminalise intentional transmission of disease. It has met with much criticism.[138] Critics maintain that criminalisation will reinforce stigmatisation of people living with HIV, will deter patients from seeking testing and counselling, and in its operation, discriminate against minority groups such as gay men and drug-users.[139] John Spencer lends his voice to a powerful defence of *Dica*:[140]

> To infect an unsuspecting person with a grave disease you know you have, or may have, by behaviour you know involves a risk of transmission, and that you know you could easily modify to reduce or eliminate the risk, is to harm another in a way that is both needless and callous. For that reason criminal liability is justified unless there are strong countervailing reasons.

There are circumstances where private interests should rightly be subordinated to the public good. This reasoning lies at the heart of public health laws. The basis of enforced treatment under public health legislation is the protection of the public. A person can be removed to hospital if precautions to prevent the infection spreading can be taken, are not being taken, and a 'serious risk of infection is thereby caused to other people'. There is no pretence that the compulsory powers are exercised solely in the 'best interests' of the patient. Where someone, albeit through no fault of his own, poses a threat to the health of others, his interest in autonomy cedes to others' interest in health and safety.

The uncooperative patient

6.24 What of the patient whose condition or conduct poses a risk of some harm or serious nuisance to others but who refuses to cooperate in measures to minimise that harm or nuisance? We have suggested that it is not appropriate to use the inherent jurisdiction protecting vulnerable patients when the patient retains capacity. And in this example, what is in issue is not protecting the individual herself but protecting others from nuisance or harm she has created. At common law an individual enjoys a right to self-defence. This is a common-law right which almost certainly survives the enactment of a public right to use force to prevent crime in section 3 of the Criminal Law Act 1967. If you are attacked by a person so mentally disordered that he could not be found guilty of any crime, you are still lawfully entitled to fend off any attacker using whatever degree of force is necessary. Might there then be circumstances

---

[138] See M Weait, 'Criminal Law and Sexual Transmission of HIV: *R v Dica*' (2005) 68 *Modern Law Review* 121.

[139] Weait (2005) 68 *Modern Law Review* 121 at 134.

[140] J R Spencer, 'Liability for Reckless Infection – Part 2' (2004) 154 *New Law Journal* 448 at 448.

174

in which treatment of a competent but confused or disturbed patient could be justified because of the harm his untreated condition poses to others? Can a patient who refuses to bathe be washed to prevent him becoming a hazard to hygiene? Such a suggestion sounds like heresy. Apart from the provisions in the Public Health Acts, the Mental Health and Mental Capacity Acts (discussed earlier), treatment of patients whose mental capacity is disputed is in theory lawful only if in the patient's 'best interests'. We should note, however, the anomalous provisions of the National Assistance Act 1948[141] that empowers community health doctors to seek to remove from their homes and place in a suitable hospital a person 'suffering from chronic disease, or being aged, infirm or physically incapacitated' and unable to care for themselves. Doctors may apply to magistrates for a warrant to remove the patient either in his own interests or *'to prevent injury to the health of, or serious nuisances to, other persons'* (our emphasis). Section 47 is controversial and many geriatricians refuse to invoke the powers under the Act. The Law Commission issued a consultation paper in 2010 addressing wholesale reform of adult social care.[142]

'Best interests' = 'exclusive interests'?

6.25   In practice there can be little doubt that healthcare professionals are imposing 'treatment' on patients which cannot be shown to be exclusively in the patients' interests. We are not suggesting that gynaecologists are sterilising women for eugenic reasons, or that surgeons are experimenting on unfortunate patients. Patients are washed against their will. Patients are sometimes given medication they would rather not have, perhaps disguised in their food. Without such stratagems, nurses struggling to care for wards catering for confused geriatric patients, or working in long-stay institutions for voluntary mental patients, might give up the struggle. Should such miscreants be tracked down and prosecuted for assault?

It is dubious whether it is ever possible to divorce the interests of the individual entirely from the interests of the carer. The example that follows is unpleasant but is an instance of a dilemma that doctors have to face, and parents may have to live with. A young woman lives at home with her father. She is physically adult and normal but has the mind of a two-year-old. She is sexually provocative and fertile. She is incontinent and it is her father who every month has to cope with her periods. None of this distresses her any more than it would a two-year-old child. Sterilisation by hysterectomy could never be said to be in her best interests, even if sterilisation per se could. Yet her father may find that he cannot cope much longer. Dealing with menstruation is the straw that breaks the camel's back. Is that young woman better off without a uterus but with her father, or with her uterus intact but in an institution? Her interests and her father's are inextricably intertwined.

[141] See s 47 of the National Assistance Act 1948, as amended by the National Assistance (Amendment) Act 1951.
[142] Law Commission Consultation Paper No 192, *Adult Social Care* (2010).

The interests of the patient must be the predominant interest to be considered. Perhaps other interests should also be taken into account? Individuals live as part of society. Society has obligations to the individual, especially the vulnerable individual. Individuals, though, have reciprocal obligations to society. Moreover, a careful review of all the decided cases on non-consensual treatment may suggest that courts do in fact take note of interests other than the patient's. If nineteen-year-old T would never have been properly aware of her pregnancy, or the birth and removal of a child, that experience may at any rate not have harmed her. Her mother and the child would certainly suffer. Would it be wrong to consider their interests? If the interests of others will inevitably be considered, would it not be better to do so openly?

Chapter 7

CLINICAL NEGLIGENCE[1]

7.1 The civil law of negligence is designed to provide compensation for one individual injured by another's negligence. Gross negligence resulting in death may be punished by the criminal courts. We consider any possible criminal liability incurred by doctors at the end of this chapter. A person seeking compensation for negligence has to establish: (1) that the defendant owed him a duty to take care; (2) that he was in breach of that duty, that he was careless; and (3) that the harm of which the victim complains was caused by that carelessness. He must satisfy all these tests to succeed. A widow succeeded in establishing that a hospital doctor was careless in not coming down to Casualty to examine her husband. He was admitted to hospital in an appalling state, which eventually proved to be caused by arsenical poisoning. He died within hours. She failed to recover any compensation from the hospital in respect of her husband's death because the evidence was that, even had he been properly attended, he would still have died.[2]

The bare bones of the law of negligence outlined above are general to everyone, in the conduct of their everyday activities and in carrying out their job. They are not special to doctors. Certain special factors about clinical negligence claims need to be introduced here. We have already mentioned the factual difficulty of proving negligence where there is a clash of medical opinion, and the effect that the need to prove fault has on the medical profession's reaction to claims against them. Doctors have become defensive. Patients used to be deferential. For a long time, English judges were unwilling to find against a 'medical man'. A brotherly solidarity bound the ancient professions of law and medicine together. Judicial attitudes have changed.[3] Claims against doctors and damages awarded against NHS hospitals have risen dramatically. The medical profession is haunted by the spectre of a malpractice crisis. In the next chapter, we explore whether it is a spectre of any substance.

[1] See generally, M A Jones, *Medical Negligence* (4th edn, 2008) Sweet and Maxwell; C J Lewis, *Clinical Negligence: A Practical Guide* (6th edn, 2006) Tottel Publishing.
[2] *Barnett v Chelsea and Kensington Hospital Management Committee* [1969] 1 QB 428.
[3] See Lord Woolf, 'Are the Courts Excessively Deferential to the Medical Profession?' (2001) 9 *Medical Law Review* 1.

Duty of care

7.2 A patient claiming against his doctor, or a hospital, generally has little difficulty in establishing that the defendant owes him a duty of care. A general practitioner accepting a patient on to her list undertakes a duty to him. A hospital and its entire staff owe a duty to patients admitted for treatment. If the patient is an NHS patient, the duty derives from the law of tort, which imposes a duty wherever one person can reasonably foresee that his conduct may cause harm to another. Where the patient is a private patient, in addition to the duty in tort, a duty arises from his contract with the doctor or the hospital. It is the same duty regardless of its origins. We look later at the circumstances in which the private patient is owed duties other than that of care. Difficulty arises where a person has not been accepted as a patient. English law does not oblige anyone to be a Good Samaritan. If someone has a coronary attack on an Inter-City express, and a doctor fails to respond to the guard's call, 'Is there a doctor on the train?' the doctor incurs no liability to the victim who dies for lack of medical treatment.[4] The law almost discourages the Good Samaritan. For if the doctor comes to the sick man's aid she undertakes a duty to him and may be liable if her skill fails her.[5]

A practical problem arises from the increasing practice of centralising casualty facilities in the larger hospitals. More and more hospitals have notices on their gates stating that they do not accept emergencies and accident victims. The notice refers the injured person to another named hospital. An accident victim whose injuries worsened because of the delay in reaching a casualty department is unlikely to succeed in a claim against the hospital which refused him admission. It never assumed any duty to him. A hospital which operates a casualty department, by contrast, is responsible for the patients who come within its doors regardless of whether they have been formally admitted to hospital. By running a casualty department, an NHS hospital undertakes to treat those who present themselves and will be liable in negligence if any failure on the part of their staff causes the patient to be sent away untreated.[6] Similarly, a GP currently owes a duty to emergency patients as well as to those on his own list. His contract with the NHS provides that he will treat visitors to his practice area falling suddenly ill. Like the hospital with the casualty ward, he undertakes to treat the genuine emergency as much as his regular patients.

In *Kent v Griffiths*,[7] the duties owed to patients by the ambulance services came before the courts. The claimant was asthmatic. She was also pregnant.

---

[4] Though she may be in breach of her professional code of conduct and may face professional disciplinary proceedings: see GMC, *Good Medical Practice* (2006), para 11.

[5] However, the standard of care which she must attain in such a case will take account of the conditions in which she volunteers to offer treatment.

[6] *Barnett v Chelsea and Kensington Hospital Management Committee* [1969] 1 QB 428.

[7] [2000] 2 All ER 74, CA. See K Williams, 'Litigation Against NHS Ambulance Services and the Rule in *Kent v Griffiths*' (2007) 15(2) *Medical Law Review* 153.

She had been exceptionally wheezy on the day in question and called her GP who telephoned for an ambulance using the 999 service. The ambulance took forty minutes to arrive despite two further anxious phone calls from the claimant's husband. On the journey to the hospital, the claimant was given oxygen. Shortly before arrival at the hospital she suffered a respiratory arrest, resulting in serious brain damage and a miscarriage. The ambulance service denied negligence. They contended that their only duty to the claimant was not by their own actions to cause her any additional injury. They had no duty to come to her aid, to 'rescue' her from the danger her illness placed her in. Earlier cases[8] involving police and fire services had found that (generally) simply failing to respond to, or respond sufficiently promptly to, a 999 call did not render those services liable in negligence. The Court of Appeal was adamant that the ambulance service was different. It is an NHS service owing equivalent responsibility to patients in need of that service to doctors and nurses. Where an identifiable patient needed and summoned the ambulance service, there was a duty to respond. Due care on the part of an ambulance service demands a reasonably prompt response. There might be cases of conflicting priorities. For example, two major road accidents take place in the same city at the same time as a winter 'flu' epidemic. The elderly 'flu' patient, whose call is given lower priority than the crash victims, is still owed a duty by the ambulance service. In the circumstances, there may be no breach of duty because, confronted by competing demands, the ambulance service responded reasonably.

Would delay by a hospital in arranging treatment breach the duty of care? If a patient is seen at an out-patients clinic and then waits so long for surgery that her cancer cannot be successfully treated, does she have a claim against the hospital? What if she could show that NHS guidelines on timely treatment had been breached? Her principal problem may well be to prove that had she been treated sooner the cancer would have been treatable. Another possible avenue of redress for patients whose health deteriorates because treatment is delayed might be to sue the authority responsible for arranging their secondary care. At the time of writing, Primary Care Trusts (PCTs) have that responsibility for all NHS patients within their jurisdiction. As we have seen in chapter 1,[9] PCTs are due to be replaced by 2013 by consortia of GPs (Commissioning Consortia – CC) who will become responsible for commissioning much of their patients' services. If a PCT or CC fails to arrange, sufficiently promptly, a cardiac bypass for a patient with clogged arteries, and he dies, could his family bring a claim in negligence? We would argue that such authorities, like the ambulance service, owe a duty to all their patients for arranging reasonably prompt and adequate secondary care for patients in need of such care.[10] That does not mean they will be liable to compensate every patient who does not obtain the treatment he needs. The demand for secondary care may

---

8   See, for example, *Capital & Counties plc v Hampshire County Council* [1997] QB 1004, CA.

9   See the discussion of the Health and Social Care Bill, above at **1.3**.

10   See M Brazier and J Beswick, 'Who's Caring for Me?' (2006) 7 *Medical Law International* 183. But see also below at **8.6**.

outstrip what can be supplied. The PCT or CC must act reasonably. If the unfortunate cardiac patient did not get his operation quickly enough because the notes are lost, or arrangements are bungled, his family should succeed. If difficult decisions about priorities for treatment have to be made, resulting in other sick patients having first call on the budget, proving negligence will be harder.

Psychiatric harm

7.3   Patients may seek to sue, not just in respect of physical harm, such as a perforated bowel in the course of surgery, but also in cases of psychiatric injury. Where additional psychiatric harm ensues directly from bungled treatment of the claimant herself, such claims have a fair chance of success.[11] In *Farrell v Merton, Sutton and Wandsworth Health Authority*,[12] the claimant suffered a horrific childbirth. She remained aware during an emergency Caesarean section; she contracted a post-operative infection and her child was born with serious brain damage. News of her child's condition was communicated inadequately and totally insensitively. She recovered compensation to include the adverse effects on her mental health of all that had happened to her.

Claims where one person alleges that negligent treatment of someone else, a close relative, caused them to suffer mental illness are harder to sustain. The law regards such people as *secondary* victims of psychiatric injury, akin to those who witness some horrific disaster, such as events at Hillsborough Football Stadium when fans were crushed to death as a result of negligence on the part of the police.[13] Just because a relative suffers injury from inadequate treatment and the effect of distress and grief makes you ill, does not suffice to create a duty owed by the defendant hospital to you. Only if you actually suffer psychiatric injury from the trauma and shock of witnessing or discovering what has happened to your relative, are you likely to be owed any duty.[14] A husband who was present and watched his wife screaming in agony because she remained awake during Caesarean surgery and saw her haemorrhaging might well succeed. A mother, coming to visit her daughter who had had routine surgery, and who, with no warning, is simply and abruptly told that her child is dead and directed to the mortuary, might be owed a duty.[15] If, in either example, husband or mother were not in any sense at the scene of the 'accident' to their beloved, but simply learned of their fate, or were told of the tragedy insensitively, they will not

---

[11]   Lewis, *Clinical Negligence: A Practical Guide*, pp 268–297; P Case, 'Secondary Iatrogenic Harm: Claims for Psychiatric Damage Following a Death Caused By Medical Error' (2004) 67 *Modern Law Review* 501.

[12]   (2001) 57 BMLR 158; and see *North Glamorgan NHS Trust v Walters* [2002] EWCA Civ 1792.

[13]   *Alcock v Chief Constable of South Yorkshire* [1991] 4 All ER 907, HL.

[14]   See *Sion v Hampstead Health Authority* (1994) 5 Med LR 170, CA.

[15]   Though see *Taylor v Somerset Health Authority* (1993) 16 BMLR 63.

recover compensation, even if, not unnaturally, the original injury to wife or daughter drives them into clinical depression.[16]

Medical examinations

7.4 Finally, a number of cases consider how far doctors examining patients, not for the patient's benefit but on the instruction of a third party, owe a duty to the patient being examined. For example, you have to have a medical examination before a job offer will be confirmed. Two different scenarios must be addressed.

(1) The doctor, had he carried out the examination with due care, would have discovered that you had early signs of cancer. Delay in diagnosis means that your cancer is now inoperable. Did the doctor who performed your 'medical' owe you a duty to alert you to your dangerous condition? There is no case directly in point but such a duty may well be found.[17]

(2) The doctor carries out the 'medical' negligently and wrongly concludes that you are unfit for the job. You lose a chance of the job. Does the doctor owe you a duty to protect you from the financial (economic) loss of not getting the job? One case suggests such a duty is owed.[18] A later judgment of the Court of Appeal is to the contrary.[19] The examining doctor owed no duty to the job applicant to protect him from economic loss. He was not responsible for looking after his job prospects.[20]

The medical standard of care

7.5 The second matter that any claimant in negligence has to prove is that the defendant was careless. A warning to the reader is called for. The diligent student who conducts search of legal databases for cases on proving clinical negligence will be overwhelmed with hundreds of cases each year. Nearly all will produce little more clarity by way of legal principle and what is in dispute will be disagreement about the facts, what happened and how reliable is memory, and/or just how to apply the current law.

The fundamental principles of law are as follows. The onus of proof is on the claimant. He must show that the defendant fell below the required standard of

---

[16] For an exceptionally generous interpretation of what may constitute trauma and shock of witnessing injury to a wife, see *Frogatt v Chesterfield and North Derbyshire Royal Hospital NHS Trust* [2002] All ER (D) 218.

[17] See D M Kloss, 'Pre-Employment Health Screening' in M Freeman, A Lewis (eds), *Law and Medicine: Current Legal Issues* (2000) OUP, vol 3.

[18] *Baker v Kaye* (1996) 39 BMLR 12.

[19] *Kapfunde v Abbey National plc* (1998) 46 BMLR 176, CA.

[20] For discussion of other circumstances where a medical examination is carried out on the instructions of a third party, see E Jackson, *Medical Law: Text, Cases and Materials* (2nd edn, 2010) OUP, pp 113–114.

care. The basic standard is that of the reasonable man in the circumstances of the defendant. A professional person must meet the standard of competence of the reasonable professional doing his job. A woman who went to a jeweller's to have her ear pierced developed an abscess because the jeweller's instruments were not aseptically sterile. The jeweller had taken all the precautions that any jeweller could be expected to take. The woman's claim failed. The defendant had done all a jeweller could reasonably be expected to do.[21] If she wanted the standard of care a surgeon could offer, she should have consulted a surgeon.

Before examining the case law in clinical negligence, we should note briefly section 1 of the Compensation Act 2006. The Act was passed as a knee-jerk reaction to much publicised claims of a 'compensation culture'. Supposedly schools were refusing to take children on school trips and local authorities were closing playgrounds to avoid any risk of liability for injury. Section 1 provides:

> A court considering a claim in negligence or breach of statutory duty may, in determining whether the defendant should have taken particular steps to meet a standard of care (whether by taking precautions against a risk or otherwise), have regard to whether a requirement to take those steps might –
>
> (a)   prevent a desirable activity from being undertaken at all, to a particular extent or in a particular way, or
> (b)   discourage persons from undertaking functions in connection with a desirable activity.

We doubt that the Act will have much effect on clinical negligence claims.[22] Unless judges decide to accept the wildest claims about defensive medicine, and determine that allowing doctors to be sued damages healthcare, the Compensation Act itself in our context needs not to be treated as a matter of great concern. However, politicians continue to believe that gold-digging compensation claims incited by greedy lawyers are damaging public service, including the NHS. The principles of law may not be affected by such rhetoric but as we shall see in the next chapter, the process of bringing a claim may be made more difficult.

The standard of care demanded of the doctor is the standard of the reasonably skilled and experienced doctor. In *Bolam v Friern Hospital Management Committee*,[23] McNair J said:

> The test is the standard of the ordinary skilled man exercising and professing to have that special skill. A man need not possess the highest expert skill, it is well established law that it is sufficient if he exercises the ordinary skill of an ordinary competent man exercising that particular art.

The defendant doctor will be tested against the standard of the doctor in his particular field of medicine. The GP must meet the standard of the competent

---

[21]   *Phillips v William Whiteley Ltd* [1938] 1 All ER 566.
[22]   See *Uren v Corporate Leisure and Others* [2010] All ER (D) 132 (Jan).
[23]   [1957] 1 WLR 582 at 586.

GP; the consultant gynaecologist the standard of the competent consultant in that specialty. As Lord Scarman put it: '. . . a doctor who professes to exercise a special skill must exercise the ordinary skill of his specialty'.[24] A patient who attends her GP complaining of an eye disorder cannot require him to have the skill of a consultant ophthalmologist. She can complain if the GP fails to refer her on to a consultant when her condition should have alerted a reasonable GP to the need for further advice or treatment.

Junior doctors

7.6   No allowance is made for inexperience. The Court of Appeal has consistently rejected arguments that standards of care should vary to allow for the degree of experience possessed by the defendant. They held an L-driver liable where, although she had done the best that could be expected of a learner, she fell short of the standard of the reasonably competent and experienced motorist.[25] In *Wilsher v Essex Area Health Authority*,[26] the appeal court considered the liability of junior hospital staff. Martin Wilsher was born nearly three months prematurely. He was admitted to a neonatal unit managed by the defendants where skilled treatment probably saved his life. He needed extra oxygen to survive. Sadly, junior doctors made an error in monitoring the oxygen levels in Martin's blood, and on two occasions, he received an excess of oxygen. It was argued by Martin's lawyers that excess oxygen caused him to develop retrolental fibroplasia (RLF), a retinal condition which left Martin nearly blind. Ultimately, the House of Lords held that the plaintiff had failed to prove that excess oxygen caused RLF in Martin and ordered a retrial.[27] The importance of the Court of Appeal's judgment lies in their exposition of the rules on negligence by junior staff. Argument by the defendants that staff concerned did their best in view of their inexperience was rejected. The law requires all medical staff in such a unit to meet the standard of competence and experience society expects from those filling such demanding posts. Their Lordships recognised the need for medical staff to train 'on the job'. They stressed that a finding of negligence on one occasion did not imply incompetence or any degree of moral culpability. Legal and moral tests of negligence may differ. Doctors may find the distinction hard to understand. One point must be made clear here. A junior doctor, who, recognising his inexperience, calls in his consultant, will have discharged his duty. Responsibility in law will move to the consultant.[28]

[24]   *Maynard v West Midlands Regional Health Authority* [1984] 1 WLR 634 at 638, HL.
[25]   *Nettleship v Weston* [1971] 2 QB 691, CA.
[26]   [1986] 3 All ER 801, CA.
[27]   [1988] 1 All ER 891; see below at **7.17**.
[28]   See *Jones v Manchester Corporation* [1952] 2 QB 852 at 871. Note that in *Wilsher v Essex Area Health Authority* [1986] 3 All ER 801, CA, Dr Wiles, the house officer, was found not negligent.

Ascertaining the standard of care: *Bolam*

7.7 How does a court ascertain the standard of skill which the doctor should have met? Let us consider the case of Mr Bolam again. He was given electro-convulsive therapy and sustained fractures. He argued that the doctor was negligent: (1) in not giving him relaxant drugs; (2) as drugs were not given, in failing to provide adequate physical restraints; (3) in not warning him of the risks involved in the treatment. We have seen that he failed in his argument that he should have been warned. As to the absence of relaxant drugs or restraints, the evidence was that while some doctors would have thought them necessary, many did not. The judge found the doctor not guilty of negligence for he acted:[29]

> ... in accordance with a practice accepted as proper by a responsible body of medical men skilled in that particular area ... a man is not negligent, if he is act-ing in accordance with such a practice, merely because there is a body of opinion who would take a contrary view.

The *Bolam* test was destined to become [in]famous. At first sight, it is unexceptionable. Courts cannot decide whether a doctor was negligent without expert evidence of 'accepted medical practice'.[30] Within any profession, genuine differences of opinion may surface. In obstetrics, doctors have different views about how best to deliver a premature breech baby. Some doctors consider that, in every case, the woman should be strongly advised to agree to an elective Caesarean section. Others believe that a trial of labour should be permitted and, only if complications ensue in labour, should surgery be resorted to. Both sides of the debate advance logical reasons for their respective judgments. Judges are not well placed to resolve such questions.

The *Bolam* test focusing on 'accepted practice' came to be applied to all claims for professional negligence. 'Responsible professional opinion' is the litmus test of liability for solicitors, accountants and architects, just as much as for doctors. There was a crucial difference. In claims against other professionals, the courts rigorously scrutinised expert evidence to ensure that evidence of professional opinion could be demonstrated to be responsible and reasonable.[31] In claims against doctors, it appeared that as long as suitably qualified expert witnesses endorsed the defendant's conduct, English judges simply deferred to the doctors. Providing expert testimony was seen to be truthful, the courts assumed that it must be responsible.[32] The key to successfully defending a claim in negligence was to find expert witnesses who would be impressive in the witness box.[33]

---

[29] *Bolam v Friern HMC* [1957] 1 WLR 582 at 587–588.

[30] See *Burne v A* [2006] EWCA Civ 24 at para 10.

[31] See, for example, *Edward Wong Finance Co Ltd v Johnson, Stokes & Master* [1984] AC 296, PC.

[32] See the account of the first instance decision in *Bolitho v City & Hackney Health Authority* [1998] AC 232, HL.

[33] Graphically illustrated in *Whitehouse v Jordan* [1981] 1 All ER 246, HL.

Trial judges who took it upon themselves to scrutinise and evaluate medical evidence faced reprimands from above. In *Maynard v West Midlands Regional Health Authority*,[34] the plaintiff had consulted a consultant physician and a surgeon with symptoms indicating tuberculosis, but she also displayed symptoms which might indicate Hodgkin's disease. The doctors decided on a diagnostic operation, mediastinoscopy. It carried a risk of damage to the vocal cords and Mrs Maynard's vocal cords were in fact damaged. She proved to have tuberculosis. She alleged that the defendants were negligent in subjecting her to the operation. Her expert witness argued that the operation should never have been done. He would have regarded her condition as almost certainly a case of tuberculosis. The defendants called a formidable number of experts who testified that the fatality rate for Hodgkin's disease if treatment was delayed justified the defendants in exposing Mrs Maynard to the risk of the mediastinoscopy. The original judge preferred Dr Hugh-Jones's evidence. The Court of Appeal and the House of Lords overruled him. Lord Scarman said: [35]

> ... a judge's 'preference' for one body of distinguished professional opinion to another also professionally distinguished is not sufficient to establish negligence in a practitioner ...

In *Maynard*, the defendants had numbers on their side. In *De Freitas v O'Brien*,[36] the expert evidence established that only a tiny minority of neurosurgeons endorsed the defendant's practice, just four or five out of two hundred and fifty doctors in that specialty. The Court of Appeal ruled that the body of opinion supporting the defendant need not be large. The perception arose that English judges would not cross swords with the doctors, however thin the evidence advanced in defence of a claim.[37]

Individual judges did on occasion attempt to assert judicial authority over medical evidence. Sir John Donaldson MR[38] emphasised that professional opinion must be '... *rightly* accepted as proper by a body of skilled and experienced medical men'. In 1968, the Court of Appeal in *Hucks v Cole*[39] rejected expert evidence in the defendant's favour. Evidence that other doctors would have followed the same practice as the defendant was 'a very weighty matter', but not conclusive. Such challenges to the supremacy of medical evidence tended to be ephemeral, apparently forgotten in the next flurry of cases.

---

[34] [1984] 1 WLR 634, HL.

[35] [1984] 1 WLR 634 at 639, HL.

[36] [1993] 4 Med LR 281, CA.

[37] Michael Jones expressed the state of play as a football score. In six medical negligence claims before the House of Lords between 1980 and 1999, the score stood at *Plaintiffs* 0 *Defendants* 6. See M A Jones, 'The *Bolam* Test and the Responsible Expert' (1999) *Tort Law Review* 226.

[38] *Sidaway v Royal Bethlem Hospital* [1984] 2 WLR 778 at 752, CA. And see Lord Bridge [1985] 1 All ER 643 at 663, HL.

[39] Reported [1993] 4 Med L R 393, CA.

Bolitho: a new dawn?

7.8   In *Bolitho v City & Hackney Health Authority*,[40] Lord Browne-Wilkinson reasserted the proper authority of the courts. *Bolitho* involved questions of causation as much as breach of duty. The facts, briefly, were these. Patrick Bolitho, aged two, was admitted to the defendant's hospital suffering from respiratory difficulties. On the second afternoon of this hospital stay, Patrick was in respiratory distress. A nurse summoned the paediatric registrar. She promised to attend as soon as possible, but did not do so. Patrick appeared to recover. At 2.00 pm, Patrick was once again having breathing problems. The registrar was called a second time, but again failed to attend. At 2.30pm, the boy collapsed; he stopped breathing and suffered a cardiac arrest, causing catastrophic brain damage. The hospital admitted negligence on the part of the paediatric registrar. She should have come to examine the child, or arranged for a suitable deputy to do so. They denied liability, however, arguing that, even if the doctor had attended Patrick prior to 2.30 pm, she would not have intubated him. Intubation offered the only prospect of averting the respiratory distress and cardiac arrest which Patrick suffered at 2.30 pm.

The trial judge accepted the doctor's evidence of fact that *she* would *not* have intubated Patrick. The question then became whether or not a competent doctor who had attended Patrick *should* have intubated the child. The *Bolam* question became the key to resolving causation. The experts were sharply divided. The plaintiff's five experts testified that Patrick's history of breathing problems was such that responsible practice required that he be intubated to prevent just the sort of catastrophe which materialised. The defendants' three experts argued that, apart from the two episodes of respiratory difficulty, Patrick seemed generally well. Intubation was distressing and not risk free for so young a child. A responsible doctor would not have intubated Patrick prior to 2.30pm. The judge ruled that, as both sets of experts represented a body of professional opinion espoused by distinguished and truthful experts, he was bound to conclude that Patrick's injury did not result from the defendants' admitted negligence. In effect, the judge asserted that he was disqualified from any form of scrutiny of expert medical evidence.

The Court of Appeal upheld the trial judge. The case proceeded to the House of Lords. Two issues fell to be resolved by their Lordships. The first, whether the *Bolam* test ever applies in determining causation, will be addressed later. The second is our present concern. Does the *Bolam* test require a judge to accept without question truthful evidence from eminent experts? Their Lordships, speaking with one voice through Lord Browne-Wilkinson, answered that question with a firm and forceful 'No'. Reviewing precedents relating to claims of negligence against other professionals, his Lordship declared that:[41]

> . . . the court has to be satisfied that the exponents of the body of opinion relied on can demonstrate that such opinion has a logical basis. In particular, in cases involving as they so often do, the weighing up of risks against benefits, the judge

[40]   [1998] AC 232, HL.
[41]   [1998] AC 232 at 242, HL.

before accepting a body of opinion as being reasonable, responsible or respectable, will need to be satisfied that, in forming their views, the experts have directed their minds to the questions of comparative risks and benefits and have reached a defensible conclusion on the matter.

Expert evidence after *Bolitho* remains of the highest importance to the success or failure of clinical negligence claims. Lord Browne-Wilkinson acknowledged that in '. . . the vast majority of cases the fact that distinguished experts in the field are of a particular opinion will demonstrate the reasonableness of that opinion'. Nonetheless, he went on to say '. . . if in a rare case, it can be demonstrated that the professional opinion is not capable of withstanding logical analysis, the judge is entitled to hold that the body of opinion is not reasonable or responsible'.[42]

Bolitho returns *Bolam* to its proper limits.[43] Doctors, like solicitors and all other professionals, are subject to legal scrutiny. The courts, not the medical profession, are the ultimate arbiters of the standard of care in clinical negligence claims. *Bolitho* has generated a plethora of academic commentary.[44] How influential has *Bolitho* been? Pessimistic commentators point out that Lord Browne-Wilkinson spoke of 'rare' cases and later noted that it will be 'very seldom' that it would be right to conclude that views genuinely held by competent experts were unreasonable. *Bolitho*, they fear, will do little to aid patients.[45] Others are concerned that *Bolitho* might go too far and stifle innovative medicine. Mason and Laurie suggest:[46]

> *Bolam* provides some protection for innovative or minority opinion or, indeed, the individual clinician's judgement call. If this protection is removed then the opinion which the cautious practitioner will wish to follow will be that which involves least risk. This may have an inhibiting effect on medical progress: after all, many advances in medicine have been made by those who have pursued an unconventional line of therapy.

We consider both fears to be unfounded. *Bolitho* did herald a new dawn, if a somewhat cloudy one![47] The proclamation of judicial authority over medical

---

42 [1998] AC 232 at 243.

43 As Andrew Grubb so nicely put it, 'Eureka!' The courts have got it at last. Expert evidence, whether of professional practice or otherwise, is not conclusive in a medical negligence case that the defendant has not been careless! A Grubb, 'Negligence, Causation and Bolam' (1998) 6 *Medical Law Review* 378, p 380; M A Jones, 'The Illogical Expert' (1999) 15 *Professional Negligence* 117.

44 See H Teff, 'The Standard of Care in Medical Negligence – Moving on from *Bolam*' (1998) 18 *Oxford Journal of Legal Studies* 473; J Keown, 'Reining in the Bolam Test' (1998) 57 *Cambridge Law Journal* 248; J Badenoch, 'Brushes With Bolam: Where Will It Lead?' (2005) 72 *Medico-Legal Journal* 127.

45 See N Glover, 'Bolam in the House of Lords' (1999) 15 *Professional Negligence* 42.

46 J K Mason and G T Laurie, *Mason and McCall Smith's Law and Medical Ethics* (8th edn, 2010) OUP (hereafter *Mason and McCall Smith*), at 139.

47 R Mulheron claims that there are now recognisable categories which flesh out the requirement that professional peer-opinion must be 'logical', 'responsible' and 'defensible'. Mulheron further articulates these categories in the hope that the law further clarifies the ambits of *Bolitho*. See 'Trumping Bolam: A Critical Legal Analysis of "Bolitho's" Gloss' (2010) 69(3) *Cambridge Law Journal* 609.

practice in *Bolitho* comes at last from the Law Lords, then the highest court in the UK and it came at a time when several other developments in the manner medical practice is regulated and audited were placing limits on unfettered clinical autonomy.[48] Simply asserting that a medical expert considers that there was no negligence is no longer a 'trump card' for defendants.[49]

What of the case law post *Bolitho*? In *Marriott v West Midlands Health Authority*,[50] the plaintiff had suffered head injuries. He was discharged from hospital but remained unwell. Eight days after the fall he was visited by the defendant GP. The GP carried out some basic neurological tests, prescribed painkillers and told the plaintiff's wife to telephone him again if her husband's condition got worse. Four days later the plaintiff collapsed and was readmitted to hospital. A large extradural haematoma was operated on and surgery revealed a skull fracture and internal bleeding. The plaintiff was left paralysed and afflicted by a speech disorder. In the claim against the GP, the crucial question was whether a responsible GP would have judged that a full neurological examination was called for and readmitted the plaintiff to hospital. The defendant's expert acknowledged that the defendant should have recognised that there was a risk that the plaintiff had a clot on the brain, but contended that the risk was so small that it was not negligent to fail to refer the plaintiff for further tests. The trial judge evaluating that evidence held that albeit the risk was small '. . . the consequences, if things go wrong, are disastrous to the patient. In such circumstances, it is my view that the only reasonable prudent course . . . is to readmit for further testing and observation'. The Court of Appeal upheld the judgment. Beldam LJ endorsed the judge's exercise in risk assessment. Whatever the expert witnesses might say, the devastating nature of the consequences of a clot on the brain were such that no responsible doctor would have subjected the plaintiff to that risk.[51] In *Burne v A*,[52] Sedley LJ stressed that:

> . . . judges are there to exercise judgment, and their judgment cannot be entirely dictated by expert evidence, even where the evidence is unopposed. The question always remains (provided a party raises it) whether the expert evidence makes sense.

Extra-judicially, both the then Lord Chancellor[53] and Lord Chief Justice[54] have indicated that judges should no longer blindly defer to medical opinion. Alas-

---

[48] See M Brazier and J Miola, 'Bye-Bye Bolam: A Medical Litigation Revolution' (2000) 8 *Medical Law Review* 85.
[49] *Mason and McCall Smith*, at 139.
[50] [1999] Lloyd's Rep Med 23.
[51] *Penney v East Kent Area Health Authority* [2000] Lloyd's Rep Med 41; *Reynolds v North Tyneside Health Authority* [2002] Lloyd's Rep Med 453; *Lillywhite v University College London Hospital NHS Trust* [2005] EWCA Civ 1466; *Manning v King's College Hospital NHS Trust* [2008] EWHC 1838.
[52] [2006] EWCA Civ 24 at para 10.
[53] Lord Irvine of Lairg, 'The Patient, the Doctor their Lawyers and the Judge: Rights and Duties' (1999) 7 *Medical Law Review* 255.
[54] See Lord Woolf, 'Are the Courts Excessively Deferential to the Medical Profession?' (2001) 9 *Medical Law Review* 1.

dair Maclean takes a less optimistic view.[55] His research into clinical negligence claims showed that out of sixty-four cases post *Bolitho*, but before 2001, *Bolitho* was only even mentioned in twenty-nine. It has been made clear that *Bolitho* in no sense reverses the burden of proof,[56] but nor was it ever designed to do so. Judges have reinforced the view that it will seldom be right to reject expert opinion as unreasonable.[57] The Court of Appeal has warned that a judge is 'not entitled to impose his own opinion regardless of the practice of the medical profession'.[58] And a tendency to presume that eminent experts will necessarily give logical evidence can be discerned in *Wisniewski v Central Manchester Health Authority*.[59]

If *Bolitho* heralds a new dawn for patient-claimants, does it endanger innovative medicine? Will doctors simply retreat into defensive practice? Will guidelines and protocols replace a sensitive and imaginative approach to the needs of particular patients? This should not happen. *Bolitho* does not seek to usurp judgments which properly rest with doctors. Judges are not empowered to decide what constitutes good medical practice.[60] What *Bolitho* does is to require expert witnesses to justify and explain the basis of their judgments.[61] It may be noted that expert evidence today is much more based on evidence and literature[62] than simple opinion.

'Responsible practice' means current practice

7.9 It has never been a defence for a doctor to say that a practice was widely accepted when he was at medical school and is therefore accepted practice, once informed medical opinion has rejected the practice.[63] A doctor clearly cannot '. . . obstinately and pig-headedly carry on with some old technique if it has been proved contrary to what is substantially the whole of informed medical opinion'.[64] Doctors must keep up to date with new developments. But there is an inevitable 'time-lag' between the making of new findings by researchers and the percolation of ideas through to doctors in the field. The doctor will be judged by the standard of awareness and sophistication to be expected of a doctor in his sort of practice. Great emphasis is placed on the professional position and the specialty of the defendant.[65] A patient who suffered from brachial palsy as a result of his arm being extended in a certain

[55] A Maclean, 'Beyond Bolam and Bolitho' (2002) 5 *Medical Law International* 205.
[56] *Smith v West Yorkshire Health Authority* [2004] EWHC 1592 (QB).
[57] *Morris v Blackpool Victoria NHS Trust* [2003] EWHC 1744; *Dunn v South Tyneside Health Care NHS Trust* [2003] EWCA Civ 870.
[58] *Ministry of Justice v Carter* [2010] EWCA Civ 694.
[59] [1998] Lloyd's Rep Med 85.
[60] *Ministry of Justice v Carter* [2010] EWCA Civ 694.
[61] Brazier & Miola (2008) 8 *Medical Law Review* 85, p 106.
[62] See *Newman v Maurice* [2010] EWHC 171.
[63] *Hunter v Hanley* (1955) SC 200.
[64] *Bolam v Friern HMC* [1957] 1 WLR 582 at 587.
[65] See *Gascoine v Ian Sheridan & Co* [1994] 5 Med LR 437.

position while he was given a blood transfusion in the course of a bladder operation brought a claim against the anaesthetist. Six months before the operation, an article had appeared in the *Lancet* condemning this practice because of the risk of brachial palsy. The claim failed. Failure to read one recent article was not negligent.[66] In 2011 the greater ease of access to medical journals via the Internet may affect judgments about how far doctors must be up to date within their specialty.

The relevant date to judge current practice must be the date of the operation or treatment, not the date the claim comes to trial. In *Roe v Ministry of Health*, a patient had become permanently paralysed after an injection of the spinal anaesthetic Nupercaine, administered in 1947. His claim against the doctors and the hospital came to trial in 1954. Before the operation, the drug had been kept in glass ampoules in a solution of phenol. The accident to the patient occurred because phenol percolated through invisible cracks in the ampoules and contaminated the Nupercaine.

No one had ever known this to happen. The claim in negligence failed. Lord Denning said: [67]

> We must not look at the 1947 accident with 1954 spectacles.

Once a tragic incident of this nature has occurred and has been attended by publicity then of course a further incident would easily be proved to be negligence. Current practice would have been shown to be wanting.

Protocols and guidelines[68]

7.10 Buzz-words in medicine today are evidence-based medicine and clinical governance. Within the NHS, the government has sought to ensure that treatment provided to patients is soundly based on good practice derived from concrete evidence. The National Institute of Clinical Excellence (NICE) is expressly instructed to investigate medical practice and provide authoritative guidelines on good practice. The Royal College of Medicine, and other doctors' organisations, increasingly draw up protocols for treatment and issue guidelines on good practice.

---

[66] *Crawford v Board of Governors of Charing Cross Hospital* (1953) *Times*, 8 December, CA. And see *Whiteford v Hunter* (1950) 94 Sol Jo 758, HL.

[67] *Roe v Ministry of Health* [1954] 2 KB 66 at 84; and see *L (a child) v West Midlands Strategic Health Authority* [2009] EWHC 259.

[68] See V Harpwood, 'NHS Reform: Audit Protocols and the Standard of Care in Medical Negligence' (1994) 1 *Medical Law International* 1; V Harpwood, 'The Manipulation of Medical Practice in Law and Medicine'; H Teff, 'Clinical Guidelines, Negligence and Medical Practice' both in M Freeman and A Lewis (eds), *Law and Medicine: Current Legal Issues*; A Samanta *et al*, 'The Role of Clinical Guidelines in Medical Negligence Litigation: A Shift from the Bolam Standard' (2006) 14 *Medical Law Review* 321.

Evidence of good practice as defined by protocol and guidelines will play a role in any claim for clinical negligence. The considered judgment of NICE, or the profession itself, will be evidence of what constitutes responsible practice. Does this mean any doctor departing from official guidelines will be proven negligent? Some doctors fear guidelines enforced by the courts will lead to a 'tick-box' approach to patient care.[69] Doctors will cease to exercise professional judgment based on the needs and circumstances of the individual patient. This should not happen. Where departure from the guidelines can be justified in the interests of the patient, the doctor discharges his duty of care. Blind adherence to guidelines or protocols would itself be negligent. *Bolitho* requires that responsible practice be demonstrably logical and defensible. Guidelines will offer some evidence of what constitutes proper treatment for the patient's condition. Evidence that the patient requires a different mode of care should not be excluded by the presence of such general guidance.[70] NICE itself put it thus:

> (H)ealth professionals, when exercising their clinical judgment, should take its guidance fully into account, but ... it does not override their responsibility for making appropriate decisions in the circumstances of the individual patient.[71]

Diagnosis

7.11 A wrong diagnosis is by itself no evidence of negligence on the part of the doctor. As a Scottish judge said:[72]

> In the realm of diagnosis and treatment there is ample scope for a genuine difference of opinion and one man is clearly not negligent merely because his conclusion differs from that of other professional men ...

A patient alleging that a wrong diagnosis was negligent must establish either that the doctor failed to carry out an examination or a test which the patient's symptoms called for, or that his eventual conclusion[73] was one that no competent doctor would have arrived at (the *Bolam* test), or was not 'capable of withstanding logical analysis' (the *Bolitho*[74] test). Not surprisingly, a doctor who failed to diagnose a broken knee-cap in a man who had fallen 12 ft on to a concrete floor was found to be negligent.[75]

---

[69] See J Warden, 'NICE to Sort our Clinical Wheat from Chaff' (1999) 318 *British Medical Journal* 416.

[70] See Brazier and Miola (2000) 8 *Medical Law Review* 85; but see B Hurwitz, 'How Does Evidence Based Guidance Influence Determinations of Medical Negligence?' (2004) 329 *British Medical Journal* 1024.

[71] National Institute for Clinical Excellence, Response to the Report of The Bristol Royal Infirmary Inquiry (2001).

[72] *Hunter v Hanley* (1955) SLT 213 at 217.

[73] See *Lillywhite v University College London Hospitals NHS Trust* [2005] EWCA Civ 1466.

[74] *Penney v East Kent Health Authority* [2000] Lloyd's Rep Med 23.

[75] *Newton v Newton's New Model Laundry* (1951) *Times*, 3 November.

The courts are readier to find negligence when a patient and his experts can point to a specific failure on the part of the doctor. A casualty doctor, who failed to examine or X-ray a drunken patient admitted with the information that he had been seen under a moving lorry, was found to be negligent when after his death the next day he was discovered to have eighteen fractured ribs and extensive damage to his lungs. It was no defence that the patient never complained of pain. The doctor should have known that alcohol would dull the patient's reaction to pain.[76] The doctor must be alert to the patient's background. A GP who failed to test for, and diagnose, malaria in a patient who had recently returned from East Africa was held liable for the patient's death. The doctor was consulted nine days after the patient's return to this country, a relative suggested malaria, but the doctor diagnosed flu. Six days later, malaria was diagnosed in hospital, where the patient died that day.[77] Failure to diagnose diabetes where the symptoms complained of by the patient should have alerted the doctor to this possibility may lead to liability.[78] Too hasty a diagnosis of hysteria or depression will often be negligent.[79]

In all the above examples, the doctor was negligent because he failed to act on information available to him and/or to perform routine tests. Where a diagnostic procedure is not routine, is costly, or painful, or risky, an additional factor has to be considered. Do the symptoms displayed by the patient justify subjecting him to the procedure? The doctor faces a legal as well as a medical dilemma. If he does not arrange for the test and the patient does suffer from some condition which the test would have revealed, the doctor may be sued for that failure. If he does arrange the test and an inherent risk of the test harms the patient, the patient may sue if the test reveals that the doctor's suspicions were groundless. We saw that that is what happened with Staff Nurse Maynard.[80] The defendants were *not* liable to her because they had followed accepted practice in going ahead with the test, despite its dangers. Doctors argue that alacrity to pin liability on them for every diagnostic error may cause patients to be submitted to more expensive and potentially risky procedures than may be strictly medically desirable.

Interpreting screening and diagnostic tests is a difficult skill, but failure to act on information that should have alerted the laboratory or the doctor to undertake further investigations may give rise to liability. So in *Penney v East Kent Health Authority*,[81] the claimants developed cervical cancer after an erroneous

---

[76] *Wood v Thurston* (1951) *Times*, 25 May.
[77] *Langley v Campbell* (1975) *Times*, 6 November; and see *Tuffil v East Surrey Area Health Authority* (1978) *Times*, 15 March. (Failure to diagnose amoebic dysentery in a patient who had spent many years in the tropics.)
[78] MDU, *Annual Report* (1990) pp 26–27.
[79] *Serre v De Filly* (1975) OR (2d) 490; and see MDU *Annual Report* (1982), pp 22–23; and (1983), p 24.
[80] *Maynard v West Midlands Regional Health Authority* [1984] 1 WLR 634; see above at 7.7.
[81] [2000] Lloyd's Rep Med 41. Note too the discussion as to the applicability of *Bolam*

negative report from a screening test. The false negative result itself was no evidence of negligence. It was admitted that abnormalities were present on the patients' slides and that any competent screener would thus have been unable to rule out that the cells were pre-cancerous. Reporting the tests as negative was therefore found by the Court of Appeal to be illogical. Although the defendants' experts sought to argue that the screeners were not negligent in their interpretation of the slides as both sets of experts agreed that the standard for a negative report was 'absolute confidence', a negative report in the face of admitted abnormalities failed the *Bolitho* test.[82]

Treatment

7.12 A claim in respect of negligent treatment may be based on an allegation that the treatment chosen was inappropriate, or that while the treatment embarked on was correct, it was negligently carried out. Doctors must ensure that they act on adequate information and supply each other with adequate information. A GP prescribing drugs must check what other medication the patient is on. Doctors must be alert to common drug reactions and actively seek relevant information from patients. A clinic which injected a woman with penicillin was held liable for her death an hour later.[83] Had they inquired of her, or examined her records, they would have been aware of her allergy to penicillin. A GP arranging for the admission of a pregnant patient to hospital, while he was treating her for a septic finger, was found negligent in not so informing the hospital. She contracted septicaemia. Had the hospital known of the state of her finger they would have put her on antibiotics straight away.[84] Doctors must be wary of relying entirely on information supplied by their colleagues. A patient was admitted for a gynaecological operation. The gynaecologist asked a general surgeon to remove what he said was a ganglion from the patient's wrist. Thus the patient would be spared two separate operations. It was not a ganglion. Surgery of that sort was inappropriate and the patient's hand was permanently paralysed. The Medical Defence Union (MDU) settled because the general surgeon should have made his own pre-operative assessment, and not relied on a colleague from another specialty.[85]

Once the doctor is properly informed and has selected his course of treatment, he must ensure that he carries it out properly. He must check the dosage of any drug. Prescribing an overdose will readily be found to be negligent.[86] He must

---

to such screening tests. And see *Farraj v King's Healthcare NHS Trust* [2009] EWCA 1203, CA.

[82] See also *Manning v King's College Hospital NHS Trust* [2008] EWHC 1838 (failure to diagnose rare tongue cancer).

[83] *Chin Keow v Govt of Malaysia* [1967] 1 WLR 813.

[84] *Hucks v Cole* (1968) 12 Sol Jo 483.

[85] MDU, *Annual Report* (1984), p 18.

[86] *Dwyer v Roderick* (1983) 127 Sol Jo 806, and see J Finch, 'A Costly Oversight for Pharmacists' (1982) 132 *New Law Journal* 176.

be sure that his handwriting is legible.[87] Care must also be taken always to read drug labelling properly. In a tragic case,[88] a senior house officer misread a label and administered potassium chloride instead of saline to a newborn infant. The baby died.

Where surgery is called for, the risk of injury is increased. Especially risky is the administration of the anaesthetic. The anaesthetist will be found to be negligent if he failed to make a proper pre-operative assessment of the patient, failed to check his equipment, failed to monitor the patient's blood pressure and/or heartbeat in the course of surgery or if, an inevitable accident having occurred, the anaesthetist fails to invoke adequate resuscitation measures. Some specific failure on the defendant's part must be pinpointed. A disturbing number of claims arose from failure to intubate the patient properly (putting the tube in the wrong place) or attaching tubes to the wrong gas so that the patient fails to receive essential oxygen.[89] Several claims have arisen from failure to anaesthetise the patient completely. Patients are paralysed and unable to communicate, but remain awake and feel pain throughout surgery.[90]

An anaesthetic tragedy of itself is generally not evidence of negligence. An anaesthetist who injected cocaine instead of procaine was found negligent,[91] as was the junior doctor who injected pentothal into an anaesthetised patient, causing his death.[92] If the wrong drug, or the wrong dosage, or a contaminated drug, is used, the patient's claim will generally be made good. The exception will be where the error cannot be laid at the anaesthetist's door. So, as we saw in *Roe v Ministry of Health*,[93] a patient who was paralysed because a then unknown risk of phenol percolating into the ampoules of local anaesthetic materialised, recovered no compensation.

Surgery must be performed with the utmost care. One judge has suggested that the more skilled the surgeon, the higher the standard of care.[94] Some errors advertise their negligence. Leaving swabs and equipment inside the patient is a good example. And the surgeon must accept responsibility for such matters and not rely on nursing staff.[95] Nor does the surgeon's responsibility end with the careful completion of surgery. He must give his patient proper post-operative care and advice. A surgeon performed a cosmetic operation just below the eye. He told his patient to inform him if bleeding occurred within forty-eight hours.

---

[87] *Prendergast v Sam and Dee* [1989] 1 Med LR 36.

[88] MDU, *Annual Report* (1989), p 32.

[89] MDU, *Annual Report* (1988), pp 28–29: (1989), pp 20–21.

[90] For example, *Taylor v Worcester and District Health Authority* (1997) 2 Med LR 215.

[91] *Collins v Hertfordshire Corporation* [1952] 2 QB 852.

[92] *Jones v Manchester Corporation* [1952] 2 QB 852.

[93] [1954] 2 QB 66, CA.

[94] *Ashcroft v Mersey Area Health Authority* [1983] 2 All ER 245 at 247. And see *Lillywhite v University College London Hospitals NHS Trust* [2005] EWCA Civ 1466.

[95] *Urry v Biere* (1955) *Times*, 19 July.

It did and the patient tried to telephone the surgeon and got no reply. The surgeon was held to be negligent.[96]

An especially important issue today concerns the need to protect patients against hospital-acquired (nosocomial) infections such as Methicillin Resistant Staphylococcus Aureus (MRSA) and Clostridium Difficile (C Diff). In a Scottish case, *Miller v Greater Glasgow NHS Board*,[97] the defendants applied to strike out a claim by a patient who alleged that she had contracted MRSA because staff had not followed an adequate hand-hygiene practice. The court refused the application, holding that protection from hospital acquired infection was an integral part of the duty owed to patients by both individual professionals and the hospital trust.[98]

Overtired, overworked doctors

7.13 If a doctor makes a mistake because she is intolerably weary, or just having a bad day, will the patient's rights be in any way affected? No, the courts rightly will not accept any argument that the doctor's duty is fulfilled if he provides an adequate service generally and only occasionally falls below the required standard of competence.[99] Judges sympathise with hard-pressed doctors. A doctor who carries on beyond the point when fatigue and overwork impair her judgment remains liable to an injured patient. The fact that the doctor was required by his employer to work such hours will not affect the patient.

The patient might, though, more appropriately proceed against the doctor's employers, the hospital. He would allege that the hospital undertook to provide him with adequate care.[100] Requiring their doctors to work to the point of utter exhaustion, or organising shifts in such a way as to prevent continuity of care, is a breach of that duty. The essence of the patient's claim would become, not that the hospital was vicariously liable for an individual doctor's negligence, but that there was a breach of a primary duty to ensure an adequate and competent service. In *Wilsher v Essex Area Health Authority*,[101] Browne-Wilkinson VC suggested that in many cases this was a more appropriate analysis of clinical negligence claims, avoiding stigmatising overworked doctors for understandable errors. But there is a risk that even fewer patients may obtain compensation if this analysis were accepted. The defendant hospital might plead in its defence the problems it faces arising from lack of resources. If patient A suffers an injury because the surgeon who operated on him was too tired to perform the surgery properly and no other surgeon was available, the hospital may argue that it could not afford to employ more, or more senior,

---

[96] *Corder v Banks* (1960) *Times*, 9 April.
[97] [2010] CSIH 40.
[98] On the direct liability of hospital trusts, see further below, ch 8.
[99] *Wilsher v Essex Area Health Authority* [1986] 3 All ER 801, CA.
[100] See *Cassidy v Ministry of Health* [1951] 2 KB 14; see ch 8.
[101] [1986] 3 All ER 801 at 833–834.

surgeons. It will be contended that, although far from ideal, the level of service was reasonable in the light of the defendants' limited budget. In one judgment, a judge expressly said that lack of resources should be taken into account in medical negligence claims.[102] But in a later case any such argument was vigorously rejected.[103]

General practice

7.14. Most patients visit their GP on average four or five times a year and make one or two hospital visits in a lifetime. While malpractice actions against GPs are becoming more common, GPs remain less vulnerable to litigation than doctors in other specialties.[104] Changes in general practice which risk jeopardising the more personal relationship between GP and patient may increase the GP's vulnerability to claims for clinical negligence. A claim against a GP may face some particular obstacles. Proving negligence, and that the patient's injury resulted from that negligence, is always difficult. Against a GP the problems multiply. How do you prove that a child's sudden deterioration resulted from the GP not visiting at once? Would immediate treatment have arrested the condition? Added to these difficulties, common complaints about general practice do not tend to be the kind of grievances that make litigation with its expense, pomp and ceremony worthwhile. Patients object to unhelpful receptionists, difficulty in getting home visits, and often simply sense a lack of sympathy. Rarely do these irritations cause injury serious enough to merit litigation.

Every GP must attain that standard of skill and competence to be expected of the reasonably skilled and experienced GP. It is no defence that she has just entered practice, or that she is elderly and infirm. Nor, as we have seen, can he be expected to have the skills or qualifications of a consultant specialist. He must exercise his judgment about when to refer a patient to a specialist, or admit him to hospital, with due care.[105] Should a GP offer additional services to his patients, for example, if he is on the obstetric list and is prepared to attend home confinements, then he must show the skill that he holds himself out as possessing. He must attain the standard, not of the consultant obstetrician, but of the specially qualified and experienced GP.

In reported cases where negligence has been proved against GPs, certain danger areas stand out. The maintenance of proper records and ensuring adequate communication with patients,[106] and with hospitals and other doctors sharing the care of a patient, is one. A failure to record and pass on to a hospital, infor-

---

[102] *Knight v Home Office* [1990] 3 All ER 237.
[103] *Brooks v Home Office* (1999) 48 BMLR 109.
[104] National Health Service Litigation Authority, *Factsheet 3* (2010).
[105] *Marriott v West Midlands Area Health Authority* [1999] Lloyd's Rep Med 23.
[106] See *Langley v Campbell* (1975) *Times*, 6 November.

mation on a patient's allergy to certain drugs, is a clear case of negligence.[107] Similarly, a failure to check exactly what treatment has been given by the hospital may result in liability. A GP was found liable for a young man's death in this case.[108] The man had gone to a cottage hospital after a lump of coal had fallen on him and crushed his finger. A nurse dressed the wound and instructed him to go to another larger hospital. Either because this was not properly explained to him or because he was in shock he did not go. He went later to his own doctor, who did not inquire as to his earlier treatment and simply put on a new dressing. At no stage did the patient receive an anti-tetanus injection and he died of toxaemia. The cottage hospital and the GP were both found to be negligent and responsible for the youth's death. The judge made his views emphatically clear:

> ... the National Health Service had been developed on the basis that a patient might well be transferred for treatment from one person to another so that the responsibility for the patient shifted ... Any system which failed to provide for effective communication was wrong and negligently wrong.

Prescription errors

7.15 Prescribing medicines is another area where GPs must be ultra-cautious, not just out of professional concern for the patient, but also in order to safeguard themselves. In 1982, a GP prescribed Migril for a Mrs Dwyer. Carelessly he wrote out a prescription for a massive overdose of the drug. A pharmacist dispensed the drug as prescribed. Mrs Dwyer became ill. A partner in the same practice attended her at home. The Migril was on a table in her bedroom, but the second doctor did not notice the bottle. Mrs Dwyer suffered gangrene as a result of the overdose. She sued both doctors and the pharmacist. All were originally found liable.[109] Mrs Dwyer received £100,000 in damages. Eventually the second doctor was exculpated on appeal. At the end of the day, the GP whose slip caused the over-prescription paid 45 per cent of the damages, and the pharmacists 55 per cent. In *Prendergast v Sam and Dee Ltd*,[110] a general practitioner prescribed Amoxil, a common antibiotic, for the plaintiff who was suffering from a chest infection. The doctor's handwriting was so atrocious that the pharmacist read the prescription as an instruction to dispense Daonil, an anti-diabetic drug. The plaintiff succumbed to hypoglycaemia and brain damage. The Court of Appeal upheld Auld J's finding that both the doctor and the pharmacist were negligent. The doctor was liable because he should have foreseen that his careless writing of the prescription might mislead the pharmacist into a dangerous error. The pharmacist was liable because the dosage prescribed and other indications on the prescription

---

[107] *Chin Keow v Government of Malaysia* [1967] 1 WLR 813.

[108] *Coles v Reading and District Hospital Management Committee* (1963) *Times*, 30 January.

[109] *Dwyer v Roderick* (1983) 127 Sol Jo 806. Recounted in 'A Costly Oversight for Pharmacists' (1982) 132 *New Law Journal* 176.

[110] [1990] 1 Med LR 36.

should have alerted him to the fact that the doctor did not intend to prescribe Daonil. Both judgments operate as timely warnings against sloppy practice. Doctors must exercise great care in writing out prescriptions. Pharmacists must exercise even greater care in checking on the doctors.

Duty to attend

7.16 A frequent complaint about GPs is that patients have difficulty getting appointments or home visits, and that receptionists take it upon themselves to decide when and if someone can see the doctor. What exactly is the GP's duty to attend his patients and who in law are his patients? What we say here relates to the regulations governing general practice in 2011. Changes that may result from the Health and Social Care Bill could alter the duties of the GP quite radically.

A GP must currently provide medical care during 'core hours' to all 'his' patients. A GP's terms of service[111] provide that his patients are firstly those who are accepted on his list.[112] Provision is made to ensure that no patient need ever be without a GP. Most importantly, the doctor's patients include persons accepted as 'temporary residents' and 'persons to whom he may be requested to give treatment which is immediately required owing to an accident or other emergency at any place in his practice area'.[113] The doctor's obligation to the health service is to provide an umbrella of cover. Wherever an NHS patient goes he should be able to see a GP. If he falls ill on holiday and can get to a doctor himself, he can go temporarily on to the local doctor's list. In dire emergency, he or his friends can call on, and count on, any GP practising in the area to come to his aid. Breach of the terms of service could lead to disciplinary sanctions.

Is there any obligation directly to the patient? Could a patient sue if denied treatment so that his condition deteriorated? A doctor on an express train can sit by and watch a fellow passenger die of a coronary. The GP's position is quite different. As far as the patients on his list are concerned, he has a continuing duty to them. A failure to attend such a patient where a competent GP would recognise the need for attendance is as much a breach of duty as giving wrong and careless treatment. Patients accepted as 'temporary residents' by a GP are in the same position for as long as they are registered with that GP.

What about 'emergency cases'? A GP's terms of service oblige her to treat such cases *in her practice area* when she is available to provide medical care. In 1955, lawyers acting for a doctor being sued by a patient on his NHS list,

---

[111] See National Health Service Act 2006, ss 83–95; National Health Service (General Medical Services Contracts) Regulations 2004, SI 2004/291; National Health Service (Primary Care) Act 1997.
[112] National Health Service (General Medical Services) Regulations, reg 15.
[113] *Ibid*, reg 15(6).

conceded that the creation of the NHS had created a legal duty on a doctor to treat any patient in an emergency, whether or not the patient was on his list.[114] Nathan and Barrowclough doubted the correctness of this concession. They commented that such a duty might reflect '. . . the standards by which the medical profession regards itself as bound and would wish to be judged [but] from the strictly legal point of view [it was] too wide'.[115] We cannot see why it is 'too wide'. The doctor has undertaken to provide an emergency service. The area and circumstances in which he must act are closely defined. The obligation on him is not unbearably onerous. Emergency patients within his practice area when he is on duty are a foreseeable class of persons to whom, by accepting the position of GP within the NHS, he has undertaken a duty, and a duty which should be legal and not merely moral.

Establishing a duty to treat will rarely be a cause of difficulty, except towards emergency cases. A patient suing a GP will find that his problems start when he seeks to prove, as he must, that the GP's failure to treat him was negligent. Some patients make intolerable demands on their doctors. The doctor is not obliged to respond immediately to every call. He may indeed be in breach of duty to his more patient patients if he always responds to the most insistent call on his services. He has to exercise his judgment. In 1953, a GP was sued when he failed to visit a child whose mother reported (a) that the child had abdominal pains, and (b) that she had previously been examined by a hospital casualty officer who had sent her home. The child proved to have a burst appendix. The judge found that the casualty doctor was negligent and the GP was not. He had acted reasonably on the information available to him.[116]

The information available to the doctor is vital in assessing his obligation to the patient. When a patient changed his address without telling his doctor and then summoned the doctor, the doctor was found not negligent when, after an attempt to visit the old address, he left to complete other calls. The judge found that he acted reasonably in assuming that if urgent treatment was needed, he would be contacted again. The doctor could not be expected to mount a search for his missing patient.[117] Similarly, information as to the patient's condition must be full and accurate. A patient may fail in any action for failure to attend if all he said to the doctor was that he felt sick and had a headache, when in fact he was feverish, vomiting and had severe abdominal pains. The courts will condemn the doctor who fails to act on information from his patient. The patient must give the doctor the information to act on. Often, information about requests for visits and appointments is not given directly to the doctor. It is channelled via the receptionist. This makes not a jot of difference to the doctor's legal obligation. His terms of service will require that he provide treatment during approved hours or, if he operates an appointments scheme, that the patient be offered an appointment within a reasonable

[114] *Barnes v Crabtree* (1955) *Times,* 1 and 2 November.
[115] P C Nathan and A R Barrowclough, *Medical Negligence* (1957) Butterworths, p 38.
[116] *Edler v Greenwich and Deptford HMC* (1953) *Times,* 7 March.
[117] *Kavanagh v Abrahamson* (1964) 108 Sol Jo 320.

time. And if the patient's condition so requires, he must be visited at home. He is responsible for his staff and must ensure that their service, as well as his, is efficient. His liability for them is absolute. Let us imagine a GP whose receptionist, in a burst of temper totally out of character, verbally abuses the mother of a seriously ill toddler and refuses to ask the doctor for a visit. The child has peritonitis and dies for lack of immediate treatment. The receptionist, not the doctor, was negligent, but as her employer, he is legally responsible for her negligence.[118]

Relating the injury to medical negligence

7.17 So far, the majority of the cases examined involved something going wrong as a result of a medical mistake. The patient's problem has been to prove that what was done, or not done, amounted to actionable negligence. Proving negligence by the doctor does not conclude the case in the patient's favour. He must also show that his injury, his worsened or unimproved condition, was caused by the doctor's negligence. He must prove causation. In practice, proving causation is often the most problematic aspect of a patient's claim. The difficulties of causation in medical malpractice cases fall into two main categories.

(1)   Can the patient convince the court that it was the relevant negligence which caused his injury, rather than the progress of his original disease or condition?

(2)   How should the courts proceed when the essence of a claim is, not that clinical negligence caused any fresh or additional injury to the patient, but that that negligence deprived him of a chance of full recovery from his original disease or condition?

In each and every case the patient must advance evidence showing that it is more likely than not that the defendant's negligence caused the injury of which he complains.

In *Kay v Ayrshire and Arran Health Board*,[119] a two-year-old boy, Andrew Kay, was rushed into hospital suffering from pneumococcal meningitis. He was negligently given a massive overdose of penicillin and nearly died as a result. Intensive efforts by hospital staff saved Andrew's life and he recovered from both the toxic overdose and from meningitis. But he was found to be profoundly deaf. His parents, on his behalf, sued the Scottish health board responsible for the hospital where Andrew had been treated. The board admitted negligence, but denied that Andrew's deafness resulted from that negligence. Deafness is often a complication of meningitis even where the disease has been correctly treated. Massive overdoses of the sort that Andrew was given are mercifully rare. So there was little available evidence of whether such an over-

---

[118] Because of the doctrine of vicarious liability; see below in ch 8.
[119] [1987] 2 All ER 417. And see *Loveday v Renton* [1990] 1 Med L Rep 117.

dose materially increased the risk that Andrew would become deaf as a result of his disease. The trial judge found in Andrew's favour, but his decision was overruled in the appeal courts. In the House of Lords, Lord Keith commented that the lack of recorded cases demonstrating the effect of overdose of penicillin '. . . cannot in itself make good the lack of appropriate evidence'.[120]

As we have seen, in *Wilsher v Essex Area Health Authority*[121] junior doctors were found to be negligent in administering excess oxygen to a very premature baby, Martin Wilsher. Martin succumbed to retrolental fibroplasia (RLF), an incurable condition of the retina causing gradual blindness. The question that went to the House of Lords was whether Martin's lawyers could prove that RLF resulted from that negligent administration of excess oxygen. The scientific evidence suggested that RLF *may* result from excess oxygen, but there were five other possible causes of RLF in very sick, very premature infants. The trial judge had held that, as negligence had been proved, the burden of disproving that that negligence caused Martin's injuries moved to the defendants. He said that as the evidence showed that the doctors were in breach of their duty to Martin and failed to take a precaution expressly designed to safeguard Martin from RLF, it was then up to them to prove that Martin's condition resulted from one of the other possible causes. The House of Lords roundly condemned such an approach, and ordered a retrial. The burden of proving causation rests on the claimant alone, and does not move to the defendant even though negligence has been proved or admitted. What is crucial for the claimant is the quality of the expert scientific evidence presented on his behalf. That evidence must, at the very least, demonstrate that it is more likely than not that the defendants' negligence materially contributed to the claimant's condition, or materially increased the risk that the claimant would succumb to such a condition.[122] Where the scientific evidence is ambivalent or suggests a variety of competing causes for the claimant's state, the action for negligence will normally fail.

Uncertainty about causation is likely to be common in many claims that essentially relate to whether the defendants' negligence caused or exacerbated disease. In *Fairchild v Glenhaven Funeral Services Ltd*,[123] claims were brought by workers who had been exposed to asbestos dust or fibres during their working lives and developed the fatal lung disease mesothelioma. The men had worked for several different employers, so pinpointing which defendant employer was responsible for the onset of the disease was nigh on impossible. Mesothelioma can result from a single asbestos fibre entering the lung. The greater your exposure to asbestos fibres, the more likely it is that this will occur. The Law Lords allowed the claim, holding all the defendant employers liable, as each of them had materially increased the risk of harm to their employees. The judges overtly invoked policy considerations to support their modified

---

[120] [1987] 2 All ER 417 at p 421.
[121] [1988] 1 All ER 871, HL.
[122]]1988] 1 All ER 871 at 882–883, per Lord Bridge.
[123] [2002] UKHL 22.

approach to, and departure from, the usual strict rules of causation.[124] Might the harsh decision in *Wilsher* thus be reconsidered? It seems unlikely. Lord Hoffmann not only declares *Wilsher* to be correctly decided in principle, but also suggests that policy reasons to protect NHS budgets could play a part in denying patient-claimants a more favourable approach to causation. He says:[125]

> The political and economic arguments involved in the massive increase in the liability of the National Health Service which would have been a consequence of the broad rule favoured by the Court of Appeal in *Wilsher's* case are far more complicated than the reasons . . . for imposing liability upon an employer who has failed to take simple precautions.

However, in *Bailey v Ministry of Defence*[126] the Court of Appeal held that in particular circumstances and in relation to cumulative causes a 'material contribution' to the claimant's injury was sufficient to establish causation in a clinical negligence claim. In such cases the 'but for' test could be modified. The claimant was a patient at a hospital managed by the Ministry of Defence. She underwent an unsuccessful procedure to remove a gallstone. The defendants admitted that following the procedure her post-operative care was inadequate, in particular a failure to resuscitate. She became progressively more ill, she was subjected to a battery of major medical interventions, and was also diagnosed as suffering from pancreatitis. Her condition deteriorated and she was eventually transferred to the renal unit of an NHS hospital where she aspirated her vomit and suffered a cardiac arrest resulting in brain damage. The issue in dispute was whether the negligent post-operative care caused the cardiac arrest and consequential brain damage. The claimant could not establish that 'but for' that negligence she would not have suffered the arrest. She was a very sick woman and her pancreatitis also contributed to her weakness. The trial judge found that the post-operative negligence contributed to her weakened state and that, but for her weakened state, she would have undergone a further intervention that would have alleviated her condition and spared her some of the later traumatic interventions to which she was subjected. The negligent care thus made a material contribution to her injury. The Court of Appeal upheld his finding. It was sufficient to show that the contribution made by inadequate care was more than negligible. Waller LJ said:

> In a case where medical science cannot establish the probability that 'but for' an act of negligence the injury would not have happened but can establish that the contribution of the negligence was more than negligible, the 'but for' test is modified, and the claimant will succeed.[127]

---

[124] Subsequently, in *Barker v Corus UK Ltd.* [2006] UKHL 22, the Law Lords ruled that each defendant should be liable only to the extent of their relevant contribution to the claimant's exposure to asbestos dust. In the specific context of claims for contracted mesothelioma, s 3 of the Compensation Act 2006 nullified that decision; discussed fully in J Murphy (ed), *Street on Torts* (12th edn, 2007) OUP, pp 145–151.

[125] [2002] UKHL 22 at para 69.

[126] [2008] EWCA Civ 883.

[127] [2008] EWCA Civ 883 at para 46.

No distinction was to be drawn between medical negligence cases and others. *Wilsher* was distinguished on the grounds that it was never established that the excess oxygen, rather than one of the five alternative causes, caused or contributed to the plaintiff developing RLF. Unlike Ms Bailey, Martin Wilsher could not meet the first condition of showing some causal link between the relevant negligence and his injury.

Modifying the 'strict rules'

7.18 In *Chester v Afshar*,[128] an earlier patient-claimant also benefited from judicial willingness to modify strict application of the rules of causation. As we have seen, Mr Afshar failed to warn Miss Chester of the 1–2 per cent risk of nerve damage in the course of spinal surgery. Miss Chester did not contend that, had she been properly warned, she would never have consented to surgery, or that she would have sought a second opinion. All she claimed was that, had she been warned, she would not have gone ahead with surgery that day. The risk of damage on any later occasion would have been just the same. Miss Chester faced the utmost difficulty in proving that, but for Mr Afshar's negligence, she would have avoided injury. The majority (3:2) in the House of Lords invoked policy grounds to assist her. Giving proper legal force to patients' rights to autonomy and dignity justified 'a narrow and modest departure from traditional causation principles'.[129]

Bolitho v City & Hackney Health Authority[130] raised a rather different question of causation. You will recall that Patrick Bolitho stopped breathing and suffered a cardiac arrest resulting in serious brain damage. The hospital admitted negligence in relation to the failure of the paediatric registrar to attend Patrick when she had been summoned to do so earlier. They denied liability because, they said, the registrar would not have intubated Patrick, had she attended him prior to his collapse. Intubation was the only means by which Patrick's respiratory failure and cardiac arrest might have been averted. The plaintiffs argued that, had Patrick been intubated, he would not have suffered injury. The defendants responded that attendance would have made no difference, medical opinion would support not intubating the child. The key question became, does the *Bolam* test play a role in causation?

Lord Browne-Wilkinson agreed with counsel for the plaintiff that 'in the generality of cases' *Bolam* plays no role in causation. *Bolitho* exemplifies an unusual problem. How do the courts address causation when the essence of the matter

---

[128] [2004] UKHL 41, discussed fully at **5.10** above.
[129] [2004] UKHL 41 at para 24 per Lord Steyn; but see to the contrary, Lord Bingham at para 9.
[130] [1998] AC 232, HL; see M A Jones, 'The Bolam Test and the Responsible Expert' (1999) *Tort Law Review* 226; A Grubb, 'Negligence Causation and Bolam' (1998) 5 *Medical Law Review* 378. And see *L (A Child) v West Midlands Strategic Health Authority* [2009] EWHC 259.

is whether something should have been done which has not been done? The factual inquiry proceeds into the 'realms of hypotheses'. The court has to ask:[131]

(1) What would the defendant have done if she had attended the boy? This is a purely factual question to which *Bolam* has no relevance.
(2) If the answer to that first question is that she would *not* have intubated, would that have been negligent?

In addressing that question, *Bolam* is central. The court had to decide if non-intubation conformed to responsible professional practice, applying their Lordships' caveat that responsible practice must be demonstrated 'logical and defensible'. In the event, the evidence of the defendants' experts that intubation of a child of Patrick's age in his circumstances was itself far from risk-free, convinced their Lordships.

Loss of a chance

7.19 When the unfortunate claimant complains not of some new injury inflicted by the defendants, but of a lost chance of recovery, his claim is even more difficult to prove. In *Hotson v East Berkshire Health Authority*,[132] the plaintiff, a school-boy of thirteen, fell heavily from a rope on which he had been swinging to the ground 12 ft below. He was taken to hospital. His knee was X-rayed and revealed no injury. No further examination was made and the plaintiff was sent home. Five days later, the boy was taken back to the same hospital and an injury to his hip joint was diagnosed and subsequently swiftly and correctly treated. The injury had traumatic consequences. The boy suffered a condition known as avas-cular necrosis. This condition, caused by a restriction of the blood supply in the region of the original injury, leads to misshapenness of the joint, disability and pain, and later in life almost certainly brings on osteoarthritis in the joint. The plaintiff's disability might have ensued from the accident in any case. But there was a 25 per cent chance that given the correct treatment immediately the plain-tiff might have avoided disability and made a nearly full recovery.

The defendant hospital admitted negligence in failing to diagnose and treat the plaintiff's injury on his first visit. Both parties agreed that prompt treatment would have offered a 25 per cent chance of avoiding permanent disability. The trial judge awarded the boy 25 per cent of full compensation for his condition, that is a sum of money to compensate him for a 25 per cent lost chance of full recovery.[133] The House of Lords quashed his judgment.[134] Their Lordships held that the plaintiff had failed to prove that it was more likely than not that avas-cular necrosis resulted from the negligent delay in treatment, because there was

---

[131] [1998] AC 232 at 240.
[132] [1987] 2 All ER 909, HL. See T Hill, 'A Lost Chance for Compensation in the Tort of Negligence in the House of Lords' (1991) 54 *Modern Law Review* 111.
[133] [1985] 3 All ER 167.
[134] [1987] 2 All ER 909, HL.

a 75 per cent chance he would have suffered from avascular necrosis, even if the treatment had been given promptly. To recover damages for the avascular necrosis, the plaintiff needed to establish at least a 51:49 likelihood that 'but for' the negligent delay in treatment, he would have made an uncomplicated recovery from his original injury. Had he succeeded in so doing, he would have been entitled to 100 per cent compensation for his disability. Their Lordships declined to say that loss of a less than 50 per cent chance of full recovery was never recoverable in a medical negligence claim. They left that question open.

The claimant in *Gregg v Scott*[135] may have hoped that his case for loss of a chance was stronger. In November 1994, his GP (the defendant) wrongly diagnosed a lump under Mr Gregg's arm as a benign lipoma. The following August, a different doctor referred him to a consultant and, in November 1995, a biopsy revealed a malignant lymphoma. The delay in diagnosis reduced Mr Gregg's chance of a 'cure' (defined as ten years in remission) from 42 to 25 per cent. Mr Gregg (unlike the young plaintiff in *Hotson*) could therefore argue that, as a consequence of the defendant's negligence, he had lost a 17 per cent chance of a 'cure'. But, alas, he could not establish that had the defendant done his job properly, he would have had a better than 50 per cent chance of a 'cure'. He was still more likely than not to face an early death even had his cancer been more promptly diagnosed. The majority of the House of Lords (3:2) applied the rules in causation strictly and found against Mr Gregg. Lord Hoffmann declared:[136]

> [A] wholesale adoption of possible rather than probable causation as the criterion of liability would be so radical a change in our law as to amount to a legislative act. It would have enormous consequences for insurance companies and the National Health Service.

One of the dissenting judges, Lord Nicholls, retorted:[137]

> It cannot be right to adopt a procedure having the effect that, in law, a patient's prospects of recovery are treated as non-existent whenever they exist but fall short of 50 per cent. If the law were to proceed in this way it would deserve to be likened to the proverbial ass . . .

How may *Gregg v Scott* be distinguished from *Chester v Afshar* and *Fairchild*? Baroness Hale seeks to contend that the latter two decisions were confined to '. . . problems which could be remedied without altering the principles applicable to the great majority of personal injury cases which give rise to no real injustice or particular problems'.[138] Their Lordships seem deeply divided on causation. Sarah Green argues cogently that distinguishing *Chester* and *Gregg* on grounds of principle cannot be done. Both are hard cases. In her view, it is *Chester* that made bad law.[139]

---

[135] [2005] UKHL 2. Contrast the facts of *Gregg v Scott* with *Manning v King's College Hospital NHS Trust* [2008] EWHC 1838.

[136] [2005] UKHL 2 at para 90.

[137] [2005] UKHL 2 at para 43.

[138] [2005] UKHL 2 at para 192.

[139] S Green, 'Coherence of Medical Negligence Cases: A Game of Doctors and Purses' (2006) 14 *Medical Law Review* 1.

Contributory negligence[140]

7.20   Could a doctor or a hospital ever plead contributory negligence and argue that the claimant's injury was in part at least his own fault? The Law Reform (Contributory Negligence) Act 1945 provides where a claimant suffers injury partly as a result of his own fault, his damages may be reduced to take account of his own responsibility for the damage. Such a case might arise if a doctor negligently prescribed a moderate overdose of a drug and the claimant exacerbated the injury from the drug by taking twice what the doctor prescribed, or drinking alcohol when he had been correctly instructed to abstain. In one reported case the claimant was wrongly told that her cervical smear test was negative but then over several years failed to attend for further tests which would have identified the cancer more swiftly. She was judged to be two-thirds responsible for her injury.[141] But what of patients whose abuse of drink or drugs, or grossly unhealthy lifestyle, made them need treatment in the first place? So that if they had not neglected their own health they would never have needed treatment and not been at risk of inadequate treatment?

Trevor Horsley was not injured by medical treatment, but by his employers' negligence in exposing him to asbestos. He was found to have contributed to his respiratory disability by having smoked heavily for thirty-five years, having received multiple warnings of the adverse effects it was having on his health.[142] Compare this case with *St George v Home Office*,[143] where the claimant was addicted to drink and drugs. On admission to prison he refused to see a doctor and was assigned to a ward in the hospital wing. He was allocated a top bunk and fell out of the bunk when he suffered a withdrawal seizure. He continued to fit for some time, developing a highly dangerous status epilepticus (status). He was transferred to an NHS hospital. As a result of his seizures he suffered permanent brain damage. The judge found that the fall triggered status, the cause of his brain damage. The defendants argued that the claimant's substance abuse contributed to his injury and damages should be proportionately reduced. Noting that this was a case on which there was no direct previous authority, the Court of Appeal agreed that the claimant was at fault. But both the judge and the appeal court held that the claimant's conduct in becoming an addict in his teens was too remote from the events in the prison that led to his fall and withdrawal seizures. It could not be said to be a cause of his negligent treatment by prison hospital staff. Counsel for the defendants had conceded that within the NHS a patient's smoking or drinking could not be invoked to hold him contributorily negligent if he suffered injury in the course of treatment related to those conditions. And it would be an odd result if doctors treating, say smokers, could say that their responsibility was less because the

---

[140]   See J Herring and C Foster, 'Blaming the Patient: Contributory Negligence and Medical Malpractice Litigation' (2009) *Professional Negligence 76*.

[141]   *Pidgeon v Doncaster Health Authority* [2002] Lloyd's Rep Med 130.

[142]   *Horsley v Cascade Insulation Services & Others* [2009] EWHC 2945 (QB), applying *Badger v The Ministry of Defence* [2005] EWHC 2941.

[143]   [2008] EWCA Civ 1068.

patient should never have needed their services. However, if a patient were to develop an illness as a result of medical negligence which is unrelated to the treatment – for example a patient with kidney disease is negligently given an overdose which damages his heart – and the injury is indivisible from that caused by, for example, poor weight management which the patient has been warned to address to avoid damage to his heart, it is possible that the claimant might be viewed contributorily negligent.

Private patients

7.21 A patient who pays for treatment enters into a contract with his doctor. They are free to set the terms of that contract, save that the doctor cannot exempt himself from liability for any injury to his patient arising from his negligence.[144] There is rarely a written contract between them. The terms will be implied from their relationship. This usually means that the doctor undertakes a duty of care to the patient. His duty of care to his private patient is usually indistinguishable from his duty in tort to his NHS patient.[145] The possibility remains of doctors agreeing to undertake a higher standard of care.

In private practice, could a doctor be found to have contracted to guarantee the desired result of treatment? This can never happen in the NHS. The doctor can only be liable in tort for a failure in care. Only rarely will a private doctor be found to have guaranteed a result in contract.[146] Where a patient is ill and seeks a cure, unless the doctor foolishly and expressly promises success in his treatment, no court will infer any term other than that the doctor will exercise skill and care. And, so far, claims by patients who have undergone private sterilisation have ultimately failed in attempts to argue that the surgeon guaranteed permanent sterility.[147]

Criminal liability

7.22 Negligence is normally a matter for the civil, not the criminal, law. However gross or culpable an act of negligence may be, negligence will not generally be a criminal offence in England, unless made so by an Act of Parliament, as in the case of careless driving. The picture changes if the victim dies. Gross negligence causing death can lead to a conviction for manslaughter. Much more than ordinary negligence, of the sort which would found a civil action for negligence, must be proved. In older cases, the negligence will be seen to derive from morally disgraceful conduct – a doctor operating while drunk or under the influence of drugs. In *R v Bateman*,[148] the Court of Appeal

---

[144] Unfair Contract Terms Act 1977, s 2.
[145] *Mary McGill v Royal Group of Hospitals* [2010] NIQB 10.
[146] See *Thompson v Sheffield Fertility Clinic* [2001] Westlaw.
[147] *Eyre v Measday* [1986] 1 All ER 488; *Thake v Maurice* [1986] 1 All ER 497, CA.
[148] (1925) 41 TLR 557.

overruled a conviction for manslaughter of a doctor whose ignorance and failure to send a woman to hospital resulted in his patient's death. The judge at the trial had failed to direct the jury properly. Criminal liability required more than the degree of negligence needed to establish civil liability. The doctor must be proved to have shown '. . . such disregard for the life and safety of others as to amount to a crime against the State and conduct deserving of punishment'.

There has been a rise in the number of doctors prosecuted for manslaughter, albeit ending, in many cases, in acquittal.[149] In *R v Prentice, R v Adomako and R v Holloway*,[150] the Court of Appeal considered two[151] appeals by doctors against conviction for manslaughter. In the first case, two junior doctors, Drs Prentice and Sulman, were convicted of manslaughter after they had wrongly injected a potent chemotherapeutic drug (vincristine) into the patient's spine, when it should have been administered intravenously. Their sixteen-year-old patient was suffering from leukaemia. Every month he received an intravenous injection of vincristine. Every other month he received a spinal injection of another powerful drug, methotextrate. The drug came down to the ward on the same trolley. Neither Dr Prentice nor Dr Sulman had ever administered such drugs before, and they were left unsupervised.

The second case involved a Dr Adomako. He was an anaesthetist. During surgery to re-attach a detached retina, Dr Adomako failed to notice, for over four minutes, that the tube administering oxygen to his patient had become disconnected. He neither noted the evidence before his eyes that the tube was no longer in place, nor did he respond to the alarm raised by the operating theatre's monitoring system. One prosecution expert described his standard of care as abysmal. The appeal court quashed the convictions of Drs Prentice and Sulman, but upheld Dr Adomako's conviction.

The Court of Appeal set the following test for gross negligence manslaughter.

(1) Did the doctor show obvious indifference to the risk of injury to his patient?
(2) Was he aware of the risk but nonetheless (for no good reason) decided to run the risk?
(3) Was an attempt to avoid a known risk so grossly negligent to deserve punishment?
(4) Was there a degree of inattention or failure to have regard to risk, going beyond mere inadvertence?

Only if at least one of these questions could be answered affirmatively should a doctor be convicted of manslaughter. In the case of Dr Prentice and Dr Sulman,

---

[149] See R Ferner and S McDowell, 'Doctors Charged with Manslaughter in the Courts of Medical Practice' (2006) 99 *Journal of RSM* 309; O Quick, 'Prosecuting "Gross" Medical Negligence: Manslaughter, Discretion and the Crown Prosecution Service' (2006) 33 *Journal of Law and Society* 421.
[150] [1993] 4 All ER 935, CA.
[151] The third appeal, *R v Holloway*, involved an electrician whose faulty wiring caused a death.

there was insufficient evidence of gross negligence deserving punishment. Dr Adomako, the Court of Appeal declared, failed to perform:

> ... his essential and in effect sole duty to see that his patient was breathing satis-
> factorily and to cope with the breathing emergency ... his failure was more than
> mere inadvertence and constituted gross negligence of the degree necessary for
> manslaughter.

Dr Adomako appealed to the House of Lords without success. His conviction was upheld.[152] The Law Lords offered no precise definition of 'medical man-slaughter'. Lord Mackay endorsed the trial judge's warning to the jury:[153]

> You should only convict a doctor of causing death by negligence if you think he
> did something which no reasonably skilled doctor would have done.

The lack of clarity about what degree of negligence constitutes 'gross' medical negligence was challenged in the Court of Appeal in *R v Misra and Srivistava*.[154] Drs Misra and Srivistava were convicted of manslaughter after a patient died because of a failure to treat a post-operative infection. The evidence established that, over a period of forty-eight hours, the doctors failed to act on information that their patient was critically ill. They did not chase up blood tests, and ignored warnings from nurses and another doctor. Part of the grounds for their appeal was that the ill-defined boundaries of gross negligence manslaughter contra-vened Article 7 of the Human Rights Convention. Article 7 requires that criminal offences must be defined in clear enough terms so that people are aware what constitutes criminal conduct. The appeal failed.[155] The Court of Appeal said that to be convicted of gross negligence manslaughter, the doctor must have failed to avert a risk of death. Other risks of lesser harm were not sufficient. Once a risk of death was established, it was for the jury to determine if the relevant negli-gence was gross. The citizen seeking to understand his potential criminal liability should be advised that, if he negligently breaches a duty of care, so as to endan-ger life, he may be convicted of manslaughter if a jury is satisfied that his negligence is gross. The appeal court judges acknowledged an element of circu-larity in their own arguments. The definition of what constitutes gross negligence remains vague and vulnerable to the subjective interpretations of juries.

When should doctors face criminal prosecution?[156] The increasingly common demand that doctors be punished for tragic mistakes causes anxiety within the

---

152 *R v Adomako* [1995] 1 AC 171, HL.
153 [1995] AC 171 at 188.
154 [2004] EWCA Crim 2375; note that subsequently the trust employing the two doc-tors was convicted of offences contravening health and safety legislation in respect of the same events: *R v Southampton University Hospitals NHS Trust* [2006] EWCA Crim 341.
155 Leave to appeal to the House of Lords was refused; *R v Misra* [2004] All ER (D).
156 See M Brazier and N Allen, 'Criminalising Medical Malpractice' in C Erin and S Ost (eds), *The Criminal Justice System and Health Care* (2007) OUP, p 15; M Brazier and A Alghrani, 'Fatal Medical Malpractice and Criminal Liability' (2009) 25 *Pro-fessional Negligence* 49.

profession. Some argue that only if there is evidence of indifference or total disregard for the patient's welfare should a doctor face criminal liability.[157] The civil law should compensate victims of mistakes. Incompetent doctors should be dealt with by the General Medical Council (GMC). Patients may lack trust in the GMC and perceive monetary compensation which comes from the NHS, not the doctor's pocket, as inadequate redress for the death of a relative. Doctors are not the only workers who risk prosecution for negligence doing their job. Train drivers and electricians, for example, meet the same fate.[158] In 2003, a teacher was jailed when his inadequate supervision of a school trip led to a child's death by drowning.[159] In all these cases, the crux of the difficulty is to determine when a fatal mistake is so bad that an otherwise law-abiding citizen deserves to be branded a criminal.

In considering the role of the criminal law in relation to medical error, it is important to reflect on the proper functions of the criminal law and its impact on doctors. If deterrence should be the primary concern, then we would need to be convinced that prosecuting doctors reduces levels of error. Or is there a risk that, fearing criminal liability, doctors might be less willing to acknowledge error? Merry and McCall Smith argue cogently that preventing error is preferable to retrospective punishment and that more thought needs to be given to learning from error, and the impact of blame.[160]

Wilful neglect

7.23   One of the anomalies of the operation of the criminal law in relation to medical malpractice is that a doctor normally only risks criminal liability if the patient dies. A doctor who is reckless as to his patient's welfare and causes serious injury short of death normally faces no risk of criminal redress. You may have read reports of investigations[161] into appalling care at some hospitals, recounting how patients were left to lie in filthy beds, dressing were not changed and patients not fed. The conduct of some staff would appear to be more morally culpable that some doctors convicted of manslaughter. Should such wilful neglect, such inhumane treatment be a criminal offence? Under the Mental Health[162] and Mental Capacity Acts,[163] wilful neglect of a mentally ill

---

[157] See A McCall Smith, 'Criminal Negligence and the Incompetent Doctor' (1993) 1 *Medical Law Review* 336.

[158] The fourth appellant in *R v Prentice, R v Adomako, R v Holloway* [1993] 4 All ER 935, CA, was an electrician whose faulty rewiring of a house resulted in the death of one of the residents.

[159] (2003) *Times*, 24 September.

[160] See A Merry and A McCall Smith, *Errors, Medicine and the Law* (2001) CUP.

[161] A shocking example is the Independent Inquiry into Care Provided by Mid Staffordshire NHS Foundation Trust, January 2005–March 2009, HC375-1.

[162] See Mental Health Act 1983, s 127.

[163] See Mental Capacity Act 2005, s 44.

or mentally incapacitated patient is a crime. Should wilful neglect of any NHS patient also be made criminal?[164]

Corporate manslaughter

7.24 Finally, we should consider how far responsibility for a dreadful medical mistake should focus more on institutions than individuals. Careful reading of virtually all the cases of accusations of medical manslaughter reveals a series of errors, many committed by people other than the doctors in the dock and compounded by inadequate systems to minimise opportunities for errors.[165] In *R v Prentice*, the two young doctors should have been supervised. The packaging of the two drugs should have given much clearer warnings about the consequences of wrongly administering vincristine. Should the hospital, rather than the doctors, have been on trial for corporate manslaughter?[166] Some of the difficulties in bringing such a prosecution may be eased by the Corporate Manslaughter and Homicide Act 2007. Section 1 of that Act provides that an NHS trust may face prosecution for corporate manslaughter if a patient dies as a result of a gross breach of a duty of care owed to the deceased, and 'the way in which its activities are managed or organised by its senior management is a substantial element in the breach'. Section 8 outlines some of factors that should be taken into account by the jury in determining whether a breach of duty was gross. The jury must consider if the evidence shows that the trust failed to comply with health and safety legislation. The jury may consider compliance with health and safety guidance and take into account 'attitudes, policies, systems or accepted practices' that were likely to have encouraged non-compliance with health and safety legislation. A trust convicted under the Act faces an unlimited fine and may be ordered to remedy the relevant breach and/or be subjected to a publicity order.[167] Any prosecution requires the consent of the Director of Public Prosecutions and at the time of writing no NHS organisation has faced a charge under the Act.[168] It will not be a panacea for all ills. Individual doctors may still face prosecution and a study of the cases shows that there may often be more than one organisation whose poor management contributes to a patient's death.[169]

---

[164] See A Alghrani, M Brazier, A M Farrell, D Griffiths and N Allen, 'Healthcare Scandals in the NHS' (2011), 34 *Journal of Medical Ethics* (230).

[165] See, in particular, the Professor B Toft, External Inquiry into the Adverse Incident that Occurred at Queen's Medical Centre, Nottingham (2001) DH.

[166] See M Childs, 'Medical Manslaughter and Corporate Liability' (1999) *Legal Studies* 316; N Allen, 'Medical or Managerial Manslaughter' in Erin and Ost, *The Criminal Justice System and Health Care* (2007), p 49.

[167] Corporate Manslaughter and Homicide Act 2007, ss 8 and 9.

[168] The first prosecution under the Act was *R v Eaton & Cotswold Geotechnical Holdings Limited* (2011) (unreported at the time of writing). See http://www.cps.gov.uk/news/press_releases/107_11/.

[169] See the case of Dr Ubani addressed in Brazier and Alghrani, *Professional Negligence* (2009) 49.

Chapter 8

MALPRACTICE LITIGATION[1]

8.1 In 2009/10, the National Health Service Litigation Authority (NHSLA)[2] received 6,652 claims for clinical negligence, a rise of 564 from the previous year. We have addressed the principles governing liability for clinical negligence. Formidable practical problems confront the patient. How can she fund a lawsuit? Whom should she sue? How quickly must she act? How do you prove negligence? What level of compensation is available? Is it worth it? There have been radical changes in the process of litigation, and more are on the way. The government has proposed that legal aid should be withdrawn for most clinical negligence claims.[3] Further reforms of the systems for costs in civil litigation have been proposed by Lord Justice Jackson,[4] and the government is consulting about implementation of the Jackson proposals.[5] We cannot predict the effect of cumulative reform on clinical negligence claims or exactly what shape those reforms will take. However, it is highly likely that seeking compensation for clinical negligence will become much more difficult and numbers of claims will fall. Finally, the radical reforms of the NHS itself promised in the Health and Social Care Bill (discussed in chapter 1) will also have an impact on litigation.

---

[1] For practical advice, see C J Lewis, *Clinical Negligence: A Practical Guide* (6th edn, 2006) Tottel Publishers. An extremely helpful, but not wholly impartial, account of the impact of malpractice litigation can be found in Chief Medical Officer, *Making Amends: A Consultation Paper Setting Out Proposals for Reforming the Approach to Clinical Negligence in the NHS* (2003) DH (hereafter CMO, *Making Amends*).

[2] See National Health Service Litigation Authority (NHSLA), *Factsheets 1–5* (2010). The NHSLA website is a rich source of information about clinical negligence claims against the NHS. See www.nhsla.com.

[3] Ministry of Justice, *Proposals for the Reform of Legal Aid in England and Wales,* Consultation Paper CP12/10, Cm 7967 (2010).

[4] Lord Justice Jackson, *Review of Civil Litigation Costs: Final Report* (2009) TSO and accessible at www.judiciary.gov.uk/publications-and-reports/reports/review-of-civil-litigation-costs/civil-litigation-costs-review-intro.

[5] Ministry of Justice, Proposals for the Reform of Litigation Funding and Costs in England and Wales, Consultation Paper CP 13/10, Cm 7947(2010).

We begin this chapter by examining the litigation process. Then we consider claims that lawsuits against doctors are damaging medicine. The spectre of the malpractice crisis is often invoked but is it a spectre with any substance?

Funding a lawsuit: public funding[6]

8.2   Few people are rich enough to meet the costs of clinical negligence claims out of their own income and savings. The majority of clinical negligence claims in the past were funded by legal aid. The success rate of such claims was low. The cost to the public purse of legal aid in personal injury claims rose rapidly. Unsurprisingly the government sought to find ways to reduce the legal aid bill. The Access to Justice Act 1999[7] removed legal aid from most personal injury claims but retained legal aid (renamed as public funding) for clinical negligence claims. In 2010, the Ministry of Justice opened a consultation proposing that public funding for most clinical negligence claims should be abolished. The Ministry of Justice took the view that most patient-claimants should be able to access alternative funding primarily via conditional fee agreements (CFAs) and so 'legal aid funding is not justified'.[8] Some limited legal aid might remain available for exceptional cases that might engage the UK's national obligations,[9] but simply because the case was one of great complexity and expense and so unlikely to secure a CFA would not of itself be enough to constitute an exception. As will be noted later, Lord Justice Jackson recommended the creation of a supplementary legal-aid scheme derived from a 'tax' on damages received by legally aided claimants and the government indicated that some clinical negligence claims might be assisted from that scheme.

Reforms in legal aid are likely to be introduced concurrently with the reform of costs more generally and CFAs in particular. Even now, when some public funding for clinical negligence claims remains available, obtaining 'legal aid' is no easy task.[10] Other proposed reforms of legal aid will make it even harder to obtain for any clinical negligence claims that escape the axe. Eligible claimants must meet a stringent means test; only adults with a very low income and minimal capital[11] will qualify. Even if the potential claimant passes the means test, her case must be strong on its merits. Children under eighteen[12] are assessed on their own, not their parents' income, so child-patients are still likely to qualify for legal aid. The state will only fund claims likely to succeed,

---

[6]   See Lewis, *Clinical Negligence: A Practical Guide* (2006), ch 3.
[7]   The Act also replaced the Legal Aid Board with the Legal Services Commission and established a Community Legal Service.
[8]   Ministry of Justice, *Proposals for the Reform of Legal Aid in England and Wales* (2010), para 4.165.
[9]   For example, cases raising issues of human rights.
[10]   See *The Funding Code* accessible from the Legal Services Commission website (www.legalservices.gov.uk/civil/guidance/funding_code.asp).
[11]   The proposed reforms will take the value of claimants' homes into account too.
[12]   Access to Justice Act 1999, s 7.

and will not usually fund a claim where damages of less than £5,000 are sought. Solicitors able to act for legally aided clients must be approved by the Legal Services Commission. Only firms who hold a franchise to do legally aided clinical negligence work can act. The franchise system has advantages for aggrieved patients. Clients can be assured that their case is in the hands of a solicitor judged competent to handle such cases. They are receiving specialist 'care'. However, the numbers of franchised solicitors may not meet demand. Lewis[13] expressed concern that fewer and fewer firms are undertaking this work. Patients may have to travel long distances, and not enough young solicitors are being trained to manage clinical negligence claims.

Conditional fee agreements

8.3 The government has made it clear that it sees conditional fee agreements (CFAs) as the primary source of future funding for clinical negligence claims but concurs with Lord Justice Jackson that CFAs need to undergo significant reform.[14] Under a CFA[15] the solicitor agrees to provide legal services on the basis that unless the claim is successful the client will pay nothing for her services. If the case is won, legislation allows the solicitor to charge up to twice the normal fee, up to a limit of 25 per cent of any damages recovered.[16] In practise, lawyers are not normally expected to take more than a 25 per cent uplift in their fees. Unsuccessful defendants may be required to meet that 'success fee'.[17] Conditional fees are often styled 'no-win no-fee' agreements. The major problems for clinical negligence claimants are two-fold. (1) Conditional fees involve risk to the lawyers. They will only take on claims if satisfied that the majority of the claims on their books will succeed. Otherwise, the firm will lose money. (2) The 'no-win no-fee' provision only covers the patient's own solicitors' costs. If the case fails, he becomes liable for the defendant hospital's, or doctor's, costs. These may be crippling. In most personal injury claims, claimants can buy insurance, after-the-event insurance (ATE), to cover them against the risk of liability for the defendants' costs, about £60k at least for anything other than a modest claim.[18] The complexity and expense of clinical negligence claims is such that insurers have been wary about entering this field. However, if the claimant wins her case, she can recover the cost of insurance premiums from the defendant, the losing party, providing the premium is set at a reasonable rate.[19]

Conditional fees must be distinguished from contingency fees, the system used to fund most claims in the USA. A contingency fee allows the claimant's law-

---

[13] See Lewis, *Clinical Negligence: A Practical Guide* (2006), p 35.
[14] Ministry of Justice, *Proposals for Reform of Civil Litigation Funding and Costs in England and Wales* (2010).
[15] Lewis, *Clinical Negligence: A Practical Guide* (2006), pp 41–49.
[16] Lewis, *Clinical Negligence: A Practical Guide* (2006), p 46.
[17] Lewis, *Clinical Negligence: A Practical Guide* (2006), p 46.
[18] Lewis, *Clinical Negligence: A Practical Guide* (2006), p 46.
[19] *Callery v Gray* [2001] EWCA Civ 1246; [2002] UKHL 28.

yers to take a proportion of the damages awarded (in some cases up to 50 per cent), but he can claim nothing if the action fails. Until Lord Justice Jackson's recent report, contingency fees had been ruled out in England. The Jackson Report makes a series of proposals to control the costs of all civil litigation and in a chapter dedicated to clinical negligence claims expresses especial concern about the impact of conditional fees on the costs to the NHS of malpractice litigation.[20] The cost of paying 'success fees' and ATE premiums has increased the costs for the NHS. Lord Justice Jackson stresses the importance of ensuring that 'the resources of the health service are not being squandered unnecessarily on litigation costs'.[21] Thus he recommended that claimants and their lawyers should no longer be able to recover 'success fees' or the cost of ATE premiums. He recommends an increase of 10 per cent in general damages to assist claimants with the financial impact of these changes. These proposals to reform CFAs have been warmly endorsed by the Ministry of Justice.[22] Lord Justice Jackson's radical proposal that contingency fees should be allowed, if renamed damages-based agreements (DBAs), has also met with a warm response from government.

The Jackson report also proposes that far more people should be encouraged to take out legal expenses insurance (also styled before-the-event (BTE) insurance), to cover them against the costs of claims in the future. Many household insurance policies offer this option. The government has as yet not taken a view on BTE insurance.[23] If legal aid is removed and CFAs become more difficult to obtain, the ability of some patients to recover compensation for a medical injury may be reduced. BTE insurance may well be an unaffordable luxury for many families.

Defending claims

8.4   Until 1990, the medical defence organisations, principally the Medical Defence Union and the Medical Protection Society, indemnified individual doctors against personal liability for clinical negligence. Each hospital, health authority, or other NHS organisation met its own costs. NHS Indemnity, introduced in 1990,[24] now provides that hospital trusts indemnify hospital doctors against liability; Trusts have taken over the cost of attending all claims

---

[20]   Lord Justice Jackson, *Review of Civil Litigation Costs: Final Report* (2009), TSO, ch 23.

[21]   Lord Justice Jackson, *Review of Civil Litigation Costs: Final Report* (2009), TSO, ch 23 at para 1.4.

[22]   Ministry of Justice, *Proposals for Reform of Civil Litigation Funding and Costs in England and Wales* (2010).

[23]   Ministry of Justice, *Proposals for Reform of Civil Litigation Funding and Costs in England and Wales* (2010), section 3.

[24]   HC (89) 34 'Claims of Medical Negligence Against NHS Hospitals and Community Doctors and Dentists'; as amended by HGG (96) 48; see M Brazier, 'NHS Indemnity: The Implications for Medical Litigation' (1990) 6 *Professional Negligence* 88; CMO, *Making Amends*, pp 53–55.

and the management of claims. The medical defence organisations continue to meet claims against GPs and claims arising in the private sector. The Medical Defence Union argues that the government should make clear that their proposed commissioning consortia (CC) will have a duty to ensure that the healthcare providers they commission have adequate indemnity arrangements in place – provisions which are currently absent from the Health and Social Care Bill 2011.[25]

In 1995, the Clinical Negligence Scheme for Trusts (CNST) was established.[26] NHS trusts could choose to join the CNST and it created a pooling arrangement to meet liabilities arising out of patient claims. 'Premiums' for trusts are worked out depending on the types of trust, the specialities offered, and their scale of operations. Membership of the CNST is voluntary, but as of 31 March 2005, all foundation trusts, NHS trusts and PCTs were members. Membership is conditional on Trusts complying with risk-management procedures prescribed by the CNST. It offers a mutual assurance system so that no individual trust risks devastation of its service because of a clutch of unfortunate losses in the courts. The reorganisation of the NHS heralded in the Health and Social Care Bill will bring about some consequential changes for the CNST.

The NHSLA [27] now administers the CNST.[28] Since April 2002, the NHSLA has dealt with all CNST claims regardless of value. The NHSLA is the driving force behind defence of claims against the NHS today. It exercises significant control over all claims, seeking to ensure swift resolution of indefensible claims and to minimise the cost to the NHS. Greater efficiency and uniformity should benefit patients as much as hospitals. The NHSLA plays an active role, not just in advising on defence of individual claims, but also in seeking to ensure that the whole litigation system is regularly kept under review. The medical defence organisations and NHS trusts were often accused of persisting in defending 'indefensible' cases. The NHSLA claims that it seeks to avoid litigation, encourage apologies and explanations, and settle appropriate claims swiftly.[29] Lawyers who act for claimants take a less rosy view of the NHSLA[30] and, as we will see, Lord Justice Jackson is critical of some of their practices. The government has launched an Industry Review to ensure that the NHSLA is run effectively and efficiently.[31]

---

[25] MDU, 'Health and Social Care Bill Needs to Specify Indemnity to Protect Patients' (Feb 2011) accessible at http://www.the-mdu.com.

[26] See CMO, *Making Amends,* p 55.

[27] See CMO, *Making Amends,* pp 55–57.

[28] For the first three years of its life, the CNST was administered by the Medical Protection Society. The NHSLA also runs the Existing Liabilities Scheme dealing with claims prior to April 1999.

[29] See NHSLA, *Report and Accounts 2010*, p 12. And see the Compensation Act 2006, s 2.

[30] See Lewis, *Clinical Negligence: A Practical Guide* (2006), pp 17–18.

[31] See DH, *Liberating the NHS: Report of the Arms Length Bodies Review* (2010).

Whom should the patient sue?

8.5   Once funding is assured, one of the first practical matters which the patient and his legal advisers must consider is whom they should sue. The legal doctrine of vicarious liability provides that when a person who is an employee commits a tort in the course of his employment, his employer is also responsible to the victim. The employer will often be better able to pay compensation than an individual employee. Let us look first at a claim by a patient who alleges that he suffered injury in the course of treatment as an NHS patient in an NHS hospital. If he can identify a particular individual as negligent he may, of course, proceed against him, be he consultant, anaesthetist, house officer, nurse, physiotherapist or hospital porter. However, he may also sue the person's employer, in the case of an NHS trust, or foundation hospital, the hospital itself. Where a hospital doctor is a defendant in the action, payment of any award of compensation made against her is guaranteed. NHS Indemnity ensures that any liability incurred by an NHS hospital doctor will be met by her employer. NHS trusts indemnify doctors directly, just as they have always done for nurses and other hospital employees. There is no practical need to bring a claim against the doctor personally. Patients who bring a claim based on the alleged negligence of a nurse rarely name the nurse personally as a defendant. Patients and their lawyers should ponder the wisdom of suing a doctor personally. As her employer will meet any award of compensation in full, there is little to gain from naming the doctor in the claim. However, suing a doctor individually may be designed not to obtain compensation, but to ensure accountability. As long as complaints and review procedures in health care are perceived by patients as inadequate, patients may go on using clinical negligence claims naming individuals as a means to ensure accountability.[32]

The employer to sue, as vicariously liable, in the case of NHS hospital treatment, will normally be the NHS trust, or foundation hospital. As privatisation creeps into the health service, this must be examined carefully. Take this example: an elderly, confused patient slips and falls on a highly polished floor. Who, if anyone, is responsible? The relevant negligence may be that a nurse failed to supervise the patient, or it may be that cleaners were careless. The nurse will be employed by the hospital. The cleaner may be the employee of a private contractor. If the patient can rely only on the doctrine of vicarious liability to make someone other than the individual nurse or cleaner liable, he may have difficulty in selecting the correct defendant. Hospital and contractor may each blame the other's employee.[33] What we now need to examine is the direct liability of the hospital to an NHS patient, what is often described as a non-delegable duty. First, the hospital will be liable for any failure of its own. A patient may suffer injury not because any particular doctor or nurse is careless, but because the system provided by the authority is inadequate. There may be insufficient med-

---

[32]   Membership of a defence organisation is no longer required of hospital doctors. Most doctors retain membership of such a body to ensure access to individual legal advice, which could be crucial if a doctor faced disciplinary or criminal proceedings.

[33]   Consider also the problem of agency nurses. They are not employed by the hospital.

ical staff to cope swiftly enough with injured patients admitted to the casualty ward. Lack of experienced staff on night duty may cause injury to a patient whose condition deteriorates rapidly, and whom the staff on duty cannot, with the best will in the world, treat sufficiently promptly. For such 'systems errors' an action will lie directly against the hospital.[34] The Court of Appeal has confirmed that hospitals have an 'organisational duty'. An NHS hospital must '. . . ensure that the hospital staff, facilities and organisation provided are those appropriate to provide a safe and satisfactory service for the patient'.[35]

Extending direct liability

8.6 May direct responsibility to NHS patients go further? When a patient is admitted for hospital treatment under the NHS, the NHS trust undertakes to provide him with reasonably careful, competent and skilled care. Should his treatment fall below that standard, the hospital is directly, not just vicariously, responsible to the patient.[36] So if an elderly patient falls on a slippery floor, and had proper care been taken that would not have happened, the hospital is liable. It matters not whether a nurse employed by the hospital or a cleaner employed by a contractor was the individual personally at fault. The hospital undertook to care for the patient. It failed and is directly liable. In *X (Minors) v Bedfordshire County Council*, Lord Browne-Wilkinson said this:[37]

> It is established that those conducting a hospital are under a direct duty of care to those admitted as patients to the hospital.

What of a patient offered a hip-replacement on the NHS whose operation is contracted out to a private hospital, or independent treatment centre? If her treatment is carried out negligently, can she sue the PCT, or if and when PCTs are abolished, the GP-led CC?[38] This could be important if, say, the private clinic goes bankrupt.

In *M v Calderdale Health Authority*,[39] M became pregnant and consulted an NHS doctor at an NHS community health centre. He arranged an abortion at a private hospital, but it was negligently performed and the woman went on to give birth to a baby boy. The health authority was found liable in negligence to M. Albeit no NHS employee was negligent, nor the health authority negli-

---

[34] See *Bull v Devon Area Health Authority* [1993] 4 Med LR 117, CA; *Robertson v East Kent Health Authority* [1999] Lloyd's Rep Med 123.

[35] *Child A v Ministry of Defence* [2004] EWCA Civ 641 at para 32.

[36] See *Cassidy v Ministry of Health* [1951] 2 KB 343, per Lord Denning at 359–360; and *Roe v Ministry of Health* [1954] 2 QB 66 at 82.

[37] [1995] 2 AC 633 at 740. And see *Miller v Greater Glasgow NHS Board* [2010] CSIH 40.

[38] See C Dyer, 'Health Bill will Destroy NHS, Says Union' (2011) 342 *BMJ* d701, recounting opposition from Unite, and the Medical Defence Union's call for the government to confirm whether CCs will bear liability to compensate patients.

[39] [1998] Lloyd's Rep Med 157.

gent in selecting the private clinic to which they contracted out abortions, they were in breach of a direct non-delegable duty to their patient. The judge summed up the position.[40]

> [M] never left the care of the first defendant. She was its patient. She never had an opportunity to divert from the route of treatment arranged on her behalf. In these circumstances she is entitled in my view to remain in the same position as a patient who remains in house relying upon the expectation of an effective provision of services.

M suggested that an NHS patient suffering injury in the private sector could sue the PCT (or CC) who contracted out her care, but it is only a decision of the county court and in *Child A v Ministry of Defence*[41] the Court of Appeal was dismissive of M, stating that the decision does '. . . not represent the current state of English law'.[42] Very briefly, Child A was born in 1998, in a German hospital while his father was serving with the British Army. Until 1996, the Ministry of Defence had run its own military hospitals in Germany. From 1996, the Ministry (via a complicated set of contracts) contracted out health care for service personnel and their families to German hospitals. A suffered brain damage in the course of his delivery. It was not disputed that his injuries were as a result of negligence. A could claim damages in Germany under German law, but his lawyers sought to sue in England and make the Ministry of Defence liable for A's injury, just as Calderdale Health Authority had been liable to M. The Court of Appeal found against him. The Ministry owed a duty to use reasonable care to provide access to suitable hospital care for service personnel and their families.[43] They had a responsibility (an organisational duty) to act reasonably to ensure care provided was on the basis of an adequate system, ie properly equipped hospitals were selected to provide care.[44] There was no 'duty to ensure that the treatment administered . . . is administered with reasonable care and skill'. There was no duty '. . . broken if one of the hospital staff, however competent, commits an isolated act of negligence in the treatment of the patient'. Such a duty (described in *A* as a non-delegable duty) would generally only lie 'in an environment over which the defendant is in control'.[45] An NHS trust hospital might well owe such a duty to all patients being treated in their hospital. The Ministry of Defence had no control over its German contractors. Does that mean that PCTs (or CCs) can similarly never be liable for treatment contracted out to the private sector? Not necessarily. Lord Phillips says that, even if PCTs did owe such a duty, it would not follow that a similar duty is incumbent on the Ministry of Defence.[46] And Department of Health Guidance expressly suggests that PCTs sending patients abroad for treatment owe those patients a duty of care that cannot be delegated.[47]

---

[40]   [1998] Lloyd's Rep Med 161.
[41]   [2004] EWCA Civ 641, CA.
[42]   [2004] EWCA Civ 641 at 52, CA.
[43]   [2004] EWCA Civ 641 at 32, CA.
[44]   [2004] EWCA Civ 641 at 32, CA.
[45]   [2004] EWCA Civ 641 at 47, CA.
[46]   [2004] EWCA Civ 641 at 54, CA.
[47]   DH, *Treating More Patients and Extending Choice: Overseas Treatment for NHS Patients* (2002).

One of us sought to argue elsewhere that PCTs should owe a direct non-delegable duty to those patients for whose care they are responsible.[48] The judgment of the Court of Appeal in *Farraj v King's Healthcare NHS Trust*[49] must, however, be considered and indicates an unwillingness to extend the limits of direct liability. Mrs Farraj knew that she and her husband carried the gene that can cause beta thallassaemia major (BTM), a serious blood disorder. The couple were in the care of an obstetrician in Jordan and a chorionic villus sample was taken from Mrs Farraj and sent for testing at the defendant hospital to determine if the foetus was affected by BTM. The hospital found that the sample was not suitable for DNA testing in its own laboratory and sent it on to an independent specialist cytogenetics laboratory, CSL. CSL were held negligent in wrongly stating that the foetus was not affected by BTM. The issue that concerns us here is could KCH (King's College Hospital) be held liable for the negligence of CSL on the grounds that they owed a non-delegable duty to the claimants. The Court of Appeal issued a decided 'no' to that question. Dyson LJ was prepared to assume that hospitals owe such a duty to the patient it treats regardless of the employment status of the staff delivering treatment.[50] But he could see no reason in this case to depart from the usual rule that a defendant can discharge his duty of care by delegating a task to a suitably competent independent contractor. Mrs Farraj was not being treated by KCH, but by a hospital in Jordan. KCH undertook no special duty to her. *Farraj* leaves open the question of whether an NHS patient who undergoes tests organised by the NHS hospital treating her could argue that the hospital owed her a non-delegable duty in respect of tests contracted out to independent laboratories. Dyson LJ only assumed and does not decide that hospitals do owe a direct duty to patients encompassing all aspects of their care and the tenor of his judgment is not favourable to an extension of direct liability.

Private patients

8.7   A private patient, who engages a private bed in an NHS hospital, contracts individually with the surgeon and anaesthetist for the surgery and the administration of the anaesthetic, and he contracts separately with the hospital trust for nursing and ancillary care. Even if the surgeon and the anaesthetist are employed by the trust when caring for NHS patients, when they act for a private patient they are acting on their own behalf, and not in the course of their NHS employment. If an error by surgeon or anaesthetist causes the patient injury, he can sue only the responsible individual. If the carelessness is that of nursing or other medical staff employed by the trust, he may sue the trust. As we shall see, this may cause problems of proof of negligence. Identifying who was the responsible individual may be nigh on

---

48   M Brazier, J Beswick, 'Who's Caring For Me?' (2006) 7 *Medical Law International* 183.
49   [2009] EWCA Civ 1203.
50   [2009] EWCA Civ 1202 at 88.

impossible, leaving surgeon and hospital to blame each other, and the patient to go uncompensated.

A patient entering a private hospital needs to consider the nature and scope of his contract. The usual arrangement is similar to that entered into by a private patient taking a private bed within the NHS. The patient engages his own surgeon and anaesthetist, who will not be employees of the private hospital. The hospital contracts to provide other medical and nursing care. Like the private patient within the NHS, the patient must proceed against the surgeon for any error of his, and against the hospital for any error by their staff. Some private hospitals and clinics will contract to provide a whole 'package' of care and treatment. When the hospital undertakes to provide total care – the operation, anaesthetic, post-operative care, etc, – then it is liable for any failure to meet the required standard of care. They are in breach of contract.[51] It is irrelevant that the surgeon, anaesthetist, or anyone else is not an employee of the hospital. The hospital is not vicariously liable for any fault of a particular person. It is directly responsible for its own breach of contract.

General practitioners

8.8 What of claims against GPs? First of all, most GPs are not employees of the NHS. A claim relating to negligence by a GP operating a single-doctor practice lies usually against that GP alone.[52] Where a GP is a member of a partnership, his partners may be sued as jointly responsible for any negligence. If it is not the doctor himself who is at fault, but a receptionist or nurse employed by the practice, the GP and his partners are vicariously liable as employers. If a receptionist refuses to allow a home visit, or refuses to allow the patient to speak to a doctor, or fails to pass any information on to the doctor, with the result that a seriously ill patient becomes sicker or even dies, the doctor, while she may be personally blameless, will be vicariously at fault and liable to the patient or his family.

When must proceedings be started?[53]

8.9 A patient contemplating an action for clinical negligence must act relatively promptly. The general rule is that all actions for personal injuries must be brought within three years of the infliction of the relevant injury. This is

---

[51] Note the Supply of Goods and Service Act 1982, s 13 (implied term that service will be carried out with care and skill); and Pt I of that Act imposing conditions as to goods supplied in the course of a contract for services; see A P Bell, 'The Doctor and the Supply of Goods and Service Act 1982' (1984) 4 *Legal Studies* 175.

[52] But a PCT might be liable if they should have known and acted on information that a GP was not providing appropriate care; see *Godden v Kent & Medway Strategic Health Authority* [2004] Lloyd's Rep Med 521.

[53] See Lewis, *Clinical Negligence: A Practical Guide* (2006), ch 26.

known as the limitation period and is laid down in the Limitation Act 1980. A claim form must be served no later than three years from the date of the alleged negligence. But sections 11 and 14 of the 1980 Act provide that where the patient originally either: (1) was unaware that he had suffered significant injury;[54] or (2) did not know about the negligence which could have caused his injury, the three-year period begins to run only from the time when he did discover, or reasonably should have discovered, the relevant facts. Where the patient knew all the relevant facts, but was ignorant of his legal remedy, the three-year limitation period runs from the time when he was, or should have been, aware of the facts.

All is not quite lost for the patient who delays beyond three years, or who is ignorant of the law. Section 33[55] of the 1980 Act gives the judge discretion to override the three-year limitation period where, in all the circumstances, it is fair to all parties to do so. The courts will examine the effect of allowing the action to go forward on both parties, taking into account, among other things, the effect of delay on the cogency of the evidence, the conduct of the parties, and the advice sought by, and given to, the patient by his lawyers and medical advisers.[56]

One further aspect of the rules on limitation must be noted. Where the injured patient is under a legal disability at the time he suffers injury, that is to say, he is under age (under eighteen) or lacks mental capacity, the limitation period does not begin to run until he reaches the age of majority, or ceases to lack mental capacity. This means that, for example, a baby might be injured at birth and the obstetrician could face an action in respect of the injury up to twenty-one years after the event. Until 1990, legal aid rules provided that if parents claimed earlier on their child's behalf, their income would be taken into account in assessing their child's eligibility for legal aid. Now that the child's income alone (if any) is relevant, parents no longer face a financial deterrent to taking action at the earliest possible stage, but, as we have seen, in many cases legal aid will simply cease to be available for medical negligence claims.

Civil justice reform: the Woolf Report

8.10 Cost, complexity and delay bedevilled, not just clinical negligence claims, but all actions for compensation in the latter part of the twentieth century. The civil justice system was perceived as inadequate. One of England's most senior judges, Lord Woolf, was commissioned to conduct a comprehensive review of the civil justice system and to recommend radical reform. He issued his Final Report in 1996.[57] Lord Woolf set out a number of admirable objectives for the

---

54 For example, he did not know for some years that he had been given blood infected by CJD; *N v UK Medical Research Council* [1996] BMLR 83.
55 See *Godfrey v Gloucestershire Royal Infirmary NHS Trust* [2003] EWHC 549.
56 See, for example, *Smith v Leicestershire Health Authority* (1996) 36 BMLR 23.
57 *Access to Justice: Final Report to the Lord Chancellor on the Civil Justice System in England and Wales* (1996) HMSO. See CMO, *Making Amends*, pp 86–87.

civil justice system. It should be just in its results, and the operation of the system should be fair to all parties. Costs should be proportionate to the nature of the case. Claims must be dealt with reasonably swiftly. The process should be understandable to everyone using it, including any litigant who chooses not to engage a lawyer, but to sue in person. The system should be responsive to the needs of litigants. There should be certainty in the way the process works. Civil justice should be adequately resourced and reasonably funded.

Four features of the Woolf reforms are central to malpractice litigation:

(1) The *Pre-Action Protocol for the Resolution of Clinical Disputes* (the *Clinical Negligence Protocol*) sought to find less adversarial and more cost-effective ways of resolving disputes about health care.

(2) In April 1999, the Civil Procedure Rules 1998[58] came into force. These Rules introduced a unified set of procedures for claims regardless of whether a claim is heard in the county court or the High Court.

(3) Integral to the Rules is the concept of case-management. Judges are given infinitely greater powers to manage cases.

(4) The rules governing expert witnesses are altered, seeking to limit the misuse of expert evidence.

The implementation of the Woolf reforms has not resulted in total success. Research commissioned by the Ministry of Justice suggests that delay is less of a problem, with cases taking less time between issuing a claim and trial or settlement.[59] But costs have risen[60] and thus, as we have seen, Lord Justice Jackson was asked to conduct a further review of civil litigation costs.

The Clinical Negligence Protocol

8.11 The Protocol set out 'ground rules' for handling disputes at their 'early stages'. It sought to encourage a greater climate of openness, to provide guidance how this more open culture can be achieved, and recommend a timed sequence of events when disputes do arise. Unfortunately the Jackson Report found that the Protocol was not working well to ensure early settlement in appropriate cases and this was contributing to an escalation of costs.

The Protocol aims to maintain or restore the relationship between the aggrieved patient and healthcare professionals and providers, and to resolve as many disputes as possible without litigation. Communication between the parties lies at the heart of the Protocol. Cases should be investigated swiftly, and records volunteered to the claimant for a reasonable period of time. Full consideration

---

[58] Civil Procedure Rules 1998, SI 1998/3132.

[59] Department of Constitutional Affairs, *Civil Justice Reform Evaluation: Further Findings: A Continuing Evaluation of the Civil Justice Reforms* (2002).

[60] J Peysner, M Severatne, *The Management of Civil Cases: The Court and the Post-Woolf Landscape* (2005) Department for Constitutional Affairs.

needs to be given to early settlement and, whether, if agreement between the parties cannot be reached, resort might be had to mediation or some other form of alternative dispute resolution.[61] The Protocol promotes a 'cards on the table' approach. Ideally, when a patient believes that she has a case in clinical negligence, within a matter of months she will be able to judge whether her belief is well founded. The defendant doctor or hospital will be in a position to settle any sustainable claim quickly. Means other than litigation of resolving genuine disputes will be reviewed. Only the truly intractable case should go to court, but more cases still seem to end in court and settlements take too long.

The Protocol focuses on pre-action events, before any claim form is issued and formal litigation begins. Requests for health records should be met within forty days at a cost no greater than if the patient requested her records under the Data Protection Act 1998. The request must provide sufficient information for the doctor or hospital to know if the injury of which the patient complains is serious and has serious consequences, and the request must be as specific as possible about which records are required. Just as the potential defendant must not keep the claimant in the dark, so the Protocol also aims to ensure that claimants and their lawyers are open and frank and do not set traps for unwary defendants. Where appropriate, on receipt of a request for records, the hospital should start to investigate the case fully.

A patient who is considering initiating litigation should send a letter of claim identifying any alleged negligence, her injuries, and any consequential financial losses. The letter or claim must identify relevant documents and give sufficient information to enable the defendant to commence investigations and evaluate the claim. The patient may choose to include an offer to settle the case, stating his valuation of what would constitute satisfactory compensation. No formal legal proceedings should be issued until three months after the letter of claim. The potential defendant must acknowledge the letter of claim within fourteen days, and within three months must provide a reasoned answer.[62] That letter of response must make it clear if the claim or part of the claim is admitted, and if admissions are binding. If the claim is denied, specific answers must be given to the patient's allegations. If additional documents are relied on, they must be disclosed. Where the patient made an offer to settle, the doctor or hospital must respond to that offer.

The Jackson Report[63] criticises three aspects of the Protocol for adding to costs in this context:

(1) There is no effective control over the costs that claimant lawyers can run up before the letter of claim or between that date and starting proceedings.

(2) There is no provision for the defendant to settle without admitting liability. Lord Justice Jackson proposes that the Protocol should be amended to accommodate this option.

---

[61] See CMO, *Making Amends,* pp 95–96.
[62] And should then notify the NHSLA.
[63] Lord Justice Jackson, *Review of Civil Litigation Costs; Final Report* (2009) TSO.

(3) Three months may be inadequate to allow the defendant to investigate the claim leading to unnecessary proceedings. The period should be extended to four months.

If the Protocol worked as Lord Woolf envisaged, patients should have no incentive to rush into litigation and both sides have every incentive to work together and not to engage in trial by battle. Lord Justice Jackson found that in too many cases this did not happen. His report is critical of the NHSLA as well as of claimants' lawyers. If parties do not cooperate and comply with the Protocol, breaches of the Protocol can result in sanctions against the parties and their solicitors. Parties may be refused extension of time to serve claim forms, or take various other steps in litigation, ie they will not be allowed to delay proceedings. Costs may be disallowed for unnecessary proceedings, eg if a patient rushes off to start formal proceedings before the three-month period has elapsed and before receiving a response from the defendants. Opinions vary on how effective sanctions have been.[64] Lord Justice Jackson recommends a tougher approach. His proposals include the following changes. Financial penalties should be imposed on any heath authority that fails, without good reason, to disclose records as required by the Protocol. The NHSLA, the Medical Defence Union, the Medical Protection Society and other organisations who act for defendants should nominate a senior officer to whom claimant lawyers could report egregious failures to produce records. The NHSLA should obtain independent expert advice before denying liability, save in relation to patently frivolous claims.

Compulsory disclosure of records

8.12 If the Protocol works, there should be no need for compulsory disclosure of records. Alas, this is not always the case. The patient seeking to compel disclosure of records will rely on section 33[65] of the Supreme Act 1981. She can apply for a court order requiring the doctor or hospital whom she plans to sue to disclose any records or notes likely to be relevant in forthcoming proceedings. Section 34[66] goes further. The court may order a person not a party to proceedings to produce relevant documents. So if the patient has started proceedings against a GP, or a private medical practitioner, but believes that the hospital or clinic holds notes of value to his claim, the hospital or clinic can be made to hand over the notes. This will help the private patient in a dilemma of whether he should properly proceed against doctor or hospital. It may also lead to the clinic being brought into the proceedings.

Three important matters on disclosure need a mention. First, the intention to bring proceedings and the likelihood that they will go ahead must be real

---

[64] See M A Shaw, 'Pre-Action Protocol for the Resolution of Clinical Disputes' [1999] *New Law Journal* 252.
[65] And see Civil Procedure Rules 1998, SI 1998/3132, r 31.16.
[66] And see Civil Procedure Rules 1998, SI 1998 /3132, r 31.7.

before the court will order disclosure. The patient must have some solid ground for thinking he has a claim. He cannot use an application for disclosure as a 'fishing expedition' on the off-chance that some evidence of negligence will come to light.[67] Resort to compulsory disclosure ought to be rare. Relevant documents should have been volunteered under the Protocol. Other avenues to discover records and information may also be pursued. A patient may always apply to see his records under the Data Protection Act 1998.[68] Or he may use the complaints procedure to explore whether he has any legal entitlement to pursue a compensation claim.[69]

Second, will the patient be able to see notes of any inquiry ordered by the hospital into his misadventure? The position is complex. If the inquiry was held mainly to provide the basis of information on which legal advice about the authority's legal liability is based, the records are protected by legal professional privilege. If the dominant purpose of the inquiry was otherwise, for example, to improve hospital procedures or to provide the basis of disciplinary proceedings against staff, then the patient may be allowed access to the notes of the inquiry.[70] That is the legal position. The Court of Appeal has expressed its disquiet about the effect such claims of legal professional privilege may have on the patient's claim. Claims of privilege can be used to frustrate the patient's attempt to find out what happened, what went wrong. In *Lee v South West Thames Regional Health Authority*,[71] a little boy, Marlon Lee, suffered a severe scald at home but he should have recovered completely. He was taken to a hospital run by health authority A and then transferred to a burns unit controlled by health authority B. The next day he developed breathing problems, was put on a respirator, and still on the respirator was sent back to A in an ambulance provided by health authority C, the South West Thames Regional Health Authority. When, three days later, the boy was taken off the respirator, he was found to have suffered severe brain damage, probably due to lack of oxygen. In her attempts to find out what went wrong, the child's mother sought disclosure of records and notes on her son prepared by staff of all three authorities. Health authority A asked South West Thames Regional Health Authority to obtain a report from their ambulance crew. South West Thames Regional Health Authority complied and forwarded the report to A. It was this report which the plaintiffs went to court to obtain access to. South West Thames Regional Health Authority had revealed its existence, but refused to hand it over to the family. They claimed it had been prepared in contemplation of litigation, and to enable legal advice to be given in connection with that litigation. So it had, but it had been prepared on the request of health authority A to obtain advice as to A's liability to the child. Reluctantly, the Court of Appeal held that the privilege attaching to the document was enjoyed by health authority A. South West Thames could not be ordered to disclose the

67 *Dunning v Liverpool Hospitals' Board of Governors* [1973] 2 All ER 454.
68 See above ch 4.
69 See below ch 9.
70 *Waugh v BRB* [1980] AC 521.
71 *Lee v South West Thames Regional Health Authority* [1985] 2 All ER 385.

report. Even had they been prepared to do so, they could not have handed over the report without A's agreement. The principle was that defendants or potential defendants should be '. . . free to seek evidence without being obliged to disclose the result of his researches to his opponent'. So a child was damaged for life in circumstances pointing to negligence on someone's part, and the law was powerless to help his mother find out what exactly caused his brain damage. The Court of Appeal expressed their disquiet and called for reform of the law. Within the doctor/patient relationship, Sir John Donaldson MR said there was a duty to answer questions put, before treatment was agreed to. Why should the duty to be frank with the patient be different once treatment was completed? In 1987,[72] he again emphasised the importance he placed on what he termed a duty of candour.

Third, the court retains the power to refuse to order disclosure where to do so would be injurious to the public interest.[73] This is unlikely to be the case where what is asked for is the patient's own medical notes. An attempt by the Secretary of State for Health to plead public interest immunity to avoid disclosure of records in the actions brought by several haemophiliac patients who had contracted HIV from contaminated blood products failed.[74]

Going to court: case-management

8.13   If attempts to resolve the claim fail, and the patient starts formal proceedings, the conduct of the case will be strictly controlled with an emphasis on enforcing time-limits and keeping costs down. The claim will be allocated to a *track*. A clinical negligence claim worth less than £1,000 would theoretically be allocated to the *small claims track*. Most such claims ought never to result in proceedings, but rather be resolved within complaints procedures. Claims worth between £1,000 and £15,000 are allocated to the *fast track*. This means that the case should be resolved within thirty weeks. The actual hearing should take one day or less and oral expert evidence is limited. Claims worth more than £15,000, or where the issues are especially complex, go onto the *multi-track*. Judges control the allocation process. Most clinical negligence claims will be multi-track. At every point, opportunities to resolve the case without further proceedings must be seized. Time-wasting and unnecessary manoeuvres by lawyers will be penalised.

Proving negligence: the role of the expert[75]

8.14   We come now to the heart of the problem. How does the patient prove negligence? How does the claimant discharge the onus of proof laid on him?

---

[72]   *Naylor v Preston Area Health Authority* [1987] 2 All ER 353.
[73]   Supreme Court Act 1981, s 35.
[74]   *Re HIV Haemophilia Litigation* (1990) 41 BMLR 171, CA.
[75]   See Lewis, *Clinical Negligence: A Practical Guide* (2006), ch 9.

He will be heavily reliant on expert testimony. He will need to put forward medical evidence to demonstrate: (1) that there was negligence on the part of the defendant, or a person for whom the defendant was responsible; and (2) that the relevant negligence caused the harm of which he complains. Obtaining expert evidence used to be a nightmare for patients. Doctors were unhappy about voicing public criticism of a colleague. Doctors in the same hospital may remain unwilling to testify against each other. However, greater openness does mean that today most patients should be able to obtain medical expert advice fairly locally. Before looking further at the rules governing medical expert witnesses, we should distinguish between 'expert' and 'professional' witnesses. The expert witness testifies as to his expert opinion on the facts of the case referred to him, a case that he will not have been involved in personally. The professional witness gives evidence about what occurred in the series of events that led to harm to the claimant on the basis of what he saw and heard.[76]

Until the Civil Procedure Rules came into force, unrestricted freedom for each side to call its own experts sometimes made a mockery of justice.[77] The Civil Procedure Rules are explicit and emphatic, the expert's primary duty is owed to the court to assist the court in matters involving his expertise, and this duty to the court '. . . overrides any obligation to the person from whom instructions were received or by whom the expert is paid'.[78] The Civil Procedure Rules also impose limits on the use of expert evidence. Expert testimony must be restricted to what is reasonably required to resolve the case.[79] The court has power to direct the appointment of a single joint expert rather than each party choosing their own experts.[80] Obviously if a single expert is to be appointed, it makes sense for the parties themselves to agree on such an expert. Lord Woolf saw no reason why, in a straightforward clinical negligence claim up to a value of £10,000, parties should not be able to agree on a single expert. Such cases may necessarily not be all that common. They are likely to be limited to cases where there is no substantial medical dispute about causation or prognosis, and perhaps all that is in issue is the appropriate measure of compensation. Many clinical negligence cases will involve disputes about whether there was negligence at all, whether the negligence caused the injuries of which the claimant complains, and what the likely prognosis for the claimant will be. Such issues may well require separate experts. Imagine a claim that a child was brain-damaged allegedly because of a mismanaged delivery. Obstetric evidence will be needed to establish if the obstetrician was negligent. Neurologists may have to be called to testify to the likely cause of the brain damage. Paediatricians and rehabilitation experts will be required to assess how the child can best be cared for into adulthood. Multiple experts may be unavoidable. Nonetheless, control of proliferation of expert evidence will be asserted by the

---

[76] The line may sometimes be blurred. See *ES v Chesterfield North Derbyshire Royal Hospital NHS Trust* [2003] EWCA Civ 1284 at para 10.

[77] See, for example, *Whitehouse v Jordan* [1981] 1 All ER 287, HL.

[78] Civil Procedure Rules 1998, SI 1998/3132, r 35(3).

[79] Civil Procedure Rules 1998, SI 1998/3132, r 35(1).

[80] Civil Procedure Rules 1998, SI 1998/3132, r 35(7).

court. Where practical, a single joint expert must be agreed in relation to any particular issue. So if there is a real and substantive dispute about whether the obstetrician was negligent, each party will probably be allowed to call its own obstetric expert, but, save in the most exceptional case, not more than one expert each. If there is no especial complexity about causation, a single expert should be agreed to address that issue. As much of the expert evidence as possible should be in writing. Oral testimony is allowable only with the permission of the court.

Where there are multiple experts, all letters, documents and instructions must be disclosed to the experts and there must be mutual disclosure of all experts' reports. Experts' meetings are encouraged. The hope may be that at such a meeting, the experts will resolve the differences between them and promote resolution of the case without proceeding to a hearing. Initially it was envisaged that experts would meet alone and conduct a quasi-scientific seminar. Lawyers and their clients were uncomfortable with such a process which could be seen as surrendering the judicial process to the doctors. Additionally, the objective of resolving proceedings more speedily might well be frustrated. The parties would not accept the experts' conclusions as binding. Consequently it is now agreed that the parties' lawyer may be present at experts' meetings.

Increasingly, questions are being asked about the expertise of experts. In a number of criminal and family law cases the accuracy and even integrity of some experts were challenged. The GMC brought disciplinary proceedings against a very senior paediatrician, Sir Roy Meadow, and found him guilty of serious professional misconduct. He challenged the finding and his erasure from the register. The Court of Appeal ultimately struck down the finding of serious misconduct but held that expert witnesses have no immunity from disciplinary proceedings when giving expert testimony.[81] This and other cases have caused great controversy[82] and the need for better training and accreditation of experts is widely agreed on. The GMC has now offered doctors guidance on giving expert evidence.[83]

May the burden of proof shift to the doctor?

8.15 While in the majority of cases the patient must prove negligence and the doctor is not called on to prove her 'innocence', are there ever occasions when that burden shifts to the doctor? There is a general rule of the law of negligence that where the defendant is in complete control of the relevant events, and an accident happens which does not ordinarily happen if proper care is

---

[81] *GMC v Meadow* [2006] EWCA 1390. And see S Devaney, 'The Loneliness of the Expert Witness' (2007) 15 *Medical Law Review* 116.

[82] See C Williams, 'The Trouble with Paediatricians' (2010) 18 *Medical Law Review* 389.

[83] GMC, *Acting As An Expert Witness* (2008).

taken, then the accident itself affords reasonable evidence of negligence. The defendant will be held liable unless he can advance an explanation of the accident consistent with the exercise of proper care. This rule is known as *res ipsa loquitur* (the thing speaks for itself).[84] *Res ipsa loquitur* can be applied in clinical negligence cases, but the courts have sometimes seemed reluctant to do so. At first, it was argued that *res ipsa loquitur* applied only where everyone of reasonable intelligence would know that that sort of accident did not ordinarily happen without negligence. As most people are not medically qualified, how could they know whether the accident to the patient was one which could, or could not, happen, if proper care was taken? The Court of Appeal said that expert medical evidence was admissible to establish what should and should not occur if ordinary care was exercised.[85] *Res ipsa* proved to be a boon in the following kind of case. Sometimes, after an abdominal operation, a swab, or even a pair of forceps, is discovered in the patient's body. Without evidence of a quite exceptional nature, it is clear that someone has been careless. *Res ipsa* may also help the NHS patient who has undoubtedly suffered because someone was negligent, either in the theatre, or in the course of postoperative care, but she cannot identify that someone. If every member of the staff who might be responsible is employed by the hospital, then an inference of negligence is raised against the hospital, who are necessarily vicariously liable for whoever may be the culprit.[86] So in *Cassidy v Ministry of Health*,[87] a patient was operated on for Dupuytren's contraction affecting two of his fingers. After the operation, the patient's hand and lower arm had to be kept rigid in a splint for up to fourteen days. When the splints were removed, the plaintiff's whole hand was paralysed. Upon finding that all the staff involved in Mr Cassidy's care were NHS employees, the court held that there was evidence of negligence against their common employer. The onus shifted to the hospital to explain how this disaster might have struck without any of its employees being negligent.

Beyond this kind of obvious bungling, *res ipsa* has limited use in clinical negligence claims. In many operations, the source of greatest danger for the patient lies not in the surgery itself, but in the anaesthetic. An anaesthetic mishap will not usually be of itself evidence of negligence, although *res ipsa* was applied in *Saunders v Leeds Western Health Authority*.[88] The patient was a four-year-old girl in otherwise perfect health who was undergoing surgery to correct a congenitally displaced hip. She suffered a cardiac arrest and consequent brain damage. Mann J said:

> It is plain from evidence called on her [the child's] behalf that the heart of a fit child does not arrest under anaesthesia if proper care is taken in the anaesthetic and surgical processes.

---

[84] See J Murphy (ed), *Street on Torts* (12th edn, 2007) OUP, pp 127–133.
[85] *Mahon v Osborne* [1939] 2 KB 14.
[86] *Roe v Ministry of Health* [1954] 2 QB 66.
[87] [1951] 2 KB 343.
[88] (1985) 82 *Law Society Gazette* 1491.

The Court of Appeal[89] has, however, made it clear that *res ipsa* will rarely be applicable in such cases and criticises the phrase itself. It can arise only when either what happened simply cannot normally happen without negligence (for example, the patient went into theatre for surgery on his left foot and comes out with unnecessary surgery having been performed on the right foot) or where expert evidence agrees, that without negligence, such an adverse outcome is highly unlikely. An unexpected outcome in itself will not raise any inference of negligence. More recent cases seek to avoid the very language of *res ipsa*, with judges preferring to take a common sense view of the facts and how far the facts call for an explanation from the defendants as to any apparent failure in the patient's care. So in *Richards v Swansea* NHS *Trust*[90] the court held that the length of the delay in moving to carry out a Caesarean section required some explanation as to why the surgery was not performed more expeditiously and when no such evidence was forthcoming, the judge held that the claimant had established the breach of a duty of care. Mason and Laurie[91] suggest that *res ipsa* as a phrase should be consigned to history and we should rather refer to a prima facie case.

Even in cases of obvious negligence, such as the forceps left in the abdomen, where the facts give rise to an inference of negligence, problems surface if one of the staff caring for the patient is not an employee of the hospital. For example, the theatre sister may be an agency nurse. Can the hospital say, 'No inference of negligence is raised against *us* because the negligent actor may well have been that nurse for whom we are not responsible'? Once again it depends on whether the hospital's liability is solely vicarious, or whether the hospital is (as we argued earlier) directly liable for any failure to measure up to the required standard of skill and care. If the hospital is directly liable, it matters not to the patient who actually employs the negligent individual. The private patient may be less fortunate. Whether he enters an NHS, or a private hospital, he will usually contract separately with the surgeon and the anaesthetist for surgery and anaesthetic. The surgeon and the anaesthetist will not be acting as employees of the hospital. If something goes wrong in the operating theatre or post-operatively and it is not clear who is to blame, *res ipsa* probably cannot be invoked. The hospital is not liable for any negligence on the part of the surgeon or anaesthetist. The patient can raise an inference of negligence against the hospital only if he can trace the relevant negligence to one of their staff. He can raise an inference of negligence against the surgeon or anaesthetist only if he can pin the relevant act on one of them personally.

If the surgeon, anaesthetist and hospital are all sued, none of them can be compelled to testify against each other. The patient will not be able to identify

---

[89] *Ratcliffe v Plymouth & Torbay Health Authority* [1998] Lloyd's Rep Med 162, CA. And see *Lillywhite v University College London Hospitals NHS Trust* [2006] EWCA Civ 1466.
[90] [2007] EWHC 487.
[91] J K Mason and G T Laurie, *Mason and McCall Smith's Law and Medical Ethics* (8th edn, 2010) OUP, p 156.

who was negligent. However, hope lies in the following statement made long ago by Lord Denning:[92]

> ... I do not think that the hospital and [the doctor] can both avoid giving an explanation by the simple expedient of throwing responsibility on to the other. If an injured person shows that one or other or both of two persons injured him, but cannot say which of them it was, then he is not defeated altogether. He can call on each of them for an explanation.

Thus robust common sense would force open any 'conspiracy of silence'.

Awards of compensation[93]

8.16 Once a patient has established that there has been negligence by the defendant as a result of which he suffered harm, what damages will he receive? There are no special rules governing clinical negligence awards. The patient's damages will be assessed to compensate her for any actual, or prospective, loss of earnings, and for the pain, suffering and disability which she has endured, and will endure. Her compensation for loss of earnings will include a sum representing any period in which she would have expected to be alive and earning but because of her injuries she will be prematurely dead.[94] Additionally, for these sums to represent what she has lost, the patient will be awarded an amount to cover extra expenses which she and her family will incur. If she requires intensive nursing care, or her house needs adapting to her invalid needs, or she requires constant attendance so that her husband gives up his job, all these expenses will be reflected in the award of damages. If the patient is dead, the damages awarded to her family will reflect the loss to them of the moneys she regularly expended on them. They recover for their loss of dependency.[95] It takes little imagination to see that if the patient dies, the burden of compensation may be reduced. Dead he suffers no pain. Dead he incurs no expenses.

Returning to the living patient, thorny problems bedevil the question of damages. The first is this. The patient must usually sue within three years. At that stage, a prognosis about future health is speculative. All his medical advisers may be able to say is something like this. The patient has a degree of brain damage. He is mildly disabled now. There is a 20 per cent chance he may deteriorate to become paralysed, and totally unable to do anything for himself, in ten years' time. The court can make an award of provisional damages based on the assumption that the prospect of further damage or deterioration will *not* materialise. Should it do so at some later date, the patient may return to

---

[92] *Roe v Ministry of Health* [1954] 2 QB 66 at 82.
[93] See CMO, *Making Amends* (2006), pp 65–76.
[94] This is known as compensation for the 'lost years'; see *Pickett v BRB* [1980] AC 136, HL. And see the Damages Act 1996, s 3.
[95] Fatal Accidents Act 1976 as amended by the Administration of Justice Act 1982.

court to ask for a further award to compensate him for the consequences of that damage or deterioration.[96]

Until recently, courts had to struggle to assess damages on a once and forever basis. The exercise was particularly difficult when estimating claims for future expenses, especially where the patient is so badly injured as to be unable to manage his own affairs. Large sums of money can be claimed to cover the cost of future care in expensive nursing homes. But there is no guarantee that that money will be so spent. The patient may be consigned to the NHS and the money deposited to grow with interest and eventually, when the patient dies, to form a windfall for relatives. The courts are alert to this danger. They will seek to ensure that the sum awarded is such as will be wholly exhausted by care of the patient, aiming to no surplus as a bonus for relatives. Plans for care must be realistic, and section 5 of the Administration of Justice Act 1982 provides that 'any saving to the injured person which is attributable to his maintenance at public expense . . . in a hospital . . . or other institution shall be set off against any income lost . . .'. A further anomaly in the law is that the claimant may be able to claim for the full cost of *any* private medical care regardless of whether such facilities are available free on the NHS.[97] Even where exactly identical surgery to alleviate the patient's condition could have been performed without charge, the claimant may demand the full cost of private care.

Once the patient's monetary losses have been quantified, consideration must then be given to how to compensate pain and suffering. Levels of compensation for those non-monetary losses have traditionally been much lower in this country than in the USA. The sum to be awarded is based on a 'tariff' system, with guidance as to what sum each category of injury should attract.[98] In 1986, the Court of Appeal ruled that £75,000 was the 'tariff' to compensate the suffering of a young woman left tetraplegic (paralysed from the neck down).[99] Incrementally that sum crept up to about £100,000. Claimants felt that £100,000 for a lifetime of suffering was ludicrously low. The Law Commission conducted a review of compensation for pain and suffering and recommended that compensation for pain and suffering should be increased dramatically, in some instances of catastrophic injury, by as much as 100 per cent.[100] In *Heil v Rankin*,[101] the Court of Appeal considered the Law Commission's proposals. An especially enlarged court agreed that more generous compensation for suffering and disability was justified. They settled on a lesser increase than that envisaged by the Law Commission. No increase should be

---

[96] See Supreme Court Act 1981, s 32A and *Chewings v Williams* [2009] EWHC 2490.
[97] Law Reform (Personal Injuries) Act 1948, s 2(4).
[98] See Judicial Studies Board, *Guidelines for the Assessment of General Damages in Personal Injuries Cases* (10th edn, 2010) OUP.
[99] *Housecroft v Burnett* [1986] 1 All ER 332, CA.
[100] Law Commission Report No 257, *Damages for Personal Injury: Non-Pecuniary Loss* (1999).
[101] [2000] 3 All ER 138.

offered in claims of less than £10,000. Graduated increases would be allowed thereafter to a maximum of about 50 per cent above prior levels of awards. Their Lordships acknowledged that the impact on the NHS of increased levels of damages played a role in motivating their caution.[102]

Other changes in the law relating to damages have also contributed to the increase in compensation payable in negligence claims against the NHS.[103] Medical skills means patients who suffer injury as a consequence of medical mistakes live much longer. Greater opportunities exist to improve their quality of life. Such benefits escalate costs. The concern generated by spiralling awards of damages is exacerbated by the fact that compensating people for injury can never be an exact science.

Claimants and defendants are often unhappy with the level of compensation awarded. For example, when negligence results in a patient's death, compensation for bereavement is only available to parents of children under eighteen, or to spouses. The level of compensation is set at £11,800. The child left desolate at the loss of her father receives no compensation for her emotional loss. The parent losing a child is told her child is worth £11,800. This amount can be seen as an insulting assessment, but can any sum compensate bereavement? Was the old rule that bereavement damages were never available preferable? When a patient survives paralysed from the waist down, will £150,000 heal her pain? Defendants also feel badly done to. Who the patient is may be crucial to the extent of their liability. Should one of us be left paralysed by an anaesthetist's mistake, the defendant hospital will have to cover the cost of future care and of equipment we will need, such as wheelchairs and alterations to our home. Providing that we can still go on lecturing, even if seated, our loss of income will be minimal. Should England's football captain suffer an identical mishap at the height of his career, his claim for loss of income could easily exceed £20m.[104] The lottery element in compensation awards was graphically illustrated by the case of Hollie Calladine.[105] Nine-year-old Hollie was awarded £700,000 in respect of brain damage caused by negligence during her birth. Much of this sum was to cover the expense of her future care. Days after the award was made, Hollie died. The hospital tried unsuccessfully to recover their damages. This sad case must suggest lump sum payments are not accurate or fair. The only equity of the system is that both sides suffer. For every case like Hollie Calladine's, there is another where claimants go grossly under-compensated by any lump sum payment. A young man of twenty-three is injured in the course of surgery. Doctors estimate he will live a further ten

---

102 [2000] 3 All ER 138 at 150.
103 See *Wells v Wells* [1999] 1 AC 345, HL; Damages Act 1996.
104 See record compensation claim in 2010 for former Commonwealth Games cyclist Manny Helmot, who was awarded £13.7m following a road-traffic accident which left him with brain injuries, mental health problems and requiring twenty-four-hour care. See http://www.claimscouncil.org.
105 See 'Legal Moves' (2001) 138 *Liability Risk and Insurance* 19.

years. He survives for twenty-five years. His compensation will be less than half of what he required.

Periodical payments – structured settlements[106]

8.17   Some of the uncertainties generated by having to assess compensation as a lump sum are avoidable by resort to reviewable periodical payments or, as they used to be described, structured settlements. The claimant receives an initial capital sum to cover actual losses already quantifiable and such matters as compensation for pain and suffering. The remainder of the money is used by the defendant to purchase an annuity for the claimant's benefit. The annuity will be flexible to adapt to the changing circumstances of the patient.[107] The income received by the patient is not taxable. The money paid out will be what he requires and no more. Should he die earlier than anticipated, payments will cease. Periodical payments avoid cases like that of Hollie Calladine. In certain cases, the periodical payments agreed or ordered can be reviewed at a later date. In ordinary personal injury claims, the defendant's insurer arranges the settlement and negotiates the purchase of annuities. As we have seen, the NHS does not insure against liability for clinical negligence on the commercial market. NHS structured settlements are usually self-financed.[108] The NHS uses its own income to arrange periodical payments, building the settlement into budgets. Tax concessions aid this process. Periodical payments in large claims may save the NHS some money. Since 2005 the courts have been able to impose a Periodical Payments Order (PPO)[109] Until 2005, structured settlements could only be established with the agreement of both parties.[110] Periodical payments may be efficient and fairer. The overall size of some awards for catastrophic injury is unlikely to drop. In 2010 there was a record personal injury claim payout of £13.7m compared to a maximum claim of £16.500 in the mid-1970s.[111]

Malpractice crisis: reality or illusion?

8.18   It will by now be apparent that bringing a claim for compensation, in any but the most straightforward of cases, is rarely easy. Yet despite the obvious difficulties associated with funding a claim and proving negligence, critics

---

[106] See J Murphy (ed), *Street on Torts* (12th edn, 2007) OUP, pp 664–666. And see A Sands, 'Periodical Payments – The Development of a Pragmatic Approach' (2006) 74 *Medico-Legal Journal* 69.

[107] A key issue is indexation to allow for inflation. See *Thompstone v Tameside and Glossop Acute Services NHS Trust* [2008] EWCA Civ 5. And see R Lewis, 'The Indexation of Periodical Payments of Damages in Tort: the Future Assured?' (2010) 30 *Legal Studies* 391.

[108] See CMO, *Making Amends*, p 74.

[109] See the Damages Act 1996, ss 2–2B (as substituted by the Courts Act 2003) and the Damages (Variation of Periodical Payments) Order 2005, SI 2005/841.

[110] See http://www.claimscouncil.org.

[111] See CMO, *Making Amends*, p 65.

of the civil justice system argue that England has succumbed to a 'compensation culture', a charge that the current government appears to endorse. Personal injury claims, it has been said, are stifling ordinary life. 'Gold-diggers' make spurious claims. Schools are afraid to let children engage in any sort of risky activity. Children are barred from conker fights without wearing goggles.[112] Lord Hobhouse suggested:[113]

> The pursuit of an unrestrained culture of blame and compensation has many evil consequences and one is certain interference with the liberty of the citizen.

In May 2010 one of the first acts of the incoming coalition government was to appoint a former Cabinet Minister, Lord Young, to review the effect of health and safety legislation in particular. While Lord Young has acknowledged[114] that there is a great deal of exaggeration in the media about a compensation culture, he aroused the wrath of lawyers acting for claimants in personal injury claims by attacking the advertising of lawyers' services and saying that they should be ashamed.[115]

In the context of clinical negligence claims, this alleged compensation culture, it is argued, results in a malpractice crisis. It has been claimed that doctors practise 'defensive medicine'. That is to say, a doctor will choose the treatment for the patient most likely to be 'legally safe' to ensure that he will not be sued by the patient. That treatment may not necessarily be medically best for the patient, and may be unnecessarily expensive and time-consuming. A common example of alleged defensive medicine is a decision to carry out a Caesarean section as soon as there is any sign of difficulty in the course of labour, rather than to run the legal risk of continuing to attempt a natural delivery. And, it is contended that the NHS is drained of resources because so many people sue.

Defensive medicine

8.19 The prospect that doctors will base decisions concerning treatment, not on their professional judgment of what is best for the patient, but on what is 'legally safest' for the doctor, does sound appalling. But is there hard evidence that doctors are being forced to practise defensive medicine?[116] The classic example often given of defensive medicine – the rise in the rate of Caesarean sections – has often been found to be explicable by many other factors. Caesarean rates rose in several countries, not all of which experienced rising

---

112 See (2006) *Times*, 18 September.
113 *Tomlinson v Congleton Borough Council* [2003] UKHL 47 at para 81.
114 HM Government, Lord Young, *Common Sense, Common Safety* (2010).
115 See 'News: Lord Young Attacks Personal Injury "Lottery"' (2010) *Law Society Gazette*, 7 October 3(1).
116 See M Jones, A E Morris, 'Defensive Medicine: Myths and Facts' (1989) 5 *Journal of the Medical Defence Union* 40, and in relation to defensive medicine in the USA, see D M Studdert, M M Mello, and T A Brennan, 'Medical Malpractice' (2004) 350 *New England Journal of Medicine* 283.

litigation rates. Nonetheless, obstetricians have voiced a subjective belief that fear of litigation makes them more ready to move swiftly to surgery rather than allow a difficult labour to proceed.[117] Then there is the question of what is meant by defensive medicine. In the House of Lords twenty-three years ago, Lord Pitt argued that the rising tide of litigation meant that doctors ordered unnecessary and sometimes painful tests, and he predicted '. . . an increase in defensive medicine with an alarming waste of resources'.[118] The difficulty is to decide when further tests and cross-checks cease to be a sensible precaution in the interests of the patient and become a waste of resources.[119]

Some of the concerns felt by doctors about defensive medicine may stem from anxiety that this country will see the excesses of malpractice litigation in the USA cross the Atlantic.[120] Before concluding that England will necessarily follow the US pattern to its extreme, differences between the two countries must be noted with the caveat that differences are less marked than was the case just ten years ago.[121]

In the USA, most medical care is provided by the private sector. If your treatment goes wrong and you suffer a medical accident, you will have to pay out more money for corrective treatment. Naturally an aggrieved patient is going to be looking to the doctor whom she perceives as responsible for the accident for the money to pay for any necessary corrective treatment. Most patients will carry private health insurance. Their insurers will be as keen as the patient to ensure that any costs, arising from medical negligence, are recovered from the doctor and his insurers. In a private health system such as that of the USA, health care is charged on a fee-for-service basis. The more tests a doctor carries out, the more money he makes. Perhaps some of the apparent evidence for 'defensive medicine' is better explained as 'expensive medicine'?

Lawyers acting for the clients in the USA act on a *contingency* fee basis. If the case fails, the client pays nothing; if the claim succeeds, the lawyer takes a percentage of the damages, normally about one-third. Such a system makes it much easier for patients to litigate, and gives lawyers a direct interest in the level of damages awarded. As we have seen, Lord Justice Jackson has suggested we should consider permitting contingency fees and not just conditional fees in England and Wales.

Awards of damages in the USA are decided not by the judge, as is the case in England, but by the jury. Even though the Court of Appeal in *Heil v Rankin*[122]

---

[117] National Sentinel Caesarean Section Audit (RCOG, 2001) (www.rcog.org.uk).
[118] HL Official Report, 10 November 1987, cols 1350–1351.
[119] See generally, P Danzon, *Medical Malpractice* (1985) Harvard University Press, Cambridge, Mass.
[120] See CMO, *Making Amends,* pp 26–27.
[121] Note suggestions that any US malpractice crisis is at least in part a creation of the medical insurers seeking to protect their profits. See N Terry, 'The Malpractice Crisis in the United States: A Dispatch from the Trenches' (1986) 2 *Professional Negligence* 145.
[122] *Heil v Rankin* [2000] 2 WLR 1173, CA. See above at **8.16**.

raised the tariff for compensation for pain and suffering in this country, levels of compensation remain infinitely more generous in the USA. Moreover, currently damages in this country are awarded solely for the purpose of compensating the patient for what he has lost as a result of the defendant doctor's negligence. A US jury is empowered in certain circumstances to double, or even treble, compensatory damages by making a further award of punitive damages, to punish the defendant for negligence.[123] Combining these factors, the Chief Medical Officer (CMO) found that while malpractice litigation consumed 0.2 percent of Gross Domestic Product in the USA, that figure was only 0.04 per cent in the UK.[124]

Financial costs to the NHS

8.20   However, the financial effects of litigation on the NHS have generated serious concern. A comprehensive study of medical litigation[125] published in 1988, demonstrated that numbers of claims against doctors doubled between 1983 and 1987. In 1999–2000, the National Audit Office[126] reported that 10,000 new claims were initiated against the NHS. The cost to the NHS had escalated. Between 1983 and 1987, the average cost of compensation doubled. And overall, litigation cost the NHS £300m.[127] In March 2000, £2.6bn was set aside to meet the cost of claims, and an estimated £1.3bn was estimated as needed to meet claims not yet reported. Since 1995–6, the cost of litigation to the NHS had increased seven-fold. In claims worth less than £50,000 in 1999–2000, costs exceeded compensation in 65 per cent of cases. One health minister was provoked to declare:[128] 'The only place for a lawyer in the NHS is on the operating table.'

The steep rise in claims has stalled somewhat. In 2004/5, the number of claims fell from 6,251 in 2003/4 to 5,609. In 2009/10, the number had risen again to 6,652. The cost to the NHS remains large; just short of £787m in 2009/10.[129] The NHSLA estimates that its total liability in relation to clinical negligence (the 'theoretical cost' of paying all outstanding claims including the incidents not yet reported to the NHSLA) amounts to £14.9bn.

How efficiently are claims dealt with? In claims of above £10,000 which were closed in 1999–2000, the time from making the claim to settlement or an

---

[123] Although Law Commission Report No 247, *Aggravated, Exemplary and Restitutionary Damages* (1997) did propose that, in exceptional cases, punitive damages should be awarded in England.

[124] See CMO, *Making Amends*, p 26.

[125] Ham *et al*, *Medical Negligence; Compensation and Accountability* (1988) Kings Fund.

[126] National Audit Office, *Handling Clinical Negligence Claims in England* (2001). But see the criticism of the NAO Report in P Fenn, A Gray and N Rickman, 'The Economics of Clinical Negligence Reform in England' (2004) 114 *The Economic Journal* 272.

[127] Ham *et al*, *Medical Negligence: Compensation and Accountability* (1988) Kings Fund, p 26.

[128] See (1998) *Guardian*, 30 April.

[129] NHSLA, *Factsheet 2: Financial Information* (2010).

award of damages was on average 5.5 years.[130] The average time to deal with a claim is now just under 1.45 years.[131] How do claims fare? In relation to claims handled by the NHSLA from 1 April 2009 to 31 March 31 2010, 40 per cent were abandoned by the claimant, 43 per cent were settled out of court, 4 per cent involved cases where a settlement required court approval and 13 per cent remain outstanding. Some of the worst problems of dealing with claims seem to be being addressed.[132]

Any judgment about whether the number of clinical negligence claims brought is excessive must be made in the context of estimates of the numbers of medical errors causing harm to patients. In one survey, 2,081 deaths were attributed to error.[133] It has been estimated that 10 per cent of 'in patient episodes' result in some injury to patients and that half of these 'adverse events' may be preventable.[134] Just under 7,000 claims for clinical negligence suggests that many patients or families who could sue do not do so.

Nevertheless, where a claim is made by an NHS patient, money to compensate an injured patient, and money to defend claims brought in respect of alleged negligence, must come out of NHS funds which might otherwise have been used to employ an extra surgeon, or pay for a new neo-natal unit, or support a programme of preventive medicine.[135] Moreover where a claimant funded by a CFA succeeds, the NHS will currently have to meet the claimant's costs, including lawyers' success fees and after-the-event insurance, as well as their own. As we have seen, Lord Justice Jackson has recommended that such costs should be irrecoverable by the claimant; a recommendation endorsed by the NHSLA. The NHSLA notes that claimants' costs are significantly higher than its own and there remains a disproportion between costs and damages paid, especially in low value claims.[136] When NHS money is used to compensate an injured patient, some benefit to society can be discerned. The disproportion between costs and compensation remains disturbing. John Harris[137] has argued that claimants in clinical negligence should compete for scarce resources with patients in urgent need of treatment. If resources for treatment are rationed, so compensation for medical accidents should be too. Costs arguments too must be kept in proportion. In absolute terms, the CMO found that just under 1 per cent of the NHS budget was expended on malpractice litigation.[138]

---

[130] House of Commons Public Accounts Committee, *Handling Clinical Negligence Claims in England*, HC 280 (2002) PAC, p 6.
[131] NHSLA, *Factsheet 3* (2010).
[132] See NHSLA, *Factsheets 1 and 3* (2010).
[133] See National Audit Office, *A Safer Place for Patients: Learning to Improve Patient Safety* (2005).
[134] See CMO, *Making Amends*, pp 31–41.
[135] See A Merry and A McCall Smith, *Errors, Medicine and the Law* (2001) CUP, p 212.
[136] NHSLA, *Report and Accounts* (2010).
[137] J Harris, 'The Injustice of Compensation for Medical Accidents' (1997) 314 *BMJ* 182.
[138] See CMO, *Making Amends*, p 26.

Wider costs to the NHS

8.21   Financial costs to the NHS are not the only cause for concern. Critics of the medical litigation process argue that it is unfair to doctors and damaging to the doctor–patient relationship. Are doctors unfairly treated? The evidence does not substantiate such a claim. Even when the rise in the number of claims was at its most dramatic, 76 per cent of legally aided claims failed. Forty per cent of all claims are still abandoned,[139] and among the 40 per cent of claims settled out of court, many will result in limited compensation to the claimant. Claimants do not seem to be 'winning' disproportionate numbers of cases. The levelling off in numbers of claims may indicate that lawyers are less willing to take on 'weak' cases and that patients struggle today to fund any claim. The Jackson reforms and the abolition of legal aid for clinical negligence claims will make it yet harder to sue for medical injury. Nor does an argument that doctors are unjustly judged by lawyers stand up to scrutiny. For in deciding whether a doctor is negligent, in the majority of cases the court relies on expert professional opinion.[140] A doctor can normally only be found to be negligent if his peers testify to his negligence. The House of Lords in *Bolitho v City & Hackney Health Authority*[141] has endorsed judicial power to disregard expert testimony in exceptional cases. Evidence of adequate practice to rebut a claim of negligence must be shown to be 'logical and defensible'. Doctors cannot really complain if courts refuse to accept evidence of 'illogical or indefensible' practice.

What is true is that many doctors have become so frightened by the spectre of a malpractice crisis that doctor/patient relationships may be damaged.[142] Evidence of defensive medicine may be disputable, defensiveness in medicine is a sad fact.[143] Doctors in 'high-risk' specialties such as obstetrics and anaesthetics are the worst affected among the profession. Doctors who are sued are concerned about:[144]

> ... the damage to their professional reputation, whether they were found negligent or not: the fact of the case was sufficient for the damage to reputation and morale.

The CMO noted:[145]

---

[139]   See NHLSA, *Factsheet 3* (2010).

[140]   *Bolam v Friern HMC* [1957] 1 WLR 582. See above at **7.5**.

[141]   [1998] AC 232, HL. See above at **7.8**.

[142]   See CMO *Making Amends*, p 76.

[143]   Hence Ian Kennedy argued many years ago that what is required to defuse any 'crisis' is better information about the law for doctors so that they will not feel constrained to practise 'defensive medicine': see 'Review of the Year 2: Confidentiality, Competence and Malpractice', in P Byrne (ed), *Medicine in Contemporary Society* (1987) King's Fund.

[144]   See CMO, *Making Amends*, p 76. And note that it has been estimated that 38 per cent of doctors who have been sued suffer clinical depression: *Making Amends*, p 43.

[145]   See *Making Amends*, p 7.

Legal proceedings for medical injury frequently progress in an atmosphere of confrontation, acrimony, misunderstanding and bitterness.

Medical litigation is difficult and unfair for patients, expensive for the NHS, and damaging to the morale of doctors. In 2006, two Acts of Parliament, discussed below, sought to address the problems.

Addressing the compensation culture

8.22 Evidence of any compensation culture[146] and, more specifically, a malpractice crisis, is mixed. What is clear is that the current litigation system satisfies neither doctors' nor patients' needs.[147] The previous government, while denying the existence of a compensation culture, nonetheless assert that the *cost* of such a belief, in terms of risk aversion, is real.[148] In 2006 two new statutes, the Compensation Act 2006 and the NHS Redress Act 2006, reached the statute book.

As we note in chapter 7,[149] unless judges decide that doctors should not be sued because of the detrimental effects it will have on health care, the Compensation Act 2006 is likely to have minimal impact on clinical negligence claims. The NHS Redress Act 2006 might have had greater effect. It gave the Secretary of State power to implement a new redress scheme for patients which would combine investigation, explanation and financial redress, without the need to go to court. In England at least the NHS Redress Scheme seems to have come to a full stop. We look more fully at how the Scheme might work in the next chapter. And we consider other means of redressing patients who have been injured in the course of their treatment.

---

[146] Better Regulation Taskforce, *Better Routes to Redress* (2004) (accessible: http://www.brc.gov.uk/downloads/pdf/betterroutes.pdf); House of Commons Constitutional Affairs Committee, *Compensation Culture,* Third Report of Session 2005–06, HC 754-1 (2006) (accessible: http://www.publications.parliament.uk/pa/cm200506/cmselect/cmconst/754/754i.pdf); House of Commons Constitutional Affairs Committee, *Compensation Culture: NHS Redress Bill,* Fifth Report of Session 2005–06, HC 1009 (2006) (accessible: http://www.publications.parliament.uk/pa/cm200506/cmselect/cmconst/1009/1009.pdf); R Lewis, A Morris and K Oliphant 'Tort Personal Injury Claims Statistics: Is There a Compensation Culture in the United Kingdom?' (2006) 14 *Torts Law Journal* 2: 158; K Williams, 'State of Fear: Britain's "Compensation Culture" Reviewed' (2005) 25 *Legal Studies* 3: 499.

[147] See CMO, *Making Amends.*

[148] House of Commons, Constitutional Affairs Committee, *Compensation Culture,* Third Report of Session 2005–06, HC 754-1 (2006), para 111.

[149] See above at 7.5. And see A Samuels, 'The Compensation Act 2006: Helpful Or Unhelpful to Doctors?' (2006) 71 *Medico-Legal Journal* 171.

Chapter 9

COMPLAINTS AND REDRESS

9.1

> The Trust failed to listen to patients' concerns, the Board did not review the substance of complaints and incident reports were not given the necessary attention.

So concluded Robert Francis QC at the publication of the *Final Report Of The Independent Inquiry Into Care Provided By Mid Staffordshire NHS Foundation Trust*.[1] Appalling standards of care, poor hygiene, inappropriate early discharge from hospital, and staff shortages between 2005 and 2009 were reported by some brave staff, but action was slow and deficient.

When injury results from medical treatment, patients or their relatives seek accountability. Such cases are not limited to the kinds of injury that would give rise to a claim for clinical negligence, but may include poor care, rudeness and a failure to have real regard for the welfare of the patient. In these and other instances patients may seek redress when they feel that health professionals have let them down. This can take a number of forms. Some may wish the responsible health professionals to be disciplined, and we examined in chapter 1 ways in which that might be achieved. When there is an injury to health, some seek financial compensation, and bring a clinical negligence claim (examined in chapters 7 and 8). Many others simply want an explanation and an assurance that the same mistake will not be repeated. In particularly serious cases of repeated error or bad practice, patients and families may demand a formal public inquiry. In other cases, the individual affected may make a formal complaint. But, as we shall see, the NHS complaints procedure has come under fire for many years. Evidence mounted up that it was failing patients, especially in terms of providing explanations for mistakes. In New Zealand, where patients are compensated without proving fault through the Accident Compensation Corporation, doctors have a legal duty of candour and adverse events are usually admitted.[2] Here, doctors fear the complaints process might lead to patients seeking compensation in the courts. And so they may be reluctant to admit errors. An inadequate complaints system causes many patients to lose

---

[1] Press Release: HC375-I (accessible at http://www.midstaffsinquiry.com/pressrelease.html).

[2] P Davis *et al*, 'Acknowledgement of "No-Fault" Medical Injury: Review of Patients' Hospital Records in New Zealand' (2003) 326 *BMJ* 79.

confidence in it, and choose to bring proceedings in court. A survey in 2000 showed that, when patients first pursued medical litigation, over 50 per cent of them primarily sought an admission of fault, action to prevent what happened to them happening to others, and an investigation of their complaint. Only 30–39 per cent of aggrieved patients initially wanted monetary compensation.[3] Some patients sue simply to find out what really happened.[4] An effective complaints system might both improve care and cut the litigation costs to the NHS.

The NHS Constitution,[5] which came into force in 2009, incorporates the right to make a complaint: but what is the substance of that right? The complaints system has been 'reformed' several times, in 1996, and again in 2003, 2006 and 2009. Further reforms will inevitably form part of the package of health reforms proposed by the government.

The NHS Constitution also reiterates the right to seek financial compensation. This is currently achieved through expensive clinical negligence litigation, examined in the previous chapter. Acting on some of the Chief Medical Officer's recommendations in *Making Amends*,[6] the NHS Redress Act 2006 is enabling legislation through which a fast-track process for small claims could have been developed. While the devolved government in Wales has developed secondary legislation[7] and issued a draft Regulation in 2010, England stalled and delayed[8] and now seems unlikely to develop a scheme based on the Act. As we have seen in chapter 8, other mechanisms to tackle the rising costs associated with negligence claims against the NHS have been proposed.

We will consider complaints mechanisms, having first outlined the ways in which services or individuals may be made the subject of a health service public inquiry in order that the NHS as a whole can benefit from the outcome of the investigation. In the second half of the chapter we will consider the (possibly defunct) NHS Redress Scheme and alternative proposals. We write without the benefit of the House of Commons Health Committee report on

---

[3] See L Mulcahy, *Mediating Medical Negligence Claims: An Option for the Future* (2000) HMSO. And see C Vincent *et al*, 'Why do People Sue Doctors? A Study of Patients and Relatives Taking Legal Action' (1994) 343 *Lancet* 1609.

[4] See M Bismark, E A Dauer, 'Motivations for Medico-Legal Action' (2006) 27 *The Journal of Legal Medicine* 55.

[5] Provided for under the Health Act 2009, s 1. See NHS, *The Handbook to the NHS Constitution* (2009), revised (March 2010).

[6] Chief Medical Officer, *Making Amends: A Consultation Paper Setting Out Proposals for Reforming the Approach to Clinical Negligence in the NHS* (2003) DH (hereafter CMO, *Making Amends*).

[7] NHS Redress (Wales) Measure 2008.

[8] Which resulted in media criticism: see N Lakhani, 'Plan to Help Victims of NHS Negligence is Left to Languish on Statute Book: Patients in England are Being Forced to Fight Lengthy and Costly Legal Battles to Receive an Apology and Explanation of What Went Wrong', *Independent on Sunday*, 30 August 2009.

Complaints and Litigation. Expected in 2011, it will explore the current short-comings, expected reforms and interface between the complaints process and clinical negligence litigation.[9]

Health Service public inquiries[10]

9.2   Dissatisfaction with the outcome of complaints procedures in a number of high-profile cases fuelled a growing demand for public inquiries. Such inquiries colour popular perceptions of the NHS as a whole, even if they address the exceptional, rather than the routine grievance. Patients and patients' organisations want a comprehensive and independent review, either of an inadequate service in general, or of the misconduct of particular individuals. They want to see the whole picture and receive assurance that action is being taken to remedy the shortcomings of the NHS and/or call to account staff whose wrongdoing caused serious harm. A number of different procedures within the NHS provide for further investigation of such NHS 'scandals'. An NHS inquiry may be established under section 2 of the National Health Service Act 2006,[11] whereby the Health Minister has a general power to do anything calculated to facilitate the discharge of his duty. In serious cases, an independent team will be drafted in to conduct the investigation. Such an inquiry will be conducted by a small committee, usually consisting of a legally qualified chairman and two medical practitioners, one from the same specialty as the person whose competence is in issue. All inquiry members will be unconnected with the hospital where the complaint originated. Copies of all documents are circulated to all parties. The complainant and the subjects of the complaint may be legally represented, and cross-examination of witnesses is allowed. The committee's findings of fact are then submitted to the staff concerned for further comment. Finally, the committee reports its findings and recommendations. The inquiry procedure can be effective, but if hospital staff refuse co-operation the procedure may break down altogether. No one can be compelled to attend the inquiry. NHS inquiries of this kind are relatively informal and lack coercive powers. The former regulator, the Healthcare Commission, reported in 2009 following such an NHS inquiry into the high mortality rates amongst patients at Mid Staffordshire NHS Foundation Trust between 2005 and 2008.[12] In an effort to achieve targets, staff numbers had been reduced. Patients were left unfed, unwashed and without medication, with grave effects on patient mortality.

---

[9]   Consultation closed 21 December 2010. See http://www.parliament.uk/business/committees/committees-a-z/commons-select/health-committee/inquiries/complaints-and-litigation/.

[10]   See K Walshe, 'The Use and Impact of Inquiries in the NHS' (2002) 325 *BMJ* 895.

[11]   Formerly National Health Service Act 1977, s 2.

[12]   Healthcare Commission, Investigation into Mid Staffordshire NHS Foundation Trust (March 2009).

At the other end of the spectrum, the Department of Health may set up a formal, independent inquiry under the Inquiries Act 2005,[13] where the matter is of sufficient public concern. When monitoring revealed poor progress in putting things right in Mid Staffordshire, the government ordered a formal, independent inquiry under the Inquiries Act 2005. The final report, referred to in the introduction to this chapter, was published in 2010.[14] A further public inquiry into the regulatory failures at Mid-Staffordshire was launched in November 2010.

The Inquiries Act 2005 gives ministers the power to convert other types of inquiry, both statutory and non-statutory, into an Inquiry Act inquiry[15] at which point the minister can change the terms of reference. The findings of an inquiry are not determinative of liability.[16] Instead the aim is to restore public confidence and ensure that mistakes are not repeated. Under section 19(4)(d) of the Inquiries Act, wide-ranging restrictions on public access may be applied according to the requirements of the particular inquiry.

Where the inquiry is held in private, people might be more willing to speak openly and honestly, but lack of openness can evoke hostile reactions. Patients involved in the many grievances caused by the conduct of Drs Neale's and Ayling's affairs pressed the Secretary of State for Health for public inquiries. Richard Neale had been struck off the register in Canada in 1985, but continued to practise in Yorkshire long after that event. He was arrogant, overly optimistic about patients' prognoses and undertook clinical procedures that were beyond his expertise. Clifford Ayling was convicted on twelve counts of indecent assaults on former patients in 2000. The Secretary of State refused a public inquiry in both cases. His decisions were unsuccessfully challenged in the courts. The resulting inquiries were private.[17] The Bristol Report[18] points out, however, that private inquiries may be counterproductive. Holding the inquiry in private may be '. . . more likely to inflame than protect the feelings of those affected by the Inquiry'. And, the Report emphasises the need for transparent, clear criteria determining when a public inquiry should be established. These warnings fell on deaf ears. In 2000, the Secretary of State

---

[13] Previously, formal statutory NHS inquiries of this kind were conducted under s 84 of the National Health Service Act 1977. S 84 inquiries could be public or partially private. One famous example is the public inquiry into children's heart surgery at the Bristol Royal Infirmary. See *Learning from Bristol – The Report of the Public Inquiry into Children's Heart Surgery at the Bristol Royal Infirmary 1984–1995*, CM 5207 (1) (2001) (hereafter *The Bristol Inquiry*).

[14] The Independent Inquiry into Care Provided by Mid Staffordshire NHS Foundation Trust, chaired by Robert Francis QC (February 2010).

[15] S 15.

[16] Inquiries Act 2005, s 2.

[17] DH, Report of the Committee of Inquiry into how the NHS Handled Allegations about the Conduct of Richard Neale, Cm 6315 (2004). DH, Committee of Inquiry – Independent Investigation into How the NHS Handled Allegations about the Conduct of Clifford Ayling, Cm 6298 (2004).

[18] At p 31.

announced a private inquiry into the murders committed by Harold Shipman. There was uproar from patients and media. A public inquiry was duly ordered in September 2000 under the Tribunals of Inquiry (Evidence) Act 1921. Patients will have less confidence in inquiries held behind closed doors. Government fears the cost of public inquiries both in cash and to the reputation of the NHS.

Aligning complaints and redress

9.3 If an individual wants a swifter, more personalised, investigation of his particular case, eg to find out why he lay on a trolley in a corridor for hours with no pain relief, he may make a complaint or, if he seeks financial redress (maybe because he fell off the trolley and broke a rib), he may initiate legal proceedings. Clinical negligence litigation has come under sustained attack in recent years. In particular, the blame culture has been perceived as adverse to the promotion of patient safety and proper accountability for error.[19] The Bristol Inquiry[20] called for the 'abolition of clinical negligence litigation, taking clinical error out of the courts and the tort system'. Litigation should be replaced by effective systems for identifying and addressing errors and new no-fault based provisions for compensation. Complaints and redress, including financial redress, should be aligned.

Responding to such criticisms, the Chief Medical Officer (CMO) circulated a Consultation Paper, *Making Amends*,[21] setting out proposals to unify complaints and redress within the NHS. Making a complaint would no longer disqualify the individual from making a claim for compensation. The report focused on changing the culture of the NHS to one of openness and learning and restoring public trust. The Report rejected the possibility of a comprehensive no-fault compensation scheme for medical accidents[22] in favour of a limited NHS redress scheme which remains, for the most part, wedded to the law of tort.

The NHS Redress Act 2006 gives the Secretary of State power to introduce a new scheme for certain claims for compensation relating to NHS hospital services. It applies in England and Wales, but remember that as yet no action has been taken to bring the Act into force in England. The promises that government would implement an NHS redress scheme once new complaints procedures were embedded,[23] have not been delivered. The 2006 Act remains

---

[19] See A Merry and A McCall Smith, *Errors, Medicine and the Law* (2001) CUP, p 217.
[20] *The Bristol Inquiry*, ch 26; and see DH Expert Group, *An Organisation with a Memory* (2000).
[21] CMO, *Making Amends*.
[22] The option of a no-fault scheme had been canvassed in the CMO's initial position paper; see *Clinical Negligence: What are the Issues and Options for Reform* (2001), DH.
[23] Lord Darzi, Hansard, 18 March 2009: col WA49.

an Act on paper only. The future of the scheme in England is uncertain. Wales now proposes an NHS redress scheme which combines investigation and where appropriate, explanation, apology and financial redress. Scotland, where the NHS Redress Act 2006 does not apply, proposes a more radical no-fault scheme. We explore all these proposals later in the chapter.[24] We now turn to the complaints process.

Complaints procedures – a troubled history

9.4   A formal NHS complaints system was introduced in 1966. There were three separate schemes, relating to primary care, clinical care and non-clinical care respectively. In 1996,[25] new procedures were introduced.

(1)   One single complaints procedure became applicable throughout the NHS. Hospital doctors, GPs and other community-based health professionals were dealt with within a unified complaints system.

(2)   A three-step process was established so that complaints were first subject to 'local resolution' which could be followed by an 'independent review' of the case, with an ultimate right to resort to the Health Service Commissioner, popularly known as the NHS Ombudsman.

(3)   The NHS Ombudsman was finally empowered to investigate complaints about clinical judgment and his jurisdiction was extended to cover GPs.

The revised NHS complaints system (1996) had a number of laudable objectives. Procedures should be responsive to complainants and seek to answer their grievances. They should enhance the quality of care and be cost effective. All processes should be accessible, be seen to be impartial, be simple and swift. Complainants need to be assured of confidentiality. NHS authorities must be accountable for the operation of complaints procedures. No-one would dissent from these sentiments. Putting principle into practice proved a harder task. Dissatisfaction with NHS complaints systems endured.[26] Patients complained that the second stage was not truly independent and that the process was complex, time-consuming and inefficient. Doctors were perceived as defensive, and mistakes were repeated.

So revisions were made in the National Health Service (Complaints) Regulations 2004,[27] which entrusted independent review to the Healthcare Commission. A number of major inquiries necessitated further reform. The Shipman Inquiry

---

[24]   Below at **9.20**.

[25]   See NHSE, *Complaints – Listening – Acting – Improving: Guidance on Implementation of the NHS Complaints Procedures* (1996), DH.

[26]   Select Committee on Health Sixth Report, *Procedures Related to Adverse Clinical Incidents and Outcomes in Medical Care*, HC 549 (1999); and see D Longley, 'Complaints After Wilson: Another Case of Too Little Too Late?' (1997) 5 *Medical Law Review* 172.

[27]   SI 2004/1768.

and two private inquiries, the Neale and the Ayling Inquiries, considered the adequacy of the NHS complaints process. The Fifth Report of the Shipman Inquiry[28] made recommendations for improvements to the system, especially in relation to general practitioners. The National Health Service (Complaints) Amendment Regulations 2006[29] were duly enacted to improve local resolution and to align the NHS and social care complaints systems. Problems endured.[30] There were at least seven different routes for complaints about health services and many were poorly signposted.[31] Only 27 per cent of people making a complaint were satisfied in the way it had been handled.[32] Further reforms were announced in 2009[33] to make the process faster and more effective and introduce a single complaints system across health and social care. Applicants now have the right to local resolution whilst simultaneously pursuing a legal claim.[34] The second stage of a three-tier complaints system was abandoned. Where previously a complainant would start with local resolution and potentially progress to the independent Healthcare Commission and finally the Health Service Ombudsman, those dissatisfied with local resolution now go straight to the Ombudsman.

Raising a concern

9.5   A distinction is drawn between concerns and complaints. A concerned individual can talk informally to the designated complaints manager, or Patient Advice and Liaison Service (PALS) staff in each trust.[35] PALS is concerned with wider patient safety issues. They will attempt to resolve the situation without the need for a formal complaint. Otherwise they can provide details of how to complain formally and refer complainants to an independent service: the Independent Complaints Advisory Service (ICAS).[36] ICAS is a free, independent and confidential service designed to help patients and relatives

---

28   *Safeguarding Patients: Lessons from the Past – Proposals for the Future,* Cm 6394 (2004) DH. And see Citizens Advice Bureau, *The Pain of Complaining* (2005), CAB recommending measures to raise standards, improve access, ensure timeliness and learn from complaints.

29   SI 2006/2084.

30   DH, *Making Experiences Count: A New Approach to Responding to Complaints* (2007) London; *National Audit Office, Feeding Back? Learning From Complaints Handling in Health and Social Care* (2008) TSO.

31   National Audit Office, *Feeding Back? Learning From Complaints Handling in Health and Social Care* (2008) TSO.

32   National Audit Office, *Feeding Back? Learning From Complaints Handling in Health and Social Care* (2008) TSO.

33   DH, *Listening, Responding, Improving – A Guide to Better Customer Care* (2009) The Stationery Office.

34   DH, *Clarification of Complaints Regulations 2009* (2010) Gateway Reference Number:13508, p 2. The complaint may be put on hold if it might prejudice a legal claim.

35   See http://www.pals.nhs.uk/.

36   Established under Health and Social Care Act 2001, s 12; replaced by National Health Service Act 2006, s 248.

make a complaint. It provides self-help guides and one-to-one support for those in greatest need. It is used in around 10 per cent of health complaints.[37]

Complaints advocacy is set to change. Local authorities, rather than the Secretary of State, will become responsible for complaints advocacy for both health and social services. It is proposed that a new consumer body, HealthWatch England,[38] will sit within the Care Quality Commission (CQC). HealthWatch England will support a network of local HealthWatches.[39] In addition to providing complaints advocacy services, they will be able to feed back concerns to HealthWatch England which can then take them forward within the CQC. There will be more emphasis on looking for trends in complaints rather than viewing them in isolation. The voice of dissatisfaction should henceforth be easier to hear. Local authorities will be able to commission the local HealthWatch or alternative complaints advocacy services.

In many cases the complaint is resolved informally, but if the individual wishes to proceed with a formal complaint there are potentially two stages to the process.

Local resolution

9.6 The first stage of the formal complaints process is to make a complaint at a local level, a process known as 'local resolution'. A complaint, which must usually be made within twelve months, may be made to any relevant NHS organisation.[40] Each organisation must have a complaints manager,[41] publicise complaints arrangements,[42] and keep records of complaints[43] which they must publish in an annual report and make available on request. A complaint can be made orally or in writing,[44] by a patient or any person affected by actions, omissions or decisions made by an NHS organisation.[45] Complaints can be made on behalf of a person where that person so requests, or has died, or is a child, or cannot make a complaint himself due to a lack of

---

[37] Parliamentary and Health Services Ombudsman, *Listening and Learning*: The Ombudsman's View of Complaint Handling by the NHS in England 2009–10 (2010) HSCIC (hereafter *Listening and Learning*), 7.

[38] Health and Social Care Bill 2011, cl 166, proposing to insert new ss 45A and 45B into the Health and Social Care Act 2008.

[39] The Health and Social Care Bill 2011, cl 170, proposes to insert a new s 223A into the Local Government and Public Involvement in Health Act 2007.

[40] And also to local authorities and other bodies listed in reg 3. This includes PCTs – previously the complainant would have had to go to the provider.

[41] The Local Authority Social Services and National Health Service Complaints (England) Regulations 2009, SI 2009/309, as amended, reg 4.

[42] SI 2009/309, reg 16.

[43] SI 2009/309, reg 17.

[44] SI 2009/309, reg 13.

[45] SI 2009/309, reg 5(1).

mental capacity.[46] At local resolution, the complaint is investigated, following which the NHS body must make a 'timely' response, including an explanation, conclusions and, where relevant, action to be taken.[47]

Quite what constitutes a 'timely' response is open to conjecture. In 2006 a twenty-day target was extended to twenty-five days.[48] The 2009 Regulations removed the target altogether. Whilst this might seem a retrograde step which is likely to increase delay, the NHS is keen to give local resolution, where the vast majority of complaints are resolved, every chance of success. Removing target time limits makes for a more flexible system and puts emphasis on the quality of the process rather than its speed. Following suit, the NHS Information Centre did not publish data on the time taken to resolve complaints at local level in its 2010 complaints statistics. However, under the new Regulations it is now possible to see how many complaints are received by each body. Some hospitals have large backlogs. We have discussed the public inquiry into the dreadful standards of care at Mid Staffordshire NHS Foundation Trust. Staffordshire County Council is helping the hospital clear its backlog of complaints and in 2010 the hospital won a grant to improve their complaints system by using local people to act as advocates for complainants.[49]

The target time limit is not the only casualty of the reforms. There were previously three stages to the complaints process. After local resolution, complainants had the right to take their case to the independent Healthcare Commission (which in 2009 was replaced by the CQC), and then on to the NHS Ombudsman. But the system was flawed. The demand for independent review was seriously underestimated and timeliness and quality suffered.[50] In 2009 the radical step was taken to remove the second stage altogether. A quicker, simpler system resulted but, as we shall see, it did not hold all the answers.

The NHS Ombudsman

9.7 Those dissatisfied with local attempts at resolution may take their complaint to the Health Service Commissioner, better known as the NHS Ombudsman. The Ombudsman is independent of both the NHS and government, and unaffected by the new Regulations. For complex or unresolved

---

[46] SI 2009/309, reg 5(2).

[47] SI 2009/309, reg 14.

[48] NHS Information Centre Press Release, 'Latest Statistics on NHS Written Complaints' (2006).

[49] BBC, *Stafford Hospital in Crisis 2007–2010*, accessible at http://news.bbc.co.uk/local/stoke/hi/people_and_places/newsid_8493000/8493964.stm.

[50] National Audit Office, *Feeding Back? Learning From Complaints Handling in Health and Social Care* (2008), 7–8 and see Healthcare Commission, *Spotlight on Complaints: A Report on Second-stage Complaints About the NHS in England* (2007).

cases, she is the 'Court of last resort'. The post was established in 1973.[51] The Ombudsman is empowered to investigate any complaint where it is alleged that a failure in the health service or maladministration in the service resulted in injustice or hardship. She still may not pursue a complaint where the person concerned may have a remedy in the courts unless she is satisfied that it is not reasonable to expect the complainant to invoke that remedy.[52] Most crucially, since 1996, the Ombudsman is empowered to investigate action taken as a result of the exercise of the professional, clinical judgment of doctors or nurses.[53] What then is the extent of the Ombudsman's power and influence today?

Complaints to the Ombudsman must be made in writing,[54] by a patient or by some responsible person acting on his behalf. Health service organisations may also refer written complaints to the Ombudsman.[55] Her powers of inquiry are extensive. She and her staff investigate in private. They will contact all hospital or primary care staff involved in the complaint and seek their comments. The Ombudsman has complete control of the investigation. If co-operation from hospital staff or administrators is not forthcoming, the production of records and documents may be ordered and staff may be compelled to testify to the Ombudsman.[56] The Ombudsman only investigates complaints where the patient can show that he has 'sustained injustice or hardship'[57] as a result of maladministration or a failure in the service, except in the case of complaints about clinical judgment where this restriction does not apply. She will only investigate a complaint if all local remedies to resolve the complaint have first been exhausted. Investigations take considerable time and resources. The Ombudsman has to select the most pressing complaints to follow up – the majority of aggrieved patients will be turned away. On completion of an investigation, the Ombudsman reports to the complainant, the relevant NHS organisation, and any individual against whom allegations were made. The report will contain a decision about whether the complaint was justified and recommend a remedy. The Ombudsman might recommend action or an apology. On rare occasions systemic change – such as staff training or changes to

---

[51] National Health Service Reorganisation Act 1973. The Ombudsman's powers are set out in the Health Commissioners Act 1993, as amended by the Health Service Commissioners (Amendment) Act 1996, National Health Service (Primary Care) Act 1997, the Health Act 1999, and the Health Services Commissioners (Amendment) Act 2000. In theory there are three separate NHS Ombudsmen. In practice, to date the post has been held by one person who is also the Parliamentary Commissioner for Administration (the general national Ombudsman). She is supported in her NHS post by a Deputy Commissioner with experience of NHS management.

[52] Health Service Commissioners Act 1993, s 4(1)(b).

[53] See V Harpwood, 'The Health Service Commissioner: The Extended Role in the New NHS' (1996) 3 *European Journal of Health Law* 207.

[54] Health Service Commissioners Act 1993, s 3. The Ombudsman has discretion to extend this time limit.

[55] Health Service Commissioners Act 1993, s 10.

[56] Health Service Commissioners Act 1993, ss 11, 12.

[57] Health Service Commissioners Act 1993, s 3(1).

policy – will be suggested, in which case the Ombudsman will send copies to relevant regulators, such as the CQC and Monitor, so that they can check progress. Sometimes compensation will be recommended for financial loss, or distress.[58] For example, when Mrs T was put on the wrong consultant's list and endured a long journey and time off work to no avail, the Ombudsman decided that it would be reasonable for the trust to pay not only travel costs (which the trust had reimbursed) but loss of earnings. The trust agreed to do so.[59]

Each year the Ombudsman makes an Annual Report to Parliament, published by HMSO and available to the public. We have seen that the 2009 Regulations, which relate to local resolution, require each NHS body to produce an annual report detailing complaint numbers and subjects, what action was taken and how many were resolved or referred to the Ombudsman. In 2010 the Ombudsman launched a consultation on how best to report this data to the public so as to improve the learning process whilst respecting privacy. In the Health and Social Care Bill 2011, the government propose that the Ombudsman's discretion to share such information is extended.[60]

The Ombudsman's activities are monitored by a Select Committee of MPs which encourage her in her work and spur her on to greater efforts on behalf of NHS patients. There have been a record number of complaints in recent years.[61] Following steady rises year on year, 2009–10 saw the largest rise in complaints about hospital and community services since records began in 1997.[62] In the same year, the Ombudsman reported 12,889 enquiries and 14,429 health complaints which is more than double received in 2008–9.[63]

The Ombudsman and clinical judgment

9.8　The exclusion of clinical judgment from review by the Ombudsman was once a most serious limitation on her effectiveness. In 1989–90, out of 470 complaints rejected as outside the Commissioner's jurisdiction, 204 related to clinical judgment.[64] The Health Service Commissioners (Amendment) Act 1996 extended her jurisdiction to embrace clinical judgment. By 2000–2001, 77 per cent of completed investigations concerned clinical judgment.[65] The

---

[58]　*Listening and Learning*, 16.

[59]　*Listening and Learning*, 16.

[60]　Pt 5, Ch 3 proposes a new s 14(2I) to the Health Service Commissioners Act 1993; 'Where the Commissioner is required by this section to send a report or statement of reasons to certain persons, the Commissioner may send the report or statement to such other persons as the Commissioner thinks appropriate.'

[61]　See D Sing, 'Ombudsman Reports Record Number of Complaints' (2004) 329 *BMJ* 192.

[62]　A rise of 13.4 per cent: The Health and Social Care Information Centre, *Data on Written Complaints in the NHS 2009–2010* (2010), HSCIC.

[63]　*Listening and Learning*, p. 13.

[64]　See tables at p 23, *Annual Report* for 1989–90.

[65]　*Annual Report* for 2000–2001, p 1.

nature of these complaints is varied. Quite a number deal with the level of care provided by junior doctors, and the adequacy of supervision and support provided for junior staff. Dealing with complaints about clinical matters is not easy. Identifying if a complaint has substance is time-consuming. Records must be obtained with the complainant's consent. Clinical advice is required and often has to be sought from specialists outside the Ombudsman's office.

Many complaints register dissatisfaction with complaint-handling at local resolution. In one case,[66] a patient saw his GP about back pain which the GP misdiagnosed. It was thought his pain was posture-related but a week later it was revealed that the patient had suffered a heart attack. When the patient complained, the GP and senior partner apologised for the delay but said it made no difference to the outcome. Afterwards they noted that in future they would 'over-diagnose' patients with chest pain, which they described as 'defensive medicine'. The Ombudsman upheld the complaint. Not only had the GP dismissed the patient's symptoms too readily, but the complaints process had been too lengthy and the comments accompanying the 'apology' inappropriate and suggestive of the fact that the practice had not learned from their mistakes. Following the decision of the Ombudsman, the practice made an action plan to prevent recurrence.

The Ombudsman and the courts

9.9   Many of the complaints dealt with by the Ombudsman could not be the subject of court action for a variety of reasons. For example, a baby was born prematurely and placed on a ventilator. Staff sought to wean him off the ventilator but soon judged that the child would not survive. A week after his birth he collapsed and died. NHS doctors were not in any sense responsible for his death; they were not negligent in their care of the infant. However, staff did not explain to the child's mother what was happening. When the consultant finally spoke to her, he said 'he had decided to let [the child] go'. His parents felt excluded from his care and lack of communication left them unprepared for his sudden death.[67]

Other investigations undertaken by the Commissioner are more likely subjects of a claim for compensation. One notorious example concerned a woman of twenty-three. She sought an abortion in 1970 and attended the hospital with her mother. The woman held a job but suffered from temporal lobe epilepsy and a degree of personality disorder. After discussion with the parents, the consultant sterilised the woman with their consent. The first the woman herself learned of the operation was when, some years later and married, she was trying to have a baby. The Ombudsman found no evidence that sterilisation was necessary for the woman's health. He judged that, acting in breach of

[66]   Ombudsman, *Being Open and Accountable – Mr K's Case* (online), accessible at http://nhsreport.ombudsman.org.uk/complainants-stories/being-open-and-accountable.html.
[67]   Case No E 1095/99–99.

DHSS guidance, which he had never read, the consultant was at fault.[68] Other more routine cases, where a claim for clinical negligence looks more straight-forward, come before the Ombudsman. A Caesarean section resulted in injury to a patient who had had problems with anaesthesia in earlier surgery. The complainant alleged that records of her previous difficulties were not trans-ferred to her obstetric records, that her own warnings were ignored, and that her complaint was badly and unsympathetically dealt with. Her first two alle-gations were of simple negligence. The Ombudsman nevertheless agreed to investigate the case in return for an undertaking that the complainant would not take legal proceedings.[69] This became common practice. The undertaking is not legally binding and there is nothing to stop a complainant assuring the Commissioner he will not sue and then launching proceedings on the basis of evidence uncovered by the Ombudsman.

Private treatment

9.10   The Health and Social Care Act 2008 established the CQC which, in April 2009, took over the regulation of health and social care, in NHS, private and voluntary organisations. All registered healthcare providers are required to publish and operate complaints procedures.[70] However, there is some vari-ation in their format because private hospitals are not required to follow the NHS complaints Regulations.[71] What of the patients receiving NHS care in an independent hospital? The patient can complain either to the provider under their complaints procedures, or to the PCT (and, in future, CCs) which commissioned the service, under the NHS complaints procedure.

Complaints about complaints

9.11   Difficulties arise within the NHS too. The phased reforms which began in 2004 improved the system, and the 2006 and 2009 reforms addressed the fragmentary nature of the complaints system. However, the Ombudsman reported after the first year of the new Regulations that significant problems remain:

> The data published here point to a clear conclusion. The NHS needs to listen harder and learn more from complaints. When it fails to do so, it is missing a rich source of insight and information that is freely and readily available and comes directly from service users.[72]

---

68   Case W 236/75-76; HC 160 (1976–77), p 23.
69   Case W 241/79-80; HC 51 (1982–83).
70   Health and Social Care Act 2008 (Regulated Activities) Regulations 2010, reg 19.
71   Members of the Independent Healthcare Advisory Service must follow their guid-ance: Independent Healthcare Advisory Services, *Making a Complaint in the Inde-pendent Sector: A Guide for Patients* (2007).
72   *Listening and Learning*, p 4.

The local resolution stage remains obscure and difficult to negotiate. Half of the complaints received by the Ombudsman in 2009–10 were inadequate or premature.[73] Dissatisfaction stemmed from inadequate responses, poor explanations and the attitude of NHS staff.[74] In one recent case the patient complained:

> Mine was a misdiagnosed TB meningitis that was missed . . . In the end, I went to litigation because I couldn't get any answers. I wanted an apology and I couldn't get any answers. Then that triggered a mental health condition in my son and he died . . . I never heard a thing. His possessions were sent home to me in a bin bag marked 'NHS household waste' . . . I am still in NHS complaints five and a half years later, unresolved.[75]

Arguably the most significant stumbling block is a lack of openness in the NHS. The Ombudsman notes, 'When things do go wrong, an apology can be a powerful remedy; simple to deliver and costing nothing'.[76] The blame culture engendered by the medical litigation system can make doctors unwilling to apologise lest it be seen as an admission of guilt. Attempts have been made to remedy this problem. Section 2 of the Compensation Act 2006 states that: 'An apology, or offer of treatment or other redress, shall not of itself amount to an admission of negligence or breach of statutory duty'.[77] The National Patient Safety Agency[78] has reiterated that: 'Saying sorry is not an admission of liability and is the right thing to do. Patients have a right to expect openness in their health care'.[79] This position is endorsed by the GMC,[80] National Health Service Litigation Authority (NHSLA)[81] and CQC.[82] But Vines questions the value of an apology which is not accompanied by an admission of guilt. First it is difficult to frame an apology stripped of factual statements or admissions of guilt which might later be used as evidence of negligence. Second, the apology might seem guarded, partial and disingenuous, and make

---

[73] *Listening and Learning*, p 13.

[74] *Listening and Learning*, p 14.

[75] Health Committee, *Complaints and Litigation – Oral Evidence* (2011) HC 786-i, Q43.

[76] *Listening and Learning*, p 4.

[77] But see P Vines, 'Apologies and Civil Liability in the UK: A View from Elsewhere' (2008) 12(2) *Edinburgh Law Review* 200 commenting on the brevity of the provision which does not define 'apology' and seems to add little to existing law.

[78] Expected to be abolished in 2013.

[79] NPSA, *Being Open: Communicating Patient Safety Incidents with Patients, Their Families and Carers* NPSA/2009/PSA003 (2009) DH, p 6.

[80] GMC, *Good Clinical Practice* (2006), para 30. 'If a patient under your care has suffered harm or distress, you must act immediately to put matters right, if that is possible. You should offer an apology and explain fully and promptly to the patient what has happened, and the likely short-term and long-term effects.' Paragraph 31: 'Patients who complain about the care or treatment they have received have a right to expect a prompt, open, constructive and honest response including an explanation and, if appropriate, an apology. You must not allow a patient's complaint to affect adversely the care or treatment you provide or arrange.'

[81] National Health Service Litigation Authority, *Apologies and Explanations: Letter to Chief Executives and Finance Directors* (2009).

[82] Care Quality Commission, *A Quality Service, A Quality Experience* (2009).

things worse. Vines extols the virtues of the systems in parts of Australia and America whereby legislation protects even those apologies accompanied by an admission of guilt.[83]

In addition to measures encouraging doctors to apologise when things go wrong, new measures to enhance institutional responsibility (considered in chapter 1) include a duty incumbent on NHS bodies to report 'incidents' such as accidents or near misses. But they must report them to the National Patient Safety Agency (in future the NHS Commissioning Board), not the aggrieved patient or his family.[84] Draft regulations on a 'duty of cooperation' seek to improve the sharing of information on NHS staff to improve patient safety.[85] Branded a 'gossips' charter' by the Medical Defence Union,[86] draft regulation 6 sets down a duty to share information about a healthcare worker, where the designated body reasonably believes it might protect patients or the public.

The government has been praised for including as one of the five domains in its outcome-based framework, 'treating people in a safe environment and protecting them from harm'. This prioritises patient safety and promises greater transparency and incentives for improvement. But there are also concerns. How will the government prevent 'gaming' – ie the over-reporting of trivial and underreporting of more serious incidents? Will higher performing providers be penalised?[87] Perhaps most importantly, the government's White Paper promises to 'require hospitals to be open about mistakes and always tell patients if something has gone wrong'[88] but will this amount to a statutory duty and how will it be enforced?

Redress

9.12 As we have seen, a significant problem endemic in the complaints procedure is the guardedness of doctors. If doctors were more open, faith might gradually be restored in the complaints process. Lack of patient confidence in the complaints system as well as a requirement for financial compensation, leads some patients to litigate. Julie Bailey, founder of Cure the NHS which was set up to represent those harmed at Mid-Staffordshire hospital, said:

> In Mid Staffordshire the majority of people that came forward to me for advice didn't want to take the litigation route. It is the same throughout the country. All

---

[83] P Vines (2008) 12(2) *Edinburgh Law Review* 200, p 222.

[84] Care Quality Commission (Registration) Regulations 2009 SI 2009/3112, reg 18.

[85] The draft Health Care Workers (Duty of Co-operation) Regulations 2010. The consultation closed in July 2010.

[86] C Dyer, 'Regulations on Sharing Concerns About Doctors are like "Gossips" Charters' (2010) 341 *BMJ* c3638.

[87] DH, *Transparency in Outcomes – A Framework for the NHS: Government Response to Consultation* (2010) ref: 15265.

[88] White Paper, *Equity and Excellence: Liberating the NHS* Cm 7881 (2010), p 3. And see NHS Constitution, s 3(b).

people want a lot of the time is answers as to what happened to their relative and why. It is a torture not knowing . . .[89]

Fear of litigation prompts a vicious cycle of little benefit to doctors, patients, or the public. The Bristol Inquiry Report[90] eloquently implored the government to abolish clinical negligence litigation and introduce no-fault compensation.

> The system of clinical negligence litigation is now ripe to review . . . [W]e take the view that it will not be possible to achieve an environment of full, open reporting within the NHS when, outside it, there exists a litigation system the incentives of which press in the opposite direction. We believe that the way forward lies in the abolition of clinical negligence litigation, taking clinical error out of the courts and the tort system. It should be replaced by effective systems for identifying, analysing, learning from and preventing errors, along with all other sentinel events. There must also be a new approach to compensating those patients harmed through such events . . . [W]e recognise that such a radical change is likely to have wide implications not least in terms of any new system of compensation . . .

So in September 2001, the CMO[91] initiated a comprehensive consultation process to explore potential options for reform of clinical negligence claims. Two years later, the Department of Health's consultation paper *Making Amends* rejected a comprehensive no-fault system of compensation on the grounds of the financial costs, problems of causation, and the scheme's perceived inability to deal with wider learning issues. The NHS Redress Act was passed and given Royal Assent in 2006. We explore its provisions below. Whilst the intention was to take 'clinical error out of the courts', as suggested in the Bristol Inquiry Report, it did not remove it from the tort system. Arguably the NHS Redress Act was not ambitious enough and, as noted above, it is questionable whether it will be taken forward in England now. Instead, Lord Young has proposed an alternative fast-track scheme.[92] But before we look at some of the detail of either scheme, let us address the debate on a no-fault compensation scheme for medical injuries.

An attack on tort

9.13   Does the tort system work? Criticism of the tort of negligence as a means of compensating for personal injury, however caused, whether by medical error or in a road accident or any other area of human activity, is far from new.[93] The tort system has been condemned as unpredictable, expensive and

---

[89]   Health Committee, Complaints and Litigation – Oral Evidence (2011) HC786-i, Q36.
[90]   See *The Bristol Inquiry*, p 367.
[91]   DH, *Clinical Negligence: What are the Issues and Options for Reform* (2001).
[92]   HM Government, Lord Young, *Common Sense, Common Safety* (2010).
[93]   See in particular, P Cane, P S Atiyah, *Atiyah's Accidents, Compensation and the Law* (7th edn, 2006), CUP.

unfair.[94] The nature of the tort system is unpredictable. The injured claimant, on whom the burden of proving negligence falls, cannot know in advance whether he will receive any monetary compensation. He cannot plan his personal finances and put his life in order. For example, a person rendered paraplegic in an accident cannot know whether he will be able to afford to convert his house to meet the limitations imposed by his new disability. Uncertainty and delay[95] may even impede his recovery.

The tort system remains expensive because of the cost of litigation. A part of the cost is borne by the state. Where the claimant is still publicly funded (though we saw in chapter 8 that a Ministry of Justice Green Paper proposes that clinical negligence be excluded from legal aid[96]), the state funds his claim, perhaps with nothing to show for it in the end. The expense hits the NHS particularly hard. Resources spent fighting costly legal battles could be better spent on improving the quality of care, so reducing the number of accidents that occur in the first place. And even if legal aid is withdrawn from claimants, the NHS still bears the cost of defending the claim and any costs or damages payable, including at present any success fee in claims funded by Conditional Fee Agreements (CFAs). Recall that in 2009/2010, the NHSLA paid out £787m in connection with clinical negligence claims, up from £769m the year before and £591m in 2005/6.[97] The legal costs in connection with claims closed that year were £163,719,971.[98]

Patients suffer in equal measure. The prohibitive price of litigation may deter claimants with a genuine case from pursuing it if legal aid is not available, and their claim is not a good enough gamble for a CFA – a problem which will be exacerbated if legal aid is withdrawn. The CMO in *Making Amends* stated that in England:[99]

> The legal and administrative costs of settling claims exceeded the money actually paid to the claimant in the majority of claims under £45,000 and took up an even higher proportion of the total amount paid out in the smaller claims.

Most of all, is the tort system fair? First, the difficulties and cost of litigation place enormous pressure on a claimant to settle for less than full compensation. Second, the dividing line between negligence and no-negligence is paper-thin.

---

[94] The Pearson Report (Report of the Royal Commission on Civil Liability and Compensation for Personal Injury) (1978) Cmnd 7054, vol 1, paras 246–263.

[95] For claims closed 1999–2000, with settlement costs exceeding £10,000, the average time from claim to payment of damages was five and a half years: House of Commons Public Accounts Committee, *Handling Clinical Negligence Claims in England*, HC 280 (2002), PAC, p 6. In 2004/5 the average was reduced to 1.44 years: *NHS Redress Bill HL 137* (2006) Research Paper 06/29, p 11.

[96] See above at **8.2**.

[97] The NHS Litigation Authority, *Factsheet 2: Financial Information*, 2009/10, accessible at http://www.nhsla.com.

[98] The NHS Litigation Authority, *Factsheet 2: Financial Information*, 2009/10.

[99] See CMO, *Making Amends*, p 69.

In *Ashcroft v Mersey Area Health Authority*,[100] Kilner Brown J reluctantly dismissed the plaintiff's claim for compensation after an operation on her ear left her with a degree of facial paralysis. He found the expert evidence on whether such damage could occur without negligence equally balanced and so the plaintiff failed to discharge the burden of proof. He commented:[101]

> Where an injury is caused which never should have been caused, common sense and natural justice indicate that some degree of compensation ought to be paid by someone.

Finally, the tort system has been attacked as unfair on the grounds that it lacks any proper moral basis. What is the justification for giving X, who can attribute his injury to human error, full compensation, and leaving Y, whose injury has some other cause, to struggle on state benefits?

The litigation system has generated blame, distrust and dissatisfaction on the part of patients and defensiveness, concealment and low morale on the part of doctors. Solicitors and claims management companies tout for business, inviting claims with advertising campaigns. The Constitutional Affairs Committee reported in 2006 that the compensation culture is a myth, but that the *cost* of the belief, in terms of risk aversion, is real.[102] Lord Young reiterates the misconceptions and calls for a common sense approach, levelling criticism primarily at health and safety legislation, but also appealing for reform to reduce and lower the costs of claims at common law.[103] Although the media has exaggerated the rise in the number of clinical negligence claims, the *size* of clinical negligence awards is increasing. Unsurprisingly, there have been several proposals for reform.[104]

Alternatives to tort

9.14   So should we abolish clinical negligence litigation? Tort is not the only means of providing compensation to victims of misadventure. Private insur-

---

[100] [1983] 2 All ER 245. And see *Nash v Richmond Health Authority* (1996) 36 BMLR 123.

[101] [1983] 2 All ER 245 at 246. See also *Wilsher v Essex AHA* (1986) 3 All ER 801 at 810 per Mustill LJ.

[102] House of Commons Constitutional Affairs Committee, *Compensation Culture*, Third Report of Session 2005–06, HC 754-1 (2006), para 111.

[103] HM Government, Lord Young, *Common Sense, Common Safety* (2010). Discussed above at **8.18**.

[104] See, for example, the Pearson Report 1978; the Kennedy Report, *The Report of the Inquiry into the Care and Management of Children Receiving Complex Heart Treatment Between 1984 and 1995* (2001) HMSO; National Audit Office, *Handling Clinical Negligence Claims in England*, HC 403 (2001); House of Commons Public Accounts Committee, *Handling Clinical Negligence Claims in England*; CMO *Making Amends*; Lord Justice Jackson, *Review of Civil Litigation Costs, Final Report* (2009) TSO; HM Government, Lord Young, *Common Sense, Common Safety* (2010).

ance is one option.[105] Another is no-fault liability. In the UK, there are various no-fault schemes, including the Industrial Injuries Scheme, the Criminal Injuries Compensation Scheme and the Vaccine Damage Payment Scheme. But they are piecemeal and incomprehensive. The case for a no-fault scheme is made out in part by the manifest deficiencies of the present system. It is beyond the scope of this book to consider whether a comprehensive no-fault scheme for all types of accidents should be introduced. In a perfect society, any person suffering from disability from whatever cause would receive appropriate financial support. The person paralysed by a stroke has identical needs to the person paralysed by a fall from a ladder or a bungled operation. That ideal would require not an accident compensation scheme, but provision of a general disability income.[106] Radical reform can never be expected to happen instantly. It must be approached incrementally. Previous editions of this book have put forward a scheme of no-fault compensation embracing two categories of medical injury:

(1) injury or illness arising from an absence of, or delay in, appropriate medical treatment[107] provided that
    (i) treatment would have prevented that injury or illness, and
    (ii) a reasonable request for medical care from a person or authority under an obligation to provide care has been made by the patient or some other person acting on his behalf;
(2) injury or illness resulting from medical treatment provided that
    (i) the injury or illness is not caused by the natural progression of disease or the ageing process, and
    (ii) the injury or illness is not the consequence of an unavoidable risk inherent in the treatment, of which the patient has received proper warning.

Category 1 would cover injury arising from failure to treat both in circumstances where the present tort of negligence would operate, and where it would not. For example, a request for treatment might be made and not acted on by the GP because at the time he acted reasonably in thinking an immediate visit was not necessary. Events prove him wrong. They do not render him negligent. Under this proposed no-fault scheme the patient would recover because he did in fact suffer as a result of lack of treatment, albeit no one was to blame.

Category 2 is more difficult to define. The intention of category 2 is that it should extend to any damage to the patient which is neither the result of the natural progression of his original disease or condition nor a consequence

---

[105] See P Cane, P S Atiyah, *Atiyah's Accidents, Compensation and the Law* (7th edn, 2006), CUP.
[106] See C Ham *et al*, *Medical Negligence: Compensation and Accountability* (1988) King's Fund Institute and Centre for Socio-Legal Studies.
[107] Treatment would be defined to include treatment given to the mother and injuring the child. Consideration of the implications of ante-natal treatment would be required, for example (1) would treatment necessary for the mother but injuring the child be excluded? (2) what about pre-conception injury to either parent?

inherent in that treatment and unavoidable if that treatment is to be success-ful. Under that last limitation, the side-effects of certain surgery and therapy would be excluded. At one level, the patient could obviously not recover compensation for pain and suffering ordinarily attendant on surgery. At another level, unpleasant and dangerous side-effects, for example, the patient's hair falling out during chemotherapy, or the risk of a stroke in some forms of brain surgery, would have to be excluded if they were inescapable in the pursuit of proper treatment. One important proviso is attached to the exclu-sion of unavoidable side-effects from compensation. The patient must have been properly warned. Failure to give proper warning, which results in injury unexpected and unconsidered by the patient, would remain a ground for com-pensation.

Avoiding definitions and drafting points may well be criticised as cowardice. The scheme above operates in a presumption of entitlement when injury fol-lows medical treatment and ensues from lack of treatment. It seeks to avoid the linguistic complications of concepts of error or mishap. Ken Oliphant[108] has argued that experience from New Zealand should make us cautious. Ini-tially at least, a compensation scheme should be based on evidence of 'medical error'. Where investigation and hindsight indicate that the patient receives less than the optimum treatment and with such treatment her injury could have been avoided, she would receive compensation. Simple evidence of an unex-pected outcome of treatment would not suffice, however serious that outcome. If a previously healthy patient suffers a cardiac arrest in the course of minor surgery, he will recover compensation if, for example, a defect is found in the anaesthetic equipment or some error was made by the anaesthetist. He will not have to show blameworthiness. If no reason for the sudden heart failure can be discovered, he has no claim in relation to that mishap.

The 'Oliphant solution' would, as he says, provide 'consistency and ease of application'. It might provoke awkward questions of causation and make it difficult to cast off the shackles of negligence. It is a notable attempt to put substance into the defining of 'medical misadventure'.

No-fault compensation abroad[109]

9.15   A growing number of no-fault compensation schemes operate abroad. We briefly outline only two,[110] the New Zealand accident compensation

---

[108] K Oliphant, 'Defining "Medical Misadventure": Lessons from New Zealand' (1996) 1 *Medical Law Review* 1, pp 30–31.

[109] In Scotland, the No Fault Compensation Review Group, set up in 2009, has con-sidered a number of different no-fault compensation schemes. See A-M Farrell, S Devaney, A Dar, *No Fault Compensation Schemes for Medical Injury – A Review* (2010), accessible at: http://www.scotland.gov.uk/Resource/Doc/924/0099427.pdf.

[110] See J Dute (ed) *et al*, 'No Fault Compensation in the Health Care Sector' (2004) 8 *Tort and Insurance Law,* covering schemes in a range of countries.

scheme, which covers medical injury within comprehensive provision for compensation for personal injury from all causes, and the Swedish Patients' Insurance Scheme, designed specifically for medical injuries. Review of New Zealand's and Sweden's experience will highlight certain problems of no-fault liability. They are problems which should be treated as an education in mistakes to avoid, rather than an indication that the concept of no-fault liability should necessarily be abandoned. In this brief review of both schemes, we concentrate on how the basic principle of no-fault liability works. Space does not allow consideration in detail of the funding and administration of either scheme. It will swiftly become apparent that defining the criteria governing eligibility to compensation is the litmus test of whether no-fault compensation can be made to work.

The New Zealand scheme was first set up in 1974 to award compensation to anyone who suffered 'personal injury by accident'. It was reformed in 2002, but links to fault-based compensation were retained. Concepts of 'medical error' and 'medical mishap' were introduced.[111] Further reform in 2005 finally broke those links.[112] In 2005, eligibility for compensation was significantly expanded to cover all 'treatment injuries'.[113] The scheme now covers most personal injuries suffered while receiving treatment from health professionals. It is a true no-fault compensation system. Claims have risen. The scheme faced a major budget shortfall in 2009 and in 2010 had a \$10.3bn net liability.[114] Whilst the scheme has been commended for providing timely compensation and effective complaints resolution, there remain concerns surrounding patient safety.[115] But the provision of a no-fault scheme does not necessarily render doctors unaccountable. A new patient safety team was introduced in order to address systemic problems and an independent health ombudsman, the Health and Disability Commissioner[116] mediates, resolves complaints and promulgates lessons for the health service.

---

[111] J Manning, 'Informed Consent to Medical Treatment: The Common Law and New Zealand's Code of Patients' Rights' (2004) 12(2) *Medical Law Review* 181.

[112] Injury Prevention, Rehabilitation, and Compensation Act 2001, s 32 (as amended by Injury Prevention, Rehabilitation, and Compensation Amendment Act (No 2) 2005).

[113] See K Oliphant, 'Beyond Misadventure: Compensation for Medical Injuries in New Zealand' (2007) 15(3) *Medical Law Review* 357.

[114] ACC, *Annual Report 2010,* p 12. The scheme has instituted change to reach its target of becoming fully funded (ie holding the assets necessary to meet all liabilities) by 2019 and achieved surplus in 2009/10. See 'ACC's Direction and Performance', accessible at http://www.acc.co.nz.

[115] See M Bismark and R Paterson, 'No-fault Compensation in New Zealand: Harmonizing Injury Compensation, Provider Accountability and Patient Safety' (2006) 25(1) *Health Affairs* 278.

[116] Created by the Health and Disability Commissioner Act 1994 (NZ). The Act was passed to implement the recommendations of Judge Cartwright: *The Report of the Committee of Inquiry into Allegations Concerning the Treatment of Cervical Cancer at National Women's Hospital and Into Other Related Matters* (1988) Government Printing Office, Auckland.

The Swedish Patients' Insurance Scheme[117] is expressly designed to provide compensation for medical injuries. Compensation is payable in respect of any injury or illness resulting from any procedure related to health care. Injury arising from any diagnostic procedure, inappropriate medication, medical treatment or surgery falls within the ambit of the Swedish scheme. But compensation for such injury is subject to three important provisos. First, the injury must be proved to result from the procedure in issue, and not from the original disease. Second, injury resulting from a risk taken by the doctor to save life or prevent permanent disability is excluded. Third, and most crucially, the claimant has to show that the procedure causing his injury was *not medically justified*. The test of whether the procedure was medically justified often reintroduces the question of negligence. Nevertheless, certain claimants who lose in England would obtain compensation in Sweden. Mrs Ashcroft, who suffered injury to a facial nerve when the surgeon accidentally cut the nerve, would recover in Sweden. The surgeon was not to blame, but cutting the nerve was not medically indicated.[118]

Examination of the problems encountered in New Zealand and Sweden must not obscure the benefits of no-fault schemes. Patients uncompensated by a tort-based system benefit in those countries. In Sweden, the investigation of the cause of a medical injury may still involve questions akin to negligence. It is an investigation. The patient will discover what happened. The opportunities for scoring points and the advantages to be gained from having the best advocate rather than the best case, do not exist.

The rejection of no-fault compensation in England

9.16   As long ago as 1978 the Pearson Commission[119] advised against abolition of tort as a means of compensating personal injuries. They made a number of specific proposals for more limited reforms. We concentrate on the proposals which relate to medical injuries. The Commission decided against recommending a no-fault scheme for all medical injuries.[120] Following its recommendations, the Vaccine Damage Payment Scheme was introduced. Strict liability for defective drugs was introduced by the Consumer Protection Act 1987.[121] That reform came not as a result of the Pearson Report, but because of pressure from Europe. The Commission's Report gathered dust. Many of its proposals went unheeded.

---

[117] Patient Injury Act 1996 (Sweden). L H Fallberg, B Borgenhammar, 'The Swedish No Fault Patient Insurance Scheme' (1997) 4 *European Journal of Health Law* 279; Patient Claims Panel (Sweden), *Patient Injury Compensation for Healthcare-Related Injuries* (2007), accessible at http://www.patientforsakring.se.

[118] *Ashcroft v Mersey Regional Health Authority* [1983] 2 All ER 245.

[119] The Pearson Report, vols 1–3.

[120] The Pearson Report, paras 1304–1371.

[121] See below ch 10.

The Bristol Inquiry Report[122] renewed the attack on tort, and in *Making Amends* the CMO also condemned the torts system in terms of both its financial and emotional ramifications, especially in relation to low-value claims.[123]

> Legal proceedings for medical injury progress in an atmosphere of confrontational acrimony, misunderstanding and bitterness. The process is anathema to the spirit of openness, trust, and partnership which should characterise the modern relationship between doctor and patient. Moreover, the whole nature of a legal dispute between two parties works against the wider interests of patients. The emphasis is on revealing as little as possible about what went wrong, defending clinical decisions that were taken and only reluctantly releasing information.

Yet, once again, the problems associated with causation, deterrence and accountability, and the financial implications of a no-fault scheme led to the rejection of a comprehensive no-fault system. Let us examine these criticisms more carefully.

Causation

9.17 The CMO, like the Pearson Commission before him, felt that distinguishing between an injury arising from treatment given and the natural progression of disease or inescapable side-effects of treatment was too difficult. This is a valid concern. But is it enough to rule out a change to no-fault compensation? Causation presents just as much of a problem within the present system. Reform of the law introducing a no-fault principle would have the following benefits. A greater number of claimants would obtain compensation to help them adapt their lives to their disabilities, or to meet financial loss resulting from death of a breadwinner. The damage done to relations between the medical profession and the public by bitter and protracted litigation would be removed. The patient would obtain compensation because he suffered injury as a result of treatment going wrong. The issue of *why* it went wrong and the doctor's competence would be for completely separate investigatory procedures. The problem of causation would still be present. Distinguishing between injury and the progression of disease (or whatever) would be made easier. The issue of causation would be investigated. It would not be part of a battle between the patient and the NHS, with the NHS having a vested interest in finding experts to deny that the patient's condition was caused by the treatment. Consideration could be given to whether the burden of proof of causation might be alleviated by requiring only proof of a reasonable possibility of causation.

Deterrence and accountability

9.18 Arguably, tort serves a valuable purpose in emphasising the accountability and responsibility of individual medical staff. It may be costly and

---

[122] See *The Bristol Inquiry*, p 367.
[123] CMO, *Making Amends*, p 7.

inefficient, it may be inequitable in whom it compensates, but if it deters medical malpractice, can we afford to abandon it? We remain unconvinced that the tort system has much systematic deterrent effect in health care insofar as individual doctors are concerned. Moreover, the alleged deterrent impact of tort often obscures the crucial question of accountability.

(1)   The tort system is capricious in its operation. Obstetricians are at high risk of a law suit. The highest payment relating to cerebral palsy in infants after an allegedly negligent delivery is £5.5m.[124] Geriatricians are hardly ever sued. This is not because obstetricians are more likely to be negligent than their colleagues in geriatrics. It is because if granny dies as a result of a negligent overdose, so little could be claimed by way of damages that it is not worth suing the responsible doctor. There will be no legal aid and nor would such a claim be a good risk for a CFA.

(2)   Even where NHS doctors are sued, the deterrent effect of tort is not direct. The damages will not come out of the doctor's pocket nor will his 'premiums' be increased. The deterrent function of tort normally operates via the insurance system. Poor drivers are deterred from carelessness and encouraged to improve because 'carelessness costs money'. NHS Indemnity means that NHS doctors do not pay any sort of insurance or indemnity. There is the emotional impact of litigation. Does the worry of being sued deter the incompetent doctor? We doubt it. Where negligence is gross and obvious, claims are settled swiftly to avoid adverse publicity. It is the cases where there truly is doubt about whether an error is negligent that drag on in the public eye. We suspect 'good' doctors worry about litigation and 'bad' doctors rarely give the possibility much thought.

(3)   Finally, there are a number of cases where, albeit there was actionable negligence, there is no moral culpability. Doctors who make mistakes after hours without sleep in under-resourced hospitals should not be blamed for their error. The tort system could operate to deter such 'negligence' only by encouraging such a doctor to refuse to treat patients at all, once he suspected he could not do so entirely competently. Such an outcome would prompt more, not less, patient suffering.

One caveat must be issued before dismissing the impact of deterrence via the tort system. Health providers are encouraged to be cost-conscious. Is there a risk that a hospital trust anxious to offer the lowest-cost appendectomy will cut corners and offer less than safe appendectomies? The fear of litigation might operate on the collective mind of the trust to deter economy measures that prejudice patients' safety. The impact of tort on providers must not be overlooked in the no-fault debate. Evaluating the extent to which providers may be influenced by the deterrent function of tort is difficult. Risk-management has a high profile within the NHS now. That is good. Hospitals review their practice and investigate adverse outcomes to try and prevent medical accidents.

[124]   CMO, *Making Amends*, p 50.

The coalition government promises a new raft of quality drivers.[125] Quality will depend on competition and greater transparency.[126] Monitors will oversee economic regulation and license NHS providers, and all providers will register with the CQC, which will assess quality of services against outcome-based standards. The proposals will reduce bureaucracy, but at what price? As GP consortia gradually have a wider array of providers from which to commission services, it is unlikely that the tension between providing cost-efficient services and high quality services will go away.[127] Arguably, fear of litigation will provide a much needed incentive to prioritise quality.

Currently a key player in risk-management is the Clinical Negligence Scheme for Trusts (CNST), which is run by the NHSLA.[128] Membership of the CNST is voluntary, but currently all PCTs and hospital trusts (and presumably in future CCs) are members. Failure to implement adequate risk-management strategies can lead to expulsion from CNST. That will mean a hospital is left to bear all its own litigation costs. CNST is the enforcer of risk-management. It operates a strategy embedded in the tort system. Put simply, NHS hospitals and other bodies are obliged to comply with risk-management or face financial disaster. Risk-management could and should survive a no-fault compensation scheme. But what would replace CNST and will it have the same 'teeth'?

Returning to accountability, does the tort system ensure that health professionals and providers are made to account for their conduct? Tort's role in ensuring accountability is minimal. The nature of adversarial litigation militates against such an outcome. If an operation goes wrong and a patient is injured, what went wrong and why it went wrong needs investigation. The professional or professionals involved should be required to explain all they can to the patient and their conduct should be evaluated to discover whether it fell below a standard of good practice and to consider what measures might be taken to avoid such an accident in future. It may well be that even though there is no negligence in the tort sense, doctors and nurses can learn from the accident and amend standard procedures in the light of that knowledge. Adversarial litigation does not encourage such an investigation of the incident. Even after the Woolf reforms, little opportunity exists in litigation to evaluate disputed practices. Doctors and nurses in the shadow of litigation clam up; they are naturally wary of admitting any doubts they may have as to what they did or did not do. If the patient fails to prove negligence, within the tort system

---

[125] See above at **1.3** and **1.15**.

[126] See C Dyer, 'NHS Reforms Could make Hospitals Safer and More Open, MPs Hear' (2011) 342 *BMJ* d787.

[127] See C Dyer, 'Health Bill Will Destroy NHS, Says Union' (2011) 342 *BMJ* d701, highlighting Unite's concerns that opening the market to 'any willing provider' will create conflicts of interest between GPs' roles as commissioners and clinicians and that abandoning the national tariff in favour of a maximum price will enhance competition on the basis of price rather than quality. See discussion above at **1.3**.

[128] Which will survive the government's cull on arm's-length review bodies, subject to an industry review to ensure it is working efficiently.

that is the end of the matter. Accountability is crucial. The tort system provides only token accountability. It is organisations such as the CQC which should help ensure the NHS learns from its mistakes.

Cost

9.19 For Mason and Laurie, cost is a major reason for the government's rejection of no-fault compensation in England.[129] The overall cost of a no-fault scheme is difficult to judge. It is not a cheap option. They estimate a total cost of £4bn annually. One article suggests that the operation of a no-fault scheme in England along the lines of the Swedish system would cost several times the cost of the current system due largely to the increase in claimants.[130] No-fault can, however, be cost-effective. In New Zealand, administrative costs in 2000/1 ran to around 7 per cent of the cost of the system,[131] ie at least 90p in every pound was paid out to victims.

The ultimate cost of a no-fault scheme will depend on the level of payments made to victims. Several hard questions need to be addressed. It would seem obvious that the payment of compensation for loss of income and cost of care should generally be by way of periodical payments rather than as a lump sum. Payments can then be adjusted to meet the claimant's current needs. Should there be a ceiling on payments? Under the tort system, a high-earning solicitor rendered unable to work obtains money to make up her actual loss of income. Should no-fault compensation be limited to sufficient to provide for the claimant's needs arising from her disability up to the 'average' standard of living?[132] What about compensation for pain and suffering? The harder a no-fault scheme tries to offer generous compensation, the harder it is to fund a scheme to meet the needs of the widest possible range of claimants. An affordable no-fault scheme will necessarily have to limit compensation payments. Typically, no-fault compensation schemes do not compensate non-pecuniary loss. Previously wealthy victims of medical accidents will not receive full compensation for their monetary loss. Their loss of income will be capped. Medical and rehabilitation costs which could be met from other sources will not be included in compensation payments.

---

[129] J K Mason and G T Laurie, *Mason and McCall Smith's Law and Medical Ethics* (8th edn, 2010) OUP, p 125. And see CMO, *Making Amends*, p 15. And see T Douglas, 'Medical Injury Compensation: Beyond No Fault' (2009) 17 *Medical Law Review* 30, who argues that, given the limited resources available, a fairer scheme might require abandoning medical injury compensation altogether, in favour of better social security and public healthcare systems and a safer NHS.

[130] P Fenn, A Gray and N Rickman, 'The Economics of Clinical Negligence Reform in England' (2005) 114 *The Economic Journal* 272 at 290.

[131] See CMO, *Making Amends*, p 98.

[132] In New Zealand, a maximum limit of 80 per cent of actual earnings. CMO, *Making Amends*, p 98.

Consider this scenario. X and Y are both paralysed in a medical accident. X, a PE teacher, who might have got nothing from the tort system because he could not prove negligence, will benefit from no-fault whatever his prior circumstances. He will gain a reasonable income (shall we say £500 a week) if he can no longer work. He will obtain money to pay for care at home over and above what the social security system may provide, and money to adapt his house to the demands of his disability. Y, who could win damages under the tort system, may lose. Assume that prior to his accident, Y was a wealthy young football star. Now he is paralysed. £500 a week could be about 5 per cent of his previous income. He will get nothing for pain and suffering. A no-fault scheme will not pay for him to have costly private care in the USA.

Proponents of social justice will argue that it is better to offer some recompense to more people than award a lottery-type damages to winners in the tort system. The problem is this. If a no-fault compensation scheme exists side by side with access to the tort system, patients such as Y will still opt for the tort system. Two options could be explored.

(1) Claimants who opt to sue in tort do so at their peril. If their claim fails, they are excluded from the no-fault scheme. That might radically lower the cost of tort claims because only the most clear-cut claims will be brought and they should be swiftly settled.

(2) Or, as in New Zealand, where a claimant is entitled to claim under the no-fault scheme a tort claim is barred altogether. No-fault becomes the exclusive route to compensation for medical accidents. Financially, and to achieve the objective of a no-fault scheme, the second option makes pre-eminent sense. But in barring access to the courts, would it violate Article 6 of the European Convention on Human Rights entitling everyone to a fair trial in determination of his civil rights and obligations?

Reforming the torts system

9.20 In *Making Amends*, the CMO rejected a no-fault medical injury scheme. Instead, the report proposed reform of the existing negligence system, incorporating four main elements:[133]

* an investigation of the incident which is alleged to have caused harm and of the harm that has resulted;
* provision of an explanation to the patient and of the action proposed to prevent repetition;
* development and delivery of a package of care providing remedial treatment, therapy and arrangements for continuing care where needed;
* payments for pain and suffering, out-of-pocket expenses and care or treatment which the NHS could provide.

---

[133] CMO, *Making Amends*, p 16.

The report provided the basis for the NHS Redress Act 2006. The Bill, introduced in 2005, was contentious. Many felt that tinkering with the torts system would not make the problems go away. Some of the measures proposed in *Making Amends* and designed to increase openness and reduce the blame culture were excluded. Though the scheme might eventually save money by cutting out the lawyer it would be costly to set up.

The NHS Redress Act 2006

9.21 The NHS Redress Act received Royal Assent in November 2006. It requires secondary legislation which, in England, now seems unlikely. It did not satisfy the proponents of no-fault compensation because whilst it was a non-adversarial scheme, it was tort-based – that is, the claimant must still be able to prove fault. It would not, initially at least, apply to PCTs (CCs in future), nor to claims before the Act was passed. At the outset, it would cover only claims of a low monetary value.[134] The proposed scheme authority, the NHSLA, raised issues of impartiality and independence – the NHSLA is traditionally the defender of the NHS's interests. There was no statutory duty of candour to enhance openness and accountability. Assistance would be provided for the individual seeking redress, most probably in the form of free independent legal advice relating to the offer and any settlement agreement,[135] and the provision of the services of jointly instructed medical experts.[136] But would lawyers and doctors be willing to work for the flat fee they would be paid under the scheme? The Act did not satisfy economists because although it would reduce delay, it would be costly to set up and would probably bring in new claims. If, as was expected, there was a £20,000 limit under the scheme, it was estimated that it would, in the first year, result in anything between a £7m saving and a cost of £48m. After ten years, it was predicted that the scheme would range between a saving of £15m and a cost of £80m.[137] Farrell and Devaney opined that, far from 'making amends', the NHS Redress Act might 'make things worse'.[138] Nevertheless, resurrection of the scheme is one alternative open to government. It would offer a preferable procedural route when compared with litigation and could potentially combine compensation with apologies, explanations and system change. One of the questions posed by the Health Committee in their review of Complaints and Litigation is to determine the government's intentions regarding the Act. There is even a Bill proposing an amendment to speed up claims resolution and cut costs.[139]

---

[134] NHS Redress Act 2006, s 2(2).
[135] NHS Redress Act 2006, s 8(2).
[136] NHS Redress Act 2006, s 8(1)(b).
[137] NHS Redress Bill Explanatory Notes, Bill 137-EN, para 52.
[138] A-M Farrell, S Devaney, 'Making Amends or Making Things Worse? Clinical Negligence Reform and Patient Redress in England' (2007) 27(4) *Legal Studies* 630.
[139] NHS Redress (Amendment) Bill, HC 96. The provisional date for the second reading is 9/9/2011.

Section 17 of the NHS Redress Act 2006 gave the National Assembly for Wales power to introduce a NHS redress scheme. Wales has been operating a successful[140] optional Speedy Resolution Scheme for low-value claims (between £5,000 and £15,000) since 2005. The NHS Redress (Wales) Measure 2008 is designed to align complaints and redress. Draft National Health Service (Concerns, Complaints and Redress Arrangements) (Wales) Regulations 2010 will, if implemented, introduce a single portal for 'concerns' which include 'an expression of dissatisfaction, a complaint, a claim for compensation and any issue arising from a patient safety incident'.[141] When a concern is raised, a responsible body would generally have thirty days to investigate the issue and make a written response. This might incorporate an apology or action taken, and include a right to take the case to the NHS Ombudsman or request further information. Draft regulation 21 would require the body to consider whether there is a 'qualifying liability in tort', in which case the redress process would be activated. It shares a number of potential flaws with the proposed English scheme, but unlike the English scheme it attempts to bring together a fragmented system of redress. The scheme constitutes a brave attempt to offer a just and unified approach to redress.

Reducing costs

9.22   In *Making Amends*, the CMO questioned whether section 2(4) of the Law Reform (Personal Injuries) Act 1948, under which claimants are permitted to claim compensation for the cost of future care in the private sector even though the NHS could adequately provide for their need, ought to be repealed.[142] But this has not been pursued. In recent times, however, emphasis on enhancing openness and reducing defensiveness have given way to new proposals to reduce the costs of litigation borne by the beleaguered NHS through civil law reform.

We explored Lord Justice Jackson's Civil Litigation Costs Review[143] in chapter 8. Lord Jackson proposes to reduce defendants' costs by replacing success fees and ATE insurance premiums (which are usually paid by the losing party) with contingency fees (paid by the claimant, supported by a 10 per cent increase in general damages). This has potential to result in huge savings for

---

[140] See M Rosser, 'The Changing Face of Clinical Negligence in Wales' (2010) 3 *Journal of Personal Injury Law* 162 at 169.

[141] Draft NHS (Concerns, Complaints and Redress Arrangements) (Wales) Regulations 2010 – Informal Explanatory note.

[142] Reiterated recently by the Medical Defence Union, *Medical Defence Union Response to Equality and Excellence* (October 2010), suggesting repeal of s 2(4) form part of the government's legislative package of NHS reforms.

[143] The Right Honourable Lord Justice Jackson, *Review of Civil Litigation Costs, Final Report* (2009) The Stationery Office.

the NHS.[144] A consultation was launched in autumn 2010.[145] It was influenced by Lord Young's report on the compensation culture which he issued in October 2010.[146] In it Lord Young laments the costly and slow medical litigation process and criticises the NHS Redress Act, which he said:

> ... missed an opportunity to improve fundamentally the way that clinical negligence claims are handled. It should have focused on improving the fact-finding phase prior to pursuit of a claim in order to facilitate faster resolution of claims and leaving it to the parties concerned, or ultimately the courts, to determine cases not resolved by the fact-finding ...[147]

To speed up the process, Lord Young recommended a fast-track scheme for low-value claims (under £25,000) which will apply both to clinical negligence and personal injury cases. It would mirror the recently introduced Road Traffic Accident Personal Injury Scheme. A web portal would enable each side to upload relevant documents on a strict time scale and for fixed fees. It offers improvements to the litigation process in terms of speed and reduced cost but moves away from the proposals in *Making Amends* which took a more holistic approach to just redress. It seems to offer a limited solution. Lord Neuberger has opined that the alternative, should it fail, is to revisit the possibility of a no-fault scheme.[148]

---

[144] J Rayner, '"Indefensible" NHS Charges Defended' (2009) 3(1) *Law Society Gazette* 2 April; C Dyer, 'Reform of Civil Litigation Rules Could Save NHS Millions of Pounds' (2010) 340 *BMJ* 308; D Locke, 'Personal Injury / Medical Negligence: New Lease of Life' (2010) 160 *NLJ* 717.

[145] Parliamentary Under-Secretary of State for Justice Jonathan Djanogly MP, Written Ministerial Statement: Ministry of Justice Reform of Civil Litigation Funding Arrangements (26 July 2010).

[146] HM Government, Lord Young, *Common Sense, Common Safety* (2010). The report was welcomed but Lord Young resigned in November 2010 over an unrelated issue.

[147] HM Government, Lord Young, *Common Sense, Common Safety* (2010), p 22.

[148] Lord Neuberger, *Costs, Management, Proportionality and Insurance*, para 26, available at http://www.judiciary.gov.uk.

Chapter 10

MEDICAL PRODUCTS LIABILITY[1]

10.1 The pharmaceutical industry once basked in the warm glow of public acclaim. The development of antibiotics, of drugs to combat high blood pressure and heart disease, of medicines to alleviate the pain of rheumatism, and later the invention of the contraceptive Pill, brought benefits to many and life itself for some.[2] Events were to change the drug companies' image. Starting with the Thalidomide tragedy, a series of disasters taught us the painful lesson that drugs can be dangerous and their use must be paid for. The list of drugs enthusiastically promoted in the first place and withdrawn from the market a few years later, amid bitter allegations that the drug in question caused injury, and even death, is long. Opren,[3] the benzodiazepine tranquillisers such as Valium,[4] human growth hormone,[5] the Pill itself,[6] and most recently the painkiller Vioxx,[7] are but a random sample of the better-known cases. Allegations of gross profit-making by multi-national drug companies have proliferated.[8] Pharmaceutical companies have been criticised for testing

---

[1] See generally S Whittaker (ed), *The Development of Product Liability* (2009) CUP.

[2] Though J Blech and G W Hajjer, *Inventing Disease and Pushing Pills* (2006) Routledge, suggest that the pharmaceutical industry is guilty of medicalising normal life processes such as birth, unhappiness and sexuality to create new markets with costly results; see P Conrad, *et al*, 'Estimating the Costs of Medicalization' (2010) 70(12) *Social Science and Medicine* 1943.

[3] Discussed later in **10.1**.

[4] See *AB v Wyeth* (1996) 7 Med LR 267.

[5] The CJD Litigation, *Newman v Secretary of State for Health* (1997) 54 BMLR 85.

[6] See *XYZ v Schering Health Care Limited and Ors* [2002] EWHC 1420 (QB). See below at **10.13**.

[7] See below **10.14**.

[8] M Goozner, *The $800 Million Pill: The Truth Behind the Cost of New Drugs* (2004) University of California Press; L Eaton, 'Drug Companies are Defrauding Healthcare Systems, Conference Hears' (2004) 329 *BMJ* 940. The IMS annual global pharma market forecast predicts 5–8 per cent annual growth up to 2014: see http://www.imshealth.com.

products destined for the West on patients in developing countries.[9] Concern about the safety of drugs has extended today to anxiety about the safety of vaccinations, medical devices (such as breast implants) and the risks posed by contaminated blood supplies[10] and other body parts.[11]

Thalidomide was developed originally by West German manufacturers Chemie Grunenthal. A British company, Distillers, bought the formula and manufactured and marketed the drug here under licence from Chemie Grunenthal. The drug was promoted as a safer alternative to existing sedatives and was expressly claimed to be suitable for pregnant and nursing mothers. Thalidomide was alleged to be the cause of gross foetal deformity. All over Europe, wherever Thalidomide had been available, babies began to be born suffering from startlingly similar deformities, notably phocomelia (flipper limbs). After a bitter campaign, Distillers and the children's parents reached a settlement to provide compensation for children recognised as damaged by Thalidomide.[12] But as they got older and their needs changed, the compensation proved inadequate. In 2010 the government finally issued a formal apology and set up a £20m support package.[13]

The anti-rheumatic drug Opren, withdrawn here in 1982, is alleged to have caused kidney and liver damage, and even death, in some of its elderly users. Patients who suffered injury took legal action on both sides of the Atlantic. In the USA, Opren sufferers secured substantial compensation payments. British victims found themselves entangled in lengthy and complex litigation. They won some preliminary skirmishes,[14] but ultimately the cost of litigation forced many of them to accept an out-of-court settlement offering only meagre compensation.[15] Other Opren victims fought on in the courts. The defendant drug company successfully contended that they took legal action too late and were barred from either benefiting from the settlement or pursuing their case further in the courts.[16]

---

[9] See S Shah, *The Body Hunters: How the Drug Industry Tests its Products on the World's Poorest Patients* (2006) The New Press.

[10] See *Re* HIV *Litigation* (1990) 41 BMLR 171, CA; *N v Medical Research Council* [1996] 7 Med LR 309; *The Creutzfeldt – Jakob Disease Litigation* (1997) 41 BMLR 157; *A v National Blood Authority* [2001] Lloyd's Rep Med 187.

[11] See J K Mason, G T Laurie, *Mason and McCall Smith's Law and Medical Ethics* (8th edn, 2010), pp 163–167.

[12] For a full and lively history of the events surrounding the Thalidomide tragedy, see H Teff and C Munro, *Thalidomide: The Legal Aftermath* (1976) Saxon House.

[13] See Parliamentary Statement, 'Government Money for Thalidomide Survivors', 15 January (2010), http://www.parliament.uk/business/news/2010/01.

[14] See, for example, *Davies v Eli Lilly and Co* [1987] 1 All ER 801, CA.

[15] In *Davies v Eli Lilly and Co* [1987] 1 All ER 801, CA, it was held that the costs of litigation must be borne proportionately by all claimants. Legally aided claims could not be used to provide 'lead' cases so that the costs would be borne by the legal aid fund.

[16] *Nash v Eli Lilly and Co* [1993] 4 All ER 383. For a full analysis of the Opren litigation, see P R Ferguson, *Drug Injuries and the Pursuit of Compensation* (1996) Sweet & Maxwell, p 14.

Costly litigation ending in minimal compensation payments was for decades the pattern for virtually all claims for drug-induced injury in England.[17]

In 1987, Parliament enacted the Consumer Protection Act. Part 1 imposed on all producers of goods strict liability for unsafe products. This Act was based on a European Community Directive[18] which required all member states to introduce such strict liability for products. In part, the intention of the Directive was to ensure fair competition between businesses in the Community. If France required French producers to meet more stringent safety laws than other member states, French businesses competed at a disadvantage to their rivals. However, much of the impetus for strict liability for unsafe goods in Europe[19] and the UK arose from a desire to give more effective protection and remedies to people who suffered injury as a result of defects in goods.

The Consumer Protection Act might be thought to make the law on drug-induced injury straightforward.[20] The drawn-out legal battle which culminated in a Supreme Court ruling in *O'Byrne v Aventis Pasteur*[21] demonstrates that this is far from the truth. O'Byrne received a meningitis vaccination which, he alleged, caused him brain damage. He mistakenly brought an action against the supplier of the vaccine, believing it to be the producer. By the time the mistake was realised, he had fallen foul of the rule that the claim must be brought within ten years of the product being put into circulation. As the supplier was a wholly owned subsidiary of the producer, O'Byrne sought to substitute the supplier defendant for the producer. The European Court of Justice held this would be permissible, provided a domestic court is satisfied that the producer controlled the supplier. The Court of Appeal was so satisfied but its decision was overturned in the Supreme Court.

A drug which causes kidney damage or foetal abnormality would be perceived by most lay observers as 'unsafe'. Defining 'defective' under the Act will be seen to be more problematical. The damage caused by some drugs takes years to manifest itself. No action under the Act is allowed more than ten years after the drug in question was put on the market.[22] Nor is a drug company's liability under the Act wholly strict, for the Act permits producers to plead a 'development risks' defence and so escape liability. Victims of drug-induced injury may

---

[17] H Teff, 'Regulation under Medicines Act 1968' (1984) 47 *Modern Law Review* 303, pp 320–322.

[18] EU Product Liability Directive 85/374/EEC. See P Shears, 'The EU Product Liability Directive – Twenty Years On' (2007) November, *Journal of Business Law* 884.

[19] For a disparaging view of the impact of the Directive, see J Stapleton, 'Products Liability in the United Kingdom: The Myths of Reform' (1999) 34 *Texas International Law Journal* 45.

[20] But see M Mildred, 'Pitfalls of Product Liability' (2007) 2 *Journal of Personal Injury Law* 141.

[21] [2010] UKSC 23. Discussed below at **10.5**.

[22] For definition of 'put into circulation', see *O'Byrne v Sanofi Pasteur MSD Ltd* (formerly *Aventis Pasteur MSD Ltd*) [2006] Case C127/0, ECJ. See H Preston, 'Liable to Change' (2006) 156 *New Law Journal* 538.

still resort to prior common-law remedies in contract and the tort of negligence. And negligence liability for drug-induced injury needs to be understood to evaluate how far strict liability under the Act is a real advance on the bad old rules under which Thalidomide and Opren victims had to play.[23]

Product liability and drugs

10.2 Whatever scheme for compensation is in operation, there are problems relating to drug-induced injury which will not go away. English law purports to treat drugs (and body products such as blood) as just another product.[24] For legal purposes, a defective drug is (in theory) little different from a defective electric blanket or kettle. In practice there are vital distinctions affecting both user and manufacturer if litigation is started. Defects in products can be of two sorts; in *design*, which means that every example of the product will prove defective, or in *construction*, which means that some but not all of the eventual products will be faulty simply because they have not been put together properly.[25] Faults in electric blankets, kettles, or even aircraft are usually construction faults.

Defects in drugs are mostly design defects. That means that a drug company facing a claim alleging their product to be defective is facing a disaster. There are going to be not just one or two claimants but a host of embittered and injured users. The cost to the company may put it out of business. The company fights back with equal vigour.

From the user's viewpoint, the greatest difficulty in any claim against the drug company is proving that the drug caused her injury. Should a new brand of electric blanket suffer a design defect, and within a week of purchase 5 per cent of users suffer an electric shock, the link between cause and effect is clear. With a new drug, the process will be nothing like so swift or sure. Consider the case of Diethylstilboestrol, a drug prescribed over fifty years ago to women threatening to miscarry. Evidence has emerged that women, *in utero* when their mothers took the drug, were affected in disproportionate numbers by vaginal and cervical cancer.[26] Delay in effect is only one of the problems. There may be uncertainty whether injury resulted from the drug taken, the

---

[23] *Richardson v LRC Products Ltd* [2000] Lloyd's Law Reports; *Abouzaid v Mothercare (UK) Ltd* [2000] EWCA Civ 348; *A v National Blood Authority* [2001] Lloyd's Rep Med 187.

[24] In contrast to West Germany, which after the Thalidomide disaster enacted a special regime of liability for injury caused by drugs.

[25] In *A v National Blood Authority* [2001] Lloyd's Rep Med 187, Burton J prefers the terminology *standard* and *non-standard* products.

[26] A particular difficulty here has been establishing which manufacturer made the actual drug taken by the mother. There were several brands of the same drug on the market; see *Sindell v Abbott Laboratories* (1980) 26 Cal 3d 588; *Mindy Hymowitz v Eli Lilly & Co* (1989) 541 NYS 2d 941 (NY, CA). See discussion of *Fairchild v Glenhaven Funeral Services Ltd* [2002] UKHL 22; *Barker v Corus* [2006] UKHL 20 and the Compensation Act 2006 below at **10.10**.

original disease, or some other natural cause. When a drug is alleged to cause foetal deformity this is a particular difficulty. Was the child's disability the result of the drug, or of some inherited disorder or disease in the mother, or one of a number of other possible causes? Then in all claims there is the problem of proving that the drug was taken by the patient in the proper dosage, and as often the same drug is manufactured under different brand names, it must be shown which brand the patient actually used.[27] Medical records are often far from perfect; memory is fallible. Finally, there is the intractable difficulty of personal idiosyncrasy. A drug beneficial to 99.9 per cent of us may be lethal to 0.1 per cent. Is that drug defective? Should the company, or anyone else, compensate the 0.1 per cent who suffers injury?

The pharmaceutical industry argues that laws which weigh too onerously on it may inhibit research.[28] Medicine would be held back and British companies would suffer loss of competitiveness. Some view this claim sceptically. Much of the competition appears aimed at producing new brands of the same basic drugs. The pace of innovation has slowed down.[29] Doctors are moving away from prescribing as freely as in the past. Any decline in the pharmaceutical industry is as likely to be due to these factors as it is to be the result of law reform to help drug-injured patients.

Consumer-buyers: most favoured claimants

10.3 A victim of drug-induced injury who bought the offending drug himself, or acquired the drug in the course of a contract, has a more effective remedy than any of his fellow sufferers. Despite the Consumer Protection Act 1987, consumer-buyers remain the most favoured claimants in England.

Two conditions are implied in every contract for the sale of goods. The goods must be of satisfactory quality.[30] This means they must meet the standard that a reasonable person would regard as satisfactory. And the goods must be reasonably fit for the purpose for which they are sold.[31] When drugs are bought over the counter they must meet these conditions just like any other goods. To take a simple example, a patient buying a bottle of cough mixture suffers internal injury because the medicine is contaminated by powdered glass. That patient recovers full compensation for his injuries from the pharmacist who sold him the medicine. The pharmacist may be entirely without fault.

---

[27] See *Sindell v Abbott Laboratories* (1980) 26 Cal 3d 588.

[28] See, for example, R A Epstein, *Overdose: How Excessive Government Regulation Stifles Pharmaceutical Innovation* (2006) Yale University Press.

[29] J Abraham, 'Regulating the Drug Industry Transparently' (2005) 331 *BMJ* 528.

[30] Sale of Goods Act 1979, s 14(2) (as amended by the Sale and Supply of Goods Act 1999); see W C H Ervine, 'Satisfactory Quality: What does it Mean?' (2004) *Journal of Business Law* 684.

[31] Sale of Goods Act 1979, s 14(3). See C Twigg-Flesner, 'The Relationship between Satisfactory Quality and Fitness for Purpose' (2004) 63 *Cambridge Law Journal* 22.

The medicine may have been supplied by the manufacturer in a sealed, opaque container. That does not matter; the medicine is neither of satisfactory quality nor fit to be sold, and the pharmacist is in breach of contract. This simple and effective remedy has a defect, however. It is normally available only when the person suffering injury from the defective drug bought it himself. Had the contaminated medicine in our example been purchased by a husband and taken by his wife, she may well have had no remedy in contract.[32] She cannot benefit from a contract to which she is not a party.

How useful is the contractual remedy in practice? A growing range of medicines are no longer available by prescription only. They have been reclassified to allow sale in pharmacies, or in many cases, just in ordinary shops.[33] Antihistamines to alleviate hay fever, similar drugs to aid sleep, antibiotic eye drops and a host of medicines to help digestive problems can now be bought over the counter. These 'deregulated' drugs are more likely to carry inherent risks of harm than the sort of cough and cold remedies available over the counter not long ago. More patients may look to their pharmacist or local supermarket for redress. Patients prescribed their medicines on the NHS remain less favoured. Such medicines will not attract conditions of satisfactory quality and fitness for purpose because there is no contract between the pharmacist and the patient into which such conditions can be implied, even though the patient will often pay for his prescription.[34] The pharmacist dispenses the drug as part of his obligation under his contract with the Primary Care Trust (GP consortium, from 2013) to provide pharmaceutical services in the area. The patient pays a statutory charge. He does not buy the drug; he pays a tax for NHS services.

By contrast, when drugs are dispensed under a private prescription, a contract does exist between the pharmacist and the patient. The patient pays the full cost of the drug directly to the pharmacist. It matters not whether the contract is one of simple sale or a contract of service under which the pharmacist provides a skilled service and incidentally supplies the drug. Quality conditions are imposed in identical terms regardless of whether goods are supplied in the course of a service or in an ordinary sale transaction.[35] The number of private prescriptions is rising. The pharmacist is exposed on the front line of liability for defective drugs. When more potent drugs become the subject of conditions of fitness, whether by prescription or an over-the-counter sale, problems of applying those conditions are likely. The question may arise as to whether a drug perfectly safe for all but pregnant women is fit to be supplied. If it is specifically aimed at pregnant women, for example, a morning sickness preparation, if it damages the woman or her baby, is clearly not fit for the purpose for which it is supplied. If it is a general medicine, such as a hay fever remedy, it could be argued that if it

---

[32] Unless she can show that her husband bought the medicine for her as her agent.

[33] See R R Fenichel, 'Which Drugs Should be Available Over the Counter?' (2004) 329 *BMJ* 182.

[34] *Pfizer v Ministry of Health* [1965] AC 512; *Appleby v Sleep* [1968] 1 WLR 948.

[35] See the Supply of Goods and Service Act 1982; A P Bell, 'The Doctor and the Supply of Goods and Service Act' [1984] *Legal Studies* 175.

carries risk to a substantial section of the community, pregnant women, then it is not of satisfactory quality, nor fit to be on general sale. This immediately raises further questions. Did the manufacturer warn of the risk to pregnant women? Is such a warning sufficient? Should the woman herself be aware of the dangers of taking drugs and avoid drugs while pregnant?

These sorts of problems inevitably plague questions of liability for defective drugs. Where a remedy lies in contract, once a court finds the drug unsafe, the claim for compensation is established. It is no defence for the retailer of the drug, or the pharmacist dispensing the drug, to argue that he personally was blameless. Nor is it any answer to the patient's claim that the state of scientific and technical knowledge at the time when the drug was produced was such that the defect could not have been discovered. There is no 'development risks' defence against a claim in contract. The liability imposed on the retailer or supplier is truly strict.

The remedy in negligence

10.4 Patients who suffer injury as a result of drugs prescribed within the NHS must look outside contract for a remedy. Prior to the Consumer Protection Act 1987 that remedy would have to be found in the tort of negligence. Gaps in the Consumer Protection Act mean that victims of drug-induced injury cannot ignore the tort of negligence.

An action in negligence arises where one person suffers injury as a result of the breach of a duty of care owed him by another. His doctor may be the first person to whom the patient turns for a remedy when he believes a drug prescribed by that doctor has harmed him. The doctor will be liable for drug-induced injury if the drug caused damage because she prescribed an incorrect dosage, or because she ought to have appreciated that that drug posed a risk to a particular patient in the light of his medical history, or where drugs have been prescribed in inappropriate and harmful combination. Similarly, if the injury to the patient results from a negligent error by the pharmacist in, for example, dispensing the wrong drug, or indicating the wrong dosage, an action in negligence lies against the pharmacist. In a number of cases, it is the cumulative negligence of both doctor and pharmacist which causes injury, as where a doctor's atrocious handwriting misled the pharmacist into dispensing entirely the wrong drug.[36] The problem for the patient is that all he knows is that he is ill and he believes the drug to be the cause. He will have no means of knowing whether an inherently 'safe' drug was prescribed for him in an unsafe and careless fashion, or whether the drug is inherently defective and harmful, however careful his doctor may be. Hence patients contemplating litigation for drug-induced injury often have to start by considering suing the doctor, the

---

[36] *Prendergast v Sam and Dee* [1985] 1 Med LR 36. And see *Dwyer v Roderick* (1988) 127 *Solicitors' Journal* 805.

pharmacist *and* the manufacturer, and hope that evidence of who was actually to blame will emerge in the course of the litigation.

Turning now to the liability in negligence of drug companies manufacturing drugs, the manufacturer of any product:

> . . . which he sells in such a form as to show that he intends them to reach the ultimate consumer in the form in which they left him with no reasonable possibility of intermediate examination, and with the knowledge that the absence of care in the preparation or putting up of the products will result in injury to the consumer's life or property, owes a duty to the consumer to take that reasonable care.[37]

There is no doubt that this duty to take care attaches as much to the manufacturer of drugs as to the manufacturer of ginger beer or any other product. The duty covers the design and formulation of the drug as well as its construction. Nor is the duty limited to the original manufacturer. Thalidomide was initially developed by a West German company and manufactured under licence here by Distillers. Distillers still owed a duty to British patients to take steps to check on the safety of the drug by testing and monitoring the formula before putting the product on the UK market.[38]

Establishing a duty to avoid negligence is not the problem. Determining what amounts to negligence is a formidable task. The potential harm caused by a defective drug is such that a very high standard of care will be imposed on the manufacturer. This is generally acknowledged. However, in England no action for personal injuries against a drug company has yet resulted in an award of damages by a court, although a claim against the National Blood Authority has, as we shall see, succeeded. What are the obstacles confronting claimants? First, the drug company must be judged by the standards for drug safety pertaining at the date when the drug was put on the market, not at the date proceedings are taken against them. Drug companies, like doctors, must not be judged negligent on hindsight alone. Today the risk to the developing foetus of drugs taken by the mother is well known to all lay women. When Thalidomide was first on the market it is far from clear that the dangers of drugs to the foetus were widely appreciated even by gynaecologists and scientists.

Consideration of the history of the Thalidomide claim[39] leads us into the second difficulty for litigants. How does a claimant obtain the evidence he will need to prove the company careless? The Thalidomide story is instructive, albeit depressing. The charge against Distillers was that they should have foreseen that the drug might harm the foetus and therefore should have conducted adequate tests before promoting it as safe for use in pregnancy and/or that once adverse reports on the drug reached them they should have withdrawn it

---

[37] *Donoghue v Stevenson* [1932] AC 562 at 599, HL.

[38] *Watson v Buckley and Osborne, Garrett & Co Ltd* [1940] 1 All ER 174 (duty imposed on distributors of hair dye).

[39] Teff and Munro, *Thalidomide: The Legal Aftermath* (1976) Saxon House, chs 1 and 2.

at once. In retrospect, the available evidence that Distillers was negligent falls into three categories. First, there was material available from 1934 onwards to suggest that drugs could pass through the placenta and damage the foetus. Second, in the 1950s a number of drug companies marketing new products had carried out tests to check the effect on the foetus mainly by way of animal experiments. Such evidence would need to have been given by experts and might not have been conclusive. The burden of proof lies on the claimant. The defendant's experts would have argued that when Thalidomide was developed it was by no means universally accepted that drugs could damage the foetus, the efficacy of animal tests would have been disputed, and it would have been strongly submitted that in any case such tests were not then current general practice.

The third and final category of evidence might have been more damning if the claimants could have got hold of it. Reports of the original testing of Thalidomide in West Germany by Chemie Grunenthal suggest that it may have been a pretty hit-and-miss affair. Fairly early on, adverse reports on the drug and concern over risk to the foetus were in the hands of Chemie Grunenthal. Some considerable time elapsed before they withdrew the drug there. Distillers acted faster, taking the drug out of circulation soon after adverse reactions were reported to them. The contents of adverse reports on a drug, the sequence and exact dates on which those reports are received, are of crucial importance to a claimant. No drug company is going to hand the reports over voluntarily. The process of discovery, of compelling a defendant to hand over documents, was seen to be complex enough in a malpractice claim against an individual doctor. In claims against a drug company, the process often became an insuperable obstacle race.

One general point on the law of negligence as it affects drug claims can be made by way of illustration from the Thalidomide case. It may ultimately prove to be the case that there is insufficient evidence that the company was negligent when they originally marketed the drug. There may be evidence, however hard to come by, that they were negligent in failing to act on adverse reports and recall the drug. Is that a breach of the manufacturer's duty? Two separate situations must be examined. Had it been proved that a child was injured by Thalidomide when the drug taken was put on the market by Distillers *after* a date by which they should have known it to be dangerous, there is no problem. The drug that injured that child was negligently put into circulation. Difficulty would arise where the drug taken by the mother had been put into circulation before Distillers should have known it was dangerous but was actually prescribed to her and taken by her after that date. There is a strong case that a manufacturer owes a further duty to monitor his product and to take reasonable steps to withdraw it if it proves unsafe.[40] Proving breach of the duty could be a nightmare. Stories of doctors continuing to prescribe, and pharmacists retaining stocks of, withdrawn drugs recur. The patient bringing

---

40 *Wright v Dunlop Rubber Co. Ltd* [1972] 13 KIR 255; *Hollis v Dow Corning Corporation* (1995) 129 DLR (4th) 609 (Canada).

such a claim may falter and sink in a sea of allegation and counter-allegation between drug company, doctor and pharmacist.

The inadequacy of negligence as an effective means of compensating victims of drug-induced injury has been demonstrated time and time again. Successive reviews of negligence as a means of remedying personal injuries resulting from any unsafe product concluded that the reform of product liability laws was essential.[41] What must now be evaluated is how effective reform by way of the Consumer Protection Act 1987 has proved to be.

Strict liability: the Consumer Protection Act 1987[42]

10.5 The concept of strict liability is simple. A claimant seeking compensation from the manufacturer of a product need prove only (1) that the product was defective *and* (2) that the defect in the product caused his injury. Strict liability is fairer to claimants because it establishes that responsibility for an injury caused by a defective product is borne by the person creating the risk and benefiting financially from the product; that is the manufacturer. The manufacturer is in the best position to exercise control over the safety and quality of the product, and can more conveniently insure against the risk of injury posed by the product. Prolonged, expensive and complex litigation should be less common with a strict liability regime.

The Act imposes liability for personal injury arising from defective products on all *producers* of goods. 'Producers' embraces a wider category of businesses involved in the marketing of drugs than simply the companies manufacturing the finished products.[43] Manufacturers of components are liable for any defect in the components. Companies importing drugs into the EU are liable under the Act as if they manufactured the drug in England. If the drug in question was manufactured in Japan, the aggrieved patient need not concern himself with the potential difficulties of suing the Japanese company abroad; he can bring his claim in England[44] against the EU company who brought the drug into the EU. A company that brand-names a drug is a producer within the Act.

---

[41] Notably the Law Commission in their report No 82, *Liability for Defective Products* (1977) Cmnd 6831, and the Report of the Royal Commission on Civil Liability and Compensation for Personal Injury (1978) Cmnd 7054 (the Pearson Report).

[42] The pharmaceutical industry repeatedly argued that drugs should remain exempt from any regime of strict liability, mainly on the grounds that: (1) scientific research and innovation would be adversely affected; (2) the nature of drug disasters meant that strict liability could have catastrophic results for the industry; (3) the difficulty of defining defect in a drug: these arguments have been consistently rejected; see Law Commission Report No 82, *Liability for Defective Products* (1977) Cmnd 6831, pp 19–21; Pearson Report, para 1274.

[43] Consumer Protection Act 1987, ss 1–2.

[44] Even if the importer is not an English company, but a company based in another EU or EFTA state, the victim will usually be able to sue here in England if he suffered injury here: see the Civil Jurisdiction and Judgments Acts 1982 and 1991 and the

Companies cannot use their name to claim the credit and the profit for a drug and when something goes badly wrong, disclaim any responsibility for that drug. Finally, any supplier[45] of a drug will be deemed to be a producer unless he identifies the source of his supply. This provision is crucial for patients. The patient may well receive his prescription or injection in a form such that he cannot possibly identify the original producer of the drug. The community pharmacist or hospital pharmacy supplying the drug must identify the producer or bear liability for the patient's injuries themselves. The intention of the European Directive,[46] on which the Act is based, and of the Act itself is that there should, as far as humanly possible, always be an identifiable producer on whom liability must rest. No company should be able to hide behind a smoke-screen.

However, if a claim is brought against the supplier in error, the claimant cannot then sue the producer unless he still falls within the ten-year time limit which starts to run when the drug is first put into circulation. A HiB vaccine produced by a French company, Aventis Pasteur SA (SA), was sold to an English subsidiary company, Aventis Pasteur MSD Ltd (MSD), who supplied it to the Department of Health, who provided it to a medical centre which then vaccinated one year-old O'Byrne. O'Byrne suffered brain damage and alleged that the vaccine had caused it. Instead of claiming against the producer, O'Byrne mistakenly brought his claim against MSD, the supplier of the vaccine. MSD successfully defended the claim on the ground that it had not produced the vaccine. By the time the mistake became apparent, O'Byrne could no longer bring a claim against the producer due to a time limit imposed by the Act – claims must be brought within ten years of the product being put into circulation.[47] The first of two preliminary rulings from the European Court of Justice confirmed that the test is objective – the fact that the reason for not bringing a claim against the producer within the time limit was a mistake as to who produced the vaccine, was irrelevant.[48] So O'Byrne sought instead to substitute his existing claim against the supplier, MSD (which was brought within the time limit) for a claim against the producer, SA. To do so, under Article 3(1) of the Directive, it was necessary to prove both that the supplier put the vaccine into circulation, and that the producer (the parent company) determined when it was put into circulation, by transferring the vaccine to MSD.[49] The argument was that the vaccine was put into circulation not when SA supplied it to MSD (in which case the case was time barred), but

Civil Jurisdiction and Judgments Order 2001, SI 2001/3929 which gave courts jurisdiction under Council Regulation (EC) 44/2001.
[45] This includes pharmacists dispensing NHS drugs even though they do not sell NHS drugs to patients.
[46] Council Directive of 25 July 1985, *Products Liability* 85/374/EC.
[47] Consumer Protection Act 1987, s 22A.
[48] *O'Byrne v Sanofi Pasteur MSD Ltd (formerly Aventis Pasteur MSD Ltd* (Case C-127/04) [2006] 1 WLR 1606.
[49] See the ECJ's second preliminary ruling: *Aventis Pasteur SA v OB* (2009) C-358/08 ECJ (Grand Chamber).

when MSD supplied it to the Department of Health under SA's control. The UK Supreme Court reached a verdict on this matter in *O'Byrne v Aventis Pasteur*.[50] Overruling the Court of Appeal, the Supreme Court held that the relationship between the two companies precluded substitution. SA could not be said to have controlled supply by MSD. The product was therefore put into circulation when SA supplied it to MSD, and consequently the action fell outside the ten-year time limit and was barred. After five related court decisions,[51] O'Byrne's case foundered.

Assuming the claimant has identified the right defendant, how do you establish that the drug is defective?[52] Section 3(1) provides that:

... there is a defect in a product ... if the safety of the product is not such as persons generally are entitled to expect;

Section 3(2) goes on to direct the judge to take into account all relevant circumstances pertaining to the safety of a product including:

(a) the manner in which, and purposes for which, the product has been marketed, its get-up, the use of any mark in relation to the product and any instructions for, or warnings with respect to, the doing of anything with or in relation to the product;
(b) what might reasonably be expected to be done with or in relation to the product; and
(c) the time when the product was supplied by its producer to another;
(d) and nothing in this section shall require a defect to be inferred from the fact alone that the safety of a product which is supplied after that time is greater than the safety of the product in question.

Determining when a drug falls within the definition is far from easy.[53] Drugs are by their nature dangerous. They are designed to do damage to the bacteria or diseased cell or whatever caused the original disease. How much safety are persons generally entitled to expect? Side-effects are often unavoidable. The court has to try to balance the potential benefit against the risk when deciding if an unwanted side-effect renders a drug defective. Distinctions may be drawn based on the condition that the drug was designed to combat. A minor tranquilliser which carried an unforeseen 5 per cent risk of liver damage could be deemed defective when an anti-cancer drug carrying identical risk would not.

---

[50] [2010] UKSC 23. See H Preston, 'The End of the Decade' (2010) 33 *Commercial Litigation Journal* 5.

[51] One each to the High Court, Court of Appeal and House of Lords and two to the European Court of Justice.

[52] See D Fairgrieve, G Howells, 'Rethinking Product Liability: A Missing Element in the European Commission's Third Review of European Product Liability Directive' (2007) 70(6) *Modern Law Review* 962 which suggests that there is a lack of consistency in Europe on the concept of defectiveness.

[53] See the thorough and excellent discussion of this problem in C Newdick, 'Strict Liability for Defective Drugs in the Pharmaceutical Industry' (1985) 101 *Law Quarterly Review* 405, pp 409–420.

Relief of moderate anxiety may be seen as insufficient to warrant the risk, whereas the battle against cancer may justify that degree of inherent danger.

Anticipated risks raise different issues. An anticipated risk must be warned against. Of course there must be some determination as to the seriousness of the anticipated risk. Consider a drug used to treat schizophrenia which may cause weight gain. Must the pharmaceutical company warn of this relatively benign potential side-effect? Class actions in America are being brought against AstraZeneca on the grounds that they should have warned that weight gain might occur in patients using Seroquel, particularly in view of the links between weight gain and type-two diabetes.[54]

What if the risk is acknowledged? Will the tranquilliser be deemed not defective if its potential danger is outlined to doctors and patients, leaving the choice to them? Clearly the warning must be taken into account. An antibiotic harmful only to the foetus will almost certainly not be defective if a warning of its risk is clearly given. Less essential drugs may remain defective even if risks are detailed in the literature supplied to doctors. The patient may never have the warning passed on to him. In such a case, though, a heavy share of liability would rest with the doctor prescribing the drug, in contravention or ignorance of warnings from the producer.

Other problems in applying this definition of 'defective' beset the patient. What of the patient who suffers injury because of an allergic reaction to the drug? The drug is perfectly safe and effective for you, but lethal to us. So might it be argued that the drug is safe for 'persons generally'? Such an argument will fail. Society, 'persons generally', demands that regard be had to the safety of all of us where, as in the case of drugs, allergic and idiosyncratic reactions are a well-known risk of the product. If risk to an individual or group is foreseeable and *not* warned of in the presentation of the product, it is defective. An individual is entitled to expect that the manufacturer will not simply ignore an identified danger to however small a group. When the risk is not foreseeable, the size and predictability of the affected group will be crucial. A sedative which causes damage to the foetus or liver damage in 10 per cent of the over-seventies will be defective. Pregnant women and the elderly are large groups of potential consumers known to be vulnerable to drug-induced injury. But what if the sedative injured only a handful of users out of millions?

Guidance on defining 'defective' is to be found in a series of judgments. In *Abouzaid v Mothercare Ltd*[55] a twelve-year-old boy was trying to attach a fleece-lined sleeping bag to his baby brother's pushchair. The sleeping bag had to be clipped on to the pushchair by passing elasticated straps round the back of the chair joined by a metal buckle. There were no instructions provided. As the boy struggled to fasten the sleeping bag to the chair, one of the straps slipped from his grasp and the metal buckle flew up and hit him in his left eye.

---

[54] 'AstraZeneca "Suppressed" Drug Test Data' (2010) *BBC News*, 26 January.
[55] [2000] EWCA Civ 348, CA.

The injury caused him to lose significant vision in that eye. The Court of Appeal found that the product was defective. There was a failure to provide instructions and the design of the product was unsafe because it could not be secured without risk. Consumers would properly expect that such a product could be used without that degree of risk. Relatively minor alterations in design would eliminate that risk.

The *Mothercare* judgment can be applied to make two key points about liability for drugs. (1) Instructions about the use of and warnings concerning possible adverse effects of drugs are crucial. Failure to warn of a known risk will, as argued earlier, render a drug defective. (2) Common sense will play its part in determining what 'people generally' may expect from a product.[56] That latter point is reinforced in *Richardson v* LRC *Products Ltd*.[57] The plaintiff became pregnant after a condom split. She sued the manufacturers, arguing that the condom failure demonstrated that the product was defective. She was unable to identify any particular construction defect in the condom or point to a risk of damage which the manufacturers should have avoided. The judge found no evidence of unsatisfactory testing of the product. The evidence was simply that, in actual use, an inexplicable number of condoms fail. Dismissing the plaintiff's claim, the judge held that the manufacturers made no claims that their (or any method) of contraception was 100 per cent safe. The fallibility of contraception is well known.

Returning to drug-induced harm, consider the following examples in the light of the above cases. You purchase Ibuprofen in a supermarket. The packet clearly warns you *not* to take the medicine if you suffer from asthma. You ignore that warning and, despite your asthma, take several tablets. An acute attack of asthma lands you in hospital. Is that pack of Ibuprofen defective? You are prescribed a cream to cure acne. No warning accompanies the product. The cream causes the eruption of a rash all over your body. Evidence emerges that that product will produce just such an allergic reaction in about 2 per cent of female users if they use the cream during pregnancy. Neither you nor your GP was aware you were pregnant at the time. Is the product defective?

A v National Blood Authority[58]

10.6 The judgment in *A v National Blood Authority* is by far the most important case yet to interpret the Consumer Protection Act 1987. It breathed new life into strict liability. The case addressed claims by patients infected with

---

[56] See also *Tesco Stores v Pollard (A Minor)* [2006] EWCA 393 where the child-resistant top on a bottle of dishwasher powder was more difficult to open than an ordinary top and therefore fell in line with reasonable expectations.
[57] [2000] Lloyd's Law Report 280. And see *Worsely v Tambrands* [2000] PIQR P 95; *Foster v Biosil* (2000) 59 BMLR 178.
[58] [2001] Lloyd's Rep Med 187. See R Goldberg, 'Paying for Bad Blood: Strict Product Liability after the Hepatitis C Litigation' (2002) 10 *Medical Law Review* 165.

Hepatitis C from blood and blood products through blood transfusions after 1 March 1988. Two important points must be made. First, the defendants (rightly) conceded that blood and body parts fell within the regime of strict liability imposed by the Consumer Protection Act. Secondly, the judge ruled that the provisions of the British legislation (the 1987 Act) must be interpreted in the light of the European Product Liability Directive. Where there were apparent inconsistencies between the two, the Directive should be preferred. The importance of this will be highlighted later.

Moving to the substance of the claims, the judge held that in determining whether the contaminated blood products were defective, what must be decided is what the *legitimate expectations* of the public were in relation to that product. People expected blood to be 100 per cent clean. Whether the relevant 'defect' in the product was *avoidable* was not the issue. The defendants had tried to argue that the public could only expect they would have done what was possible to screen blood and avoid contamination. In more diplomatic language, the judge effectively declared this to be nonsense. He said:

> ... it is as inappropriate to propose that the public should not 'expect the unattainable' – in the sense of tests and precautions which are impossible – at least unless it is informed as to what is unattainable or impossible as it is to reformulate the expectation as one that the producer will not have been negligent or will have taken all reasonable steps.[59]

The judge marked a clear boundary between negligence and strict liability. He went on to say a distinction needs to be made between *standard* and *non-standard* products, a distinction analogous to design and construction defects. Establishing that a standard product was defective would continue to be difficult. The infected batches of blood were non-standard. They could only not be defective if it could be shown the public were made aware of the risks. In this instance, this was not the case. Unlike condoms, which most people know do and can split for no apparent reason, most of us assume that blood will not cause us to succumb to serious, even fatal, disease.

Development risks[60]

10.7 In *A v National Blood Authority*,[61] the Blood Authority had another weapon. If the contaminated blood was defective, they argued they were not liable because they could invoke the development risks defence.[62] A

---

59   [2001] Lloyd's Rep Med 167 at 216.
60   The Consumer Protection Act, s 4 outlines a number of defences which will only rarely be relevant in claims for drug-related injuries. For example, in *Piper v JRI (Manufacturing)* [2006] EWCA (Civ) 1344, a replacement hip sheared into two but the manufacturer was not liable because 'the defect did not exist in the product at the relevant time'.
61   [2001] Lloyd's Rep Med 187.
62   See s 4(1)(e).

'development risks' defence amounts to this. The manufacturer will not be liable if he can prove that the state of scientific and technical knowledge at the time when he put the product into circulation was not such as to enable the existence of the defect to be discovered.[63]

The scope of the development risks defence in the UK looks broad. The European Directive on Products Liability framed the defence in terms of the scientific and technical knowledge generally available. Section 4(1)(e) of the Consumer Protection Act 1987 provides:

> ... the state of scientific and technical knowledge was not such that a producer of products of the same description as the product in question might be expected to have discovered the defect.

The test in the Act appears to be what was the knowledge and practice of the pharmaceutical industry at the time. The European Commission challenged the British Act, alleging that the UK had improperly sought to broaden the defence allowed by the Directive. The challenge failed.[64] The European Court of Justice allowed the British interpretation of the Directive. The result might have been depressing.[65] Academic research may reveal significant concerns about the safety of a novel drug. If that research has not permeated industry, the 'development risks' defence could still avail the drug companies creating a test little different from 'old' negligence rules. So, in *A v National Blood Authority* the defendants argued: (1) that as at the relevant time there was no effective test to screen blood for Hepatitis C, the development risks defence applied; and, (2) that the 1987 Act provided that producers of analogous products must at the relevant time have been aware of and able to eliminate the relevant risk. Construing the Act in the light of the Directive, the judge dismissed both arguments. The defence applies only where the very existence of the defect was unknown and undiscoverable.[66]Authorities responsible for blood supplies at the relevant time were aware of the risks of contamination. That no method of screening for Hepatitis C had yet been developed was irrelevant. The wording of section 4(1)(e) of the 1987 Act was inappropriate. The Directive made it clear that once knowledge of a risk was accessible to manufacturers, the risk was known. A single article in an obscure Chinese journal ('the Manchurian exception') might not suffice.[67] General knowledge accessible to the academic and commercial communities would.[68]

---

[63] The European Directive Art7(e) permitted states to incorporate a development risks defence.

[64] *Commission v UK* (Case C-300/95) [1997] All ER (EC) 481.

[65] Discussed in C Hodges, 'Developing Risks: Unanswered Questions' (1998) 61 *Modern Law Review* 560; M Mildred and G Howells, 'Comment on Development Risks: "Unanswered Questions"' (1998) 61 *Modern Law Review* 570.

[66] And see *Richardson v LRC Products Ltd* [2000] Lloyd's Rep Med 280.

[67] [2001] Lloyd's Rep Med 187 at 220–221.

[68] See G Howells and M Mildred, 'Infected Blood: Defect and Discoverability: A First Exposition of the EC Product Liability Directive' (2002) 65 *Modern Law Review* 95.

If *A v National Blood Authority* is followed in the higher courts, the Consumer Protection Act 1987 may make a difference.[69] A producer invoking the development risks defence will have to establish that the defect in the drug, or device, or bodily product, was undiscoverable and the onus will lie on him to prove this.

Until 2010 it seemed likely that Burton J's decision in *A v National Blood Authority* would come under review in a group litigation on anti-epileptic drugs. The claimants were children whose mothers took the anti-epileptic drug, Epilim, in pregnancy. The mothers were warned of potential adverse effects to their foetuses but were reliant on the drug to control their epilepsy. They took the drug out of necessity. Is the drug 'defective' within the meaning of the Act? Preliminary hearings were unable to reach a conclusion on the matter.[70] The case was expected to come to trial in November 2010, but after a six-year battle, legal aid was withdrawn weeks before the case was due to come to trial. It seems inevitable that the case will now be abandoned.[71]

Collective actions

10.8 Class or 'collective' actions where members of a larger faction sue on behalf of the whole group, are common in the USA, but rarer and more limited[72] in the UK. One recent example is an action by around 200 women treated for incontinence problems at Liverpool Women's Foundation NHS Trust. Allegedly, the Trust failed to heed consultant George Rowland's complaints that he was feeling overwhelmed.[73] Patients complained of sub-standard care and after-care. Innovatively, the NHS Litigation Authority (NHSLA) has agreed special terms in order to keep costs down and aid access to justice. Reportedly, if the claimants win, their lawyers will not claim success fees, and if the NHSLA win, it will not recover costs.[74]

The most common procedural method for a collective action is the Group Litigation Order,[75] but this is more a method of case management rather than a

---

[69] For a contrary view, see J Stapleton (1999) 34 *Texas International Law Journal* 45 and J Stapleton, 'Bugs in the Anglo-American Products Liability' (2002) 53 *South Carolina Law Review* 1225.

[70] [2007] EWHC 1860, [2009] EWHC 95 (QB).

[71] J Meikle, 'Families Lose Legal Aid in Epilepsy Drug Damages Case' (2010) *Guardian*, 9 November.

[72] See, for example, *Emerald Supplies Ltd v British Airways plc* [2010] EWCA Civ 1284.

[73] N Lakhani, 'Women Launch Class Action Against "Target Obsessed" NHS' (2010) *Independent on Sunday*, 9 May, 16.

[74] C Baski, 'Class Action Protocol Drawn up for NHS Litigation' (2010) *Law Society Gazette* 20 May.

[75] Civil Procedure Rules, r 19.10: A Group Litigation Order ('GLO') means an order made under r 19.11 to provide for the case management of claims which give rise to common or related issues of fact or law (the 'GLO issues').

representative action.[76] As we shall see, actions which have been successful abroad have stalled or failed in the UK, for both legal and financial reasons. In 2008 the Civil Justice Council (CJC) sought to make it easier to bring a collective action in any type of civil case.[77] Access to justice might be enhanced by allowing individuals to opt out of group litigation rather than requiring them to opt in. But the previous administration insisted that it was preferable to develop rules that are specific to each sector.[78] Pressure for change from the CJC is matched by pressure from Europe where there are increasing numbers of new judicial and non-judicial collective consumer redress mechanisms.[79] In 2008 the European Commission adopted a Green Paper on Consumer Collective Redress and the European Parliament backed proposals to facilitate cross-border consumer collective redress. Any resulting Directive, if indeed things progress that far, is likely to stop short of a US-style class action, both in deference to opposition from industry and due to the perception that it would contribute to a compensation culture.

vCJD-contaminated blood products

10.9 When bovine spongiform encephalopathy (BSE) was linked to new variant Creutzfeldt-Jakob Disease (vCJD), a class action was mounted against the government.[80] It petered out when a no-fault compensation scheme, run by the national CJD Surveillance Unit, was put in place in 2001 in the wake of the BSE Inquiry.[81] The scheme has been criticised for its complexity and the extensive discretion given to Trustees, but an application for judicial review of the Department of Health's decision to reject radical amendment failed.[82]

In 2004, the Secretary of State announced a similar ex-gratia compensation scheme for people infected with Hepatitis C from NHS blood or blood prod-

---

[76] Civil Justice Council, *Improving Access to Justice through Collective Actions* (2008), p 24.

[77] Civil Justice Council, *Improving Access to Justice through Collective Actions* (2008).

[78] Ministry of Justice, *The Government's Response to the CJC's Improving Access to Justice through Collective Actions* (2009). And see White Paper, *A Better Deal for Consumers: Delivering Real Help Now and Change for the Future*, Cm 7669 (2009).

[79] Civic Consulting (Lead) and Oxford Economics, *Evaluation of the Effectiveness and Efficiency of Collective Redress Mechanisms in the EU – Part I: Main report* (2008), p 4: 'In the last few years, new collective redress mechanisms have been established in Germany (2005), the Netherlands (2005), Bulgaria (2006), Finland (2007), Greece (2007), and Denmark (2008). The most recent mechanism, which is expected to come into force in 2009, is the Italian group action.'

[80] See, for example, 'Families of CJD Victims Will Sue for Millions' (2001) *Telegraph*, 19 June.

[81] See http://collections.europarcHIVe.org/tna/20090505194948/http://bseinquiry.gov.uk/report/index.htm.

[82] See *R (McVey) v Secretary of State for Health* [2010] EWHC 437 (Admin).

ucts.[83] In *R (Moore) v Skipton Fund Ltd*[84] M applied for judicial review of the terms of the scheme. During the course of medical treatment, M was infected with Hepatitis C in 1987. Very occasionally, the immune system clears the body of the disease. In the vast majority of this small number of cases, this occurs in the early acute stage of the disease, in which case no compensation is payable. M's body was clear of the disease and, according to the scheme, she bore the burden of proving, with 'robust medical evidence', that this occurred in the later chronic stage of the disease if she were to be paid compensation. M could not prove this and complained that such proof was, in her case, scientifically impossible. Her application failed. Parker J held that, given the statistical improbability of the disease clearing after six months, and the low risks of long-term problems if it cleared before that time, it was right that M must demonstrate that she had suffered the chronic stage of the disease.

More recently, fears have arisen surrounding the contamination of blood products with vCJD. In 2003, it was found that a blood donor may have transmitted vCJD to a patient who underwent a blood transfusion.[85] The National Blood Service[86] now asks anyone who has received blood products since 1980 not to donate blood.[87] A donor history is taken from potential or definite vCJD cases, and their blood products recalled. White blood cells (which are thought to carry vCJD) are removed. Plasma is imported from countries with few or no cases of BSE. All children born after 1996 receive this plasma. Since 2005, donors and donees who are identified as being 'at-risk' for public health purposes are informed of the public health precautions they and their healthcare staff should take. Around 6,000 patients, many of them haemophiliacs, have been told they are 'at risk'. For them the uncertainty has the potential to blight their lives. There is no test and no cure for this fatal disease. Researchers are developing a test which will diagnose vCJD earlier and potentially allow blood screening.[88] But if the result is positive, should donors be made aware of the results? Researchers have developed a blood-screening test for vCJD. But if the result is positive, should donors be made aware of the results? Will anyone consent to giving blood any more?[89] At the time of writing, a private member's bill, the Contaminated Blood (Support for Infected and Bereaved Persons) Bill 2010/11,[90] aims to provide additional support for families and patients infected by contaminated blood products. It includes measures to test blood donors for various conditions, including vCJD, and for

83 DH, 'Details of Hepatitis C Ex-Gratia Payment Scheme Announced' 2004/0025.
84 [2010] EWHC 3070 (Admin).
85 See, for example, C A Llewelyn, *et al*, 'Possible Transmission of Variant Creutzfeldt-Jakob Disease by Blood Transfusion' (2004) 363 *Lancet* 417.
86 Part of the NHS Blood and Transplant Authority, a Special Health Authority established by the NHS Blood and Transplant Order 2005, SI 2005/2529.
87 And see DH, *Better Blood Transfusion*, HSC 2007/001.
88 J E Edgeworth *et al*, 'Detection of Prion Infection in Variant Creutzfeldt-Jakob Disease: A Blood-Based Assay' (2011) *Lancet* (online publication), 3 February.
89 'Blood Test for vCJD Unrealistic' (2008) *BBC News*, 20 October.
90 A similar Bill in 2009/10 did not progress beyond the first reading in the House of Commons.

prion-filtration of donated blood. Anyone infected would be eligible for non-means tested compensation, as would family carers. The Bill will receive its second reading in February 2011.

In the mean time, for those who go on to develop vCJD, the compensation fund will provide for those victims who on the balance of probabilities:

> . . . contracted vCJD as a result of (i) exposure to bovine product(s) purchased in the UK which came from cattle reared and slaughtered in the UK or (ii) otherwise as a result of exposure in the UK to BSE or vCJD . . .[91]

Acceptance of compensation does not preclude legal action.[92] For those infected, a possible class action exists if it can be demonstrated that the government was aware of the potential risk but took no action because of the cost of alternative synthetic products.[93]

The UK also sold blood products abroad.[94] The wording of the Trust Deed clearly encompasses cases where infected meat products are exported, but it seems that transmission of vCJD from blood products contaminated in the UK will not result in ex-gratia compensation unless *exposure* occurred 'in the UK'. Whilst the compensation fund may deter UK citizens from pursuing legal action, there is no such luxury for someone infected by exported blood products.

Causation

10.10 The claimants in *A v National Blood Authority* were lucky in one respect. They knew who had supplied the 'defective' blood. Where a claim relates to a drug, a potential claimant may well have taken the drug over several years and not be able to trace which of several drug companies manufactured the drug that caused his injury. An analogous problem arose in *Fairchild v Glenhaven Funeral Services Ltd*[95] facing workers who contracted the industrial disease, mesothelioma. They could show that their illness was caused by exposure to asbestos dust or fibres. They established that their employers were negligent in exposing them to asbestos. However, as they had worked for several companies during their working life, they could not pin-

---

[91] *vCJD Main Trust Deed* (2002). See: http://www.cjdtrust.co.uk/cjdtrustdeeddoc02 .pdf at para. 1.12.2.

[92] *vCJD Main Trust Deed* (2002), para B.

[93] For an examination of products liability for pathogenically infected products, see J Stapleton (2002) 53 *South Carolina Law Review* 1225. For tortious liability arising from public health initiatives, see R Martin, 'Public Health and the Scope of Potential Liability in Tort' (2005) 21 *Professional Negligence* 39.

[94] J Meikle, R Evans, 'British Blood Products May Pose vCJD Risk in 14 Countries' (2006) *Guardian,* 14 May.

[95] [2002] UKHL 22. See also *Gregg v Scott* [2005] UKHL 2. These cases are discussed in ch 7.

point which employer was actually responsible for their disease, which can be caused by a single fibre entering the lung. The Law Lords ruled that as each defendant employer had increased the risk to the affected workers, causation was established against all of them. In the USA, in *Sindell v Abbott Laboratories*,[96] it has been held that where patients are exposed to risk from a defective drug manufactured by several different companies, each company is held liable in proportion to its market share. Lord Hoffmann in *Fairchild* did not consider that the industrial disease claims before the Law Lords and claims against drug companies were the same. He said that the risk from consuming a drug bought in one shop is not increased by the fact it can be bought in another shop. With respect, he overlooks the possibility of drug-induced injury caused by prolonged or incremental use of a medicine. However, more importantly, he signalled that, even if *Fairchild* does not conclusively determine that the *Sindell* rule prevails in England, he looked at the possibility with some favour. He described the market share approach against several drug companies as 'imaginative' and suggested that such a possibility would be looked at if a claim came before the House of Lords.'[97]

Lord Hoffmann implemented this approach in *Barker v Corus*[98] which also involved a mesothelioma victim employed by a number of employers who had breached their duty of care and exposed the employee to asbestos. Lord Hoffmann stated:

> In my opinion, the attribution of liability according to the relative degree of contribution to the chance of the disease being contracted would smooth the roughness of the justice which a rule of joint and several liability creates. The defendant was a wrongdoer, it is true, and should not be allowed to escape liability altogether, but he should not be liable for more than the damage which he caused and, since this is a case in which science can deal only in probabilities, the law should accept that position and attribute liability according to probabilities.[99]

Consequently Corus were liable according to the probability of risk they created. They were not liable for the probability of risk created by the first, insolvent employer. This meant that Mr Barker went under-compensated. Those employed by a single solvent employer, however, could be assured of 100 per cent compensation. The government responded with the Compensation Act 2006, section 3 of which reverses the effect of *Barker* for mesothelioma victims and provides that compensation will be joint and several. Victims of mesothelioma can seek full compensation from any solvent negligent employer. The negligent employer will then be able to claim back contributions from other responsible persons under the Civil Liability (Contribution) Act 1978. *Barker* remains an authoritative decision in non-mesothelioma cases,[100] though the ambit of the decision was restricted. In cases where the damage results

[96] (1980) 607 P 2d 924.
[97] [2006] UKHL 20 at para 74.
[98] [2006] UKHL 20. Examined in ch 7.
[99] [2006] UKHL 20 at para 43.
[100] *Sienkiewicz v Grief* [2009] EWCA 1159.

from a single agent, and multiple factors have increased the damage, or the risk of damage, it remains to be seen how widely the decision will be construed.[101] The *Sindell* rule might still find favour in a case involving prolonged or incremental use of a medical product.

In chapter 5, we examined a case which has potentially wider implications for product liability. In *Chester v Afshar*[102] Miss Chester underwent surgery on the advice of Mr Afshar, her surgeon, during which she suffered nerve damage to her legs. The operation was performed with due care but even so, there was a 12 per cent risk of nerve damage. Miss Chester was not warned of the risk. Had she been so warned, she would have deferred the operation, but on the balance of probabilities, it could not be said that she would have withheld consent. Did the lack of causation defeat her claim? The majority held that it did not. Lord Hope stated:

> To leave the patient who would find the decision difficult without a remedy, as the normal approach to causation would indicate, would render the duty useless in the cases where it may be needed most. This would discriminate against those who cannot honestly say that they would have declined the operation once and for all if they had been warned. I would find that result unacceptable. The function of the law is to enable rights to be vindicated and to provide remedies when duties have been breached.[103]

Once again, it remains to be seen whether this approach will be applied in wider contexts.[104] If the same practical justice is applied to product liability, it seems that a failure by the manufacturer or supplier to warn a patient of side-effects or adverse reactions may result in liability, even if the claimant cannot prove that he would not have used the product if he had been properly warned.[105]

Prevention better than cure?[106]

10.11 The Thalidomide tragedy prompted new laws to vet drugs before they could be marketed in the UK. The Medicines Act 1968 provided for the licensing and monitoring of drugs. In 1998 a similar system was set up to regulate

---

[101] See M Jones, 'Proving Causation – Beyond the "But For" Test' (2006) 22 *Professional Negligence* 251.

[102] [2004] UKHL 41.

[103] [2004] UKHL 41 at para 87.

[104] *Chester* was distinguished in a claim for negligent financial advice: *Beary v Pall Mall Investments* [2005] EWCA Civ 415. See J Stapleton, 'Occam's Razor Reveals an Orthodox Basis for *Chester v Afshar*' (2006) 122 *Law Quarterly Review* 426.

[105] See L Jones, '*Chester v Afshar*: Effect of Product Liability' (2005) 5(1) *Health and Safety Law* 12–14.

[106] For a fuller account, see P Feldschreiber (ed), *The Law and Regulation of Medicines* (2008) OUP; G Appelbe, J Wingfield, *Dale and Appelbe's Pharmacy, Law and Ethics* (9th edn, 2009) Pharmaceutical Press; S Shorthose, *Guide to EU Pharmaceutical Regulatory Law: Annual Manual* (2010) Kluwer Law International.

medical devices (for example diagnostic tests or intra-uterine devices) and in 2003 both systems were brought under a single agency: the Medicines and Healthcare Products Regulatory Agency (MHRA). The licensing process (described below) has evolved to take into consideration the increasing relevance of European regulations.[107]

No medicine[108] may be manufactured, imported or marketed without a licence. The Clinical Trials Directive[109] (chapter 15) requires three different types of licence in the development of an investigational medicinal product. First, the companies manufacturing and distributing the medicines are required to have 'manufacturer's and wholesale dealer's licences'; second, 'clinical trial authorisations' are required in order to develop new products; and third, a 'marketing authorisation' is required before the product can be marketed.

There are various routes to marketing authorisation: the MHRA oversees UK marketing authorisation and the European Medicines Agency (EMA) gives 'centralised' authorisation valid in all EU and EEA-EFTA states. In addition, there are systems by which marketing authorisation can be obtained in several EU countries concurrently.

The EMA was established in 1995[110] to harmonise and streamline licensing across Europe. It has a staff of around 500 and is based in London. One of its committees is called the Committee for Medicinal Products for Human Use (CHMP)[111] which licenses human medicinal products for distribution across the EU. Some drugs must be authorised by this route.

In other cases, a product can be licensed in the UK only, via the MHRA. In addition to a staff of around 700, the MHRA also supports expert advisory bodies, such as the Committee on the Safety of Devices and the Commission on Human Medicine (CHM).[112] The CHM reviews licensing applications and produces an independent assessment. It will review the safety, quality and efficacy of the healthcare product but will not consider its efficacy in comparison with any existing product. The CHM does not exist to prevent copies, sometimes referred to as 'me-too' drugs.

---

[107] Directive 2001/83/EC relating to medicinal products for human use, amended by Directives 2002/98/EC, 2003/63/EC, 2004/24/EC and 2004/27/EC.
[108] As to what constitutes a medicine, see MHRA, *A Guide to What is a Medicinal Product* (2007) MHRA Guidance Note 8.
[109] 2001/20/EC, implemented in the UK by the Medicines for Human Use (Clinical Trials) Regulations 2004, SI 2004/1031.
[110] The original European Medicines Evaluation Agency was renamed in 2004.
[111] Established by Regulation 726/2004, replacing the Committee for Proprietary Medicinal Products (CPMP).
[112] Established under s 2 of the Medicines Act 1968. The terms of reference are set out in s 3 as amended by the Medicines (Advisory Bodies) Regulations 2005. The CHM replaced the Committee on the Safety of Medicines in 2005.

Once marketing authorisation is obtained, the product manufacturer must show that the product is cost effective before the NHS will make it available. The MHRA then subject the product to a lifetime of checks and inspections, operating systems to control product information, advertising,[113] pharmacovigilance and potentially reclassification (for example, if a prescription drug is made available in pharmacies or ordinary shops). Marketing authorisations are granted for periods of up to five years after which they must be renewed.

The CHM 'promote the collection and investigation of information relating to adverse reactions for human medicines'.[114] The EMA promulgates guidance to enhance consistency and transparency.[115] Post-marketing surveillance systems include the 'yellow card scheme' which concerns adverse reactions to medicines and Adverse Incidence Reports regarding devices. On the basis of these systems the CHM makes recommendations regarding safety issues and the minimisation of risk and less urgent issues are communicated via a regular bulletin.

Section 28 of the Medicines Act 1968 empowers the Minister to revoke an existing licence. Several grounds for revocation are established, of which the most important is where:

> ... medicinal products of any description to which the licence relates can no longer be regarded as products which can safely be administered for the purposes indicated in the licence, or can no longer be regarded as efficacious for those purposes ...

The decision to withdraw a drug from the market is no longer solely a matter for the manufacturer. A manufacturer aggrieved by the refusal or revocation of a product licence may seek a review by the CHM. No product licence can be refused or revoked without consultation with the CHM. A manufacturer whose product has been approved by the CHM, but who is refused a licence by the Minister, has a right to a further hearing. If he chooses, as he may, to reject their advice, he must set up an independent inquiry before which the manufacturer may state his case.[116]

---

[113] Prescription drugs cannot be advertised directly to the public. Medicines (Advertising) Regulations 1994, SI 1994/1932, as amended.

[114] As do the Advisory Board on the Registration of Homeopathic Products and Herbal Medicines Advisory Committee.

[115] European Commission, Detailed Guidance on the Collection, Verification and Presentation of Adverse Reaction Reports Arising from Clinical Trials on Medicinal Products for Human Use (2006). See also European Commission, Public Consultation: Draft Detailed Guidance on the Collection, Verification and Presentation of Adverse Reaction Reports Arising from Clinical Trials on Medicinal Products for Human Use (June 2010) produced in response to the Public Consultation on the Functioning of the Clinical Trials Directive (2009).

[116] Medicines Act 1968, s 21(5).

Off-label drug use

10.12 Drugs are sometimes used 'off-label' – that is, in an unapproved form or dosage. For example, a drug licensed for use in adults might be used 'off-label' to treat a child with a related illness when no licensed treatment exists.[117] The alternative would be to refuse the child treatment until a clinical trial can be carried out and marketing authorisation received. Clearly this would be too late for the patient. In other cases, a patient might suffer a rare disease and a trial would not be financially viable. As a result, some 'off-label' drug use is sanctioned, but the drug company should not actively market the drug for this use. However, it has been alleged that the profits attainable by marketing a drug for unlicensed use might justify the fines imposed upon the company if they are caught.[118]

A lacuna in the law relating to off-label drug use was revealed in 2008. The anti-depressant drug, Seroxat, was licensed for use in adults, but frequently used off-label to treat teenagers. GlaxoSmithKline was alleged to have withheld clinical trial data showing that Seroxat was ineffective and potentially unsafe for those under the age of eighteen.[119] However, the regulations controlling safety information did not extend to off-label drug use and as a result the case against the drug company was weak. Nevertheless, the MHRA was much criticised for its decision not to prosecute, especially as other countries responded far more harshly.[120] In 2009 the Medicines for Human Use (Marketing Authorisations Etc) Amendment Regulations 2009[121] extended the requirement to provide safety information to encompass off-label drug use.

---

[117] See Royal College of Paediatrics and Child Health, *The Use of Unlicensed Medicines or Licensed Medicines for Unlicensed Applications in Paediatric Practice* (2010).

[118] D Evans, 'When Drug Makers' Profits Outweigh Penalties' *Washington Post*, 21 March 2010: 'Since May 2004, Pfizer, Eli Lilly, Bristol-Myers Squibb and four other drug companies have paid a total of $7bn in fines and penalties. Six of the companies admitted in court that they marketed medicines for unapproved uses. In September 2007, New York-based Bristol-Myers paid $515m – without admitting or denying wrongdoing – to federal and state governments in a civil lawsuit brought by the Justice Department. The six other companies pleaded guilty in criminal cases.'

[119] L McGoey, E Jackson, 'Seroxat and the Suppression of Clinical Trial Data: Regulatory Failure and the Uses of Legal Ambiguity' (2009) 35 *Journal of Medical Ethics* 107. For comparable US cases, see allegations that AstraZeneca illegally marketed Seroquel for uses not approved by the FDA between 2001 and 2006: US Dept of Justice, accessible at http://www.justice.gov/opa/pr/2010/April/10-civ-487.html.

[120] D Batty, 'Seroxat' (2008) *Times*, 6 March; 'Critics of the MHRA and the pharmaceutical industry point to the tougher penalties faced by firms overseas. In the USA, GSK was sued by the New York state attorney general, Eliot Spitzer, and settled for $2.5m (£1.25m) and an agreement to publish all its trial results – negative or positive – on a publicly available database.'

[121] SI 2009/2820.

Holding regulators to account

10.13 The MHRA authorises, inspects, surveys and enforces the use of medicines and devices, aiming to protect, promote and improve public health. But does the system adequately represent patient's interests? Critics fear that drug regulators lack transparency and favour efficacy over patient safety. As long as drug companies evaluate their own products the public interest will not be served. The MHRA, they complain, is 'unaccountable, slow, and lacking the necessary expertise'.[122] The 2005 House of Commons Select Report on the Pharmaceutical Industry[123] was critical of the MHRA's close proximity to industry, its over-reliance on trust and its failure to properly scrutinise licensing data,[124] concluding:[125]

> In view of the failings of the MHRA, we recommend a fundamental review of the organization in order to ensure that safe and effective medicines, with necessary prescribing constraints, are licensed.

Can aggrieved patients sue the regulators? The possibility of governmental liability for drug-induced injury was aired even in the Thalidomide days. The Health Minister, Sir Keith Joseph, dismissed suggestions that the government could be liable. He argued further that, even when the elaborate licensing provisions of the 1968 Act were in force, the legal liability for any defect in the drug rested on the manufacturers alone.[126] The patients injured by the anti-arthritic drug, Opren, sought compensation from the Health Minister and the erstwhile Committee on Safety in Medicines (CSM) as well as from the drug company.[127] They contended that the government and the CSM had been negligent both in originally licensing the drug and for continuing to allow it to be marketed after its dangers should have become apparent to the Ministry and the CSM. The Opren case against the government was ultimately abandoned.

Another claim against the CSM was mounted in *Smith v Secretary of State for Health (on behalf of the Committee for Safety of Medicines)*.[128] In May 1986, seven-year-old Amanda Smith caught chickenpox and was given one aspirin tablet on two consecutive days by her mother, who followed the advice on the label. Amanda's condition worsened. She developed spastic tetraplegia and was eventually diagnosed with Reye's Syndrome. In June 1986, the CSM issued a warning that aspirin should not be given to children under the age of twelve except on medical advice because it could trigger Reye's Syndrome. They had met in March 1986, but delayed the warning so as to cooperate with the drug companies. No interim warning was made. Was the CSM negligent? Morland J held that it was not. There was no breach of statutory duty or com-

---

[122] F Godlee, 'Can we Tame the Monster?' (2006) 333 *BMJ* 333.
[123] HC 42-I, 2005.
[124] HC 41-I (2005), p 4.
[125] HC 41-I (2005), p 5.
[126] HC Deb Vol 847, Cols. 440–441, 29 November 1972.
[127] The claim against the CSM was dropped.
[128] [2002] EWHC 200 (QB).

mon law duty of care. The decision by the CSM was a discretionary policy decision which is not, Morland J held, justiciable in private law, even if there was fault in the timetabling of the warning.[129]

In *XYZ and Others v Schering Health Care Ltd*,[130] the CSM was once again under fire, but this time from the drug companies. The case involved a group action by claimants alleged to have suffered cardio-vascular injuries as a result of taking certain brands of the combined oral contraceptive ('the Pill'). In 1995, the CSM circulated a warning to prescribers of 'the Pill' that three as yet unpublished articles indicated a two-fold increase in risk of venous-thromboembolism. The defendants argued that the letter was ill-considered and that the ensuing 'Pill scare' was a public health disaster. Mackay J held that there was not in fact a two-fold increase in risk and on that basis the claimants lost their case. Nor was the advisability of the CSM's letter under review in this case. Regulators have the unenviable task of deciding when it is appropriate to 'act as though a given association were causal rather than to continue to assume that it is not'.[131]

Could a claim against the CHM, in effect for negligently monitoring drugs and/or blood products, succeed? In *Smith*, Morland J did not rule out the possibility. Neither the Secretary of State nor the CHM enjoys blanket immunity from a common law suit.[132] Improper exercise of duty such as the postponing of a meeting 'because it clashed with the Epsom Derby meeting'[133] would clearly be considered negligent. Beyond that, claimants would have to persuade the court that it was 'just, fair and reasonable' for the CHM to be subjected to a duty of care to individual patients and that the decision was not discretionary or policy-based. Two particular questions will pose problems for claimants. The court will seek to ask whether the scheme of regulation established by the Medicines Act, and now heavily influenced by European legislation, was designed to provide a right to compensation to those injured by unsafe drugs. And given that the primary responsibility for the medicine still rests with the drug company, should the government be liable for their wrongdoing?

Claims brought abroad

10.14 The majority of drug companies are multinationals. Drugs are not confined within national borders. British women who suffered injury as a result of using the Dalkon Shield IUD sued the manufacturers in the USA and recovered compensation from a settlement fund set up when the company

[129] [2002] EWHC 200 (QB) at para 93, per Morland J.
[130] [2002] EWHC 1420 (QB).
[131] [2002] EWHC 200 (QB) at para 19, per Mackay J.
[132] *Stovin v Wise* [1996] AC 923, HL at 937–941, per Lord Nicholls.
[133] *Smith v Secretary of State for Health* [2002] EWHC 200 (QB), para 95.

went bankrupt.[134] When can an injured patient resort to a foreign court and why should he want to?

When a claim has a foreign element, a set of rules known as private international law, or conflict of laws, comes into play. These are excessively complex and we give only the barest outline of the relevant law. Essentially, when a claim for negligence is brought, the claimant can sue in any country where a relevant act of negligence occurred, or in the country where the drug company is based.[135] There may be more than one such country. So in the case of a defective drug, negligence may have occurred both in the country where it was carelessly manufactured and in the country where it was carelessly marketed as safe[136] and injured the claimant. It is on the basis of the careless manufacture of the device in the USA that the women suing over the Dalkon Shield were able to go to court in the USA. Where there is a dispute over whether an action should be allowed to go ahead, the law of the country where the claimant is trying to sue determines whether it should do so.

Why should anyone want to sue abroad? After all, if they took the drug here and were injured here they can bring their claim in their homeland on the basis that it was here the drug caused them harm. There are three reasons why claimants may opt for the hassle of a foreign lawsuit. First, the procedural rules in the foreign courts may be more favourable to claimants. They may be able to conduct a 'collective (or class) action' more effectively than in England. Second, there remain financial incentives to sue in the USA if you can. Not only is liability for drugs strict, but awards of damages are made by juries, and are generally much higher than English judge-made awards. The contingency fee system may offer more favourable access to the courts than conditional fees do here. And finally a threat to sue in the USA may prompt the defendants into offering a more generous settlement than would otherwise have been the case.

However, legal action abroad is fraught with difficulties. When the pharmaceutical giant, Merck, withdrew the drug Vioxx from the market because of links to cardiovascular problems such as heart attacks,[137] successful claims were brought in Australia and the USA. However, legal aid was refused in the UK, and law firms were unwilling to risk action based on a conditional fee

---

[134] See Ferguson, *Drug Injuries and the Pursuit of Compensation* (1996) Sweet & Maxwell, pp 6–8.

[135] These complex rules are neatly summarised in A Saggerson, 'PI Litigation across Jurisdictions: Summary of Service Regimes' (2002) 6 *Personal Injury* 3.

[136] *Distillers Co (Biochemicals) Ltd v Thompson* [1971] AC 458. Where a New Zealand mother was allowed to sue the British company Distillers in New Zealand over Thalidomide manufactured here; the essence of the negligence alleged was failure to warn her, in New Zealand, of the danger to her baby.

[137] See, for example, T Nesi, *Poison Pills: The Untold Story of the Vioxx Drug Scandal* (2008) Thomas Dunne Books, USA; H M Krumholz *et al*, 'What have we Learnt from Vioxx?' (2007) 334 *BMJ* 120.

arrangement.[138] As a result, UK citizens took their case to the American courts, but this too was unsuccessful: US juries could not be expected to understand our complex regulatory system.[139]

Vaccine damage: a special case?

10.15 Vaccine damage has received special treatment because of the distinction in social effect between vaccines and other drugs.[140] Generally the benefit and risk of taking a drug rests with the individual patient alone. No one else suffers directly if he does not take the drug. No one else benefits directly if he does. With a vaccine the position is different. If a child is immunised, the child himself benefits from the immunity conferred and his friends and schoolfellows benefit from the elimination of the risk that he will pass that disease on to them. Consequently, vaccination of young children against diseases such as tetanus, diphtheria, polio, measles, meningitis C and whooping cough is actively promoted by the Department of Health. The whooping cough vaccine caused outcry and distress, and concerns about the MMR vaccine generated similar controversy. A number of children healthy before vaccination have, their parents claim, suffered severe and lasting brain damage as a consequence of receiving the vaccine. More recently, however, the scientific claims that the MMR vaccine had such an effect have been largely discredited and the doctor who led the research was found guilty of serious professional misconduct by the General Medical Council (GMC).[141]

What remedies have the parents of a vaccine-damaged child? First they may, as a number of parents of children allegedly damaged by whooping cough vaccine have done, seek to use the tort of negligence to obtain compensation. The advantage of this course is that, if the claim was successful, their children would receive full compensation for any disability caused by the vaccine. One problem is whom to sue. The crux of the question is often whether the risk of the vaccine to a child is greater than the risks posed by contracting the disease itself. An action against a doctor for negligently using a reputable vaccine is likely to fail because, even if some doctors and experts condemn its use, a substantial body of informed opinion still backs the vaccine. A negligence action is usually only viable if some special feature of the child's history should have ruled out routine vaccination, or if symptoms at a first vaccination, indicating that further vaccination was unwise, were missed. Suing the manufacturers will run into the problem of the risk/benefit ratio of the product. The

---

[138] J Dreaper, 'UK Vioxx Cases Await Court Hearing' (2006) *BBC News*, 11 April.
[139] *In re Vioxx Litigation*, 395 NJ Super 358, 373–74 (Sup Ct NJ, App Div, 2007):See J Robins, 'Stars and Gripes' (2006) 46 *Litigation Funding* 4–6, discussing New Jersey Court decision to reject UK class action for alleged injuries suffered as a result of using Vioxx.
[140] See, in particular, the Pearson Report, ch 25.
[141] GMC, *Dr Andrew Wakefield: Determination on Serious Professional Misconduct and Sanction*, May 2010. Accessible at http://www.GMC-uk.org.

manufacturers dispute the level of risk from the vaccine and will argue that the overwhelming benefit to the community of vaccination outweighs any risk to a very few. They will contend that, properly used, the vaccine is not defective. In relation to the whooping cough vaccine, the companies deny that the vaccine does indeed cause brain damage. In *Loveday v Renton*,[142] a judge held that the claimants failed to prove that the pertussis (whooping cough) vaccine caused the child's brain damage. Attempts to recover compensation for vaccine injuries through claims in negligence have generally proved unsuccessful in England.[143] The MMR litigation has cost in the region of £15m. In 2004, the High Court rejected an application for a judicial review of an earlier decision to withdraw legal aid on the basis that the claims were unlikely to succeed and would cost the public a further £10m.[144] The Legal Services Commission is clamping down on funding. Unless there is a good chance that the case will succeed and unless the claim is based on solid research, group actions such as the MMR Vaccine Group Litigation and Gulf War syndrome are less likely to receive funding in the future.[145]

The problems of litigation deter many parents from going to court. Successive reviews of the issue of compensation for vaccine damage recognised that it is an example of injury where compensation via the tort of negligence, or the Consumer Protection Act 1987, may be inappropriate. There may prove to be no negligence on anyone's part because the benefit to the majority is held to justify the risk to a small minority. Yet it is scarcely fair that those who suffer damage should bear the whole burden of disability alone. On the recommendation of the Pearson Commission, Parliament enacted the Vaccine Damage Payments Act 1979 to provide for a no-fault compensation scheme for vaccine-damaged individuals. The current amount payable is £120,000.[146] Claims for payments under the Act are made initially to the Department of Health. If the Department official responsible is not satisfied that the claim is made out, the claimant may ask for the decision to be reviewed by an independent medical tribunal. The decision of the tribunal is final. The making of a payment under the 1979 Act does not debar a claimant from also suing for negligence in respect of the vaccination.

The Act remains a target of criticism.[147] Successful cases are rare.[148] £120,000 may sound a substantial amount. If a child is so damaged that he will never be

---

[142] [1990] 1 Med LR 117.

[143] Though parents in Ireland succeeded: see *Best v Wellcome Foundation* [1993] 2 IR 421.

[144] See C Dyer, 'Commission Withdraws Legal Aid for Parents Suing over MMR Vaccine' (2003) 327 *BMJ* 641.

[145] G Langdon Down, 'Practice Area: Product Liability: Productive Work' (2004) April *Law Society Gazette* 22.

[146] The Vaccine Damage Payments Act 1979 Statutory Sum Order 2007, SI 2007/1931.

[147] See S Pywell, 'The Vaccine Damage Payment Scheme – A Proposal for Radical Reform' (2002) 9 *Journal of Social Security Law* 73.

[148] See 'Vaccine Damage Payments' (2004) 27 *Consumer Law Today* 4(5)(1) and '£3.5 Million Paid Out in Vaccine Damages' (2005) *BBC News*, 16 March. One successful

able to care for himself and earn his own living, it falls far short of his needs. A successful tort claim would result in a multimillion-pound award. The Act remains a compromise. It has not replaced tort with an adequate compensation mechanism. Critics complain that the ever-present problem of causation of drug-induced injury is simply ignored in the Act. The claimant must establish on the balance of probability that his disablement resulted from the vaccine.

example is a £90,000 award in 2010. Robert Fletcher's parents contended that the MMR injection at thirteen months caused him to suffer epilepsy and brain damage (though not autism, as the tribunal was careful to note). His case was turned down in 1997, but on appeal the tribunal (by a majority) awarded compensation.

Part III

MATTERS OF LIFE AND DEATH

Chapter 11

CONTRACEPTION, PREGNANCY AND CHILDBIRTH

Reproductive autonomy and reproductive health

11.1 In *Rees v Darlington Memorial Hospital NHS Trust*[1] the majority of the House of Lords concurred with Lord Millett in *McFarlane v Tayside Health Board*[2] in his endorsement of a legal right of reproductive autonomy. A woman who gave birth to a child after a failed sterilisation had, he said, suffered a legal wrong – 'the denial of an important aspect of [her] personal autonomy, viz the right to limit the size of [her] family'.[3] While just over fifty years ago judges sought to limit individuals' freedom to plan their families, today English law leaves such matters to personal choice. In 1954, Lord Denning MR said of vasectomy:

> Take a case where a sterilisation operation is done so as to enable a man to have the pleasure of sexual intercourse without shouldering the responsibilities attached to it. The operation is plainly injurious to the public interest. It is degrading to the man himself. It is injurious to his wife and any woman who he may marry, to say nothing of the way it opens to licentiousness, and unlike other contraceptives, it allows no room for a change of mind on either side. It is illegal, even though the man consents to it . . .[4]

In 2002, Munby J[5] resoundingly declared that contraception was a matter for personal choice and conscience, and no business of the law. The judge declared that it was:

> . . . not any part of the responsibilities of public authorities – let alone of the criminal law – to be telling adult people whether they can or cannot use contraceptive devices of the kind which I have been considering.

---

[1] [2003] UKHL 52, HL.
[2] [1999] 4 All ER 961, HL. Discussed at **11.12** below.
[3] [2003] UKHL 52 at para 123.
[4] *Bravery v Bravery* [1954] 3 All ER 59 at 67–68.
[5] *R (on the application of SPUC) v Secretary of State for Health* [2002] 2 FLR 146.

11.2 Contraception, Pregnancy and Childbirth

This chapter will examine several aspects of how the law implements or fails to implement broad notions of reproductive autonomy, embracing choices about whether or not to conceive or beget a child, and choices that may face women in the course of pregnancy. We also look at a number of practical legal questions relating to contraception, pregnancy and childbirth, and consider issues of reproductive health given that for most prospective parents the priority will be the birth of a healthy infant.

Contraceptives: patients' rights

11.2 An infallible contraceptive has yet to be invented.[6] Contraceptives, such as the Pill and the IUD, carry a price-tag. They pose some risk to women's health. Contraception is a medical as well as a social issue. And it largely concerns women for, except for the still experimental male 'Pill',[7] the more sophisticated contraceptives which pose medical risk are used by women. Women seek two sorts of protection from the law. First, they require definition of the doctor's obligation to assist them to avoid pregnancy at the least possible risk to health. In *Wooton v J Docter Ltd*,[8] for example, a pharmacist negligently gave a patient the wrong type of contraceptive pill and she became pregnant. But as the correct pill and the pill given in error had the same hormone levels, it was held that the error had not caused or materially contributed to the pregnancy. Second, they demand information, and greater control of their reproductive and sexual lives.

A doctor advising a woman on contraception owes her the same duties as in any other area of medicine. He must offer her competent and careful advice. He must perform any technical procedure, for example, inserting an IUD, skilfully.[9] He must obtain her consent to any invasive procedure and ensure that she is competent to give it.

Modern contraceptive treatments have not just generated moral controversy. They have resulted in litigation where use of contraceptive methods has resulted in adverse effects for women. Several million dollars in compensation were paid out to women who suffered injury through use of the Dalkon shield, an IUD which caused substantial pelvic injuries to patients.[10] The injectable contraceptive Depo-Provera led to a number of lawsuits in the UK. The use of

---

[6] For an overview of the efficacy of contraceptives, see: J-J Amy, V Tripathi, 'Contraceptives for Women – An Evidence Based Overview' (2009) 339 *BMJ* 1136.

[7] Though significant progress has been made recently: Y Gu *et al*, 'Multicenter Contraceptive Efficacy Trial of Injectable Testosterone Undecanoate in Chinese Men' (2009) 94 *Journal of Clinical Endocrinology and Metabolism*, 1910.

[8] [2008] EWHC Civ 1361.

[9] For example, making a 20-cm incision to perform a hysterectomy when a 15-cm incision was appropriate constituted negligence: *Brown v Scarborough and North East Yorkshire Healthcare NHS Trust* [2009] EWHC 3103 (QB).

[10] See above at **10.14**.

Depo-Provera in its early years offers a classic example of how not to approach contraceptive advice and treatment.

Depo-Provera is a synthetic form of a natural hormone, which acts like most brands of the Pill to prevent eggs developing and makes the womb hostile to any fertilised embryo. One injection is effective for at least three months. Doctors may advise the use of the drug for women for whom the Pill is a health risk, women who are considered too unreliable to be trusted to use other means of contraception and where pregnancy should be completely ruled out, for example when a woman has just been vaccinated against rubella. Increasingly women choose Depo-Provera for its convenience. Depo-Provera can produce unpredictable and unpleasant side-effects, including severe and irregular bleeding. Complaints were made that: (1) some women were injected with the drug without ever being told of its nature; and (2) even where Depo-Provera was expressly prescribed and described as a contraceptive, inadequate explanation of its potential side-effects was given. Fears were voiced that Depo-Provera might be 'forced' on inarticulate, or not particularly intelligent, women.[11]

A Salford woman, Mrs Potts, won £3,000 damages[12] after she was injected with Depo-Provera concurrently with a vaccination against rubella. She suffered severe bleeding. The injection was given days after the delivery of her third child, and she thought that it was a routine post-natal 'jab'. The aim of her doctor was laudable, to protect her from pregnancy while the vaccine might harm any unborn child. He had no right to deprive her of her choice of whether or not to accept or decline a controversial drug. Women must be told the nature of the drug offered to them, and if their right to choose is to be effective they must have its advantages and disadvantages explained to them. The judge awarding Mrs Potts's compensation said: 'She should have been given the choice, and she was entitled to know beforehand what the decision entailed'. The same holds true of any contraceptive treatment.[13]

A doctor prescribing contraception must be properly informed about the current stage of research and knowledge about different types and brands and their risks to particular patients. In the 1980s and 90s, scare stories about the Pill, including risks of cancer, heart disease and thrombosis, hit the headlines with monotonous regularity.[14] More recently, lowered hormone levels have led to a safer Pill. Young women remain at elevated risk, especially if they

---

[11] When Depo-Provera and Norplant (a slow release capsule injected into the arm) were first licensed in the USA, they were used as sentencing alternatives as a pregnancy restriction for drug and alcohol addicts and child abusers, though most cases were overturned on appeal. See J Mertus, S Heller, 'Norplant Meets the New Eugenicists: The Impermissibility of Coerced Contraception' (1992) 11 *St Louis University Public Law Review* 359.

[12] See (1983) *Guardian* 27 July, p 4.

[13] See, for example, *Local Authority v A* [2010] EWHC 1549 (Fam), discussed at **6.4** above.

[14] See **10.1** and **10.13** above for relevant claims arising under the Consumer Protection Act 1987.

smoke or are obese, but a 2010 study indicates health benefits for older women, in terms of lowered rates of cancer and heart disease.[15]

What information is the user entitled to? Clearly both the doctor and the drug company manufacturing the contraception are required to give the woman sufficient information to enable her to make an informed choice about whether to use, or continue to use, that method of contraception. We would argue that in the light of *Bolitho v City & Hackney Health Authority*,[16] and *Pearce v United Bristol Healthcare NHS Trust*,[17] women must be advised of any risk that the contraception poses to them which a sensible woman would consider material to a reasonable decision about what sort of contraception to use.[18]

What about contraceptives which simply fail? We shall see later that the House of Lords has ruled that parents cannot recover compensation for the cost of bringing up a normal, healthy child.[19] Might a failed contraceptive method be viewed as 'defective' under the Consumer Protection Act 1987? In *Richardson v LRC Products Ltd*[20] it was held that evidence that a condom split was not by itself sufficient to prove that product defective. The fallibility of condoms was well known. The manufacturer never guaranteed 100 per cent success.

Sterilisation

11.3 When a further pregnancy or the burden of caring for more children may endanger a woman's health, therapeutic sterilisation may be advised. Non-therapeutic sterilisation is increasingly sought as a method of permanent birth control, both by older couples who feel that their family is complete and by younger people adamant that they never wish to reproduce.[21] A new innovative technique has reduced the need for invasive surgery and general anaesthetic. Small silicone implants are placed in the fallopian tubes by hys-

---

[15] P C Hannaford, *et al*, 'Mortality Among Contraceptive Pill Users: Cohort Evidence from Royal College of General Practitioners' Oral Contraception Study' (2010) 340 *BMJ* 1136.

[16] [1997] 4 All ER 771.

[17] [1999] PIQR P 53; see above **5.7**.

[18] But see *Vadera v Shaw* (1999) 45 BMLR 172, CA. Discussed in R Goldberg, 'The Contraceptive Pill Negligence and Causation: Views on *Vadera v Shaw*' (2001) 8(3) *Medical Law Review* 316.

[19] See *McFarlane v Tayside Health Board* [1999] 4 All ER 961, HL.

[20] [2000] Lloyd's Law Reports 280.

[21] Amid fierce criticism, Barbara Harris reportedly attempted to extend her 'Project Prevention' (see www.projectprevention.org) to English cities. The project (inter alia) offers money to drug addicts willing to undergo sterilisation, in the hope of reducing the number of babies born with drug withdrawal symptoms. See J Doward, 'Anti-Drugs Campaigner Barbara Harris Brings Crusade to Sterilise Addicts to UK' (2010) *Observer*, 30 May.

teroscope.[22] The woman's own tissue then grows around the implants, rendering her infertile. A plethora of private clinics offer female sterilisation and vasectomy at a price. Patients refused sterilisation within the NHS must resort to that private sector if they can meet the cost.

A doctor undertaking sterilisation must ensure that the patient understands and agrees to what is to be done. Operating without any consent is obviously a battery. Nor should sterilisation be automatically performed concurrently with some other gynaecological operation to which the patient has consented. The doctor may correctly judge, in the course of some other form of surgery, that a woman should not risk pregnancy again. He cannot act 'in her best interests' without her agreement. In *Devi v West Midlands Area Health Authority*,[23] a married woman of thirty-three who already had four children entered hospital for a minor gynaecological operation. Her religion outlawed sterilisation or contraception. In the course of the operation the surgeon discovered her womb to be ruptured and sterilised her there and then. She received £4,000 damages for the loss of her ability to conceive again and £2,700 damages for the 'neurosis' caused by the knowledge of what had been done to her. The choice whether to accept sterilisation is the patient's. It may be more convenient to sterilise the patient on the spot. It is unlikely to be so immediately necessary as to justify acting in an emergency without consent.

A doctor who has obtained consent may still be liable for negligence if he fails to discuss properly with the patient the implications of the operation in a manner consistent with good medical practice. The doctor must not only give the patient sufficient information on which to make up her mind, but do so at a time when she is in a fit state to make a reasoned decision.[24] In *Thake v Maurice*, Mr Thake decided to have a vasectomy and paid £20 for the operation. The judge found that the defendant never warned Mr and Mrs Thake of the small but real risk that nature would reverse the surgery. She did not discover her pregnancy until it was nearly five months advanced. The couple sought compensation from the defendant surgeon. As Mr Thake had paid for his vasectomy, unlike an NHS patient, he had a contract with the surgeon. The trial judge held[25] that Mr Thake had agreed to an operation that he understood would render him irreversibly infertile. That is what he contracted for. The defendant was in breach of contract if he failed to achieve that aim. By failing to warn Mr Thake of the risk of natural reversal of the vasectomy, he *guaranteed* to make him sterile. He was responsible for the financial loss to the family occasioned by the birth of the unplanned infant. The Court of Appeal[26] held by a majority that the surgeon never guaranteed to make Mr Thake sterile. Neill LJ found that no reasonable person would have understood the defendant as

---

[22] NICE, *IPG315 Hysteroscopic Sterilisation by Tubal Cannulation and Placement of Intrafallopian Implants: Guidance* (2009).

[23] [1980] 7 *Current Law* 44.

[24] *Wells v Surrey Area Health Authority* (1978) *Times*, 29 July.

[25] [1984] 2 All ER 513.

[26] [1986] 1 All ER 497, and see *Eyre v Measday* [1986] 1 All ER 488.

giving a binding promise that the operation would achieve its purpose. They nevertheless unanimously found for Mr Thake on grounds enabling NHS patients as well as private patients to sue if they are not warned of the risk of nature reversing sterilisation of either sex. They held that failure to warn of this risk was negligent.

Moreover, if sterilisation is proposed on therapeutic grounds, the patient's consent must necessarily be based on adequate and careful advice as to the medical need for sterilisation. In *Biles v Barking Health Authority*,[27] a woman was advised to undergo sterilisation on the grounds that she was suffering from a severe and probably fatal kidney complaint. That diagnosis was proved later to be mistaken and negligent. Mrs Biles recovered damages of £45,000, which included the cost of a failed attempt to reverse the sterilisation and the cost of IVF treatment to try to enable her to have a child of her own, despite her surgically blocked fallopian tubes.

Involuntary sterilisation[28]

11.4   No statute in England ever provided for the compulsory sterilisation of mentally ill or disabled patients. In chapter 14 we discuss a number of cases of involuntary sterilisation of minors. In 1989, in *F v West Berkshire Health Authority*,[29] their Lordships ruled that sterilisation of an adult woman with mental disability was not unlawful if that operation was in her 'best interests'. In theory, a woman may not be sterilised in the interests of society, of her potential children, or on eugenic grounds. She may be sterilised only where she lacks the capacity to make decisions on childbearing for herself, and to protect her health and welfare.

The Mental Capacity Act 2005 governs the law surrounding adults and young persons[30] who lack mental capacity. It is examined in detail in chapter 6. Much of the Act and the accompanying Code of Practice[31] enshrine principles developed by the common law. In *F v West Berkshire HA*,[32] protection from liability to carers and health professionals was granted through the application of the doctrine of necessity. Section 5 of the Mental Capacity Act 2005 performs a similar role, granting a 'general authority' to act in the best interests of the patient lacking mental capacity and setting conditions that must be

---

[27] See M Puxon, A Buchan, 'Damages for Sterility' (1988) 138 *New Law Journal* 80.

[28] See further above at **6.6–6.7**.

[29] [1989] 2 All ER 545, HL.

[30] The Mental Capacity Act 2005 applies largely to persons of age sixteen and over who lack capacity (see s 2(5)). For those under sixteen, persons with parental responsibility can consent on their behalf. Disputes are resolved under the Children Act 1989; the Mental Health Act 1983 or under the jurisdiction of the High Court. In the case of young persons between the ages of sixteen and eighteen, there is overlap between the Mental Capacity Act 2005 and the Children Act 1989.

[31] Mental Capacity Act 2005, Code of Practice, updated April 2007.

[32] [1989] 2 All ER 545, HL.

satisfied before liability can be avoided. The Act defines what constitutes a lack of capacity in section 2(1):

> ... [A] person lacks capacity in relation to a matter if at the material time he is unable to make a decision for himself in relation to the matter because of an impairment of, or a disturbance in the functioning of, the mind or brain.

The Code of Practice gives guidance on how to make that judgment. The requirement of an 'impairment or disturbance' sets the 'diagnostic threshold' for lack of capacity. In addition to this, it must be demonstrated that the person is 'unable to make a decision';[33] the test is decision-specific. The protection of the incapacitated person's health or welfare is more complex. The Act endorses the common law position that the 'act done, or decision made ... must be done, or made, in his best interests'.[34] In *DH NHS Foundation Trust v PS*,[35] for example, a patient suffering from a learning disability did not have the capacity to consent to a hysterectomy necessary to treat cancer of her uterus. The High Court was able to sanction the operation on the basis that it was in her best interests.

Conversely, in a case emerging as this book goes to press, the Court of Protection was unable to authorise sterilisation of twenty-one-year-old P because it could not ascertain that she lacked capacity.[36] The case was heard in open court due to the legitimate public interest. P, who has learning difficulties, was pregnant with her second child. P had previously refused a contraceptive injection and her mother argued that P was unable to make decisions about contraception. P's mother, who cared for P and her child, felt that she and P would not be able to cope with any more children. Further children would necessitate adoption which, she argued, would devastate P. P's mother wanted the sterilisation to be performed at the same time as P's Caesarean section. Hedley J refused. A further hearing, expected to take place in May 2011, will determine whether or not P can make a decision herself. If not, the court will decide whether treatment is appropriate and what form (sterilisation or a contraceptive implant) it might take.

The Mental Capacity Act 2005 requires that consideration is given to the least restrictive means by which the best interests of an individual lacking capacity can be met.[37] There is evidence that, even before the Act came into force, judges are already endorsing this principle. In *Re S (Medical Treatment: Adult Sterilisation)* (1998),[38] a twenty-two-year-old woman lived with her parents.

---

[33] Mental Capacity Act 2005, s 2(1).
[34] S 1(5). See also s 4 which lists factors relevant to the determination of an individual's best interests. See above ch 6.
[35] [2010] EWHC 1217 (Fam).
[36] The case is unreported at the time of writing. There is extensive media coverage. See, for example, K McVeigh, 'Mother's Legal Plea to Sterilise her Daughter Remains Unresolved' (2011) *Guardian*, 15 February.
[37] Mental Capacity Act 2005, s 1(6).
[38] [1998] 1 FLR 944.

She was meticulously cared for and well supervised. The arrangements for her care at home, at the day centre which she attended, and when she was in respite care, meant that the risk of her engaging in sexual intercourse or being subject to sexual assault was exceptionally low. Her mother feared that S might be a victim of a sexual assault, and that especially as her parents grew older and less able to care for her, some care worker might take advantage of her. Johnson J refused to authorise sterilisation. The risk of pregnancy must be balanced against the risks and distress of surgery. That risk in S's case was, at the time of the hearing, no more than speculative. The case that S's interests and welfare demanded immediate surgery was not made out.

As we saw in chapter 6, the House of Lords in *F v West Berkshire Health Authority*[39] found that there was no jurisdiction enabling them to require doctors to seek a declaration before sterilising an adult woman. No declaration was required provided that two practitioners are of the opinion that the operation is a therapeutic necessity.[40] Does the Mental Capacity Act 2005 clarify the situation? At the extremes of the spectrum, the Act is clear. The Code of Practice on the Mental Capacity Act 2005 advises that a court order be sought in all cases of non-therapeutic sterilisation. The Act also gives authority to the decision-maker to act when there is a therapeutic necessity. Thus, the Code of Practice acknowledges that there may be situations when treatment should be given without delay[41] and the duties incumbent on the decision-maker under sections 4(6) and 4(7) to consult others when determining whether treatment is in the best interests of the person lacking capacity exist only 'if it is practicable and appropriate'. Where the procedure is therapeutic but not urgent, the waters remain murky. As we saw in chapter 6, the definition of best interests under the Act is not synonymous with non-negligent care. The decision-maker is required to look beyond the clinical need of the person lacking capacity, to her wider welfare issues. Consequently it is likely doctors and carers will seek reassurance from the Court of Protection that any therapeutic (but not urgent) sterilisation they propose for an adult lacking capacity is in her best interests.

Conception to birth

11.5 Medical care begins long before a baby is born. Research into the growth of the foetus in the womb has established the crucial importance of good ante-natal care.[42] In the next sections we explore whether a parent or child can claim for injury sustained before birth.

---

[39] [1989] 2 All ER 545, HL.
[40] See *Pembrey v GMC* [2003] UKPC 60.
[41] Mental Capacity Act 2005, Code of Practice, 2007, para 6.5.
[42] The Thalidomide tragedy highlighted the vulnerability of the developing foetus. See above **10.1**.

Can parents sue?

11.6 The parents of a child injured before birth may be able to recover for their loss at common law. The doctor caring for the mother in pregnancy owes her a duty in relation to her own health and in respect of the health of the developing foetus. The damage which she will suffer if she bears a disabled child, the emotional trauma[43] *and* the financial burden of the extra expense such a child entails are readily foreseeable and recoverable. But will she be able (1) to prove negligence, and (2) to prove that the child's disability resulted from that negligence? One rare success occurred in a recent group litigation,[44] where Akenhead J found a local authority to have been negligent in allowing harmful dust to contaminate the environment during their reclamation of a British Steel complex. The dust contained heavy metals and dioxins and was found to be teratogenic – exposed to pregnant women, it caused some babies to suffer birth defects.[45]

Proving negligence is, as we have seen, no easy task in any malpractice claim. A claim in relation to the birth of a disabled child has two special problems of its own. First, if the claim lies against the doctor, it has to be established that he should have been aware of the risk posed to the foetus by drugs he prescribed or treatment he gave. Second, where a mother becomes ill in pregnancy, or the pregnancy itself is complicated, the interests of mother and child may conflict. An ill or injured pregnant woman may need treatment known to carry risk to the child. For example, a woman injured in an accident may need surgery which can only be carried out under general anaesthetic. The anaesthetic may harm the baby.[46] The doctor's duty to the mother, his patient, is this. He must consult and advise her, giving her sufficient information about her needs and the risk to her baby. If she chooses to reject a particular course of treatment for the sake of the baby he cannot impose it. He must in any case aim at a course of action which will benefit the mother with minimum risk to the child. Even if it can be shown that the doctor has failed in his duty to the mother, that he was negligent, establishing that the infant's disability resulted from that negligence is likely to be even more difficult.[47] Despite immense advances in knowledge concerning the development of the embryo, pinpointing the exact cause of the birth defect remains extremely difficult. Success in a claim for negligence depends on proof that it is more likely than not that the relevant negligence caused the injury. All a claimant with a damaged child is

---

[43] *S v Distillers Co* [1970] 1 WLR 114.

[44] *Corby Group Litigation v Corby DC* [2009] EWHC 1944 (TCC). The contamination was also found to constitute a public nuisance.

[45] An out-of-court settlement was reached in 2010: S Adams, 'Council to Pay Out Millions to Birth Defect Children' (2010) *The Telegraph,* 17 April.

[46] Another example is *Multiple Claimants v Sanifo-Synthelabo* [2007] EWHC 1860 (QB), [2009] EWHC 95 (QB), discussed below at **11.8**.

[47] On the difficulties in proving causation of birth defects, see the Report of the Royal Commission on Civil Liability and Compensation for Personal Injury (1978) Cmnd 7054 (the Pearson Report), paras 1441–1452.

likely to be able to prove is that a drug she took or treatment she received may have caused the defect in the baby. However, the cause may be inherited disease, a problem that the mother suffered in pregnancy, or some unknown cause. The parents may well fail to satisfy the burden of proof.

Congenital Disabilities (Civil Liability) Act 1976

11.7 This Act, passed to give rights and a remedy to children born disabled as a result of human fault, is ambitious, complex and largely irrelevant. It is ambitious in that it sought to provide a scheme to protect children, not just against injury in the womb, but against any act at any stage of either parent's life which might ultimately result in a disability affecting a child. Its complexity we outline in succeeding sections. It is irrelevant because it fails to address the central problem in this type of claim. How do you prove that the disability resulted from an identified act of negligence? Just as his mother's claim is likely to founder for lack of proof of the cause of the disability, so is the child's. If Parliament intends and desires to give children disabled by human act a remedy, it must consider whether retaining the normal burden of proof in actions by mother and child is practical.

The Act applies to all births after 1976 and purports to provide a comprehensive code of liability for disabled children in respect of damage caused to them before birth. Under the Act the child's mother[48] is generally exempt from any liability to her child. The father is offered no such immunity. The Act entirely replaces the common law and it would not be possible for a child unable to recover under the Act to argue that liability exists at common law. So, for example, a child seeking to sue his mother, exempt under the Act, must fail, however reckless her conduct in pregnancy and however clear it might be that she caused him to be born disabled.

The scheme of the Act is this. The child must be born alive.[49] He must establish that his disabilities resulted from an 'occurrence' which either: (1) affected the mother or father in her or his ability to have a normal healthy child (preconception event); or (2) affected the mother during her pregnancy; or (3) affected mother or child in the course of its birth. At this first hurdle, proving the cause of the disability, many claims will fail. Where proof of cause is forthcoming the child faces further obstacles. It is not enough to show that the person responsible for the occurrence was negligent. The child must prove that the person responsible for the occurrence was liable to the affected parent. The child's rights are derivative only. The likelihood is that the occurrence at the time caused the parent no harm. The Act provides that it is no answer that the parent affected suffered no visible injury at the time of the occurrence pro-

---

[48] Under s 2, she is liable for injuries caused through negligent driving of a vehicle on the road.

[49] Where the child is not born alive, the mother may be able to claim for the pain and suffering of miscarriage or stillbirth.

viding there was '. . . a breach of legal duty which, accompanied by injury, would have given rise to the liability'. The breach of duty is the negligence of the defendant in relation to the affected parent's reproductive capacity. Sandra Roberts recovered £334,769 in compensation for catastrophic damage she suffered during her mother's pregnancy.[50] A blood transfusion administered to her mother seven years before her birth rendered her parents rhesus incompatible, creating danger for any child of theirs. The hospital knew of Mrs Roberts's condition. They failed to act to prevent or minimise the risk to Sandra. This was negligent care for the mother and thus created a right to compensation for mother and via her for Sandra. Other cases are less straightforward.

Drugs and damage to the foetus

11.8 Let us take first what appears to be a simple case, the sort of case the Act was intended to remedy. A pregnant woman takes a drug prescribed for her by her GP that damages her baby so that he is born disabled.

The child can prove that his disability results from the effect of the drug on the foetus. He will have to show that the doctor was negligent towards his mother. It must be proven that: (1) the doctor knew or ought to have known that she was pregnant, and therefore was in breach of duty to her in prescribing a drug which might damage her baby; and (2) that he ought to have been aware of the risk posed by the drug. It will be no defence for the doctor to answer that, far from injuring the mother, the primary effect of the drug benefited her by ameliorating the symptoms of some common ailment, or helping her to relax or sleep. The doctor's responsibility to her embraces taking care to avoid harm to the child she carries. Two difficulties arise. First, a GP is judged by the standard of the reasonable, average GP. He is not expected to be an expert on embryology or drug-related damage. Proving that he ought to have been aware of the risk of the drug may be awkward. Second, the doctor may be aware of the risk to the baby, but argue that the risk to mother and child of not prescribing the drug is greater. Perhaps the mother might argue that, given the uncertainty surrounding the effect of medicines on foetal development, only exceptionally should *any* drug be prescribed to a pregnant woman by her GP. Advice should be sought from the specialist obstetrician. However, is it reasonable to deny pregnant women basic medicine for minor ailments and is the cost to the NHS of multiple referrals to obstetricians justifiable? The focus ought to lie on ensuring that all doctors give women adequate advice about the potential risks of drugs in pregnancy.

Doctors are not the only potential source of compensation for a drug-damaged child. Could the child sue the drug company? The company's liability is governed by the Consumer Protection Act 1987 which we examined in chapter 10. The crucial questions will be: is the drug defective?; and did it cause the

---

[50] (1986) *Times*, 26 July. The hospital conceded liability.

relevant injury to the foetus? There can be little doubt that if the company can be shown to be aware of a risk of foetal damage, yet still marketed the drug with *no* warning of that risk, the drug is defective. The unborn baby is most vulnerable to harm in the earliest stages of pregnancy. The mother may not know that she is pregnant. Warnings about the use of many non-prescription medicines in pregnancy are routine, but futile if a woman is unaware of her pregnancy. Might a drug be defective simply because it poses a risk of foetal harm? Clearly that cannot generally be the case with many prescription drugs. The benefit such drugs offer when properly prescribed outweigh the remote chance of unwitting foetal harm. Over-the-counter, non-prescription medicines might be looked at differently. If a cough remedy poses a substantial risk of harm, greater than other similar products, for relatively small benefit, that product might be found to be defective.[51]

In *Multiple Claimants v Sanifo-Synthelabo*[52] pregnant women took the anti-epileptic drug, Epilim, despite warnings that it could cause foetal abnormalities. Some of their children mounted a class action to test whether the product is defective within the meaning of section 3 of the Consumer Protection Act 1987 and also whether their disabilities result from an 'occurrence' within the meaning of sections 1(2)(a) or 1(2)(b) of the Congenital Disabilities (Civil Liability) Act 1976. The children argue that their disabilities result from the drug. Sanifo-Synthelabo argues that the 'occurrence' is the epilepsy itself. Legal aid was withdrawn in November 2010 and the case seems likely to founder.

Suing a doctor

11.9 We have already mentioned the potential liability of the mother's GP in prescribing drugs for her. She will meet other doctors during ante-natal visits. One special feature of suing a doctor under the Act needs note: section 1(5) of the 1976 Act, 'the doctors' defence'. Section 1(5) of the Act provides:

> The defendant is not answerable to the child, for anything he did or omitted to do when responsible in a professional capacity for treating or advising the parent, if he took reasonable care having due regard to the then received professional opinion applicable to the particular class of case; but this does not mean that he is answerable only because he departed from received opinion.

The aims of those who sought the inclusion of those words 'then received professional opinion' were probably twofold. First, they quite reasonably wanted it made clear that hindsight as to the effect of a drug or course of treatment should not prejudice a doctor, and second, less reasonably, they did not want the courts to adjudicate on the adequacy of received opinion. As the defendant's standard of care will always be tested by what was expected of the competent practitioner at the time of the alleged breach of duty, that first objective was met at common law. Second, perhaps doctors sought to ensure

---

[51] See above at **10.4**.
[52] Preliminary hearings include [2007] EWHC 1860 (QB), [2009] EWHC 95 (QB).

courts would not seek to evaluate 'received professional opinion'. In 1976, it is likely that no court would have done so. The judgment of the House of Lords in *Bolitho v City & Hackney Health Authority*[53] now requires that responsible professional opinion be demonstrably 'logical and defensible'. We see no reason why section 1(5) should not be susceptible to similar judicial scrutiny.

Ante-natal screening[54]

11.10   Ante-natal screening to diagnose foetal abnormalities has become routine. Just some of the more common procedures are looked at here.[55] In amniocentesis a needle is inserted, through the mother's abdomen and the uterine wall, into the sac surrounding the foetus. A small amount of the amniotic fluid surrounding the baby is removed. Tests on the fluid will indicate whether a number of abnormalities are present, including spina bifida and Down's syndrome. Cultures from the fluid may be grown which will disclose the child's sex. A mother who underwent amniocentesis and was told that she carried a spina bifida or Down's syndrome baby could then opt for an abortion. A mother who knew she was a carrier of haemophilia and learned that she carried a male child might similarly seek a termination. There are medical problems with amniocentesis. It cannot be performed before the fourteenth week of pregnancy and is often delayed until the sixteenth week. It carries about a 1 per cent risk of causing a miscarriage. It sometimes causes the mother acute discomfort. It is expensive, reserved largely for mothers at special risk of producing a disabled infant, in particular those over thirty-five or where blood tests suggest some abnormality in the baby. Chorionic villus testing, whereby early placental cells are removed and analysed, is possible earlier in pregnancy, at about ten to twelve weeks. But there is a slightly greater risk of miscarriage and chorionic villus testing does not detect neural tube defects (such as spina bifida). Increasingly doctors are seeking to limit the number of women who need to undergo invasive tests of this sort by using simple blood tests to identify high-risk pregnancies. A blood test to discover raised alpha-protein levels, an indication of possible spina bifida, has been available for several years. A blood test identifying increased risk of Down's syndrome is available. Only women whose blood tests indicate possible foetal abnormalities will then have to undergo the invasive procedures of amniocentesis or chorionic villus testing. Finally, ultra-sound scans are now routinely used to check on the growth and development of the foetus and will in certain cases

---

[53]   [1997] 4 All ER 771.

[54]   For a more comprehensive account of ante-natal screening and genetic counselling, see J K Mason and G T Laurie, *Mason and McCall Smith's Law and Medical Ethics* (8th edn, 2010) (hereafter *Mason and McCall Smith*) OUP, ch 7.

[55]   See Royal College of Obstetricians and Gynaecologists, *Amniocentesis and Chorionic Villus Sampling* (2010).

reveal the presence of such deformities as spina bifida without the need to submit the pregnant woman to risky or invasive tests.[56]

What are the legal implications of amniocentesis and chorionic villus testing? First, they involve an invasion of the mother's body. Her consent is essential and should be obtained expressly and in writing. Second, the risk that a healthy baby may be lost should be communicated to the parents. The duty of the obstetrician caring for the mother must embrace offering her the information on which to make such a crucial decision.[57] Tests should be carried out and analysed with due care. Negligence in offering or carrying out ante-natal screening may result in claims by both mother and child. They will contend that had adequate care been provided for the mother in pregnancy, she would have elected to terminate the pregnancy. The mother would have avoided the burden of a disabled child.[58] The child would have avoided the harm of her disabled existence. In neither case is the essence of the claim a claim for wrongful disability. Unlike the examples discussed earlier in this chapter, the defendants' negligence is not responsible for causing disability to a foetus normal at conception. The defendants' negligence is responsible for the birth of a child who, but for his negligence, would not have been born. The mother seeks compensation for a wrongful birth, a birth which, if properly advised, she would have chosen to avoid. The child sues in respect of wrongful life, a life, her counsel argues, she would have chosen not to endure. Both claims, as we will see, face major obstacles.

Non-invasive pre-natal genetic diagnosis (NPGD) is under development.[59] The pregnant woman's plasma is tested for a range of single gene disorders and Down's syndrome. Not only could this vastly reduce the risk to both woman and foetus, but it could be conducted at around seven weeks' gestation. But cell-free foetal DNA testing raises new ethical issues. It might potentially be

---

[56] For example, in *P v Leeds Teaching Hospital NHS Trust* [2004] EWHC 1392, a routine scan revealed a foetal bladder anomaly. P was referred for a specialist scan and was told that the foetus had a minor, correctable condition. On birth, P's son had a major bladder and bowel deformity. P was awarded damages due to the high standard owed by the specialist on the basis that P would, on the balance of probabilities, have opted for a termination has she known the real extent of her son's condition.

[57] Though the duty does not necessarily extend to ensuring that the patient understands the advice: see *Al Hamwi v Johnston* [2005] EWHC 206. The decision is criticised, in J Miola, 'Autonomy Rued OK' (2006) 14(1) *Medical Law Review* 108.

[58] See, for example, *Farraj v King's Healthcare NHS Trust* [2006] EWHC 1228, where a private laboratory responsible for culturing a chorionic villus sample and the trust responsible for carrying out DNA testing were held liable when a hereditary condition was missed.

[59] See Human Genetics Commission, *Advice on Free Foetal DNA Testing* (2008), encouraging further research and evaluation; and C F Wright, L S Chitty, 'Cell-Free Fetal DNA and RNA in Maternal Blood: Implications for Safer Antenatal Testing' (2009) 339 *BMJ* 2451; C Wright, *Cell-Free Foetal Nucleic Acids for Non-Invasive Prenatal Diagnosis, Report of the UK Expert Working Group* (2009) PHG Foundation.

available to significantly higher numbers of women; the non-invasiveness raises the possibility that the informed consent process might be less rigorous;[60] and there are eugenic concerns on the basis that it will be possible, in theory, to use it to determine the gender and other characteristics of the foetus.

Wrongful life

11.11 A classic claim for wrongful life is recounted in *McKay v Essex Area Health Authority*.[61] The plaintiffs in *McKay* were a little girl, born disabled as a result of the effect of rubella suffered by her mother early in pregnancy, and her mother. When Mrs McKay suspected that she had contracted rubella in the early weeks of her pregnancy, her doctor arranged for blood tests to establish whether she had been infected. As a result of negligence by either her doctor or by laboratory staff, Mrs McKay was wrongly informed that she had not been infected by rubella. She continued with the pregnancy. Had she known the truth, she would, as her doctor was well aware, have requested an abortion under the Abortion Act 1967. The little girl was born in 1975, before the Congenital Disabilities Act 1976 was passed. The Court of Appeal had to decide the position at common law. They said that no action lay where the essence of the child's claim was that but for the negligence of the defendant she would never have been born at all. The child's claim was thrown out, although her mother's claim was allowed to proceed. The case is not solely of historical interest. The judges further said that under the Act no child born after its passing could pursue such a claim.

In the view of the Court of Appeal, the Act[62] can never give rise to a claim for 'wrongful life'. Ackner LJ, considering section 1(2)(b) of the Act, said that the relevant 'occurrence' has to be one that affected the mother in pregnancy 'so that the child *is born* with disabilities which would not otherwise have been present'. Clearly under the Act, then, where the breach of duty consists of carelessness in the conduct of the pregnancy or the birth, the claim must relate to disabilities inflicted as a result of the breach of duty by the defendants. Where the essence of the claim is that the child should never have been born at all, it lies outside the scope of section 1(2)(b). A claim by the child that amniocentesis should have been performed, or that subsequent tests were negligently conducted so that the pregnancy continued, and he was born disabled, will fail.

---

60 D Schmitz *et al*, 'Commentary: No Risk, No Objections? Ethical Pitfalls of Cell-Free Fetal DNA and RNA Testing' (2009) 339 *BMJ* 2690.

61 [1982] 2 All ER 771.

62 It has been argued that the Act does not apply to a 'wrongful life' claim. The Act provides a scheme to compensate for disability inflicted by human error, not to a claim for allowing a disabled foetus to be born at all. See J Fortin, 'Is the "Wrongful Life" Action Really Dead?' [1987] *Journal of Social Welfare Law* 306.

The effect of the judgment in *McKay* is that in England a child injured before birth may claim only compensation for *wrongful disability* that is against a defendant whose conduct actually caused his disability. He cannot sue for *wrongful life*. The Court of Appeal gave three main reasons for ruling out such claims. (1) It was not possible to arrive at a proper measure of damages representing the difference between the child's disabled existence and non-existence.[63] (2) The law should not impose a duty on doctors to abort, to terminate life *in utero*.[64] (3) To impose any duty to abort would be to violate the sanctity of life and to devalue the life of handicapped persons.[65] The second and third reasons are difficult to sustain in the light of the fact that the court did allow Mrs McKay to pursue her *wrongful birth* action.

Wrongful birth[66]

11.12 In *Udale v Bloomsbury Health Authority*,[67] Jupp J held that the birth of a healthy child could not be allowed to create a claim in damages. He argued that the child, when he came to know of the award, might feel unwanted and the family's relationship could be disrupted. Doctors might put pressure on women to have abortions. Children were a blessing, and any financial loss was offset by the joy of their birth.

A series of judgments from the Court of Appeal firmly rejected Jupp J's invocation of policy to refuse parents compensation in such a case.[68] Damages amounting to the cost to the family of raising an unplanned child appeared to be readily endorsed in claims for wrongful conception. Two decisions of the House of Lords restored English and Scottish law to the position declared by Jupp J in *Udale*, albeit on different grounds. It was held in *McFarlane v Tayside Health Board*[69] that compensation for the cost of bringing up a healthy child will not be awarded. Such a loss is categorised now as irrecoverable economic loss. *McFarlane* is difficult to analyse.[70] Five Law Lords rejected the parents' claim. Five sets of very different reasons are advanced by their Lordships.

---

63   [1982] 2 All ER 771 at 782, 787 and 790.
64   [1982] 2 All ER 771 at 787.
65   [1982] 2 All ER 771 at 781.
66   See J K Mason, *The Troubled Pregnancy: Legal Rights and Wrongs in Reproduction* (2007) CUP.
67   [1983] 2 All ER 522.
68   See *Emeh v Kensington & Chelsea Health Authority* [1984] 3 All ER 1044, CA; *Thake v Maurice* [1986] 1 All ER 479, CA.
69   [1999] 4 All ER 961, HL. See also *Greenfield v Irwin (A Firm)* [2001] 1 FLR 899.
70   See J K Mason, 'Unwanted Pregnancy: A Case of Retroversion?'(2000) 4 *Edinburgh Law Journal* 191; J Weir, 'The Unwanted Child' (2000) 59 *Cambridge Law Journal* 238; L Hogano, 'Misconceptions about Wrongful Conception' (2002) 65 *Modern Law Review* 883; J K Mason, *The Troubled Pregnancy: Legal Rights and Wrongs in Reproduction* (2007) CUP, ch 4; N Priaulx, *The Harm Paradox: Tort Law and the Unwanted Child in an Era of Choice* (2007) Routledge Cavendish.

The facts of the case are straightforward. Mr and Mrs McFarlane had four children. Mr McFarlane had a vasectomy. Six months after his operation, the surgeon told him that his sperm count was negative and he and his wife could dispense with contraception. The couple relied on that advice. Mrs McFarlane became pregnant. They alleged that the surgeon was negligent and sought compensation (1) for Mrs McFarlane's pain and distress in pregnancy and labour, and (2) for the costs of bringing up their healthy daughter, Catherine.

Four out of the five Law Lords[71] held that Mrs McFarlane could recover damages for the pain and discomfort of pregnancy and any immediately consequential financial loss to her. All agreed that the more substantial claim for the cost of raising Catherine should fail. All tried to avoid Jupp J's forthright reliance on policy to categorise such claims as repugnant to the public interest.[72] Lord Slynn appeared to accept that the blessings conferred by healthy children come in tandem with substantial burdens. He rejected the argument that courts should regard the financial costs of raising a child as offset by the joys of parenting. He claimed not to be concerned by possible psychological consequences to a child of learning that she is unwanted because her parents received damages for her wrongful conception. His speech focused on his finding that doctors are not responsible for the economic loss entailed in child rearing. Doctors owe a duty of care to prevent pregnancy and the consequential physical effects on the mother. It is not fair, just or reasonable to extend that responsibility to the costs of rearing the child.[73] Lord Hope took a somewhat similar approach. He appeared exercised by the potential scale of claims for wrongful conception. If such a claim is allowable, it would relate to the actual costs to particular parents of raising that child. Thus a claim by wealthy aristocrats might extend to the cost of nannies, ponies, public school and so on. The extent of liability would be disproportionate to the negligence.[74]

Lord Hope and Lord Steyn both, unlike Lord Slynn, adverted to the benefits of parenthood. Lord Hope declared:[75]

> ... it would not be fair, just or reasonable, in any assessment of the loss caused by the birth of a child, to leave these benefits out of account. Otherwise the [claimant] would be paid far too much. They would be relieved of the costs of rearing the child. They would not be giving anything back to the wrongdoer for the benefits. But the value attached to their benefits is incalculable. The costs can be calculated but the benefit, which must in fairness be set against them, cannot. The logical conclusion, as a matter of law, is that the cost to the [claimant] of

---

[71] Lord Millett dissented on this point.

[72] More recently, see the Irish High Court case: *Byrne v Ryan* [2007] IEHC 206, where a plaintiff who underwent a negligently performed sterilisation was awarded damages for the pain and inconvenience relating to the pregnancies and birth of two children, and a second sterilisation operation, but not for raising the two children. See C Craven, 'Recoverability of Damages for Pregnancy and Children: Variations on the Theme of *Byrne v Ryan*' (2008) 3(1) *Quarterly Review of Tort Law* 8.

[73] [1999] 4 All ER 961 at 978, HL.

[74] [1999] 4 All ER 961 at 985, HL.

[75] [1999] 4 All ER 961 at 985, HL.

meeting their obligations to their child during her childhood are not recoverable as damages.

Lord Steyn contended that his rejection of the parents' claim was not on policy grounds. He '. . . would avoid those quicksands'.[76] He saw the question as one of distributive justice. He stated that he was 'firmly of the view that an overwhelming number of ordinary men and women' would reject claims such as the McFarlanes'. He argued that if claims by a child for wrongful life should be rejected as repugnant to the value of human life, so should a claim by parents for its wrongful conception.[77] Lord Steyn may have sought to avoid the quicksands of public policy but became immersed in them none the less.

Lord Clyde treated the claim as one of *quantum* of damages. Like Lord Hope, he was exercised by questions of proportionality. There could be significant differences in the level of awards depending on parental lifestyle. The expense of bringing up the child would be disproportionate to any wrongdoing and go beyond reasonable restitution.[78] Lord Millett, uniquely, sought to reject both claims by the parents, the claim for the mother's pain and suffering in pregnancy, as well as the claim for the cost of raising Catherine. Lord Millett was forthright in his views.[79]

> In my opinion, the law must take the birth of a normal healthy baby to be a blessing, not a detriment. In truth it is a mixed blessing. It brings joy and sorrow, blessing and responsibility. The advantages and disadvantages are inseparable. Individuals may choose to regard the balance as unfavourable and take steps to forego the pleasures as well as the responsibilities of parenthood. They are entitled to decide for themselves where their own interests lie. But society itself must regard the balance as beneficial. It would be repugnant to its own sense of values to do otherwise. It is morally offensive to regard a normal, healthy baby as more trouble and expense than it is worth.

The only damages Lord Millett would allow was a nominal sum to represent the loss of the parental freedom to limit the size of their family. He proposed £5,000. Lord Millett stands alone in the openness of his opinion that it is just unacceptable to society to compensate parents for having a child, however hard they had tried to avoid further pregnancies. His honesty should be commended. The reasons advanced by his colleagues are not convincing.

Will *McFarlane* affect a claim by parents of a disabled child who can establish that, had the child's disability been diagnosed *in utero*, the mother would have terminated the pregnancy? The Law Lords in *McFarlane* expressly restricted their decision to claims concerning healthy infants. Yet consider the approval Lord Steyn bestows on the following statement from an Australian textbook:[80]

---

[76] [1999] 4 All ER 961 at 998, HL.
[77] Ibid.
[78] Ibid.
[79] [1999] 4 All ER 961 at 1005, HL.
[80] F Trindade and P Cane, *The Law of Torts in Australia* (2nd edn, 1993) OUP, p 434.

... it might seem inconsistent to allow a claim by the parents, while that of the child, whether *healthy or disabled*, is rejected (our emphasis). Surely the parents' claim is equally repugnant to ideas of the sanctity and value of human life and rests, like that of the child, on a comparison between a situation where a human being exists and one where it does not.

Lord Steyn comments[81] '... the reasoning is sound. Coherence and rationality demand that the claim by the parents should also be rejected.'

So can a distinction between a claim for wrongful birth of a healthy child, and wrongful birth of a disabled child be sustained? The Court of Appeal endorsed such a distinction in *Parkinson v St James and Seacroft NHS Hospital Trust*,[82] ruling that where a disabled child is born as a consequence of clinical negligence his parents may recover the additional costs occasioned by his disability. The relevant negligence in *Parkinson* ensued from a bungled operation to sterilise the mother. The surgeon failed to secure a clip effectively to Mrs Parkinson's left fallopian tube. She conceived again ten months after the operation. The case for compensation covering the costs resulting from a child's disability when the alleged 'wrong' is a failure to prevent the birth of a disabled infant looks stronger. Doctors expressly advising potential parents about the risks of conception, and screening women in pregnancy, undertake that responsibility expressly to avoid the birth of a disabled child. The 'harm' to the parents of the birth of a child with spina bifida, or damaged by rubella,[83] is just what the doctors seek to prevent. Only a limited group of people (parents whose children were unfortunately born disabled) could bring a claim and Brooke LJ saw no difficulty with the proposition that the doctor assumed responsibility for the disastrous economic consequences of the birth of such a child. '[O]rdinary people would consider that it would be fair for the law to make an award in such a case provided that it is limited to the extra expenses associated with the child's disability.'[84] Both Brooke LJ and Hale LJ[85] constructed elegant examples to distinguish the case of the disabled child from *McFarlane*. Hale LJ proposed a model of 'deemed equilibrium' whereby the costs and benefits of a healthy child balance each other out. The reader may ponder whether the appeal court did not in reality simply regard *McFarlane* as wrongly decided.[86] Unable to say so forthrightly, the judges sought to mitigate its worst effects. The parents' damages, however, will be limited to the add-

---

[81] [1999] 4 All ER 961 at 978.
[82] [2001] Lloyd's Rep Med 309, CA.
[83] As in *Hardman v Amin* [2000] Lloyd's Rep Med 498.
[84] [2001] EWCA Civ 530 at para 50; and see Hale LJ at para 82.
[85] Note Hale LJ's analysis of the nature of the loss and injury. Are the costs consequent on the birth of an unplanned child, disabled or not, truly pure economic loss?
[86] The Australian High Court rejected *McFarlane* in *Cattanach v Melchior* [2003] HCA 38. Queensland and New South Wales have legislated to counteract the effects of this case. For analysis, see J K Mason, *The Troubled Pregnancy: Legal Rights and Wrongs in Reproduction* (2007) CUP, p 125.

itional costs of raising a child with his particular disability.[87] Before *McFarlane*, English courts awarded such parents the whole cost of childrearing.[88] Compensation in such cases of wrongful birth will now relate only to the additional cost of caring for the disabled child.[89] Compensation may still be considerable. It can and should include cost of care beyond the child's minority.[90] 'Good' parents will seek to provide for their disabled children into adulthood.

The tangled web of case law following *McFarlane* may be morally disturbing to some people. Refusing to compensate parents for the unplanned birth of a healthy child, Lord Millett said in *McFarlane*:[91]

> There is something distasteful, if not morally offensive, in treating the birth of a normal healthy child as a matter of compensation.

He regarded childbirth as akin to a balance sheet. The joys of parenthood offset financial costs. Mutual support of parent and child, the support perhaps of the parent in old age offset the burdens of parenting. Distinguishing the healthy and disabled child might seem to suggest the latter is a 'curse' not a 'blessing'. In *Parkinson*, Hale LJ took a pragmatic approach. She said of the disabled child that:[92]

> This analysis treats a disabled child as having exactly the same worth as a non-disabled child. It affords him the same dignity and status. It simply acknowledges that he costs more.

If cost is key, then what of the wrongful birth of a healthy baby to a disabled parent? In *Rees v Darlington Memorial Hospital NHS Trust*, the Court of Appeal[93] allowed the claim of a visually impaired woman whose negligent sterilisation led to the birth of a healthy child. The claimant suffered from retinitis pigmentosa. She had only very limited vision in one eye. She elected to be sterilised because she did not want children and judged that her virtual blindness

---

[87]   For guidance on what constitutes 'disability', see [2001] EWCA Civ 530 at para 91 per Hale LJ.

[88]   *Salih v Enfield Health Authority* [1991] All ER 400 (though note that, if the parents would in any case have gone on to have a healthy child, the damage would be restricted to the costs incurred by the child's disability).

[89]   *Rand v East Dorset HA* [2000] Lloyd's Rep Med 181; and see *Anderson v Forth Valley Health Board* (1997) 44 BMLR 108 (Scotland).

[90]   *Nunnerley v Warrington Health Authority* [2000] Lloyd's Rep Med 170; and see R Glancy, 'Damages for Wrongful Birth: Where Do They End?' (2006) 3 *Journal of Personal Injury Law* 271–279.

[91]   [1999] 4 All ER 961 at 1003, HL.

[92]   *Parkinson v St James and Seacroft NHS Hospital Trust* [2001] Lloyd's Rep Med 309 at 325, CA. It should be noted Hale LJ seems less than convinced of Lord Millett's general reasoning that the joys of a healthy child outweigh the costs. And see *Hardman v Amin* [2000] Lloyd's Rep Med 498. *Mason and McCall Smith*, p 348, argue that Lady Hale's opinion, which is based on bodily integrity, can be applied equally to the disabled and healthy child. 'The feeling remains that one or other decision [*McFarlane* or *Parkinson*] must be wrong.'

[93]   [2002] 2 All ER 177.

would prevent her looking after a child. Hale LJ[94] distinguished *McFarlane* on a number of grounds, relying on the pragmatic 'deemed equilibrium' model she first set down in *Parkinson*. Unlike the healthy parent of a healthy child, but like the parent of any disabled child, the claimant incurred extra costs in bringing up a child. The compensation awarded to her was not compensation for the cost of the child per se, but the costs occasioned by her own disability. *McFarlane*, it was held, applied only to healthy parents.

The case proceeded to the House of Lords,[95] where the Law Lords had an opportunity to revisit their judgment in *McFarlane*. They refused to do so. By a four:three majority, they overturned the decision of the Court of Appeal. Though, for reasons of public policy it is unacceptable to view a healthy child as a financial liability, the Law Lords put a 'gloss' on the *McFarlane* ruling. As we noted at the start of this chapter, the Law Lords in *Rees* belatedly endorsed Lord Millett's proposal in *McFarlane* that an award of general damages was appropriate to mark the injury to the claimant. Lord Bingham proposed that, in addition to the award for pregnancy and birth, a conventional figure of £15,000 should be awarded to reflect that the defendant's negligence constituted a legal wrong causing the parents to suffer a loss of autonomy. The majority agreed. Elevated costs of rearing a healthy child as a result of parental disability are not recoverable. 'General damages' are all such parents can hope for.[96]

Hale LJ's 'deemed equilibrium' was rejected on the basis that the costs and benefits associated with the birth of a child were unquantifiable and consequently impossible to balance. Alasdair Maclean argues that, though correct, this leaves no legal basis for the 'gloss' on *McFarlane*.[97] Whilst there may be public policy grounds for the avoidance of general negligence principles in wrongful birth cases, even after two House of Lords decisions, sound legal reasoning remains elusive. Perhaps, as Emily Jackson suggests,[98] the Law Lords in *Rees* were simply creating their own novel scheme of compensation to acknowledge the legal wrong whilst limiting the pay-out. On the other hand the 'gloss' may be viewed, as Lord Steyn suggested in his dissenting judgment, as 'a radical and most important development which should only be embarked

---

[94] Note the difference in reasoning between Hale and Robert Walker LJ. Consider whether poverty is a 'disability' deserving at least some compensation for an unplanned child. Walker LJ dissented, comparing a hypothetical woman driven to 'crisis in health terms' by the birth of a fifth child following a negligent sterilisation, with a similar crisis on the part of a disabled parent. For both, the recovery of the costs of caring for the healthy child might alleviate the crisis. Why should the law treat the two differently?

[95] [2003] UKHL 53.

[96] But see V Chico, 'Wrongful Conception: Policy, Inconsistency and the Conventional Award' (2007) 8 *Medical Law International* 139.

[97] A Maclean, 'An Alexandrian Approach to the Knotty Problem of Wrongful Pregnancy: *Rees v Darlington Memorial Trust* in the House of Lords' [2004] 3 *Web Journal of Current Legal Issues*. And see P Cane, 'Another Failed Sterilisation' (2004) 120 *Law Quarterly Review* 181.

[98] E Jackson, *Medical Law: Text, Cases and Materials* (2nd edn, 2010) OUP, p 747.

on after rigorous examination of competing arguments'.[99] On this view, the majority in *Rees* overstepped the limits of judicial discretion.

Rees has implications for the status of *Parkinson*. Though Lord Hutton approved of the decision,[100] Lord Bingham was critical of it.[101] The refusal of the majority to make a calculation of costs based on benefits and detriments in the case of a healthy child is arguably equally applicable to the disabled child.[102] *Parkinson* was applied in *Farraj v King's Healthcare Trust and Cytogenetic Data Services*.[103] Mrs Farraj, who was pregnant with her third child, was the carrier of a recessive gene which can cause beta thalassaemia major. Her husband was also a carrier, creating a strong chance that any child of theirs would suffer from the disease. Mrs Farraj thus underwent chorionic villus testing. Their second child had the blood disorder and they intended to terminate the pregnancy if the foetus was a carrier. The test result was negative, but proved to be a false negative. Sadly, baby Abdullah inherited the disorder. The laboratory had failed to identify that the sample was poor quality, or ask for a second sample. They were held liable and the couple were able to claim expenses related to the child's disability.

Children damaged by pre-conception events

11.13   The Congenital Disabilities (Civil Liability) Act 1976 purports to protect children against pre-conception injury,[104] not just injury *in utero*. This could happen where the father or mother is affected by radiation or drugs so that the sperm or egg carries a serious defect. Or the child may be damaged if doctors mismanage a previous pregnancy, for example if they fail to take note of and treat rhesus incompatibility in the mother and the second child is born brain damaged.[105] The Act intended to cover such cases, providing as it does that the relevant occurrence may be one which affected either parent in his or her ability to have a healthy child. But it may be argued that, if the claim is that

[99] Per Lord Steyn (dissenting) *Rees v Darlington Memorial Hospital NHS Trust* [2003] UKHL 52 at para 43. See also Lord Hope's judgment.

[100] [2003] UKHL 53 at para 96.

[101] [2003] UKHL 53 at para 9.

[102] See A Maclean [2004] 3 *Web Journal of Current Legal Issues*: 'Unless one is prepared to argue that having a disabled child is not – as a matter of policy – a blessing, which might be interpreted as devaluing the disabled, then the calculation is no more possible for the birth of a disabled child than it is for the birth of a healthy child . . . [I]f x cannot be balanced against y then nor can x be balanced against y + x.'

[103] [2008] EWHC 2468 (QB). See also Scottish case: *JS v Lothian Health Board* [2009] CSOH 97.

[104] Including injury caused by infertility treatment: see Congenital Disabilities (Civil Liability) Act 1976, s 1A, as amended by the Human Fertilisation and Embryology Act 1990, s 44(1).

[105] See American cases: *Yeager v Bloomington Obstetrics and Gynaecology, Inc* 585 NW2d 696 (Ind, 1992); *Lazenvnick v General Hospital of Munro City Inc*, F Supp 146 (Md, 1980).

the child was born disabled because one of his parents is incapable of creating a healthy infant, his claim is essentially that he should never have been born at all, and that it is an action for 'wrongful life' and is barred under the Act. We think this is a mistaken view of the Act. The child's claim in the case of a pre-conception occurrence rests on the hypothesis that *but for* that occurrence he would have been born normal and healthy, and that his actionable injury is therefore the difference between the life he might have had and the life he must now perforce endure. In *McKay*,[106] the child sought to maintain that her actionable injury was life itself, and as such her claim was not and would not be sustainable. What *McKay* does clarify in cases of *pre-conception* injury is that a doctor who is not responsible for that original injury cannot be liable under the Act if he fails to diagnose the child's disabilities in pregnancy, and fails to perform an abortion in such circumstances.

Pre-pregnancy advice and genetic counselling

11.14 Women planning a child often seek advice before allowing themselves to conceive. For a healthy woman, this may be simply a check that she is immune from rubella. Another may seek reassurance that pregnancy will not damage her own health, for example, if she has a history of cardiac disease. Couples in whose family genetic disease is prevalent, or couples who already have a child with a genetic disease, may need specialised genetic counselling.

In all these cases, those counselling the woman undertake a duty to her in relation not only to her own health and welfare, but also in relation to the birth of a healthy child. If she is given the green light to go ahead with a pregnancy and suffers at the end of it the trauma and additional financial burden of a damaged child, she may have a claim in negligence.[107] She and the child's father will be able to claim the additional cost to them of caring for a disabled child. Proving negligence may not be easy. Not only must she show that the doctor failed to take into account factors relating to her medical history or genetic background, or failed to conduct tests that would have alerted him to the danger, she must show that a reasonably competent doctor would have discovered the risk.[108] If a woman requests a test for immunity from rubella, is brushed aside, and subsequently contracts the disease in pregnancy, her claim should succeed. The enormous publicity given to the Department of Health campaign

---

[106] *McKay v Essex Area Health Authority* [1982] 2 All ER 771.

[107] See *Parkinson v St James and Seacroft University Hospital NHS Trust* [2001] EWCA Civ 530, CA; *Hardman v Amin* [2000] Lloyd's Rep Med 458; *Enright v Blackpool Victoria Hospital NHS Trust* [2003] EWHC 100 (QB); *Farraj v King's Healthcare NHS Trust* [2006] EWHC 1228; *FP v Taunton and Somerset NHS Trust* [2009] EWHC 1965 (QB).

[108] See, for example, *Constable v Salford and Trafford HA and Kerr* [2005] EWHC 2967 (QB) where a failure to re-test a woman for chlamydia which allegedly caused her son to be born prematurely, was not shown to have caused or materially contributed to his prematurity.

to eradicate the risk to the unborn child posed by rubella is such that any GP must be aware of and guard against the risk. If the sister of a haemophiliac consults her doctor and explains her brother's condition, and he fails to refer her for counselling with the result that she bears a haemophiliac son, she too should succeed.[109] Beyond these obvious examples of want of competence, the medical profession is much divided on the value of pre-conception advice. Some doctors run special clinics and advise special diets and total abstinence from alcohol when attempting to conceive. Significant evidence of the relationship of such regimes to the reduction of risk to the child, and their acceptance by the profession at large, will be needed before a claim based on the lack of such detailed guidance could succeed. Finally, the claimant must also establish that had she received proper advice she would not have allowed herself to become pregnant when she did.

Has the disabled child a remedy? We must distinguish three types of cases where negligent pre-pregnancy advice results in the birth of a disabled child. In the first case, the relevant negligence may be that the woman was encouraged to become pregnant when, had proper care been taken, she could have been advised never to contemplate pregnancy because of the risk to *any* child she might bear. The child's action in such a case will fail because the essence of his claim is that he should never have been born at all. It is a claim for 'wrongful life'.

In the second instance, the negligence may have been in failing to counsel the mother properly on precautions to take, or the timing of pregnancy. Such a claim raises an awkward problem. For example, a woman is not tested for immunity to rubella, or the test is negligently conducted. She is wrongly told that she has immunity. She becomes pregnant, contracts the disease and the child is born disabled. Had she been properly advised, she would have been vaccinated against the disease and advised in the strongest of terms to delay pregnancy for three months after the vaccination. The actual child born would never have been born. The particular set of genes in the egg and sperm that went to create him would never have met. A literal interpretation of *McKay* would deny the child a remedy on the ground that that unique individual would never have been born had his mother had proper advice. It would seem a harsh result, but the conclusion that it follows from the interpretation of the Act by the Court of Appeal in *McKay* is difficult to resist. Examples of this sort could be multiplied endlessly. A parent might be undergoing treatment for venereal disease. He or she is carelessly advised that pregnancy is now safe. It is not. Treatment was not complete. The particular child born disabled would not have been born, had proper advice been given. A woman knows a little of a family history of genetic disease affecting the males in her family. She seeks counselling. She should have been advised of the risks to male children and been offered pre-implantation genetic diagnosis (PGD) so that she could, if she wished, have ensured she did not give birth to a male child. A disabled male child cannot sue under the Act, for had PGD or amniocentesis been offered and accepted, that boy would not exist.

[109] See *Anderson v Forth Valley Health Board* (1998) 44 BMLR 108.

Finally, there is one limited class of case where the child's action based on allegedly careless pre-pregnancy advice may succeed. That is where adequate counselling advice would have enabled that very child to be born hale and hearty. Realistic examples are difficult to think of. Perhaps one example concerns the relationship between maternal diet before conception and spina bifida. There is evidence that folic acid supplements may reduce the likelihood of spina bifida. The child could contend that, had his mother been advised to follow that regime, his disability would not have developed. He would have been born, but not born disabled. Such a child claims for his disabilities, not wrongful life. He overcomes the first problem in his claim against medical staff, but will he be able to prove that the treatment if given would have prevented his disability?

What if a parent realises the risk?

11.15 Alas, further problems confront the child whose claim is based on pre-conception injury. Section 1(4) of the 1976 Act provides that in such cases, if the affected parent is aware of the risk of the child being born disabled, the defendant is not liable to that child. Responsibility for knowingly running the risk of creating a disabled baby rests with his parents, and whatever the degree of fault, the original creator of the risk is relieved of liability to the child. There is one exception to this rule. Where the child sues his father, the fact that the father is aware of the risk of begetting an abnormal child will not defeat the child's claim as long as his mother is ignorant of the danger. This raises a nice question. A young man suffers contamination by toxic chemicals at work through the negligence of his employers. He is warned that his reproductive capacity has been damaged, that he is likely to beget abnormal offspring and is advised never to have children. He ignores the warning, marries and tells his wife nothing. A disabled child is born. The child cannot sue his father's original employers. Even if they were in breach of duty to his father, 'the affected parent', the father's knowledge of the risk is a defence. Can the child sue her father? The answer has to be no. This child, like the plaintiff in *McKay*,[110] can only claim against her father that she should never have been born at all. His father's condition at the time of the relevant 'negligence', begetting the child, was such that he could not beget a normal child. The father's 'negligence' was in creating him, not in inflicting a disability which but for some act or omission on his part would not have been present. We will consider a little later if fathers can ever be liable for causing pre-natal injury to their own children.

Must a mother consider abortion?

11.16 Section 1(7) of the 1976 Act offers a partial defence whereby if the affected parent shared responsibility for the child being born disabled, the child's damages may be reduced. For example, the child's disabilities may be diagnosed

---

[110] *McKay v Essex Area Health Authority* [1982] 2 All ER 771.

when the mother has an ultra-sound scan, or amniocentesis, before his birth. Once the mother knows of the potential damage to her child, she will, under the 1967 Abortion Act, be entitled to an abortion on the grounds that there is substantial risk that the child, if born, would be seriously handicapped. Assuming that it is the mother who is the affected parent, does she share responsibility for the child being born disabled, if she refuses an abortion? In *McKay v Essex Area Health Authority,* refusing to allow the child's claim that she should have been aborted, Ackner LJ said that he could not accept:[111]

> ... that the common law duty of care to a person can involve, without specific legislation to achieve this end, the legal obligation to that person, whether or not *in utero*, to terminate his existence. Such a proportion runs wholly contrary to the concept of the sanctity of human life.

Applying Ackner LJ's proportion to a submission that a mother should have accepted abortion, advanced by the defendant responsible for inflicting the disabilities suffered by the child, such a submission must fail. To impose an *obligation* on a mother to undergo an abortion is more repugnant to the concept of the sanctity of human life than to impose an obligation to abort on a doctor.

In *Emeh v Kensington, Chelsea and Fulham Area Health Authority,*[112] the plaintiff brought a wrongful conception claim, long before *McFarlane.*[113] An operation to sterilise her was carried out negligently by the first defendant and she became pregnant again. She was offered, but refused an abortion. The trial judge held that once she elected to continue the pregnancy, the pregnancy ceased to be unwanted, and that the birth of the child was the result of her own actions and not a consequence of the defendant's negligence. Her refusal to consider an abortion was so unreasonable as to eclipse the defendant's wrongdoing. The Court of Appeal overruled him.[114] Mrs Emeh did not become aware of her pregnancy until it was about seventeen to eighteen weeks advanced. Refusing an abortion at that stage in pregnancy could not be considered unreasonable. Whether the Court would have taken a different view had the pregnancy been less advanced remains open to question. Waller LJ laid great stress on the increased risk, discomfort and hospitalisation entailed in abortion at twelve weeks plus.[115] Slade LJ was emphatic that abortion should generally never be forced upon a woman. He said:[116]

> Save in the most exceptional circumstances, I cannot think it right that the court should ever declare it unreasonable for a woman to decline to have an abortion in a case where there is no evidence that there were any medical or psychiatric grounds for terminating the particular pregnancy.

111 [1982] 2 All ER 771 at 787.
112 (1983) *Times,* 3 January.
113 *McFarlane v Tayside Health Board* [1999] 4 All ER 961, HL.
114 [1984] 3 All ER 1044.
115 [1984] 3 All ER 1044 at 1048.
116 [1984] 3 All ER 1044 at 1053.

Slade LJ's condemnation of judicially enforced abortion is endorsed in *McFarlane* by Lords Slynn,[117] Steyn[118] and Millett. Lord Millett declares[119] that it is morally repugnant to suggest that it is unreasonable not to have an abortion.

Some slight doubt, however, lurks in the kind of cases we are currently considering. If a foetal abnormality is diagnosed in pregnancy, and caused by the defendants' prior negligence, does this constitute *medical* grounds to terminate the pregnancy, and constitute the sort of exceptional circumstances Slade LJ refers to? Certainly the foetal injury would entitle the mother to choose to abort the child. We cannot see that it could require her to do so or risk a reduction to her child's compensation for the disability he suffers. Section 1(7) of the 1976 Act envisages the sort of case where a pregnant woman ignores medical advice and exacerbates her child's disability by drinking, smoking or failing to take precautions advised by her doctors. The mother actively contributes to the disability. That is very different from refusing abortion. Assume a court was prepared to entertain this defence, how will they assess the mother's decision? Is it some totally objective test? Or must the woman's own moral views and religious affiliation be considered? Given that the Court of Appeal has finally confirmed that no women can be forced to undergo a Caesarean section to protect the life or health of the foetus, to 'force' a woman to 'kill' her foetus would be illogical.[120] Maternal autonomy demands that pregnant women's choices in this delicate arena of moral controversy should be respected.

Maternal immunity: discriminating against fathers?[121]

11.17 We noted earlier that, save in respect of road accidents on public roads, mothers remain immune from claims under the 1976 Act.[122] Fathers enjoy no such formal immunity. A pregnant woman who drinks so heavily that her child is born with foetal alcohol syndrome or whose drug habit is such that her baby is born addicted to crack cocaine cannot be sued by her child. The Law Commission,[123] recommending that mothers be exempted from claims for pre-natal injury, offered a number of reasons for maternal privilege. They considered that a claim against the mother would have little practical utility. She, unlike the father, was unlikely to have funds to meet an award of damages. Suing 'mum' would disturb the parental bond and in practice would only happen where a father used his child's claim as a weapon in parental dispute.

---

[117] [1999] 4 All ER 961 at 970, HL.

[118] [1999] 4 All ER 961 at 976, HL.

[119] [1999] 4 All ER 961 at 1004, HL.

[120] *St George's Healthcare NHS Trust v S* [1998] 3 All ER 673, CA.

[121] See generally, R Scott, *Rights, Duties and the Body: Law and Ethics of Maternal-Fetal Conflict* (2001) Hart Publishing; E Jackson, *Regulating Reproduction: Law, Technology and Autonomy* (2001) Hart Publishing, pp 140–160.

[122] See above at **11.7**.

[123] Discussed fully in P Pace, 'Civil Liability for Pre-Natal Injuries' (1977) 40 *Modern Law Review* 193.

The first of these two reasons looks rather outdated now when many more women have independent means. The second applies equally to fathers. Other reasons remain more compelling.[124]

How could an equitable standard of reasonable pregnancy conduct be set? Women are beset by contradictory advice about what they should and should not eat, drink or do. Though objectively one might agree that the reasonable mother-to-be should give up smoking, for example, achieving that standard is more difficult for some than others. The harassed mother of four struggling alone in poverty may know that she ought to quit smoking but struggles to do so. Most importantly, potential liability for foetal injury would in practice constitute a significant invasion of pregnant women's liberty and privacy. The threat of possible redress by the child could be used by partners and doctors to impose their judgment of foetal welfare. Given evidence of the foetus's vulnerability in early pregnancy, when a woman may not know she is pregnant, as Sheila McLean has said, the law would in effect demand that '. . . fertile, sexually active women of childbearing age should act at all times as if they were pregnant'.[125] Finally, pragmatically, we should remind ourselves that a claim under the 1976 Act can only arise if a child is born alive. Maternal liability under the 1976 Act could simply provide an incentive to abort. A woman fearing, perhaps for little reason, that she has harmed her child could ensure that he was never born at all.

If there remains a case for maternal immunity, consideration must at least be given to paternal immunity. In 1976, the kind of harms men might do their unborn children were perceived as crude and obvious wrongdoing. A father who beats his partner up so badly that he injures both her and the child in the womb elicits little sympathy. What science can now tell us about how lifestyle from an early age may affect human gametes is cause for concern. Studies have shown that heavy smoking in teenage years could increase the risk of a man's child born years later succumbing to certain cancers. Whether fathers ought to be constrained by law in their pre-conception conduct must be questionable. Paternal liability unearths a further quirk of the 1976 Act. Even absent maternal immunity, in what sort of circumstances could either parent be liable for pre-conception injury? Liability under the Act is derivative only. The defendant must be liable in tort to the affected parent. Consider this example. A man is a heavy drug-user in his youth in an era when such drug use is known to damage sperm. Later he begets a child born disabled because of his damaged gametes. To be liable to the child, he must be liable to her mother. To be liable to the mother, the courts would have to find that men have a duty of care to their future partners to ensure that they protect those partners' reproductive health. Imagine the outcry if the law declared that women must order their lives to safeguard their husbands' right to have healthy children.

---

[124] See M Brazier, 'Parental Responsibilities, Foetal Welfare and Children's Health' in C Bridge (ed), *Family Law: Towards the Millennium* (1997) Butterworths, p 263.
[125] See S A M McLean, *Old Law, New Medicine* (1999) Pandora Press, p 66.

Criminal liability[126]

11.18   Before concluding that pregnancy conduct can never be subjected to legal redress, the decision of the House of Lords in *A-G's Reference (No 3 of 1994)*[127] must be considered. A father attacked his pregnant girlfriend and injured his child in the womb. The baby was born alive but subsequently died of her pre-natal injuries. The father was charged with his daughter's murder. Following his acquittal, the Attorney-General referred the case to the Court of Appeal to determine whether murder or manslaughter can be committed where a foetus is injured *in utero*, but is subsequently born alive only to die later of pre-natal injuries. In a convoluted judgment, the Court of Appeal answered yes to both questions.[128] The House of Lords partially upheld their judgment on very different grounds. The Law Lords endorsed earlier judgments[129] that a charge of murder or manslaughter can be sustained where a foetus injured *in utero* is born alive and later dies as a consequence of those injuries. On the facts of this case, their Lordships held that a charge of murder could not be sustained, but that a charge of manslaughter could. Murder could not be committed in this case because there was no express design to harm the foetus 'or the human person which it would become'.[130] However, manslaughter could be established in this instance. In his assault on the mother, the father committed an unlawful and dangerous act likely to cause harm to the child, and the event resulting in her death. Such conduct constituted unlawful act type manslaughter. The implications of *A-G's Reference (No 3 of 1994)* are that:

(a)   a person whose unlawful and dangerous conduct results in foetal injury followed by the birth of a child 'doomed to die' commits manslaughter;

(b)   gross and culpable negligence in relation to the foetus may similarly, where the child is born alive and subsequently dies, constitute manslaughter;

(c)   a deliberate attempt to harm or kill the foetus directly could in such cases amount to murder.

Finally Lord Mustill[131] suggests any violence against the foetus resulting in harm short of death may engage criminal responsibility.

At no point do any of the Law Lords consider maternal criminal responsibility. Their reasoning leaves pregnant women open to such liability in a range of scenarios. The pregnant woman who continues to abuse illegal drugs so that

---

[126]   See E Cave, *The Mother of All Crimes* (2004) Ashgate.

[127]   [1997] 3 All ER 936. See S Fovargue, J Miola, 'Policing Pregnancy: Implications of the Attorney-General's Reference (No 3 of 1994)' (1998) 6 *Medical Law Review* 265 and E Cave, ibid.

[128]   [1996] 2 All ER 10, CA; discussed in M Seneviratne, 'Pre-Natal Injury and Transferred Malice: The Invented Other' (1996) 59 *Modern Law Review* 884.

[129]   *R v West* (1848) 175 ER 329; *R v Senior* (1832) 168 ER 1298.

[130]   [1997] 3 All ER 936 at 949 per Lord Mustill.

[131]   [1997] 3 All ER 936 at 942.

her child is born damaged by those substances and dies of their effect could be said to commit unlawful act type manslaughter. The woman whose heavy abuse of alcohol results in a child so dreadfully harmed by foetal alcohol syndrome that he lives only a short while could be seen as criminally negligent. If Lord Mustill's statement about harm short of death is right, even if her child does not die, the mother could be charged with causing him grievous bodily harm.

The sorts of illegal or reckless behaviour which might engage criminal liability might seem to create a case for endorsing criminal responsibility for egregiously bad behaviour in pregnancy. The moral obligation to have due regard for the welfare of a child whom a mother elects to bring to term is incontrovertible. Whether the invocation of the criminal law would in practice enhance foetal welfare or simply offer means of coercing pregnant women and stigmatising unfortunate mothers is to be doubted.[132]

Once the baby is born alive, a mother who deliberately kills her baby will not necessarily have committed murder or manslaughter if 'the balance of her mind was disturbed by reason of her not having fully recovered from the effect of giving birth to the child'. Section 1(1) of the Infanticide Act 1938 provides a partial defence. In *R v Gore*[133] G hid her pregnancy and abandoned her baby, which sadly died due to lack of medical attention. At the time, section 1 stipulated that '. . . notwithstanding that the circumstances were such that but for this Act the offence would have amounted to *murder*, she shall be guilty of felony, to wit of infanticide' (italics added).[134] Her parents argued[135] that the elements of murder (including the requisite mens rea) must be proved, but the Court of Appeal held not. There is no requirement in the Act of proof of intention to kill. In 2006 the Law Commission expressed concern that a negligent act which falls short of gross negligence manslaughter might lead to prosecution.[136] Section 57 of the Coroners and Justice Act 2009[137] made minor amendments to section 1 of the Infanticide Act.[138] It now refers to 'murder or

---

[132] See Fovargue and Miola [1998] 6 *Medical Law Review* 265; M Brazier, 'Parental Responsibilities, Foetal Welfare and Children's Health' in C Bridge (ed), *Family Law: Towards the Millennium* (1997) Butterworths; Cave, *The Mother of All Crimes* (2004) Ashgate; M Brazier, 'Liberty Responsibility and Maternity' (1999) 52 *Current Legal Problems* 359.

[133] [2007] EWCA Crim 2789. See A Ashworth, 'Infanticide' (2008) *Criminal Law Review* 388.

[134] Infanticide Act 1938, s 1(1) prior to amendment.

[135] G was deceased and her parents appealed on her behalf.

[136] See Law Commission, *Murder, Manslaughter and Infanticide* No 304 (2006); and Ministry of Justice, *Murder, Manslaughter and Infanticide: Proposals for Reform of the Law* (2008).

[137] Which came into force October 2010. See A Samuels, 'The Coroners and Justice Act 2009' (2010) 174(17) *Criminal Law and Justice Weekly* 250.

[138] Infanticide Act 1938, s 1(1), as amended: 'Where a woman by any wilful act or omission causes the death of her child being a child under the age of twelve months, but at the time of her act or omission the balance of her mind was disturbed by reason

manslaughter' and ensures that no-one can be charged with infanticide unless a homicide is committed.

Childbirth: how much choice?[139]

11.19 In future, ectogenesis may allow the foetus to be gestated in an artificial womb.[140] Our great-grandmothers gave thanks if they survived the perils of childbirth. Today medical technology offers a whole range of sophisticated devices to monitor mother and baby and ensure safe delivery. Increasingly, many women reject the panoply of machinery found in many hospital labour wards. Accepting the necessity of 'high-tech' birth for a minority of difficult cases, the natural childbirth movement has campaigned for the medical profession to be more willing to let nature take its course. For a number of women the ideal is delivery at home in the comfort of familiar surroundings.

What role does the law play? Childbirth remains a professional monopoly. The law denies a woman, unable to persuade a doctor or midwife to attend her at home or a hospital to comply with her wishes concerning the birth, the choice of seeking alternative help.[141] For it is a criminal offence for a person, other than a registered midwife or a registered medical practitioner, to attend a woman in childbirth. And any person means any person. In 1982, a husband was convicted of delivering his own wife and fined £100.[142] Nor is the unqualified attendant the only potential 'criminal'. The mother herself, if she procures the other's services – in ordinary English, if she asks for help – may be guilty of counselling and procuring a criminal offence. So her choice is to accept the medical help available or give birth alone. Giving birth alone is not an attractive option and one not free of legal hazard, not to speak of medical risk, for if the baby dies, the mother may face prosecution for manslaughter.[143] Gross

of her not having fully recovered from the effect of giving birth to the child or by reason of the effect of lactation consequent upon the birth of the child, then, if the circumstances were such that but for this Act the offence would have amounted to murder or manslaughter she shall be guilty of felony, to whit of infanticide, and may for such offence be dealt with and punished as if she had been guilty of the offence of manslaughter of the child.'

[139] See J Jomeen, 'Choice in Childbirth – A Realistic Expectation?' (2007) 15(8) *BMJ* 485.

[140] A Alghrani, 'Regulating the Reproductive Revolution: Ectogenesis – A Regulatory Minefield' in M Freeman (ed), *Law and Bioethics: Current legal Issues* (2008) OUP, vol 11, pp 303–329.

[141] Nurses, Midwives and Health Visitors Act 1979, s 17. An exception is made for emergencies to protect family, policemen and ambulance crew from liability for helping in emergencies. For thorough discussion of the monopoly on childbirth, see J M Eekelaar, R W J Dingwall, 'Some Legal Issues of Obstetric Practice' (1984) *Journal of Social Welfare Law* 258, and J Finch, 'Paternalism and Professionalism in Childbirth' (1982) 132 *New Law Journal* 995, 1011.

[142] For further discussion of this case, see Finch (1982) 132 *New Law Journal* 995.

[143] See A-G's Reference (No 3 of 1994) [1997] 3 All ER 936.

negligence by attendants in the delivery of a baby has resulted in criminal conviction where the baby died.[144] The issue where an unattended mother was on trial would be whether refusing medical attendance was sufficiently culpable negligence in relation to the safety of her child.

The rationale for legislation which makes professional attendance at childbirth compulsory may appear self-evident. If a person refuses to seek medical help for any other life-threatening condition he physically harms himself alone. A woman refusing medical attention in childbirth puts her baby at risk. The legislation originally enacted to require professional attendance at childbirth was intended to outlaw the 'Sarah Gamps' – elderly and often dirty local women who made their living as unqualified midwives.[145] Today's legislation has moved a long way from that point. It may by chance be correct, but it needs proper consideration whether a husband delivering his wife, or a mother her daughter, should be branded as criminal when all goes well and mother and baby thrive.

Hospital birth

11.20 How far does a woman retain control of her labour? Save in an emergency, explicit consent is required for any invasive examination or procedure in labour.[146] That does not mean that the midwife must obtain a written consent for every vaginal examination, or that explicit consent to wiping the woman's brow is called for. Any significant procedure must where possible proceed with the woman's agreement. Most midwives regard treating mothers as partners in labour as simply good practice. One of the most controversial issues of hospital birth is the use of episiotomy. A small cut is made in the vagina to assist delivery and prevent tearing. One of its advantages is said to be that the deliberate cut will heal better than a random tear. In some hospitals, episiotomy became routine. It was performed regardless of any necessity for it. The number of episiotomies has fallen.[147] Many women will enter the labour ward confused and a little overwhelmed. They will have given no express instructions. Episiotomy without express consent is unlawful. It is not an inevitably necessary invasion of the mother's body, as are the contacts by the midwife when she feels the abdomen and assists the baby's exit. Episiotomy is a greater invasion of the body than any contacts implicitly authorised simply by seeking professional aid. The skin is cut. A wound, however small, is made. The law should uphold the mother's right to control what happens to her.

---

[144] *R v Senior* (1832) 1 Mood CC 346; and see *R v Bateman* (1925) 19 Cr App R 8.
[145] See Finch (1982) 132 *New Law Journal* 995 at 995–996.
[146] Though see the contrary view expressed by Eekelaar and Dingwall (1984) *Journal of Social Welfare Law* 258.
[147] See Royal College of Obstetricians and Gynaecologists, *Management of Third-and Fourth-degree Perineal Tears Following Vaginal Delivery* (2007).

Childbirth can be an unpredictable process. Midwives and obstetricians sometimes have to respond swiftly to an unforeseen emergency. The woman may be in acute pain, perhaps a little panicky, or significantly affected by doses of painkilling drugs which cause some mental confusion. Doubts may surface about her decision-making capability, and/or time to seek consent may truly be limited. The Court of Appeal[148] has suggested that if the woman is temporarily incompetent to make decisions for herself, health professionals may do whatever is required in her best interests. Defining the borderline between capacity and mental incapacity in such cases is tricky. It is too easy to assume women are incompetent. 'Birth plans' offer a partial solution to such dilemmas. Women, ideally in consultation with their midwives, outline how they wish to be treated if certain emergencies materialise. 'Advance decisions'[149] should have just as great force and authority at childbirth as in the life-threatening circumstances in which they are more usually invoked. The controversy over whether the law should compel medical attendance in childbirth would be much less substantial if the woman's rights in hospital were fully protected.

It goes without saying that a mother suffering injury as a result of carelessness in the management of childbirth is entitled to compensation for negligence. She will recover compensation for her pain and suffering and for the shock and grief consequent on the death of a baby, or the birth of a disabled child. Her damages may also include any effect of the mismanaged delivery on her prospects of future childbearing.[150] Where obstetric negligence results in the birth of a disabled infant, the child too has a claim. The most common case centres on allegations that the baby suffered brain damage as a consequence of oxygen starvation during delivery. The parents argue that the obstetric team failed to act on signs of foetal distress and perform a Caesarean section as swiftly as the circumstances required. The child is born with cerebral palsy. Very often the core of the dispute is not whether clinical negligence can be proven, but whether causation can be established. Such cases are expensive, slow and worryingly common. The NHS Litigation Authority (NHSLA) reports the value of claims made against each medical speciality. The highest value claims by far (totalling £4,386,700 since 1995) are in obstetrics and gynaecology.[151] Little wonder the Chief Medical Officer gave serious thought to a special no-fault scheme to compensate birth injuries.[152]

Maternal autonomy/foetal welfare

11.21 The child injured by obstetric negligence will have a claim against doctors and midwives who failed him. What are his rights if his mother refuses a

---

[148] *Re MB (An Adult) (Medical Treatment)* [1997] 2 FCR 541, CA.
[149] See ch 6.
[150] *Kralj v McGrath* [1986] 1 All ER 54.
[151] NHSLA, Factsheet 3: Information on Claims (2010).
[152] CMO, *Making Amends – Clinical Negligence Reform* (2003), Rec2. However, there are, at present, no plans to take this recommendation forward.

course of action that will benefit him and thus causes him injury? In theory the child's rights are governed by the Congenital Disabilities (Civil Liability) Act 1976, albeit the Act appears to go unnoticed in the relevant case law. The 1976 Act covers not just injury to the child in the womb but also any occurrence which *affected mother or child in the course of its birth*. It has been argued that the 1976 Act reduced the child's rights.[153] Liability under the Act arises only where the defendant would have been liable in tort to the affected parent. Where a failure by the defendant caring for the mother, eg failure to proceed quickly enough to Caesarean section, is in no way the responsibility of the mother, no problem is caused to the child. The duty to the mother embraces care of her child. A breach of duty to her which injures the child creates rights for both her and her child.

The thrust of the argument that the Act reduced the child's rights lies in these sorts of circumstances. The child is believed to be at risk. Doctors recommended Caesarean section. The mother refuses and the child is born suffering brain damage. The child will not be able to sue the doctor. The doctor is not liable to the mother. The child cannot sue his mother, for the Act grants immunity to mothers.[154] If there is no duty directly to the child, a doctor cannot after the Congenital Disabilities (Civil Liability) Act 1976 advance his duty to the child as a defence to acts done to the mother.[155] Where there is still a direct duty to the child, the doctor might contend that, in exceptional circumstances, he could, for example, proceed to Caesarean section without consent in order to save the baby. That begs the fundamental question of whether doctors ought ever to be allowed to prioritise the child's welfare above his mother's right to autonomy, to make her own choices about her childbirth.

In 1998, the Court of Appeal in *St George's Healthcare NHS Trust v S*[156] finally ruled that in English law no mentally competent woman could be required to submit to a Caesarean section or any other form of obstetric intervention to which she objected. Neither pregnancy nor labour diminished the woman's rights of self-determination. Judge LJ put the position succinctly:[157]

> ... while pregnancy increases the personal responsibilities of the pregnant woman it does not diminish her entitlement to decide whether or not to undergo medical treatment.

Six years of uncertainty were ended. In 1992, in *Re S*,[158] the then President of the Family Division had ruled that doctors could carry out a Caesarean on a woman whose own life and that of her child were imminently imperilled by an

---

153 Eekelaar and Dingwall (1984) *Journal of Social Welfare Law* 258, p 265.
154 Congenital Disabilities (Civil Liability) Act 1976, s 1(2).
155 Eekelaar and Dingwall (1984) *Journal of Social Welfare Law* 258, p 265.
156 [1998] 3 All ER 673.
157 [1998] 3 All ER 673 at 692.
158 [1992] 4 All ER 671.

obstructed labour. Several other cases[159] followed where courts, often in hurried hearings in circumstances of dire emergency, ordered Caesarean surgery despite maternal objections. In a number, but not all, of these cases the mother's mental capacity was questionable. In 1997, in *Re MB (Adult: Medical Treatment)*,[160] the Court of Appeal said that if a woman retained mental capacity she retained the right to make decisions about surgery for herself but found on the facts that MB's needle phobia rendered her temporarily incompetent.

The theory of the law is this. Unless a woman lacks the mental capacity to make her own decisions about labour, her freedom to determine what is and is not done to her is unimpaired. This is confirmed in Department of Health guidance which states:

> If an adult with capacity makes a voluntary and appropriately informed decision to refuse treatment (whether contemporaneously or in advance), this decision *must* be respected, except in certain circumstances as defined by the Mental Health Act 1983. This is the case even where this may result in the death of the person (and/or the death of an unborn child, whatever the stage of the pregnancy).[161]

In practice, the temptation to seek grounds to find her capacity to be impaired is great.[162] Judge LJ in *St George's* is emphatic in his endorsement of maternal autonomy. The mother's wishes should be respected even if her thinking process is '. . . apparently bizarre and irrational and contrary to the views of the overwhelming majority of the community at large'. Yet in *Re MB*, Butler-Sloss LJ suggested a woman might suffer temporary incapacity induced by confusion, shock, pain or drugs. Or fear might paralyse the will.[163] Finding any of these factors in childbirth will not be hard.

The situation is altered little by the Mental Capacity Act 2005.[164] The Act codifies the test for capacity in section 2. Capacity is judged at the 'relevant time'. Its temporary nature is irrelevant. However, neither a condition (such as

---

[159] *Rochdale Healthcare NHS Trust v C* [1997] 1 FCC 274; *Norfolk and Norwich (NHS) Trust v W* [1996] 2 FLR 613; *Re L (An Adult: Non Consensual Treatment)* [1997] 1 FCR 609; *Tameside & Glossop Acute Services Trust v CS* [1996] 1 FLRC 762.

[160] [1997] 2 FLR 426.

[161] DH, *Reference Guide to Consent for Examination or Treatment* (2nd edn, 2009), ch 1, para 44.

[162] See *Bolton Hospitals NHS Trust v O* [2003] 1 FLR 824.

[163] Note that the DH, *Reference Guide to Consent for Examination or Treatment* (2009), ch 1, para 46, recognises that withdrawal of consent during a procedure may be non-capacitous (and therefore not valid) if brought on by 'pain, panic and shock'.

[164] See ch 6.

pregnancy) nor an aspect of the person's behaviour (such as irrationality) can establish a lack of capacity under the Act.[165]

In the case of a pregnant woman, it must be demonstrated that the pregnant woman is unable to make the particular decision as a result of an impairment or disturbance of the mind. The Code of Practice on the Mental Capacity Act 2005 recognises a wide range of factors which can lead to such impairment, including drugs and delirium.[166] Consequently, it will remain the case that doctors may have little difficulty in demonstrating a temporary lack of capacity during labour.

Is the theory right? Or ought the foetus at the point of birth to be more highly valued? The difficulty of using law to enforce a duty to the foetus is well illustrated in *Re F (In Utero)*,[167] where a local authority unsuccessfully tried to make a foetus a ward of court. The mother was a thirty-six-year-old woman who suffered from severe mental disturbance, but she was not 'sectionable' under the Mental Health Act 1983. She refused ante-natal care and had disappeared by the time the local authority started proceedings to make the foetus a ward of court. There was concern for the child's welfare. Refusing to extend the wardship jurisdiction to unborn children, the court advanced the following reasons for their decision. (1) In English law the foetus has no legal personality until it is born, and has an existence independent of the mother. (2) To extend the wardship jurisdiction to the foetus with its predominant principle that the interests of the ward are paramount would create inevitable conflict between the existing legal interests of the mother and her child. Is the mother to be 'sacrificed' for the child? (3) There are immense practical difficulties in enforcing any order against the mother. If she is, for example, refusing to consent to an elective Caesarean and is not already in hospital, will the police be called on to go and arrest her? (4) There would be problems with the limit of such a jurisdiction. Mothers can do most harm to their unborn children early in pregnancy by, for example, alcohol and drug abuse. Yet up to twenty-four weeks into pregnancy a mother may well be able to obtain a legal abortion. Would a woman who wants her baby be subject to coercive measures in the baby's interests, yet free to destroy it should she change her mind? May LJ concluded that in the light of these problems any such radical extension of the wardship jurisdiction was a matter for Parliament and not for the courts themselves. In the event, and unbeknownst to the court, while they were hearing the action, the mother had already safely given birth to a healthy child.

Parliament should reject any proposal to extend the wardship jurisdiction to unborn children or to endorse non-consensual obstetric interventions.[168] Over and above those reasons given by the Court of Appeal, such a proposal should

---

[165] Mental Capacity Act 2005, s 2(3)(b).
[166] Mental Capacity Act 2005 Code of Practice, updated April 2007 at 4.11.
[167] [1989] 2 All ER 193.
[168] As the Royal College of Obstetricians and Gynaecologists itself has done; see RCOG, *Law and Ethics in Relation to Court-Ordered Obstetric Intervention* (2006).

be thrown out on the grounds of the damage it would do to ante-natal care generally. Obstetricians, knowing that they could in the end coerce their patients, would become less willing to inform and persuade, to rely on patience rather than compulsion. Women, knowing that they could be forced against their will to submit to blood transfusion or surgery may opt out of formal obstetric care and far more babies could be born damaged as a result. The law must continue to recognise the pregnant woman's autonomy and her sovereignty over her own body. In no other circumstances can one person be required to submit to any medical procedure to benefit another's welfare. Once a child is born, neither of his parents could be forced to donate even a drop of blood to him however trivial the discomfort to them or great the child's need. Caesarean surgery remains major invasive surgery with significant risks and pain for the patient.[169]

---

[169] See L Miller, 'Two Patients or One? A Problem of Consent in Obstetrics' (1993) *Medical Law International* 97.

Chapter 12

ASSISTED CONCEPTION[1]

12.1 It has been estimated that about one in seven couples have difficulty conceiving naturally and seek medical help.[2] The birth of the first 'test-tube' baby, Louise Brown,[3] in 1978 gave hope to many childless couples. Since then, the pace of development in the reproductive technologies has been relentless. Reproductive medicine no longer focuses exclusively on the management of physiological infertility. Single women can be assisted to have a child without resort to sexual intercourse. Same-sex couples can be helped to have a child. Couples who are fertile, but know that they, or one of them, is a carrier of a genetic disease can be helped to have a healthy child, by way of preimplantation genetic diagnosis (PGD) whereby embryos are screened to avoid implanting any embryos with the defective gene. Couples who already have one sick child can seek PGD together with tissue typing, to attempt to create a 'saviour sibling' for their sick child. Each and every development in the reproductive technologies attracts controversy. For everyone who rejoices at what doctors can now do, there are those who condemn the advances in medicine as unnatural, contrary to the will of God, or destructive of 'normal family life'.

Louise Brown's birth did not only generate moral controversy. Concerns arose about the safety of the 'new' technologies. Fears grew about the competence of practitioners and basic issues, such as hygienic storage of human gametes.[4] In response, the government established a Committee under Dame Mary Warnock (now Baroness Warnock) which reported in 1984 and recommended legislation to regulate these emerging reproductive technologies.[5] After years of delay, Parliament enacted the Human Fertilisation and Embryology Act

---

[1] E Jackson, *Regulating Reproduction: Law, Technology and Autonomy* (2001) Hart.
[2] Human Fertilisation and Embryology Authority, *Facts and Figures* (2008), p 3.
[3] Who gave birth to her own first child without fertility treatment in 2006.
[4] There is a (possibly apocryphal) story about one clinic storing sperm in the same fridge as milk for staff coffee breaks.
[5] Report of the Committee of Inquiry into Human Fertilisation and Embryology (1984) Cm 9314 (The Warnock Report).

1990.[6] That Act entrusted the primary responsibility for regulating the reproductive technologies in the UK to the Human Fertilisation and Embryology Authority (HFEA).

The 1990 Act and the HFEA were once seen as the model for effective regulation of assisted conception and embryo research, but in recent years the 1990 Act and the HFEA have been subjected to increasingly intense criticism.[7] It is scarcely surprising that a statute enacted in 1990 no longer met the needs of scientific developments, undreamed of twenty years before. The Act generated prolific litigation.[8] The paternalist structure of regulation was perceived as outdated and incompatible with a human rights culture, especially section 13(5) of the Act requiring that consideration be given to a child's 'need for a father'. Liberal critics of the 1990 Act attacked it as insufficiently responsive to reproductive autonomy.[9] Conservative critics charged that the Act permitted the degradation of human embryos and children, reducing them to mere means to an end.[10] In 2005, the Department of Health launched a review of the 1990 Act[11] and a White Paper[12] proposing substantial reforms was published in December 2006. Some fertility specialists had argued that there was no longer any need for special regulation of reproductive medicine. This argument for wholesale deregulation was rejected by the government. Instead the 1990 Act was heavily amended by the Human Fertilisation and Embryology Act 2008 and that Act also introduced radical new rules relating to parenthood, allowing female same-sex couples to achieve the status of legal parents when they seek fertility treatment together. The 2008 Act preserved the central role of the HFEA, rejecting earlier proposals to merge the HFEA with the Human Tissue Authority (HTA). Then in 2010 the coalition government announced that the HFEA and the HTA were to be abolished and their functions transferred to other bodies by the end of this Parliament.[13] The detail of how regulation will work after the

---

[6] The Act reached the statute book only after vitriolic debate in Parliament and the publication of two further reports by the government, a general consultation document early in 1987 and a White Paper later that year. See *Legislation on Human Infertility Services and Embryology* (1987) Cm 46; *Human Fertilisation and Embryology: A Framework for Legislation* (1987) Cm 259.

[7] See, in particular, the House of Commons Science and Technology Committee Fifth Report of Session 2004–5 *Human Reproductive Technologies and the Law* HC-7-1, vol 1.

[8] See, for example, *R (Quintavalle) v Human Fertilisation and Embryology Authority* [2003] 2 All ER 105; *R (Quintavalle) v Human Fertilisation and Embryology Authority* [2005] 2 All ER 555, HL.

[9] See E Jackson, *Regulating Reproduction: Law, Technology and Autonomy* (2001) Hart.

[10] See J Laing, D A Oderberg, 'Artificial Reproduction, the "Welfare Principle" and the Common Good' (2005) 13 *Medical Law Review* 328.

[11] DH, *Review of the Human Fertilisation and Embryology Act – A Public Consultation* (2005) ref: 269640; Report on the Consultation on the Review of the Human Fertilisation and Embryology Act 1990 (2006).

[12] Review of the Human Fertilisation and Embryology Act – Proposals for Revised Legislation (including the Establishment of the Regulatory Authority for Tissue and Embryos) (2006) Cm 6989.

[13] DH, *Liberating the NHS: A Review of Arm's Length Bodies* (2010).

demise of the HFEA is far from clear. At the time of writing,[14] it appears that the powers currently exercised by HFEA are to be shared between the Care Quality Commission (CQC), a new research regulator[15] and the Health and Social Care Information Centre. The cumulative impact of the 1990 and 2008 Acts and a substantial body of case law means that we have to compress into this chapter material that could fill more than one book. The combination of the 1990 and 2008 Acts creates a maze of rules through which we struggle to navigate.

Regulating human fertilisation and embryology

12.2　The primary responsibility for regulating the reproductive technologies in the UK remains for the present with the HFEA, operating as a statutory licensing authority, and established by section 5 of the Human Fertilisation and Embryology Act 1990. Schedule I to the Act prescribes the authority's membership with a strong emphasis on a partnership between lay representation and expert input. Neither the chairman nor the deputy chairman may be a medical practitioner, or professionally involved in embryo research or assisted conception. At least one-third, but fewer than half, of the members must be persons so involved in research or infertility treatment. When the powers of the HFEA are transferred to other more generalist bodies, a substantial body of experience and expertise may be lost.

The HFEA was granted impressive powers, many of which focused on the power to license clinics to undertake fertility treatments. We envisage that the licensing powers currently vested in the HFEA will be taken over by the CQC if the HFEA is indeed abolished. Section 3 of the Human Fertilisation and Embryology Act 1990 makes it a criminal offence to bring about the creation of an embryo outside the human body, or keep or use such an embryo,[16] except in pursuance of a licence granted by the HFEA. Any infertility treatment requiring the creation of an embryo by means of in vitro fertilisation (IVF), that is the creation of a 'test-tube' embryo, must be licensed. An embryo in vitro is defined to include embryos where the process of fertilisation started outside the woman's body.[17]

Section 4 of the Human Fertilisation and Embryology Act 1990 prohibits any storage of gametes (sperm or eggs), and the use of donor sperm or eggs, without a licence from the HFEA. Any infertility treatment involving artificial

---

[14]　And see above at **1.16**.

[15]　See the proposals for the Health Research Agency: Academy of Medical Sciences, *A New Pathway for the Regulation and Governance of Health Research* (2011) discussed below at **15.5**.

[16]　See *A-G's Reference (No 2 of 2003)* [2004] EWCA Crim 785.

[17]　S 1(2). But Gamete Intra Fallopian Transfer (GIFT), where eggs and sperm are mixed in the laboratory and then placed in the woman's body, would seem to remain outside the Act unless donor gametes are used, as fertilisation does not begin until the sperm and eggs unite within the body.

insemination by donor (DI) or egg donation is unlawful unless licensed by the HFEA. There is a limited exception to the rule relating to sperm. DI can be undertaken outside a licensed clinic if the sperm is 'partner-donated sperm which has neither been processed nor stored'.[18] The amendments to the 1990 Act have introduced much stricter controls on DI, designed to control the growing number of 'businesses' offering both access to fresh donated sperm and 'sperm sorting', a process that offers a crude form of primary sex selection. Often based on Internet sites, sperm was advertised to women who wanted a child but no relationship with a man. Given that the sperm was fresh and the sites were not based in any form of medical environment, health risks were high. Any such enterprise must now be licensed in the new category of 'non medical fertility services'. Two men have already been convicted of supplying sperm from an unlicensed site.[19] One question that arises is, does the new law effectively ban self-insemination in such cases as a lesbian woman asking a friend to donate sperm to her with which she inseminates herself, or a commissioning father providing sperm for self-insemination by a surrogate mother. A literal reading of the Act might suggest that it does, for in such cases the sperm is not partner donated. Mason and Laurie,[20] however, argue that the man providing sperm on the basis of a private agreement with a woman who is a friend or a potential surrogate falls outside the ban in section 4 as he is not 'providing treatment services'. We tend to agree but wonder about the possible case of a man who widely advertises his own services as a sperm donor?

Sections 3 and 4 of the Human Fertilisation and Embryology Act 1990 also outlaw a number of specific procedures, for example, keeping an embryo after the appearance of the primitive streak (fourteen days), placing an embryo in an animal and the use of embryos for reproductive cloning. One of the fiercest debates around the 2008 Act centred on the creation of human/animal hybrids. The Act permits a number of techniques in relation to research only and within strict limits. Those issues are dealt with further in the next chapter. One point must be made here. Only 'permitted' embryos and gametes may be placed in a woman in the course of fertility treatment.[21] Permitted gametes must have been produced or extracted from a human male or female and the nuclear or mitochondrial DNA of the gamete must not have been altered.[22] Permitted embryos must be created from permitted gametes. Thus no form of embryo created from the mixing of human and animal material may be used in fertility treatment.

---

[18] See s 4(1)(b)(ii). And see s 1(5): sperm is to be treated as partner donated if the donor and the recipient declare that they have an 'intimate physical relationship'.

[19] HFEA Press Release, 17 September 2010.

[20] J K Mason and G T Laurie, *Mason and McCall Smith's Law and Medical Ethics* (8th edn, 2010) OUP (hereafter *Mason and McCall Smith*), p 260.

[21] S 3(2).

[22] S 3ZA. But see s 3ZA(5), allowing regulations to amend the definition of permitted egg and embryo to legalise treatment to prevent the transmission of serous mitrochondrial disease.

Licensing fertility treatment

12.3 Any clinic that offers IVF or artificial insemination (AI) is subject to the control of the HFEA, and we assume will in future be subject to the CQC. A clinic cannot operate lawfully without a licence and its staff and procedures are strictly monitored and controlled. Failure to comply with HFEA guidelines about, for example, safety procedures, numbers of embryos to be implanted,[23] selection of donors or assessment of patients may lead to forfeiture of that licence.

The Human Fertilisation and Embryology Act 1990 only provided a basic framework of rules governing assisted conception in the UK. The Act entrusted to the HFEA extensive powers to fill in the details of those rules and to regulate both the ethical and practical problems of assisted conception; powers the CQC may inherit. The HFEA has to operate within the framework set by Parliament, but many crucial decisions were left to them. So, the HFEA has had to consider: should ovarian tissue be harvested from foetuses?; should sister-to-sister egg donation be banned?; should egg sharing be permitted? And these were examples of the HFEA's less contentious business. The developments in the techniques of assisted conception continually posed novel problems for the HFEA. The ethics of sex selection constantly troubled the HFEA. The controversy relating to PGD exposed the HFEA to attack on several fronts. Other ethical dilemmas facing the HFEA fade almost into insignificance in comparison with the debate surrounding human cloning. The HFEA found itself making policy in relation to deeply divisive social questions generated by the rapid developments in reproductive medicine. The rewards for its efforts were charges that the unelected Authority had usurped the role of Parliament.[24] In the government review that proposes the abolition of the HFEA, it is stated that policy issues should be relocated in government, with Ministers taking a more significant role rather than unelected 'quangos'. It is difficult to see how legislation making the changes to the 1990 Act will be able to split policy functions between the CQC and the Department of Health and we would express some caution about the impact of political pressures on issues of moral controversy.

Crucial to the role played by the HFEA was its Code of Practice setting out the general 'rules' within which clinics must work. Clinics that violate the Code may lose their licence. The 8th edition of the Code was published in 2009. Grand ethical issues faced the HFEA. Their everyday difficulties are apparently more mundane. How often should gametes from one donor be used? The more often sperm from one donor is used, the higher the risk of unwitting incest. No single donor is to be used for more than ten inseminations.[25]

---

[23] See *R (on the application of the Assisted Reproduction and Gynaecology Centre) v Human Fertilisation and Embryology Authority* [2002] EWCA Civ 20.

[24] See, in particular, the Report of the House of Commons Science and Technology Committee.

[25] See Human Fertilisation and Embryology Authority, *Code of Practice* (8th edn, 2009), paras 11.35–11.40.

The HFEA has long sought to reduce the number of multiple births resulting from IVF.[26] The more embryos replaced in the woman, the greater the risk of multiple pregnancies. Such pregnancies increase the risk of premature labour with adverse consequences for mothers, babies and over-stretched neonatal units within the NHS. The current guidance requires all clinics to aim to reduce any multiple births and to consider when it might be appropriate to move to Single Embryo Transplants. Some fertility specialists vehemently oppose what they see as paternalistic interference with clinical freedom. If the woman considers that increased chances of pregnancy outweigh the risk of multiple pregnancies, those doctors argue that the number of embryos replaced is none of the HFEA's business. An attempt to strike down this policy by way of judicial review failed.[27]

Another dilemma for the HFEA surrounded clinics with poor success rates. Live birth rates per cycle using fresh eggs remain on average about 33.1 per cent for women under thirty-five, falling to 12.5 per cent for women aged between forty and forty-two.[28] Small, less well-equipped centres achieve much less success. All clinics are regularly inspected. The HFEA publishes information enabling patients to know about the track record of each clinic. Ensuring patients receive information designed to help them to determine whether and where to seek treatment might seem uncontroversial. Alas for the HFEA, this is not the case. Clinics complain about the criteria used to grade them. It is claimed that some clinics turn away older women, or couples with complex fertility problems, to inflate their success rates.[29]

The HFEA became a target for attack. The ethical decisions entrusted to it go to the heart of differences in our society. The role of the HFEA as a regulator of fertility practice was sometimes overlooked. The HFEA received little credit for the job it did in ensuring 'quality control' of reproductive medicine at a time when in some other European countries assisted conception was wholly unregulated. British patients, lucky enough to gain access to treatment, could be reasonably assured that they would be treated by competent practitioners and protected by standards enforced by the HFEA.[30] A series of serious errors, however, contributed to the HFEA coming under attack for incompetence, as much as for its policy-making role. In one incident, evidence emerged that the sole embryologist who was working for two clinics had engaged in a range of malpractice. A number of frozen embryos had been allowed to thaw. The embryologist knew this, but did not disclose this disaster to his colleagues.

---

[26] Human Fertilisation and Embryology, *Code of Practice* (8th edn, 2009), paras 7.1–7.8.

[27] *R (on the application of the Assisted Reproduction and Gynaecology Centre) v Human Fertilisation and Embryology Authority* [2002] EWCA Civ 20.

[28] See Human Fertilisation and Embryology Authority, *Facts and Figures 2008,* p 5.

[29] See *Understanding Clinic Success Rates* (2006) HFEA accessible at www.hfea.gov.uk/cps/rde/xchg/SID-3F57079.

[30] See M Brazier, 'Regulating the Reproduction Business?' (1999) 7 *Medical Law Review* 166.

Several women underwent procedures which they believed involved implanting 'their' embryos. In fact, no embryo was within the substances inserted in the women. The embryologist was convicted of assault as well as several charges of fraud.[31] Another mistake came to light in *Leeds Teaching Hospital NHS Trust v A*.[32] A white couple, Mr and Mrs A, were receiving IVF treatment. Mrs A gave birth to mixed-race twins. It emerged that failure to monitor the sperm used to create the embryos implanted in Mrs A led to the use of sperm from Mr B who was black. Mr and Mrs B were also undergoing treatment at the same clinic. Such errors may have made it harder for the HFEA to fight off its sentence of death from government.

In vitro fertilisation (IVF): opening Pandora's box?

12.4 Before 1978 and the birth of Louise Brown, doctors were limited in what they could offer a couple who could not have a child. Women might be offered drugs to help them ovulate or undergo surgical investigations and procedures. Where the man was infertile, donor insemination (DI) had been practised for decades. In vitro fertilisation (IVF), the medical advance that led to the passing of the first Human Fertilisation and Embryology Act in 1990, created a whole new range of possibilities for those who sought to have a child. IVF of itself provokes relatively few ethical[33] or legal dilemmas. IVF offers a woman who ovulates normally, but whose fallopian tubes are absent or damaged, and so cannot conceive naturally because the eggs that she produces cannot travel to meet sperm and be fertilised, the chance of her own child. Eggs are removed from the woman and fertilised in the laboratory with sperm taken from her husband, or partner or a donor. The embryo, or embryos, thus created are carefully tested and then implanted in the mother's womb. IVF is used in a number of other instances, including cases of 'unexplained infertility'. The woman ovulates, her fallopian tubes are clear and her partner provides healthy sperm, yet no pregnancy results. No questions of family law normally arise from IVF on its own. That child has the same relationship to her parents as if she were naturally conceived. But the ability to fertilise eggs outside the woman opened Pandora's box. No longer was it only sperm that could be donated, eggs could be too. And as reproductive medicine developed, social attitudes changed. Individuals who were not infertile, single women and same-sex couples sought treatment as did women past the normal age of childbearing. The difficult questions posed by IVF relate to whom should have access to 'fertility' treatment, how to define parenthood once donor gametes are used, to IVF and the many issues that arise from developments in IVF that allow selection of embryos.

---

[31] See (2003) *Guardian*, 16 January. And see *A-G's Reference (No 2 of 2003)* [2004] EWCA Crim 785.

[32] [2003] 1 FLR 1091.

[33] IVF is still opposed by the Roman Catholic Church on the grounds that it separates the conjugal act and the creation of a child: see E Jackson, *Medical Law: Text, Cases and Materials* (2nd edn, 2010) OUP, p 763.

Before looking at access to treatment, we might just ask what happens even in a straightforward IVF if a mistake is made, and the woman's eggs are inseminated by the 'wrong' sperm from someone else's husband or partner, as occurred in *Leeds Teaching Hospital NHS Trust v A*.[34] As we noted earlier, sperm from Mr B (intended for treatment of his wife, Mrs B) was in error used to fertilise eggs from Mrs A (who was undergoing treatment with her husband Mr A). The mistake became apparent only when Mrs A gave birth to mixed-race twins.[35] Who was the twins' father? Which couple should bring up the children? Section 28(2) of the Human Fertilisation and Embryology Act 1990 deemed a husband to be the legal father of his wife's child born as a result of sperm donation, if he consented to her undergoing donor insemination. This was of no help to Mr A as he patently did not consent to donor insemination of his wife. Nothing in the 1990 Act assisted Mr A in his claim to become the legal father of his wife's children. Mr B was their genetic father. Dame Elizabeth Butler-Sloss P ruled that, although he had not consented to the use of his sperm to fertilise Mrs A's eggs, Mr B, as the genetic father, should be treated as the legal father of the twins. Nonetheless, she had ruled that Mr and Mrs A should retain 'custody' of the children. The twins should stay with the 'parents' who had settled them in a loving home. Mr A could apply for a parental responsibility order or the couple could apply to adopt the twins. At some point when they were older, their origins should be explained to them and contact with Mr B arranged.

Access to fertility treatment: the welfare of the child

12.5 An increasing number of women who have no male partner want to have a child. They may be seeking to raise the child alone or be part of a same-sex couple wanting to create a family. During the passage of the first Human Fertilisation and Embryology Act, attempts were made in Parliament to outlaw DI for women without a male partner. A compromise was embodied in section 13(5) of the Act, which provided, apparently innocuously, that a licence-holder treating a woman must take into account the welfare of any child who may be born as a result of treatment, *including the need of that child for a father*.[36] Section 13(5) was viewed by many commentators as outdated and unnecessary.[37] The House of Commons Select Committee on Science and Technology concluded that the requirement to consider the need for a father

---

[34] [2003] 1 FLR 1091. And see A Bainham, 'Whose Sperm Is It Anyway?' [2003] *Cambridge Law Journal* 566.

[35] It is suggested that this is not a unique error, but one which became apparent because the couples involved had different racial origins; see (2002) *Guardian*, 8 July.

[36] A number of MPs and peers (in 1990) hoped that the HFEA would ban DI, and other forms of assisted conception, for all single women, save in the most exceptional circumstances.

[37] See, for example, E Jackson, 'Conception and the Irrelevance of the Welfare Principle' (2002) 65 *Modern Law Review* 176.

was[38] 'offensive to many' and constitutes 'unjustified discrimination against unconventional families'. The Select Committee went further and recommended abolition of the welfare principle. In the event the welfare principle survives in an amended form now requiring that clinics must still take account of the 'welfare of any child who may be born as a result of the treatment (*including the need of that child for supportive parenting*) and of any other child who may be affected by its birth'. Section 13(5) as amended would seem to look more favourably on any couple seeking treatment, heterosexual or not, than a single woman. The HFEA Code of Practice that had long sought to attenuate the effect of the provision when it focused on the need for a father now seeks to limit the impact of the current wording. Clinics must assess each patient individually and gauge whether 'there is a risk of significant harm or neglect to any child'.[39] Clinics should operate on a presumption of providing treatment to those seeking help to conceive whether they be heterosexual couples, lesbian couples or single women. Only if there is evidence of risk of serious harm to a future child should treatment be refused. In considering the statutory need for supportive parenting, clinics should regard this as a commitment to the health and well-being of the child that all prospective parents may be presumed to have. The HFEA has de facto virtually eliminated the need to demonstrate any specific family structure before being granted access to fertility treatment. Lacking a partner is of itself no bar.

Access to fertility treatment: post-menopausal mothers

12.6 Much of the debate on the welfare principle has focused on its application to single and gay women. But another area of controversy concerns older women seeking treatment. Egg donation offers women the opportunity to extend their reproductive lives. Several babies have been born to women who have undergone the menopause. Eggs are collected from a donor and implanted in the post-menopausal woman whose womb has been restored to a pre-menopausal state by hormone treatment. Success rates are low; nonetheless, in 2006, a British woman of sixty-two gave birth as a result of such treatment in Russia, and in Spain a woman of sixty-nine had twins. The crux of the question should not be the post-menopausal state of the woman. Some women suffer a premature menopause in their twenties. Few argue that they should be denied help. The question is whether women over fifty, or even sixty, should be assisted to have a child. France prohibits treatment of women past the normal age of childbearing. Those opposed to treating older women focus on the child. If a woman gives birth at sixty-two, she will be eighty before her child is legally an adult. It is more likely that her health will decline, or that the child will face the death of his mother, than if she were merely forty. Given the

---

[38] See House of Commons Science and Technology Committee, *Human Reproductive Technologies and the Law,* para 101.

[39] Human Fertilisation and Embryology Authority, *Code of Practice* (8th edn, 2009), para 8.2.

HFEA Guidance, the crux of the question becomes, does the age of the mother pose 'a risk of serious harm or neglect to the child'? Others point out that men fairly often beget children in their fifties and later. Is it discriminatory to prohibit helping women to do what nature permits men to do? Perhaps what we should ask is whether to create a child at an age when the chances are your ability to care for that child are diminishing is morally responsible for either men or women? Then we need to consider if it is ethical to assist another person to do something irresponsible.[40] The age of the partner may be a key factor. Many older fathers have much younger wives. So would the risk assessment to the child be different if the prospective mother of sixty-two had a partner aged forty-five? And if the age of the mother is relevant to the welfare of the child, should it follow that treatment would be refused if the man's age was such that he may well not be alive to nurture his child to adulthood?

Access to treatment on the NHS

12.7 The liberal guidance from the HFEA, and in particular their advice that only a risk of significant harm or neglect to a potential child should 'disqualify' a woman or a couple from receiving treatment, grants clinics a broad discretion about whom to treat. But private treatment costs a great deal of money and many prospective parents are unable to pay such sums, or nearly bankrupt themselves to do so. For them the real problem is not access to any clinic but access to treatment funded by the NHS. It has been argued that section 13(5) never made much difference in practice to the range of patients private clinics will treat.[41] IVF treatment is largely provided in the private sector, with very limited NHS facilities for those who cannot pay for treatment. NHS clinics had to make hard choices, choices that may now fall to Primary Care Trusts (PCTs) or GP consortia. Practice varied, but many clinics operated criteria based on the likelihood that patients would be good parents.[42] Some followed adoption guidelines used by local services departments. Most offered treatment only where neither partner has any existing children. Many operated upper age limits as low as thirty-five for the women. Courts were reluctant to interfere. Mrs Harriott was refused IVF because of a criminal record for prostitution offences and because she and her husband had been rejected as prospective adoptive or foster parents by Manchester social services department. The clinicians referred her case to the hospital's informal ethical advisory committee, who endorsed their decision. She sought judicial review of that decision, alleging that the grounds for refusing her treatment were unreasonable and unlawful. The judge held that decisions on IVF treatment could be reviewed by a court. If a patient was refused treatment on grounds, say, of

---

[40] See M Brazier, 'Liberty, Responsibility, Maternity' (1999) 52 *Current Legal Problems*, p 359.

[41] G Douglas, 'Assisted Reproduction and the Welfare of the Child' (1993) *Current Legal Problems* 46.

[42] See D Savas and S Treece, 'Fertility Clinics: One Code of Practice?'(1998) 3 *Medical Law International* 243.

religion or ethnic origin, such a refusal would be clearly unlawful. Public bodies and officials, including clinicians taking decisions within the NHS, must act reasonably and not on the basis of irrational prejudices. In Mrs Harriott's case, however, the judge found that the grounds for regarding her to be an unsuitable parent were reasonable.[43] Mrs Seale and her husband were refused NHS treatment because at thirty-seven she was 'too old'. The authority argued that thirty-five was a sensible cut-off point because the older the woman, the less the chances of establishing a successful pregnancy. Given a tight budget, the NHS should concentrate on treating women most likely to benefit from treatment. The judge agreed.[44] Conditions set by NHS clinics varied widely.

Decisions about who gets access to treatment on the NHS rest with those who fund NHS care. At present that is the PCTs, but government reforms proposed in the Health and Social Care Bill[45] will transfer that power to the GP consortia. Criteria by which PCTs decided to fund fertility treatment have varied widely. Where you live might determine whether you were 'too old' to be treated or whether you were 'unsuitable'. In 2003, NICE recommended that every infertile couple should be offered three cycles of IVF within the NHS with an upper age of forty for the woman.[46] The government reduced that to one cycle. Some PCTs still refused to fund fertility treatment at all, and as cuts bite, more PCTs remove funding for fertility treatments.[47] British couples may look with envy at France. France provides generous public funding for fertility treatment. Couples of childbearing age are unlikely to be turned away.[48] However, treatment is limited to heterosexual couples of reproductive age. Single women, lesbian couples or post-menopausal mothers are excluded. British patients have considerable 'freedom' if they can pay. Income is not an impediment in France.

Access and prisoners

12.8 A particular issue of access arises in the context of couples where the man is serving a prison sentence. English law does not permit conjugal visits and so if a couple wish to have a child while the male partner remains in prison, he has to be able to access the facilities to 'donate' sperm to his wife or partner. The Home Office placed substantial restrictions on any attempt to facilitate artificial insemination (AI) by prisoners and two prisoners refused permission

---

[43] *R v Ethical Advisory Committee of St Mary's Hospital, ex p Harriott* [1998] 1 FLR 512.

[44] *R v Sheffield Area Health Authority, ex p Seale* [1994] 25 BMLR 1.

[45] See above at **1.3**.

[46] NICE, *Fertility Assessment and Treatment for People with Fertility Problems* (2004). Accessible at www.nice.org.uk/pdf/CS011niceguidelines.pdf.

[47] DH, *Primary Care Trust Survey – Provision of IVF in England 2007* (2008).

[48] See M Latham, 'Regulating the New Reproductive Technologies: A Cross-Channel Comparison' (1998) *Medical Law International* 89.

to access AI challenged the Secretary of State, contending that this violated their rights to family life (Article 8) and to found a family (Article 12). The first case failed in the Court of Appeal, the court holding that such restrictions were justifiable in the public interest under Article 8(2). The Court noted that the wife would in this case still be of childbearing age when her husband was eligible for parole.[49] Founding a family was merely delayed and not prevented. In the second case, Mrs Dickson would be past childbearing age before her husband would be free. Her husband's challenge to the refusal of AI succeeded before the Grand Chamber of the European Court of Human Rights.[50] The UK government argued that as Mr and Mrs Dickson had married while he was in prison and had never lived together, the relationship had never been tested in a normal environment and there were concerns about the welfare of any child. Moreover, the public had a legitimate concern that the punitive element in the prison sentence would be circumvented by allowing him to father a child. The ECtHR was unimpressed. Mr Dickson's conviction deprived him of some of his rights to private life, but rules made by the Minister and not sanctioned by Parliament, that effectively denied him and his wife any prospect of conception, did not represent a fair balance between the public and private interests involved.

Gamete donation and parental status: meaning of 'father'

12.9   While IVF itself does not create any particularly knotty legal problems, the capacity to fertilise eggs outside the womb and the expansion of those who can access treatment has generated a host of legal questions, many of them relating to gamete donation when IVF involves the use of donated gametes, for example where the woman cannot ovulate and/or her partner produces no sperm. If a woman is treated with donated eggs, who is the child's legal mother? If a woman is treated with donated sperm, who is the father? Where it is the man who is infertile, couples have long been offered the opportunity to have a child using sperm from another man, by artificial insemination by donor (DI). DI long precedes the development of IVF. In its most basic form, DI is so simple that it can be, and often is, performed without medical assistance. But we should note that there are many instances when donor sperm will now be used in conjunction with IVF. In any such a case, who is the child's legal father? Two sets of rules now operate. If the woman was treated using donor sperm before April 2009, section 28 of Human Fertilisation and Embryology Act 1990 still applies. If the couple were married, were treated in a licensed clinic and the husband fully and freely consented, section 28(2) deems the child to be the husband's child[51] and gives the husband all the usual

---

49   *R v Secretary of State for the Home Department, ex p Mellor* [2001] EWCA Civ 472.
50   *Dickson v UK* (2007) 46 EHRR 41.
51   In cases where the husband's consent is disputed, it would be for him to prove that he did not consent.

privileges of fatherhood, including an entitlement to contact with his child should the marriage break down.[52]

Section 28(3) of the Human Fertilisation and Embryology Act 1990 related to unmarried heterosexual couples who sought DI together because the male partner was infertile. Whenever donor sperm were used in the treatment of a woman and a man together by a person to whom a licence applies, the man was to be treated as the father of the child.[53] The intent of section 28(2) and (3) was to bestow the legal rights and responsibilities of fatherhood on the social father, the man who seeks a child with his wife or partner. The apparent simplicity of these provisions about legal paternity is misleading. The notion of the couple treated together posed endless points of tricky interpretation. Evidence that at the time the mother received DI she was living with a male partner was not sufficient. The social father himself was unlikely to receive any treatment, though he would have undergone fertility tests at an earlier date.[54] Several legal cases ensued that are dealt with fully in the fourth edition of this work.[55] What was clear was the law was not satisfactory.[56]

Sections 35 to 41 of the Human Fertilisation and Embryology Act 2008 thus provide new rules on the meaning of 'father' whenever a woman is treated with donor sperm after April 2009. The position of a married couple has changed little. Section 35 provides that if a married woman is treated with donor sperm as part of IVF or simple DI, her husband will be the legal father of the child unless he did not consent to the use of donor sperm or DI. The section applies regardless of whether fresh or frozen sperm is used, whether the woman is treated in a licensed clinic or elsewhere or simply self-inseminates, and whether the woman is treated in the UK or abroad. The position is more complicated when a couple are unmarried. The 'agreed fatherhood conditions' in sections 36 and 37 apply. If the woman is treated in a licensed clinic in the UK and no man is deemed to be the father by virtue of section 35, nor any female civil partner is deemed to be parent by virtue of section 42, fatherhood is conferred by agreement. A man will be deemed to be the legal father of the child if he has given notice in writing to the clinic that he consents to be treated as the father and the woman has given notice in writing that she agrees that he shall be the father of her child, and neither party has withdrawn such consent.

---

[52] *Re CH (Contact: Parentage)* [1996] 1FCR 768.
[53] This means that if he and the mother register the birth of the child together, they share parental responsibility for the child. Should they not do so, to gain parental responsibility for the child, the 'social' father must either enter into a formal agreement with the mother to do so, or seek a court order to share parental responsibility with the mother; see s 4 of the Children Act 1989 as amended by the Adoption and Children Act 2002.
[54] *Re B (Parentage)* [1996] FLR 15; *Re Q (Parental Order)* [1996] 1 FLR 369.
[55] See, for example, *U v W (A-G Intervening)* [1998] Fam 29; *Re R (A Child) (IVF: Paternity of a Child)* [2003] 2 AC 621, HL.
[56] See C Lind, 'In Re R (Paternity of IVF Baby) – Unmarried Paternity under the Human Fertilisation and Embryology Act 1990' (2003) 15 *Child and Family Law Quarterly* 327.

There does not seem to be any requirement as such that the man and the woman must be living together or be partners. So a single woman planning to bring her child up largely alone could, if she so wished and he agreed, nominate a friend to act as the child's legal father. When sections 35 and 36 apply, the sperm donor need fear no parental responsibility to his genetic offspring for the husband or the agreed father and no other man is to be treated as the father. But we should note that if DI is carried out outside the UK, or outside a licensed clinic within the UK, and the woman is not married or has no civil partner, the donor will remain the legal father of the child. So if X agrees to help out a friend and gives her sperm for her to self-inseminate, he remains as much the legal father of the child as if the child were conceived naturally.

Gamete donation: the meaning of 'mother'

12.10 IVF created the possibility to treat women who do not ovulate, with donated eggs. Such a woman could have eggs implanted that were donated by another and fertilised with her husband's or partner's sperm, thus enabling her to bear a child. But who is the child's legal mother – the donor or the woman who gives birth? Legally if not physiologically, motherhood is simpler to define than fatherhood, and the new rules in the Human Fertilisation and Embryology Act 2008 do not alter the law. Section 27 of the Human Fertilisation and Embryology Act 1990, applying to a woman treated before April 2009, and section 33, applying to women treated after that date, both set out a simple rule: the woman who carries the child 'as the result of the placing in her of an embryo or sperm and eggs; and no other woman' is the legal mother. Thus if a woman is treated with donor eggs, the donor has no claim on or responsibility to the child. But it also means that if a surrogate carries a child, even using eggs provided from the commissioning mother, it is the surrogate and not the woman who seeks to have the child via surrogacy who is in law the mother. Finally we must note that in the case of embryo transplant or 'adoption' the child may have no genetic link with either parent. If both are infertile, an embryo may be created from donated sperm and eggs or have been a surplus embryo donated by another couple. The woman who carries the child will be the mother and the rules above will determine if her husband or partner is the legal father.

Gamete donation: same sex couples

12.11 The Human Fertilisation and Embryology Act 1990 made no express provision for the growing number of cases where a same-sex couple sought fertility treatment to have a child together. One partner in a lesbian couple might seek DI or IVF with donated sperm with a view to bringing up the child with her partner. The partner would have no legal status in relation to the child unless she later sought to adopt her. The Human Fertilisation and Embryology Act 2008 makes express provision for such couples. The provisions are modelled as closely as possible on those applying to heterosexual couples. Section 42 provides that when two women are in a civil partnership and one becomes pregnant via IVF or DI, the other partner will be treated as a parent of the child unless she did not consent to the treatment of her partner. Section 42 applies whether in the UK or abroad, and to self-insemination as much as treatment in a licensed clinic. Sections 43 and 44 deal with lesbian couples not party to a civil partnership and provide that a second woman can be treated as a parent of the child by virtue of 'agreed female parenthood conditions'. Thus the prospective other parent and the woman being treated must both give notice in writing that they consent to the second woman being treated as a parent of the child. The parenthood provisions only apply if the woman is treated in a licensed clinic in the UK. As with heterosexual couples, when a second woman is treated as the other parent by virtue of the Act, the sperm donor has no legal relationship with his genetic child. But if the couple are not in a civil partnership and perhaps ask a gay male friend to provide sperm for self-insemination, once again the 'partner' obtains no parental status and the sperm donor is in law the father of the child.

Despite the breadth of the new provisions in the 2008 Act, they do not cover all the permutations of parenthood that modern medicine can facilitate.[57] They address only female same-sex couples and make no provision for trans-sexuals. Male couples have to navigate the murky waters of the law governing surrogacy. If two men agree with a surrogate that she will bear a child for them created by the fertilisation of her eggs with sperm from one of them, the latter will be the father of the child and the surrogate the mother. The other partner will, as we shall see later, have to seek an adoption or parental rights order.

Artificial insemination by husband (AIH) or partner (AIP)

12.12   There are rare cases where, although a woman's husband or partner is fertile, he cannot beget a child because he is incapable of normal intercourse. His sperm may be used to impregnate his wife or partner by artificial means.[58] Or the man may produce some sperm, but not sufficient healthy and mobile sperm to achieve fertilisation in the usual way. Such a couple may be helped by Intra Cytoplasmic Sperm Injection (ICSI). A single sperm is injected into the cytoplasm (outer casing) of the woman's egg. IVF is combined with AIH. Concerns have been expressed about the safety of ICSI.[59] The child's legal status will be just the same as if she were conceived naturally. Where normal intercourse was not possible, so that a marriage has never been consummated, AIH

---

[57]   See S McGuinness, A Alghrani, 'Gender and Parenthood: The Case for Realignment' (2008) 16 *Medical Law Review* 261.

[58]   And see *Dickson v UK* [2008] 46 EHRR 41 (above at **12.8**) where a prisoner challenged the refusal by the prison authorities to allow him to arrange to provide sperm to enable his wife to become pregnant.

[59]   Do resulting children face a greater risk of genetic disease? Will some born via ICSI be themselves infertile? See S Mayor, 'Technique for Treating Infertility May Be Risky' (1996) 313 *BMJ* 248.

will not prevent the wife from petitioning the court to annul the marriage,[60] although on policy grounds, the court may refuse a decree if they consider that in having the child the wife approbated the marriage. The child will remain a marital child even if his parents' marriage is later annulled, for they were married when he was conceived and non-consummation only renders a marriage voidable. It does not mean that the marriage was never valid.

AIH or AIP may also be resorted to when a man has banked sperm, for example in advance of chemotherapy for cancer. If he survives and thrives and the couple agree to treatment using the stored sperm no problems arise, but what if he dies and the woman seeks treatment with his sperm? Or she asks a doctor to take sperm from a dying or just dead partner?

Posthumous gamete donation

12.13 The issue of posthumous donation made headlines in the case of Diane Blood. Diane and Stephen Blood had been married for four years before Mr Blood was struck down with meningitis. He lapsed into a coma and died. Shortly before his death, at Mrs Blood's request, doctors used electro-ejaculation to take sperm from her dying husband which was then stored at a licensed fertility clinic. The HFEA instructed the clinic not to treat Mrs Blood, nor to release her husband's sperm to her so that she could seek treatment abroad. The HFEA ruled that the recovery and storage of Stephen Blood's sperm was unlawful under the Human Fertilisation and Embryology Act 1990. The taking of sperm did not comply with Schedule 3 to the 1990 Act which imposed a mandatory requirement for written 'effective' consent. No such written consent had ever been given by Mr Blood, although his widow argued that they had planned to start a family, and that Stephen had told her that in the kind of tragic circumstances which ultimately overtook him she should do just as she did.

Mrs Blood challenged the HFEA by way of an application for judicial review, alleging that it was the HFEA who were acting unlawfully. The High Court upheld the HFEA, but Mrs Blood succeeded in the Court of Appeal.[61] The appeal court agreed that the taking of sperm without Mr Blood's written consent was unlawful. It contravened the 1990 Act, and constituted a common law assault. The court expressed sympathy with Mrs Blood. She had acted in good faith. There should be no question of prosecution. Nonetheless, treatment in the UK would be unlawful. However, the Court of Appeal held that the HFEA had failed to give sufficient consideration to EU law.[62] Section 24 (4) of the Human Fertilisation and Embryology Act 1990 permitted the HFEA

---

[60] *L v L* [1949] P 211.

[61] [1997] 2 All ER 687, CA. See D Morgan and R Lee, 'In the Name of the Father? *Ex parte Blood* Dealing with Novelty and Anomaly' (1997) 60 *Modern Law Review* 84.

[62] See T Hervey, 'Buy Baby: The European Union and Regulation of Human Reproduction' (1998) 18 *Oxford Journal of Legal Studies* 207.

to issue directions authorising the export of sperm. Articles 59 and 60 of the Treaty of Rome guarantee certain fundamental freedoms, which include a right to receive services. Such a right is not absolute, but any limitations on that right must be justified. Given that the Court's ruling that taking sperm without written consent was unlawful, the Court said that the circumstances of Mrs Blood's case would not be repeated. The Court of Appeal directed the HFEA to reconsider Mrs Blood's request to export sperm. They did so and granted her permission to take her husband's sperm to Belgium where she finally received treatment and gave birth to a healthy son, Liam, followed some years later by a second son. The narrow grounds of the appeal court's ruling in Mrs Blood's favour left domestic law unchanged. No woman in a similar position would benefit. Unless the deceased then had given formal written consent to storing and use of his sperm,[63] no British clinic could treat his widow or former partner. But the judicial optimism that there would be no repeat of the *Blood* case proved ill founded. In *L v Human Fertilisation and Embryology Authority*,[64] L's husband died suddenly in the course of a minor operation. L obtained an order that it was lawful to retrieve sperm from his body and the sperm was then stored at a licensed clinic. L sought to argue that the absolute rule that prevented her using the sperm contravened both EU law and Article 8 of the ECHR. She failed. The judge found that while the retrieval of the sperm fell outside the Act and indeed, immediate use of the sperm might have done so too, he had no power to declare that continued storage of the sperm was lawful. The power vested in the HFEA to allow the sperm to be exported meant that EU Treaty rights were not violated and later the HFEA authorised the export of the sperm retrieved from L's husband so that she, like Mrs Blood, could seek treatment abroad.

After the *Blood* case, Professor Sheila McLean conducted an extensive review of the law on consent and removal of gametes, but recommended only limited changes in the law.[65] One change did, however, result from the review and Mrs Blood's campaign to have her dead husband recognised as her sons' father. The Human Fertilisation and Embryology (Deceased Father) Act 2003 amended section 28(6) of the Human Fertilisation and Embryology Act 1990 to allow the name of the deceased (genetic) father to be entered on the child's birth certificate. That Act has now been repealed and sections 28(5) A–I of the 1990 Act as amended by the Human Fertilisation and Embryology Act 2008 address questions of post-mortem fatherhood in relation to women treated before April 2009 and sections 39–41 address children born as a result of treatment after that date. Under both Acts the written consent of the husband or partner remains an essential pre-condition to lawful treatment. Assuming that such a consent is present and the woman is successfully treated and bears a child, she has forty-two days to elect to have her deceased husband or partner

---

[63] A number of children have been born after posthumous AIH where the requisite written consent had been given.

[64] [2008] EWHC 2149.

[65] Review of Common Law Provision Relating to the Removal of Gametes and of the Consent Provision in the Human Fertilisation and Embryology Act 1990 (1998).

treated as the father of the child in the sense that his name will be entered into the Register of Births. However, the child born in such circumstances remains ineligible to inherit from his genetic father's estate.

The 2008 Act has not substantially changed the law and the *Blood* case leaves more questions unanswered than it resolves. If Stephen Blood's sperm had been lawfully stored, would Diane Blood have been able to demand treatment? It seems unlikely; the ultimate decision remains with the clinician. In the context of private treatment, a widow might seek to argue that she has a contractual right to AIH. The possibility remains of attempts to contend that the frozen sperm form part of the deceased husband's estate. Should a court accept that sperm can be classified as 'property' and 'inherited' by the wife, it would logically follow that she could demand 'her' sperm, but she could still not require the DI clinic to inseminate her.[66] In the light of the underlying philosophy of the 1990 and 2008 Acts, it seems at first sight unlikely that such a 'property' argument would succeed. But consider the judgment of the Court of Appeal in *Yearworth v North Bristol NHS Trust*.[67] The claimants sued in negligence after sperm banked in advance of treatment for cancer was negligently allowed to thaw. The appeal court held that for the purposes of a claim in negligence the men enjoyed property rights in that sperm and could be awarded damages for the damage to their property.

Gamete donation: supply and demand

12.14 For many prospective parents seeking fertility treatment, access to suitable donated gametes is crucial to their treatment. Both eggs and sperm are in short supply and so there have been several proposals to increase supply, many attracting controversy. Eggs donors are especially hard to recruit. Unlike sperm donation, egg donation is attended by some risk to the donor. Egg donation requires a surgical procedure, an invasion of the donor's body. The woman will be given drugs to induce her to supra-ovulate, to produce several eggs at once. Supra-ovulation carries risks to the health and in a very, very few cases to the life of the woman. A woman undergoing IVF runs identical risks. She does so to have 'her' baby. Egg donors are asked to risk harm with no prospect of benefit to themselves. Healthy volunteers who agree to participate in medical research are invited to act in a similarly altruistic manner. What might be done to improve the supply of both eggs and sperm? All we can do here is offer a few examples.

In its submission to Warnock long ago, the Royal College of Obstetricians and Gynaecologists (RCOG) suggested that eggs might 'conveniently' be collected from patients undergoing sterilisation or hysterectomy. Such action might be seen as avoiding unnecessary surgical *interference* by using women already

---

[66] See the discussion in I Kennedy and A Grubb, *Medical Law: Text and Materials* (3rd edn, 2000) Butterworths, pp 1308–1315.
[67] [2009] EWCA Civ 37; discussed below at **18.9**.

scheduled for surgery. The procedure for collecting eggs is relatively simple and risk-free. The risks centre on supra-ovulation. A woman asked to donate eggs concurrently with other surgery is in effect asked to agree to a further risky and, for her, unnecessary procedure. Will she be in a proper state of mind to give a full and free consent? Will she feel constrained to 'help out' the doctor treating her?[68] Of particular concern has been the practice of offering free sterilisation to women who agree to be donors. Waiting lists for NHS sterilisations can be lengthy. For a woman to be offered a private sterilisation free of charge is a powerful inducement to agree to donate eggs.

If inducements are to be contemplated at all, why do we not simply pay gamete providers? Direct payment to buy eggs, sperm or embryos is currently unlawful in the UK unless authorised by directions from the HFEA.[69] The HFEA used to allow a 'fee' for eggs or sperm of up to £15. In response to requirements in the EU Tissue Directive[70] to promote wholly altruistic tissue donation, the HFEA limited recompense to gamete donors to expenses and loss of income. Sums of around £15 for sperm donors and considerably more to egg donors are lawfully paid by way of expenses, but there must be no profit to the donor. The HFEA has launched a major consultation on several issues relating to donation including the question of whether more substantial payments should be authorised.[71] To encourage a greater pool of egg providers, the reward would need to run into thousands of pounds. In the USA, payments of $50k are not unknown in order to attract tall, healthy, highly intelligent college students to sell their eggs.[72] The HFEA still uses cautious language speaking only of expenses, compensation and benefits in kind.

One such benefit in kind is 'egg sharing'. If an open 'egg market' is not allowed in the UK, does 'egg sharing' operate as a covert market? Women who are undergoing egg collection as part of their own IVF treatment agree to donate a proportion of their eggs to others. In return, they receive free IVF. 'Egg sharing' avoids subjecting the donor to risks unrelated to her own treatment.[73] But does the invitation to 'egg sharing' operate as a questionable inducement to women who could never afford private fertility treatment? Unless they agree to 'egg sharing', some women have no chance of treatment by IVF. How might a donor feel if she learns that the recipient of her eggs had a successful pregnancy, when she did not?

---

[68] See *Mason and McCall Smith*, p 269.
[69] See s 12(e) of the Human Fertilisation and Embryology Act 1990.
[70] Directive on Setting Standards of Quality and Safety for the Donation, Testing, Processing, Preservation, Storage and Distribution of Human Tissues and Cells (Directive 2004/23/EC).
[71] Press Release, *HFEA Launches Public Consultation on Sperm and Egg Donation* (17 January 2011) accessible at http://www.hfea.gov.uk/6285.
[72] See E Jackson, *Medical Law: Text, Cases and Materials* (2nd edn, 2010) OUP, pp 789–790.
[73] See Human Fertilisation and Embryology Authority, *Code of Practice* (8th edn, 2009), paras 21.1–12.32.

For women who have to undergo medical treatment that may compromise their fertility or women who simply want to preserve and freeze eggs to allow them to delay motherhood, it is now possible for them to store their own eggs (or a portion of ovarian tissue) for future use. Freezing eggs proved more difficult than freezing sperm.[74] More damage is caused when the eggs are thawed. Freezing sections of ovarian tissue may be more successful in the long term. When the woman wishes to contemplate pregnancy, the ovarian tissue (with eggs intact) is simply re-implanted.

Most of the problems surrounding storing eggs and ovarian tissue taken from the intending mother herself are generated by questions about the safety of the procedure. For example, if ovarian tissue is taken from a woman about to undergo chemotherapy for cancer, is there a risk of re-implanting cancer cells in her? Legal and ethical dilemmas are not absent. If a child of seven is about to undergo chemotherapy, can her parents authorise surgical removal of ovarian tissue in case their daughter once an adult, wants to have children? Is such a procedure in the child's interests? Perhaps that will depend on the depths of immediate risk and distress posed to the child by additional surgery. The prospect of adult women choosing to 'bank' eggs for future use appals some people. Storing eggs avoids some of the practical and moral problems that arise if embryos are stored.[75]

It is technically possible to collect immature eggs from foetuses.[76] Aborted female foetuses could be collected, 'their' eggs harvested and subjected to a process of maturation. A plentiful supply of eggs would be secured. Controversy over such a possibility led to amendment of the Human Fertilisation and Embryology Act 1990. Section 3A now bans treatment using eggs derived from foetuses. Research can still lawfully continue.

Ovarian tissue might be taken from dead women, just as kidneys and other organs are taken from cadaver donors. Such a process would need to meet the legal conditions currently provided for by both the Human Tissue Act 2004 *and* Schedule 3 to the 1990 Act.

Storing gametes and embryos

12.15 The capacity to freeze and store gametes and embryos has been crucial to the improvement of success rates in fertility treatment.[77] Storage of gam-

---

[74] Though note that children have been born using frozen eggs.

[75] No question of destroying embryos arises if a woman decides later that she does not wish to have children. And a woman who stores her eggs avoids the fate that overtook Natalie Evans. See *Evans v UK* [2006] ECHR discussed below at **12.15**.

[76] See HFEA, *Donated Ovarian Tissue in Embryo Research and Assisted Conception* (1994).

[77] The first British baby to 'start life' as a frozen embryo, was born in Manchester in 1985.

etes and embryos is lawful only if licensed by the HFEA.[78] Storage has generated its own ethical and legal conundrums. The 1990 Act (as amended) now prescribes a maximum statutory storage period of ten years for both gametes and embryos.[79] Freezing inevitably means that at the end of the storage period there will be embryos left unused. The Act requires that such embryos be 'allowed to perish'.[80] In 1996, the first storage period for embryos (then set at five years) came to an end, and thousands of embryos were to be disposed of. In many cases, clinics had lost all contact with the gamete donors (or parents). A public outcry greeted the fate of what the media styled the 'orphan embryos'. The government used powers under the Human Fertilisation and Embryology Act 1990 to extend the storage period for embryos from five to ten years in certain cases[81] and it is now ten years in all cases. But the furore around 'orphan embryos' remains instructive. If embryos can be equated to orphan children, they should not be created doomed to die. If children, these 'orphans' should have been offered to other infertile couples for adoption. If embryos are morally insignificant, they should be put to some good use, whether that use was to help other infertile couples or forward research.

As to the fate of embryos in storage prior to their expiry date, the Human Fertilisation and Embryology Act 1990 requires anyone storing gametes or embryos to decide what may or may not be done with those embryos before any treatment begins. The donors of the genetic material jointly decide its fate in foreseeable circumstances. But what if they disagree? In *Evans v Amicus Healthcare Ltd*,[82] Natalie Evans wanted to be able to have 'her' frozen embryos implanted to establish a pregnancy. Her former partner, Howard Johnson, refused to agree and sought to have the embryos destroyed. Some years earlier, Ms Evans had been diagnosed with pre-cancerous tumours in both ovaries. She was advised to have her ovaries removed. As the cancer was growing slowly, there was time for her and her partner to undergo IVF and freeze embryos for future use. Ms Evans enquired about the possibility of freezing her eggs and was told that success rates using frozen eggs were much lower than where frozen embryos were used. Her partner reassured her that they would not split up, but would go on to have children together when she was fully recovered and clear of cancer. Both partners signed the necessary forms consenting to storage of the embryos. A year later, the relationship broke down and Mr Johnson notified the clinic that he withdrew his consent to storage of the embryos and asked that they be destroyed. Ms Evans was prepared to undertake that she would never make a financial claim for child support and argued that the stored embryos offered her her only chance to have a child genetically related to her.

---

[78] S 4.
[79] See s 14(3)(4). S 14(5) allows for reduction or extension of these periods by regulations.
[80] S 14(1)(c).
[81] Human Fertilisation and Embryology (Statutory Storage Period for Embryos) Regulations 1996, SI 1996/375.
[82] [2004] EWCA Civ 727.

The obstacle confronting Ms Evans, when persuasion failed to change her former partner's mind, lay in Schedule 3 to the Human Fertilisation and Embryology Act 1990. To summarise, any continuing storage of the embryos and any use (ie implantation) of the embryos required the 'effective consent' of both the parties who had contributed the gametes creating the embryos. 'Effective consent' means a consent 'which has not been withdrawn'. Mr Johnson had withdrawn his consent to continued storage of the embryos and never gave any consent to Ms Evans to use the embryos on her own. Wall J held that Schedule 3 made it clear that the continuing consent of both parties was required and that either party was free to withdraw that consent.[83] The Court of Appeal upheld his judgment.[84] Throughout the litigation in England, Ms Evans argued that if Schedule 3 was interpreted to require Mr Johnson's continuing consent, the 1990 Act was incompatible with Ms Evans' rights under Articles 8, 12 and 14 of the European Convention on Human Rights. Her rights to family life and to found a family were violated by an absolute rule that denied her her only chance to have a genetically related child. The Court of Appeal held (inter alia) that any interference with Ms Evans' right to private and family life under Article 8(1) was justifiable within the terms of Article 8(2). Permitting implantation without Mr Johnson's consent would violate his Article 8 rights. Justification for violating the father's right to self-determination and autonomy could not be based on any claim that violation was necessary to protect Ms Evans' right:[85]

> The need, as perceived by Parliament, is for bilateral consent to implantation … To dilute this requirement in the interests of proportionality, in order to meet Ms Evans' otherwise intractable biological handicap, would create new and even more intractable difficulties of arbitrariness and inconsistency.

Ms Evans took her case to the ECtHR. She lost again in both the European court of first instance[86] and the Grand Chamber.[87] The Court noted that there is no consensus among Convention states, or internationally, as to how to regulate consent to implantation of embryos. A number of states conform to the UK model, allowing consent to be withdrawn up to the time of implantation. Others limit the male partner's right of veto. Ms Evans sought to argue that her circumstances were exceptional and precluded the Court from deciding that this vexed question of consent fell within the margin of appreciation allowed to member states. Destruction of the embryos destroyed her right to reproduce. Permitting the consent regime in the Human Fertilisation and

---

[83] [2003] EWHC 2161 (Fam).

[84] [2004] EWCA Civ 727; see A Alghrani, 'Deciding the Fate of Frozen Embryos' (2005) 15 *Medical Law Review* 244.

[85] [2004] EWCA Civ 227 at para 69 per Thorpe LJ.

[86] [2006] 1 FCR 585 (ECtHR). The House of Lords declined to hear Ms Evans' appeal. See T Annett, 'Balancing Competing Interests Over Frozen Embryos: The Judgment of Solomon' (2006) 14 *Medical Law Review* 425; C Lind, '*Evans v United Kingdom* – Judgments of Solomon: Power, Gender and Procreation' (2006) 18 *Child and Family Law Quarterly* 576.

[87] [2008] 46 EHRR 34.

Embryology Act 1990 to stand was not necessary or proportionate. The position of women and men could not be equated. Mr Johnson might suffer some violation of his right to determine his reproductive fate. Ms Evans' right was obliterated. Despite sympathy from the European judges, the Court held that the UK regime was based on a clear and principled rule and fell within the margin of appreciation. The Grand Chamber concurred.

The 2008 Act made one small change to help anyone finding themselves in the same position as Natalie Evans, amending Schedule 3 to the 1990 Act to provide that if one party withdraws consent to storage of embryos, a one-year 'cooling off' period should be introduced before the embryos have to be destroyed.[88] Within that year, the hope is that the parties can reach some agreement about the future of the embryos.

Pre-implantation genetic diagnosis (PGD)

12.16 Advances in reproductive medicine have helped not only infertile couples, but also couples who risked transmitting a genetic disease to their children. Much progress has been made in a short time. Initially a woman who was a haemophilia carrier could avoid giving birth to an affected son by opting for egg donation. PGD offers such a woman the chance to have her own genetic child. Embryos are created by IVF, and PGD is used to screen out embryos affected by the relevant genetic disease. Only healthy embryos are selected for implantation. In some cases, PGD involves sex selection for medical reasons, for example, screening out male embryos potentially susceptible to haemophilia. As PGD develops, doctors become more able to refine the screening process and identify affected, and unaffected, embryos.

The Human Fertilisation and Embryology Act 1990 made no express provision for PGD and it was the HFEA that developed the framework within which PGD could lawfully be offered to couples at risk of transmitting a genetic disease. Not everybody applauded this development and PGD has been criticised both on the grounds that it involves deliberate destruction of embryos and that in screening out disabled embryos it discriminates against disabled people and reinforces negative images of disability.[89] Pro-life groups challenged the legality of PGD, arguing that the HFEA had no power to license a treatment for couples who could have children without assistance. The Court of Appeal[90] confirmed that HFEA policy permitting PGD was lawful under the Act in that for couples affected by a risk of transmitting such disease PGD constituted treatment 'for the purpose of assisting women to carry children'. A process that enabled the woman to become pregnant free from the fear that

---

88 See Sch 3, para 4A(4).
89 See R Scott, 'Choosing Between Possible Lives: Legal and Ethical Issues in Pre-Implantation Genetic Diagnosis' (2006) *Oxford Journal of Legal Studies* 153.
90 *R (on the application of Quintavalle) v Human Fertilisation and Embryology Authority* [2003] 3 All ER 257, CA.

her child would be affected by a serious genetic disease was one that assisted her to carry a child. Amendments to the 1990 Act now set out a statutory framework for PGD modelled on HFEA policy. The provisions are lengthy and complex and we do no more than set out the basics here. Schedule 2 1ZA to the Act now provides that PGD may be licensed to establish if the embryo has a defect affecting its capacity to result in live birth, in any case where there is a particular risk that the embryo may have a gene, chromosomal or mitochondrial abnormality, or to establish gender where there is a particular risk of a serious gender-related condition. In cases where PGD is licensed in relation to an abnormality in the embryo, it must further be shown that there is significant risk that, if born, the person would have or develop a serious disability or illness. It is clear that not every genetic anomaly will qualify as 'serious'. The ends of the spectrum are easy to discern. You could not license PGD to screen out red hair. Dreadful diseases, for example, Tay-Sachs where the child born is condemned to early disability and death while little more than an infant, clearly meet the test. Other conditions will provoke debate and prospective parents may have different perceptions about both risk and seriousness. The HFEA *Code of Practice* places a great deal of emphasis on consultation with the couple and their subjective judgment of the condition that they seek to avoid for their child.[91] Whether this approach meets the conditions now laid down in the Act remains to be seen.

What about late onset diseases where a child is born healthy but carries a gene that results in serious illness later in life? For example, if BRAC1, the gene predisposing family members to breast cancer, is present in the prospective mother, can she seek PGD to ensure that any child she bears is free of that gene? The amended Act once again endorses the prior policy of the HFEA in permitting PGD for late onset disease[92] in including not just persons who will be born with a genetic disease but also those who may develop such a disease.[93]

PGD and 'saviour siblings'

12.17 It was the development of the ability to use PGD as the first step to offering treatment to a sick child that provoked especial controversy, what is popularly described as the creation of 'saviour siblings'. Parents who have a child already afflicted by a potentially fatal genetic disorder can seek to have

---

[91] HFEA *Code of Practice* (8th edn), paras 10.4–10.6; and see R Scott, C Williams, K Ehrich and B Farsides, 'The Appropriate Extent of Pre-implantation Genetic Diagnosis: Health Professionals' and Scientists' View on the Requirement for a Significant Risk of a Serious Genetic Condition' (2007) 15 *Medical Law Review* 320.

[92] HFEA, *Choices and Boundaries* (2006).

[93] Note that PGD to establish if a person is a carrier of a genetic abnormality is not permitted as such by the amended Sch 2 but tests for a recessive condition may disclose that there are embryos which are not affected by the disease themselves but are carriers and could lawfully then not be selected for implantation.

another baby whose stem cells, taken from her umbilical cord, could 'cure' her brother or sister. PGD is combined with tissue typing the embryos via Human Antigen Tissue Typing (HLA). By this means, a baby is created who is both unaffected by the genetic disorder in question, and an exact tissue match for the sick sibling. Opponents of PGD/HLA argued that it was wrong to create a baby purely as a means to an end. But desperate parents often make several attempts to have a baby naturally to achieve just that end – a tissue match for a sick child. Nothing in the original 1990 Act addressed this question. The HFEA struggled to deal with the dilemma. The Authority gave a clinic permission to treat Zain Hashmi. Zain suffered from *beta thallasaemia* (BT), a genetic disease. His family could provide no compatible stem cell donor. So his parents sought PGD with HLA. Charlie Whitaker suffered from Diamond Blackfan Anaemia (DBA). His parents also wanted to use PGD with HLA to create a 'saviour sibling' for Charlie. The HFEA said no. The Hashmi embryo was itself at risk of BT. DBA is not thought to be a genetic disease, so the HFEA initially argued that Whitaker embryos could not be screened as they would obtain no benefit. The distinction between the two cases met vigorous criticism.[94] The HFEA changed its mind.

Meanwhile pro-life groups challenged the legality of the HFEA decision to allow PGD with HLA in the Hashmi case. Ultimately, the House of Lords[95] ruled in favour of the HFEA, confining themselves to an exercise in statutory interpretation and seeking to side-step moral controversy. Now amendments to the Human Fertilisation and Embryology Act 1990 give statutory backing to the use of PGD/HLA to create saviour siblings. Schedule 2, para 1ZA, expressly allows testing on the embryo to ascertain if the tissue of the embryo would be compatible with an existing sibling who suffers from a serious illness that could be treated by umbilical cord cells, bone marrow or other tissue from the child to be born. Other tissue is expressly defined to exclude solid organs. But while this prohibition would mean that tissue typing could not go ahead were there an intent to resort to organ donation at the time of the creation of the saviour embryo, it would not of itself make it unlawful to authorise organ donation later if all other measures had failed. A living transplant from a minor would however require approval under the Human Tissue Act 2004 and that would be unlikely to be forthcoming.[96]

PGD: selecting for 'disability'

12.18 As the 2008 Act made its way through Parliament, a new controversy erupted. PGD is normally used to screen out certain sorts of serious disease or disability. What if a couple wanted to screen in a particular condition, for

[94] See S Sheldon and S Wilkinson, 'Hashmi and Whitaker: An Unjustifiable and Misguided Distinction' (2004) 12 *Medical Law Review* 137.
[95] *R (on the application of Quintavalle v Human Fertilisation and Embryology Authority* [2005] 2 All ER 555, HL.
[96] See below **17.5**.

example a deaf couple wanted to ensure that their child was also deaf?[97] They want their child to be part of their community and challenge society's notion of deafness as disability. Sections 13(8)–(10) of the Human Fertilisation and Embryology Act 1990 as amended now provide that embryos known to have a serious abnormality 'must not be preferred to those not known to have such an abnormality'. Nor must a gamete donor known to carry such an abnormality be preferred to one who is not. Note the limits of the statute. First, is it clear that deafness would qualify as sufficiently serious under the Act? If it did, note that the Act does not ban implantation of the 'deaf embryo' – just that it cannot be selected if there are unaffected embryos created at the same treatment. We assume that the couple could choose to have none implanted and try again for the embryo of their choice.

PGD: social sex selection

12.19   It may be that at the root of concerns about PGD lies discomfort with the notion of parents having a free choice of what kind of children they have – the prospect of 'designer babies'. The UK legislation as it relates to PGD is heavily based on a medical model, so testing an embryo to establish its gender is allowed to avoid the birth of a child with a sex-linked genetic disease. But should the law allow sex selection for non-medical reasons? A couple with three sons want a daughter to 'balance' their family.[98] A single woman wants only female children. Despite strong support for lifting any ban on social sex selection, the law is now clear. It is unlawful to use PGD to test for gender save in the context of gender-linked disease.[99] Nor can techniques based on sperm sorting be allowed, that is separating X and Y sperm and using only Y sperm to inseminate the woman wanting a son and vice versa. The legislation now prohibits any use of sperm without a licence, save as we have seen for partner-donated sperm that has not been processed. Sorting will constitute processing. The debate will continue.

What should the child be told?

12.20   Does a child born after the use of donor gametes have a right to know the identity of his genetic parents? An adopted child has, at eighteen, a right of access to his original birth certificate and so has the opportunity to trace his natural parents.[100] If an adopted child may trace his birth mother and genetic father, should children born from gamete donation be afforded a similar right? Until August 2005, anonymity protected all gamete donors, while affording

---

[97]   See J Savulescu, 'Deaf Lesbians, "Designer Disability" and the Future of Medicine' (2002) 325 *BMJ* 771.

[98]   S Wilkinson, ' Racism and Sexism in Medically Assisted Conception' (1998) 12 *Bioethics* 25.

[99]   Sch 2, para 1ZB.

[100]   Adoption Act 1976, s 51(2).

some limited rights to children born as a result of donation. Section 31 of the 1990 Act required the HFEA to keep a register detailing the provision of treatment services and the use of gametes. At the age of eighteen a person could, after proper counselling, request information from that register, Section 31(4)(b) provided that information *must* include information about whether or not the applicant and a person whom he proposes to marry are related. Section 31(4)(a) provided that such other information relating to the applicant 'as the Authority is required by regulations to give' shall be made available to him. The wording of section 31(4)(a) was such that the HFEA would be free to decide that the information should include the *identity* of the child's genetic parents, the gamete donors. Section 31(5), however, ensured that any removal of anonymity could not be retrospective. If anonymity prevailed when sperm was donated, a later change in the rules will not give children access to the identity of the donor. Regulations removing anonymity from gamete donors were brought into force in April 2005,[101] and are now consolidated in the heavily amended section 31 of the Human Fertilisation and Embryology Act 1990. The 'new' section 31 provides that a person will, at the age of eighteen, acquire the right to information about the identity of donor parents.[102] An offer of counselling must be made to the applicant before any information is released. But the new rules cannot apply retrospectively, so no pre-existing donor risks losing his or her anonymity. Anyone donating now is aware that his or her offspring may be able to trace them and make contact and the HFEA has a power to warn donors when requests for information are made.

Clinics fear that loss of prospective anonymity will exacerbate the acute shortage of gamete donors. Some children will acquire the right to know the identity of a genetic parent at the expense of couples who remain childless for lack of donors. The removal of anonymity to donors was prompted by powerful arguments that the child's interests in private and family life require that she has access to such information. A person's psychological well-being is, it is claimed, intimately connected to a sense of identity and heritage. If donation is seen as an ethical, altruistic act, why must it be kept secret? If adopted children need to know the identity of their genetic parents, why are the needs of children born from gamete or embryo donation less pressing?[103] Granting a young man who had spent a miserable childhood in care access to all the files held on him, the European Court of Human Rights declared[104] that '. . . everyone should be able to establish details of their identity as individual human beings'. And in *R (on the application of Rose) v Secretary of State for Health*,[105] Scott Baker J held that Article 8 of the European Convention on Human Rights was relevant to

---

[101] Human Fertilisation and Embryology Authority (Disclosure of Donor Information) Regulations 2004, SI 2004/1511.

[102] And about possible half-siblings.

[103] But see K O'Donovan, 'What Shall We Tell the Children? Reflections on Children's Perspectives and the Reproduction Revolution' in R Lee and D Morgan (eds), *Birthrights: Law and Ethics and the Beginning of Life* (1989) Routledge.

[104] *Gaskin v UK* [1990] 1 FLR 167.

[105] [2002] EWHC 1593.

the question of what access to information children born via assisted conception should enjoy.

Liability for disability

12.21 What if fertility treatment results in the birth of a disabled infant? This could happen for several reasons. In DI, the donor may turn out to be the carrier of some disease or genetic disorder. Babies have been born abroad suffering from HIV contracted from donor sperm. An error may be made in the laboratory, damaging an IVF embryo. Or treatment, such as ICSI, might in years to come be shown to produce abnormalities manifesting themselves only when the children reach maturity.

Parents will be able to maintain an action against the doctors and the clinic if mother or child is injured by negligence. Clearly, if the mother herself suffers any injury, for example, in the course of collecting eggs, she may recover compensation for that injury. The woman accepted for treatment expects care, not only in relation to herself, but also in the 'production' of a healthy infant. If, by negligence, the child is born disabled, damage to the parents is readily foreseeable. Both mother and father will suffer emotional trauma and face the added expense of bringing up a disabled child.[106] Is there a problem if the parents cannot pinpoint exactly who was negligent? It may be impossible for them to know if the embryo was damaged by the gynaecologist removing the eggs and implanting the embryo, or by the scientists in the laboratory. In NHS clinics, the NHS trust owes a direct duty to the parents and is responsible for negligently failing to discharge that duty. In the private sector, patients should ensure that the clinic similarly undertakes a contractual duty to provide and underwrite the whole course of treatment. Exactly what the contractual terms agreed with a private clinic entail may be crucial. A couple successfully sued a private clinic who implanted three embryos in the woman after she had specifically stated that no more than two embryos should be replaced. The clinic was held liable for breach of contract and responsible for the birth of a third child.[107] One final point relating to actions by parents is that, while they may have legal redress if a damaged baby is born, there will be no legal remedy if no baby is born. Neither NHS nor private clinics undertake more than to attempt to assist conception using all due skill and care.

What of an action by the child? He will need to rely on the right of action in respect of pre-natal injuries enacted in the Congenital Disabilities (Civil Liability) Act 1976.[108] The Human Fertilisation and Embryology Act 1990 expressly amends the 1976 Act to allow for an action arising out of negligence in the process of assisted conception. Section 44 inserts into the 1976 Act a section

---

[106] See *Parkinson v St James and Seacroft University Hospital NHS Trust* [2001] 3 All ER 97, CA.

[107] *Thompson v Sheffield Fertility Centre* (2000) 24 November (unreported) (QBD).

[108] See above at **11.7**.

1A which provides for an action if a child carried by a woman as a result of the placing in her of an embryo, or sperm and eggs, or DI, is born disabled, and the disability results from negligence in the selection, or keeping or use outside the body, of the relevant embryo or gametes. Providing the defendant is answerable in tort to one or both parents, he is liable to the child. The sorts of cases envisaged by section 1A are just the sort of examples mentioned earlier – the child born HIV-positive because doctors failed to screen donors adequately, the child born damaged by some technical error in his creation, and the child born disabled because a defective embryo was negligently implanted in the mother. A further extension to the rights of the child is made in section 35(4) of the 1990 Act, again amending the 1976 Act, to provide that injury to the reproductive capacity of the genetic parent gives rise to a derivative action under the 1976 Act for the child. Sections 34 and 35 of the 1990 Act make extensive provision for disclosure of information necessary to any action by parent or child for damages occasioned by assisted conception.

One difficulty facing an action by the child remains. Is the essence of his action for 'wrongful life', or 'wrongful disability'? If the former, no action can lie.[109] Much will then turn on how it is alleged the child came to suffer injury. If it is claimed that gametes and embryo were originally healthy, but damaged by some act of the doctors or scientists treating the mother, the claim is for 'wrongful disability'. It is on a par with a claim that a healthy foetus was damaged *in utero* by drugs given to the mother. But what if the alleged negligence is that infected sperm was used to inseminate the mother or a defective embryo was implanted in her? Such a claim must logically be classified as a 'wrongful life' claim. Assume these facts: a clinic negligently fails to check donors for HIV; Baby X is born with HIV from contaminated sperm; had the clinic exercised due care in the collection of sperm, that individual, Baby X, would never had been born at all. Similarly, if a defective embryo is not screened and discarded in the laboratory, any action the child brings is for 'wrongful life'. His parents could, 'but for' the relevant negligence, have had a healthy child. He would not have been that child.

Both parents and children seeking compensation for disability will face problems proving negligence where it is difficult to isolate the cause of the damage to the child. A baby resulting from DI, born HIV-positive, or afflicted by a genetic disease carried by the father, poses no legal problem in a claim by his parents. Competent screening should have discovered the disease or defect and that sperm should never have been used to inseminate the mother. Linking a defect to an error in the laboratory will be less easy. An action based on abnormalities manifesting themselves later in life is almost bound to fail. If in 2015 it is shown that freezing embryos produces cancer in the late teens and early twenties, the defence to any claim in negligence will be that responsible professional opinion, endorsed by countless official reports, believed freezing to be safe in 1995 when the child was born.

---

[109] See *McKay v Essex Area Health Authority* [1982] 2 All ER 771, CA, discussed above at **11.11**.

Finally, if parent or child has a right to sue and proves negligence, are there defences open to the doctor based on the parents having agreed to run the risk of a damaged child? Section 44(3) of the Human Fertilisation and Embryology Act 1990 provides that an action by the child shall fail if either or both parents knew of the risk of their child being born disabled '. . . that is to say, the particular risk created by the act of omission'. So if the mother is known to carry a genetic disease herself and is counselled that it would be better to use donor eggs for an IVF pregnancy, yet insists on a child who is genetically hers, she cannot turn round and sue the doctors who carried out her wishes if her genetic problem is inherited by her child. However, it would be no defence for a defendant simply to say, 'Well, parents know that this is a relatively new and risky process, so I am not liable.' The parents must be aware of the particular risk of harming their child. Often the risk of harm arises from the increased danger of a multiple pregnancy. A parent who was not fully counselled on this risk might argue that not warning of that particular risk was negligent. To succeed in an action she would then have to prove that had she been warned she would not have gone ahead with the treatment.

Reproductive cloning

12.22　Human reproductive cloning is illegal in the UK. It does not matter how the 'clone' is created. When Parliament enacted the Human Fertilisation and Embryology Act 1990, the intent was to ban any form of reproductive cloning and the assumption was that section 3(1)(d) outlawed any form of human cloning. Replacing the nucleus of an embryo with the nucleus of a cell taken from any other person or embryo was prohibited. The development of cell nuclear replacement (CNR), heralded by the birth of Dolly the sheep, highlighted the inadequacy of section 3(1)(d). Placing the donated nucleus into an emptied egg still fell outside the prohibition. As we shall see in the next chapter, the government sought to permit the HFEA to license the use of CNR in developing stem cell therapies, often referred to as therapeutic cloning.[110] Reproductive cloning was condemned.[111] Pro-life groups, however, challenged the regulations, arguing that CNR embryos fell outside the 1990 Act altogether because the embryos were not created by fertilisation. Their victory at first instance[112] led to the Human Reproductive Cloning Act 2001 prohibiting the implantation in a woman of an embryo 'created otherwise than by fertilisation'.[113] That Act has now been repealed. The amendments to the 1990 Act made by the 2008 Act make it clear that embryo is defined to include

---

[110] See Human Fertilisation and Embryology (Research Purposes) Regulations 2001, SI 2001/188.

[111] HFEA/HGAC, *Cloning Issues in Reproduction, Science and Medicine* (1998).

[112] *R (on the application of Quintavalle) v Secretary of State for Health* [2001] 4 All ER 1019.

[113] And see *R (on the application of Quintavalle) v Secretary of State for Health* [2003] 2 All ER 113, HL.

embryos created by fertilisation or 'any other process capable of resulting in an embryo'.[114] Only 'permitted embryos' may be implanted in a woman and that excludes any cloned embryo.[115]

Several arguments are advanced for,[116] and against, reproductive cloning.[117] Safety is a concern that all parties in the debate share. Mammalian cloning has shown a high rate of birth defects and miscarriage. But research might overcome this hurdle to permitting cloning. Other arguments centre on the impact on the cloned child of her means of production. She will (it is said) lack a unique genetic identity, but so does any identical twin. If she is a clone of her mother, she will see her genetic future mapped out from birth. Moreover, she may be condemned to live more generally in her creator's shadow – a copy, not a daughter. If she is a clone of a dead sibling, her parent(s) may not value her, but rather the ghost of her sister. Yet environment shapes us as much as our DNA. A clone of either of the authors would grow up in different times and with different parents. Confusion about relationships is another problem for a clone. A clone of Emma Cave would have Emma for her mother? Or would Emma's mother be mother to the clone? The Emma clone would be truly fatherless. The debate goes on. Yet Mason and Laurie[118] 'suspect that the days of the outright prohibition on reproductive cloning are numbered'.

Surrogacy

12.23   Where a woman is unable to carry a child herself, perhaps because she has undergone a hysterectomy or has endured several miscarriages, surrogacy may be her and her partner's only hope for a child. Surrogacy can take a number of forms. In *partial surrogacy*, a surrogate agrees with the commissioning couple to undergo artificial insemination with the man's sperm. She agrees to carry any resulting child, and to hand the child over to the genetic father and his wife or partner, immediately she is born. In the past, surrogates have practised self-insemination privately,[119] and as we have seen, amendments to the Human Fertilisation and Embryology Act 1990 have imposed stricter controls on the use of fresh sperm. However, we would argue that a purely private arrangement between the commissioning father and the surrogate still falls outside the need for a licence and note that even if that were not the case, a pregnancy could still be established via normal sexual relations.

---

[114] S 1(1).

[115] S 3(2).

[116] See, notably, J Harris, *On Cloning* (2004) Routledge.

[117] Summed up in E Jackson, *Medical Law: Text, Cases and Materials* (2nd edn, 2010) OUP, pp 818–826.

[118] *Mason and McCall Smith*, p 249.

[119] See M Brazier, A Campbell and S Golombok, *Surrogacy: Review for Health Ministers of Current Arrangements for Payments and Regulation* (1998) Cm 4068 (hereafter referred to as Surrogacy Review).

IVF offers a couple where the woman ovulates, but cannot safely carry a child to term, the chance of a baby who is genetically theirs. Eggs are taken from the woman, fertilised in the laboratory with sperm from the man, and the embryo implanted in the surrogate. The surrogate once again carries the child and agrees to hand her over at birth. The surrogate is literally a 'hostess' for the couple's embryo. This practice may be styled *full surrogacy*, although Mason and Laurie prefer the term *womb leasing*.[120]

Who are the parents?

12.24   The first legal question we need to address is who in English law are the mother and father of a child born as result of a surrogacy arrangement. As will become clear, in both partial and full surrogacy the couple will need to seek a parental order or adopt the child if they are both to become the legal parents of the child, and moreover to obtain a parental order the couple will need to establish that both legal parents consent to the granting of the order. In relation to both partial and full surrogacy, the surrogate who carries the child is the legal mother[121] and the wife or female partner in the commissioning couple has no legal relationship with the child, even if her eggs are used and she is the genetic mother of that child. If the surrogate is married and her husband consented[122] to her participation in the surrogacy arrangement, the surrogate's husband will be the legal father of the child whenever and wherever the surrogate was inseminated or the embryo implanted in her body.[123] If the surrogate is not married and practised self-insemination using donor sperm from the commissioning father, he will be the legal as well as the biological father of the child. But if the surrogate was treated in a licensed clinic before April 2009 then it may be that her partner, if she has one, will be the legal father or the child will be legally fatherless.[124] After April 2009, theoretically the agreed fatherhood conditions could apply and the surrogate could nominate her partner as the 'father'.[125] Note that the surrogate cannot give notice that the commissioning father be the legal father of the child as the agreed fatherhood conditions exclude the donor of the sperm.[126]

The complexity of the provisions on parenthood and the mistaken belief by many commissioning couples that biological parenthood will confer legal

---

[120] *Mason and McCall Smith*, p 283.

[121] See Human Fertilisation and Embryology Act 1990 (as amended), s 27; and Human Fertilisation and Embryology 2008, s 33.

[122] So it may be that the commissioning couple will want to try and show that the husband did not consent; see *Re G (Surrogacy: Foreign Domicile)* [2007] EWHC 2814.

[123] See Human Fertilisation and Embryology Act 1990 (as amended), s 28; and Human Fertilisation and Embryology Act 2008, s 35.

[124] Human Fertilisation and Embryology Act 1990 (as amended), s 28.

[125] See Human Fertilisation and Embryology Act 2008, ss 36–38.

[126] Human Fertilisation and Embryology Act 2008, s 36(d).

status on them has resulted in a raft of cases before the Family Division, many relating to surrogacy arrangements entered into abroad.

Parental orders and adoption

12.25   Prior to the Human Fertilisation and Embryology Act 1990 the only way that a commissioning couple could both acquire parental responsibility for 'their' child was to seek to adopt the child, going through exactly the same process of assessment and scrutiny as any other couple seeking to adopt a child not genetically related to them. As we will see, section 95 of the Adoption Act 2002 bans payments in relation to adoptions and normally the legal parents of the child must both consent to the adoption. The courts have the power to dispense with parental consent in adoption proceedings if it is unreasonably withheld. But commissioning couples, especially in full surrogacies, were unhappy at being obliged to adopt their own genetic child and so, late in its passage through Parliament, section 30, introducing 'parental orders', was inserted in the 1990 Act to help some commissioning couples in surrogacy cases.[127] It provided for a simpler and faster procedure, other than adoption, by which some couples could acquire parental rights over 'their' child. Parental orders are now governed by section 54 of the Human Fertilisation and Embryology Act 2008 which empowers the court to order that the commissioning couple be treated in law as the parents of the child, but *only* in a limited number of circumstances:

(1)   The couple must be married, or civil partners, or 'living as partners in an enduring family relationship'.

(2)   The child must have been conceived from either the placing of the embryo, or sperm and eggs in the woman, or by DI. And the eggs or sperm or both must come from the couple. There must be a genetic link with at least one partner in the commissioning couple. Children conceived by natural intercourse between the surrogate and the husband are not within the ambit of section 54.[128]

(3)   Normally the application must be made within six months of the birth of the child.

(4)   At the time of the making of the order, the child must be living with the couple, one or both of whom are domiciled in the UK.

(5)   The surrogate (and the 'legal father' if not the commissioning 'father')[129] must have given full and free consent not less than six weeks after the birth. Section 54 is of no relevance if the surrogate changes her mind and is not willing to hand over the child. Nor is it a backdoor route to enforcing a surrogacy contract. Unlike adoption the court cannot dispense with the consent of a legal parent on the grounds that it is unreasonably withheld but section 54(7) does provide that consent is not

---

[127]   See *Re W (Minors Surrogacy)* [1991] 1 FLR 385.
[128]   As was the case in *Re an Adoption Application (Surrogacy)* [1987] 2 All ER 826.
[129]   On which see *Re Q (Parental Order)* [1996] 2 FCR 345.

required from a legal parent who cannot be found or is incapable of giving consent.

(6) No payments (other than for expenses reasonably incurred)[130] must have been made to the surrogate unless authorised by the court. Until the passing of the 2008 Act, only married couples could apply for parental orders and section 54(11) allowed partners who were unable to apply under the 1990 Act but qualified under the 2008 Act six months grace to make a retrospective application for a parental order. Parental orders may be simpler than adoption, but still pose a number of hurdles for a couple to surmount.

Prohibiting 'commercial' surrogacy

12.26 Surrogacy where no money changes hands is lawful in the sense that no crime is committed. The Surrogacy Arrangements Act 1985 made it a criminal offence for anyone to play any part in setting up a surrogacy arrangement on a commercial basis and advertising or compiling information to promote or assist surrogacy arrangements was also made criminal. The ban applied equally to partial and full surrogacy. Section 59 of the Human Fertilisation and Embryology Act 2008 has amended the Surrogacy Arrangements Act to allow reasonable payments to be made to non-profit-making bodies and for such non-profit agencies to place advertisements. Under the Act, no offence is committed by a woman herself seeking to become, or becoming, a surrogate, nor is any offence committed by the man or the couple who persuade her to carry a child. The 1985 Act (as amended) is limited to banning the activities of any commercial agencies or individuals aiming to make a profit out of arranging surrogacy. A fertility specialist who helps in establishing a full surrogacy even in the private sector incurs no criminal liability so long as he does not involve himself in arranging the introduction of couple and surrogate.

Although the surrogate and the couple engaging her services do not commit any offence under the Surrogacy Arrangements Act 1985 even if she is paid for what she does, the law still seeks to prevent any payment suggesting that the child has been bought. As we have seen, the commissioning couple need either to adopt the child or obtain a parental order, and it is a criminal offence to give or receive any payment in relation to the adoption of a child, the grant of consent to adoption, or the handing over of a child with a view to its adoption, unless that payment is authorised by a court.[131] Any payment beyond 'reasonable expenses' (again unless authorised by the court) will debar the couple from obtaining a parental order.[132] And if barred from obtaining a parental

---

[130] But note payments of £12,000 and more have been deemed reasonable expenses; *Re C (Application by Mr and Mrs X under s 30 of the Human Fertilisation and Embryology Act)* [2002] EWHC 157.

[131] See Adoption Act 2002, s 95.

[132] S 54(8).

order the couple's only option is to adopt but if they try to adopt the child and money paid to the surrogate is found to include a sum in payment for her agreement to the adoption and handing over the child, the surrogate and the couple may all face prosecution. Moreover, the Adoption Act 1976 further provides that the court may order the infant to be removed to a place of safety 'until he can be restored to his parents or guardians or until other arrangements can be made for him'. The courts have struggled for decades to dilute the rigour of laws of which many couples are simply unaware.

How to respond to such a surrogacy case was a dilemma which confronted Barnet Social Services in 1985. Kim Cotton had agreed to carry a child for a childless couple from abroad. She was artificially inseminated with the husband's sperm. The arrangements were made through an agency paid £13,000 by the father, of which the surrogate received £6,500. At the relevant time, the Surrogacy Arrangements Act 1985 had not yet been enacted. The baby was born and the mother prepared to hand her over. Barnet Social Services stepped in. The child was made a ward of court. Latey J[133] had to decide on her fate, and set the precedent for pragmatic compassion that his judicial colleagues have followed since. He said that the crucial issue before him was what was best for this baby. The methods used to create the child and the commercial aspects of the case raised delicate problems of ethics, morality and social desirability. They were not for him to decide. Careful inquiries showed that the father and his wife were eminently suitable to be parents. The judge granted them custody of the baby and permission to take her abroad with them to their home. The question of adoption, and the illegality of any payment under the Adoption Act 1976, did not arise in that case.

Two years later, Latey J adjudicated on the consequences of another surrogacy arrangement where all the parties desired to abide by that arrangement.[134] Mr and Mrs A arranged for Mrs B to carry a child for them. The child was conceived by natural sexual intercourse between Mr A and Mrs B. Mrs B was to be paid £10,000.[135] A baby was born and handed over to Mr and Mrs A after birth. They sought to adopt the child, as they then had to do to acquire parental rights. Were they in breach of the Adoption Act 1976 and so at risk of losing their child? Latey J found they were not. He held that the payments were *not* to procure Mrs B's consent to adoption. At the time of the agreement this was not in the parties' minds. The payments were in the nature of expenses for Mrs B, recompense for her time and inconvenience. Furthermore, the judge held that, even if he were wrong and the payments *were* illegal payments, he had power to ratify those payments retrospectively. Payments authorised by the court are not unlawful. As a matter of pure legal reasoning, Latey J's

133 *Re C (A Minor)* [1985] FLR 846.
134 *Re an Adoption Application (Surrogacy)* [1987] 2 All ER 826. And see *Re Q (Parental Order)* [1996] 1 FLR 369.
135 In the event, Mrs B accepted only £5,000 of the agreed fee, having co-authored a book on her experience of surrogacy.

grounds for finding the payments made by Mr and Mrs A to Mrs B were lawful may well be faulty. What is clear is that the judge saw no reason to upset an arrangement which had worked, or to remove the child, now two, from the only parents it had known.

The problem of payments to the surrogate remains a source of difficulty. In *Re X and Y (Foreign Surrogacy)*,[136] the commissioning couple entered into an agreement with a married woman in the Ukraine. She gave birth to twins after being implanted with a donor egg fertilised by the commissioning father's sperm. The couple were able to bring the children back with them to the UK by special leave of the immigration authorities. Under Ukrainian law, the surrogate and her husband had no legal relationship with the twins but under UK law, they were the legal parents and both had to consent before the grant of any parental order. Hedley J managed to find that there was such a consent from the Ukrainian husband. But the surrogate had been paid substantial sums of money: 235 Euros a month during pregnancy and a lump sum of 25,000 Euros on the live birth, 80 per cent of which was paid on the delivery of her consent to hand over the twins. Such payments were lawful in the Ukraine. The couple conceded that the sums paid exceeded reasonable expenses. Hedley J first prioritised the welfare of the twins as requiring that they be considered to be lifelong members of the applicants' family. Then he considered if the money paid was so disproportionate to reasonable expenses that for him to grant the parental order would be an affront to public policy. Noting that the couple had always acted in good faith and had made no attempt to defraud the authorities he felt able to grant the order.

Later in *Re S (Parental Order)*,[137] the same judge granted an order despite a payment of $23,000 to a Californian surrogate, identifying three issues relating to public policy. The court must ensure that a surrogacy arrangement is not used to circumvent the childcare laws in the UK to allow an order in favour of people who would not be approved as parents in England. The court should be astute not to be involved in anything that looks like a simple payment to buy a child abroad and to ensure that the sums of money offered are not such that they overbear the will of the surrogate. In *Re L (A Minor)*[138] Hedley J faced a case where there could be no doubt that the payments made exceeded even the most generous interpretation of reasonable expenses. The commercial surrogacy arrangement entered into by a British couple in Illinois was lawful under the law of Illinois and unlawful under the Human Fertilisation and Embryology Act 2008 in the UK. Nonetheless the judge used his powers under section 54(8) of the Act to authorise the payment retrospectively and grant the parental order. He was careful to stress that the couple acted in good faith, unaware of the law here. He described the authorised payment as 'compensation' and stressed that each case must be scrutinised on its own facts. But when the welfare of the child was at stake, Hedley J stressed that the good of the

---

[136] [2008] EWHC 3030 (Fam).
[137] [2009] EWHC 2977 (Fam).
[138] [2010] EWHC 3146 (Fam).

child must be accorded priority and that 'if it is desired to control commercial surrogacy arrangements, those controls need to operate before the court process is initiated'.[139]

'Custody' of the baby

12.27   As the cases above show, if the surrogate is content to hand the baby over, the courts will help the commissioning couple to become the parents of the baby. What if she changes her mind? First, it is absolutely clear in England that surrogacy agreements are not enforceable as contracts. The commissioning couple cannot sue the surrogate for breach of contract, or ask a court to order performance of a contract. Nor can the surrogate sue if she does not receive any agreed payments. Section 1A in the Surrogacy Arrangements Act 1985 provides quite simply that:

> No surrogacy arrangement is enforceable by or against any of the persons making it.

It does not matter by what means the child was created, be it sexual intercourse, DI or IVF, the arrangement is not an enforceable contract.

That still leaves open the question of what happens if the surrogate wants to keep the baby. In England, if the surrogate changes her mind and refuses to surrender the child, she will usually be allowed to keep the child. In *A v C*[140] as long ago as 1978, a young woman agreed to have a baby by DI and hand over the child to the wealthy father and his partner. She was to be paid £3,000. When the child was born she refused to give him up. The father sought care and control. The trial judge found that the mother should be allowed to keep the child, but granted the father limited access. The Court of Appeal removed his rights of access, condemning the whole arrangement as 'irresponsible, bizarre and unnatural'. Nor does it seem that greater tolerance of surrogacy has altered judicial policy where surrogates change their minds. In *Re P (Minors) (Wardship: Surrogacy)*,[141] Sir John Arnold P refused to order a surrogate mother to hand over twins born as a result of her artificial insemination by the father. It would seem that in England, a surrogate would be deprived of her baby only if she were an unfit mother who would not be allowed to keep the child however it had come to be conceived. Surrogacy is an arrangement couples enter into at their peril. If all goes to plan, they will get 'their' baby. If the arrangement breaks down, the law will not in most cases assist them in a battle with the surrogate. Most recently in *Re T (A Child) (Surrogacy: Residence Order)*[142] Baker J refused to make a residence order in favour of the commissioning father after a surrogacy agreement broke down in acrimony.

---

[139] [2010] EWHC 3146 (Fam) at para 10.
[140] [1985] FLR 445 (FD and CA).
[141] *Re P (Minors) (Wardship: Surrogacy)* [1987] 2 FLR 421.
[142] [2011] EWHC F 33 (Fam).

But there are exceptions. If the surrogate hands over the child, who is settled into the couple's home, but later changes her mind about consent to adoption or a parental order, the court has on two occasions at least overruled the surrogate's refusal of consent.[143] The welfare of the child once he or she is established in a 'new' family will override any claims of the surrogate.

Re N (A Child)[144] is another exceptional case and a cautionary tale of the perils of surrogacy. We do no more than summarise the basis of this complex case. Mrs P agreed to carry a child for Mr SJ and his wife TR. Mrs P underwent artificial insemination with SJ's sperm and became pregnant but deceived SJ, telling him she had miscarried so that she could keep the child, N. She had perpetrated just the same fraud on another couple some years earlier, giving birth to a child, C. The Court of Appeal upheld the judgment by Coleridge J that N, now aged eighteen months, should live with his biological father and his wife.[145] A residence order in favour of SJ with contact for Mr and Mrs P was most likely to give N a happy home into which to mature as a happy balanced adult. Mrs P's fraud was relevant to her suitability as a parent but the judge in favour of SJ must not be seen as a penalty for breaking the surrogacy agreement. In relation to the older child, C, an agreement was reached before the court hearing that C, who was nearly six, should remain with Mr and Mrs P and at an appropriate time be told of her biological paternity and contact with her genetic father arranged. Both children were made wards of court.

Foreign surrogacies

12.28 An increasing number of the cases reaching the courts relate to couples who go abroad to find a surrogate in a jurisdiction where more young women may be prepared to act as surrogates, or the rules on parenthood may be more favourable to the couple and controls on payment less rigorous. *Re X and Y (Foreign Surrogacy)*[146] (discussed above) has shown that it is UK rules on legal parenthood that will apply and the problems that may cause. We have also seen that judges will take a fairly lenient view of payments so as not to disrupt an established relationship between the commissioning couple and the child.[147] Other couples have faced more serious problems. If the child is born abroad and the commissioning couple are not in law her parents, how can they lawfully bring her home to the UK? Can they only apply for such an order when the child has a home with them in this country? The immigration authorities will grant exceptional leave to allow the child into the UK if at least one partner has a genetic link to the child and it is likely that a parental

---

[143] *Re MW (Adoption: Surrogacy)* [1995] 2 FLR 759; *C v S* (1996) SLT 1387.
[144] [2007] EWCA Civ 1053.
[145] *Re P (Surrogacy: Residence)* [2008] 1 FLR 177.
[146] [2008] EWHC 3030 (Fam); and see *Re S (Parental Order)* [2009] 2977 (Fam).
[147] As in *Re L (A Minor)* [2010] EWHC 3146 (Fam).

order will be granted. In *Re K (Minors)*[148] twins were born as a result of a commercial surrogacy arrangement in India entered into by a British couple. The children were handed over to the couple, but remained for most of the time with their Indian grandparents, while the couple sought to bring them home to the UK. An application for parental order was listed before Hedley J who ruled that as the children were not in this country he could not progress the applications and declined to issue any directions to the immigration authorities. He noted that without the children's presence in the UK, no welfare assessment could be made and expressed concern about the issues that might arise in relation to the monies paid to the surrogate and her husband. He also questioned whether the payments would be at a level that the court would be unable to accept as reasonable expenses or exercise their powers to authorise. Finally, the judge warned that the strict six-month time limit to apply for a parental order may create problems with foreign surrogacies.

Problems may also arise when couples come from abroad to seek a surrogacy arrangement in the UK. A Turkish couple made such an arrangement and the child was handed over to them but they were not domiciled in the UK and so ineligible to apply for a parental order. The judge was able to exercise a power under the Adoption and Children Act 2002 to confer parental responsibility on the couple to permit them to take the child home to Turkey and adopt the child there.[149]

Surrogacy in need of reform

12.29   Simply reading in full the cases[150] mentioned above will show that for all the parties concerned surrogacy arrangements can be perilous. The courts do their best to protect the interests of the child, sometimes stretching the letter of the law to breaking point. Many couples are unaware of the law relating to surrogacy and the potential exists for exploitation of all parties by an unscrupulous or unbalanced individual. Some couples and surrogates do not seem to have been offered sound advice.

How serious is the problem? The number of surrogacy arrangements is impossible to ascertain accurately. In 1998,[151] it was estimated that there were about fifty to eighty births in the UK arising from surrogacy arrangements. Surrogacy had not, as the Warnock Report had hoped, 'withered on the vine'.[152] In one well-publicised case in 1996, a young woman agreed to carry a child for a Dutch couple in return for £12,000 expenses. Like Mrs P[153] many years later,

---

[148] [2010] EWHC 1180 (Fam).
[149] *Re G (Surrogacy: Foreign Domicile)* [2007] EWHC 844.
[150] In particular read *Re P (Surrogacy: Residence)* [2008] 1 FLR 179.
[151] See Surrogacy Review.
[152] Surrogacy Review, para 2.23.
[153] See *Re N (A Child)* [2007] EWCA Civ 1053, discussed above at **12.27**.

she changed her mind and first she told them that she had had an abortion. Later she said that she was still pregnant but planned to keep the baby. Around the same time, one of the leading US surrogacy agents arrived in Britain advertising his commercial surrogacy service. In 1998, the government set up a review[154] of payments for and regulation of surrogacy.

The Surrogacy Review made a number of recommendations. The most controversial proposal was that the prohibition on paying surrogates for their services should be maintained, and given teeth. A new Surrogacy Act should define expenses to exclude covert payments. Unless pregnancy causes the surrogate to give up work, it is difficult to see how genuine expenses resulting from pregnancy can add up to more than a couple of thousand pounds. Any agency which introduced couples and surrogates or offered advice on surrogacy would have to be registered with the Department of Health. A Code of Practice would be developed which agencies must abide by, setting out a model of good practice for couples and surrogates. The Code would seek to ensure frank exchanges of information and offer independent counselling to all involved. Multiple surrogacy would be discouraged. Parties who complied with the Code would be able to obtain a parental order swiftly. Where the Code was not followed, the lengthier process of adoption would be required with provision for a full investigation of the circumstances of the arrangement. The proposed Surrogacy Act would reinforce a philosophy of surrogacy as a gift relationship, and set in place regulations which would seek to safeguard the interests of all parties. Prohibition on payments was vigorously opposed by the major surrogacy agency COTS (Childlessness Overcome Through Surrogacy) and a number of eminent scholars. The most telling criticism of the *Surrogacy Review* came from Michael Freeman[155] who argued, first, that surrogates are entitled to payment and, second, that a ban on payment will drive surrogacy underground, increasing risks of exploitation and harm to the children.

There is, however, agreement that some sort of regulation of surrogacy is needed. The form of regulation will never be settled, however, unless the vexed question of payment is resolved. The arguments are finely balanced. We expect and receive payment for the use of our brains. Why should a surrogate not be paid for the use of her uterus? But should bodily services or body parts be traded? Can you buy children?[156] Proponents of payment argue that paying a surrogate for reproductive labour is not buying a child. Yet what couple would pay if the child is not surrendered? Most pro-payment campaigners argue that surrogacy contracts should remain unenforceable.[157] Is that logical? If the use

---

[154] Surrogacy Review.

[155] M Freeman, 'Does Surrogacy Have a Future after Brazier?' (1999) 7 *Medical Law Review* 1.

[156] See M Brazier, 'Can You Buy Children?' (1999) 11 *Child and Family Law Quarterly* 345.

[157] With the honourable exceptions of COTS and *Mason and McCall Smith*, at 8.116.

of the uterus is no different from manual or intellectual labour, why should the surrogate not be obliged to honour her contract?

No immediate action followed the report of the *Surrogacy Review*. Presumably in an attempt to improve the quality of advice available on surrogacy, the Human Fertilisation and Embryology Act 2008 has, as we have seen, made provision for lawful payments to non-profit-making agencies. We doubt whether that small step alone will suffice and suggest that a comprehensive review of the law and practice relating to surrogacy is urgently needed. Permitting regulated payments may prove to be the price for protecting children and the families they come from and go to.

A right to reproduce?

12.30 The practical questions raised by assisted conception are many and varied. At the heart of those questions lies the intractable problem of whether individuals enjoy a right to reproduce, and just what such a right entails. Articles, 8, 12 and 14 all touch on this problem. The ECtHR in *Evans*[158] and *Dickson*[159] has acknowledged that Article 8 rights to private life are engaged in laws regulating reproductive medicine and access to treatment. Article 12 speaks of a 'right to marry and found a family'.[160] Article 14 prohibits unjustifiable discrimination, so a woman denied fertility treatment might argue that barriers to treatment discriminate against her just because she is infertile. The first difficulty of a rights-based argument in the context of fertility treatment is this. As Wall J noted in his first instance judgment in *Evans*:[161]

> The right to found a family through IVF can only, put at its highest, amount to a right to have IVF treatment. Self-evidently it cannot be a right to be treated successfully.

Evans illustrates another difficulty too. Had the ECtHR held that Ms Evans had a claim to a right to procreate that entitled her to demand the implantation of the frozen embryos against the will of her former partner, his right *not* to procreate would be violated. Even when no such conflict arises it is unclear just what a right to procreate entails. Does it manifest a right to reproductive autonomy, ie to reproductive choice? Would that include a right to abortion?[162]

And see E Jackson, *Medical Law: Text, Cases and Materials* (2nd edn, 2010) OUP, pp 851–854.

[158] *Evans v UK* (2008) 46 EHRR 34.

[159] *Dickson v UK* (2007) 46 EHRR 41; and see *SH and Others v Austria* (Application No 55813/00) 15 November 2007.

[160] But Art 12 has seemingly been relegated to the sidelines by the ECtHR: see M Eijkholt, 'The Right to Found a Family as a Stillborn Right to Procreate?' (2010) 18 *Medical Law Review* 127.

[161] [2003] EWHC 2161 (Fam) at para 263.

[162] See *A, B and C v Ireland* [2010] ECHR 25579/05.

Is it a positive as well as a negative obligation?[163] The ECtHR seems at present to go little further than this. Article 8 is engaged in claims touching on reproduction and the right to respect for decisions 'to become and not become a parent'.[164] But any such claim must be weighed against the countervailing public interests in Article 8(2) and in the stormy waters of debates on reproduction the Court will allow states a more than generous margin of appreciation.[165]

---

[163] A question skilfully ducked in *Dickson v UK* [2008] 46 EHRR 41.
[164] *Dickson v UK* (2008) 46 EHRR 41 at para 71.
[165] See *A, B and C v Ireland* [2010] ECHR 25579/05.

Chapter 13

ABORTION AND EMBRYO RESEARCH

13.1 The legal and moral status of the human embryo continues to attract controversy. For the devout Roman Catholic and many others, if a life given by God begins at conception, the deliberate destruction of an embryo, be it in the course of embryo research, or by abortion, is the equivalent of killing you or us. The destruction of the embryo can only be justifiable, if at all, where the mother's life is at risk. Even in this case, abortion is still not lawful in some countries.[1] In 2010, three women went to the European Court of Human Rights (ECtHR) to challenge Irish laws that failed to provide access to safe and lawful abortion for women whose health was imperilled by pregnancy. The ECtHR, as we shall see, allowed one of the three claims but stopped well short of ruling that draconian restrictions on abortion violated Article 8 of the Convention.[2]

If the human embryo has, as others contend, no greater moral status than a mouse embryo, neither research nor abortion is morally wrong. 'Gradualists' argue that the embryo acquires increasing moral claims as it develops in the womb. For many feminists, a right to abortion is part and parcel of a woman's rights over her own body.

The present English laws[3] on abortion and embryo research represent an attempt to reach a compromise in a debate in which there is no consensus. In 1990, Parliament, in the first Human Fertilisation and Embryology Act, sanctioned embryo research up to fourteen days, and permitted abortion in certain cases up to the moment of birth. 'Pro-life' campaigners continued to fight to ban research and restrict abortion. In recent years, the principal thrust of the campaign to restrict abortion in the UK has centred on attempts to reduce the

---

[1]   See R Sifris, 'Restrictive Regulation of Abortion and the Right to Health' (2010) 18 *Medical Law Review* 185.

[2]   *A, B and C v Ireland* [2010] ECHR 25579/05. See below at **13.17**.

[3]   On the history of abortion law in England, see J Keown, *Abortion, Doctors and the Law* (1988) CUP.

time limit for legal abortions. In Parliamentary debates on the Human Fertili-sation and Embryology Act 2008, further attempts were made by 'pro-life' groups to reduce time limits while 'pro-choice' groups sought to remove the requirement that two doctors must approve any termination of pregnancy. Both attempts to hijack the Bill to change the law on abortion failed. The 2008 Act in its amendments to the 1990 Act does make some substantial changes to the law governing embryo research, principally to address the development of stem-cell therapies and the vexed question of human/animal hybrid embryos. At the time of writing, the fate of the current research regulator, the Human Fertilisation and Embryology Authority (HFEA) is unknown. The coalition government proposes to abolish the HFEA and transfer its functions to other authorities; in the case of embryo research we assume that this will be the new research regulator, the Health Research Agency.[4]

Criminal abortion[5]

13.2   The law relating to criminal abortion is still to be found in sections 58 and 59 of the Offences Against the Person Act 1861. Strictly speaking, all that the Abortion Act 1967 does is create defences to charges under the 1861 Act. Section 58 of that Act makes it a criminal offence punishable by a maximum of life imprisonment: (1) for any woman, being with child, unlawfully to do any act with intent to procure a miscarriage; and (2) for any other person unlawfully to do an act with intent to procure the miscarriage of any woman. Self-induced abortion by the woman herself is criminal only if the woman is in fact pregnant. Any act by a third party is criminal regardless of whether or not the woman can be proved to be pregnant. This limited protection afforded to the woman extends only to cases where she acts entirely alone. If she seeks help from a doctor, or any other person, she may be charged with aiding and abetting that person to commit the offence of criminal abortion[6] or of con-spiracy with him to commit that offence.[7] Section 59 makes it an offence to 'unlawfully supply or procure any poison or other noxious thing, or any instrument or thing whatsoever, knowing that the same is intended to be unlawfully used or employed with intent to procure the miscarriage of any woman'.

A possible lacuna in the law is to be seen in the extraordinary case of *Regina v A*.[8] Mr A set up a deliberate scheme of deception to seek to ensure that his young wife (to whom he was unhappily married) underwent an abortion

---

4   See above **1.16, 12.1** and below **15.5**.
5   See, generally, S Sheldon, *Beyond Control: Medical Power and Abortion Law* (1997) Pluto; E Lee (ed), *Abortion: Whose Right?* (2002) Hodder and Stoughton.
6   *R v Sockett* (1908) 72 JP 428. In 1927, a girl of thirteen was prosecuted for attempt-ing to induce an abortion on herself by taking laxative tablets and sitting in a hot bath.
7   *R v Whitchurch* (1890) 24 QBD 420.
8   [2010] EWCA Crim 1949.

without her consent or even her knowledge. Mrs A spoke no English and he took her to two clinics attempting to deceive doctors into believing that his wife wanted a termination. Both attempts failed and the wife was very upset when she discovered on the second occasion that she was booked into an abortion clinic. She finally managed to escape from her husband who was convicted under section 59 of the Offences against the Person Act 1861. His conviction was, however, overturned in the Court of Appeal. The appeal court rejected the argument that A had sought to procure a 'thing', ie surgery, contrary to section 59 and found many of the grounds for the prosecution to be unsustainable. Additionally the court noted that, on the information available to them, the doctors, had the deception succeeded, might have acted lawfully in terminating the pregnancy. So A walked free after trying to terminate his wife's pregnancy against her will, yet the letter of the law seems to prevent women who seek to terminate an unwanted pregnancy from so doing.

The rigour of the law has always been tempered by a defence to a charge of criminal abortion by a doctor that he acted to preserve the life or health of the mother.[9] At no time in England was abortion absolutely prohibited so as to require the mother to be sacrificed for her unborn child. In *R v Bourne*,[10] acquitting a doctor of a charge of criminal abortion, the judge suggested that there might be a *duty* to abort to save the 'yet more precious' life of the mother. The extent of the defence available to doctors was unclear. Some doctors interpreted this defence liberally to include the mother's mental health and even happiness. Others would intervene only to prevent a life-threatening complication of pregnancy endangering the woman. Abortion on the grounds that the foetus suffered from some serious disability was not lawful. Illegal abortion flourished. Several thousand women were admitted to hospital for treatment after back-street abortions. The Abortion Act 1967 was introduced to bring uniformity into the law, to clarify the law for the doctors, and to stem the misery and injury resulting from unhygienic, risky, illegal abortions.

The Abortion Act 1967

13.3 The Abortion Act 1967 provides that abortion may be lawfully performed under certain conditions.[11] A pregnancy may be terminated by a registered medical practitioner if two registered medical practitioners are of the opinion, formed in good faith, that one of four grounds specified in the Act are met. They are:

(1) The pregnancy has not exceeded its twenty-fourth week and the continuance of the pregnancy would involve risk to the life of the pregnant woman, or of injury to her physical or mental health, or that of the

---

[9] *R v Bourne* [1939] 1 KB 687.
[10] *R v Bourne* [1939] 1 KB 687 at 693.
[11] See s 1 as amended by Human Fertilisation and Embryology Act 1990, s 37.

existing children of her family, greater than if the pregnancy were terminated. This is sometimes described as the 'social' ground for abortion.
(2)   The termination is necessary to prevent grave permanent injury to the physical or mental health of the woman.
(3)   The continuance of the pregnancy would involve risk to the life of the pregnant woman, greater than if the pregnancy were terminated.
(4)   There is a substantial risk that if the child were born it would suffer such physical or mental abnormalities as to be seriously handicapped.

No time limit restricts termination of pregnancy on any of these latter three grounds. In assessing any risk to the health of the woman or her children, account may be taken of the woman's actual or reasonably foreseeable environment. Exceptionally, one registered medical practitioner may act alone when he is of the opinion that an abortion is immediately necessary to save the life of the woman, or to prevent grave permanent injury to her physical or mental health. Save in an emergency any termination of pregnancy must be carried out in a National Health Service (NHS) hospital or a place (clinic) approved by the Department of Health.[12] Section 4 of the Act provides that no person shall be under any duty to participate in the performance of an abortion if he has a conscientious objection to abortion, save where immediate treatment is necessary to save the life of the woman or to prevent grave permanent damage to her health.[13]

Abortion on demand or request?[14]

13.4   Ninety-one per cent of abortions[15] are carried out before thirteen weeks, and 75 per cent at under ten weeks. Critics claim that abortion is available on demand, and that the Abortion Act 1967 is not being properly applied. Gynaecologists prepared to perform an abortion on the request of the pregnant woman rely on statistics which appear to show that statistically the risk of abortion in the first twelve weeks of pregnancy is less than the risk of childbirth. Therefore any abortion performed in that period meets the requirement of the Act that the continuance of the pregnancy poses a greater risk to the health of the woman than does termination. Such statistics include women for whom pregnancy poses exceptional risk, such as very young girls, or older women. The individual patient's risk will often be much less than any statistical 'average'. The issue has never been tested in court.

---

[12]   Abortion Act 1967, s 1(3).
[13]   See *Janaway v Salford Area Health Authority* [1988] 3 All ER 1051, HL, discussed below **13.15**.
[14]   This issue is fully discussed in J K Mason and G T Laurie, *Mason and McCall Smith's Law and Medical Ethics* (8th edn, 2010) OUP (hereafter *Mason and McCall Smith*), at 9.58–9.65.
[15]   DH, *Abortion Statistics, England and Wales 2009* (2010).

A successful prosecution against a doctor performing an abortion on demand would have to establish: (a) that the statistics indicating that abortion posed less risk than childbirth were invalid; and (b) that the doctor on trial did not believe them to be valid and so failed to act in good faith. In view of the fact that only one successful prosecution has ever been brought against a doctor for performing an abortion purportedly under the 1967 Act in bad faith,[16] such a course would appear a clumsy means of regulating or eliminating abortion on demand or request. However, the Abortion Act confers on women no right to abortion. By making doctors the 'gatekeepers' for the Act, abortion in England is a privilege granted or withheld at the doctors' discretion.[17]

Post-coital birth control

13.5   The Abortion Act 1967 envisaged that once a diagnosis of pregnancy had been made, the doctor faced with a request for an abortion would consider and weigh any risk to the woman or the child. Post-coital contraceptive drugs (emergency hormonal contraception), if taken by a woman within seventy-two hours of intercourse, ensure that any fertilised egg will not implant in the womb. This, inaptly named, 'morning-after' pill is not the only means by which a fertilised egg may be disposed of at a stage before pregnancy can be confirmed. An intra-uterine device (IUD) fitted within a similar time after intercourse will have the same effect.[18]

Post-coital contraception raised the question of where the line is drawn between contraception and abortion. Post-coital contraception works before the fertilised egg can implant in the womb. The crucial legal issue, in relation to the use of post-coital contraception, is whether a drug or a procedure which prevents implantation is an act done to procure a miscarriage.[19] Is there a carriage of a child by a woman before implantation takes place? If not, to prevent that event occurring cannot be an act done to procure a miscarriage. Many fertilised eggs fail to implant naturally and no one suggests that a miscarriage has occurred. The opponents of post-coital birth control responded that the fertilised egg is present within the body of the woman; thus she carries it within her. Therefore there is a carriage of a child, and any act removing that

---

[16]   *R v Smith (John)* [1974] 1 WLR 1510, CA.

[17]   The history of abortion in England from well before the 1967 Act is marked by 'medicalisation'; see J Keown, *Abortion, Doctors and the Law* (1988) CUP.

[18]   In *R v Price* [1969] 1 QB 541, a prosecution for criminal abortion was brought against a doctor who inserted an IUD into a woman who was some months pregnant. The prosecution failed because it was not proved that he knew her to be pregnant.

[19]   As long ago as 1983, the Attorney-General expressed his opinion that prior to implantation there is no pregnancy and so means used to prevent implantation do *not* constitute procuring miscarriage. HC Official Report, 10 May 1983, cols 238–239. In 1991, a judge dismissed a prosecution for criminal abortion based on the insertion of an IUD, agreeing with the Attorney-General that until implantation there is no pregnancy: *R v Dhingra* (1991) unreported.

child from her womb is an act done to procure a miscarriage.[20] As at least 40 per cent of implanted embryos abort spontaneously, the arguments based on spontaneous loss of fertilised eggs are irrelevant.

In 2000, a version of the 'morning-after' pill (Levonelle) was deregulated to allow sale over the counter in pharmacies. Women no longer needed a prescription to obtain post-coital birth control.[21] The Pro-Life Alliance unsuccessfully sought judicial review, arguing that the free availability of such a drug contravened the 1861 Act because the drug procures miscarriage. Munby J poured scorn on their case, and forcefully held that no pregnancy is established until the fertilised egg is implanted in the uterus.[22] 'Miscarriage' today means the termination of an established pregnancy, whatever it may have meant in 1861.

Emergency hormonal contraception must not be confused with 'medical abortion'[23] and the 'abortion pill'. Mifepristone (RU-486) and misoprostol (prostaglandin) are drugs which are administered orally in the first nine weeks of pregnancy, and will, in most women, induce a complete miscarriage. A small percentage of women require a surgical abortion to complete the evacuation of the uterus.[24] The use of mifepristone is lawful only within the conditions laid down in the 1967 Act. The development of the drug does not liberalise the law on abortion. Section 37(3) of the Human Fertilisation and Embryology Act 1990 permitted its routine use in England by authorising the Secretary of State for Health to approve clinics prescribing the drug. The woman will need to attend an approved clinic to take mifepristone, which blocks the hormones necessary to maintain pregnancy. She must then return two days later to receive misoprostol, which causes the uterus to contract. The practice of many clinics is to allow women to take the misoprostol and return home so they can 'miscarry' in privacy. This usually occurs four to six hours later. Some women fear that contractions will start on the journey home, whilst others object to the inconvenience and stress of having to attend the clinic twice and lose control over the timing of their miscarriage. The British Pregnancy Advisory Service (BPAS) challenged the Department of Health's interpretation of section 1(3) of the Abortion Act 1967 which requires that 'any treatment for the

---

[20] See J Keown, 'Miscarriage: A Medico Legal Analysis' [1984] *Criminal Law Review* 604.

[21] See Prescription Only Medicines (Human Use) Amendment (No 3) Order 2000, SI 2000/3231.

[22] *R (on the application of Smeaton v Secretary of State for Health and Others* [2002] 2 FLR 146. See J Keown, 'Morning After Pills, Miscarriage and Muddle' (2005) 25 *Legal Studies* 302.

[23] Forty per cent of abortions in England and Wales are now 'medical abortions'; see DH, *Abortion Statistics, England and Wales 2009* (2010).

[24] The woman will be asked to agree to undergo surgical abortion should the drug fail to work before she is given mifepristone. She cannot be forced to go through with the surgical procedure should she later change her mind. But, providing she has been properly warned of the risk of failure and possible adverse effect on the embryo, neither she nor any child damaged by the drug could sue in respect of their injuries. See R P Jansen, 'Unfinished Feticide' (1990) 16 *Journal of Medical Ethics* 61–70.

termination of pregnancy' is carried out in an approved clinic or hospital. BPAS brand the rule 'medically unnecessary' and call for women to be allowed to take the second part of the treatment, the misoprostol, at home.[25] BPAS argue that clinics would comply with section 1(3) were they to administer the mifepristone and prescribe and issue the misoprostol at the same visit. The Abortion Act, they claim, was designed to make abortion safe, and there is evidence from other countries that their proposed method is both safe and convenient. The Department of Health contests this interpretation, arguing that 'any treatment for the termination of pregnancy' covers the prescription *and* the administration of the abortion drugs.

Mason and Laurie, who for the most part support lawful abortion, express concerns that link emergency hormonal contraception and the 'abortion pill'. They fear both 'will inevitably come to be regarded as a safe form of contraceptive back-up', blurring the distinction between preventing new life and taking life.[26] We are less pessimistic. What mifepristone does do is to place responsibility for ending her pregnancy on the woman taking the drug. She cannot evade responsibility by seeing the abortion as something done to her. The procedure involves experiencing the pain and distress of a miscarriage. The loss of the embryo will be very evident to her. It is no more likely to be used lightly than recourse to surgical abortion.

The status of the embryo and embryo research: the debate[27]

13.6 The development of in vitro fertilisation (IVF) offered not just new means to overcome infertility, but also the capacity to develop medicine in several directions via research on embryos in the laboratory. The process of IVF generates far more embryos than will ever be implanted in a maternal womb; what should happen to the 'spare embryos'? The possibilities opened up by embryo research prompted renewed controversy about the nature and status of early human embryos, whether the embryo is located in a Petrie dish or a woman's uterus. John Harris argues that it cannot:[28]

> . . . be morally preferable to end the life of an embryo *in vivo* than it is to do *in vitro*.

The law regulating abortion in England sanctions the destruction of nearly 200,000 embryos every year.[29] The original advocates of embryo research asked how society can logically accept abortion yet ban research. If the embryo

---

[25] BPAS, Press Release (13 January 2011).

[26] *Mason and McCall Smith*, at 9.91.

[27] See generally, A Dyson and J Harris (eds), *Experiments on Embryos* (1989) Routledge.

[28] J M Harris, *The Value of Life* (1985) Routledge & Kegan Paul, p 117.

[29] The total number of abortions in 2009 in England and Wales was 189,100 but note that this was a fall from 195,296 in 2008; see DH, *Abortion Statistics, England and Wales: 2009* (2010).

can be destroyed at its mother's request, how can it be unethical to destroy it in the course of beneficial scientific research? Both camps in the debate on embryo experiments link the questions of abortion and research.[30]

At the heart of the debate lies the question of the moral status of the developing embryo. When does it acquire the same right to protection as we enjoy? We will for the moment assume that the embryo is created the 'old fashioned' way via fertilisation, rather than Cell Nuclear Replacement (CNR). Is it at fertilisation, when a new unique genetic entity comes into being?[31] Or is it at some later stage in embryonic development? This might be at fourteen days, when the primitive streak forms,[32] or when brain activity, brain life, is first discernible at eight to ten weeks.[33] Or is it much, much later, after birth? One school of philosophy argues thus.[34] Humanity is just another species of animal and as such has no greater moral status than any other animal. What gives rise to moral rights is not being a human animal, but being a *person*. It is the capacity to value your own existence which gives a person rights, including the right to life. Embryos, and newborn infants, lack that capacity and so are *not* persons. So at no stage of embryonic or foetal development, inside or outside the womb, does the embryo or foetus have moral status.

Each ethical school of thought marshals impressive arguments in support of its thesis. Argument that the embryo enjoys full human status from fertilisation is an argument often resting on theological grounds. If you believe that human life is divinely created in the image of God, and that human beings possess an immortal immaterial soul, you are unlikely to find any argument based on personhood acceptable. The crucial moment when the embryo acquires humanity becomes ensoulment. Traditionally that moment might be seen as fertilisation, but a number of eminent Christian theologians argued for a later date – either the appearance of the primitive streak as marking clear individuality, as this is the latest date that twinning can occur and when it is possible to distinguish embryonic and placental cells, or the beginning of brain life.[35] Any concept of human life as special per se is irrelevant to those who support

30   See M Brazier, 'Embryos' "Rights": Abortion and Research', in M D A Freeman (ed), *Medicine, Ethics and Law* (1988) Stevens, pp 9–23.

31   See O O'Donovan, *Begotten Not Made* (1984) OUP; A Holland, 'A Fortnight of My Life is Missing: A Discussion of the Status of the Pre-embryo' (1990) 7 *Journal of Applied Philosophy* 25.

32   As the Warnock Report concluded: see Report of the Committee of Inquiry into Human Fertilisation and Embryology, pp 63–64.

33   See, in particular, M Lockwood, 'When Does a Life Begin?' in M Lockwood (ed), *Moral Dilemmas in Medicine* (1988) OUP.

34   See J M Harris, *The Value of Life* (1985) Routledge, pp 18–25; and 'Embryos and Hedgehogs: on the Moral Status of the Embryo', in Dyson and Harris (eds), *Experiments on Embryos* (1989) Routledge, p 65; and see J Glover, *Causing Death and Saving Lives* (1977) Penguin.

35   See G R Dunstan, 'The Moral Status of the Human Embryo: A Tradition Recalled' (1984) 10 *Journal of Medical Ethics*, 38; Keith Ward, 'An Irresolvable Debate?', in Dyson and Harris (eds), *Experiments on Embryos* (1989) Routledge, p 106.

the personhood thesis. J K Mason advances a rather different argument, one which allows a clearer demarcation between abortion and embryo research. Mason contends that the crucial factor that brings an embryo within the moral community of humankind, and so entitles it to protection, is implantation.[36] Implantation in the womb connects the embryo to its mother and grants it capacity for meaningful development. The embryo in the Petrie dish is no more than a 'laboratory artefact'.[37]

How should the law respond to such a divergence of moral opinion? Consensus is impossible to attain. Proponents of embryo research argued that no one is compelled to participate in research. A liberal democracy should respect divergent moral views. But that is anathema to 'pro-life' groups. It is rather like saying that if a sufficient number of people decide redheads are not human and have no moral claim on society, anyone who holds that belief may kill off any redhead he meets. Of course, no 'pro-redhead' will be required to join in the slaughter! So what is the difference between redheaded adults and embryos? On any analysis, the redhead enjoys moral and legal rights. She is without doubt a person. The embryo's true nature is unprovable. One of the authors of this work happens to believe that from fertilisation the embryo is *very probably* of the same moral value as herself. It is a unique being created in the image of God, in whom she believes. She cannot prove that belief. But then nor can those who maintain that humanity is just another animal species prove their contention. The verdict on the nature of the embryo must be 'not proven'.

What consequences should the 'not-proven' nature of the embryo have for its legal status? It must be accorded recognition and respect. If its claims to rights conflict with the claims of an entity whose status is beyond doubt, its claims may be subordinated to that entity's. Thus if there is a conflict between the claims of the embryo and the rights of the mother, indubitably a legal person, the mother's rights take precedence. A belief that the embryo must be respected as fully human from fertilisation requires that a woman rejects abortion as an option for herself. As that belief is unprovable, she cannot legitimately enforce it on other women.[38] Embryo research, by contrast, gives rise to no such direct conflict of rights. The question becomes whether society can legitimately destroy an entity which may be fully human in nature and status. The embryo should be given the benefit of the doubt. Justifications have always been advanced for permitting the killing of indubitably human persons in certain cases. It might be argued that the public 'good' expected from embryo research

---

[36] J K Mason, *Medico-Legal Aspects of Reproduction and Parenthood* (2nd edn, 1998), p 234; *Mason and McCall Smith*, at 8.74.

[37] J K Mason, *Human Life and Medical Practice* (1988) Edinburgh University Press, p 94.

[38] For a powerful argument that even if the embryo is presumed to enjoy full human status, abortion remains defensible, see J Jarvis Thompson, 'A Defence of Abortion', in R M Dworkin (ed), *The Philosophy of Law* (1977), p 112. But note the response by J M Finnis, 'The Rights and Wrongs of Abortion', in the same book, p 129.

justifies destruction of these 'maybe' human persons. The onus of proof lies on those who advocate research.

What are the 'goods' which may flow from research? They include improvement in fertility treatments, particularly IVF, the development of more effective means of contraception, the detection and 'cure' of genetic defects and disease, and, with the development of stem cell therapies, 'therapeutic cloning', the use of pluripotent stem cells retrieved from early embryonic tissue to transplant into sick adults and children. The potential for stem cell therapies has become the most disputed issue in this debate by 2011. How much could be achieved without research on live human embryos is hotly disputed. A further issue arises from research on induced pluripotent stem (IPS) cells. It is suggested that the need for stem cells harvested from embryos could be eliminated by retrieving adult stem cells and manipulating those cells to operate like embryonic stem cells. There would then be no need for embryonic stem cells.[39] It is difficult for a layperson to evaluate the scientific debate, partly because scientific opinion on the merits of research seems to depend on what stance the scientist takes on the ethics of research. However, if the 'pro-research' camp confronts some difficulty establishing that the manifest benefit of research justifies the destruction of arguably human embryos, the 'anti-research' camp has a fundamental problem of its own. If an embryo is arguably human, it is wrong to destroy it, to experiment on it for a purpose not designed to benefit it, so that it must ultimately perish. If it is wrong to destroy embryos for research purposes, it must also be wrong to destroy them in the course of infertility treatments using IVF. As long as 'spare' embryos are created, surplus embryos are doomed to die. To return to a practice of harvesting only one egg from the woman, and so creating and implanting just one embryo, was thought to be a fatal blow to IVF.[40] It is difficult to argue that it is ethical to destroy embryos to alleviate infertility and yet unethical to destroy embryos in order to improve our knowledge and treatment of genetic disease. Those who opposed research should logically also have opposed IVF.[41]

Embryo research: the Human Fertilisation and Embryology Act 1990 (as amended)

13.7 At this point the reader may be advised to apply a cold flannel to his or her head! To begin to understand the regulation of embryo research in the UK,

---

[39] See E Jackson, *Medical Law: Text, Cases and Materials* (2nd edn, 2010) OUP, pp 641–643.

[40] Clinicians are now suggesting that modern treatment may achieve much greater success with single embryo transplant (SET) at less risk to the woman. However, even with SET multiple embryos will be created and stored and so the issue of the fate of the 'spare' embryo remains moot.

[41] See M Brazier, 'The Challenge for Parliament: A Critique of the White Paper on Human Fertilisation and Embryology', in Dyson and Harris (eds), *Experiments on Embryos* (1989) Routledge, p 142.

we need to examine the Human Fertilisation and Embryology Act 1990 as amended by the later 2008 Act, trace a little of the history of the intervening years, and finally consider the effect of impending changes to the regulation of research as whole.[42] We can do little more than introduce the legislation. One initial point should be made. The UK legislation now distinguishes sharply between those 'permitted embryos', 'permitted eggs' and 'permitted sperm' that can be used in fertility treatment and those embryos and gametes that can at this stage be used only for research and the development of stem cell therapies.

The 1990 Act was, and remains, based on a compromise advanced in the Warnock Report of 1984.[43] The human embryo should be accorded special status and treated with respect[44] but that 'status' fell far short of the status to be accorded to any born human. Legislation thus permitted research on embryos but only if licensed by the HFEA, subject to a strict limit of fourteen days, and a number of other prohibitions.

It is thus a criminal offence punishable by up to ten years' imprisonment to bring about the creation of an embryo (outside the human body) or to keep or use an embryo except in pursuance of a licence.[45] The current licensing authority remains the HFEA at the time of writing, but as we have seen the government is proposing to transfer the functions of the HFEA to other bodies and in the case of embryo research, we assume that this will be the new overarching research regulator.[46] The substantive provisions of the Act are not due to change. So no embryo may be created or kept without a licence, or used after the appearance of the primitive streak, that is, fourteen days from the day the gametes were mixed, '. . . not counting any time during which the embryo was stored'.[47] The 1990 Act expressly prohibited certain activities, focusing on seeking to ban cloning and attempts to create human/animal hybrids. As we will see, the amendments in the Human Fertilisation and Embryology Act 2008 both now provide for 'therapeutic cloning' and for what are now called 'human admixed embryos'. But while the HFEA may now license research in these fields, the Act in its rules on permitted embryos ensures that no cloned or hybrid embryo may be implanted in a woman.[48] Other restrictions remain. Human embryos or gametes may not be implanted in animals, nor may animal embryos be inserted in humans.[49] A non-human primate could not be used as a surrogate to gestate a human embryo. The genetic structure of an embryo

---

[42] See Academy of Medical Sciences, *A New Pathway for the Regulation and Governance of Health Research* (2011); discussed fully below at **15.5**.

[43] Report of the Committee of Inquiry into Human Fertilisation and Embryology (1984) Cmnd 9314 (the Warnock Report) and see above at **12.1**.

[44] Baroness Warnock has since regretted that her committee endorsed any notion of respect for the embryo; see E Jackson, *Medical Law: Text, Cases and Materials* (2nd edn, 2010) OUP, p 628.

[45] See s 3(1). Any prosecution under the Act will require the consent of the DPP: s 42.

[46] See above **1.16** and below **15.5**.

[47] S 3(3)(a).

[48] See ss 3 and 3ZA.

[49] See s 3(2) and s 3(3)(b).

may not be altered '... except in such circumstances (if any) as may be specified in ...' regulations to be made by the HFEA.[50]

The original rules governing embryo research in the Act centred on two principles. We suggest that while the 2008 amendments changed the application of those principles, they remain fundamental to UK legislation:

(1)   The Act implicitly accepts that respect is due to the embryo from fertilisation, but that up until the development of the primitive streak, the 'goods' to be expected from research outweigh the interests of the embryo.

(2)   The Act sought to allay fears of a science-fiction nightmare in which scientists freely create all sorts of clones, hybrids and other monsters. It should be noted that until the enactment of the Human Fertilisation and Embryology Act 1990 embryos *in vitro* enjoyed no legal protection at all. The wording of abortion legislation prohibiting 'procurement of miscarriage' meant that in theory 'test-tube' embryos could then be grown and destroyed at will.

Subject to the express prohibitions above, the HFEA was given a remarkably free hand by the Act. Legislation allows embryos to be created solely for research purposes. Schedule 2 outlines what a research licence may authorise. First the HFEA must be satisfied that the proposed research is necessary and desirable for an authorised purpose. Five specific purposes were originally set out in the Human Fertilisation and Embryology Act 1990:

(1)   promoting advances in the treatment of infertility;
(2)   increasing knowledge about the causes of congenital disease;
(3)   increasing knowledge about the causes of miscarriage;
(4)   developing more effective techniques of contraception;
(5)   developing methods for detecting the presence of gene or chromosomal abnormalities in embryos before implantation.

Those five specific purposes may be regarded as justification for the destruction of embryos, aimed at improving medicine and increasing human happiness, designed to reassure those who were doubtful about, but not adamantly opposed to, research. To those named purposes was added an apparently innocuous phrase – 'or for such other purposes as may be specified in regulations'.

Embryo research and 'cloning'

13.8   From 1990 to about 1998 the fury of the embryo research debate abated. The birth of Dolly, the cloned sheep, changed all that. Dolly was created by a process of cell nucleus replacement (CNR). The nucleus of an adult cell was inserted into an emptied egg cell. The egg cell was then subjected to an electrical impulse so it began to divide and develop as an embryo. The embryo was implanted in a surrogate 'mother'. There is no scientific reason why this

---

[50]   Sch 2, para 3(4).

process could not (in theory) be replicated in humans. Two principal purposes could drive the development of CNR in humans.

(1) Obviously attempts could be made to create a child, a copy of its lone parent sharing most of his or her DNA. Many British scientists abhor the notion of 'reproductive cloning'. A number of eminent ethicists argue no case has been made out sufficient to justify banning 'reproductive cloning'.[51] As we saw in the last chapter, reproductive cloning is prohibited in the UK.

(2) Stem cells could be collected from the cloned embryo. Embryonic stem cells retain their pluripotency. That means they can be cultured to develop into different sorts of tissue, or even potentially grown into organs. 'Therapeutic cloning', or stem cell therapy as it is more usually styled today, may offer a tantalising range of scientific benefits. For example, assume that a patient has a neurological disease. An embryo could be created by CNR using DNA from one of the patient's own cells. Stem cells taken from the resulting embryo could be used to create tissue to repair her damaged brain. As the cells used were 'hers', there would be no risk of rejection.

In 1998, the HFEA joined the Human Genetic Advisory Commission (HGAC) to consider the ethics of cloning in both its guises. Their Report[52] recommended that regulations under the Human Fertilisation and Embryology Act 1990 should be extended to allow the HFEA to authorise procedures:

(a) to extract embryonic stem cells for research on the possible treatment benefits in a wide range of disorders by replacing cells which have become damaged or diseased; and

(b) to conduct research into the treatment of some rare but serious inherited disorders carried in maternal mitochondria.

A further consultation led by the Chief Medical Officer[53] endorsed the recommendations of the HFEA and HGAC. Both ruled out reproductive cloning as beyond the pale. 'Good' cloning would be allowed. 'Bad' cloning would be banned. Regulations to permit stem cell therapy were approved by Parliament in January 2001.[54] These regulations purported to authorise the following additional research purposes:

---

[51] See, for example, J Harris, 'Goodbye Dolly? – The Ethics of Human Cloning' (1997) 23 *Journal of Medical Ethics* 353.

[52] HFEA/HGAC, *Cloning Issues in Reproduction, Science and Medicine* (1998). And see J Harris, *Clones, Genes and Immortality* (1998) OUP.

[53] Expert Group of the CMO, *Stem Cell Research: Medical Progress and Responsibility* (2000) DH. See also House of Lords, *Stem Cell Research* (2002) HL 83(i); Nuffield Council on Bioethics, *Stem Cell Therapy: A Discussion* (2000).

[54] The Human Fertilisation and Embryology (Research Purposes) Regulations 2001, SI 2001/188. Such was the public concern about their regulations that they were immediately reviewed (and in the event approved) by a Select Committee of the House of Lords; see above House of Lords, *Stem Cell Research*.

- increasing knowledge about development of embryos;
- increasing knowledge about serious disease;
- enabling such knowledge to be applied in developing treatment for serious disease.

The Regulations were made on an assumption that CNR fell within the Human Fertilisation and Embryology Act. Pro-life groups challenged the regulations, arguing that embryos created by CNR fell wholly outside the 1990 Act and were not covered by section 3(3)(d) which had been intended to ban cloning. Section 3(3)(d) only barred replacing a nucleus of a cell taken from an embryo with a nucleus taken from any person or an embryo. CNR removes the nucleus from an egg cell, not an embryo. The government argued that nonetheless reproductive cloning was effectively outlawed because the HFEA would never license any attempt at reproductive cloning. So to do so would be a crime, because creating an embryo without an HFEA licence is a crime. But 'embryo', for the purpose of the unamended 1990 Act, was defined as follows:[55]

> embryo means a live human embryo where fertilisation is complete.

If CNR is used to create the embryo, *fertilisation* never takes place.[56] CNR involves propagation not fertilisation. Did it fall outside the 1990 Act and so CNR 'cloning' (for either therapeutic or reproductive purposes) could take place without a licence?

The All-Party Pro-Life Alliance challenged the regulations allowing stem cell therapy. They argued that the regulations were ultra vires because an embryo created by CNR was not an embryo within the definition provided in the Human Fertilisation and Embryology Act 1990. Crane J agreed that an embryo created otherwise than by fertilisation fell outside the Act.[57] The government rushed through the Human Reproductive Cloning Act 2001. That Act made implanting a CNR embryo in a woman a criminal offence. The status of the regulations governing stem cell therapy remained in limbo. The Court of Appeal came to the government's rescue.[58] The House of Lords upheld the Court of Appeal.[59] In both courts, moral controversy was translated into an exercise in statutory interpretation. Lord Bingham declared[60] that the '... basic task of the court is to ascertain and give effect to the true meaning of what Parliament has said in the enactment to be construed'. The 1990 Act must '... be read in the historical context of the situation which led to its enactment'. Parliament, their Lordships concluded, never intended to distinguish between

---

55 S 1(1)(a).
56 See M Brazier, 'Regulating the Reproduction Business?' (1999) 8 *Medical Law Review* 166.
57 *R (Quintavalle) v Secretary of State for Health* [2001] 4 All ER 1019.
58 *R (Quintavalle) v Secretary of State for Health* [2002] 2 A11 ER 625, CA.
59 [2003] 2 A11 ER 113. The House of Lords, however, did also confirm that s 3(3)(a) of the Act did not impose an absolute prohibition on CNR.
60 [2003] 2 All ER 113 at 118.

live embryos produced by fertilisation, and embryos produced without fertilisation. Parliament, in 1990, would have been unaware that the latter process was possible. The fundamental purpose of section 3(1)(a) of the Act was to provide protection for embryos created outside the human body.[61]

> The protective purpose was plainly not intended to be tied to the particular way in which an embryo might be created.

As we shall see, the amendments in the Human Fertilisation and Embryology Act 2008 give statutory endorsement to the earlier regulations allowing and controlling stem cell therapies. What of the moral arguments? Does it follow that anyone who in 1990 was sceptical about the legitimacy of embryo research should be outraged by developments allowing stem cell therapies, 'therapeutic cloning'? It is no more than a logical outcome of permitting research at all. If the 'goods' of more successful fertility treatments justified destroying embryos, it is difficult to say that the 'good' of helping seriously ill patients does not. The argument may be raised that use of embryos is not essential to achieve that end. Adult stem cells could be treated to recover pluripotency. It might just take longer to do the research. CNR forces some reconsideration of the basis of opposition for embryo research. Embryos created from fertilisation of egg by sperm result (normally) in the creation of a unique new genetic entity. What is the nature of an embryo created by CNR using our nuclei, our DNA? If used solely for stem cell therapy, is it different from taking a skin graft from a leg to treat burns on an arm.

Amendments to the Human Fertilisation and Embryology Act 1990 now clarify the status of CNR embryos and give statutory endorsement to the development of stem cell therapies. First, section 1(b) redefines an embryo as 'an egg that is in the process of fertilisation *or is undergoing any other process capable of resulting in an embryo*' (our emphasis). Thus CNR embryos are 'captured' by the Act and so would be embryos created by any other process as yet unknown. Schedule 2, para 3A to the 1990 Act (as amended) formally extends the list of purposes for which the HFEA may grant a research licence adding to the original five:

- increasing knowledge about serious disease or other serious medical conditions;[62]
- developing treatments for serious disease or other serious medical conditions;
- increasing knowledge about the cause of any congenital disease or other congenital condition that does not fall within paragraph (a).

But it is crucial to remember that for a licence to be granted for any of these purposes (and/or for the use of human admixed embryos), the applicant must

---

[61] [2003] 2 All ER 113 at 126 per Lord Steyn.
[62] The addition of serious conditions to serious diseases in the Act is to cover research into treatment for such conditions as spinal injury.

establish that the use of embryos is necessary.[63] Those opposed to embryo research will no doubt seek to argue that it is not necessary, as the objectives above could be met by using adult stem cells (IPSC).

Human admixed embryos

13.9   Before the amendments to the Human Fertilisation and Embryology Act 1990, once the regulations to permit stem cell therapies had been declared lawful by the courts under the unamended Act, the HFEA granted licences to allow the use of embryos to develop stem cell therapies, but scientists immediately faced a resource problem. Developing CNR embryos needs a plentiful supply of eggs to 'empty' and into which the nucleus can be inserted to create embryos, from which embryonic stem cells can then be cultured. Human eggs for the purposes of egg donation in fertility treatment are in short supply, never mind human eggs for research such as this. However, human eggs are not necessary for the purpose. A cow or rabbit egg will do just as well. Sometimes referred to as cytoplasmic hybrid embryos, the resulting embryo remains more than 99.9 per cent 'human'. Only the mitochondrial DNA from the animal egg remains and any stem cells retrieved are 100 per cent human.[64]

The possibility of creating human/animal hybrids sparked new controversy and initially the government indicated that it would use new legislation to ban any research entailing any element of hybridisation, stating in its White Paper that the 'Government will propose that the creation of hybrid or chimera embryos *in vitro* should not be allowed . . .'[65] Scientists criticised the government's proposal to ban the procedure, arguing it was based solely on unreasoned expressions of public revulsion and the opinions of certain religious groups.[66] The use of rabbit eggs to develop human embryonic cells will not create a creature half-rabbit, half-human. The cloned embryo will never develop into a living animal of any species. The HFEA launched a consultation on the matter and the government changed its mind.[67] Thus the 2008 Act amended the 1990 Act to permit the HFEA to license research on what the Act now terms human admixed embryos. It is worth repeating that the Act still prohibits implanting any such embryo in a woman and equally bans implanting a human admixed embryo in any animal.[68] Section 4A defines human admixed embryos to include not only the cytoplasmic hybrids described above

---

[63]   Human Fertilisation and Embryology Act 1990, Sch 3A.

[64]   See E Jackson, *Medical Law: Text, Cases and Materials* (2nd edn, 2010) OUP, pp 634–635.

[65]   Review of the Human Fertilisation and Embryology Act (2006) Cm 6989, para 2.85.

[66]   See (2007) *Times,* 5 January.

[67]   When the 2008 Act had been passed but was not yet in force, the HFEA granted two licences to permit research using cytoplasmic hybrid embryos. An application for judicial review to strike down the licences failed: see *R (on the application of Quintavalle and the CLC) v HFEA* [2008] EWHC 3395 (Admin).

[68]   S 4A(4).

but a range of other embryos created by mixing animal and human gametes. So human/animal hybrids mixing human and animal gametes are allowed as are transgenic embryos in which animal DNA has been introduced, and chimeras where a human embryo has been altered by the addition of animal cells. And finally provision is made for other hybrid/chimeras subject to the condition that the animal DNA is not predominant.[69]

Artificial gametes

13.10   Developments in stem cell research open up the possibility that scientists may be able to manipulate stem cells to create artificial gametes. That is to say that stem cells taken from an infertile man or woman could be used to create functioning sperm and eggs, even that stem cells from a male could be used to create artificial eggs and vice versa. Research into the development of artificial gametes remains lawful in the UK but section 3ZA of the Human Fertilisation and Embryology Act 1990 prohibits the use of any artificial gametes in treatment by providing that only permitted sperm and eggs may be so used and defining such gametes as extracted from the testes of a man or ovaries of a woman with no alteration of the nuclear or mitochondrial DNA of sperm or eggs.

Replacing the Human Fertilisation and Embryology Authority (HFEA)

13.11   If proposals to abolish the HFEA go ahead, its licensing functions in relation to research are likely to move to the Health Research Agency proposed by the Academy of Medical Sciences.[70] But we note that in their Report (at paragraph 7.3), the Academy acknowledges the role of the HFEA in facilitating debate and that it has earned the confidence of researchers. No recommendations are made about the regulation of embryo research and in chapter 9 the Academy sets out the role of the HFEA in its pathway for regulation and governance of health research. The HFEA may live to fight another day?

Embryo to foetus: foetus to baby

13.12   An embryo *in vitro* will not be allowed to develop beyond fourteen days from fertilisation. What of the embryo *in vivo*, growing and developing in his mother's womb? By twelve weeks, the embryo will, if seen on an ultrasound scan, bear a distinct resemblance to a baby[71] and from then on will

---

[69]   See *Mason and McCall Smith*, pp 252–253.
[70]   Academy of Medical Sciences, *A New Pathway for the Regulation and Governance of Health Research* (2011).
[71]   On which see D Kirklin, 'The Role of Medical Imaging in the Abortion Debate' (2004) 30 *Journal of Medical Ethics* 426.

usually be termed a foetus. In many legal systems, the protection given to the embryo/foetus is extended as the pregnancy progresses, and the foetus develops. Thus, in France, abortion is allowed on demand up to ten weeks' gestation, and from then is permissible only on the grounds of risk to the mother's health. In the USA, the Supreme Court in *Roe v Wade*[72] declared that any restriction on abortion in the first twelve weeks of pregnancy was unconstitutional, as a violation of the pregnant woman's right to privacy. States may regulate abortion to protect maternal health from twelve to twenty-four weeks, and from viability (between twenty-four and twenty-eight weeks) the interests of the foetus take precedence over the interests of the mother. *Roe v Wade* adopts an openly gradualist approach to the conflict of rights between the mother and her unborn child.

In England, the Abortion Act 1967 originally set no limit to the time when an abortion might lawfully be performed. Section 5(1) provided instead that nothing in the Act should affect the provisions of the Infant Life (Preservation) Act 1929 protecting the viable foetus. Under that Act, any person who with intent to destroy the life of a child capable of being born alive causes the child to die before it has an existence independent of the mother is guilty of child destruction. The foetus was deemed to be capable of being born alive at twenty-eight weeks.[73] The objective of the 1929 law was to protect the foetus in the course of delivery,[74] and to safeguard any foetus who, but for improper intervention, could have been born alive.

But what was meant by 'capable of being born alive'? In *C v S*,[75] a young man, seeking to stop his girlfriend aborting their child at eighteen weeks, argued that at eighteen weeks a foetus was 'capable of being born alive'. It is fully formed and its heart may beat for a second or so after expulsion from the mother. At eighteen weeks there is no prospect of a baby breathing independently of its mother even with the aid of a ventilator. The Court of Appeal found that to be 'capable of being born alive' a foetus must be able, on delivery, to breathe either naturally or with mechanical aid. The fight to limit late abortions returned to Parliament. Anti-abortion campaigners persuaded the government to agree to the introduction of an amendment to what was to become the Human Fertilisation and Embryology Act 1990, an amendment designed to reduce the time limit for abortions. Their attempt misfired, and after a night of confusion, section 37 of the Human Fertilisation and Embry-

---

[72] (1973) 93 S Ct 705. Though since *Roe v Wade*, anti-abortion campaigners have ceaselessly sought to reverse the decision or limit its impact; see *Mason and McCall Smith*, at 9.74–9.79.

[73] Albeit at twenty-eight weeks the foetus was deemed to be capable of being born alive, that did *not* mean an earlier abortion was necessarily lawful. It would be for the prosecution to prove *that* foetus was capable of being born alive.

[74] Thus closing a lacuna in the abortion laws.

[75] [1987] 1 All ER 1230. A somewhat different interpretation was offered in *Rance v Mid-Downs Health Authority* [1991] 1 All ER 801.

ology Act 1990 emerged. Section 37 produced a liberalisation, rather than restriction, of abortion laws in England.

Section 37 amended the Abortion Act 1967 to provide that the time limit for lawful abortions carried out on grounds of risk to the physical or mental health of the woman or her existing children (so called 'social abortions') is twenty-four weeks. In the other three cases, there is *no* time limit, ie an abortion may be performed right up to the end of the pregnancy. Abortion up to birth is lawful when: (1) termination is necessary to prevent grave permanent injury to the physical or mental health of the mother; or (2) continuance of the pregnancy threatens the life of the mother or (3) there is a substantial risk that if the child is born it would suffer from such physical or mental abnormalities as to be seriously handicapped.

It is the third of these cases which has proved most controversial. The Infant Life (Preservation) Act 1929 permitted action necessary to save the life of the mother, even if doing so inevitably entailed the destruction of the child; preventing grave permanent injury to her health was also almost certainly permissible.[76] Such cases of a stark choice between mother and child are few and far between in modern medicine. Permitting abortion up to forty weeks on grounds of foetal handicap was novel. In debate in Parliament, that provision seemed to be regarded as covering only the most grave of disabilities, perhaps where a woman was found late in pregnancy to be carrying an anencephalic child incapable of surviving more than a few hours after birth. However, the wording of section 37 is identical to the general foetal handicap ground provided for in the 1967 Act. So, if Down's syndrome or spina bifida is diagnosed, however late into pregnancy, may the foetus lawfully be destroyed? The wording of the Act is vague.[77] The Royal College of Obstetricians and Gynaecologists (RCOG) offer doctors further guidance.[78] They shy away from prescription, considering that 'it would be unrealistic to produce a definitive list of conditions that constitute serious handicap'. The RCOG emphasises the need for the parents and the doctor to weigh the potential suffering of the child, the suffering of the mother, the burden on the family, and the severity of the handicap affecting the foetus. The 2010 report does set a minimum threshold advising that the child must have a physical or mental disability which would cause 'significant suffering or long term impairment of their ability to function in society'. The RCOG acknowledges that in applying these criteria to actual cases, foetal medicine specialists take different moral views.

---

[76] See *R v Bourne* [1939] 1 KB 687.
[77] See E Wicks, M Wyldes and M Kilby, 'Late Termination of Pregnancy for Fetal Abnormality: Medical and Legal Perspectives' (2004) 12 *Medical Law Review* 285; S Sheldon and S Wilkinson, 'Termination of Pregnancy for Reasons of Foetal Disability: Are there Grounds for a Special Exception in Law?' (2001) 9 *Medical Law Review* 85.
[78] Royal College of Obstetricians and Gynaecologists, *Termination of Pregnancy for Fetal Abnormality in England, Scotland and Wales* (2010).

In 2004, the Reverend Joanna Jepson challenged the decision by West Mercia Police not to investigate a complaint that doctors had authorised the termination of a pregnancy at twenty-eight weeks of a foetus with bilateral cleft lip and palate. She obtained leave to apply for judicial review.[79] The hearing was postponed while police conducted further investigations. The Crown Prosecution Service reviewed the evidence and decided not to pursue a prosecution. Reverend Jepson took no further action.[80] The CPS found that doctors acted in good faith on the basis of appropriate expert opinion. Much was made of the importance of consultation in the absence of a precise definition of serious foetal handicap.[81] It seems that, in effect, serious handicap may come to be defined subjectively – do the parents and the doctors consider the relevant handicap to be serious? The impact of section 37 of the Human Fertilisation and Embryology Act 1990 is that in England children capable of being born alive may be killed, providing they are disabled. The protection afforded to the viable foetus by the Infant Life (Preservation) Act 1929 is withdrawn from the disabled foetus. A medical practitioner acting within the provisions of the amended and extended Abortion Act 1967 cannot be convicted of child destruction. The 1929 Act remains in force, but applicable only to *unlawful* late abortions, and those cases where a violent attack on a pregnant woman kills the child within her.

Late abortions on grounds of foetal handicap are not the only source of controversy in relation to time limits to termination of pregnancy. As we shall see in the next chapter, developments in the care of extremely premature babies mean that a small number of babies born before twenty-four weeks' gestation survive. The twenty-four-week limit for 'social abortions' is under attack. It is argued that it is not ethically justifiable to destroy a foetus which may have the capacity to survive independently outside its mother's womb. A 'viable' foetus should acquire a right to survive.

The issue of foeticide brings the debate on late abortions into a sharp focus. Doctors aborting a foetus late on in pregnancy will seek to ensure that they use means that will destroy the foetus before it emerges from the mother. For if a child is born alive, nothing in the Abortion Act 1967 authorises her destruction. Accounts are given of premature infants left to die in the sluice room adjacent to the operating theatre where an abortion was attempted.[82] What are the legal rules applicable when an attempted abortion results not in a dead

---

[79] *Jepson v The Chief Constable of West Mercia Police Constabulary* [2003] EWHC 3318.

[80] C Dyer, 'Doctor Who Performed Late Abortion will Not be Prosecuted' (2005) 330 *BMJ* 668.

[81] See R Scott, 'The Uncertain Scope of Reproductive Autonomy in Pre-implantation Genetic Diagnosis and Selective Abortion' (2005) 13 *Medical Law Review* 291; R Scott, 'Interpreting the Disability Ground of the Abortion Act' (2005) 64 *Cambridge Law Journal* 388.

[82] See S K Templeton and L Rogers, 'Babies that Live after Abortions are Left to Die' (2004) *Sunday Times,* 20 June.

foetus, but a living, albeit sick, infant? The child once born alive is protected by the law. Any positive act to destroy it is murder. Failure to offer the child proper care *with the intention that it shall die* on the part of persons with an obligation to care for the child is equally murder.[83] Failure to offer the child proper care out of incompetence or carelessness is manslaughter. The theory is clear. Reality is more problematical. A doctor who embarks on an abortion undertakes the care of the mother, and to relieve her of her unwanted child. Yet the criminal law imposes on him an obligation to the child. His position none-theless is clearly distinct from that of the doctor undertaking safely to deliver a mother of a desired child. And what of the child born disabled? The doctor sets out to abort on the grounds of the substantial disability affecting the child, but if the child survives, must he then use all his efforts to save her? This leads us into the question of medical care of the disabled newborn baby, his rights and those of his parents, a minefield we enter in chapter 15.

Unsurprisingly, obstetricians try to avoid entering that minefield. Advice from the RCOG recommends foeticide in all terminations of pregnancy at a gesta-tional age of more than twenty-one weeks and six days, unless the foetal abnormality is such that early neonatal death is inevitable.[84] In practice, this means that foetal medicine specialists administer a fatal injection of potassium chloride into the foetal heart before beginning the process of terminating the pregnancy. Foeticide has become a routine part of late termination of preg-nancy. It is performed not only to ensure that the foetus is born dead, but also to ensure that the foetus suffers no pain in the course of the termination.[85] Not all women agreeing to termination of pregnancy for a serious abnormality want also to agree to foeticide. The RCOG recognises that in cases where a lethal abnormality is present, foeticide may not be appropriate.

Selective reduction: selective foeticide

13.13 So far, discussion of the legality of abortion has proceeded on the basis that the procedure used terminates the woman's pregnancy completely. There are cases where only selected foetuses in a multiple pregnancy are destroyed, and the pregnancy continues to term when the woman delivers her surviving children. Selective reduction, or selective foeticide, may be advised either when the woman has a multiple pregnancy and is unlikely to carry all the foetuses

---

[83] *R v Hamilton* (1983) *Times,* 16 September. In 1983, a consultant gynaecologist was charged with attempted murder. Police had been informed that a baby had been left on a slab to die for some time before being transferred to a paediatric unit. The alle-gation against the doctor was that he performed an abortion on the basis of an esti-mate of twenty-three weeks' pregnancy and, when the baby proved to be of thirty-four weeks' gestation, left it without attention, intending it to die. The pros-ecution was dismissed by magistrates for lack of evidence.

[84] RCOG, *Termination of Pregnancy for Fetal Abnormality* (2010), pp 29–31.

[85] See RCOG, *Fetal Awareness: Review of Research and Recommendations for Prac-tice* (2010).

safely to term, or when one of two or more foetuses is disabled. The 'surplus' or disabled foetuses will, using foetoscopically directed procedures, be killed. The dead foetuses are not expelled from the uterus, but become 'foetus papyraceous', and emerge on delivery of its healthy brothers and sisters. Selective reduction to destroy a disabled twin was quietly practised for years. The development of IVF and consequent increase in multiple pregnancies brought the procedure to public attention. Until recently, in a number of fertility clinics, to maximise the woman's chances of pregnancy, several embryos were implanted. If she conceived quadruplets or more, the risk was that the babies would be delivered prematurely and in the worst case scenario *all* might fail to survive. Selective reduction offered the prospect of one or two healthy children being born safely.

The deliberate destruction of selected foetuses raised ethical and legal problems. Legal debate focused on whether selective reduction was lawful.[86] Section 37(5) of the Human Fertilisation and Embryology Act 1990 legalises selective reduction, if performed for one of the grounds on which termination of the whole pregnancy is lawful. Thus, if foetuses are destroyed on grounds of foetal handicap, or because a multiple pregnancy poses a risk to the mother's health, selective reduction is as lawful as ending the pregnancy altogether would be. The anomalous situation is this. Where multiple pregnancy occurs, the underlying reason for wanting to destroy foetus A and B is to maximise the prospects of a healthy birth for foetuses C and D. The ground that would need to be invoked is that permitting abortion to safeguard the health of any 'existing children' of the pregnant woman. Can foetuses C and D be regarded as 'existing children'? The whole philosophy of English law relating to the status of the foetus is that a foetus is not for legal purposes a child.

Section 37(5) grants legal recognition to a much disputed procedure.[87] If foetuses can be selected and destroyed in effect as part and parcel of infertility treatment, the message from Parliament seems to be that unborn life is little more than a means to an end. The foetus itself counts for little. The parents' desire for children justifies its destruction. Does selective killing of disabled foetuses with legal blessing reinforce the second-class status of the disabled foetus?

Nurses and abortion

13.14 Nurses are increasingly involved in the process of termination of pregnancy. A particular concern for nurses in relation to second-trimester terminations, is abortions in the middle months of pregnancy. The Abortion

---

[86] See J Keown, 'Selective Reduction of Multiple Pregnancy' (1987) 137 *New Law Journal* 1165; D P T Price, 'Selective Reduction and Foeticide: The Parameters of Abortion' [1988] *Criminal Law Review* 199.

[87] R Lee and D Morgan, *Human Fertilisation and Embryology: Regulating the Reproductive Revolution* (2000) Blackstone, pp 252–256.

Act 1967 provides for circumstances when a pregnancy may lawfully be terminated by a registered medical practitioner, a doctor. In 1967, all lawful abortions were carried out by surgical means. The surgeon removed the foetus and ended the pregnancy. By 1972, medical induction of abortion was introduced as the standard method of terminating pregnancies in the second trimester. A doctor inserts a catheter into the woman's womb. Later, a nurse attaches the catheter via a flexible tube to a pump, which feeds the hormone prostaglandin through the catheter and induces premature labour. The nurse administers another drug via a drip in the woman's arm to stimulate her contractions. The immature foetus is born dead. The substances that cause the abortion are administered by the nurse. The nurse in effect terminates the pregnancy.

The Royal College of Nursing was doubtful whether a pregnancy terminated by a nurse was lawfully terminated. Might nurses face prosecution for conducting criminal abortions? The Department of Health and Social Security issued a circular upholding the legality of medical inductions of abortion. The Royal College of Nursing went to court for a declaration that the circular was wrong in law. The College lost in the High Court, won in the Court of Appeal and finally lost by three to two in the House of Lords.[88] The majority of their Lordships held that the Act must be construed in the light of its social purposes, first, to broaden the ground on which abortions may lawfully be obtained, and second, to secure safe and hygienic conditions for women undergoing abortion. The Act contemplated the participation of a team of hospital staff involved in the overall treatment of the woman, and exonerated them all from criminal liability if the abortion was carried out within the terms of the Act. It was not necessary for a doctor to perform every physical act leading to the termination of the pregnancy. Provided a doctor accepts full responsibility for every stage in the treatment, a nurse acting under his instructions and in conformity with accepted medical practice does not act unlawfully when she administers the drugs which terminate the pregnancy in an induced abortion.

Conscientious objection

13.15 A vital component of the compromise on which the Abortion Act 1967 was based was the right of conscientious objection. Section 4 provides that no person shall be under any duty 'to participate in any treatment authorised by this Act to which he has a conscientious objection'.[89] It is for the person objecting to prove that their objection rests on grounds of conscience. And, in the case of abortion, the professional's conscience does not relieve him of any duty to intervene to save the life of the mother or to prevent grave permanent injury to her health.

---

[88] *Royal College of Nursing v DHSS* [1981] AC 800.
[89] S 38 of the Human Fertilisation and Embryology Act 1990 confers a similar right to refuse to participate in embryo research or any of the infertility treatments regulated by that Act.

In *Janaway v Salford Area Health Authority*,[90] the House of Lords was asked to determine *who* was entitled to rely on the right of conscientious objection. Mrs Janaway was a devout Roman Catholic employed as a secretary. She refused to type abortion referral letters and the authority dismissed her. She challenged her dismissal as unlawful because, she argued, she was entitled to rely on the right of conscientious objection provided for by section 4 of the Abortion Act 1967. Her action failed. The Law Lords ruled that the term 'participate' in section 4 meant actually taking part in treatment designed to terminate a pregnancy. Mrs Janaway was not asked to do anything that involved her personally in the process of abortion. Yet she was an essential cog in the wheel. Abortion was as repugnant to her as murder. For Mrs Janaway, however irrational others might perceive her views to be, her employers were asking her to type out a death warrant.

The House of Lords' restrictive interpretation of the right to conscientious objection has other consequences too. A healthcare professional may legitimately refuse to carry out, or assist at, an abortion. He cannot withdraw from any contact with abortion advice. Consider this example. A woman of over thirty-five receives her ante-natal care from an obstetrician adamantly opposed to abortion. He never discusses with her whether, in view of her age, she should undergo amniocentesis to test for Down's syndrome. The prevalence of Down's syndrome increases in mothers over thirty-five. If she gives birth to a Down's baby, the mother may sue the obstetrician for negligence.[91] If, as we strongly suspect, the overwhelming body of responsible professional opinion regards amniocentesis (or other available tests for Down's) as routine for pregnant women over thirty-five, the obstetrician's right to conscientious objection will be of no avail to him. If his duty of care (as defined by his peers) extends to advice on amniocentesis, then even though that advice on amniocentesis is almost inevitably an act preparatory to abortion, he must fulfil that duty, for it involves no active participation in the process of ending a pregnancy.[92]

The right to conscientious objection is limited in scope and in practice difficult to exercise. Hospitals are wary of staff who will not participate in what has become a fairly common operation. It is said that nurses face greater risk to their career prospects if they declare their conscientious objection to abortion.[93] Paradoxically, there remain areas of England where abortion within the NHS is difficult to obtain. Is that a violation of women's rights caused by giving undue precedence to the professional's right to his conscience? The irony is that consultants and GPs can avoid involvement in abortion without having to invoke the right to conscientious objection. The doctor simply refuses to certify that a ground specified in the Act is made out. The woman

---

[90] [1988] 3 All ER 1051, HL.

[91] See above at **11.10**.

[92] And doctors opposed to abortion should at least refer the patient to another doctor; see *Barr v Matthews* (2000) 52 BMLR 217. Failure to do so may violate GMC Guidance; see GMC, *Personal Beliefs and Medical Practice* (2008).

[93] See *Mason and McCall Smith*, p 332.

can then only try to find another more sympathetically inclined doctor. Her only remedy against the first practitioner would lie if she could prove that to refuse her an abortion was a breach of the duty of care owed to her. If the doctor is a consultant or a GP, no one can order him to participate in an abortion.

Fathers and abortion[94]

13.16   Has the father of the unborn child any say in whether or not the child be aborted? In 1978, in *Paton v British Pregnancy Advisory Service*,[95] a husband tried to prevent his wife having an abortion. She had been concerned about her pregnancy and consulted her doctor, but did not consult her husband. She obtained a certificate from two registered medical practitioners that the continuance of the pregnancy would involve risk to her health. So an abortion could lawfully proceed. Her husband intervened. He went to court to ask for an injunction (an order) to prevent the abortion from being carried out without his consent. The court refused an injunction. The judge said that the 1967 Act gave no right to the husband to be consulted. In the absence of such a right under the Act, the husband had 'no legal right enforceable at law or in equity to stop his wife having this abortion or to stop the doctors from carrying out the abortion'.

The abortion went ahead. The husband went to the European Commission of Human Rights, arguing that the Act and the judge's decision infringed the European Convention on Human Rights. He argued that his right to family life and the unborn child's right to life had been infringed. The Commission dismissed his claim.[96] They said that where an abortion was carried out on medical grounds, the husband's right to family life must necessarily be subordinated to the need to protect the rights and health of the mother. The unborn child's right to life was similarly subordinate to the rights of its mother, at least in the initial months of pregnancy. In *C v S*,[97] the Court of Appeal, having held that the abortion of a foetus at eighteen weeks did not contravene the Infant Life (Prevention) Act 1929, refused the father any right *qua* father or a guardian of the unborn child to challenge the proposed abortion. In England, husbands have no standing to oppose an abortion agreed to by the wife, nor has a father any right to intervene to 'save' the foetus, nor can anyone argue that the foetus itself has legal personality so enabling him to act as its 'guardian' and stop an abortion.

---

[94]   See M Fox, 'Abortion Decision-Making – Taking Men's Needs Seriously' in E Lee (ed), *Abortion Law and Politics Today* (1998) Macmillan, p 198; S Sheldon, 'Unwilling Fathers and Abortion: Terminating Men's Child Support Obligations' (2003) 66 *Modern Law Review* 175.

[95]   [1979] QB 276.

[96]   [1980] 3 EHRR 408.

[97]   [1987] 1 All ER 1230. And see *Kelly v Kelly* 1997 SLT 896 (Scotland).

One issue remains open. The father in *Paton* reluctantly accepted that the doctors' certificate as to the need for the abortion was issued in good faith. Had he challenged the certificate, could he have asked for an injunction to prevent an unlawful abortion taking place? The judge in *Paton* did not have to decide this point. He expressed the view that an injunction would not be granted. The supervision of abortion and the issue of the doctors' good faith is left to the criminal law and a jury. The Court of Appeal in *C v S*[98] endorsed that opinion.

Foetal status: *Vo v France* and *A, B and C v Ireland*

13.17 The vexed question of foetal status, and whether the unborn child can assert a right to life, came before the ECtHR once in *Vo v France*.[99] The applicant, Mme Vo, attended hospital in France for an ante-natal appointment in the sixth month of her pregnancy. Mme Vo was originally from Vietnam and spoke little French. A terrible error led to a doctor mistakenly supposing her to be another woman with a similar name. This other patient was scheduled to have a contraceptive coil removed. The doctor then proceeded to attempt to remove a non-existent coil from the pregnant Mme Vo. He pierced the amniotic sac and a week or so later the pregnancy had to be terminated on health grounds. The foetus was found to be between twenty and twenty-one weeks' gestation.

Mme Vo began a number of civil and criminal proceedings against the doctor and the hospital. For our purposes, the crucial process was an attempt to bring a criminal prosecution against the doctor for involuntary homicide, what in this country would be styled gross negligence manslaughter. The French courts held a non-viable foetus could not be the subject of homicide. Mme Vo argued that French law violated Article 2 of the Human Rights Convention by failing to protect the life of her unborn child.

The majority of the ECtHR dodged the central question of foetal status.[100] They held that the question of when a right of life accrued fell within the margin of appreciation allowed to contracting states. This was a question unresolved among European countries, and there was no European consensus on scientific and legal definitions of the beginning of life. Additionally, even if the foetus in *Vo* was entitled to such protection under Article 2, its rights were sufficiently protected by the rights the mother enjoyed to protection from assault and injury. It was not desirable to address the question of whether an unborn child was a person for the purposes of Article 2 in the abstract. Read-

---

[98] [1987] 1 All ER 1230 at 1243.

[99] [2004] 2 FLR 577; see J K Mason, 'What's in a Name?: The Vagaries of *Vo v France*' [2005] *Child and Family Law Quarterly* 97. And see *Evans v UK* (2008) 46 EHRR 34.

[100] See K O'Donovan, 'Taking a Neutral Stance on the Legal Protection of the Fetus' (2006) 14 *Medical Law Review* 115.

ing the dissenting opinions within the Court will demonstrate that the human rights judges in Strasbourg are as divided in their judgments on foetal status as society in general.

In *Vo*, the margin of appreciation operated to deny any specific protection for the foetus under the European Convention on Human Rights. In *A, B and C v Ireland*[101] it was invoked to accept laws in Ireland to protect the unborn. The three applicants challenged Irish laws that only permit a lawful abortion in Ireland when the mother's life is at risk, and even in that case while a termination of pregnancy is permissible in theory, in practice the lack of clear legislative guidance on the criteria for a lawful abortion means that it is impossible to access abortion even in such a case. Applicants A and B advanced evidence that the absence of legal abortion in Ireland, forcing them to travel to the UK, damaged their health and thus violated their rights under Article 8 of the Convention. C contended that the absence of lawful abortion in Ireland endangered her life.[102] C's claim succeeded on the narrow grounds that as Irish law permitted abortion to save the mother's life, the state's failure to implement that right granted her by Irish law breached C's right to respect for her private life.[103] A and B's claims failed. While the prohibition on abortion even on health grounds amounted to an interference with their private rights, the interference was justified under Article 8(2). It fell within the margin of appreciation within which Ireland should be permitted to judge the value to be attached to unborn life.

Girls under sixteen

13.18 The Abortion Act made no special provision for abortion involving girls under sixteen. In 1981, a fifteen-year-old girl who already had one child became pregnant again while in local authority care. She wanted an abortion. Her doctors believed that the birth of a second child would damage her mental health and endanger her existing child. The girl's father objected. Abortion was contrary to his religion. The local authority applied to have the girl made a ward of court and thereby seek the consent of the court to the operation. Butler-Sloss J authorised the abortion.[104] She said that while she took into account the feelings of the parents, she was satisfied that the girl's best interests required that her pregnancy be ended. Her decision was approved by the House of Lords in *Gillick v West Norfolk and Wisbech Area Health Authority*.[105] *Gillick* would suggest that as long as the girl is mature enough to understand what abortion entails physically and emotionally, the doctor may go ahead on the basis of her consent alone. Nor are doctors under any obligation to inform her parents. The *Gillick competent* girl is as entitled to

---

[101] [2010] ECHR 25579/05.
[102] *A-G v X* [1992] 2 CMLR. And see *Tysiac v Poland* (2007) 45 EHRR 42.
[103] And see *Tysiac v Poland* (2007) 45 EHRR 42.
[104] *Re P (A Minor)* (1981) 80 LGR 301.
[105] [1985] 3 All ER 402, HL.

confidential treatment as the adult woman.[106] If the girl is insufficiently mature to make a decision for herself, the doctor must act in her best interests. Should her parents refuse consent to abortion, doctors and social workers may seek to go to court[107] and ask a judge to decide on the conflict between medical and parental opinion. Her wishes will be considered, but not treated as decisive. A doctor who ignores parental views will not be guilty of an offence of criminal abortion. He may face legal action by the girl's parents in the civil courts, or, in an extreme case, prosecution for an assault on her.

What of a case where parents want their daughter to have an abortion but she refuses? The Court of Appeal in *Re W (A Minor) (Medical Treatment)*[108] ruled that a doctor may lawfully proceed with treatment of any young person under eighteen with parental consent. He simply needs a valid consent either from his young patient herself, or from her parents. *Gillick competent* children and minors under eighteen can authorise their own treatment, but not veto treatment. In theory, a gynaecologist could elect to override his patient's refusal to terminate her pregnancy as long as her parents endorsed the abortion. However, to force an abortion on a girl must question whether either doctor or parents act in her interests. Lord Donaldson in *Re W* considered it unthinkable that doctors would use the law to coerce young girls into abortion.[109]

Mentally incapacitated women

13.19 In *T v T*,[110] a woman of nineteen became pregnant. She was said to have a mental age of two, was doubly incontinent and incapable of any comprehensible speech. The problem for her mother and her doctors was that T was quite incapable of giving her consent to the proposed abortion and, as she was an adult, no one else could authorise treatment on her behalf. Wood J granted a declaration that performing an abortion on T was not unlawful if that operation was considered to be in her best interests and in conformity with good medical practice. Termination of pregnancy in such a case will now be governed by the Mental Capacity Act 2005, discussed earlier in chapter 6. The fundamental test will continue to be whether, in all the circumstances, abortion is in the best interests of the woman. In determining her best interests, regard must be had for any views of feelings the woman herself expresses, or has expressed, in the past. The impact on her must be fully evaluated. The timing of the proposed abortion may be crucial. In 2002, a judge refused to authorise an abortion close to the twenty-four-week limit for 'social abortions'.[111]

---

[106] *Axon v Secretary of State for Health* [2006] EWHC 37.

[107] See *Re B (A Minor) (Wardship: Abortion)* [1991] 2 FLR 226 (Hollis J authorised abortion for twelve-year-old-girl).

[108] [1992] 4 All ER 627, discussed below at **14.21**.

[109] [1992] 4 All ER 627 at 635.

[110] [1988] 1 All ER 613.

[111] *Re SS (Medical Treatment: Late Termination)* [2002] 1 FLR 445. Contrast with *D v NHS Trust (Medical Treatment: Consent: Termination)* [2003] EWHC 2793.

A moral mess?

13.20 The debate on the morality of abortion continues. Consensus on the moral claims of the human embryo remains unattainable. The law in England is clear on one matter: the embryo/foetus has no legal personality or rights of its own until birth. It is recognised as an entity whose status deserves protection, but not as a legal person with rights equal to yours or mine. The question thus becomes how much protection should the embryo/foetus be afforded and at what cost to maternal rights and interests? And should that protection increase with gestational age? Today the law recognises two classes of foetus. Disabled foetuses are denied any protection from destruction even once capable of surviving birth. 'Normal' foetuses acquire a qualified right to birth at twenty-four weeks, dependent on their survival posing no grave risk to the mother. Up to twenty-four weeks, the fate of the 'normal' foetus rests in the hands of its mother's doctors. Whatever the intentions of the 1967 Abortion Act, in practice it has conferred the authority to grant or withhold abortion to the medical profession. If the fate of the embryo/foetus cannot in our community be decided on the basis of consensus as to its moral status, would it be better to leave women to make the decision on abortion? Can it be right on any analysis that a woman's entitlement to abortion and her child's claim to life should depend on where in the country a woman happens to live?

Chapter 14

DOCTORS AND CHILDREN

14.1 In this chapter, we examine the law governing doctors' relationships with child patients. The courts are often asked to determine the fate of sick children when doctors and parents disagree about how best to care for the child. Several cases have attracted much publicity. Charlotte Wyatt's parents sought assurances that, if their very sick baby daughter stopped breathing, she would be re-ventilated. Charlotte's case was considered by the courts on no less than six occasions.[1] Doctors caring for a baby known as MB wanted to switch off his ventilator and let him die peacefully. His parents objected and the judge refused to authorise removing MB from respiratory support.[2] Baby OT's parents also sought continuation of treatment but were unsuccessful both in their argument that the treatment was in their baby's best interests[3] and the procedural argument that the emergency application did not give them the time they needed to present their case.[4] The courts continue to struggle with the question of blood transfusions for the children of Jehovah's Witnesses. May a doctor insist on administering a transfusion against the parents' wishes? Some cases involve, not disagreement between doctors and parents, but disputes between parents themselves. Should a little boy be circumcised as his Muslim father wishes, when his mother vehemently opposes circumcision? On the opposite side of the coin, are there limits to treatment to which a parent may agree on behalf of the child? For instance, may a mother, learning that her four-year-old daughter is a likely carrier of haemophilia, have the child subjected to genetic testing for carrier status, or even sterilised? As a child matures, common sense dictates that she be allowed to take more decisions for herself. *Gillick*[5] appeared to establish a right to adolescent autonomy. It proved to be an odd sort of 'right', a right to say yes but not to say no.[6]

1   *Re Wyatt* [2004] EWHC 2247, [2005] EWHC 117, [2005] EWHC 693, [2005] EWHC 2902, [2006] EWHC 319; *Wyatt v Portsmouth NHS Trust* [2005] EWCA Civ 1181.
2   *An NHS Trust v MB* [2006] EWHC 507 (Fam).
3   *Re OT (A Baby)* [2009] EWHC 635 (Fam).
4   *Re OT (A Baby)* [2009] EWCA Civ 409.
5   *Gillick v West Norfolk and Wisbech Area Health Authority* [1985] 3 All ER 402, HL.
6   See *Re R (A Minor)* [1991] 4 All ER 177, CA; *Re W (A Minor)* [1992] 4 All ER 627, CA.

14.2 *Doctors and Children*

We begin by looking at the legal position where everyone would agree that the child is too young to make any sort of decision about medical treatment for herself. Then we explore the vexed issues surrounding adolescents.

At the threshold of viability[7]

14.2 The birth of such a very sick baby is a tragedy. The joy of normal childbirth is replaced by fear for the baby's and the family's future. Until relatively recently, two factors, to some extent, mitigated the parents' dilemma. Little could be done for the baby. Most extremely premature babies died at birth. Many severely disabled infants survived only a few weeks or months after birth. Their parents suffered the pain of bereavement, but were spared anxiety about the child's future. In any case, whether the child lived or died, the decision was made by 'God or nature'. The parents could do nothing about it. Developments in neonatal intensive care enable doctors to prolong the lives of babies born at ever earlier stages in gestation. And babies born later in pregnancy, but affected by severe abnormalities, can also be 'saved'. The evidence, however, suggests that although these babies' lives are prolonged, many babies will not survive to leave the neonatal intensive care unit and go home. A proportion of those who do survive will be affected by severe impairments. In a recent study, survival of babies born at twenty-two to twenty-four weeks was 53 per cent compared with 90 per cent for those born at twenty-five to twenty-seven weeks.[8] An earlier study[9] showed that of those babies born at twenty-three weeks who survived to their sixth birthday, 25 per cent or so were affected by severe disability. At twenty-two weeks, just two babies survived at all. Babies born nearer to the usual term of pregnancy, or at term, may also suffer from severe abnormalities, for example, the baby's brain may not have developed properly or she may be born with virtually no bowel. Some congenital conditions such as Edwards Syndrome mean that babies can survive only with intensive care, and are unlikely, whatever is done for them, to live for more than a short time. Parents may be faced with agonising decisions about the treatment of their baby within minutes of her birth.

The dilemma about how to care for a very sick person, whether prolonging life is always the right course of action, is not exclusive to babies. The problem arises equally acutely in relation to the terminally or chronically ill adult, or an

---

[7] See, generally, Nuffield Council on Bioethics, *Critical Care Decisions in Fetal and Neonatal Medicine* (2006) (hereafter NCOB Report).

[8] B E Stephens *et al*, 'Special Health Care Needs of Infants Born at the Limits of Viability' (2010) 125(6) *Pediatrics* 1152. See also T Markestad *et al*, 'Early Death, Morbidity, and Need of Treatment Among Extremely Premature Infants' (2005) 115 *Pediatrics* 1289, indicating that just 16 per cent of babies born at twenty-three weeks survive, and only 44 per cent of those born at twenty-four weeks.

[9] See the discussion of the EPICure 1 study in the NCOB Report. EPICure 1 looked at babies born at twenty-two to twenty-five weeks' gestation in 1995. EPICure 2 is looking at babies born in 2006 and seeks to determine how effective advances in neonatal care have been. Accessible at www.epicure.ac.uk.

older child irreversibly injured in an accident. Nonetheless, there are special features surrounding any discussion of the care of sick babies. The conscious adult patient can speak for himself. The decision about any continuation of treatment may be his. Even if unconscious, he may earlier have expressed his wishes should the question arise. The baby cannot express any preference. Her parents may give their views. Should parental wishes be decisive? Parents' views are crucial, but children have interests too. The baby's plight is different from that of a newly disabled adult. She does not move from full health to disability. She does not experience a dramatic drop in her expectations of life. A life of disability is all that she can know. Nor will her parents be as able to speak for her as for an older child. The older child (even at three or four years old) will have indicated what gives her pleasure and what causes her pain. So for over a quarter of a century now, a number of doctors, lawyers and philosophers have argued that questions about how to treat newborn babies raise somewhat different issues to the more general questions about when to give priority to prolonging life.

For doctors, one critical factor has been the evidence that certain kinds of intervention have poor long-term results. While some parents will want doctors to do everything possible to keep their baby alive, others who discover at birth that their baby is severely disabled may be perplexed by suggestions that their newborn baby must now be subjected to aggressive measures to keep him alive. The Abortion Act 1967 permits the termination of pregnancy when there is a substantial risk that the child, if born, will be severely disabled. Some people ask why a child who could have been actively destroyed if his disability had been diagnosed in pregnancy, must be the subject of intensive life-saving measures if his disability goes unnoticed until birth. Some philosophers argue that it is irrational that the law should allow the killing of a foetus at thirty-eight weeks into pregnancy, but insist on saving the baby prematurely delivered at twenty-four weeks. What moral difference does the journey through the birth canal make?

The concept of the sanctity of each and every human life is under attack. Forceful arguments are advanced[10] that the value of life lies in its quality and its contribution to society, rather than in any intrinsic merit in life itself. The newborn baby is no more a 'person' than the embryo or the foetus. Such arguments are equally forcefully rebutted.[11]

Proposals for reforms of law and practice

14.3   Debate about whether the law should make special provision in relation to newborn babies is not new. The prosecution of Dr Leonard Arthur for

[10]   See J Glover, *Causing Death and Saving Lives* (1977) Penguin, ch 12. See also ch 2 of this book.
[11]   See, in particular, J K Mason, *Human Life and Medical Practice* (1988) Edinburgh University Press, ch 6.

murder prompted calls for new legislation as long ago as 1981.[12] Broadly similar proposals were made by Mason and McCall Smith in the first edition of *Law and Medical Ethics*,[13] and survived with amendments to the sixth edition of that work.[14] Legislation aimed solely at clarifying the law concerning withholding and withdrawing treatment may be of limited utility. What is meant by 'worthwhile quality of life'? What degree of pain and suffering renders life unbearable?

Another question in relation to changing the law to try to clarify when doctors may lawfully withhold or withdraw treatment is this. If it is lawful to withhold life support from a baby, 'allowing her to die', should it also be lawful to take active steps to end her life swiftly and painlessly? Is there any moral difference between the two? What of the baby whose condition is agonising and likely to be fatal who hangs on to life? In 2007 it was reported that Dr Michael Munro had administered a muscle relaxant, pancuronium, to two babies who were suffering agonal gasping, a type of paroxysmal distress which often precedes death. Both babies were born prematurely and as a result of the health problems they endured, the decision was taken to withdraw treatment. Because Dr Munro's primary motivation was a desire to relieve suffering, the GMC found him not guilty in a fitness to practise hearing.[15] Dr Munro had the full support of both sets of parents.

In the Netherlands,[16] the Groeningen Protocol[17] was developed to permit doctors to act to end the life of a baby in the most exceptional circumstances. To put it crudely, the Protocol allows neonatal euthanasia. It is not formally part of Dutch law. A team of physicians, including a doctor who is not directly involved in the care of the baby, must confirm that the baby's condition is such that he is subjected to unbearable suffering, and that his condition is untreatable. If the parents consent,[18] high doses of opiates such as morphine are used to induce the death of the baby gently over one to two days. Immediately

---

[12] See, for example, draft 'Limitation of Treatment Bill' discussed by D Brahams (1981) 78 *Law Society Gazette* 1342.

[13] J K Mason and R A McCall Smith, *Law and Medical Ethics* (1st edn, 1985) Butterworths, p 89.

[14] (2002) Butterworths, p 390.

[15] See O Dyer, 'Doctor Cleared of Act "Tantamount to Euthanasia"' (2007) 335 *BMJ* 67. And see J Goodman, 'The Case of Dr Munro: Are there Lessons to be Learnt?' (2010) 18(4) *Medical Law Review* 564 supporting the outcome of the case but pointing out potential 'slippery slope' concerns.

[16] See S Moratti, 'End of Life Decisions in Dutch Neonatology' (2010) 18(4) *Medical Law Review* 471.

[17] See E Verhagen, P J Saver, 'The Groeningen Protocol – Euthanasia in Severely Ill Newborns' (2005) 352 *New England Journal of Medicine* 959; H Lindemann *et al*, 'Ending the Life of a Newborn: The Groeningen Protocol' (2008) 38(1) *Hastings Center Report* 42.

[18] Though the ethical validity of this requirement is questioned by J M Appel, 'Neonatal Euthanasia: Why Require Parental Consent' (2009) 6(4) *Journal of Bioethical Inquiry* 477.

lethal injections of substances such as potassium chloride are not used. After the baby's death, a report should be[19] made to the coroner, and a committee of five members, including an ethicist and a lawyer, scrutinise the decision to check that the treatment of the baby meets the conditions set out in the Protocol. The 'killing' of the baby remains a criminal offence, but if the Protocol is followed, doctors will not be prosecuted.

If legislation allowing active neonatal euthanasia were to be enacted in the UK, a series of difficult decisions would need to be taken. Do we accept some distinction in the value of the life of the newborn baby, and the older child or adult? If so, where is the line to be drawn? Is it seventy-two hours, or twenty-eight days, or later? The Abortion Act 1967 may have altered perceptions of the sanctity of life. Debate has ebbed and flowed for centuries as to the status and humanity of the unborn. Abortion, although severely punished, was never equated with murder in England. Birth is a relatively clear dividing line. No other distinction can be as clear. So how (if at all) could legislation, expressly and exclusively designed to allow ending the lives of newborn babies, be justified? Do we regard the parents as standing proxy for their child in any decision as to treatment? If so, why draw the line at twenty-eight days? Older children develop chronic disease, are disabled in accidents, or are discovered to suffer from severe disabilities later in childhood.

One other possibility to be considered is whether, without changing the law, clearer guidelines relating to the resuscitation of extremely premature babies would be helpful.[20] In light of increasingly consistent case law, this is the approach recommended by Mason and Laurie in the 2010 edition of their book.[21] Indeed, societies and professional bodies in many countries produce such guidance.[22] Practice in the UK varies considerably. Some neonatal units will try and discuss what to do with the parents before the birth where this is possible. Others resuscitate all babies born after twenty-three weeks, admit the baby to neonatal intensive care, and then review his prospects. A few units will seek to resuscitate a baby born at twenty-two weeks, or even below. The extent of parents' involvement in such decisions also varies.[23] Resuscitation of such a very premature baby raises questions of the ethics of attempting to resuscitate a baby who is highly likely to die whatever is done for her. And when a baby does

---

[19] The committee was set up in 2007. It expected to deal with around fifteen to twenty cases a year. By 2010 there had been only one case, raising questions about the extent to which cases are reported. See S Buiting *et al*, 'Dutch Experience of Monitoring Active Ending of Life for Newborns' (2010) 36 *Journal of Medical Ethics* 234.

[20] See the NCOB Report.

[21] J K Mason and G T Laurie, *Law and Medical Ethics* (8th edn, 2010) OUP (hereafter *Mason and McCall Smith*), at 15.53.

[22] M S Pignotti *et al*, 'Perinatal Care at the Threshold of Viability: An International Comparison of Practical Guidelines for the Treatment of Extremely Preterm Births' (2008) 121(1) *Pediatrics* 193.

[23] See K J Griswold *et al*, 'An Evidence-Based Overview of Prenatal Consultation with a Focus on Infants Born at the Limits of Viability' (2010) 125(4) *Pediatrics* 931.

survive on a ventilator, but the long-term prognosis is dire, decisions to withdraw intensive care may be even more painful than decisions to institute care.

Finally, the question of use of resources raises its ugly head. It is a question of two parts.

(1) Should money spent on intensive care of babies unlikely to survive be spent elsewhere, say on treatment for early breast cancer?

(2) Would money spent on Baby A born at twenty-two weeks be better spent on B, born a little later? The limited number of places in neonatal units means that doctors sometimes have to arrange for a baby to be transported hundreds of miles to a neonatal unit far away because there is no capacity to care for him nearer the family home.

In the Netherlands,[24] professional guidelines advise against the resuscitation of a baby born before twenty-five weeks unless the parents press very strongly for resuscitation and doctors have grounds to judge that the particular baby has an exceptional chance of survival. The Nuffield Council on Bioethics[25] examined ethical, social and legal issues arising in relation to critical care decisions in neonatal medicine. Among a number of recommendations, the Report proposed guidelines for deciding whether to institute neonatal intensive care. The guidelines suggest that below twenty-two weeks no baby should be resuscitated, except within an approved clinical research study. Between twenty-two and twenty-three weeks, the general practice would be not to institute intensive care unless the parents, fully informed, reiterate requests for resuscitation. Between twenty-three and twenty-four weeks, precedence should be given to parental wishes, and from twenty-four weeks, the presumption should be that full intensive care for the baby should be instituted.[26]

The courts and sick infants

14.4 For the present, legal principles governing the medical care of newborn babies and small children must be discerned from the judgments of the courts.

---

[24] See Dutch Paediatric Association, *To Treat or Not to Treat? Limits for Life-Sustaining Treatment in Neonatology* (1992) Utrecht, Netherlands; F J Walther, 'Withholding Treatment: Withdrawing Treatment and Palliative Care in the Neonatal Intensive Care Unit' (2005) 81 *Early Human Development* 905; NCOB Report, p 135; and J Dorscheidt, 'End of Life Decisions in Neonatology and the Right to Life of the Disabled Newborn Child: Impressions from the Netherlands' in L Clements, J Read (eds) *Disabled People and the Right to Life: The Protection and Violation of Disabled People's Most Basic Human Right* (2007) Routledge Cavendish, ch 9.

[25] NCOB Report. For commentary, see A Morris, 'Selective Treatment of Irreversible Impaired Infants: Decision-Making at the Threshold' (2009) 17(3) *Medical Law Review* 347.

[26] Similar recommendations are in place internationally. See M S Pignotti *et al,* 'Perinatal Care at the Threshold of Viability: An International Comparison of Practical Guidelines for the Treatment of Extremely Preterm Births' (2008) 121(1) *Pediatrics* 193.

Professional guidelines seek to translate them[27] and the GMC requires that these are taken into account and that doctors seek a second opinion where doubts or uncertainties arise.[28] The focus in any case referred to court is the individual baby.[29] Flexibility has advantages, but may result in some parents feeling that judgments are too subjective and governed by the moral and personal viewpoints of the chosen judge. Doctors worry about lack of certainty. They are concerned that decisions to withhold or withdraw treatment (even when agreed with parents) could subject them to possible criminal liability for murder or manslaughter.

The fundamental principle governing withholding life-saving treatment from young children was settled in *Re B* in 1981. It concerned an infant girl, Alexandra, born suffering from Down's syndrome and an intestinal obstruction. In a normal child, simple surgery would have been carried out swiftly with minimal risk to the baby. Without surgery, the baby would die within a few days. Her parents refused to authorise the operation. They argued that God or nature had given their child a way out. The doctors contacted the local authority and the child was made a ward of court. A judge was asked to authorise the operation. He refused to do so. The authority appealed, and the Court of Appeal[30] ordered that the operation go ahead. Counsel for the parents submitted that in this kind of decision, the views of responsible and caring parents must be respected and that their decision should decide the issue. The Court of Appeal rejected the submission, holding that the decision must be made in the best interests of the child.

In the same year that the Court of Appeal held that Alexandra must be treated and live, Dr Arthur faced trial for murder.[31] A baby was born in the hospital where Dr Arthur was consultant paediatrician. The baby suffered from Down's syndrome. His parents did not wish him to survive. He died sixty-nine hours after his birth. The prosecution alleged that Dr Arthur ordered nursing care only and prescribed a drug to suppress the baby's appetite and so starve him to death. They claimed that, apart from Down's syndrome, the baby was

---

27. For example, Royal College of Paediatrics and Child Health, *Withholding and Withdrawing Life-Sustaining Treatment in Children. A Framework for Practice* (2004) (currently under review); BMA, *Withholding and Withdrawing Life-Prolonging Medical Treatment: Guidance for Decision Making* (2007); NHS, *Toolkit for High Quality Neonatal Services* (2009).

28. GMC, *Treatment and Care Towards the End of Life: Good Practice in Decision Making* (2010), para 94.

29. See GMC, *Treatment and Care Towards the End of Life: Good Practice in Decision Making* (2010), para 90: '. . . You must also consider the role and responsibilities of parents and others close to them, but your primary duty is to the child or young person who is your patient.'

30. *Re B (A Minor) (Wardship: Medical Treatment)* [1981] 1 WLR 1421, CA.

31. (1981) 12 BMLR 1. See also 'Dr Leonard Arthur: His Trial and Its Implications' (1981) 283 *BMJ* 1340; H Benyon, 'Doctors as Murderers' [1982] *Criminal Law Review* 17; M Gunn and J C Smith, 'Arthur's Case and the Right to Life of a Down's Syndrome Child' [1985] *Criminal Law Review* 705.

otherwise healthy, and that his death resulted from starvation and the effect of the drug causing him to succumb to bronchopneumonia. Defence evidence established that: (1) the baby suffered from severe brain and lung damage; (2) Dr Arthur followed established practice in the management of such an infant; (3) that in the first three days of life, normal babies take in little or no sustenance and usually lose weight (which the dead baby had not done). The baby patently did not starve to death. The judge directed that the charge be altered to attempted murder. Summing up, the judge stressed that there is '. . . no special law in this country that places doctors in a separate category and gives them special protection over the rest of us'. He emphasised that, however severely disabled a child may be, if the doctor gives it drugs in an excessive amount so that the drugs will cause death, then the doctor commits murder. He highlighted the distinction between doing something active to kill the child and electing not to follow a particular course of treatment which might have saved the infant. Considering the ethical arguments on terminating newborn life, the judge reminded the jury that if ethics and the law conflict, the law must prevail. Nonetheless his Lordship concluded:

> . . . I imagine that you [the jury] will think long and hard before deciding that doctors of the eminence we have heard in representing to you what medical ethics are and apparently have been over a period of time, you would think long and hard before concluding that they in that great profession have evolved standards which amount to committing crime.

The jury acquitted Dr Arthur.

A confused picture emerges. A baby with Down's syndrome was ordered to be saved, yet Dr Arthur was not guilty of a crime in relation to his treatment of a severely damaged Down's infant. The acquittal of Dr Arthur tells us little about the law. The confusion over the pathological evidence may have irretrievably prejudiced the jury against the prosecution's case. The baby's multiple abnormalities should have been irrelevant to the reduced charge of attempted murder. When Dr Arthur ordered nursing care only, he thought that he was dealing with a Down's baby as entitled to survive as Alexandra. Did the jury see it that way? As Mason puts it: 'Murder, in the popular sense of the word, was the one thing of which Dr Arthur was certainly innocent.'[32]

Deliberate killing

14.5 In all but one exceptional instance, illustrated by the case of the Manchester conjoined twins, it is indisputable that neither doctor, nor parents, nor anyone else may do any *act* intended *solely* to hasten the death of the disabled baby. The deliberate killing of any human being is murder. The moment that the child has an existence separate from his mother,[33] the moment he has

---

[32] J K Mason, *Human Life and Medical Practice* (1988) Edinburgh University Press, p 63.
[33] Some dispute exists as to the moment in childbirth when this occurs. The child need not have breathed apparently. See *R v Poulton* (1832) 5 C & P 329, and *R v Brain*

independent circulation, even though the afterbirth may not yet fully have been expelled from the mother's body, he is protected by the law of homicide. It has on occasion been faintly argued that a grossly malformed child, 'a monstrous birth', should not be regarded in law as human. We shall see that this argument was advanced unsuccessfully in the conjoined twins case.[34] Defining humanity, other than by virtue of human parentage, is an impossible and unacceptable task. Does 'monstrous' refer to appearance, in which case an intelligent infant of appalling mien could legitimately be destroyed? Does it cover lack of intelligence, or lack of a brain?[35] Both are almost impossible to measure at birth.

Nonetheless, in *Re A (Minors) (Conjoined Twins: Separation)*,[36] the Court of Appeal authorised the killing of the weaker of two conjoined twins. Jodie and Mary were born in Manchester after a scan in their native Malta revealed their condition. Their parents came to this country in the hope of surgery to separate and save both children. The girls were joined at the pelvis. Each had her own arms and legs as well as a brain, heart and lungs. Mary's brain was said to be 'primitive', her heart was defective, and she had no functioning lung tissue. Mary remained alive only because a common artery allowed Jodie's heart to circulate oxygenated blood to both infants. Left conjoined, the strain on Jodie's organs would result in the death of both children within three to six months. Surgery to separate the girls would result in Mary's death within minutes of separation. Surgery would kill Mary.[37] Doing nothing would result in the death of both girls. The parents were devout Roman Catholics. They refused to consent to surgery because they believed that it would be a sin to 'murder' Mary and that their children's fate must be subject to God's will. The hospital applied to the court for authority to overrule the parents' objections.

The Court of Appeal ruled that surgery should go ahead. What follows can only be a summary of their Lordship's complex, and not always unanimous, reasoning. Let us deal first with the question of how it could be said to be lawful to kill Mary. Mary, the judges agreed, was in law a person whose right to life was entitled to respect. She was not to be regarded as non-human, a monster or, as some had suggested, a 'tumour' attached to Jodie's body.[38] Ward and

---

34. (1834) 6 C & P 349; *A-G's Reference (No 3 of 1994)* [1997] 3 All ER 936, HL. And see NCOB Report 5.

   Re A (Minors) (Conjoined Twins: Separation) [2000] Lloyd's Rep Med 425 at 464–465.

35. How would you classify the status of a baby born with anencephaly?

36. [2000] Lloyd's Rep Med 425. The names given to the girls to preserve their anonymity, but the ban on identifying the family was later lifted.

37. For an eloquent discussion of the issues raised by surgery to separate conjoined twins prior to *Re A*, see S Sheldon, S Wilkinson, 'Conjoined Twins: The Legality and Ethics of Sacrifice' (1997) 2 *Medical Law Review* 149.

38. Though note Mason's interesting argument that as Mary had no independent lung function she should have been classified as stillborn: J K Mason, 'Conjoined Twins: A Diagnostic Conundrum' (2001) 5 *Edinburgh Law Review* 226.

Brooke LJJ[39] accepted that surgery to separate the twins constituted killing Mary. However much their doctors wished the case to be different, in cutting off Mary's blood supply by clamping the common artery, they 'intended' Mary's death. Unless some lawful excuse justified their conduct, the doctors were exposed to liability for murder. The Court found such excuse. They found that excuse in the doctrine of necessity.[40] Brooke LJ cited the analogy of the captain of a ship about to capsize. He had to choose who entered the lifeboats. The judge continued:[41]

> He would not be guilty even though he kept some of the passengers back from the boat at revolver-point and he would not be guilty even though he had to fire the revolver.

Doctors caring for the conjoined twins had duties to both girls. Surgery would involve an assault, a fatal assault on Mary. To save Jodie, it was justifiable. It was necessary to avoid an inevitable and irreparable evil. It was no more than what was necessary to preserve Jodie's life. Given Mary too would die without surgery, the evil of her inevitable death was not disproportionate. A finding that surgery did not constitute murder did not conclude the question of the twins' fate. The more important question revolved around who had the right to make the crucial decision. Doctors wanted to operate. The parents objected. Before going on to look at the question of who decides, we must first consider the more common case, where what is at stake is not actively killing a child, but withholding treatment from her.

Withholding and withdrawing treatment

14.6 To what extent does the law require parents and doctors to provide treatment to prolong the baby's life? Before any failure to treat a child can engage *criminal* liability, it must be established that a duty to act was imposed on the accused. Parents are under a duty to care and provide for their dependent children. Failing to provide proper care, including medical aid where necessary, will result in a conviction for wilful neglect of the child, provided that the parent was aware of the risk to the child's health.[42] Should the child die, the parents may be convicted of manslaughter.[43] Parents who are aware of the danger to a child's health, but who do not seek medical aid because of religious or other conscientious objection to conventional medicine, have no defence to criminal prosecutions for neglect or manslaughter.[44] Parents who deliberately withhold sustenance and care from a child, intending him to die,

---

[39] [2000] Lloyd's Rep Med 425 at 456, 466–467. Robert Walker LJ sought to argue that Mary's death resulted not from surgery but her own inability to sustain life (at 510).

[40] Ward LJ advanced, and preferred, a doctrine of quasi self-defence.

[41] [2000] Lloyd's Rep Med at 474.

[42] Children and Young Persons Act 1933, s 1(1).

[43] *R v Lowe* [1973] QB 702.

[44] *R v Senior* [1899] 1 QB, 823.

may be guilty of murder.[45] Finally, a range of other legal remedies is available to local authority social services departments. Failure to provide medical aid, risking significant harm to the child, is a ground for taking a child into care.[46]

What of the doctor? If he is under a duty to treat a baby then, like the parent, should the child die, he could be prosecuted for manslaughter if his omission resulted from neglect, or for murder if he intended the infant to die. Once the doctor accepts the baby as a patient, he assumes a duty to that baby to give him proper medical care. Nor is it likely that a paediatrician could, should anyone ever want to, evade responsibility by refusing to accept a child as a patient after his birth. His contract with the NHS imposes on him an obligation towards the children born in his hospital, giving rise to a duty to the individual infant.[47]

Parents and doctors have a duty to provide medical aid, but what is the scope of that duty? Where a child is suffering from severe abnormalities, may proper medical care be defined as keeping her comfortable, but withholding life-prolonging treatment? Two factors play a vital role in the decision as to whether to treat an acutely ill child. What do her parents desire? What is the practice of the medical profession in the management of her kind of illness or disability?[48] The answer to the second question is that in many instances, doctors will explain the treatment available, give a prognosis as to the child's future, and accept the decision taken by the parents. Yet, as we have seen, the Court of Appeal in the case of Alexandra ordered surgery to remove an intestinal blockage against her parents' wishes. The baby would be affected by the mental and physical disabilities attendant on Down's syndrome. If treated, she could expect the same quality of life as any one of the many other Down's babies born each year. She would suffer no pain from her disability, and the evidence suggests that properly cared for Down's children lead happy lives. The surgery needed to save Alexandra was simple and without risk. Her proposed treatment had a purpose, the baby was not inevitably dying, and the treatment was in no way unduly burdensome. *Re B*[49] signalled that the legality of withholding treatment is dependent on the degree of a child's disability and the degree of suffering continued life may cause her. Some sort of balance between the pain of prolonged life and the finality of death has to be struck.[50] In striking that balance, the law, in appropriate cases, allows doctors and parents to conclude that it is not in the interests of the baby to intervene to prolong her life.

---

[45]   *R v Gibbons and Proctor* (1918) 13 Cr App Rep 134.

[46]   Children Act 1989, s 31(2).

[47]   See Beynon [1982] *Criminal Law Review* 17, at 27–28.

[48]   See GMC, *Treatment and Care Towards the End of Life: Good Practice in Decision Making* (2010), para 106.

[49]   *Re B (A Minor) (Wardship: Medical Treatment)* [1981] 1 WLR 1421, CA.

[50]   In GMC, *Treatment and Care Towards the End of Life: Good Practice in Decision Making* (2010), para 93.

What though, of withdrawing treatment already instituted? A baby may be resuscitated at birth, or an older child put on a ventilator after a traumatic injury, but tests later show that the child is never likely to leave hospital, or even to survive off the ventilator. It is thought his best interests are best served by allowing him to die peacefully in his parents' arms. Can doctors lawfully switch off the ventilator? Or is that an act hastening death and so murder? We shall see later that the House of Lords[51] has ruled that switching off a ventilator, or withdrawing life-sustaining treatment from a patient of any age, does not constitute an act hastening death. Discontinuing life support is 'no different from not initiating it in the first place'. In a case directly concerned with the care of a baby in intensive care, the judge stressed that[52] '... there is no legal distinction between withholding or withdrawing life support ... the best interests test applies equally to both situations'.[53] Where withdrawal of treatment includes the withdrawal of artificial nutrition and hydration, the GMC advise that a second medical opinion is sought.[54] The Royal College of Paediatrics and Child Health acknowledged in 2004 that there are situations where continued treatment might not be in the best interests of the child. It lists five situations when doctors and family might consider withholding or withdrawing life-sustaining treatment: the brain dead child; the child in a persistent vegetative state; the 'no chance' situation (where treatment would delay death but not alleviate suffering); the 'no purpose' situation ('where the patient may be able to survive with treatment, [but] the degree of physical or mental impairment will be so great that it is unreasonable to expect them to bear it'); and the 'unbearable' situation (where 'the child and/or family feel that in the face of progressive and irreversible illness further treatment is more than can be borne').[55] The list is not intended to form 'rigid rules' – the family and medical team will need to take a view of the child's overall situation when reaching a decision.

'Best interests': a balancing exercise[56]

14.7 The decision must be made in the 'best interests' of the child and case law has evolved to give a fuller picture of the balancing exercise required. In 2006 Holman J produced a tenfold summation in *An NHS Trust v MB*.[57] An abridged version is repeated here:[58]

---

[51] *Airedale NHS Trust v Bland* [1993] AC 789, HL. See below at ch 19.

[52] *Airedale NHS Trust v Bland* [1993] AC 789 at 866 per Lord Goff.

[53] *An NHS Trust v MB* [2006] EWHC 507 (Fam) at para 20.

[54] See GMC, *Treatment and Care Towards the End of Life: Good Practice in Decision Making* (2010), para 106.

[55] Royal College of Paediatrics and Child Health, *Withholding or Withdrawing Life Sustaining Treatment* (2004), pp 10–11.

[56] See S Elliston, *The Best Interests of the Child in Healthcare* (2007) Routledge Cavendish.

[57] [2006] EWHC 507 (Fam) at paras 106–107.

[58] [2006] EWHC 507 (Fam) at para 16, based on *Wyatt v Portsmouth Hospital NHS Trust* [2005] EWCA Civ 1181 at para 87.

i) ... It is the role and duty of the court to ... exercise its own independent and objective judgment. ii) The right and power of the court ... only arises because the ... child lacks the capacity to make a decision for himself ... iv) The matter must be decided by the application of an objective approach or test. v) That test is the best interests of the patient. Best interests ... include, non-exhaustively, medical, emotional, sensory (pleasure, pain and suffering) and instinctive (the human instinct to survive) considerations ... vii) Considerable weight ... must be attached to the prolongation of life ... But it is not absolute, nor necessarily decisive ... ix) All these cases ... depend entirely on the facts of the individual case. x) The views and opinions of both the doctors and the parents must be carefully considered ... [Parental] ... views may have particular value because they know the patient and how he reacts so well; ... [Parental] wishes, however understandable in human terms, are wholly irrelevant to consideration of the objective best interests of the child save to the extent in any given case that they may illuminate the quality and value to the child of the child/parent relationship.

Let us review some of the case law. In *Re C (A Minor) (Wardship: Medical Treatment)*,[59] a baby had been made a ward of court shortly after birth on grounds of her parents' inability to care for her. C suffered from an exceptionally severe degree of hydrocephalus, and the brain itself was poorly formed. She appeared to be blind and virtually deaf. At sixteen weeks she was, apart from her enlarged head, the size of a four-week baby. It was said to be inevitable that she would die in a matter of months at most. The judge made an order that leave be given to 'treat the ward to die'. This infelicitous phrase caused an outcry, being wrongly interpreted by some of the media as sanction for active euthanasia. The Court of Appeal affirmed his judgment, deleting the unfortunate phrase. Lord Donaldson MR saw C's case as very different from that in *Re B*. C was inevitably dying. Her life appeared to offer her no pleasures. The court ordered: 'The hospital authority be at liberty to treat the minor to allow her life to come to an end peacefully and with dignity ...'. Seventeen years later another case, also confusingly called *Re C*,[60] concerned a baby who became blind and deaf as a result of meningitis. She survived only with the support of a ventilator, suffered repeated convulsions and was likely to die in the next two years, or perhaps sooner. She had a 'very low awareness of anything'. Her parents and doctors both wished to withdraw life support and let C die. The judge authorised removing the baby from life support.

Re J (A Minor) (Wardship: Medical Treatment)[61] is a more difficult case. J was born thirteen weeks prematurely at a birth weight of 1.1 kg. He nearly died several times, but was saved by medical skill. He was found to have severe brain damage: 'A large area of fluid filled cavities where there ought to have been brain tissue'. J was said to be likely to develop paralysis, blindness and probable deafness. Unlike either baby C, his life expectancy might extend to his late teens. If he developed an infection, must he be treated? If he suffered a further episode of cyanosis and collapse, must he be resuscitated? The Court of Appeal found that he need not. Lord Donaldson regarded *Re B* as near to

[59] [1989] 2 All ER 782, CA.
[60] *Re C (a baby)* [1996] 2 FLR 43.
[61] [1990] 3 All ER 930, CA.

binding authority that a balancing exercise should be performed in assessing the course to be adopted in the best interests of the child. The exercise must seek to reflect the 'assumed' view of the child. In deciding whether the prolonged life of the child will be 'demonstrably awful',[62] the child's perspective on life is the crucial test. He will know no other life, and the amazing adaptability and courage of disabled people must be considered.[63]

> But in the end there will be cases in which the answer must be that it is not in the interests of the child to subject it to treatment which will cause increased suffering and produce no commensurate benefit, giving the fullest possible weight to the child's, and mankind's, desire to survive.

Note that in *Re J* (as in *Re C* (1996)), there was no disagreement between J's parents and doctors. The application to court was undertaken to ensure that any decision to withhold treatment was lawful so neither parents nor doctors would risk prosecution.

English judges have shown themselves prepared to accept that appropriate care for a terribly sick child is not always to prolong his life. Does the Human Rights Act 1998 make any difference, enforcing as it does the right to life enshrined in Article 2 of the Human Rights Convention? In *A National Health Service Trust v D*,[64] a baby was born with irreversible lung disease and multi-organ failure. D was in the process of dying and the trust sought a declaration that it would be lawful not to resuscitate him if he stopped breathing. The judge held that as long as any decision not to resuscitate D was made in his best interests, there was no violation of Article 2. Article 3 which prohibits cruel or inhuman treatment entails a right to be allowed to die with dignity.

Disputing best interests

14.8 The most difficult cases arise when parents and doctors disagree about the best interests of a baby. Professional guidelines place great emphasis on working in partnership with parents.[65] In many cases the decision can be postponed until consensus between doctors and parents is reached.[66] In other cases the court is called upon to determine the child's best interests. The GMC hails this a 'constructive way of thoroughly exploring the issues and providing

---

[62] See J Read and L Clements, 'Demonstrably Awful: The Right to Life and the Selective Non-Treatment of Disabled Babies and Young Children' in L Clements and J Read (eds), *Disabled People and the Right to Life: The Protection and Violation of Disabled People's Most Basic Human Right* (2007) Routledge Cavendish, ch 8.

[63] [1990] 3 All ER 930 at 938, CA.

[64] (2000) 2 FLR 677.

[65] GMC, *Treatment and Care Towards the End of Life: Good Practice in Decision Making* (2010), paras 95, 107.

[66] See, for example, A Verhagen *et al*, 'Conflicts About End-Of-Life Decisions in NICUs in the Netherlands' (2009) 124 *Pediatrics* 112.

reassurance for the child and parents that the child's interests have been properly considered in the decision',[67] though sadly the court's involvement sometimes signifies a breakdown in the relationship between parents and doctors.

As we have seen in the case of the conjoined twins, *Re A*,[68] such disagreement was present. Having decided that ending Mary's life was not unlawful, the court had to address whose judgment on the interests of the two little girls should determine their fate. Their Lordships stressed that while the decisions of devoted and responsible parents should be treated with respect, the court retained power to intervene to protect the paramount welfare of the child. The conjoined twins case was unique because Jodie's welfare depended on Mary's demise. The parents, however, had other separate concerns about Jodie. They feared[69] that she would be profoundly disabled, unable to walk, likely to have to undergo several more operations during her infancy and possibly doubly incontinent. Their view was that it was not in the interests of either child to operate. The Court of Appeal disagreed. There was a reasonable prospect that Jodie could lead a relatively normal life. Mary, Ward LJ said, was 'beyond help'. Surgery might shorten her brief life. Without surgery she would still die. The '. . . least detrimental choice, balancing the interests of Mary against Jodie and Jodie against Mary permit the operation to be performed.'[70]

Jodie's prospects, it might be said, were not 'demonstrably awful'. Will the courts always rule in favour of continuing a child's life unless it is either likely to involve unbearable suffering, or will be such that the child will have virtually no ability to enjoy any of the senses, or use any of her abilities? In *Re T* (1997),[71] T was born with biliary atresia, a life-threatening liver disease. Without a liver transplant, he would die at about two and a half years of age. Earlier surgery when he was three and a half weeks old had failed, and the baby suffered great pain and distress. His parents, both health professionals, adamantly opposed transplant surgery. Fearing intervention by social services, the parents fled abroad. The local authority intervened seeking a court order requiring the family's return to England and that the transplant go ahead. The parents argued that if their son had the transplant, even if the operation was successful, he would be subjected to further pain and distress, he would have to take anti-rejection drugs for the rest of his life and might face repeated surgery. They

---

67 GMC, *Treatment and Care Towards the End of Life: Good Practice in Decision Making* (2010), para 108.
68 [2000] Lloyd's Rep Med 425, discussed above at **14.5**.
69 These fears have not materialised. Surgeons expected 'Jodie' to be able to walk, to avoid incontinency and even to be able to bear children. S Laville, 'Siamese Twin Jodie is Making Progress' (2000) *Telegraph,* 9 November.
70 [2000] Lloyd's Rep Med 425 at 455.
71 *Re T (A Minor) (Wardship: Medical Treatment)* [1997] 1 All ER 906, CA, discussed in M Fox and J McHale, 'In Whose Best Interests?' (1997) 60 *Modern Law Review* 600.

thought that his best interests were better served by a short, happy life and a peaceful death. The Court of Appeal ruled that the parental views should prevail. The parents in *Re T* were entitled to withhold life-saving treatment from their child. The essence of the court's ruling in *Re T* was that on the 'unusual facts' of the case, any presumption that the best interests of the child are to prolong his life was rebutted. The trial judge, ordering the transplant, had given insufficient weight to the mother's views. Best interests are not limited to clinical considerations.[72] If the operation was ordered against her will, her son's welfare would be compromised. Her commitment to his care was an integral part of any successful recovery post-transplant. Deprived of her care (ie taken into care) he would suffer. If she reluctantly complied with the court order, family problems would beset child and parents. The mother would have to return to, and remain in, England reluctantly. It was not clear whether the father would give up his job and return with her. If not, problems would arise in terms of financial and emotional support for mother and son. Butler-Sloss LJ, finding that the mother's view could not be considered unreasonable, said this:[73]

> The mother and child are one for the purposes of this unusual case and the decision of the court to consent to the operation jointly affects the mother and it also affects the father. The welfare of the child depends on his mother. The practical considerations of her ability to cope with supporting the child in the face of her belief that this course is not right for him, the requirement to return probably for a long time to this country, either to leave the father behind and lose his support or to require him to give up his present job and seek one in England were not put by the judge into the balance when he made his decision.

Is *Re T* an aberration? Consider Butler-Sloss LJ's language. She says 'mother and child are one' and that the child's welfare depends on his mother. Where the child remains with loving parents, is this not usual rather than unusual? A sick child always requires extra parental commitment. Why, you might ask, did a similar analysis not apply to Jodie, the stronger of the conjoined twins? Are there other singular features of *Re T*? All the judges emphasise that the parents were themselves health professionals. Did this give their views extra weight? More importantly, and what is truly unusual about *Re T*, is that any court order would also have needed to drag the family back from the other side of the world. Would *Re T* have had the same outcome if the parents had never left England?[74]

Re T was affirmed in *LA v SB, AB and MB*.[75] Doctors argued that surgery was the optimal treatment for six-year-old MB, who was suffering around 100

---

[72] See GMC, *Treatment and Care Towards the End of Life: Good Practice in Decision Making* (2010), para 90.

[73] [1997] 1 All ER 906 at 914–915.

[74] This seems to be the tenor of Roch LJ's judgment.

[75] [2010] EWCA Civ 1744, per Wall P at 2: 'As the most recent case cited to me was the decision of the Court of Appeal in *Re T (Wardship: Medical Treatment)* [1997] 1 FLR 502 (and in particular the judgment of Butler-Sloss LJ (as she then was)) I thought it sensible to revisit the point to see if the law needed to be moved on. In my judgment, it does not.'

epileptic seizures a day. The seizures were thought to be causing permanent developmental problems and posed a risk to his life, but his parents objected to surgery in preference for drug treatment. Sir Nicholas Wall P refused the local authority's application[76] on procedural grounds. The matter was between the hospital and the parents and when the hospital was invited by the court to intervene, it declined to do so. Though surgery remained the optimal treatment, it was not the only treatment and talks between the hospital and the parents could be resumed. Were MB's best interests served by this judgment? Surgery had an 85 per cent chance of stopping the seizures and MRI scans had already demonstrated irreversible harm. We must await an application from the hospital if MB is to be given a chance of optimal treatment.

Scruple or dogma?[77]

14.9 *Re T* and *LA* are unusual cases where parents refuse to consent to treatment for their child because of their judgments about the medical outcome. More common are cases where parents who are Jehovah's Witnesses refuse to consent to blood transfusions. Transfusions violate a fundamental tenet of Witnesses' faith.[78] The kinds of cases which reach the courts are well illustrated by *Re S* (1993).[79] S was four and a half and suffering from T-cell leukaemia. His parents agreed to intensive chemotherapy. Doctors argued that transfusion of blood products was essential to maximise the prospects of successful treatment and saving S's life. Without resort to blood, the chances of successful treatment were significantly reduced. His parents objected not just on religious grounds. They raised concerns about the safety of blood products. Their lawyers argued that S's relationship with his family might suffer, for his parents would believe that his life had been prolonged by an 'ungodly act'. Thorpe J dismissed the parental objection. The child's welfare required he be given the best chance of prolonged life. He was unimpressed by talk of problems in the family later in life. Reconciling *Re S* and *Re T* is nigh on impossible. In a series of cases, while judges now show some understanding of the dilemma confronting Jehovah's Witness parents, in the end the courts endorse the child's interest in survival and overrule parental objections.[80]

---

[76] Made under s 100 of the Children Act 1989 for leave to invoke the court's inherent jurisdiction or alternatively for permission to apply for a specific issue order.

[77] See C Bridge, 'Religion, Culture and Conviction – the Medical Treatment of Young Children' (1999) 11 *Child and Family Law Quarterly* 1, and 'Religion, Culture and the Body of the Child' in A Bainham, S D Sclater and M Richards, *Body Lore and Laws* (2002) OUP, p 265; J McHale, 'Health and Health Care Law, Faith(s) and Beliefs: New Perspectives and Dilemmas' 9(4) (2009) *Medical Law International* 279; M Fox, M Thomson, 'Older Minors and Circumcision: Questioning the Limits of Religious Actions' 9(4) (2009) *Medical Law International* 283.

[78] Although the Council of Elders does seem to have softened slightly its opposition to transfusions, leaving the matter more to the conscience of the believer.

[79] *Re S (A Minor) (Medical Treatment)* [1993] 1 FLR 376.

[80] *Re E (A Minor)* (1990) 9 BMLR 1; *Re O (A Minor) (Medical Treatment)* (1993) 4 Med LR 272; *Re R (A Minor)* [1993] 2 FLR 757.

Perhaps part of the key to apparently contradictory decisions about parents' rights to determine the treatment of their young children can be found in the judgment of Waite LJ in *Re T* (1997).[81] He contrasts cases where parental opposition to treatment is '. . . prompted by scruple or dogma of a kind which is patently irreconcilable with principles of health and welfare widely accepted by the generality of mankind' and '. . . highly problematic cases where there is a genuine scope for a difference of opinion'. Ward LJ, in the conjoined twins' case, says[82] that that was not a case where the parents' opposition to surgery to separate the girls was 'prompted by scruple or dogma'. How much weight should parents' religious beliefs carry? Parents will argue that Article 8 of the Human Rights Convention (endorsing their right to family life) and Article 9 (guaranteeing religious freedom) mean that their views should be conclusive. Both Articles are qualified. The parents' 'rights' must be balanced against the children's interests. Caroline Bridge has argued that in delaying treatment, so prolonging a child's suffering, in attempts to meet parents' convictions, the child's interests are undervalued.[83]

Responsibilities not rights?

14.10 One consistent message can be elicited from English case law about the medical treatment of young children. The common law only confers on parents those rights they need to fulfil their responsibilities to provide adequate medical care for their children. Lord Templeman summed up the position in *Gillick v West Norfolk and Wisbech Area Health Authority*:[84]

> Where the patient is an infant, the medical profession accepts that a parent having custody and being responsible for the infant is entitled on behalf of the infant to consent or to reject treatment if the parent considers that the best interests of the infant so require. Where doctor and parent disagree, the court can decide and is not slow to act, I accept that if there is no time to obtain a decision from the court, a doctor may safely carry out treatment in an emergency if the doctor believes the treatment to be vital to the survival or health of the infant and notwithstanding the opposition of a parent or the impossibility of alerting the parent before the treatment is carried out.

In a genuine emergency,[85] doctors may proceed without parental consent or court authority. So if a child is brought into casualty bleeding to death after a

---

[81] *Re T (A Minor) (Wardship: Medical Treatment)* [1997] 1 All ER 906.

[82] *Re A* [2000] Lloyd's Rep Med 425 at 454; and see *Re C (A Minor) (Medical Treatment)* [1998] 1 FLR 384.

[83] See C Bridge, 'Parental Powers and the Medical Treatment of Children' in C Bridge (ed), *Family Law: Towards the Millennium* (1997) Butterworths, p 321. Note that in *An NHS Trust v MB* (discussed below at **14.11**), Holman J accords some weight to the parents' Muslim beliefs.

[84] [1985] 3 All ER 402 at 432.

[85] As Lord Scarman put it in *Gillick v West Norfolk and Wisbech Area Health Authority* [1985] 3 All ER 402 at 410, HL: 'Emergency, parental neglect abandon-

road accident and his Jehovah's Witness parents refuse to agree to a blood transfusion, the hospital can overrule them if delay threatens the child's life. Dire necessity justifies their action.

The decision of the European Court of Human Rights in *Glass v UK*[86] issues a warning to doctors not to stretch the definition of emergency, and places a strong emphasis on a presumption of the parents' right to make decisions about the treatment of their young children. David Glass suffered from multiple disabilities. In 1998, he suffered a series of infections after a tonsillectomy. Doctors believed that David had little awareness of, or pleasure in, his surroundings, and that he was dying. They decided that if David stopped breathing he would not be resuscitated, and administered diamorphine to relieve any distress. His mother vehemently objected both to the administration of diamorphine and the doctors' decision not to resuscitate David. On one occasion she successfully resuscitated David herself. The relationship between David's family and doctors deteriorated into acrimony and violence. Mrs Glass unsuccessfully challenged her son's treatment in the English courts.[87] She eventually took his case to the European Court of Human Rights in Strasbourg, and won. The Court ruled that administering diamorphine to David against the wishes of his mother violated Article 8 of the Human Rights Convention. Doctors violated David's right to respect for his privacy, notably his bodily integrity. Where children are too young, or otherwise unable, to make their own decisions about medical treatment, doctors must normally seek consent from the parents who speak on their child's behalf. Where doctors considered that parents were not acting in the child's interests, they must seek authority from a court before overruling the parents, except where intervention was immediately necessary to save the child's life.

The court can respond quickly where an emergency application is made. However, this gives little time to parents to prepare their case. In *Re OT (A Baby)*,[88] which we examine further in the next section, OT's parents argued that an emergency application was procedurally unfair. They claimed it breached baby OT's rights under Article 8. This submission was not accepted by the court. Parker J held that the parents had had adequate time to prepare their case and given the serious nature of OT's condition it was 'imperative now to reach a conclusion'.[89] The parents were refused permission to appeal.[90]

---

ment of the child or inability to find the parent are examples of exceptional situations justifying the doctor proceeding to treat the child without parental knowledge or consent'.

[86] [2004] 1 FLR 1019, ECtHR.
[87] *R v Portsmouth NHS Trust v Glass* (1999) 50 BMLR 269, CA.
[88] [2009] EWHC 635 (Fam).
[89] [2009] EWHC 635 (Fam) at 7.
[90] [2009] EWCA Civ 409.

Disputing best interests: parental demands

14.11 *Glass v* UK[91] reiterated that doctors may not unilaterally override the wishes of a child's parents. Courts retain the authority to do so. We have seen that courts will rarely endorse a parental refusal of treatment offering to a child a realistic prospect of continued life. Other cases present the reverse scenario. Parents want doctors to continue treating a child for whom the doctors judge there is little (if any) hope of meaningful survival.

In *Re C (A Minor) (Medical Treatment)*,[92] Orthodox Jewish parents argued that their sixteen-month-old daughter with spinal muscular atrophy should continue to be ventilated. Doctors argued that continued ventilation was futile. The child was dying. Ventilation would only prolong her life by a few days. The parents' faith dictated that every effort be made to preserve the spark of life. The court declined to interfere with the doctors' clinical judgment. *Re C* can be explained in several ways. English courts have on several occasions refused to order doctors to carry out treatment which in their clinical judgment they consider inappropriate.[93] It can persuasively be argued that prolonging a child's suffering cannot be in her interests.[94] Is *Re C*, however, another case where judges may have been tempted to dismiss the parents' case as 'scruple and dogma'?

More recently, in *Re OT (A Baby)*,[95] nine-month-old OT suffered from mitochondria, a progressive neuro-metabolic genetic condition. He was unable to swallow and dependent on a ventilator. He had suffered irreversible brain damage. Doctors felt that continued treatment was futile and would cause him distress. Both parents felt strongly that treatment of their son should be continued. They argued that he was aware of them and still enjoyed pain-free periods. The court accepted the expert evidence and made the declarations sought by the hospital trust. Sadly, this led to OT's immediate death in March 2009.

Charlotte Wyatt's parents' received a more sympathetic hearing from Hedley J. Their religious faith and determination to prolong their daughter's life were given careful consideration. Charlotte was born at twenty-six weeks' gestation. She needed to be ventilated for most of her first three months of life. She suffered severe infections and both her breathing and brain functions had steadily deteriorated. The damage was probably irreparable. She was believed at the first hearing to be blind and deaf and incapable of voluntary movement.

---

[91] [2004] 1 FLR 1019, ECtHR.

[92] [1998] 1 FLR 384. And see *Royal Wolverhampton Hospitals NHS Trusts v B* [2000] 2 FLR 953; *A National Health Service Trust v B* [2000] 2 FCR 577; *Re MM (Medical Treatment)* [2000] 1 FLR 224.

[93] *R (Burke) v GMC* [2005] EWCA Civ 1003.

[94] See *Superintendent of Family and Child Services and Dawson* (1983) DLR (3d) 610.

[95] [2009] EWHC 635 (Fam). See S Burns, 'The Right to be Kept Alive' (2009) 153(17) *Solicitors Journal* 11. See also *Re K (A Minor)* [2006] EWHC 1007 (Fam).

On five occasions, Hedley J was asked to adjudicate in disputes between her parents and her doctors,[96] and on one occasion, the case went to the Court of Appeal.[97] The dispute concerned not the current care of the child, but a contingency that might arise. Should Charlotte stop breathing, must she be re-ventilated? Her fundamentalist Christian parents were adamant that everything be done to prolong her life. They sought a miracle. Her doctors considered that the pain and distress likely to ensue from ventilation would only prolong the process of her dying. The trust sought a declaration that doctors were not obliged to re-ventilate Charlotte. At the original hearing in 2004, experts suggested that Charlotte had no more than a 5 per cent chance of surviving the winter of 2004–5. Charlotte defied the odds. Her parents' and her doctors' perception of what sort of life Charlotte could enjoy differed radically. The doctors saw a baby with severe brain damage, unable to respond to stimulation other than pain. Her parents believed (and believe) that she responds to them, that she feels pleasure.

Hedley J emphasised the presumption in favour of prolonging life, but acknowledged that, in assessing the best interests of a sick child, there is this balancing exercise to be performed. He quoted Taylor LJ in *Re J (A Minor) (Wardship: Medical Treatment)*,[98] asking would '. . . the child in question, if capable of exercising sound judgment . . . consider the life to be intolerable'? Hedley J expressly declined to utilise 'intolerability' as a supplementary test, or a replacement test, for best interests. Examining the nature of her current existence and the risks and distress entailed in a tracheotomy, the judge concluded (in October 2004) that further aggressive treatment, even if necessary to prolong Charlotte's life, was not in her best interests. Rejecting her parents' views, Hedley J acknowledged that her parents knew her best. He had to regard their 'intuitive feelings', but he reminded himself '. . . they may project those on Charlotte'. So in three hearings, the judge granted and continued the declaration sought by the trust.

Charlotte survived, and in October 2005, the judge lifted his declaration.[99] The judge found that given her improved condition, it could no longer be said that ventilation would inevitably be futile or wholly inappropriate. Whether ventilation was in Charlotte's best interests would depend on her condition at the relevant time when a decision must be made. Charlotte's improved condition was such that one would expect that decisions about her care would fall to be determined by normal principles of law and clinical practice. However, the relationship between her parents and the hospital had been, at times, openly hostile. Professionals feared retribution if they made a decision opposed by the Wyatts. The trust sought a declaration that in the event of irreconcilable disagreement, the professionals' decision would be lawful and final. This wide

[96]   *Re Wyatt* [2004] EWHC 2247, [2005] EWHC 117, [2005] EWHC 693, [2005] EWHC 1181, [2005] EWHC 2902, [2006] EWHC 319.
[97]   *Wyatt v Portsmouth NHS Trust* [2005] EWCA Civ 1181.
[98]   [1990] 3 A11 ER 930 at 945.
[99]   *Portsmouth NHS Trust v Wyatt* [2005] EWHC 2293 (Fam).

declaration, Hedley J refused to grant. Instead he sought to reinforce that the usual principles relating to the medical care of infants must apply. If a decision whether or not to intubate (or provide other treatment) arose, her parents and doctors must seek to agree on what constitutes her best interests. They must seek to work in partnership. No doctor was compelled to administer treatment he considered not to be in the child's best interests or an affront to his conscience; though he should not prevent other clinicians from so doing. Hedley J concluded by urging the parties to work together. In 2006, the case returned to court. Charlotte developed an infection and her condition had worsened again. The judge reaffirmed that doctors have no obligation to intubate or ventilate her, should she stop breathing.

The protracted litigation relating to Charlotte Wyatt, highlights three rather different issues about the role of the law.

(1) Hedley J declined to replace the best interests test with any test of 'intolerability' or 'significant harm' that might give more force to parental judgments. He preferred to retain the traditional 'balancing exercise' of best interests.

(2) The length and bitterness of the litigation spelled out a cruel lesson concerning the consequences of a breakdown in trust between families and professionals.

(3) Medical prognosis is not always accurate. Charlotte defied medical expectations and improved, but the converse can also happen. Court declarations sought by hospital trusts may vary in their specificity and may need to be revisited. In *Re B (A Minor)*,[100] the court issued a declaration concerning the future treatment of twenty-two-month-old B who had a deteriorating illness and was not expected to reach the age of five. If, in future, she deteriorated considerably, she should not be given intensive resuscitation. Obiter dicta, Coleridge J suggested that a short joint experts' report might be attached to broader declarations made in similar circumstances, so that new and existing doctors might have much-needed guidance and elaboration.

In *An NHS Trust v MB*[101] Holman J refused to authorise doctors to withdraw life support from baby MB, against the strongly voiced objections of his parents. MB was eighteen months old; he had the most severe form of spinal muscular atrophy and breathed only with the aid of a ventilator. He would inevitably die within the next twelve months or so. His parents refused to consent to switching off the ventilator except as a test to see if he could breathe independently. They also wanted MB to have a tracheotomy to allow the baby to be ventilated outside hospital. The doctors sought to withdraw the endotracheal tube and, with the aid of sedatives, allow MB a pain-free dignified

---

[100] [2008] EWHC 1998 (Fam).
[101] [2006] EWHC 507 (Fam). See M Jonas, 'The Baby MB Case: Medical Decision Making in the Context of Uncertain Infant Suffering' (2007) 33(9) *Journal of Medical Ethics* 541.

death. The medical evidence unanimously supported this course of action, as did the guardian appointed by the court to represent the baby. His parents gave evidence that MB responded to them, that he enjoyed stories, songs and his favourite TV programmes. The Muslim father believed that the decision about when, or if, his son dies, must be left to God. The judge refused the parents' request for an order for further invasive treatment to prolong MB's life. He refused the doctors' request to withdraw ventilation. He attempted a balancing exercise in which the crucial feature was that MB retained some significant cognitive function. MB was (or might be) still able to function at some level like any other infant, recognising his mother and taking simple pleasures from touch, light and sound. The suffering he might endure as a consequence of all the invasive, intrusive treatments keeping him alive was in the judge's view balanced by these benefits.

The judgment in *An NHS Trust v MB* poses difficult questions. If MB's cognitive function is the *key* factor tipping the balance in favour of continuing to ventilate him, those questions include the following. MB's parents fought to keep him alive. What of a baby whose medical condition is identical to MB, but whose parents want him to be allowed to die – does that tip the balancing exercise the other way?[102] If MB does have the cognitive function to distinguish him from earlier cases where ventilation was withdrawn, is his suffering maybe all the greater? What weight do we put on cognitive function? Does mental disability make a life less worth living than even grave physical abnormalities? Why was this case decided differently from Baby C who was also dying of spinal muscular atrophy?[103]

Not just life or death

14.12 Difficult decisions about the medical care of young children are not exclusively confined to decisions relating to life-sustaining treatment. In *Re C (HIV test)*,[104] a baby was born to an HIV-positive mother. She had declined conventional treatment for HIV, rejected treatment in pregnancy which might have diminished the risk of transmitting HIV to the child, and intended to breastfeed. Both parents refused to agree to an HIV test for their baby. They argued that any possible treatment for the child (were she HIV-positive) could be more toxic than beneficial, and that sero-positive status would stigmatise the child. The local authority, applying for an order to test the child, relied on medical opinion that the child was at a 25 per cent risk of having contracted HIV and that effective medical care of the child required knowledge of her HIV status. The Court of Appeal upheld the trial judge's view that the child's

---

[102] Consider *Re RB (A Child)* [2009] EWHC 3269 (Fam). After a six-day hearing RB's father accepted the views of the medical team that withdrawal of treatment was in his son's best interests. The ten-paragraph judgment endorses the parental decision. See further G Douglas, 'Medical Treatment' (2010) 40 (Feb) *Family Law* 139.

[103] [1998] 1 FLR 384.

[104] [2000] Fam 48, CA.

interests should allow the HIV test. The parents sought to assert their right to respect for family life enshrined in Article 8 of the European Convention on Human Rights. As the trial judge noted, such a claim is swiftly countered by consideration of the child's own rights and the needs of his health and welfare expressly recognised in Article 8(2).[105]

Resolving 'conflicts of rights' is not easy. Disputes between parents can be just as complex as disagreements between doctors and parents. In *Re J (Child's Religious Upbringing and Circumcision)*,[106] a devout Muslim father sought a court order to circumcise his five-year-old son. The child's non-Muslim mother objected. The couple were estranged. The father argued that circumcision would identify child with father and establish the boy within the Muslim community. He invoked his right under Article 9 of the European Convention on Human Rights to freedom of religion. The mother's religious adherence to Christianity was said to be notional only. There were no medical grounds for circumcision. The courts found for the mother, influenced by the pain and distress circumcision might cause the boy. In *Re C (Welfare of the Child: Immunisation)*,[107] two fathers applied for court orders that their daughters should receive the MMR vaccine. Both girls lived with their mothers who considered the MMR vaccine to be unsafe. The Court of Appeal upheld the trial judge's ruling that vaccination was in the girls' best interests. The judges considered that the medical evidence of both the efficacy and safety of the MMR vaccine was overwhelming. They dismissed the contrary evidence out of hand.

Re J (1999) and *Re C* (2003) came to court because the parents disagreed about the interests of their children. It illustrates one of the anomalies of the law. If the principle is that treatment necessary for the welfare of the child should be carried out and nothing contrary to his interest should be done, is circumcision, even with both parents' agreement, lawful?

The limits of parental consent

14.13 As parental rights to determine medical treatment of their child derive from the parental duty to obtain adequate medical care for them, those rights cannot be unfettered. In Skegg's words, a parent may give '. . . a legally effective consent to a procedure which is likely to be for the benefit of the child, in the sense of being in the child's best interests'.[108] Routine treatment or surgery for an existing physical condition, diagnostic procedures or preventative measures such as vaccination, pose no problem. The benefit is there for all to see. More intricate and even risky procedures cause little difficulty. Not all parents

---

[105] See L Haggar, 'Some Implications of the Human Rights Act 1998 for the Medical Treatment of Children' (2003) 6 *Medical Law International* 25.

[106] [2000] 1 FRC 307.

[107] [2003] 2 FLR 1095, CA.

[108] See P D G Skegg, 'Consent to Medical Procedures on Minors' (1973) 36 *Modern Law Review* 370 at 377.

might agree to complex heart surgery on a baby, but if doctors and parents weigh risk and benefit, and conclude in favour of going ahead, they have exercised their respective duties properly. Problems surface in relation to medical or surgical procedures not immediately called for to treat or prevent ill-health. Two classic issues are dealt with later – whether a child can donate organs or tissue (in chapter 17), and when children can be used for medical research purposes (in chapter 15). Sterilising minors raises interesting questions about the limits of parental and judicial authority.

Re D[109] concerned a girl aged eleven. She suffered from Soto's syndrome and was afflicted by epilepsy and a number of other physical problems. The girl also had some degree of learning disability. Her mother was anxious about her future and considered that she would never be capable of caring for a child, that having a child would damage her, that she might all too easily be seduced and would be incapable of practising any form of contraception. Accordingly she sought to have her sterilised before these risks should materialise. The girl's paediatrician agreed, and a gynaecologist was found who was ready to perform the operation. An educational psychologist involved with the child disagreed and applied to have the child made a ward of court. Heilbron J ordered that proposals for the operation be abandoned. Her function, she said, was to act as the 'judicial reasonable parent', with the welfare of the child as her paramount consideration. She found that medical opinion was overwhelmingly against sterilisation of such a child at eleven. The irrevocable nature of sterilisation, the emotional impact on the girl when she discovered what had been done to her, her present inability to understand what was proposed, coupled with evidence that her mental development was such that she would one day be able to make an informed choice for herself on childbearing, all led the judge to conclude that the operation was '... neither medically indicated nor necessary. And that it would not be in [the girl's] best interests for it to be performed'.[110]

None the less, in *Re B* (1987),[111] the House of Lords sanctioned the sterilisation of seventeen-year-old Jeanette. Jeanette was more profoundly disabled than D. She was said to have a mental age of five or six, with a more limited capacity to communicate. She had no understanding of the link between sexual intercourse and pregnancy. Those caring for her testified that, apart from sterilisation, no means of reliable contraception would be suitable for Jeanette. If she became pregnant, delivery might well have to be by Caesarean section, and the girl had an unbreakable habit of picking and tearing at any wounds. Despite her profound disability, Jeanette was sexually mature. The Law Lords held that the legality of the proposal to sterilise Jeanette must depend only on whether sterilisation would '... promote the welfare and serve the best interests of the ward'.[112] Consideration of eugenics and whether sterilising Jeanette

---

[109] [1986] 1 All ER 326.
[110] [1986] 1 All ER 326 at 335.
[111] [1987] 2 All ER 206.
[112] [1987] 2 All ER 206 at 213, per Lord Bridge.

would ease the burden on those caring for her was irrelevant.[113] Their Lordships concluded that as Jeanette: (1) would never be capable of making any choice for herself on whether to have a child; (2) would never even appreciate what was happening to her; and (3) would suffer damage to her health if she ever became pregnant, she could lawfully be sterilised by occlusion of her fallopian tubes (not hysterectomy). Lord Templeman, however, suggested that the radical nature of sterilisation was such that a girl of eighteen should never be sterilised without the consent of a High Court judge.[114]

> A doctor performing a sterilisation operation with the consent of the parents might still be liable to criminal, civil or professional proceedings. A court exercising the wardship jurisdiction emanating from the Crown is the only authority which is empowered to authorise such a drastic step as sterilisation after a full and informed investigation.

Following *Re B*, a number of subsequent cases appeared to evidence judicial willingness to authorise sterilisation of young girls fairly readily. In 2007 doctors sought legal advice regarding the proposed hysterectomy of fifteen-year-old Katie Thorpe, who had a mental age of eighteen months. Her mother feared that menstrual bleeding would frighten and confuse her, and adversely affect her dignity.[115] There is no record of the case reaching the courts. Parallels were drawn between the request to treat Katie and the controversial[116] treatment of Ashley X in America. Ashley had the mental age of a three-month-old baby and could not walk, talk or swallow. Her breast buds and uterus were removed and she was treated with hormones designed to keep her small. The intention was to enhance her quality of life – to improve her care by making her more mobile. The media reported that a hospital ethics committee supported the decision.[117]

Recent decisions relating to the proposed sterilisation of adult women indicate that: (a) judges are more ready to scrutinise any proposal to sterilise a woman more rigorously; and (b) that where other surgery, such as hysterectomy, will result in infertility, cases where reasonable people might disagree on what was best for the patient ought to go before a judge.[118]

What *Re B* reaffirms in the context of children's treatment generally is that parental powers are limited. Albeit parents honestly believe they are acting in their child's interests, if they propose to authorise some irreversible or drastic measure, their authorisation alone will not make that measure lawful. It must

---

113 [1987] 2 All ER 206 at 213 at 219 per Lord Oliver.
114 [1987] 2 All ER 206 at 213 at 214.
115 C Dyer, 'Mother Asks Surgeons to Perform Hysterectomy on Daughter with Cerebral Palsy' (2007) 335 *BMJ* 743.
116 Some of the ethical debates are recited in D S Diekema, N Fost, 'Ashley Revisited: A Response to the Critics' (2010) 10(1) *American Journal of Bioethics* 30, which supports the treatment.
117 C Ayres, 'Parents Defend Decision to Keep Girl a Child' (2007) *Sunday Times*, 4 January.
118 See *Re S* (*Adult Patient: Sterilisation*) [2000] 3 WLR 1288 discussed above at **6.7**.

be shown to be in the child's interests. No mother could authorise the sterilisation of her four-year-old daughter because that daughter was a haemophilia carrier. She has no right to deprive her child of the right to make that decision herself. The child's best interests include her potential right to autonomy. It seems unlikely that parents could authorise a vasectomy on even the most severely mentally disabled son.[119] For such an operation would not be in his interests, albeit it benefited society. Similarly, no parent, however strong or genuine his commitment to medical research might be, could lawfully authorise the entry of his healthy child into a research trial posing real and substantial risk to that child's health.

Procedures to protect children

14.14 We do not examine in any detail the procedural means by which disputes about the care or treatment of a child come before the courts. One or two brief points about parental responsibility and family law procedures are noted here.[120] When a child's parents are married, both parents share parental responsibility for her. When the parents are unmarried, they share parental responsibility if either they jointly register the child's birth, or they subsequently enter into a formal agreement to share parental responsibility. Or a father may seek a court order conferring parental responsibility on him where the mother is not voluntarily prepared to share legal responsibility for the child.[121] Normally, in relation to medical treatment, the consent of one parent to the treatment of their young child suffices.[122] If a mother takes her five-year-old for a booster vaccination, the doctor does not need to delay matters by ensuring that the father also agrees to vaccination. The courts have, however, made it clear that where some major or irreversible decision needs to be made about a child's treatment, or where there is disagreement between the parents sharing parental responsibility, both parents' consent is required and/or the case must be referred to the court.[123]

Should a father without parental responsibility, or other relatives, such as grandparents, local social services or any other third party, have concerns about a child's medical treatment, a number of means exist by which a dispute concerning the child's welfare can be adjudicated by a court. The child could be taken into care or made a ward of court,[124] but that is rare these days. The

---

[119] See *Re A (Medical Treatment: Male Sterilisation)* [2000] 1 FCR 193 CA, discussed above at **6.7**.

[120] See J Bridgeman, *Parental Responsibility, Young Children and Healthcare Law* (2007) CUP.

[121] See s 4 of the Children Act 1989 as amended by the Adoption and Children Act 2002.

[122] GMC, *Treatment and Care Towards the End of Life: Good Practice in Decision Making* (2010), para 104.

[123] See *Re J (Child's Religious Upbringing and Circumcision)* [1999] 2 FLR 1004 CA.

[124] In which case the court will acquire control over all aspects of the child's life and upbringing.

inherent jurisdiction of the court can be invoked, or an order sought under section 8 of the Children Act 1989. Section 8 orders are diverse in kind. Of particular relevance here are 'specific issue orders' and 'prohibited steps orders'. If an unmarried father (who does not have parental responsibility) strongly believes that surgery to correct a hideous birthmark is in his child's interests and her mother opposes surgery solely because she believes that her child's deformity was 'God's will – a punishment for being born out of wedlock', he may seek a 'specific issue order'.[125] Should he seek to prevent the performance of purely cosmetic surgery which his child's mother wants because she wants the child to be a model, he could apply for a 'prohibited steps order' to prevent surgery.

Sometimes the machinery to protect children from inappropriate 'treatment' operates fairly randomly. In the course of the judgment in *Re D* (above), it emerged that two similar sterilisation operations on mentally disabled girls had already been performed in Sheffield. D was lucky. Her psychologist was persistent and chance took D's dilemma to the High Court. Despite judicial pronouncements that sterilisation of girls under eighteen must always be a matter for the courts, girls have been sterilised by hysterectomy for 'hygienic' reasons, without judicial approval. These cases involve girls who cannot in any sense cope with menstruation. They may refuse to wear sanitary protection. It is not clear beyond doubt that such an operation is in the girl's interests, though it is certainly in her carers' interests. The Court of Appeal considers such 'borderline' cases should always go before a judge.[126] However, the problem in protecting such girls is: who will know what happened? Only if some interested third party intervenes will the matter reach the light of day in time to prevent the procedure going ahead.

Consider female circumcision, mutilation of a girl child's genitalia to comply with cultural norms. Parliament intervened to ban the practice in the UK, in the Prohibition of Female Circumcision Act 1985, now repealed and replaced by the Female Genital Mutilation Act 2003. One might have thought that such mutilation of a child was indubitably an assault on her. In Parliamentary debates on prohibition of female circumcision in 1985, Lord Hailsham rightly argued that genital mutilation of a child was already a crime, assault occasioning actual bodily harm. But who would tell the authorities, who will prosecute? Besides which, had the common law been faced with the question of female circumcision, difficult questions would arise in answering the question of the girl's best interests. What if she agreed, wishing to fall in with the custom of her community? What of arguments that the girl's mental well-being required that she meet the customs of her people? If ritual male circumcision is permissible, why not female circumcision, if carried out by surgeons in aseptic conditions?

---

[125] As the fathers did in *Re C (Welfare of the Child: Immunisation)* [2003] EWCA Civ 1148.
[126] *Re S (Adult Patient: Sterilisation)* [2000] 3 WLR 1288, CA.

The views of the child

14.15   What of a child's own wishes? Once a child can communicate, she will in many cases have an opinion of her own. Most four-year-olds object robustly to injections, dental treatment and anything likely to cause them discomfort. At four, the case that the child cannot form any sensible judgment about the pros and cons of treatment may well be made out. At eight, ten and twelve the child acquires greater maturity, albeit most doctors and parents would be reluctant to bow to the child's judgment. What must be remembered, however, is that the balance of the child's best interests will be (radically) affected by his willingness or otherwise to participate in treatment. Obtaining assent even from very young children is good practice.[127] Forcible treatment which may involve restraining, even detaining the child, requires strong justification. And as the child reaches her teens, becomes what is rather pompously called a 'mature minor', the legal picture changes. GMC guidance states that: 'Parents are usually the best judges of their children's best interests and should make important decisions up until children are able to make their own decisions.'[128]

Family Law Reform Act 1969

14.16   The Family Law Reform Act 1969 reduced the age of majority from twenty-one to eighteen. When the 1969 Act was before Parliament it was unclear what effect, if any, a consent to medical treatment given by a minor might have. Many sixteen- and seventeen-year-olds live, or spend considerable periods of time, away from their parents. Some are married and parents themselves. Section 8 of the 1969 Act clarified the law concerning sixteen- to eighteen-year-olds and empowered them to consent to their own medical treatment. Sub-sections (1) and (2) of section 8 provide:

(1)   The consent of a minor who has attained the age of sixteen years to any surgical, medical or dental treatment which, in the absence of consent, would constitute a trespass to his person shall be as effective as it would be if he were of full age: and where a minor has by virtue of this section given an effective consent it shall not be necessary to obtain any consent for it from his parent or guardian.

(2)   In this section 'surgical, medical or dental treatment' includes any procedure undertaken for the purposes of diagnosis, and this section applies to any procedure (including, in particular, the administration of an anaesthetic) which is ancillary to any treatment as it applies to that treatment.

---

[127]   See United Nations Convention on the Rights of the Child 1989, Art 12(1): 'States Parties shall assure to the child who is capable of forming his or her own views the right to express those views freely in all matters affecting the child, the views of the child being given due weight in accordance with the age and maturity of the child.'

[128]   GMC, *0-18 Guidance for all Doctors* (2007), para 21.

So far, so good; once a person is sixteen he can consent to treatment himself. That does not mean that any parental consent relating to their children under eighteen is always ineffective. If the child of sixteen or seventeen is incapable of giving consent, for example, because he lacks mental capacity, his parents may still act on his behalf until he comes of age. Section 8 went on in sub-section (3) to provide:

(3)   Nothing in this section shall be construed as making ineffective any consent which would have been effective if this section had not been enacted.

The majority of lawyers and doctors interpreted section 8(3) in this way. The common law had never directly determined when, if at all, a child could give effective consent to medical treatment. The assumption was that the law gave effect to consent by a minor provided she or he was sufficiently mature to understand the proposed treatment or surgery.[129] Sixteen was the average age at which doctors judged patients to be old enough to give consent without consulting parents on every occasion. Nevertheless, many doctors regarded themselves as free to treat children under sixteen without parental approval, if the individual child appeared sufficiently intelligent and grown up to take the decision on treatment alone. Before 1969, every case turned on the doctor's assessment of the particular minor in her surgery. The 1969 Act freed the doctor from doubt and risk where the patient was over sixteen. She no longer had to consider the maturity of a patient over sixteen. She could assume adult status and capability. Sub-section (3), it was argued, simply preserved the status quo for the under-sixteens. Doctors could continue to treat a child under sixteen as long as that child was mature enough to make his own judgment. This assumption, that there had always been a limited freedom to treat children under sixteen without parental consent, and that what sub-section (3) did was preserve that freedom, was at the heart of the *Gillick* saga and its sequels in *Re R* and *Re W*.

The *Gillick* case

14.17   The *Gillick* saga has its origins in a circular issued by the DHSS in 1974, outlining arrangements for a comprehensive family planning service within the NHS. Statistics on the number of births and induced abortions among girls under sixteen led the DHSS to conclude that contraceptive services should be made more readily available to that age group. The essence of their advice was that the decision to provide contraception to a girl under sixteen was one for the doctor. He might lawfully treat, and prescribe for, the girl without contacting her parents. He should not contact parents without the girl's agreement. In 1980, the DHSS revised its advice. The revised version stressed that every effort should be made to involve parents. If the girl was adamant that her parents should not know of her request for contraception, the principle of confidentiality between doctor and patient should be preserved.

[129] See Skegg (1973) 36 *Modern Law Review* 370, pp 370–375.

This amended advice from the DHSS did not satisfy critics. Victoria Gillick sought assurances that none of her daughters would be given contraceptive, or abortion advice, or treatment without her prior knowledge and consent until they were sixteen. Those assurances were refused, and Mrs Gillick went to court seeking declarations: (1) against her health authority and the DHSS to the effect that their advice that children under sixteen could be treated without parental consent was unlawful and wrong; and (2) against her health authority to the effect that medical personnel employed by them should not give contraceptive and/or abortion advice and/or treatment to any child of Mrs Gillick's under sixteen without her prior knowledge and consent. Mrs Gillick's concern was with contraception and abortion for under-sixteens. She had no axe to grind in respect of other forms of medical treatment. The trouble is that contraception cannot be isolated from more general questions. Mrs Gillick's counsel challenged the assumption that the common law permitted medical treatment of children under sixteen in the absence of parental consent.

Children under sixteen and consent to treatment: *Gillick* competence

14.18 At first instance, Woolf J[130] endorsed the view that once a child was able to understand what was entailed in proposed treatment, he or she could consent to such treatment. Any physical contact involved in treatment would not constitute battery. Mrs Gillick appealed and, in a complex judgment, the Court of Appeal[131] found for her. Not only was any treatment of a child under sixteen potentially battery unless authorised by a parent, but giving children advice or information about contraception without parental knowledge could constitute an infringement of parental rights. After the Court of Appeal decision, no doctor could (save in emergency) safely see a child under sixteen in her clinic or surgery without parental knowledge. The DHSS appealed to the House of Lords. By a majority, the House of Lords held that the original advice circulated by the DHSS was not unlawful and that a child under sixteen can in certain circumstances give a valid consent to medical treatment, including contraception or abortion treatment, without parental knowledge or agreement.[132]

The general problem of consent

14.19 The majority of their Lordships rejected the Court of Appeal's finding that consent given by a child under sixteen was of no effect. Like Woolf J, they accepted the view that the Family Law Reform Act 1969 had left that question open. The matter was for the common law to determine. The common law was not static, fossilised in eighteenth-century notions of the inviolable rights of the *paterfamilias*. Judge-made law must meet the needs of the times. Parental rights derived from parental duties to protect the person and property of the

---

130 [1984] 1 All ER 365.
131 [1985] 1 All ER 533.
132 [1985] 3 All ER 402, HL.

child. Modern legislation qualified and limited parental rights by placing the welfare of the child as its first priority. Parental rights being dependent on the duty of care for – and maintenance of – the child, they endured only so long as necessary to achieve their end. As Lord Scarman put it: '. . . the parental right yields to the child's right to make his own decisions when he reaches a sufficient understanding and intelligence to be capable of making up his own mind on the matter requiring decision'.[133]

Their Lordships argued that the common law had never regarded the consent of a child as a complete nullity. Were that the case, intercourse with a girl under sixteen would inevitably be rape. That is not so. Provided the girl is old enough to understand what she is agreeing to, intercourse with her consent will not be rape. Parliament, to protect girls under sixteen from the consequences of their own folly, enacted a separate offence of unlawful sexual intercourse with girls under sixteen in the commission of which the girl's consent is irrelevant. If the girl validly consented, that is the only offence committed, and not the more serious crime of rape.[134]

Moving from the general issue of consent by children to the problem of consent to medical treatment, the House of Lords saw no reason to depart from the general rule. Lord Fraser thought it would be ludicrous to say that a boy or girl of fifteen could not agree to examination or treatment for a trivial injury. Importantly, Lord Templeman, who dissented on the specific issue of contraceptive treatment, agreed that there were circumstances where a doctor could properly treat a child under sixteen without parental agreement. He concurred that the effect of the consent of the child depended on the nature of the treatment and the age and understanding of the child. A doctor, he thought, could safely remove tonsils or a troublesome appendix from a boy or girl of fifteen without express parental agreement. *Gillick* establishes that a child below sixteen may lawfully be given general medical advice and treatment without parental agreement, provided that child has achieved sufficient maturity to understand fully what is proposed. The doctor treating such a child on the basis of her consent alone will not be at risk of either a civil action for battery or criminal prosecution.

The special problems of contraception and abortion

14.20   Lord Templeman, however, dissented on the specific issue of contraception. He did not accept that a girl under sixteen has sufficient maturity and

---

[133] [1985] 3 All ER 402 at 422, HL.

[134] In another context, just a year before the *Gillick* hearing, the House of Lords had considered the crime of kidnapping as it related to children under sixteen. They held that the central issue was the agreement of the child, not either parent, to being taken away by the accused. In the case of a young child, absence of consent could be presumed. With an older child, the question was whether he or she had sufficient understanding and intelligence to give consent. See *R v D* [1984] 2 All ER 449.

understanding of the emotional and physical consequences of sexual intercourse to consent to contraceptive treatment. His Lordship put it thus:[135]

> I doubt whether a girl under the age of sixteen is capable of a balanced judgement
> to embark on frequent, regular or casual sexual intercourse fortified by the illu-
> sion that medical science can protect her in mind and body and ignoring the
> danger of leaping from childhood to adulthood without the difficult formative
> transitional experiences of adolescence. There are many things a girl under six-
> teen needs to practise but sex is not one of them.

The majority of his colleagues disagreed. They conceded that a request by a
girl under sixteen for contraception, coupled with an insistence that her parents not be told, posed a problem for the doctor. Assessing whether she is
mature enough to consider the emotional and physical consequences of the
course she has embarked on is not easy. But that question should be left to the
clinical judgment of the doctor. Lord Fraser set out five matters the doctor
should satisfy himself on before giving contraceptive treatment to a girl below
sixteen without parental agreement. They are:[136]

> . . . (1) that the girl . . . will understand his advice; (2) that he cannot persuade her
> to inform her parents . . .; (3) that she is very likely to begin or continue having
> sexual intercourse with or without contraceptive treatment; (4) that unless she
> receives contraceptive advice or treatment her physical or mental health or both
> are likely to suffer; (5) that her best interests require him to give her contraceptive
> advice or treatment or both without the parental consent.

Lord Fraser's formula failed to satisfy Mrs Gillick. She regarded it as inadequate in two respects. First, in a busy surgery or clinic, has any doctor sufficient
time to embark on the investigation and counselling of the girl necessary to
fulfil the criteria laid down? Second, underlying the judgments of the majority
is acceptance of the view that, as significant numbers of young girls under sixteen are going to continue having sexual intercourse regardless of whether
they have lawful access to contraception, it may be in their best interests to
protect them from pregnancy by contraceptive treatment. Mrs Gillick disagreed. She contended that if access to contraception without parental
agreement were stopped, at least the majority of young girls would: (a) be
deterred from starting to have intercourse so young by fear of pregnancy and/
or parental disapproval; and (b) would have a defence against pressure from
their peers to 'grow up' and sleep with someone. Both sides in the debate on
'under-age' contraception agree that early sexual intercourse increases the
danger of disease to the child, be it cervical cancer or venereal disease. Most
agree about the emotional damage the child risks. They are no nearer agreement how girls under sixteen may best be protected than on the day Mrs
Gillick first went to court. The decision to allow emergency contraception
(morning after pill) to be sold over the counter in local pharmacies reignited
controversy.

[135] [1985] 3 All ER 402 at 432, HL.
[136] [1985] 3 All ER 402 at 413, HL.

What about abortion? The greater part of the Law Lords' decision concentrated on contraception. The rules for abortion on girls under sixteen are the same. If a girl is intelligent and mature enough to understand what is involved in the operation, the doctor, if the girl insists on not telling her parents, or if they refuse to agree to an abortion, may go ahead on the basis of the girl's consent alone. The House of Lords endorsed the approach of Butler-Sloss J in an earlier case.[137] A fifteen-year-old girl, with one child already, became pregnant again while in the care of the local authority. She wanted an abortion. Doctors considered that the birth of a second child would endanger the mental health of the girl and her existing child. Her father objected. Abortion was contrary to his religion. The local authority applied to have the girl made a ward of court and so seek the court's consent to the operation. The judge authorised the operation. She said the decision must be made in the light of the girl's best interests. She took into account the parents' feelings, but held that they could not outweigh the needs of the girl.

Mrs Gillick had, however, a second line of attack. The Sexual Offences Act 1956 made it a criminal offence 'to cause or encourage . . . the commission of unlawful sexual intercourse with . . . a girl for whom [the] accused is responsible'. So Mrs Gillick argued that providing contraception for a girl under sixteen amounted to 'encouraging' that crime. The Law Lords dismissed this second claim too. The Sexual Offences Act 2003 replaces the 1956 Act. It creates a raft of new criminal offences and toughens up the law relating to unlawful sexual relations with people under sixteen. But sections 14 and 73 of the Act provide express protection for doctors and nurses providing contraceptive advice or treatment, abortions, or indeed any health care relating to the young person's sexual health. No offence of facilitating a child sex offence, of aiding and abetting unlawful sexual intercourse is committed if the person acts either: (1) to protect the child from sexually transmitted diseases; (2) to protect the child's physical safety; (3) to prevent a girl becoming pregnant or to promote the child's emotional well-being.

A right to say no?

14.21   For several years, *Gillick* was assumed to have established that once young people acquired the necessary maturity to consent to treatment, what Lord Donaldson was later to style *Gillick competence*,[138] they acquired a right to determine what medical treatment they received. They had a right to say no, as much as a right to say yes. Recall Lord Scarman's words in *Gillick*,[139] '. . . the parental right yields to the child's right to make his own decision when he reaches a sufficient understanding and intelligence to be capable of making up his own mind on the matter requiring a decision'. Subsequent judgments of the Court of Appeal rejected that apparently logical conclusion. Adolescent

---

[137] *In Re P (A Minor)* (1982) 80 LGR 301.
[138] See *Re R (A Minor)* [1991] 4 All ER 177, CA.
[139] [1985] 3 All ER 402 at 422, HL.

autonomy is little more than myth, for no young person under eighteen – no minor – has a right to refuse treatment.[140] Parental powers to authorise treatment against their offspring's will endure, concurrently with extensive judicial powers to order minors to submit to treatment others deem necessary for their welfare.

In *Re R*, R[141] was a fifteen-year-old girl suffering from acute psychiatric problems. Her condition fluctuated. At times she appeared rational and lucid. However, she lacked insight into her illness. During her lucid phases she refused medication and became psychotic once again. R was in care, and the local authority responsible for her sought judicial guidance seeking authority to administer anti-psychotic drugs without R's consent. The Court of Appeal agreed with the trial judge that R was not *Gillick competent*. Her illness prevented her from fully understanding the need for drugs to control her condition. R could lawfully be treated against her will. In this particular case, the court authorised her treatment via its wardship jurisdiction. But the local authority as her legal guardian could equally have provided a proxy consent on R's behalf. The interest of *Re R* lies in Lord Donaldson's dicta. He went on to say that even were R *Gillick competent*, she would still have no power to veto treatment. A *Gillick competent* minor could consent to, but not refuse, treatment. Consent was akin to a key which 'unlocked the door to treatment', making the doctor's action lawful, but not obligatory. Once a young person became *Gillick competent* she became a keyholder. Her parents remained keyholders until she reached eighteen. They could still authorise treatment on her behalf. Doctors faced with willing parents but unwilling children were not obliged to treat the child, indeed might choose not to. They could lawfully elect to act on the basis of the parents' consent alone. The problem was one of ethical and clinical judgment for the physician.[142]

Re R was not well received.[143] In *Re W*,[144] Lord Donaldson was unphased by his critics. W was a sixteen-year-old girl. She was critically ill with anorexia nervosa and had had a tragic childhood. The local authority sought guidance whether W could, if it proved necessary, be moved to a specialist unit and force-fed. As W was sixteen, she was empowered to consent to treatment by virtue of section 8 of the Family Law Reform Act 1969. The Court of Appeal ruled that section 8 on its wording solely empowered a minor over sixteen to give an 'effective consent' to treatment. Section 8(3)[145] preserved the concurrent parental power to authorise treatment and the inherent powers of the courts to act to protect a minor's welfare. Lord Donaldson regretted only one

---

140 See C Bridge and M Brazier, 'Coercion or Caring: Analysing Adolescent Autonomy' (1996) 15 *Legal Studies* 84.

141 *Re R (A Minor)* [1991] 4 All ER 177, CA.

142 See *Re R (A Minor)* [1991] 4 All ER 177 at 184.

143 See, for example, A Bainham, 'The Judge and the Competent Minor' (1992) 108 *Law Quarterly Review* 104.

144 [1992] 4 All ER 627.

145 See Balcombe LJ at 639.

part of his dicta in *Re R*: his use of the keyholder metaphor. For as he acknowledged keys can lock as readily as unlock. In *Re W* he preferred to compare consent to a flakjacket, saying pithily:[146]

> ... I now prefer the analogy of the legal 'flak jacket' which protects from claims by the litigious whether [the doctor] acquires it from his patient who may be a minor over the age of sixteen, or a '*Gillick competent*' child under that age or from another person having parental responsibilities which include a right to consent to treatment of the minor. Anyone who gives him a flak jacket (ie consent) may take it back, but the doctor only needs one and so long as he continues to have one he has the legal right to proceed.

Re R and *Re W* make a nonsense of *Gillick*. They are explicable on their facts. There are powerful grounds to argue that both R and W lacked mental capacity regardless of their age. Their illness deprived them of the understanding and capacity to make a decision about treatment. Were they adults, they would be found to lack capacity applying sections 1 and 2 of the Mental Capacity Act 2005.[147] The same is true of the young people involved in a number of similar cases where judges ruled that an adolescent could not veto treatment.[148]

Consider *Re E*.[149] E was fifteen and shared his parents' Jehovah's Witness faith. He was seriously ill with leukaemia. Doctors advised that to maximise the prospects of successful chemotherapy, E should receive transfusions of blood products. E, like his parents, refused to agree to transfusions. The boy was made a ward of court. The judge authorised transfusion. He acknowledged that E was highly intelligent, mature for his age and well informed about his illness. Nonetheless, he held that E was not *Gillick competent*. He lacked insight into the process of dying. He could not turn his mind to the effect of the manner of his death or its effect on his family. How many adults enjoy such insight? Understandably, courts seek to protect young people from decisions that may endanger their life. In E's case, the outcome is tragic. Treatment at fifteen resulted in a temporary remission. At eighteen he relapsed, refused treatment and died believing that he had participated in an ungodly act. Then in *Re M (Child: Refusal of Medical Treatment)*,[150] a girl of fifteen-and-a-half refused to consent to a heart transplant. Her refusal was overridden by Johnson J. One of M's reasons for refusing surgery was said to be the prospect of life-long medication. Were her reasons for refusing a transplant much different from those of T's parents in *Re T (A Minor) (Wardship: Medical Treatment)*?[151]

---

[146] [1992] 4 All ER 627 at 635.
[147] See above ch 6.
[148] For example, *South Glamorgan County Council v B & W* [1993] 1 FLR 574; *Re S (A Minor) (Consent to Medical Treatment)* [1994] 2 FLR 1065; and see Bridge and Brazier (1996) 15 *Legal Studies* 84.
[149] *Re E (A Minor)* (1990) 9 BMLR 1.
[150] [1999] 2 FLR 1097.
[151] [1997] 1 All ER 906, CA.

The courts have distorted common sense and ethics in attempts to avoid the implications of *Gillick*. Judges have even gone so far as authorising restraint and detention of young people to ensure that they comply with treatment.[152] All this can be done without resort to the Mental Health Act 1983 (as amended by the Mental Health Act 2007), or the amended provisions of the Mental Capacity Act 2005, which at least build in some safeguards for adult patients.[153]

Confidentiality and children under sixteen

14.22 Do young people seeking treatment independently of their parents have any right to confidentiality? A young girl, embarking on a sexual relationship and considering seeking contraception, probably does not think so much about her capacity to give consent to treatment, as 'Will the doctor tell my mum?' The thought that a doctor may be free to give contraceptive advice to a child without the parents even knowing what is proposed was perhaps at the heart of Mrs Gillick's concern. The disruption of family life, and the danger that the girl might omit to give the doctor information on other drugs she might be taking, worried many caring parents. The Law Lords' decision in *Gillick* did not expressly address confidentiality. The assumption on which most doctors[154] and lawyers proceeded was that a *Gillick competent* minor had as much of a claim to a right of confidentiality, as he had a right to grant an independent consent to any treatment proposed by his doctor. Twenty years after *Gillick*, Mrs Axon challenged this assumption.[155] She argued that the parent of a child under sixteen had a right to be notified if a health professional proposed to offer advice or treatment relating to abortion or contraception to a child under sixteen. The parents' responsibility for the welfare of their children justified a limited exception to the usual duty of confidentiality to patients. The parents' right to respect for their privacy and family life under Article 8 of the European Convention on Human Rights granted them a right to such information about their child. Silber J[156] rejected Mrs Axon's case: A *Gillick competent* minor has the same right to confidentiality as any adult patient. This is reflected in recent guidance from the

---

[152] See *Re C (Detention: Medical Treatment)* [1997] 2 FLR 180.

[153] See C Bridge, 'Adolescents, and Mental Disorder: Who Consents to Treatment' (1997) 3 *Medical Law International* 51.

[154] GMC, *Confidentiality: Protecting and Providing Information* (2000) at para 38. Superseded by GMC, *0–18 years: guidance for all doctors* (2007), para 51, which states that disclosures when a child lacks capacity to consent should only be made if they are in the best interests of the child.

[155] She sought judicial review of DH Guidance, *Best Practice Guidance for Doctors and Other Health Professionals on the Provision of Advice and Treatment to Young People under Sixteen on Contraception, Sexual and Reproductive Health.*

[156] *R (on the application of Axon) v Secretary of State for Health* [2006] EWHC 37 (Admin). See J Loughrey, 'Can you Keep a Secret?' (2008) 20(3) *Child and Family Law Quarterly* 312.

Department of Health.[157] Nevertheless it remains good practice to involve parents, 'unless the young person specifically wishes to exclude them.'[158] If the doctor considers that his young patient is not *Gillick competent*, the GMC advises that he first seek to persuade her to involve her family, but ultimately he may disclose information to an appropriate person (usually the girl's parents). Could a doctor justify disclosure without consent in relation to a *Gillick competent* young patient? A difficult dilemma arises if the doctor suspects that the girl is being subjected to sexual abuse. Might public interest justify his action, especially if he suspected that other children might also be at risk from abuse?

A quite different dilemma relating to children's confidentiality has arisen as a result of the recent proliferation of genomics companies offering direct to consumer genetic tests. The tests may, for example, provide evidence of genetic ancestry, paternity or health issues. There is little to stop parents purchasing the tests for use on their children,[159] and the implications for the child may be considerable. In August 2010 the Human Genetics Commission published a Common Framework of Principles, a voluntary code which recommends the deferral of genetic tests until the child has the capacity to decide for herself. The Commission advises that where a genetic test is clinically indicated, it should be organised by healthcare professionals who can put in place necessary screening and after care.[160]

Human rights[161]

14.23 The most recent court case on adolescent treatment refusals was in 2003,[162] three years after the Human Rights Act 1998 came into force. No mention was made in that case of Article 12 of the United Nations Convention on the Rights of the Child[163] or Article 8 of the European Convention on Human Rights, which protects the right to respect for private and family life.

---

[157] DH, *Reference Guide to Consent for Examination of Treatment* (2nd edn, 2009), ch 3, paras 2–11.

[158] DH, *Reference Guide to Consent for Examination of Treatment* (2nd edn, 2009), ch 3, para 5.

[159] See M Henderson, 'DNA Tests May Threaten your Child's Rights: Watchdog Warns Parents Against "Unethical" Step' (2010) *Times*, 4 August.

[160] Human Genetics Commission, *Common Framework of Principles* (2010), at 6.9.

[161] See J Fortin, *Children's Rights and the Developing Law* (2009) CUP; S Choudhry, J Wallbank, J Herring, *Rights, Gender and Family Law* (2010) Routledge Cavendish.

[162] *Re P (Medical Treatment: Best Interests)* [2003] EWHC 2327 (Fam).

[163] Art 12(1) 'States Parties shall assure to the child who is capable of forming his or her own views the right to express those views freely in all matters affecting the child, the views of the child being given due weight in accordance with the age and maturity of the child.' See A MacDonald, 'Bringing Rights Home for Children: Arguing the UNCRC' (2009) *Family Law* 1073. Note that in 2010 the National Assembly of Wales proposed a 'Rights of Children and Young Persons (Wales) Measure' to increase regard to the UN Convention on the Rights of the Child 1989 (UNCRC).

The Convention gives a wide margin of appreciation and a human rights challenge to the refusals cases is by no means inevitable.[164] However, both Conventions are 'living instruments'. In *Axon,* Silber J reflected that children's rights are being given increased significance in the European Court of Human Rights jurisprudence.[165] Silber J relied on Article 8 to show that the mature minor's right to a private and family life not only outweighed the parental right but extinguished it.[166] This view was criticised,[167] but arguably Article 8 has new significance for the mature minor. This is reflected in section 43 of the Mental Health Act 2007.[168] It limits the rights of doctors and parents to override the competent decision of a relevant young person refusing to be admitted to hospital. In 2009 the media reported that thirteen-year-old Hannah Jones's decision to withhold consent to a heart transplant was respected, even though her life was likely to be shortened as a result.[169] Hannah's parents supported her decision. The trust, satisfied that Hannah understood the implications of her decision, dropped their application to the High Court to authorise the treatment against Hannah's will.[170] Fortunately Hannah later changed her mind and a successful heart transplant was performed. The decision in Hannah's case can be contrasted sharply with *Re M (Medical Treatment: Consent),*[171] where, as we have seen, the court authorised a heart transplant against the wishes of the fifteen-year-old patient.

Protection of individual autonomy does not hold universal appeal.[172] Beyleveld and Brownsword have demonstrated that the doctrine of consent has limitations,[173] and Maclean recommends a relational view of autonomy in informed consent.[174] Recent professional guidance stresses the importance of doctors, parents and children making decisions together to foster trust, openness

---

[164] See *Mason and McCall Smith,* at 4.28.

[165] See *Yousef v The Netherlands* (2003) 36 EHRR 345. See also *Johansen v Norway* (1996) 23 EHRR 33 and *Hoppe v Germany* [2003] 1 FCR 176.

[166] *R (on the application of Axon) v Secretary of State for Health* [2006] EWHC 37 (Admin) at 132.

[167] See A Hall, 'Children's Rights, Parents' Wishes and the State: The Medical Treatment of Children' (2006) 36 *Family Law* 317; J Fortin, 'Children's Rights – Substance or Spin?' (2006) 36 *Family Law* 36, 757.

[168] See ch 36 of the Code of Practice to the Mental Health Act 1983, as amended 2008. And see W Cheng, 'Making Decisions on Behalf of Children: Parents' Rights under the New Mental Health Legislation' (2010) *Family Law* 973.

[169] E Grice, 'Hannah Jones: "I Have Been in Hospital Too Much"' (2008) *Telegraph,* 12 November.

[170] M Cornock, 'Hannah Jones, Consent and the Child in Action: A Legal Commentary' (2010) 22(2) *Paediatric Nursing* 14.

[171] [1999] 2 FLR 1097. M later relented and consented to the procedure and subsequent treatments.

[172] J Bridgeman, *Parental Responsibility, Young Children and Healthcare Law* (2007) CUP, p 21.

[173] Beyleveld and Brownsword, *Consent in the Law* (2007) Hart Publishing.

[174] And see A Maclean, *Autonomy, Informed Consent and Medical Law: A Relational Challenge* (2009) CUP.

and confidence.[175] Others warn that the minor's autonomy must be balanced with his welfare and his future interests,[176] and with the rights of parents.[177] Much depends on the clinical setting and medical history of the child. A ten-year-old who has battled cancer for years might have a higher level of capacity than a fifteen-year-old suffering the sudden onset of disease. It might be contrary to the best interests of a thirteen-year-old to force upon her an unwanted heart transplant, but be in the best interests of a seventeen-year-old to endure coercive treatment for anorexia nervosa.[178]

Re R and *Re W* leave the law in a contradictory and unsatisfactory state and are subject to challenge.[179] Indeed, guidance from the Department of Health recognises that a test case is needed on treatment refusals by mature minors.[180] The challenge is likely to focus on the ability of parents to provide the consent their competent child withholds. The court's inherent jurisdiction to authorise coercive treatment in the best interests of the child is more readily justifiable. Though Article 8(1) is engaged, the breach is likely to be permissible if the child's life depends on it, both under Article 8(2) and Article 2, which protects the right to life. The courts' *parens patriae* jurisdiction is justifiable, but due consideration should be given to the child's capacity.[181] The Supreme Court of Canada reached this conclusion in 2009 in *AC v Manitoba (Director of Child and Family Services)*.[182] The Manitoba statute which (unlike in England and Wales) allows competent minors of sixteen and over to withhold consent to medical treatment, but enables the court to authorise treatment in the best interests of competent children under the age of sixteen, was upheld as consti-tutional. The capacity of children under the age of sixteen would be a relevant factor when determining their best interests, to the extent that:

> In some cases, courts will inevitably be so convinced of a child's maturity that the principles of welfare and autonomy will collapse altogether and the child's wishes will become the controlling factor.[183]

---

[175] GMC, *0 to 18 Years: Guidance for All Doctors* (2007); British Medical Association, *Consent Tool Kit* (2008); British Medical Association, *Parental Responsibility* (2009); DH, *Reference Guide to Consent for Examination of Treatment* (2009).

[176] See L Friedman Ross, 'Against the Tide: Arguments against Respecting a Minor's Refusal of Efficacious Life-Saving Treatment' (2009) 18(3) *Cambridge Quarterly of Healthcare Ethics* 302.

[177] See, for example, *K v UK* (2010) 51 EHRR 14 where the ECtHR held that a father's Art right was breached when, (wrongly) suspected of child abuse, he was denied access to his nine-year-old daughter in hospital.

[178] See, for example, J Tan *et al*, 'Attitudes of Patients with Anorexia Nervosa to Compulsory Treatment and Coercion' (2010) 33 *International Journal of Law and Psychiatry* 13.

[179] See R Taylor, 'Reversing the retreat from Gillick? *R (Axon) v Secretary of State for Health*' (2007) 19(1) *Child and Family Law Quarterly,* 81 and E Cave, 'Adolescent Con-sent and Confidentiality in the UK' (2009) 16(4) *European Journal of Health Law* 309.

[180] DH, *Reference Guide to Consent to Examination of Treatment* (2009), para 8.1.

[181] See E Cave, 'Maximisation of Minors' Capacity' (2011) *Child and Family Law Quarterly* (forthcoming).

[182] 2009 SCC 30.

[183] 2009 SCC 30 at 87, per Abella J.

Arguably the welfare test has been used to undermine the autonomy principle enshrined in *Gillick*, but it might also be used as a mechanism through which developing autonomy rights are protected.[184] Much will depend on the doctor's and the court's assessment of the particular child's capacity. Alongside the question of whether the courts should override a competent decision by a minor, the question of how to determine capacity warrants renewed consideration.

Health services for children

14.24   Professor Sir Ian Kennedy called for improvements in the state of health and health care of children in 2001.[185] Until 2007 his calls for improvement fell on deaf ears. In 2007, seventeen-month-old Peter Connelly, perhaps better known as Baby P, died in Haringey, London. He had suffered over fifty injuries over a period of months, during which time he was seen by social workers and NHS health professionals. Subsequent reports and inquiries reveal that children's services had let him down.[186] In 2009, Professor Sir Ian Kennedy led a review of children's services, which was published in 2010.[187] The report details startling variations in the quality of children's services. Mortality rates are too high, as are the rates of teenage pregnancy and low birth-weight babies. GPs too frequently have limited training in paediatrics and children too frequently have to travel too far to access the services they need. The government has reacted with an engagement document,[188] promising to raise the priority of children's health by personalising services, providing better and more age-appropriate information and enhancing transparency with the publication of outcome-related statistics. In law and policy, it seems, children's rights and health are beginning to receive the recognition they deserve.

---

[184] See E Cave, 'Maximisation of Minors' Capacity' (2011) *Child and Family Law Quarterly* (forthcoming).

[185] *Learning from Bristol: The Report of the Public Inquiry into Children's Heart Surgery at the Bristol Royal Infirmary 1984–1995*, Command Paper: CM 5207.

[186] Care Quality Commission, *Review of the Involvement and Action Taken by Health Bodies in Relation to the Case of Baby P* (2009); Ofsted, *Healthcare Commission and HM Inspectorate of Constabulary, Joint Area Review: Haringey Children's Services Authority Area* (2009).

[187] Professor Sir Ian Kennedy, *Getting it Right for Children and Young People: Overcoming Cultural Barriers in the NHS so as to Meet their Needs* (2010).

[188] DH, *Better Health for Children, Young People and their Families* (2010).

Chapter 15

HEALTHCARE RESEARCH[1]

15.1 In 2006, six healthy volunteers at Northwick Park Hospital were rushed to Critical Care after suffering an adverse reaction in a phase 1 clinical trial.[2] At least four of them suffered multiple organ failure, and it is feared that they may have suffered permanent damage to their immune systems. The drug, TGN1412, was a monoclonal antibody designed to treat leukaemia and rheumatoid arthritis. Volunteers were paid £2,000 to volunteer. The MHRA concluded that the reaction resulted from an 'unpredicted biological action' of the drug in humans. It found no deficiencies in the manufacturers' work, the formulation of the drug or its administration to the participants.[3] An independent Expert Scientific Review, chaired by Professor Duff, was less sympathetic:[4]

> Our conclusion is that the pre-clinical development studies that were performed with TGN1412 did not predict a safe dose for use in humans, even though current regulatory requirements were met.

The system was at fault. The expert group made twenty-two recommendations to improve the safety of first-in-man clinical trials.

The shocking incident at Northwick Park continued a trend of diminishing confidence in the regulation of research. In 1981, an elderly widow, Mrs Wigley, died from the effects of an experimental drug she had been given subsequent to an operation for bowel cancer. She died, not from bowel cancer, but from bone-marrow depression induced by the drug. Without her knowledge or consent she had been entered in a clinical trial of the new drug. In 2000, inquiries were held into allegations that research was carried out on newborn babies

---

[1] For an international perspective on medical research, see A Plomer, *The Law and Ethics of Medical Research: International Bioethics and Human Rights* (2005) Cavendish. And for an excellent practical guide, see H Biggs, *Healthcare Research Ethics and Law: Regulation, Review and Responsibility* (2009) Routledge-Cavendish.

[2] DH, *Expert Scientific Group on Phase One Clinical Trials* Final Report (2006) HMSO.

[3] MHRA, *Investigations into Adverse Incidents during Clinical Trials of TGN1412 Final Report* (May 2006), para 6.

[4] DH, *Expert Scientific Group on Phase One Clinical Trials* Final Report (2006), p 2.

without parental consent in a hospital in North Staffordshire.[5] Scandals surrounding retention of body parts originated in Bristol and Liverpool with evidence of children's body parts being retained for research without their parents' consent or knowledge.[6] And in 2010 Andrew Wakefield was struck off the medical register for serious professional misconduct relating to research into the alleged link between autism and the triple MMR vaccine.

Medical research was acquiring a bad reputation. Yet every time any one of us receives a prescription for antibiotics we benefit from research performed on others in the past. It is becoming a human guinea pig oneself, or letting one's child be so used, that may be an unattractive prospect. However, if medicine is to progress to combat cancer and continue the battle against diseases such as diabetes and multiple sclerosis, new drugs and procedures must be subject to trials.

In this chapter, we examine the role the law does and should play in the control of medical research involving human participants. Two European Directives, the Clinical Trials Directive 2001[7] and Good Clinical Practice (GCP) Directive 2005,[8] instigated change across Europe. They enabled clinical trials to take place in more than one country, with a single permission, and enhanced the safety of research participants. Some felt they went too far and stifled research. States were inconsistent in their interpretation of the Clinical Trials Directive. Its remit was arguably too wide, leading to disproportionate regulation of some research. Research generates not only medical advances but also increased revenue. It has become apparent that the regulation and governance of research is 'discouraging academic and commercial health research sponsors from conducting their studies in the UK'.[9] The emphasis shifted and reforms focused on facilitating good research. We shall see that the ethical review process has been reformed and streamlined. It still has some way to go. Most recently the government endorsed the Academy of Medical Sciences[10] 2011 report calling for the creation of a single research regulator, the Health Research Agency (HRA), to replace the 'numerous approval and permissions processes, coordinated by multiple bodies with overlapping responsibilities'. The HRA is intended to enhance the UK's research profile and make it a more attractive place to undertake commercial research. The Academy recommends that the HRA establish and manage:

- a new National Research Governance Service to streamline NHS governance arrangements; and

---

[5] See below at **15.6**.
[6] See below **18.2**.
[7] EC 2001/20.
[8] (EC) 2005/28 implemented in Medicines for Human Use (Clinical Trials) Amendment Regulations 2006, SI 2006/1928.
[9] AcMedSci, *A New Pathway for the Regulation and Governance of Health Research* (January 2011), chaired by Sir Michael Rawlins.
[10] AcMedSci, *ibid.*

- a single system for ethical review, covering research of both a general (such as clinical trials) and specialist (such as embryo research or genetic research) nature.

We explore each of these later in this chapter. The overarching question is this: will the reformed system achieve an appropriate balance between the facilitation of good research and the protection of the rights and interests of research participants? In particular:

(1) The authority to carry out research on the human adult derives from that person's consent. The first crucial question thus becomes: how satisfactory are the principles governing consent to participation in clinical research?

(2) The law on medical treatment demands that the physician respects the confidences of his patient. How does this translate into medical research?

(3) And, finally, what provision does the law make for an individual suffering injury in the course of her participation in such clinical research?

Clinical research[11] may be classified in a number of ways. Non-intrusive research involves no direct interference with the participant, for example, research into medical records, epidemiological research. Intrusive research may be non-invasive, for example, psychological inquiries, or invasive, involving actual contact with the patient's body, for example, taking blood, administering drugs, testing new surgical techniques. Some research is combined with medical care, sometimes referred to as 'therapeutic research'. Some utilises volunteers who agree to participate in a research project not likely to confer any personal benefit to them. In previous versions of the Declaration of Helsinki[12] such research was categorised as 'non-therapeutic', and special restrictions recommended, but the distinction was abandoned in 2000.[13] It is not always logical to be more permissive of 'therapeutic' than 'non-therapeutic' research. Some research (such as pathogenesis and pathophysiology, or if a patient is at risk, but currently healthy[14]) does not fit neatly into either category.[15] Consequently, the category of 'non-therapeutic research' was removed and a new category of

---

[11] This chapter will focus on clinical research. Wider aspects of healthcare research (including sociological research) are not covered here. See N Mays, C Pope (eds), *Qualitative Research in Health Care* (3rd edn, 2006) Blackwell. Also P Moule, G Hek, *Making Sense of Research: An Introduction for Health and Social Care Practitioners* (4th edn, 2011) Sage.

[12] The Declaration is an international ethical guideline. The 1996 version is endorsed in the Medicines for Human Use (Clinical Trials) Regulations 2004, SI 2004/1031, Sch 1, Pt 2, para 1.

[13] World Medical Association, *The Declaration of Helsinki: Ethical Principles for Medical Research Involving Human Subjects*, WMA General Assembly, Edinburgh, October 2000 (hereafter Declaration of Helsinki). Clarifications were added in 2002, 2004 and the Declaration was amended in 2008.

[14] See, for example, R Pierce, 'Complex Calculations: Ethical Issues in Involving At-Risk Healthy Individuals in Dementia Research' (2010) 36 *Journal of Medical Ethics* 553.

[15] See, for example, RJ Levine, 'The Need to Revise the Declaration of Helsinki' (1999) 341 *New England Journal of Medicine* 531.

'research combined with medical care' was introduced. The concepts remain broadly the same. The boundaries are still difficult to draw. Generally, the more invasive the research and the smaller the potential benefit to the participant, the greater are the ethical problems.

Research governance

15.2 Responsibility for the regulation of clinical research in the NHS is shared by local NHS research and development (R&D) management and NHS research ethics committees (RECs). In 2006 the National Institute for Health Research (NIHR) was created[16] to 'improve the health and wealth of the nation through research'. The NIHR manages public funding of research, seeking to enhance our international profile and facilitate effective (and efficient) research.[17]

Special rules apply to Clinical Trials of Investigational Medicinal Products (CTIMPs) which constitute around 15 per cent of research applications.[18] CTIMPs cannot commence without the authorisation of both an ethics committee and the UK licensing authority,[19] the MHRA. The MHRA[20] provides the relevant assessment for clinical trials of medicines and devices. It must make its assessment within sixty days of receiving the application. If the MHRA gives approval and the clinical trial commences, then the MHRA takes on a monitoring role. As we saw in chapter 10, the MHRA goes on to provide marketing authorisation (licences), inspect the marketing processes and is also responsible for surveillance and enforcement. The MHRA's responsibilities in authorising CTIMPs are dual. First it subjects proposals to a scientific assessment to ensure that participants are safe. These are followed up with routine and triggered Good Clinical Practice Inspections. The Academy of Medical Sciences recommends that the MHRA make efforts to improve the consistency and proportionality of their clinical trials regulations,[21] but ultimately much will depend on the proposed revisions of the Clinical Trials Directive (see **15.5**). The second goal is to make the UK an attractive place to conduct research.[22] The two goals do not always sit comfortably together.[23]

---

[16] Following R&D Directorate, DH, *Best Research for Best Health* (2006) ref: 6050, which sets down the goals for NHS R&D to 2011.

[17] See NIHR, *Embedding Health Research* – Annual Report 2009/10 (2010).

[18] DH, *Report of the Ad Hoc Advisory Group on the Operation of NHS RECs* (2005), para 3.2.

[19] Medicines for Human Use (Clinical Trials) Regulations 2004, SI 2004/1031, reg 11(3).

[20] The MHRA subsumed the old Medicines Control Agency.

[21] AcMedSci, *A New Pathway for the Regulation and Governance of Health Research* (January 2011), rec 6.

[22] See MHRA, *Business Plan for 2006–7* (2006), at 10.

[23] See *Expert Scientific Group on Phase One Clinical Trials* Final Report, and criticism of the MHRA in 10.13.

More worrying than the possible shortcomings of the MHRA was the limited governance of research which does not fall within the ambit of the Clinical Trials Regulations. The Department of Health took steps to address this deficiency in its *Research Governance Framework for Health and Social Care*.[24] Now all NHS organisations engaging in research are required to meet standards and manage risk through reporting, inspecting and reviewing internal systems. Compliance is monitored by the Care Quality Commission (CQC) as part of its general review of performance. The *Framework* has improved patient safety, but because trusts implemented the *Framework* on an individual basis, inconsistencies, delays and duplication in the R&D permissions process emerged. The Academy of Medical Sciences[25] calls for a co-ordinated UK approach and recommends that a new National Research Governance Service is created as part of the proposed HRA. The Academy further proposes that the NIHR should develop a new system to assess trusts in their managing, approving and undertaking of research, and use it to inform its funding decisions.[26] Trusts would have an additional incentive to make consistent and timely R&D permissions.

Research ethics committees (RECs)

15.3 The Clinical Trials Regulations require that CTIMPs have prior regulatory and ethical approval. Embarking on a trial without the prior sanction of a relevant ethics committee is a criminal offence.[27] We will say more about the constitution of ethics committees under the Clinical Trials Regulations shortly. First it is important to note that outside the remit of the Clinical Trials Regulations a researcher contravenes no law in carrying out research without ethical approval. However, other sanctions and ethical guidance[28] deter any such practice. One of the conditions for NHS R&D permission is the approval of a REC. An NHS employee failing to seek approval from the relevant REC is likely to be disciplined by his employing trust. Outside the NHS, researchers may face disciplinary action by professional regulatory authorities. Conducting research without ethical review may constitute impaired 'fitness to practice'. In 2007, the General Medical Council (GMC) instigated disciplinary action against Andrew Wakefield, the author of a 1998 *Lancet* paper linking autism and the MMR vaccine. Among ten counts of serious professional misconduct, was the claim that children underwent research procedures without prior approval from an ethics committee. Dr Wakefield was struck off the medical

---

[24] (2nd edn, 2005); annex updated 2008.

[25] AcMedSci, *A New Pathway for the Regulation and Governance of Health Research* (January 2011), rec 2.

[26] AcMedSci, *A New Pathway for the Regulation and Governance of Health Research* (January 2011), rec 4.

[27] AcMedSci, *A New Pathway for the Regulation and Governance of Health Research* (January 2011), rec 4.

[28] See Declaration of Helsinki (2008), Art 15; Council of Europe, *Additional Protocol to the Convention on Human Rights and Biomedicine, Concerning Biomedical Research* (2005), art 9 (the UK is not a signatory).

register in 2010.[29] Journal editors also play a monitoring role. One of the functions of the Committee on Publication Ethics[30] is to ensure that its members do not publish studies unless guidelines on ethical review are followed.

A number of ethics committees exist outside the NHS. These include ethical review committees set up by universities, private hospitals and pharmaceutical companies. Within the NHS, RECs comprise lay and medical individuals who advise as to the ethics of any NHS healthcare research and 'protect the dignity, rights, safety and well-being of all actual or potential research participants'.[31] They can also consider private-sector research if requested to do so. The number of RECs has been reduced in recent years and there are now around 100. RECs include up to eighteen members from a balanced age and gender distribution. There should be a mixture of expert and lay members, the latter constituting at least one third of the membership.[32] The quality of the people who volunteer to serve on NHS ethics committees, and their ability to exercise judgment, is fundamental to the process.

A troubled history

15.4 The Department of Health first recommended that district health authorities establish local research ethics committees (LRECs) in 1975. More detailed formal guidance was issued in 1991.[33] Each local health authority was required to set up at least one, and there were over 200 LRECs in all. Due to limited guidance and coordination, the review process was often inconsistent. Multi-centre researchers fared worst, facing a diversity of procedures and outcomes. In an effort to improve the system, multi-centre research ethics committees (MRECs) were introduced in 1997.[34] MRECs performed a single ethical review of research taking place in more than one research site and then passed the protocol on to LRECs to consider relevant local matters. The process remained unwieldy. The Central Office for NHS Research Ethics Committees (COREC) was established in 2000, to improve the system, issue guidance to RECs, manage the budget and appoint MRECs.[35] Strategic health

---

[29] GMC, *Wakefield: Determination on Serious Professional Misconduct and Sanction* (2010) 24 May. See D J Opel *et al*, 'Assuring Research integrity in the Wake of Wakefield' (2011) 342 *BMJ* d2.

[30] See http://www.publicationethics.org.uk/.

[31] *Governance Arrangements for NHS Research Ethics Committees* (2001), para 2.2.

[32] See NRES, *CT Regulations – Membership of Ethics Committees*, version 4.1 (July 2009).

[33] DH, *Local Research Ethics Committees* HSG (91) 5. Replaced by the *Governance Arrangements for NHS Research Ethics Committees* (2001). The Royal College of Physicians also issues guidelines for ethics committees: RCP, *Guidelines on the Practice of Ethics Committees in Medical Research with Human Participants* (4th edn, 2007).

[34] DH, Multi-centre Research Ethics Committees, HSG (97) 23. Replaced by the *Governance Arrangements for NHS Research Ethics Committees* (2001).

[35] The National Research Ethics Service took over from COREC in 2007.

authorities took on the role of appointing authority for LRECs. In 2001, the Department of Health issued *Governance Arrangements for NHS RECs* (GAfREC), an updated version of which has been long awaited and repeatedly postponed since 2007. Researchers stepped up political pressure, aimed at reducing the level of bureaucracy and facilitating research, and as a result, the National Patient Safety Agency took over responsibility for COREC in 2005.

The implementation of the Clinical Trials Directive 2001,[36] in the Medicines for Human Use (Clinical Trials) Regulations 2004 wrought further changes on the system. In each member state, the decision of one REC is valid for the whole of that country, thereby enabling research to cross borders within Europe. In addition to requiring standards of good clinical practice,[37] the Directive demands the approval of a statutorily recognised REC before research can commence or a protocol can be amended. In the UK, the approval of both a recognised REC and the licensing authority, the MHRA, is necessary.[38] The remit of RECs was tightened.[39] In summary, the committee can consider the relevance of the trial and its design; the balance of risks and benefits; the protocol; the suitability of the investigator and the facilities; the information sheet and procedure for obtaining informed consent; indemnity, insurance and compensation arrangements and payments to the participant and investigator. Ethics committees are not required to concern themselves too much with legal and scientific evaluations.[40]

Under the Regulations, RECs require independent statutory authority, provided by the UK Ethics Committee Authority (UKECA).[41] Rather than giving all RECs statutory authority as occurred in some countries,[42] the Ethics Committee Authority recognises certain RECs appointed by a range of authorities including strategic health authorities, the National Research Ethics Service (NRES), universities and independent institutions. Other NHS RECs, established under the *Governance Arrangements for RECs*, together with other independent ethics committees, may only review applications that do not relate to CTIMPs.[43] The failure to give statutory authority to all RECs led to a complex system at a time when researchers felt stifled by bureaucracy. Medical

---

36 (EC) 2001/20.
37 Medicines for Human Use (Clinical Trials) Regulations 2004, SI 2004/1031 Pt 4. See also Commission Directive (EC) 2005/28.
38 Medicines for Human Use (Clinical Trials) Regulations 2004, SI 2004/1031, reg 12.
39 Medicines for Human Use (Clinical Trials) Regulations 2004, SI 2004/1031, reg 15.
40 *Governance Arrangements for NHS Research Ethics Committees* (2001), para 2.6.
41 Medicines for Human Use (Clinical Trials) Regulations 2004, SI 2004/1031, reg 5.
42 There therefore remain different REC systems in Europe, which creates inconsistency; see R Hernandez *et al*, 'Harmonisation of Ethics Committees' Practice in 10 European Countries' (2009) 35 *Journal of Medical Ethics* 696; and H Davies *et al*, 'Standards for Research Ethics Committees: Purpose, Problems and the Possibility of Other Approaches' (2009) 35 *Journal of Medical Ethics* 382.
43 'Recognised' RECs include Type 1 RECs which can review research involving healthy volunteers, and Type 3 RECs can review other CTIMPs and other research. 'Authorised' RECs are established under the *Governance Arrangements for NHS*

professionals are hardened to the prolific use of acronyms, but the comprehension of new researchers must be sorely tested by a system in which UKECA-recognised NHS RECs review CTIMPs aided by MHU(CT) Regulations, whilst both UKECA-recognised and GAfREC-authorised NHS RECs review non-CTIMPS, aided by GAfREC and SOPs, promulgated by the NRES.

Nor were researchers' fears that the process stymied research calmed by the introduction of a common application form[44] in 2004. An *ad hoc* review was launched. Its results were published in 2005.[45] In response, the 'National Research Ethics Service' (NRES) was launched in 2007, taking over the head-office function from COREC. Researchers want a proportionate response to their research. If the research poses few or no ethical issues, it should be dealt with swiftly. Researchers do not want to duplicate their applications. A National Research Ethics Advisory Panel was set up to (amongst other things) aid REC chairs, determine strategy and arbitrate ethical debates. In 2009 a new research site procedure assessment was introduced to eliminate duplication.[46] Pilot studies to test early advice procedures and a fast-track 'proportionate review service' were launched in 2007 and 2009. A new version of the Standard Operating Procedures[47] incorporating these measures is expected in May 2011. A new, integrated version of GAfREC,[48] harmonising requirements in England, Scotland and Wales, is expected imminently.

In the meantime, researchers remain frustrated.[49] The complex regulatory system was developed in a piecemeal fashion. It requires duplication and is felt to be onerous. In 2008 a Wellcome Trust and Medical Research Council workshop called for greater trust in researchers. Lessons from Nordic countries indicate that a less complex system, where researchers are trusted to put the participants first, can work. In summary it was stated that:

> Although it would be unrealistic, at least in the short term, to change existing regulation in a fundamental way, regulators should aim to keep the regulatory burden to a minimum.[50]

Research Ethics Committees (2001). They are not recognised by the UK Ethics Committee Authority and can review research other than CTIMPs.

[44] The *Integrated Research Application System* (IRAS) v. 3.0 (2010) is a single application form for permissions for healthcare research in the UK.

[45] DH, *Report of an Ad Hoc Advisory Group on the Operation of NHS Research Ethics Committees* (2005). See A J Dawson, 'The Ad Hoc Advisory Group's Proposals for Research Ethics Committees: A Mixture of the Timid, the Revolutionary and the Bizarre' (2005) 31 *Journal of Medical Ethics* 435.

[46] NPSA, *Transfer of Site-Specific Assessments for NHS Sites* (2009).

[47] Standard Operating Procedures for Research Ethics Committees in the United Kingdom v 4.1 (2010).

[48] NPSA, *Governance Arrangements for Research Ethics Committees: A Proposed Harmonised Edition* (2009).

[49] N Fudge *et al*, 'Streamlined Research Governance: Are we There Yet?' (2010) 341 *BMJ* 4625.

[50] MRC / Wellcome Trust, *Workshop: Regulation and Biomedical Research* (2008), 1.

The future

15.5 The government do not perceive radical change to research regulation to be 'unrealistic'. In 2010 the Academy of Medical Sciences recommended further streamlining of research regulation.[51] Following this, a report on arm's-length bodies in July 2010 proposed 'radical simplification'.[52] The review expressed the intention to abolish the NPSA by 2012 and create a single research regulator to oversee governance and ethical review of all NHS research.[53] It recommended that the Gene Therapy Advisory Committee should be brought under the umbrella of the NRES. More controversially, as we examined in chapters 12 and 18, the research functions of the Human Tissue Authority and Human Fertilisation and Embryology Authority would be transferred to the new regulator. A consultation by the Academy of Medical Sciences, reporting in 2011, is supportive of the proposals.[54] It recommends that the NRES continue to operate the established structure of RECs. Its role will be expanded – the NRES will provide more advice and set up training for researchers. The new research regulator, the HRA, will introduce a streamlined system for giving the approval and licences required in specialist research.

The government has pledged to reduce the number of arm's-length bodies, so the Academy explored in depth whether it was necessary to introduce a new one. One possibility would be to make the MHRA the new single research regulator. The Academy rejected this option on the ground that the MHRA currently deals only with clinical trials and would find the transition to a wider research remit and to working with non-commercial researchers difficult. Furthermore, public confidence would be limited by virtue of the MHRA's role in licensing drugs for the pharmaceutical industry.

The reforms will require legislative change. At the time of writing, a Public Bodies Bill and a Health and Social Care Bill 2011 are working their way through Parliament. But regulatory reform in Britain can only go so far. The Clinical Trials Directive does not promulgate minimum standards – member states should not add to or detract from the requirements of the Directive (though it will be argued later that, in practice, they do so). In Europe the Clinical Trials Directive has been labelled 'arguably the most criticised piece of legislation in the Union *acquis* on medicines'.[55] In 2009 it was scrutinised in a

---

[51] Academy of Medical Sciences (hereafter Ac Med Sci), *Reaping the Rewards: A Vision for UK Medical Science* (2010).

[52] DH, *Liberating the NHS: Report of the Arm's-Length Bodies Review* (2010), para 3.22.

[53] The Health and Social Care Bill 2011, Pt 10, proposes provisions to this effect.

[54] AcMedSci, *A New Pathway for the Regulation and Governance of Health Research* (2011).

[55] European Commission, Roadmap: Legislative Proposal on a Regulation/Directive Amending the Clinical Trials Directive 2001/20/EC (2010), 1.

public consultation.[56] In 2011 the Academy of Medical Sciences urged the government to exert their influence on the European Commission for speedy revision. The Academy recommends that the scope of the Directive should be limited so that approval and monitoring are proportionate to risk and that reporting of adverse events is simplified and duplication eliminated.[57] Legislation to amend the Directive is expected in late 2011.[58] Whether reforms are addressed through new guidelines, amendment to the Directive, or its replacement with a Regulation, remains to be seen. A Regulation would not need to be transposed into national laws, so avoiding problems of unharmonised translation but rendering the system less flexible.

The ongoing reform of the ethical review process, both in the UK and Europe, focuses on the facilitation of good research; efficiency, effectiveness and proportionality are of key importance. Article 6 of the Declaration of Helsinki states that: 'In medical research involving human subjects, the well-being of the individual research subject must take precedence over all other interests'; sentiments echoed in Article 2 of the European Convention on Human Rights and Biomedicine.[59] Both the Good Clinical Practice Directive and the Clinical Trials Directive refer to the Helsinki Declaration (albeit to a previous version[60]) as do the Clinical Trials Regulations 2004. Because there is potential for drug companies to make handsome profits and researchers to benefit in terms of career advancement, it is particularly important that the rights and interests of research participants are safeguarded. This begs the question: how well do the Clinical Trials Regulations protect research participants? We attempt to answer that question in the next sections.

Consent to participation in trials[61]

15.6 In 2000, allegations were made, albeit later largely not proven,[62] surrounding research carried out a decade before on premature babies at North

---

[56] European Commission, Safe, Innovative and Accessible Medicines: a Renewed Vision for the Pharmaceutical Sector (2008); European Commission, Assessment of the Functioning of the Clinical Trials Directive 2001/20/EC (2009); European Commission, Assessment of the Functioning of the Clinical Trials Directive 2001/20/EC: Summary of Responses to the Public Consultation Paper (2010).

[57] AcMedSci, *A New Pathway for the Regulation and Governance of Health Research* (2011), rec 5.

[58] European Commission, Roadmap: Legislative Proposal on a Regulation/Directive Amending the Clinical Trials Directive 2001/20/EC (2010).

[59] Art 2: 'The interests and welfare of the human being shall prevail over the sole interest of society or science.' See also GMC, *Good Medical Practice* (2006), para 71.

[60] They make reference to the 1996 version. See E Cave, C Nichols, 'Reforming the Ethical Review System: Balancing the Rights and Interests of Research Participants with the Duty to Facilitate Good Research' (2007) 2 *Clinical Ethics*, 181.

[61] See GMC, *Consent to Research* (2010).

[62] See Editorial, 'Babies and Consent: Yet Another NHS Scandal' (2000) 320 *BMJ* 1285.

Staffordshire Hospital. It was claimed the research was conducted without parents' consent.[63] Since 1964 the Declaration of Helsinki has sought to protect research participants' rights by demanding rigorous consent procedures. Special rules apply to CTIMPs under the Clinical Trials Regulations 2004. Schedule 1, Pt 2, para 9 requires that 'subject to the other provisions of this Schedule relating to consent, freely given informed consent shall be obtained from every subject prior to clinical trial participation'. The Regulations go on to require that informed consent:

(a)   is given freely after that person is informed of the nature, significance, implications and risks of the trial; and

(b)   either:

    (i)   is evidenced in writing, dated and signed, or otherwise marked, by that person so as to indicate his consent, or

    (ii)   if the person is unable to sign or to mark a document so as to indicate his consent, is given orally in the presence of at least one witness and recorded in writing.[64]

Though informed consent of the participant is a prerequisite for ethical approval in most types of medical research, the Clinical Trials Regulations and, outside their remit, ethical codes of conduct, accept limited circumstances where alternative safeguards are acceptable. Self-evidently someone may be unable to consent by virtue of being a child or suffering from mental incapacity. In such circumstances, we shall see that other safeguards are put in place to protect the research participant.[65] Even in relation to competent adult participants, there may be trials where low risks justify research without consent. Thus, in some cases of epidemiological research (such as the collection of statistics on measles, for example) where the individual participant cannot be identified, an ethics committee might decide that obtaining consent is unnecessary.[66] Even in epidemiological trials, however, if data is not fully anonymised, consent should usually be obtained.[67] Article 24 of the Declaration of Helsinki

---

[63]   M P Samuals, D P Southall, 'Negative Extrathoracic Pressure in Treatment of Respiratory Failure in Infants and Young Children' (1989) 299 *BMJ* 1253. There was a subsequent NHS review: NHS Executive, *West Midlands Regional Office Report of a Review of the Research Framework in North Staffordshire Hospital NHS Trust* (2000).

[64]   Sch 1, Pt 1, para 3(1) implementing Art 2(j) of Directive (EC) 2001/20. See also Sch 1, Pt 3 which sets out conditions of informed consent.

[65]   See below **15.8** and **15.9**.

[66]   GMC, *Confidentiality* (2009), paras 40–44.

[67]   But see Declaration of Helsinki (2008), Art 25: 'For medical research using identifiable human material or data, physicians must normally seek consent for the collection, analysis, storage and/or reuse. There may be situations where consent would be impossible or impractical to obtain for such research or would pose a threat to the validity of the research. In such situations the research may be done only after consideration and approval of a research ethics committee.' See also National Health Service Act 2006, ss 251–252; formerly Health and Social Care Act 2001, s 60, discussed below at **15.15**.

outlines the importance of adequate information and Article 22 stresses the importance of voluntariness. What does this mean in practice?

In any research on human beings, each potential participant must be adequately informed of the aims, methods, sources of funding, any possible conflicts of interest, institutional affiliations of the researcher, the anticipated benefits and potential risks of the study and the discomfort it may entail. The participant should be informed of the right to abstain from the study or to withdraw consent to participate at any time without reprisal. After ensuring that the participant has understood the information, the researcher should then obtain the participant's freely given informed consent, preferably in writing. If the consent cannot be obtained in writing, the non-written consent must be formally documented and witnessed.

The requirement of adequate information for consent to treatment has already been addressed in chapter 5. We have seen that, gradually, the English courts are moving away from an exclusively professional standard of information disclosure. In the context of research, we would argue that the 'prudent patient' test governs what researchers must disclose to research participants.[68] A House of Commons Review led to new guidance on the framing of information sheets.[69] The formal guidance offered to researchers is overtly patient-centred. Only rarely, we would suggest, could it be logical or defensible[70] to depart from such unequivocal guidance.

The volunteer is not free to accept any risk whatsoever. RECs will carefully assess the risk involved before sanctioning a research project. Special measures have been put in place to protect volunteers in first-in-man phase 1 drug trials after the Northwick Park disaster in 2006.[71] New guidance for effective communication between ethics committees and the MHRA has been issued[72] and additional guidance relates to safety issues in phase 1 trials[73] and, in the light

---

[68] *Governance Arrangements for NHS Research Ethics Committees* (2001), paras 9.17 and 10.6. Under the NHS plan, the 'good practice in consent initiative' seeks to review consent procedures to ensure a patient-centred standard.

[69] See House of Commons Health Committee, *The Influence of the Pharmaceutical Industry*, Fourth Report of Session 2004–5, HC 42-I (2005). See also NPSA, *Guidance for Researchers and Reviewers: Information Sheets and Consent Forms* v. 3.5 (2009). And see Royal College of Physicians, *Guidelines on the Practice of Ethics Committees in Medical Research with Human Participants* (2007), at 5.46–5.49 and GMC, *Consent to Research* (2010), paras 4–8.

[70] 'The use of these adjectives – responsible, reasonable and respectable – all show that the court has to be satisfied that the exponents of the body of opinion relied upon can demonstrate that such opinion has a logical basis': per Lord Browne-Wilkinson, *Bolitho v City and Hackney Health Authority* [1998] AC 232 at 778.

[71] See P Ferguson, 'Clinical Trials and Healthy Volunteers' (2008) *Medical Law Review* 23 and see above at **15.1**.

[72] COREC, *Memorandum of Understanding Between MHRA, COREC and GTAC* (2006).

[73] European Medicines Agency, Committee for Medicinal Products for Human Use,

of the manufacturers' limited liability insurance, the appropriate level of clinical trials' insurance.[74]

Ethics committees will consider whether the volunteers are truly volunteers. Do medical students feel under compulsion to assist in trials mounted by their teachers? Do patients feel obliged to 'help' their doctor if he asks them to participate in research that is not related to their medical care?[75] Where resort is had to volunteers outside the medical schools and hospital patients, payments are often made in this country. Amounts paid are usually relatively modest but may still constitute an inducement to impoverished students and the unemployed.[76] The principles of law are clear. Any degree of compulsion renders any written consent given invalid.[77] Proving compulsion might be the difficulty for a medical student. And for an unemployed 'volunteer', economic compulsion arising from his circumstances rather than any misconduct by the research team is as yet unrecognised in English law. Article 26 of the Declaration of Helsinki provides that where any suspicion of duress might arise, an independent physician unconnected with the research project should seek the participant's consent.[78] The issue of free and full consent is central to the propriety and legality of clinical trials.[79] The definition of what constitutes a proper consent is, as we have seen, far from easy.

Innovative therapy

15.7 There is another difficulty too. The line between experimenting on a patient and doing your utmost for him is blurred.[80] For example, if a doctor caring for patients with AIDS attempts a novel treatment as a last resort, knowing

Guideline on Strategies to Identify and Mitigate Risks for First-In-Human Clinical Trials with investigational Medicinal Products (2007).

[74] See Royal College of Physicians, *Guidelines on the Practice of Ethics Committees in Medical Research with Human Participants* (2007), para 4.19: '... a contract which accepts liability regardless of fault should be used for each participant'.

[75] Department of Health and the Royal College of Physicians of London guidelines both require patient consent forms to state expressly that whether or not the patient agrees to take part in the trial will not affect his medical care and that the patient is free to withdraw from the trial at any time.

[76] See Wilkinson and Moore, 'Inducements in Research' (1997) 11 *Bioethics*, 373 who argue that inducements are acceptable and promote individual autonomy; A Wertheimer, F Miller, 'Payment for Research Participants – A Coercive Offer?' (2008) 34 *Journal of Medical Ethics* 389; and J McMillan, 'Coercive Offers and Research Participants – A Comment on Wertheimer and Miller' (2010) 36 *Journal of Medical Ethics* 383.

[77] *Re T (Adult: Refusal of Medical Treatment)* [1992] 4 All ER 649.

[78] And see Royal College of Physicians, *Guidelines on the Practice of Ethics Committees in Medical Research with Human Participants* (2007), paras 10.12–10.21.

[79] See L Doyal, J S Tobias (eds), *Informed Consent in Medical Research* (2000) BMJ Publishing.

[80] See J K Mason and G T Laurie, *Law and Medical Ethics* (8th edn, 2010) OUP(hereafter *Mason and McCall Smith*), p 627.

that there is no conventional treatment which will prolong the patient's life, has she crossed that line and made her patient a research-participant?

In *Simms v Simms and An NHS Trust*[81] it was held to be lawful to administer experimental treatment that had never been tested on humans to two patients suffering from new variant Creutzfeldt-Jakob Disease. Both lacked the mental capacity to give consent themselves. Both faced a dismal prognosis given their degenerative and terminal condition. The risks of treatment were unknown but as some benefit was possible, Butler-Sloss P held that administration of the drug, Pentosan Polysulphate, by intracerebral infusion was in the best interests of the patients. *Simms* establishes that the use of innovative therapies in the best interests of the patient is not necessarily unlawful.

Jonathan Simms' father fought for the treatment which might effect an improvement in his son's terrible condition. In *An NHS Trust v J*, the patient's family opposed the administration of innovative therapy.[82] J was in a persistent vegetative state (PVS) after suffering a brain haemorrhage three years earlier. Against the wishes of her family, withdrawal of artificial hydration and nutrition was postponed so that an innovative therapy could be administered. Two research papers had indicated that the insomnia drug Zolpidem sometimes enhanced neural responses in PVS patients. Experts held out little hope that it would work in J's case, but saw no harm in trying. The family disagreed. J had extensive neurological damage. Heightened awareness, if it could be brought about, would bring to her only distress. Sir Mark Potter P accepted the expert opinion that the therapy was in J's best interests and ordered it to proceed.[83]

In Europe regulations have been introduced to enhance consistency and transparency in the compassionate use of unauthorised medicinal products. Under Article 83[84] the European Medicines Agency's Committee on Human Medicinal Products can provide an opinion. It did for the first time in 2010 where two applications concerned the compassionate use of medicines to treat influenza.[85] The CHMP issued guidance as to when Zanamivir and Tamiflu IV (a new, unauthorised intravenous treatment) should be given, and at what dosage.

Children in medical research programmes

15.8 When can a child give her own consent to participation in a trial? When can she withhold that consent? If the child is incapable of giving an effective

---

[81] [2002] EWHC 2734 (Fam). See J Harrington, 'Deciding Best Interests' [2003] 3 *Web Journal of Current Legal Issues*.

[82] [2006] All ER (D) 290. See further **19.16**.

[83] See guidance in DH, *Reference Guide to Consent for Examination or Treatment* (2nd edn, 2009), ch 1, para 41.

[84] In accordance with EC Regulation 726/2004, Art 83.

[85] EMA45566/2010; EMA110920/2010.

consent, may a parent give consent on her behalf? Once again, the answers depend on whether or not the study is governed by the Medicines for Human Use (Clinical Trials) Regulations 2004.[86]

For studies that fall outside the ambit of the Act, the House of Lords' ruling in *Gillick*[87] empowers a minor to consent to medical treatment when he or she has reached an age and individual maturity to judge what the treatment entails and assess its benefit and disadvantages. In the case of research combined with medical care, the test might be the same, though professional guidelines encourage the involvement of parents.[88] If the child is over sixteen, the Family Law Reform Act 1969, which empowers minors over sixteen to consent to medical treatment, will offer protection to the medical team.

What of research that confers no direct benefit on the child? There is no apparent reason why the *Gillick* ruling should not apply. The basis of the judgment is not limited to medical treatment alone but concerns the general capacity of older children to make decisions for themselves. Whenever researchers wish to include in such research a research participant under eighteen, only the *Gillick* test can grant the minor herself authority to consent to participate in the trial. Section 8 of the Family Law Reform Act 1969, empowering young people between sixteen and eighteen to consent to medical treatment, is strictly limited to therapeutic and diagnostic interventions.[89] Lord Donaldson considered it to be 'highly improbable'[90] that a *Gillick competent* minor could consent to a procedure of no benefit to himself. Nevertheless, recent Department of Health guidance encourages parental involvement, but recognises that young people and children may provide a valid consent to research which is of no direct benefit to them, provided they are *Gillick competent*.[91]

What about younger children?[92] The law is unclear as to whether parental consent to research of no benefit to the child is of any effect.[93] Paediatricians

---

[86] See E Cave, 'Seen But Not Heard? Children in Clinical Trials' (2010) 18 *Medical Law Review* 1.
[87] *Gillick v West Norfolk and Wisbech Area Health Authority* [1984] QB 581.
[88] Medical Research Council, *Medical Research Involving Children* (2nd edn, 2007), para 5.3.1.a; GMC *0-18* (2007), para 38: '... If they are able to consent for themselves, you should still consider involving their parents, depending on the nature of the research'; and see Royal College of Paediatrics and Child Health, 'Guidelines for the Ethical Conduct of Medical Research Involving Children,' (2000) 82 *Ethics Advisory Committee in Archives of Disease in Childhood* 177.
[89] *Re W (A Minor) (Medical Treatment)* [1992] 4 All ER 177 CA at 635 and 647, CA.
[90] [1992] 4 All ER 177 at 635, CA.
[91] DH, *Reference Guide to Consent for Examination of Treatment* (2nd edn 2009), ch 3, paras 3–5.
[92] Neonatal research poses particular problems: see S A Mason and C Megone, *Informed Consent in European Neonatal Research* (Ashgate, 2001).
[93] See, for example, the American case *Grimes v Kennedy Kreiger Institute*, Nos 128, 129, Sept Term, 2000, cert den 2001, in which the Appeal court in Maryland ruled that parents cannot consent to their child's participation in non-therapeutic research.

emphasise the need for some degree of carefully controlled research on children.[94] Children respond differently to drugs, they suffer from illnesses not afflicting adults and, above all, their suffering when afflicted is particularly poignant. The GMC (2007) states that children can be involved in research that has either 'potential benefits for children or young people generally, as long as the research does not go against their best interests or involves only minimal or low risk of harm ... or potential therapeutic benefits for them that outweigh any foreseeable risks ...',[95] a position endorsed in guidance issued by the Department of Health in 2009.[96]

In law, research can only be carried out on children if it is in their best interests. How can research of no benefit to the child ever be in his best interests? Do best interests include the interests of the community?[97] The House of Lords in *S v S*[98] were asked to authorise a blood test on a child to determine his paternity. Lord Reid described the parental power to authorise such a test in this way:

> Surely a reasonable parent would have some regard for the general public interest and would not refuse a blood test unless he thought that would clearly be *against the interests of the child* [our italics].

Arguably where any risk to the child is minimal, parents may authorise any procedure which is not perceived as *against* the interests of the child. However, the Clinical Trials Regulations 2004, which will cover most research projects on healthy children, take a different, altogether more restrictive, stance. In the event that the courts were asked to decide whether or not a parent could consent to his child taking part in research outside the ambit of the Clinical Trials Regulations, that did not confer any direct benefit to the study group, it is likely that the courts would take a similar line.

The *Gillick* ruling does not apply to CTIMPs. The Clinical Trials Regulations 2004[99] require that in CTIMPs, the written consent of the person with legal responsibility[100] for the child is obtained. In addition the child should be 'given information according to his capacity of understanding' whereupon his refusal to participate or request to withdraw from the trial must be 'considered'. Thus the Regulations do not require the child's informed consent even if he is capable of giving it. The weight given to his refusal or request to

---

[94] See S Conroy, J McIntyre, I Choonara, T J Stephenson, 'Drug Trials in Children: Problems and the Way Forward' (2000) 49 *British Journal of Clinical Pharmacology* 93.

[95] GMC 0-18(2007), para 37.

[96] DH, *Reference Guide to Consent for Examination or Treatment* (2nd edn, 2009), ch 3, para 28.

[97] P Lewis, 'Procedures that are Against the Medical Interests of Incompetent Adults' (2002) 22(4) *Oxford Journal of Legal Studies* 575 asks whether we should be more honest and accept a utilitarian calculus that sometimes the incompetent person's interests are not paramount.

[98] [1972] AC 24, HL.

[99] See Sch 1, Pt 4.

[100] The 'person with legal responsibility' will usually be a parent, guardian, or the court.

withdraw will depend on his capacity and possibly on the effect withdrawal will have on his health. As we saw in chapter 14, competent children are not always entitled to decline treatment that might save them from death or serious injury. But research is by nature experimental – it is difficult to predict the outcome for an individual patient, especially in an RCT.[101] Should competent children have a stronger right to withdraw or object? The Council of Europe's draft guidelines for ethics committees[102] recommend that in addition to parental consent, competent children should assent to their inclusion in research and their objections should be respected.

Research poses a more awkward problem where it is not combined with medical care. The Clinical Trials Regulations 2004 state that children should only be enrolled in research where it 'can only be carried out on minors' and, more prohibitively, that 'some direct benefit for the group of patients involved in the clinical trial is to be obtained from that trial'.[103] Research of no direct benefit to the group of trial participants cannot be sanctioned, notwithstanding: the consent of both child and legal representative; that the research poses minimal risk to the child; and that it will benefit children in the future. This is unproblematic provided the trial involves a drug that is already licensed in adults, because it will be possible to establish direct benefit to the group. In phase 1 trials (which test very small doses of the treatment), designed to combat diseases which affect only children, however, it is much harder to establish direct benefit.[104]

And there is another, perhaps bigger, problem in paediatric medicine. Too many drugs which are licensed for use in adults are not licensed for use in children.[105] This frequently results in drugs being prescribed for children 'off-label'.[106] More good quality paediatric clinical trials are needed. In an attempt to tackle this problem, the EU Regulation on Paediatric Medicines 2006[107]

---

101 E Cave, 'Seen But Not Heard? Children in Clinical Trials' (2010) 18 *Medical Law Review* 1.
102 Council of Europe *Draft Guide for Research Ethics Committee Members* CDBI/INF(2009) 6, fig 6.2.
103 Medicines for Human Use (Clinical Trials) Regulations, 2004, SI 2004/1031, Pt 4, paras 9, 10.
104 See E Cave, 'Seen But Not Heard? Children in Clinical Trials' (2010) 18 *Medical Law Review* 1.
105 A Svobodník *et al,* 'How to Improve Children's Research', *Applied Clinical Trials* (2010), February, 46: 'Children and adolescents represent about 25% of the European population, however, most medicines given to children are used off-label. In hospital paediatric wards this is around 45% and in the neonatal intensive care setting this can be as high as 90%.'
106 See Royal College of Paediatrics and Child Health, *The Use of Unlicensed Medicines or Licensed Medicines for Unlicensed Applications in Paediatric Practice* (2010).
107 EU Regulation on Medicinal Products for Paediatric Use Regulation (EC) No 1901/2006. See also European Commission, Guidance on the Information Concerning Paediatric Clinical Trials to be Entered into the EU Database on Clinical Trials (EudraCT) and on the Information to be Made Public by the European Medicines

requires that new medicines (and some existing drugs) are tested on children in accordance with an agreed Paediatric Investigation Plan (PIP)[108] in order to produce information for the drug label.[109] In addition, new networks have been established to facilitate paediatric trials.[110] But are the new rules and incentives sufficient?[111] The 2009 review of the Clinical Trials Directive confirmed that significant barriers to paediatric research remain. Too frequently ethics committees and insurers automatically perceive paediatric clinical trials as high risk. In addition there are practical problems 'such as the transfer of children from specialist hospitals to other, non-specialised, hospitals, the need to adapt pill sizes to children, and training in GCP for nurses',[112] which make paediatric clinical trials burdensome. Reform of the Directive is likely to emphasise the need to facilitate paediatric research.

Adults who lack mental capacity

15.9   As problematic as the question of research involving children is the question of research involving mentally ill, mentally disabled, or unconscious patients. The Clinical Trials Regulations 2004 deal with clinical trials and the Mental Capacity Act 2005 with other research.[113] Consistency between the two was inevitably too much to ask and there is evidence of confused interpretation of the law by RECs.[114] In 2010 the NRES released an on-line tool kit offering practical advice on the confusing legal requirements.[115]

According to the Mental Capacity Act 2005 (discussed fully in chapter 6), capacity is now assessed in a decision-specific test made at the relevant time. Where a person lacks capacity, her best interests, determined by reference to her previous wishes and the views of family and carers, will dictate the appropriate course of action. There is a notable exception to this rule: according to

Agency (EMEA), in Accordance with Art 41 of Regulation (EC) No 1901/2006, (EC) 2009/C 28/01.

[108] But see K Megget, 'The problem with PIPs' (2009) 4(6) *Clinical Discovery* 10.

[109] There are exceptions, for example if the illness does not affect children or the drug may be unsafe for them.

[110] See European Medicines Agency, *European Paediatric Research Network Ready to Start* EMA/273427/2010 (2010).

[111] European CRO Federation, 'Testing Medicines for Children in Europe' (2009) July *Good Clinical Practices Journal* 10.

[112] European Commission Assessment of the Functioning of the Clinical Trials Directive 2001/20/EC: Summary of Responses to the Public Consultation Paper (2010), p 14.

[113] Also see Mental Capacity Act 2005 (Loss of Capacity During Research Project) (England) Regulations 2007, SI 2007/679. And see guidance in DH, *Reference Guide to Consent for Examination or Treatment* (2nd edn, 2009), ch 2, paras 31–33.

[114] See M Dixon-Woods, E Angell, 'Research Involving Adults who Lack Capacity: How have Research Ethics Committees Interpreted the Requirements?' (2009) 35 *Journal of Medical Ethics* 377.

[115] Available at https://connect.le.ac.uk/alctoolkit/.

section 32(8), the duty to consult is waived if treatment is urgent or consult-ation is impracticable.

Special rules are put in place to govern research. Section 30 states that intru-sive research[116] is lawful if an 'appropriate body'[117] (normally a REC) agrees that the research is safe and relates to the person's impairing condition and that it cannot be done as effectively using people who have the requisite men-tal capacity to consent. In addition, the research must produce a benefit to the person that outweighs any risk or burden, or it will derive new scientific know-ledge[118] and it is of minimal risk to the person and can be carried out with minimal intrusion or interference with their privacy.[119]

Let us compare this with the arrangements for clinical trials under the Clinical Trials Regulations 2004. According to these Regulations, a clinical trial can only recruit adults lacking mental capacity if it relates 'directly to a life-threatening or debilitating clinical condition from which the subject suffers'[120] and '[t]here are grounds for expecting that administering the medicinal product to be tested in the trial will produce a benefit to the subject outweighing the risks or produce no risk at all'.[121] Note that this test is stricter than the test applied under the Clinical Trials Regulations to children; there the benefit need only apply to the group as a whole, rather than to the individual participant. This is probably due to the necessity to prioritise research on children whose physiology is quite dif-ferent to adults. It is also somewhat more restrictive than the equivalent section dealing with adults lacking capacity in the Mental Capacity Act 2005. Under that Act, the benefits do not necessarily have to outweigh the risks provided the study derives new scientific knowledge and is of 'minimal risk'. Under the Clin-ical Trial Regulations the research must either benefit the participant or produce 'no risk at all'.[122]

---

[116] In essence, intrusive research is research that would normally require consent. The Mental Capacity Act 2005, s 30(2) states: 'Research is intrusive if it is of a kind that would be unlawful if it was carried out – (a) on or in relation to a person who had capacity to consent to it, but (b) without his consent.'

[117] Mental Capacity Act 2005, s 30(4). Defined in Mental Capacity Act 2005 (Appropri-ate Body) (England) Regulations 2006, SI 2006/2810, reg 2: '[T]he 'appropriate body' is a committee (a) established to advise on, or on matters which include, the ethics of intrusive research in relation to people who lack capacity to consent to it; and (b) which is recognised for those purposes by the Secretary of State.'

[118] Mental Capacity Act 2005, s 31(5).

[119] Mental Capacity Act 2005, s 31(6).

[120] Medicines for Human Use (Clinical Trials) Regulations 2004, SI 2004/1031, Pt 5, para 11.

[121] Medicines for Human Use (Clinical Trials) Regulations 2004, SI 2004/1031, Pt 5, para 9. Note that the requirements are not as stringent as those relating to a minor whereby some direct benefit for the group of patients is required (Pt 4, para 10).

[122] See Medical Research Council, *Medical Research Involving Adults who Cannot Consent* (2007) which gives guidance on assessing risk and other decisions relevant to research on adults lacking capacity; Royal College of Physicians, *Guidelines on the Practice of Ethics Committees in Medical Research with Human Participants* (2007), paras 4.32–4.36; GMC, *Consent to Research* (2010), paras 25–29.

Emergency research

15.10 Section 32(9) of the Mental Capacity Act 2005 provides an exception
to the requirement to obtain consent where there is either 'prior agreement of
a registered medical practitioner not involved in the trial or the researcher acts
in accordance with a procedure approved by the appropriate body at the time
the research project was approved'.[123] An ethics committee will be unlikely to
sanction research without the prior agreement of a medical practitioner, save
in one situation: emergency research. Emergency research involves participants with life-threatening conditions who cannot give consent. It might, for
example, compare two methods of treatment of stroke on admission to hospital. Were it not for section 32(9), emergency research would be severely
restricted.

No such exception was to be found in the original Clinical Trials Regulations
2004. Schedule 1, Pt 4, para 4 (relating to minors) and Schedule 1, Pt 5, para
4 (relating to adults lacking capacity) required that the prior consent of a legal
representative must always be obtained where the proposed research participant lacks the capacity to give consent. Ideally, the legal representative will be
a 'personal' one; a carer or family member. Otherwise a professional legal representative might be sought: 'A person not connected with the conduct of the
trial who is (a) the doctor primarily responsible for the adult's medical treatment, or (b) a person nominated by the relevant healthcare provider (e.g. an
acute NHS Trust or Health Board)'. Whilst this posed few problems in most
cases, it presented insurmountable difficulties for some types of emergency
research.

This was highlighted in the international TROICA trial[124] comparing two
types of emergency treatment given when patients suffering cardiac arrest
were brought into hospital by ambulance. In many cases a personal representative could not be immediately located and, given that treatment often had to
be administered within minutes by ambulance personnel, it was impracticable
to utilise a professional representative. The ambulance personnel could not
perform this role due to lack of independence. Yet the research was clearly
valuable. Other countries across Europe had interpreted Article 5(a) of the
Clinical Trials Directive more flexibly and the TROICA trial had been sanctioned. In England, the MHRA, concerned at the potential ill-effects on
emergency medicine, or perhaps at missing out on lucrative research, proposed
an amendment in August 2005 sanctioning *deferred* consent. Accordingly, it
was proposed that consent could be obtained within twenty-four hours of
commencing the research treatment. The Medical Research Council thought
this was not enough time and suggested seventy-two hours. But would this

---

[123] See GMC, *Consent to Research,* paras 33–35.
[124] Thrombolysis in Cardiac Arrest: a prospective, randomised, double-blind, placebo-
controlled, multicentre, parallel-group comparison trial led by Boehringer Ingelheim
GmbH to evaluate the efficacy of tenecteplase during CPR as compared with standard treatment in patients suffering from out-of-hospital cardiac arrest.

constitute a contravention of the Clinical Trials Directive? Beyleveld and Pattinson[125] argue that the provisions in the Directive 'unequivocally rule out both ... no consent and deferred consent approaches to emergency research on medicinal products'; that the position taken in the original Clinical Trials Regulations was correct. They argue that the duty to put the research participant before the interests of science prevents a purposive interpretation of the Directive.

Nevertheless, the Medicines for Human Use (Clinical Trials) Amendment (No 2) Regulations 2006[126] promulgates a new interpretation of Article 5(a) of the Directive. The 'deferred consent' model proposed by the MHRA was abandoned for a 'no consent' model. Accordingly an exception to the requirement that a legal representative gives consent on behalf of an adult who lacks capacity is created when:

(i)   treatment is required urgently;

(ii)   the nature of the trial also requires urgent action;

(iii)   it is not reasonably practicable to meet the conditions in paragraphs 1 to 5 of Part 5 (obtaining consent etc); and

(iv)   an ethics committee has given approval to the procedure under which the action is taken.

We now join a number of European countries awaiting a test case which will determine whether this flexible approach to interpretation of the Directive is legal. Would it not have been better to argue for the amendment of the Directive?[127]

Randomised controlled trials[128]

15.11   At the heart of much modern medical research lies the randomised controlled trial (RCT). Patients suffering from the same illness are divided into two groups and subjected to different treatments. Most commonly, either (a) one group will receive the conventional treatment, and another be given the experimental and, hopefully, more effective treatment, or (b) one group will be given a new drug, and the other a placebo.[129] For an outsider there are a number of

---

125   See D Beyleveld, S Pattinson, 'Medical Research into Emergency Treatment: Regulatory Tensions in England and Wales' [2006] 5 *Web Journal of Current Legal Issues*.

126   SI 2006/2984.

127   See Beyleveld, Pattinson [2006] 5 *Web Journal of Current Legal Issues*. Note that the European Commission Assessment of the Functioning of the Clinical Trials Directive 2001/20/EC: Summary of Responses to the Public Consultation Paper (2010), p 14 recognises that: 'Most respondents agreed that the situation as established by the CTD [in relation to emergency research] was unsatisfactory.'

128   For trenchant criticism of randomised clinical trials, see J Penston, *Fiction and Fantasy in Medical Research: The Large Scale Randomised Trial* (2003) London Press.

129   Note that the Declaration of Helsinki (2008), Art 32 states: 'The benefits, risks, burdens and effectiveness of a new intervention must be tested against those of the best

worrying features to RCTs. First, there is again the question of consent. Second, there is concern that the control group is denied a chance of superior treatment.[130] In particular, public anxiety was highlighted by a trial involving 3,000 women at risk of conceiving a spina bifida baby. Studies had shown that similar women appeared to suffer a reduced incidence of carrying a spina bifida baby if treated with special vitamin supplements. The trial involved randomising the women into four groups. One group received the full treatment under trial, another part only of the supplement, a third the other element of the supplement, and the fourth a placebo. Why should any woman at risk be denied a treatment which *might* help her avoid a spina bifida conception? Further criticism of randomised trials includes this point, that while the control group in a test may be denied a benefit, people are also concerned at the risk to the experimental group. And finally, who controls and monitors RCTs?

There are doctors and researchers who believe that the RCT is most effective if conducted 'blind', that is the patient is told nothing at all.[131] The issue then is whether consent to treatment given generally is negated by unwitting participation in the RCT. The law will decide the issue on how closely related the RCT is to the condition under treatment and whether consent to treatment impliedly includes consent to what was done in the trial. At best, a patient asked to take part in an RCT will be told just that. The nature of the trial and the purpose of random allocation may be explained. Exactly what will be done to the patient cannot be explained, by virtue of the very nature of an RCT. Consent on the strength of a proper explanation of the trial and free acceptance by the patient of its random basis would appear both sufficient and necessary. Entering the patient in a random test with no explanation and no consent places the doctor at risk of an action for battery if the patient finds out. Fears that patients, if properly informed, will refuse to participate are natural. The erosion of personal freedom resulting from allowing 'blind' trials is not justified by those fears. A patient who will not agree to, or cannot understand the implications of, a trial should not be entered in that trial.[132]

current proven intervention, except in the following circumstances: The use of placebo, or no treatment, is acceptable in studies where no current proven intervention exists; or where for compelling and scientifically sound methodological reasons the use of placebo is necessary to determine the efficacy or safety of an intervention and the patients who receive a placebo or no treatment will not be subject to any risk of serious or irreversible harm. Extreme care must be taken to avoid abuse of this option.' See also *Additional Protocol to the Convention on Human Rights and Biomedicine, Concerning Biomedical Research* (2005), Art 23(3).

[130] The ethical acceptability of placebo-controlled research is usually based on either the concept of 'equipoise' or minimal risk. See Royal College of Physicians, *Guidelines on the Practice of Ethics Committees in Medical Research with Human Participants* (2007), at 5.15; 5.18 and ch 6.

[131] And see *Mason and McCall Smith*, p 623, on the ethical implications of a blind, randomised controlled trial on the treatment of Parkinsonism.

[132] See the useful discussion in S J Edwards *et al*, 'Ethical Issues in the Design and Conduct of Randomised Controlled Trials' (1998) 2 *Health Technology Assessment* 1.

The RCT is particularly hard on participants in research to test a new therapy, where existing treatments have failed. In those circumstances the Royal College of Physicians suggested that Zelen's design might be appropriate.[133] Instead of randomising participants *after* consent has been taken, randomisation occurs before (and thus without) consent. At this point patients are told which treatment they have been assigned and can choose whether to remain in the trial or seek alternative (including possibly the experimental) treatment. Alternatively, only those patients who are offered the experimental treatment might be told that there is an alternative, existing treatment which they can take if they prefer to opt out of the trial.

Apart from the questions of consent, the other means by which the courts may be invoked to consider the RCT arise when something goes wrong, and a participant suffers injury. Will the law enable him to obtain compensation?

Compensation for mishap

15.12 The Clinical Trials Directive requires that both sponsor and lead investigator are insured or indemnified before research can commence. Under the research governance framework, the sponsor of research is responsible for ensuring that appropriate insurance and indemnity arrangements are in place. In the NHS, R&D management permission, required at every research site before research can start, should not be granted unless NHS indemnity arrangements are in place.[134] Unlike salaried employees of the NHS, many GPs and other independent practitioners must make their own indemnity or insurance arrangements with their professional bodies or the Medical Defence Union to protect themselves and their staff. In both cases, however, the NRES advises[135] that RECs leave the matter of indemnity and insurance in NHS research to the research governance process. They should, however, concern themselves with the adequacy of indemnity and insurance in research on private patients where the NHS research governance arrangements do not apply.

At present, compensation for personal injury suffered as a participant in a clinical trial is available only either to a participant who can prove negligence on the part of the operator of the trial, or on an ex gratia basis. Indemnity for non-negligent harm (caused through no discernible fault of an individual or institution involved) cannot be purchased by NHS bodies, and universities are

---

[133] Royal College of Physicians, *Guidelines on the Practice of Ethics Committees in Medical Research with Human Participants* (2007); M Zelen, 'A New Design for Randomised Clinical Trials' (1979) 300 *New England Journal of Medicine* 1242.

[134] Special rules apply to trials involving healthy volunteers. The Royal College of Physicians, *Guidelines on the Practice of Ethics Committees in Medical Research with Human Participants* (2007), at 4.19, recommends that 'a contract which accepts liability regardless of fault should be used for each participant'.

[135] COREC, *Guidance for RECs on GP Indemnity* (2006).

finding the costs of such arrangements increasingly prohibitive.[136] A claim in negligence may arise in two contexts in an RCT. First, a participant from the control group may complain that he was denied an improved prospect of cure. Second, participants from the experimental group may allege that unjustifiable risks were taken. Neither is likely to succeed. As long as conventional treatment of the control group remains proper medical practice, the control has no claim in negligence. As long as the novel procedure was a properly conducted piece of research, carried out in conformity with a well-founded and responsible body of medical opinion, the subject of that procedure is likely to fail.

Next, what about the case where something goes disastrously and unexpectedly wrong? The participant will not know why. It may be an inherent risk in the trial, it may be that the staff conducting the trial were negligent. The patients in the Northwick Park debacle[137] quickly ran into difficulties in their legal action. Not only did the MHRA conclude that the reaction was an 'unpredicted biological action', but TeGenro, the German manufacturer, offered an interim payment but then filed for bankruptcy with only limited insurance. Whilst the NHS will meet their immediate medical needs, the injured participants went under-compensated.

In principle, carelessness by the research team, be it in selecting participants on the basis of their previous medical history, or in the conduct of the trial or in monitoring of the effects of the trial, creates a remedy for the patient. Moreover, he also may have in theory a possible remedy against the ethics committee which approved the trial. It has been held that ethics committees can be subject to judicial review.[138] Arguably committees recognised by the UKECA have sufficient legal personality to be a defendant in a civil law suit. However, for those which lack statutory recognition, both the appointing strategic health authority and each individual ethics committee member have direct legal responsibilities to research participants.[139] Though there has yet to be an English case in which an ethics committee or committee member is held liable for acts or omissions in their ethics committee proceedings, now that committee

---

[136] In the European Commission Assessment of the Functioning of the Clinical Trials Directive 2001/20/EC: Summary of Responses to the Public Consultation Paper (2010), para 10.3, 'an EU-wide insurance was suggested and advocated as a "silver bullet" for academic research'.

[137] See above at **15.1**.

[138] *R v Ethical Committee of St. Mary's Hospital (Manchester), ex p H* [1988] 1 FLR 512.

[139] On liability of ethics committees, see M Brazier, 'Liability of Ethics Committees' (1990) 6 *Professional Negligence,* 186 and E Pickworth and M Brazier, 'Fees and Research Ethics Committees' (1999) 151 *Bulletin of Medical Ethics,* 18. The Royal College of Physicians, *Guidelines on the Practice of Ethics Committees in Medical Research with Human Participants* (2007), para 4.9, states: 'NHS employees serving on a REC are provided with indemnity for such work. Members who are not NHS employees should be issued with a form of indemnity on appointment (see SOPs 2.42). In the absence of such an undertaking, new members may wish to reconsider their participation.'

members have detailed guidance on good practice, this possibility should not be discounted. The court would consider whether the committee acted negligently in approving a hazardous trial and failed in its duty to safeguard the interests of patients and volunteers. The claimant's problems lie in proof of negligence, just as any other patient-claimant's do.[140] And they are more acute: if proving negligence in the operation of standard procedures is difficult, how much more difficult is it to prove negligence in embarking on novel procedures?

No-fault compensation

15.13 Is the present law adequate as a means to provide compensation for injury suffered as a participant of medical research? Over thirty years ago the Pearson Commission[141] recommended that:[142]

> Any volunteer for medical research or clinical trials who suffers severe damage as a result should have a cause of action, on the basis of strict liability, against the authority to whom he has consented to make himself available.

To date, the Department of Health and the pharmaceutical industry have operated ex gratia compensation schemes. The injured participant's legal rights remain, in general, dependent on the vagaries of the law of negligence. When a research participant suffers injury in a drug trial, he may, of course, gain some slight advantage from the regime of strict liability imposed on drug companies by the Consumer Protection Act 1987. He still has to prove that his injury resulted from a defect in the drug, and that it was that defect which caused his injury. If the drug company chooses to dispute liability, once again the matter is clumsily resolved by adversarial proceedings.[143] An individual, volunteer or patient, who agrees to subject himself to risk in the cause of medical science and the better health of the community deserves better than this.

Extra-legally, drug companies in the UK recognise the research participants' moral right to compensation independent of proof of fault. The Association of British Pharmaceutical Companies (ABPI) operates an ex gratia scheme whereby any healthy volunteer in a drug trial mounted by an ABPI member will receive compensation for any injury arising from that trial. However, many drug trials relate to drugs manufactured by foreign companies. Such companies may not be ready to accept the ABPI guidelines. Department of Health guidance provides that ethics committees should be adequately reassured about 'whether there is provision in proportion to the risk for compensation/treatment in the case of injury/disability/death of a research participant attributable to participation in the research; the insurance and

---

[140] See ch 8 on the problems of litigation.
[141] See above, **9.16.**
[142] Royal Commission on Civil Liability and Compensation for Personal Injury, Cmnd 7054 (HMSO, 1978), paras 1340–1341.
[143] For the problems of establishing strict liability under the 1987 Act, see ch 10.

indemnity arrangements'.[144] Further, the Royal College of Physicians advises RECs that 'sponsors and investigators must have insurance or indemnity cover to meet their potential liabilities arising from research'.[145]

Patients agreeing to participate in research, and volunteers involved in non-drug trials, remain outside this informal no-fault provision. And the ex gratia nature of the ABPI scheme means that compensation remains dependent on the drug companies' generosity and is in no sense a right enjoyed by research participants.

The case for no-fault compensation of persons injured in the course of research has long received wide support among doctors.[146] The burden of compensating those injured in the course of research to benefit us all should have a wide base. A fund could be financed from all bodies promoting research, from the profession, the pharmaceutical industry and the Department of Health. The prospects for introduction of a scheme to compensate medical research victims along these lines may be brighter than prospects for a general no-fault scheme for all victims of medical accidents. Practical problems of definition, administration and finance will be faced, but with a will most difficulties could be overcome. A scheme limited to injury suffered as a research participant will confront one very real problem. Exactly who would be entitled to benefit under the scheme? Would eligibility be confined to healthy volunteers, such as those in the Northwick Park hospital disaster? The moral case for automatic compensation for that group is overwhelming. Volunteers put their health on the line with no hope of personal benefit. But what of patients used as participants in research into conditions unrelated to their illness? Should eligibility depend on the lack of any conferral of benefits from the research? Or should it extend to all research participants? If it did, the problem of deciding eligibility moves to determining when a patient suffers injury as a result of a research enterprise, as opposed to in the course of general health care which may include resorting to some novel procedure. These potential problems are not insuperable. They illustrate perhaps that a general scheme of compensation embracing all victims of medical mishap is to be preferred.

A second problem occurs where the threat of litigation is removed without the introduction of stringent measures to ensure accountability. In New Zealand in 1988, a public inquiry revealed a horrific tale.[147] An individual gynaecologist was convinced that orthodox opinion on cervical smear tests was wrong.

---

[144] *Governance Arrangements for NHS Research Ethics Committees* (2001), para 9.15(l).

[145] Royal College of Physicians, *Guidelines on the Practice of Ethics Committees in Medical Research with Human Participants* (2007), para 4.10.

[146] See J M Barton *et al*, 'The Compensation of Patients Injured in Clinical Trials' (1995) 21 *Journal of Medical Ethics* 166.

[147] Commission of Inquiry into the Treatment of Cervical Cancer and Other Related Matters at National Women's Hospital (New Zealand, 1988), chaired by Judge Sylvia Cartwright.

A positive smear, he believed, was not a precursor of cervical cancer. No action should be taken until an actual malignancy was apparent. He recruited thousands of women into his trial, using manifestly inadequate consent procedures. Many, many women suffered dreadfully when cancer did develop and by that stage of the disease they had to undergo painful invasive surgery. For years no other doctor dared speak out and challenge the investigator. New Zealand operates a no-fault system of compensation. The cervical smear trial started before that system was introduced. It will never be possible to know whether the knowledge that no patient could sue for their injuries either reinforced the investigator in his blind faith in his misguided theory, or deterred his colleagues from taking action earlier, even if only out of self-protection. Recourse to court is a clumsy weapon, but it must not be taken from the research participant without affording him other safeguards. Litigation may provoke distrust, leading to public demand for all-embracing and stringent statutory controls on research. Abolishing legal liability in clinical research may provoke a scandal that will have the same effect unless existing controls are seen to operate effectively.

Research misconduct

15.14 Monitoring guards against research misconduct, which has been the subject of public outcry in recent years.[148] Career promotions are dependent on research publications and competition is fierce. In 1995, a high-ranking obstetrician and gynaecologist made headline news when it was discovered that he had forged a number of papers.[149] Two years later a former secretary of the Royal College of Physicians in Edinburgh was struck off the medical register for research misconduct.[150] In 2002, a GP falsified research data.[151] Professional groups are subject to disciplinary action by the relevant regulatory bodies, such as the GMC and the Nursing and Midwifery Council. The Medical Research Council promulgates *Good Research Practice* guidance[152] and operates a Scientific Misconduct Policy.[153] In relation to clinical trials (CTIMPs) it is an offence to provide false or misleading information when requesting authorisation of an opinion from a REC.[154] We have seen that the

---

[148] See M Farthing, R Horton, R Smith, 'Research Misconduct: Britain's Failure to Act' (2000) 321 *BMJ* 1485.

[149] S Lock, 'Lessons from the Pearce affair: Handling Scientific Fraud' (1995) 310 *BMJ* 1547.

[150] C Dyer, 'Consultant Struck Off Over Research Fraud' (1997) 315 *BMJ* 205.

[151] C Dyer, 'GP who Falsified Research Data Found Guilty of Professional Misconduct' (2001) 323 *BMJ* 1388. More recently see BBC News, *South Korea Clone Scientist Convicted*, 26 October 2009; C Dyer, 'Surgeon is Suspended for Misleading his Supervisor over his Research' (2010) 341 *BMJ* 4969.

[152] Medical Research Council, *Good Research Practice* (2000, updated 2005).

[153] Medical Research Council, *Scientific Misconduct and Policy and Procedure* (updated 2008).

[154] Medicines for Human Use (Clinical Trials) Regulations 2004, SI 2004/1031, reg 50. Penalties are set out in reg 52.

MHRA perform routine and triggered Good Clinical Practice Inspections during which they will be alert to potential research misconduct. In addition, an NHS Counter Fraud and Security Management Service operate to combat fraud in the NHS. Fraud, however, is only one species of research misconduct. The Committee on Publication Ethics[155] promulgates guidelines and a code of conduct for journals but not all misconduct comes to the attention of journal editors. A panel for Research Integrity in Health and Biomedical Sciences was set up in 2006,[156] but its role is promotional and advisory. Investigations of research misconduct remain in the hands of employers or sponsors. Overall there remains a substantial imbalance between the monitoring of clinical trials and the monitoring of other research. The Academy of Medical Sciences urges the government to introduce a National Research Governance Service. The chief aim is to streamline the process and ensure that governance is proportionate, but the Academy also recognises the need to ensure that poor quality or fraudulent research is prevented or stopped.[157] Participants deserve the reassurance of a comprehensive monitoring system.

Confidentiality and medical research[158]

15.15 The Academy draws attention to aspects of the regulatory process that it believes are operating inappropriate constraints on health research. One such 'problem area' is access to patient data. The Data Protection Act 1998 (implementing the European Directive 95/46/EC on the processing of personal data into UK law) came into effect in March 2000. The Directive has been criticised as outdated, unclear and overly burdensome.[159] It will be reviewed in late 2011.[160]

Under the Data Protection Act 1998, an Information Commissioner registers the names of data controllers and a description of the processing of data by each. Medical researchers are among those who must in most cases register with the Commissioner. In addition to registration, researchers must also comply with the complex provisions of the Act which demand special conditions to be attached to the processing of 'sensitive data' (including all personal health data). The Act requires that explicit consent is obtained before personal health data is processed, but an exception is made in the case of medical research. However, the Act demands that 'personal data shall be processed

---

[155] See http://www.publicationethics.org.uk/.
[156] See UK Research Integrity Office, *Code of Practice for Research: Promoting Good Practice and Preventing Misconduct* (2009).
[157] AcMedSci, *A New Pathway for the Regulation and Governance of Health Research* (2011), at 2.3.2.
[158] The common law duty of confidentiality and the Data Protection Act 1998 are explored in more detail in ch 4.
[159] Rand Europe, *Review of the European Data Protection Directive* (2009).
[160] Ministry of Justice, Call for Evidence on the Data Protection Legislative Framework. Closed 6 October 2010.

fairly and lawfully'. This arguably places a duty on the researcher to apply the principles enshrined in the common law duty of confidentiality. Arguably it goes further still.

The common law duty of confidentiality, which applies independently of the Act, is equally open to misinterpretation in relation to medical research. To advance the development of medicine and to enable research when completed to benefit other patients, the results of research must be published. Does publication of research findings amount to a breach of confidence to the patient? First, the patient, if he has given full and free consent to his participation in a trial may at the same time agree to information about him being disclosed once the trial is completed and a report is prepared. This must be the preferable course of action. Whether in law disclosure in the course of a research project of confidential information about a patient without his consent amounts to an actionable breach of confidence depends yet again on the nebulous test of whether that disclosure can be justified by the public interest in the advancement of the relevant research.

The GMC[161] requires that where practicable, researchers seek consent and anonymise data, and always keep disclosures to a minimum. It provides special requirements for researchers dealing with medical records and advises on the reporting of research data. Prior to 1999 it was generally assumed that it was not necessary to obtain the participant's consent to release data, provided that data was fully anonymised. In such a case neither the researcher nor any other individual can trace the data to a given research participant. The Data Protection Act 1998 does not apply when data is fully anonymised because the data is not considered 'personal'. The matter was put to the test in *R v Department of Health, ex p Source Informatics Ltd*[162] which involved pharmacists who sold fully anonymised data to industry. Latham J held at first instance that such disclosure might breach confidentiality on the basis that consent could not be implied because the data was used for commercial purposes and was therefore not in the public interest. However, researchers breathed a sigh of relief when the decision was overturned in the Court of Appeal where it was held that confidence would not be breached where the confider's identity was not disclosed.

What is clear is that disclosure should be limited to information strictly necessary to the project and that the anonymity of the patient must be protected. The NHS Ombudsman upheld a complaint from a young man who discovered in a medical textbook a full-face frontal picture of his naked body. There are various means of achieving 'anonymity', a much abused term. Full anonymisation offers greatest protection to research participants' confidentiality; however, the research cannot then be linked to either the individual's past medical history or his future treatment. In most research projects a system of

---

[161] GMC, *Confidentiality* (2009), paras 40–50; GMC, *Good Practice in Research* (2010), paras 31–32.
[162] [1999] 4 All ER 185, [2000] 1 All ER 786, CA.

data coding is preferred. The codes can be broken in the event of adverse reaction and results can be linked to the individual's past medical history. A significant problem lies in aggregating data so they can be coded or anonymised. Who should perform this task?[163] In 2008 a Data Sharing Review recommended that the legal framework on data sharing be simplified.[164] 'Safe havens' should be developed where identifiable data can be coded by approved researchers. The Academy for Medical Sciences' 2011 review encourages the government to take these suggestions forward. In addition to the establishment of 'safe havens', the review recommends that:

> Accredited investigators and research team members should be considered part of a clinical care team to enable identifying patients eligible for approved studies. The UK Data Protection Act should be reviewed to identify and amend aspects requiring clarification and to inform proposed revisions to the EU Data Directive.[165]

There is one limited exception to the rule that identifiable data cannot be used in research without consent. As we saw in chapter 4, the controversial sections 251–252 of the National Health Service Act 2006[166] enable the Secretary of State to support the use of confidential patient information to improve the patient's medical care or in the public interest without the patient's consent provided there is no reasonably practicable alternative. The approvals process is carried out by the National Information Governance Board through its Ethics and Confidentiality Committee. The Board considers:

- the feasibility of doing the research or other activity with patients' consent or by using anonymised or coded information; and
- whether the use of identifiable information would benefit patients or the public sufficiently to outweigh patients' right to privacy.[167]

Consequently, where it can be demonstrated that research is in the public interest, that anonymised patient data will not suffice and that it is impracticable to seek consent, an application may be made under the National Health Service Act 2006, ss 251–252, for approval of the research. However, the research must still comply with data protection legislation.

The Freedom of Information Act 2000 heralded a new age of transparency. The interface between this and the Data Protection Act 1998 was put to the test in a Scottish case in 2008.[168] Mr Collie asked the Scottish Common Services Agency to release details of the incidence of childhood leukaemia between the years 1990 and 2003, for the Dumfries and Galloway postal area, so that

---

[163] See J Strobl, E Cave, T Walley, 'Data Protection Legislation: Interpretation and Barriers to Research' (2000) 321 *BMJ* 890.

[164] R Thomas, M Walport, *Data Sharing Review Report* (2008), rec 17.

[165] AcMedSci, *A New Pathway for the Regulation and Governance of Health Research* (2011), p 63, and see rec 8–10.

[166] Previously Health and Social Care Act 2001, s 60.

[167] See GMC, *Confidentiality* (2009), para 45.

[168] *Common Services Agency v Scottish Information Commissioner* [2008] UKHL 47.

he might undertake epidemiological research. The Agency replied that some of the data was incomplete and that other data was sensitive and subject to the common law duty of confidentiality. Because the low incidence of childhood leukaemia and small geographic area might lead to identification, the information could not be released. Mr Collie took his case to the Scottish Information Commissioner, who issued a decision in 2005.[169] He was satisfied that individual children might be identified and that disclosure would breach the Data Protection Act. The Commissioner asked that the Agency provide the information to Mr Collie in an alternative form. The First Division of the Court of Session refused the Agency's subsequent appeal and the case proceeded to the House of Lords where the appeal was allowed. The case was remitted back to the Commissioner to determine whether or not the data could be sufficiently anonymised and thus released to Mr. Collie. The data must be presented in a form that either was not personal data, or did not contravene the principles of the Data Protection Act. In 2010, the Commissioner decided that this was achievable and directed the Agency accordingly.[170]

Genetic privacy[171]

15.16   Genetic research generates significant public concern.[172] Some deem it 'unnatural' or unethical. Others worry about the implications for their right to privacy under Article 8 of the European Convention on Human Rights. As we saw in chapter 4, Article 8 is transforming the law of confidentiality. Tighter controls on medical data were ushered in by the Data Protection Act 1998. It became harder for researchers to access the data they desire. They are required to protect the identity of participants and to prove that any non-consensual use of confidential data is in the public interest. Genetic profiling is playing an ever increasing role in research. Much controversy has been created by the UK Biobank project.[173] It is funded by the Department of Health, Scottish Executive, Medical Research Council and Wellcome Trust and aims to collect both data and samples on the health of 500,000 volunteers[174] and analyse it over a period of thirty years. Consent of participants will be sought, but because it is

[169] Scottish Information Commissioner, *Mr Michael Collie and the Common Services Agency* (CSA), Decision 021/2005.

[170] Scottish Information Commissioner, *Mr Michael Collie and the Common Services Agency* (CSA), Reference No: 200500298 (2010).

[171] See G Laurie, *Genetic Privacy: A Challenge to Medico-Legal Norms* (2002) CUP; H Widdows and C Mullen, *The Governance of Genetic Information: Who Decides?* (2009) CUP.

[172] Medical Research Council, *Public Perceptions of the Collection of Human Biological Samples* (2000).

[173] See *Mason and McCall Smith*, at 240; S M C Gibbons, 'Regulating Biobanks: A Twelve-Point Typological Tool' (2009) 17(3) *Medical Law Review* 313.

[174] UK Biobank announced that it had reached the goal of recruiting 500,000 participants in July 2010. See http://www.ukbiobank.ac.uk/.

not possible to predict all future research uses, the consent will be general rather than specific.[175]

In chapter 18, we examine the law relating to the human body and its parts and the effects of the Human Tissue Act 2004. The doctrine of consent is central to the legislation. An exception exists for health-related research on living people where the tissue is unidentifiable and the project has received ethical approval[176] in accordance with the Human Tissue Act 2004 (Ethical Approval, Exceptions and Licensing and Supply of Information about Transplants) Regulations 2006. The REC must consider how tissue is to be disposed of and the means by which relatives are informed of results.[177] Another exception exists by virtue of section 7(4) of the 2004 Act which confers on the Secretary of State a power to deem consent to be in place, though it is envisaged that this will only be used where there is an overwhelming public interest in doing so.[178]

The Genetic Interest Group[179] (renamed Genetics Alliance UK in 2010) expressed concern that insignificant weight is attached to the public interest in research. Concessions to research in the Human Tissue Act 2004, it claimed, are 'piecemeal, diffident and on occasion, virtually secret'. Could we be heading for a policy of 'ask or anonymise' that applies to both human tissue and data? Might the public interest threshold be set so high as to inhibit valuable research? It is unlikely. As we demonstrated in chapter 4, the right to privacy under Article 8(1) is not absolute. It can be limited under Article 8(2):

> ... in the interests of national security, public safety or the economic well-being of the country, for the prevention of disorder or crime, for the protection of health or morals, or for the protection of the rights and freedoms of others.

Though there has been little case law on Article 8(2) in the context of medical confidentiality,[180] the House of Lords in *R (S & Marper) v Chief Constable of South Yorkshire Police*[181] indicates how readily the judiciary will put the public interest before that of the individual. It was held that the retention and use of DNA and fingerprints by the police, after a suspect had been cleared of the offence, did not offend Article 8. Four of the Law Lords held that Article 8(1) was not invoked. Baroness Hale held that though there was an interference

---

[175] See *UK Biobank Ethics Governance Framework* v. 3.0, 2007, para B1.

[176] By an authorised research ethics committee: see the Human Tissue Act 2004 (Ethical Approval, Exceptions from Licensing and Supply of Information about Transplants) Regulations 2006, SI 2006/1260, reg 2.

[177] See HTA, *Code of Practice 9: Research* (2009). Brought into force by Directions 002/2009.

[178] For additional guidance on research involving human tissues, see GMC, *Consent to Research* (2010), paras 36–39, and Royal College of Physicians, *Guidelines on the Practice of Ethics Committees in Medical Research with Human Participants* (2007), paras 4.37–4.41, and ch 7.

[179] Genetics Interest Group, *Human Rights, Privacy and Medical Research* (2006), at 3.

[180] Though see Strasbourg cases *MS v Sweden* (1997) 28 EHRR 313 and *Z v Finland* (1997) 25 EHRR 371 protecting children's medical confidentiality.

[181] [2004] UKHL 39.

with privacy within the meaning of Article 8(1), it was justified as proportionate under Article 8(2). The information would not be made public and individuals were not identifiable to the 'untutored eye'. The retention of the samples to be used as comparators was appropriate.

The government will not shackle researchers. Research is lucrative. Let us not forget that it also advances medicine and saves lives. In England and Wales, regulation and review of research is going through a period of unprecedented change. The Health and Social Care Bill 2011 proposes a new section 131 to the NHS Act 2006 imposing a duty incumbent on the NHS Commissioning Board both to promote research and utilise its results to improve the health service. We have seen that a proposed new research regulator, the HRA, will further streamline the regulatory process. Efforts to facilitate good research have been matched by significant improvements in the level of participant safety. Provided this equilibrium is maintained (and as domestic reform proposals and reforms of the Clinical Trials and Data Protection Directives unravel this cannot yet be assumed), the changes are to be celebrated.

Chapter 16

DEFINING DEATH

16.1 The single certainty in human life is that we shall die. Death cannot be evaded, albeit it may be delayed. Fifty years ago there would have been little debate about how to define death. Nonetheless there is ample evidence that our ancestors feared that their physicians and their families might mistakenly anticipate their demise and one might find oneself buried alive.[1] Today, as we shall see, medical technology has created real questions about just how we identify the threshold between dying but alive, and death itself. The development of transplantation played a major role in prompting doctors to rethink definitions of death. It would be wrong to conclude that a desire to maximise the number of viable organs suitable for transplant is the only or the most important factor in the imperative need to define the moment of death.[2] The question is far from straightforward and a legal definition of death is required for several purposes.

Defining death[3]

16.2 Defining death is difficult because, biologically, death is a process and not an event. Different organs and systems supporting the continuation of life cease to function successively, and at different times. The need to determine an exact or, at best, approximate time of death is important for many reasons. The law often requires such a finding.[4] Establishing the date of death may be important for property purposes. Until death is established, steps cannot be

---

[1] See J Bondeson, *Buried Alive: The Terrifying History of our Most Primal Fear* (2001) Norton.

[2] See C Machado, J Korein, Y Ferrer *et al*, 'The Concept of Brain Death Did Not Evolve to Benefit Organ Transplants' (2007) 33 *Journal of Medical Ethics* 197.

[3] For an excellent analysis of all the medical and ethical conundrums surrounding a definition of death, see J K Mason and G T Laurie, *Mason and McCall Smith's Law and Medical Ethics* (8th edn, 2010) OUP (hereafter *Mason and McCall Smith*), pp 521–528.

[4] The old common law 'year and a day' rule which required that if a person was

taken to obtain probate or letters of administration to that person's estate, and the interest of a beneficiary under a will is usually dependent upon the beneficiary surviving the testator. In some cases, when the testator and the beneficiary die at around the same time, it is important to know when each death took place. When two relatives die in a common accident, there may be a legal presumption that the elder died before the younger, unless evidence can be established as to the precise time of death of either; and the property consequences of this decision are significant.[5] There may also be tax factors. If a person gives away property before his death, that property may be free from inheritance tax, or be subject to less tax, only if he survives the gift for a specified period. There have been many stories written involving relatives of such donors going to great lengths to postpone or conceal the 'true moment' of death so that the donor 'survives' beyond the relevant statutory period for tax purposes. If the victim has a claim for damages for the injuries sustained, the amount of damages will differ substantially between cases where the victim is comatose yet living, or dead.[6] And, self-evidently, doctors cannot remove organs for transplant under the rules governing cadaver donations unless the donor is legally dead.

Determining whether a person was dead once posed little difficulty. Historically, the key factors in the process used to determine whether death had occurred were the cessation of breathing and the cessation of heartbeat. Thus, the irreversible cessation of heartbeat and respiration implied death of a patient as a whole, although that did not necessarily imply the immediate death of every cell in the body. Doctors accepted and used traditional methods of establishing death. When someone's heart stopped beating and he stopped breathing, he was dead. Advances in medicine gradually demonstrated that this was not a valid test for all purposes: elective cardiac arrest during open-heart surgery, for example, or cases of spontaneous cardiac arrest followed by successful resuscitation. The heart stops but the patient is not dead. Machines such as mechanical ventilators or respirators have effected major improvements in techniques of resuscitation and life support for those who are desperately ill or injured. Where these efforts are successful and the patients recover, one may praise the advances in medical techniques. Sometimes such measures do not provide any satisfactory outcome, for example, where the person's heart continues to beat on the machine long after breathing has stopped but his brain is irreversibly damaged. In such circumstances, keeping a body 'alive' on a machine can be as undesirable as it is pointless. It is distressing to relatives. It can have an adverse effect on nursing staff morale; the cost of maintaining the patient in such intensive care is high, and the use of machines in these cases can mean that other patients, better able to benefit from them, may be denied access to them. Developments in life support made rethinking death inevitable.

charged with murder his victim must have died within a year and a day of the unlawful act was abolished by the Law Reform (Year and a Day Rule) Act 1996.

[5]   See Law of Property Act 1925, s 184.
[6]   See *Lim Poh Choo v Camden and Islington Area Health Authority* [1980] AC 174.

Nonetheless, a significant trigger to rethinking our definition of death was the development of transplantation, which highlighted the need for speed in diagnosing death and removing organs from the body. Thus, pressures developed to consider a redefinition of death based upon a new concept of 'irreversible brain damage' or 'brain death'. This concept can be illustrated dramatically by considering a guillotine victim. Nobody would consider the body, after the head has been severed, to represent an individual living being; yet the decapitated body could be resuscitated and the organs kept 'alive' for a considerable period. In most cases, brain death follows the cessation of breathing and heartbeat in the dying process, but occasionally that order of events is reversed. This occurs as a result of severe damage to the brain itself, from perhaps a head injury or a spontaneous intracranial haemorrhage. In such cases, instead of failure of such vital functions as heartbeat and respiration eventually resulting in brain death, brain death results in the cessation of spontaneous respiration; normally followed within minutes by cardiac arrest. If, however, the patient is supported by artificial ventilation, the heartbeat can continue for some days and this will, for a time, enable the function in other organs, such as the liver and kidneys, to be maintained.

This condition of what was then described as a 'state beyond coma' or 'irreversible coma' or 'brain death' was first advanced as a new criterion of death in 1968 in an influential report of an ad hoc Committee of the Harvard Medical School.[7] In such cases (it was said) a doctor could pronounce as dead a 'comatose' individual who had no discernible central nervous system activity; and then the ventilator could be switched off. The Harvard doctors stated that judgment of the existence of the various criteria of death was solely a medical issue. Using words such as coma or comatose was unhelpful and raised suspicion that concepts of death were being manipulated to make it easier to declare a patient 'dead'.[8]

Public opinion was unwilling to surrender control of such matters lightly to the medical profession. Unease was expressed about the relationship between attempts to redefine death and the needs of transplant surgeons to ensure that organs taken from a deceased person should be taken as soon as possible after death. In 1975, the British Transplantation Society expressed concern at the poor quality of cadaver kidneys being transplanted, mainly because of delay between the determination of death and the removal of the kidneys from the body. It was also important, for transplantation, that a ventilator should not be switched off permanently, but rather that the body be kept on the machine to preserve the quality of the organs until they were required. Two major fears were voiced. First, was the pressure to redefine death being made simply to enable transplant surgeons to obtain better results? Could it be said, for example, that potential transplant donors might be designated 'dead' at a point of time earlier than if they were not potential donors? Second, was it ethically or legally permissible to remove organs from a donor before the ventilator had

---

[7] 'A Definition of Irreversible Coma' (1968) 205 *Journal of the American Medical Association* 337.

[8] See *Mason and McCall Smith*, pp 524–525.

been turned off? Because of doubts such as these, the British Transplantation Society recommended that the death of a potential organ donor should be certified by two doctors, neither of whom was a member of the transplant team and, most important, that the decision to stop a ventilator should be made quite independently of transplant considerations.

From the late 1970s the medical establishment in Britain[9] agreed that 'brain death'[10] or, preferably, 'brain-stem death' (which is the 'irreversible loss of brain-stem function') could be diagnosed with certainty; and in these circumstances, the patient is dead whether or not the function of some organs, such as a heartbeat, is still maintained by artificial means.

Some commentators, however, continued to reject the notion that 'death' could be equated with 'irreversible loss of brain stem function'.[11] They argued that only the cessation of the heartbeat truly indicated the end of life. Claims were made of 'mistakes'. Were patients being diagnosed as brain dead who were not 'really' dead? Or were the few reported examples of such mistakes simply cases where the appropriate criteria for determining brain death had not been properly implemented? Was it possible that organs were being taken for transplant before a patient had died? The validity of procedures to establish 'brain-death' had never, some argued, been rigorously tested. Short-cuts in procedures were too often prompted by pressure from the transplant team anxious to 'get at' organs swiftly. In January 2011, the Chief Rabbi, Lord Sachs, re-ignited controversy relating to brain death. He issued a rabbinical ruling that only 'cardiac death' was acceptable as the definition of death in Orthodox Jewry.[12] The consequences for organ donation are discussed in the next chapter.[13]

Official endorsement of 'brain-stem death' is now to be found in a comprehensive Code of Practice issued by the Academy of Medical Royal Colleges.[14] The Code notes that '[D]eath involves the irreversible loss of those essential characteristics which are necessary to the existence of living human persons and thus the definition of death should be regarded as the irreversible loss of

[9]   See Conference of Medical Royal Colleges and their Faculties in the UK, 'Diagnosis of Brain Death' (1976) 2 *BMJ* 1187; and 'Memorandum on the Diagnosis of Death' (1979) 1 *BMJ* 332; C Pallis, D H Harley, *ABC of Brainstem Death* (2nd edn, 1996) BMJ Books.

[10] For an analysis of the confusing terms in debates on 'brain death' see *Mason and McCall Smith*, pp 524–525.

[11] See M Evans, 'A Plea for the Heart' (1990) 3 *Bioethics* 227; and note that in Japan 'brain-stem death' has only recently been accepted as a lawful definition of death in the late 1990s: see J Wise, 'Japan to Allow Organ Transplants' (1997) 314 *BMJ* 1298.

[12] And see A Bedir, S Aksoy, 'Brain Death Revisited: It is not "Complete Death" According to Islamic Sources' (2011) 37 *Journal of Medical Ethics* 290–294.

[13] (2011) *Guardian,* 14 January.

[14] Academy of Medical Royal Colleges, *A Code of Practice for the Diagnosis and Confirmation of Death* (2008).

consciousness combined with the irreversible loss of the capacity to breathe'. Brain-stem death is defined as follows:

> 2.1 Death following the irreversible cessation of brain-stem function
>
> The irreversible cessation of brain stem function (brain-stem death) whether induced by intra-cranial events or the result of extra-cranial phenomena, such as hypoxia, will produce this clinical state and therefore irreversible cessation of the integrative function of the brain stem equates with the death of the individual and allows the medical practitioner to diagnose death.

Importantly, the Code of Practice also sets out detailed and careful instructions for rigorous criteria for tests to confirm death.[15]

The law

16.3   There is still no statutory definition of death in the UK. There is, however, little doubt that there is sufficient judicial authority to support a definition of death based on 'brain-stem death'. The question first arose where persons accused of murder claimed that it was not they who killed the victim, but the hospital team who disconnected the life-support machine. The courts did not react favourably, even though they side-stepped the issue as to what, in law, constitutes death. In *R v Malcherek; R v Steel*,[16] the Court of Appeal dealt with two such cases. The first defendant had stabbed his wife, who was taken to hospital and put on a life-support machine. When it was found she had irreversible brain damage, the ventilator was disconnected and shortly after that all her bodily functions ceased. The second defendant attacked a girl, causing her multiple skull fractures and severe brain damage. She too was taken to hospital and put on a life-support machine, which was disconnected when the doctors concluded that her brain had ceased to function. The Court of Appeal upheld the trial judges' decisions in each case not to leave the issue of causation to the jury, pointing out rather tartly that it was not the doctors, but the accused who were on trial. The Court took the crucial evidence to be that the original criminal acts by the defendants were continuing, operating and substantial causes of the death of their victims. In the ordinary case where treatment is given by bona fide competent and careful medical practitioners, evidence is not admissible to show that the treatment would not have been administered in the same way by other medical practitioners. Without exploring the definition of death, the Court was not prepared to allow assailants to shelter behind technical arguments challenging standard medical procedures. Lord Lane CJ did go slightly further, saying:[17]

> . . . whatever the strict logic of the matter may be, it is perhaps somewhat bizarre to suggest . . . that where a doctor tries his conscientious best to save the life of a patient brought to hospital in extremis, skilfully using sophisticated methods,

---

[15]   Academy of Medical Royal Colleges, *A Code of Practice for the Diagnosis and Confirmation of Death* (2008), chs 4–6.

[16]   [1981] 2 All ER 422. And see *Finlayson v HM Advocate* 1978 SLT 60.

[17]   [1981] 2 All ER 422 at 429.

drugs and machinery to do so, but fails in his attempt and therefore discontinues treatment he can be said to have caused the death of the patient.

Re A[18] settles the matter. A two-year-old boy suffered a serious head injury. Doctors struggled to save his life and he was put on a ventilator. His condition deteriorated and tests established that he was, undoubtedly, brain-stem dead. His parents vehemently opposed the decision to switch off the ventilator. The hospital sought a declaration that doctors in disconnecting the child from the ventilator did not act unlawfully. Endorsing the definition of brain-stem death then encapsulated in a Department of Health Code of Practice, the judge declared that the child was for all purposes legally dead. The House of Lords in *Airedale NHS Trust v Bland*[19] lent further authority to a legal definition of death dependent on proof of 'brain-stem death'.

Should there be a statutory definition of death?

16.4   The case for a statutory definition of death is less compelling than when such arguments were first advanced,[20] as the courts have introduced a degree of certainty into the debate. Had there been a statutory definition of death in 1976, a definition based upon the long-standing medical criteria of irreversible cessation of breathing and heartbeat, then the medical redefinition of death to take into account irreversible cessation of brain function would have no legal effect in those cases where there was a difference in time between the two definitions, until the existing definition had itself been changed by statute. As long as the matter is treated as a question of medical fact, changes in medical approach can be accommodated within the law without any requirement for further legislation.

Those in favour of legislation, however, regard the very ease with which, without legislation, definitions of death can, and have, altered as a source of disquiet. Doctors, supported by judges, changed the goalposts. Visceral fears that doctors continue to be eager to declare A dead to give B her organs have not gone away.[21] A debate on a statutory definition of death would allow wide public involvement in that debate, and an opportunity for public education. Such a debate could also encompass other difficult issues surrounding defining death. There are those who argue that patients in a persistent vegetative state (PVS), such as Tony Bland,[22] are not dying but dead. The destruction of the cortex and consequent loss of all cognitive function rendered Tony Bland, in that ghastly

---

[18]   [1992] 3 Med LR 303; and see *Mail Newspapers plc v Express Newspapers plc* [1987] FSR 90; *Re TC (A Minor)* (1993) 2 *Medical Law Review* 376.

[19]   [1993] 1 All ER 821, HL see below at **19.10**.

[20]   For example, see Fourteenth Report of the Criminal Law Reform Committee, *Offences Against the Person* (Cmnd 7844, 1980).

[21]   See J M Appel, 'Defining Death: When Physicians and Family Disagree' (2005) 31 *Journal of Medical Ethics* 641.

[22]   *Airedale NHS Trust v Bland* [1993] 2 All ER 821, HL; see below **19.10**.

phrase, a 'human vegetable'. He had irreversibly lost personhood, and those capacities which made him distinctively human. Should we modify the definition of death so that patients in this state are also regarded as dead?[23] Some argue that this is the most sensible and most compassionate way of dealing with these persons. Criteria based on 'brain-stem death' would be replaced by a concept of 'cognitive death'. But is this a decision that unelected judges should take by choosing to endorse flexible and developing definitions of death as valid if they accord with medical practice? Would a definition of death based on 'cortical or cognitive death' be comprehensible or acceptable to the public?

Formulating a statutory definition of death is not straightforward. Early attempts provided for alternative definitions: the long-established traditional definition and the new definition. This, it was said, would lead the public to believe that there are two separate phenomena of death, one being primarily for transplantation purposes. The American Uniform Brain Death Act (1978) served as a model for a number of states in the USA. It provides simply that 'for legal and medical purposes, an individual who has sustained irreversible cessation of all functioning of the brain, including the brain stem, is dead. A determination under this section must be made in accordance with reasonable medical standards'. It is difficult to see what this would add to English law, were it to be enacted. Such a statute would simply repeat and reinforce the Academy of Medical Royal Colleges' Code currently operated voluntarily by the medical profession. Any doctor violating that Code today by acting on a concept of 'cognitive death' in relation to his patients would have difficulty in justifying his action in any subsequent legal or disciplinary proceedings. Section 26(2)(d) of the Human Tissue Act 2004 empowered the Human Tissue Authority (HTA) to prepare a Code of Practice in relation to the definition of death, but for the purposes of that Act only. No such Code has as yet been developed by the HTA. The HTA is one of the many arms'-length bodies threatened with abolition or merger at present.[24] While the HTA, if it survives, may be well placed to consult widely in relation to preparation of such a Code, it is regrettable that their Code of Practice would be narrowly focused within the 2004 Act. This could reinforce fears that a different standard applies where the primary question is removal of organs and tissue from the body.[25]

Open debate about how we define death would allow two other questions to be explored, those relating to anencephalic infants and pregnant women. In anencephalic babies, criteria for 'brain-stem death' are unworkable. An anencephalic baby is born lacking a higher brain. He is bound to die, usually in a matter of days and, were his interests alone to be considered, such an infant would not be ventilated. Other babies are born with intact brains, but defective hearts or kidneys. Doctors may want to use organs from the anencephalic

---

[23] See the arguments discussed in P D G Skegg, *Law, Ethics and Medicine* (1995) Clarendon Press.

[24] See above at **1.16** and below at **17.2**.

[25] See C Machado *et al*, 'A Definition of Human Death Should Not be related to Organ Transplants' (2003) 29 *Journal of Medical Ethics* 201.

baby to save the life of a baby with other defective organs. If they allow the anencephalic baby to die 'normally', simply by ceasing to breathe, his organs will deteriorate so rapidly as to be useless. If the anencephalic baby is to be used as an organ donor, he must be ventilated. That poses a problem in defining when he dies. Tests for 'brain-stem death' are not applicable to newborn babies,[26] and there is some evidence that, if ventilated, an anencephalic infant's brain stem may remain active, 'alive', for some considerable period of time. If 'brain-stem death' is inapplicable to anencephalic babies, should we accept that the lack of any higher brain function renders the baby, so to speak, born dead?[27] Or is that confusing active euthanasia with defining death?

One objection, regardless of how we define death in such cases, is that in ventilating an anencephalic baby to retrieve her organs we use her solely as a means to an end. A similar problem surrounds ventilating brain-dead pregnant women.[28] If a pregnant woman suffers head injuries during pregnancy and brain-stem death is diagnosed, should her corpse be ventilated to allow the foetus the opportunity to be delivered alive? Who should make such decisions? Where a woman has herself contemplated such a possibility and in an advance directive expressed her wish that her body be sustained so her child can live, the outcome might seem clearer. She has authorised the use of her body for that purpose. But such a use of a dead body is not contemplated in the Human Tissue Act 2004. The temptation for doctors wishing to comply with the 'dead' woman's instructions might be to fall back on earlier definitions of death based on cessation of heartbeat and declare that this woman is thus not dead. What of instructions not to ventilate her 'corpse' from a woman in the later stages of pregnancy when a few further days in the womb might give the foetus a fighting chance of survival? Absent any instruction from the woman herself, does her husband, partner or parent have a right to determine whether or not the foetus survives? Or is this a case where an independent foetal interest can be asserted? Whatever your conclusion, the notion of 'brain-dead incubators'[29] challenges our understanding of death, and could undermine confidence in established definitions of brain-stem death.

The brutal reality may be that, however death is defined, and whether such a definition is enshrined in statute or not, diagnosing death will always be a matter of concern. Few people wish their final moments to be cut short by others. Accepting the death of someone close to you is more than an exercise in logic.

---

[26] See Working Party of the British Paediatric Association, *Diagnosis of Brain-Stem Death in Infants and Children* (1991) endorsed in the Academy of Medical Royal Colleges, *Code of Practice for the Diagnosis and Confirmation of Death* (2008), para 6.2 and Appendix 4.

[27] See the Report of the Working Party of the Medical Royal Colleges, *Organ Transplantation in Neonates* (1988) sanctioning such a course of action.

[28] See *Mason and McCall Smith*, pp 530–532. And see D Sperling, *Management of Post Mortem Pregnancy: Legal and Philosophical Aspects* (2000) Ashgate.

[29] See N S Peart, A V Campbell, A R Manara, 'Maintaining a Pregnancy Following Loss of Capacity' (2000) 8 *Medical Law Review* 275.

Chapter 17

ORGAN AND TISSUE TRANSPLANTATION

17.1 This chapter explores legal questions surrounding organ and tissue transplantation. It focuses solely on transplantation. Closely related questions relating to organ retention for the purposes of education and research are dealt with in chapter 18.[1] The Human Tissue Act 2004,[2] which came into force in September 2006, is now the primary legislation regulating transplantation in those countries. Its origins owe more to the controversy surrounding revelations about the practice of organ retention than the needs of transplant medicine itself.[3] The Act is complex and difficult to understand.[4] In the context of transplantation, a fundamental principle embodied in the Act is that all donations, including cadaver donations, must be based on 'appropriate consent'.

Certain sorts of tissue transplantation, such as blood donation and skin grafts, have been routine for many decades. Tens of thousands of lives have been saved by bone-marrow transplants. Despite the number of lives saved, solid organ donation has had a stormy history. Debates involving clinical, ethical, scientific, financial and resource considerations continue to rage. The Human Tissue Act 2004 has not stilled controversy. Public response to transplantation has often been erratic, influenced by publicity given to dramatic successes and

---

[1]   For a masterly analysis of legal and ethical issues relating to all uses of human tissue, see D Price, *Human Tissue in Transplantation and Research* (2009) CUP. And for a range of proposals addressing strategies to increase the supply of donor organs, see A-M Farrell, D Price and M Quigley (eds), *Organ Shortage: Ethics Law and Pragmatism* (2011) CUP.

[2]   The Act does not apply in Scotland (save for s 45, prohibiting the taking and analysis of DNA samples without consent). The Human Tissue (Scotland) Act 2006 is the governing Act in Scotland.

[3]   See below at **18.2**. As Mason and Laurie rightly say '. . . the 2004 Act was born under the wrong star': J K Mason and G T Laurie, *Mason and McCall Smith's Law and Medical Ethics* (8th edn, 2010) OUP (hereafter *Mason and McCall Smith*), p 548.

[4]   For an overview of the Act, see D Price, 'The Human Tissue Act 2004' (2005) 68 *Modern Law Review* 798; M Brazier and S Fovargue, 'A Brief Guide to the Human Tissue Act 2004' (2006) 1 *Clinical Ethics* 26.

failures. For example, in the early days of heart transplants, stories which described transplant surgeons as 'human vultures', and claims of organs allegedly removed from bodies before 'real death' had occurred, contributed to excite concern and hostility. On the other hand, the media can be effective in publicising the benefit of transplantation and creating favourable public awareness about transplant medicine.

Scientific developments in transplantation continue to be amazing. The principal problem remains the discrepancy between supply and demand,[5] even though in the UK the number of donors is rising. As National Health Service Blood and Transplant (NHSBT) reported, in 2009–10, 8,000 patients were registered on the 'active' waiting list as in need of a transplant, and 2,545 more patients are on the 'suspended' list, that is to say that they need a transplant but are not currently fit enough for surgery. Yet in that same year deceased organ donation rose by 7 per cent from 809 donors in 2008/9 to 959, and the number of living donors rose by 10 per cent to 1,026, making 2009/10 a record year for organ donation. Nonetheless 552 people still died in the UK in 2009/10 for want of a transplant,[6] and compared to countries such as Spain the UK falls well short of the optimum number of cadaver transplants.[7] Three factors must be noted. Live donors now play a central role in organ donation; very often one single cadaveric donor is the source of multiple transplants, and the criteria for selecting cadaver donors are less stringent.[8] Such was the degree of concern about rates of organ donation that the government convened the Organ Donation Task Force (ODT) which issued its first report in 2008 setting out a strategy designed to achieve an increase of 50 per cent in cadaver donation within five years.[9] The ODT was then asked by government to reconvene specifically to look again at the case for amending the Human Tissue Act 2004 to introduce a system of presumed consent (sometimes styled an 'opt-out' system) for cadaver donations. Perhaps to the surprise of the government, the ODT's second report recommended against moving to presumed consent at present.[10] Proponents of presumed consent argue that doctors should be allowed to remove organs from the dead unless the deceased had registered an objection to organ donation. Attempts to introduce presumed consent during the passage of the Human Tissue Act had also failed. However, those who press its case are unlikely to give up easily.

---

[5] See the analysis in B New, M Solomon, R Dingwall, J McHale, *A Question of Give and Take? Improving the Supply of Donor Organs for Transplantation* (1994) Kings Fund Institute. But note that far more people are considered eligible to receive a transplant than used to be the case.

[6] NHSBT, *Transplant Activity in the UK 2009/10* (2010).

[7] See D Price, *Human Tissue in Transplantation and Research* (2009) CUP, p 15.

[8] See A Cronin, 'Making the Margins Mainstream: Strategies to Maximise the Donor Pool' in Farrell, Price and Quigley (eds), *Organ Shortage: Ethics, Law and Pragmatism* (2011) CUP, p 104.

[9] *Organs for Transplant: A Report from the Organ Donation Taskforce* (2008) (hereafter ODT Report 1).

[10] *The Potential Impact of an Opt Out System for Organ Donation in the UK: An Independent Report from the Organ Donation Taskforce* (2008) (hereafter ODT Report 2).

Another strategy to increase the supply of organs focuses on living donors, with many ethicists advocating a 'market' in organs. But for the present, the emphasis endorsed in both reports of the ODT is on increasing the numbers of organs available for transplant by focusing on much better systems of identifying and recruiting potential organ donors and improving ways of maintaining the quality of organs removed from deceased donors. In December 2011, the government proposed that all new applicants for a driving licence should be required to state whether or not they would agree to donate their organs after death, introducing a form of 'mandated choice'. In the future it may become possible to 'grow' new organs from stem cells,[11] and the possibility of xenotransplantation, using genetically modified organs harvested from non-human animals, remains on the agenda, but looks less likely to materialise than five years ago. At present there remains a pressing need for organs donated by human donors.

Before examining the law in more detail, one or two points need to be understood about the mechanics of transplantation. First, the organ must be suitable for transplant – that means it must be healthy. The person from whom the organ is removed must be free of any systemic disease and the organ must retain a reasonable 'shelf-life'. Most deaths occur in the elderly. Organs are now taken from an increasingly older range of cadaver donors, but those who die of progressive organ failure, common in the very old, are unsuitable donors. Second, the organ must remain viable – in good condition. Either the transplant must take place a very short time after its removal from the donor, or means must be found to preserve it while it is transported to the potential recipient. Finally, there must be a tissue match between donor and recipient. Improvements in drugs used to prevent rejection of 'alien' organs have made it possible to use a wider range of donors with less emphasis on the perfect tissue match but a live transplant from a close relative is still an optimal choice. A healthy sibling may be able to provide a matched organ that can be transplanted within minutes of its removal from the donor.

The Human Tissue Act 2004 – an overview

17.2   The Human Tissue Act 2004 now regulates most of the issues relating to the removal, retention and use of human body parts and tissue.[12] It repeals all previous legislation, including the Human Tissue Act 1961 and the Human

---

[11]   See D Price, *Human Tissue in Transplantation and Research* (2009) CUP, pp 7–8.

[12]   S 53 of the Act adopts the term 'relevant material' and defines such material as '. . . material other than gametes, which consists of or includes human cells'. Embryos outside the human body, hair and nail clippings, are expressly excluded from the Act. This very broad definition covers more than organs, such as kidneys, and tissue, such as bone marrow, but does not mean that every section of the Act applies to every speck of 'human material': see D Price, 'The Human Tissue Act 2004' (2005) 68 *Modern Law Review* 798, at 800.

Organ Transplants Act 1989.[13] The 2004 Act regulates all aspects of human transplantation, whether the organs (or tissue) are removed from the living or the dead. However, scanning the Act itself, the reader will find surprisingly few direct references to transplantation. The Act sets out rules for twelve scheduled purposes involving the use of human organs and tissue. Transplantation is just one of the twelve.[14] For the most part, the broad rules which the Act imposes apply generally to transplantation. Only a few sections of the Act apply exclusively to transplants. The Act itself offers no more than a framework to regulate transplantation. The details are supplied by regulations to be made by the Department of Health, and Codes of Practice promulgated by the Human Tissue Authority (HTA).

The HTA was central to the Act,[15] and was established to regulate all matters concerning the removal, storage, use and disposal of human tissue (except for gametes and embryos).[16] The HTA is also the competent authority in the UK for the implementation of the European Union Tissue and Cells Directive.[17] We shall see that the Authority has a number of special responsibilities in relation to transplants. The HTA must have a majority of lay members. Its remit in the context of this chapter was principally to regulate transplantation. Another authority, the NHS Blood and Transplant (NHSBT),[18] was charged with operational matters relating to transplantation, and required to encourage donation and ensure the quality of the transplant service. The HTA has, however, also played a role in working to increase the number of organs made available for transplant when, on 26 April 2006, the HTA promulgated a new policy designed to increase the numbers of living donors by allowing new kinds of altruistic donation.[19] We saw in chapter 12 that in the government's review of arm's-length bodies, the Human Fertilisation and Embryology Authority (HFEA) was destined for abolition with its functions divided up between other bodies such as the Care Quality Commission and a new research regulator. The Academy of Medical Sciences has proposed the creation of a Health Research Agency to undertake the latter role.[20] The HTA faces the same fate.[21] Exactly which body will take over the functions described below remains to be seen. The role that the HTA plays in approving and monitoring

---

[13]   The Act also repeals the Human Tissue Act (Northern Ireland) 1962; the Corneal Tissue Act 1986 and the Anatomy Act 1984.

[14]   See Sch 1, Pt 1(7).

[15]   See ss 13–15 and Sch 2. Note that although different legislation (the Human Tissue (Scotland) Act) applies in Scotland, the HTA will perform various roles in Scotland.

[16]   Already regulated by the Human Fertilisation and Embryology Authority; see above at **12.2**.

[17]   See the Human Tissue (Quality and Safety for Human Application) Regulations 2007, SI 2007/1253.

[18]   Which survives the proposed cull of arm's-length bodies proposed in DH, *Liberating the NHS: Report of the Arms Length Bodies Review* (2010).

[19]   HTA, Press Release (26 April 2006).

[20]   Academy of Medical Sciences, *A New Pathway for the Research and Governance of Health Research* (2011), discussed above at **15.1, 15.2, 15.5**.

[21]   DH, *Liberating the NHS: Report of the Arms-Length Bodies Review* (2010).

live transplants looks hard to reassign and it should be noted that groups unhappy with the substantive provisions of the Human Tissue Act 2004 are making efforts to amend the legislation. In its report on the regulation of research, the Academy of Medical Sciences shares some of those concerns and recommends that the definition of 'relevant material' within the Act be amended to exclude plasma, serum, urine, faeces and saliva.[22] Should the Academy's proposals be accepted, there will be changes relating to the law addressing retention of, and research using, human tissue but no substantive change in the law governing transplantation.

The Human Tissue Act 2004, currently 'policed' by the HTA, rests on a number of central tenets. Explicit consent to most forms of the use of organs and tissue is required. Criminal penalties attach to certain breaches of the Act. A number of activities relating to the removal and use of tissue, and the conduct of post-mortem examinations, have to be licensed. Transplants do not require a licence, but certain kinds of transplant activities will require special approval from the HTA.

Live donor transplantation

17.3 For one person to subject himself to an unnecessary procedure for the benefit of another requires courage and altruism. A distinction must be made between donation of regenerative and non-regenerative organs. The blood donor undergoes temporary discomfort. His body replaces the blood he has lost. Blood and bone marrow are regenerative tissue. Some non-regenerative organs, such as the heart, are impossible for a living donor to donate in normal circumstances. However, what are possible are domino transplants, involving 'swaps' of heart and lungs. For example, a cystic fibrosis patient may need a heart and lung transplant. She receives a heart and lung from a cadaver organ. Her own healthy heart can, if she consents, be transplanted into another patient.[23]

The most common non-regenerative organ donated by a living person remains the kidney. There were 1,037 living kidney donors in 2009/10.[24] Techniques allowing transplants of lobes of the lung and segments of liver have increased the utility of live donations, but at a cost. The risk of death in a live kidney donation is about 1:3000 but rises to 1:100 for living liver donations.[25] The donor agrees to major surgery and accepts a significant risk to his own health.

---

[22] Academy of Medical Sciences, *A New Pathway for the Regulation and Governance of Health Research* (2011), para 7.4.

[23] As a domino transplant involves treatment of both patients, such procedures are not as such regulated by the HTA, but the HTA nonetheless gives guidance on good practice: see HTA, Code of Practice: *Donation of Organs, Tissue and Cells for Transplantation,* Code 2 (2009) (hereafter Code of Practice, Code 2), paras 27–28.

[24] See NHSBT, *Transplant Activity in the UK 2009/10* (2010).

[25] See ODT Report 1, para 1.7.

In 2009/10 there were twenty-three living liver donors.[26] The ODT commented that the acceptance of such risks to healthy people demonstrated 'the critical shortage of deceased donors'.[27] But it is not clear that living donation should be seen as second best and a mark of failure to recruit enough cadaver donors given that the live donations achieve better results in terms of the length of time that the transplanted organ continues to function, especially if the recipient received the organ without having to endure dialysis.

The law needs to be designed to ensure that such a donation is informed, truly voluntary, and not the result of coercion. And the British tradition has been that the donation of body products should be just that, a gift, not a sale. No part of a person's body should be treated as a commodity subject to the pressures of the market.[28] Section 32 of the Human Tissue Act 2004 continues the prohibition on sale of organs (or other bodily material) for transplantation, a ban initially imposed by the Human Organs Transplant Act 1989.[29] Markets remain illegal in the UK. Whether this should be so, we discuss later.

Adult donors

17.4 In the early days of transplantation, doubts were cast about whether it was lawful for a person to agree to donate a solid organ, such as a kidney, to another during his lifetime. As we have seen, inflicting actual bodily harm on another person can constitute a crime regardless of consent.[30] By 1995, the Law Commission[31] could say with confidence that '... once a valid consent has been forthcoming, English law now treats as lawful donation of regenerative tissue and also non-regenerative tissue not essential to life'. The Human Tissue Act 2004 provides a statutory basis for live donation of organs and tissue for transplantation.

Sections 1 and 3 of the Act provide in effect that it is lawful to remove organs from a living adult for transplant with, but only with, his *appropriate* consent. The law empowers a person to choose to give a kidney, or a lobe of her lung, or segment of liver, to another in need of a transplant. But what is an appropriate consent? Living donors are often closely related to the potential recipient. The potential donor may be the best match as a person whose com-

---

[26] See NHSBT, *Transplant Activity in the UK 2009/10* (2010).

[27] See ODT Report 1, para 1.7.

[28] See R M Titmuss, *The Gift Relationship: From Human Blood to Social Policy* (1971) Allen & Unwin.

[29] This Act was rushed through Parliament as a hasty response to a scandal involving the sale of human kidneys by four impoverished Turkish citizens in circumstances where it seemed highly likely that the 'vendors' were cruelly exploited.

[30] See *R v Brown* [1993] 2 All ER 75, HL.

[31] Law Commission Consultation Paper No 139, *Consent in the Criminal Law* (1995) HMSO, para 8.32.

patibility is such that a relative's life can be saved.[32] In such circumstances, the psychological pressure can be enormous. It becomes crucially important to establish that the donor did give a genuinely free and informed consent. The Act itself does not define what appropriate means. That task is left to the HTA, which has set out guidance on consent in two key Codes of Practice.[33] Both Codes emphasise the need for good communication. The potential donor must be given information about what will be done to her and the risks to her. She must be given reliable information about the chances of success. She must be warned about some of the risks of tissue typing. Tests might reveal that apparent siblings are not full siblings. A donor could discover that her supposed father is not after all her biological parent. Donors should be offered counselling, given time to make a decision and reassured that they are free to withdraw consent at any time up to the operation.

Nor is the donor's consent alone sufficient to make a live organ donation lawful. Under the Human Organs Transplant Act 1989, where the donor and recipient were not closely genetically related, it was a criminal offence to remove an organ for transplant without the authorisation of the Unrelated Live Transplant Authority (ULTRA). This rule was primarily designed to prevent covert sales of organs. The 1989 Act banned such sales, but the legislators suspected that organ vendors and purchasers might seek to bypass the ban. ULTRA had the task of ensuring that all apparently altruistic donations between strangers were truly altruistic. The law would be enforced, and potential donors could be protected from coercion or exploitation.

Section 33 of the Human Tissue Act 2004 extends the powers of the new HTA to oversee all live donations, including those between family members. The HTA must be satisfied that no money has changed hands and that other conditions prescribed by regulations are met.[34] All potential donations, whether by a stranger, a friend, or a sister, will be scrutinised. Is this right? The need to ensure a tissue match between donors and recipients means doctors will normally prefer a living donor closely related to the potential recipient. Close genetic relationships maximise the chances of a successful transplant. It might be argued that if we (as adults) choose to give a kidney, or a segment of liver, to a dying sibling, this is nobody else's business. Within the family, emotional pressure may be as potent a threat to our free will as poverty could be were sales of organs allowed. Questions must also be asked about donors' understanding of risk. As we have seen, the risk to a donor giving a kidney is small, but the donor of a liver segment faces a 1:100 risk of death.

---

[32] In one American case a court, not surprisingly, refused to *order* the only possible donor to submit to a bone-marrow transplant; *McFall v Shimp* (1978) 10 Pa D & C 3d.

[33] See Code of Practice, Code 2 (2009); and HTA, Code of Practice: Consent, Code 1 (2009) (hereafter Code of Practice, Code 1).

[34] See the Human Tissue Act 2004 (Persons Who Lack Capacity to Consent and Transplants) Regulations 2006, SI 2006/1659.

The regulations made under section 33 of the Human Tissue Act 2004 need to be read together with the HTA Code of Practice, Donation of Organs, Tissue and Cells for Transplantation.[35] Doctors responsible for any potential live donor of a solid organ, or part of an organ, or bone marrow, must refer the case to the HTA. The HTA must satisfy itself that the organ or bone marrow is not being sold. All live donations must be scrutinised to ensure a genuinely free consent has been given by the donor. The HTA will appoint Independent Assessors (IA) who will interview potential donors and recipients, satisfy themselves that the conditions set out by the HTA are fully met, and report to the HTA. The IA will be specially trained and senior health professionals. The Regulations and the Code of Practice distinguish between different kinds of live donation. When the donor and the recipient are genetically related or known to each other, what the HTA describes as 'genetically related donation' or 'emotionally related organ donation',[36] the IA simply reports to the HTA and on the basis of his approval, the donation may lawfully go ahead. Three other sorts of live donation involving competent adults are then identified, and more closely regulated. The first two involve an 'exchange' of donated organs.[37]

(1)   In a 'paired donation' a kidney will be removed from donor A and given to someone who is a stranger to him. In return, a kidney removed from donor B will be given to a relative or close friend of donor A. Assume your husband needs a kidney transplant but you are not a suitable tissue match. If you agree to donate your kidney to B, a relative of B will provide a kidney for your spouse.

(2)   'Pooled donations' involve a linked series of 'paired donations'. For example, donor A gives a kidney to the son of donor B. Donor B gives a kidney to the husband of donor C. Donor C's kidney is given to the wife of donor A. These 'exchange' donations increase the likelihood of live donations. Should a brother be dying of renal failure and none of his relatives are a tissue match, his family could volunteer to give an organ to someone else for whom one of them is a match. And then, in exchange, directly or indirectly, a relative of the recipient will donate an organ to the brother.

In both the above kinds of donation, two IAs must make a report which is then considered by a panel of at least three members of the HTA. The panel will decide whether or not to approve the donation.

(3)   Finally, there are what the HTA describes as 'altruistic non-directed donations', wholly altruistic donations, where the donor gives an organ with no conditions, and no expectation of any exchange benefiting those close to her.[38] A rigorous procedure is set out to monitor such altruistic donations. The donor must undergo medical, surgical and psychiatric assessments. She must be interviewed by an Independent Assessor who will make recommendations to an HTA panel of at least three members.

---

[35] Code of Practice, Code 2.
[36] The IA must seek evidence to prove the relevant relationship.
[37] See SI 2006/1659, reg 1.12, and Code of Practice, Code 2, para 26.
[38] See Code of Practice, Code 2, paras 65–92.

Child donors

17.5 More difficult questions arise where organs or tissue are to be taken from children. Should children ever be used as organ donors?[39] In the USA, the courts sanctioned such a course of action nearly fifty years ago. The cases involved three sets of minor twins aged nineteen, fourteen and fourteen respectively. In each case, the healthy twin was willing to donate a kidney to his dying brother, but it was not clear whether the law permitted this. Applications were made to the court for guidance. The court focused on the psychiatric evidence given to show that each donor had been fully informed about the nature of the procedure and also that, if it were not possible to perform the operation and the sick twin were to die, there would be a resulting grave emotional impact of the surviving twin. This enabled the court to be satisfied in each case that the operation was for the benefit not only of the recipient but also of the donor, and that accordingly a parent was capable of giving consent to such a 'therapeutic' procedure, just as he could to any other medical treatment needed by his child.[40]

In England, until the Human Tissue Act 2004, this was a 'grey' area of law. It became routine practice for parents to authorise bone-marrow donations (and skin grafts) from a healthy child to a sick sibling. Solid organ donations from one living child to another appear to have been ruled out by the transplant community itself. Bone-marrow donations[41] proceeded on the basis that the harvesting of bone marrow involves some discomfort, but minimal risk, for the donor child. The psychological benefit of a sibling's survival or well-being was said to outweigh any distress to the donors. The balance of burdens and benefits made the 'donation' a procedure in the best interests of the child and so an intervention parents could properly authorise. But how does a parent make an impartial evaluation of the interests of one child when the life of another of her children is at risk?

The Human Tissue Act 2004 clarifies the law, and the HTA has ensured that any donation by a person under eighteen is scrutinised by both the HTA and the courts. We deal first with children too young to consent on their own behalf. Where it is proposed to use such a child as a living donor, such a donation will require appropriate consent from a person with parental responsibility for the child.[42] That means in most cases consent from his parents.[43] It will not be strictly necessary for both parents to consent, even when they share

---

[39] See D Price, A Garwood-Gowers, 'Transplantation from Minors: Are Children Other People's Medicine?' (1995) 1 *Contemporary Issues in Law* 1.

[40] Curran, 'A Problem of Consent: Kidney Transplantation in Minors' (1959) 34 *New York University Law Review* 891.

[41] See now HTA, Code of Practice: Donation of Allogeneic Bone Marrow and Peripheral Blood Stem Cells for Transplantation, Code 6 (2009) (hereafter Code of Practice, Code 6). We do not address this Code in detail but note that the level of scrutiny of bone-marrow donations by young children has been increased.

[42] See Human Tissue Act 2004, s 2(3).

[43] Where parents are married or register the birth of the child together they automatically share parental responsibility. In other cases, the unmarried father will need

parental responsibility for the child, but we submit that the nature of the procedure is such that a court would be likely to wish to ensure that both parents agreed to the donation.[44] Parental authorisation alone will not suffice to make a donation by a minor lawful, even to a sibling. First the approval of a court must be obtained and then just as with adult donors, the donation will need to be scrutinised by the HTA. Regulations made under the Act require that any proposal to use a child[45] as a solid organ donor must be referred to the HTA for advice, and considered by a panel of three members of the Authority.[46] The HTA also states that 'Children can be considered as living organ donors only in extremely rare circumstances'.[47]

What of older children? The younger American twins were fourteen. Even if legally not of an age to give independent consent, at fourteen the child can be a party to the decision. Many fourteen-year-olds would be considered *Gillick competent* in this country if what was in issue was therapeutic treatment.[48] Section 2(2) of the Human Tissue Act empowers the *Gillick competent* minor to donate organs and tissue. If a minor of fifteen or seventeen is considered sufficiently mature and intelligent to weigh up the benefits or risks of donating an organ, her consent will authorise the donation. As with younger children, the approval of a court must first be sought and then the proposed donation will be further scrutinised by the HTA. Doctors and the HTA will be anxious to ensure that any such decision is fully understood by the young person and not subject to undue pressure from the family. So, as is the case with younger children, all proposed live donations of organs[49] involving *Gillick competent* minors will be examined by a panel of three from the HTA. The more mature teenager, not her parents, can decide to offer a kidney to her brother. The HTA will exert a more intense scrutiny of her decision than if she were eighteen. Should a minor be allowed to donate a kidney? If a beloved twin needed such a transplant, it is not difficult to suggest that the physical risk to a willing donor is outweighed by the emotional benefit.

Mentally incapacitated 'donors'

17.6 In the USA, in *Strunk v Strunk*[50] a twenty-eight-year-old married man who was dying of a fatal kidney disease sought the permission of the court for a kidney donation from his twenty-seven-year-old brother, who was said to

either to seek an order granting him such parental responsibility or enter into a formal agreement with the mother.

44 See above at **14.14**.
45 SI 2006/1659, reg 12(2)(a).
46 See Code of Practice, Code 2, paras 47–49, 69–70.
47 Code of Practice, Code 2, para 47.
48 Prior to the Human Tissue Act 2004, it was doubtful whether any minor was legally competent to consent to organ donation. See *Re W (A Minor) (Medical Treatment)* [1992] 4 A11 ER 627 at 635 and 647.
49 For regulation of bone-marrow donations, see Code of Practice, Code 6, paras 70–86.
50 (1969) 35 ALR (3d) 683.

have a mental age of six and who was detained in a mental institution. The Kentucky court emphasised the emotional and psychological dependence of the mentally disabled sibling on his brother, and that his well-being would be jeopardised more severely by the loss of his brother than by the removal of a kidney. Accordingly, it applied a doctrine of 'substituted judgement', to allow the court to act as they believed the mentally disabled brother would have acted had he possessed all his faculties, and gave consent on behalf of the donor. Subsequent cases in the USA stressed that in authorising organ donation on behalf of a mentally disabled adult the court must be fully satisfied that the interests of the donor will be served by the transplant. The benefits to him of his sibling's, or relative's, survival must be real, not speculative.[51]

Before the Human Tissue Act 2004 came into force, in *Re Y*,[52] Connell J granted a declaration that bone-marrow donation from a severely learning disabled woman of twenty-five to her thirty-six-year-old sister, who was dying of leukaemia, was lawful. Of the elder sister's relations, only her learning disabled sister proved to be a compatible donor. She was, it was agreed, incapable of giving consent to the procedure. The relationship between the sisters themselves was not especially close. The older sister's illness had meant that visits had become fewer. The relationship between the younger sister and her mother was close, as was the relationship between mother and her older, sick daughter. The judge found that if the older daughter died, her death would have an adverse impact on the mother. She would be less able to visit Y and much occupied in caring for her grandchild if the child's mother died. If the transplant went ahead, the 'positive relationship' between Y and her mother would be enhanced, as would the relationship between the sisters. The risk and discomfort to Y would be minimal. Accordingly it was in Y's best interests to allow the bone-marrow transplant to go ahead. Connell J made it clear that he was not setting a precedent for kidney 'donation' by a learning disabled person. He said:

It is doubtful that this case would act as a useful precedent where the surgery involved is more intrusive than in this case . . .

Should he have sanctioned a transplant which amounts to enforced donation? The 'benefit' to Y seems somewhat remote on the facts of the case.

Regulations[53] made under section 6 of the Human Tissue Act 2004 provide that organs or tissue can be removed from a person lacking mental capacity for transplant if, but only if, such a procedure is in that patient's best interests. Any such proposal must first receive approval from the Court of Protection[54] and must then be referred to and scrutinised by the HTA. It is difficult to see how the discomfort and surgery needed to remove a solid organ could be justified

---

51 See *Re Peslinski* 226 NW 2d 180 at 181 (Wisconsin); *Re Richardson* (1973) 284 So 2d 185.
52 *Re Y (Mental Incapacity: Bone Marrow Transplant)* [1997] Fam 110.
53 See SI 2006/1659 and Code of Practice, Code 2, paras 50–53, 78–83.
54 Code of Practice, Code 2, para 50, and see the Department of Constitutional Affairs, *Mental Capacity Act: Code of Practice* (updated April 2007), para 6.16.

by a supposed emotional benefit. If the proposed donor cannot comprehend what is done to her, the balancing exercise becomes somewhat mythical.

Cadaver transplantation

17.7 Although the number of live donations is rising fast, the need for much greater numbers of cadaver donors remains acute. As we shall see later,[55] a person has no legal right at common law to determine what shall happen to his body after his death. A body, or part of it, cannot ordinarily be the subject matter of ownership, and normally it is the legal duty of the close relatives of a deceased or those who are in 'lawful possession' of the body to arrange for its disposal at the earliest opportunity. So it is not legally possible for a person to impose a duty upon others that she be cremated after death. All she can do is to indicate that she desires to be cremated, and her executors or family are free to comply with or ignore such a wish as they see fit. At common law, a person had no legal power to donate organs from his body after his death; equally nobody has any right to interfere with a corpse, and any such interference would be a criminal act.[56] It was feared that cadaver transplantation might be illegal. Legislation was needed.

In 1952, the Corneal Grafting Act, later amended by the Corneal Tissue Act 1986, authorised the removal and use of eyes for therapeutic purposes in some circumstances. This statute attracted little publicity, nor was there much more public interest when, in 1961, the Human Tissue Act 1961 widened the law to cover any other parts of the body. Although the 1961 Act served as a model for similar legislation in many other countries, it proved to be unsatisfactory in almost every respect. It is repealed and replaced by the Human Tissue Act 2004.

Before examining the provisions of the 2004 Act in more detail, we need to address the problems with which the Act engages. What should be the basis on which organs can lawfully be removed from a dead body for transplant into another person? How can the law maximise the numbers of organs made available for transplant and ensure that organs can be removed and transplanted in a state likely to be 'fit for purpose'? The philosopher John Harris[57] proposed a radical and simple solution. Organ retrieval from the bodies of the dead should be lawful without any need for either the authorisation of the deceased or any consent from her family. The dead person has no interests sufficient to outweigh the needs of a patient whose life depends on a transplant.

---

[55] See below at **18.4**.

[56] In *R v Lennox-Wright* [1973] Crim LR 529, an unqualified person removed eyes from a cadaver for further use in another hospital. He was successfully prosecuted for contravening Human Tissue Act 1961, s 1(4), which prohibited removal save 'by a fully registered medical practitioner'.

[57] J Harris, 'The Survival Lottery' (1975) 50 *Philosophy* 81.

Organ conscription would replace organ donation. Harris[58] himself recognises that such a radical proposal would be highly unlikely to gain parliamentary support and so has also endorsed a doctrine of 'presumed consent' as second best.

'Presumed consent', sometimes referred to as 'opt-out' or 'contracting out', means in effect that the law should allow organs to be removed for transplant unless the deceased had expressly put on record, for example, on a public register, that he had objected to such use. Relatives would lose any right of veto. Such a law, which now exists in a number of European countries, should, in theory, enable surgeons to acquire all the organs they need, unless there happened to be a dramatic change in public attitude so that large numbers of people go to the trouble of registering their objections.

'Presumed consent' is, however, a much more complex issue than first appears and what we can say here is merely introductory.[59] Regimes of 'presumed consent' differ considerably, with the majority, whatever the letter of the law, operating a system of 'soft' presumed consent. Relatives are still consulted and if they object, their objections are normally respected. Very few countries implement 'hard' presumed consent and simply remove organs unless the deceased's name is entered on the register of objectors. A trans-national comparison suggested that donation rates improved by 25–30 per cent if the law of the country allowed presumed consent. In Belgium, law reforms introducing 'presumed consent' rules for organ donation resulted in a significant increase in the number of cadaver organs transplanted. Belgium offers a particularly interesting test case for law reform. Laws implementing 'presumed consent' were implemented in one part of the country, but not universally.[60] Spain has the most successful cadaver donation programme in Europe and the law endorses presumed consent.[61] But in Spain the system is markedly 'soft' with the family still permitted to refuse to allow the donation to go ahead. And study of the Spanish model suggests that only many years after the introduction of laws on presumed consent did donation rates rise. The major factor in the Spanish success is a well resourced and highly organised system for identifying potential donors and obtaining the family's agreement.[62]

Two other options should be noted: 'mandated choice' and 'required request'. In the first, the law requires that each citizen places on record whether he consents or objects to the removal of his organs after death. The proposal by the

---

58 J Harris, 'Law and Regulation of Retained Organs: The Ethical Issues' (2002) 22 *Legal Studies* 527.

59 For a full discussion of the issue, see D Price, *Human Tissue and Transplantation and Research* (2010) CUP, ch 5. And see ODT Report 2.

60 See I Kennedy *et al*, 'The Case for 'Presumed Consent' in Organ Donation' (1998) 351 *Lancet* 1650.

61 A Abadie, S Guy, 'The Impact of Presumed Consent Legislation on Cadaveric Organ Donation: A Cross Country Study' (2006) 25 *Journal of Health Economics* 599.

62 M Quigley, M Brazier, R Chadwick *et al*, 'The Organs Crisis and the Spanish Model: Theoretical Versus Practical Consideration' (2008) 34 *Journal of Medical Ethics* 223.

UK government that all new applicants for a driving licence should be required to make such a choice looks like a variant of mandated choice.[63] 'Required request' focuses on the role of doctors rather than the deceased and the family. It is suggested that one of the main reasons for the shortfall in donor organs is the failure by doctors to ask relatives to agree cadaver organ donations. A number of American states[64] enacted legislation requiring hospital staff to request permission from the deceased's family to remove suitable organs. The King's Fund Report[65] suggested it was unlikely to work and might result in undue pressure being placed on families.

The enactment of the Human Tissue Act 2004 ruled out reforms based on 'conscription', 'presumed consent', 'mandated choice' or 'required request', and the two reports of the ODT also rejected reform of the Act relating to consent to donation. The controversy generated by revelations that organs had been retained for research, education and diagnosis without consent, created a climate in which new laws even appearing to endorse an element of coercion would not command support. Explicit consent thus becomes the fundamental condition for all cadaver donations as much as donations by living donors.

Beating- and non-beating-heart donors

17.8 Whatever the legal rules governing consent to donation, any principled basis for donation must also take account of the practical need for the shortest possible period between removal of an organ and its transplantation into the intended recipient. We noted earlier that a successful transplant requires that the organ to be transplanted remains viable – ie it has not, to put it brutally, begun to decay in the time between removal from the dead donor and implantation in the recipient. When a beating-heart donor is used, the donor will usually have been on a ventilator and diagnosed as brain-stem dead. Oxygen will have continued to perfuse his organs up to the time that the heart or kidney is removed. However, the number of potential donors who are diagnosed as brain-stem dead while on a ventilator remains small.[66]

Beating-heart donors (now referred to as donors after brain death: DBD) are patients whose initial condition resulted in them being placed on a ventilator in the hope that treatment could be instituted to prolong their lives. Once they are diagnosed as brain-stem dead, but with the heart still beating, arrangements may be made for organ donation. In the 1990s, elective ventilation was seen as a possible solution to the problem and implemented at a hospital in Exeter. Elective ventilation would involve patients dying from strokes or similar condi-

---

[63] See D Price, *Human Tissue in Transplantation and Research* (2009) CUP, pp 82–87.
[64] I Kennedy and A Grubb, *Medical Law* (3rd edn, 2000) Butterworths, pp 1048–1057.
[65] New, Solomon, Dingwall, McHale, *A Question of Give and Take; Improving the Supply of Donor Organs for Transplantation*, (1994) Kings Fund Institute, pp 60–63.
[66] Although the NHSBT reported a 2 per cent rise in such donors in 2009/10: see *Transplant Activity in the UK 2009/10* (2010).

tions being transferred to the intensive-care unit and ventilated until brain-stem death occurs. In this way, their organs are maintained in optimum condition for organ retrieval. Patients would be brain-stem dead when organs are removed, but not legally dead when ventilated. Ventilation would be performed *solely* to enable the patient to become a potential organ donor and confer no benefit on him. Is elective ventilation lawful? The practice was abandoned well before the enactment of the Human Tissue Act 2004 on the grounds that the ventilation of the dying patient constituted an assault on her. There is nothing in the Human Tissue Act 2004 expressly authorising or prohibiting elective ventilation. But is such a procedure an assault in all cases? At the time a decision is made to transfer the patient to intensive-care he is unlikely to be able to consent to such a procedure himself. And so it is argued that the transfer to benefit the potential organ recipient is unlikely to be judged to be in his interests[67] and might fall foul of section 4 of the Mental Capacity Act 2005.[68]

Should elective ventilation be lawful? The Law Commission's original report on the treatment of adults lacking mental capacity suggests that with proper safeguards, such a procedure could be ethical and lawful. The Mental Capacity Act 2005 does not expressly implement this proposal. Perhaps two cases should be differentiated. If I choose, not just to carry a donor card, but to indicate that were I to suffer a stroke or other cerebral incident and recovery of consciousness was not possible, I should be ventilated to maximise my utility as an organ donor, that advance directive is as entitled to respect as any other. If I have expressed no such wish, should I, while still alive, be used as means to other ends even with my family's concurrence? The Mental Capacity Act 2005 gives statutory force to advance refusals of treatment but not alas in this context, advance requests. Could one argue nonetheless that if we have expressly requested elective ventilation to bolster our wish to be organ donors, then that procedure does, paradoxically, become something done in our best interests? We would agree with Price that the time has come to revisit the troubled topic of elective ventilation.[69]

Efforts to maintain the rate of organ donation in the UK now depend ever more heavily on the use of non-heart-beating donors,[70] now sometimes referred to as donors after cardiac death (DCD). The donors' hearts would have stopped and death would be diagnosed by the traditional cardio-respiratory criteria. DCD donors can only donate non-vital organs such as kidneys and corneas. The statement by the Chief Rabbi for England in January 2011 that Jewish law only recognised a definition of death based on traditional cardio-respiratory criteria

---

[67] See J V McHale, 'Elective Ventilation – Pragmatic Solution or Ethical Minefield?' (1995) 11 *Professional Negligence* 23.

[68] See above **6.10**.

[69] D Price, 'End of Life Treatment of Potential Organ Donors: Paradigm Shifts in Intensive and Emergency Care' (2011) 19 *Medical Law Review* 86–116.

[70] In 2009–10, the number of DCD (non-heart-beating donors) rose to 336, an increase of 17 per cent on the previous year, see NHS BT, *Transplant Activity in the UK 2009/10* (2010), p 1.

will limit the numbers of organs that may be donated from within the Orthodox Jewish community.[71]

Any organs removed from a DCD donor need to be rushed to the recipients as lack of oxygenation will swiftly trigger the start of decay. Cold perfusion of the organ (or the whole body) will extend the time in which organs remain viable. Such a procedure needs to be done as soon as the heart stops beating, at a time when it cannot be ascertained if the deceased had consented to donation and relatives are not at the scene. Section 43 of the Human Tissue Act 2004 allows hospitals, or other relevant authorities, to take whatever steps are immediately necessary to preserve parts of the body for transplantation. What is done must be the minimal and least invasive steps possible. It means this: a young man is brought into hospital after suffering inevitably fatal brain injuries in a road accident. His heart stops before his family can be contacted or even his identity ascertained. Doctors may lawfully use cold perfusion to preserve his organs until either it can be shown he had consented in advance to organ donation, or his family can be contacted.[72]

But could other steps (short of elective ventilation) be taken earlier, prior to the patient's death, to increase the potential that the dying patient could become an organ donor? Such steps could include delaying for a short time the withdrawal of treatment, and measures such as administering drugs close to the point of death to protect the viability of the organs destined for donation.[73] The steps taken would, however, be in the interests of the potential organ recipient and not in the clinical interests of the dying patient. Thus some doctors argue that doing anything to the patient before his death is unethical and unlawful given that patient's inability to consent for himself and his right to be treated in his own best interests. But 'best interests' embrace more than narrow clinical considerations and for the many dying patients who wish to be organ donors, interventions to assist in the realisation of that wish once there is no hope of recovery, are part and parcel of their best interests.[74] Such a view is gaining increasing official sanction.[75]

The Human Tissue Act 2004

17.9   As we have reiterated, the 2004 Act adopts a principle of explicit consent for cadaver donation; Parliament expressly rejected calls to introduce a

[71]   See above **16.2**.
[72]   Code of Practice, Code 2, paras 123–132.
[73]   Fully discussed in D Price, 'End of Life Treatment of Potential Organ Donors: Paradigm Shifts in Intensive and Emergency Care' (2010) 18 *Medical Law Review* (forthcoming).
[74]   See J Coggon, M Brazier, P Murphy, D Price and M Quigley, 'Best Interests and Potential Organ Donors' (2008) 336 *BMJ* 1346.
[75]   ODT Report 1, paras 4.13–4.15; D Price, 'End of Life Treatment of Potential Organ Donors: Paradigm Shifts in Intensive and Emergency Care' (2010) 18 *Medical Law Review* (forthcoming).

system of presumed consent for transplant purposes. Removal of organs and tissue after death for the purposes of transplantation are governed by rules identical to those applying to removal of tissue after death for those other purposes, such as medical research or education. When the proposed donor died over the age of eighteen, removal of organs for transplantation will be lawful if:

(1) the deceased himself gave appropriate consent before he died; *or* if he gave no consent, but nor did he veto organ donation;

(2) consent is given by the deceased's nominated representative – that is a person expressly nominated by the deceased to make decisions about the use of his body parts before his death; *or* if the deceased neither made his own decision about donation, nor did he nominate a representative;

(3) consent is given by a close family member or friend – what is described as 'a person who stood in a qualifying relationship with the deceased before his death'.[76]

Let us take each case in turn. When the deceased has made his own decision about donation of organs after his death, the Human Tissue Act 2004 provides that his consent alone is sufficient to authorise the transplant team to take his organs.[77] In theory, the objections of his family carry no weight. But there are two difficulties. First, the 2004 Act prescribes no formalities to govern post-mortem donations for transplant.[78] There is no requirement that directions be given in writing. So, extra-legal measures to ensure easy access to information about donors are crucial. The first-named author has carried a donor card for decades. It resides in her handbag. Should she be killed in a road accident, the handbag will not necessarily accompany her to the casualty unit where she is declared brain-stem dead. A 1992 survey showed only 27 per cent of people had donor cards and only one in five carried their card with them at any time.[79] The NHS Organ Donation Register is thus of paramount importance. Just over 17m potential donors were registered at the end of March 2010.[80] Where donation is a possibility, the first job for staff at the hospital where the potential donor dies is to check the register. When evidence of the deceased's wishes is available, his wishes should not be subject to any family veto. The objections of a grieving widower do not in law override his wife's authorisation. Implementing such a policy in practice will be harder. The HTA urges doctors to discuss this dilemma sensitively with the family. They should be encouraged to accept the deceased's wishes. Their last sentence of advice on this matter is telling: 'There may nevertheless be cases in which donation is inappropriate and each case should be considered individually'.[81] We hope

---

76 S 3(6).
77 And equally his veto will prohibit any removal of organs for transplant.
78 Unlike donation for anatomical examination or public display, see below **18.7**.
79 New, Solomon, Dingwall, McHale, *A Question of Give and Take: Improving the Supply of Donor Organs for Transplantation* (1994) Kings Fund Institute.
80 See NHSBT, *Transplant Activity in the UK 2009/10* (2010), p 69. Of 959 deceased donors in 2009–10, 30 per cent were on the register.
81 Code of Practice, Code 2, para 100.

that this compassionate sentiment will not routinely be allowed to override the gift of life offered by the deceased.

The second means of authorising organ donation is by way of a nominated representative. The Human Tissue Act 2004 requires any such nomination to be in writing and witnessed. It may be asked why one should delegate such a task to someone else?[82] If a person has given the thought to donation required to make a nomination, you might expect her to express her own wishes directly. One reason for nominating a proxy may be a case where the potential donor is aware of divisions in his family about organ donation. The family might belong to a faith where more orthodox adherents rule out organ donation. The deceased may wish to ensure that authority to decide about uses of his body rest with a relative who shares his own views. The HTA stresses that in such a case it is the nominated representative whose decision is crucial and he cannot be overruled by other family members, but advises that doctors should ensure that the representative and the family have discussed the question of donation.[83]

In this absence of express authorisation by the deceased or a proxy chosen by him, the power to donate organs falls to the family. The Act sets out a hierarchy of relatives.[84] Whilst the 1961 Act spoke vaguely of the need to ascertain that no 'surviving relative' objected to the removal of organs for transplant, the 2004 Act requires the consent of a relative (or exceptionally, a friend) if no directions have been given by the deceased, or his chosen proxy. Staff seeking consent should first approach the deceased's spouse or partner.[85] If he or she declines to make a decision, or the deceased had no spouse or partner, those seeking consent then work their way through the following list:[86] (1) parent or child; (2) siblings; (3) grandparent or grandchild; (4) nephews or nieces; (5) step-parents; (6) half-siblings; (7) friend of longstanding. In what will often be the case, where more than one individual falls into any of these categories, the consent of one person alone will suffice to make removal of organs for transplant lawful.[87] Both authors are married, so our cases would be easy; our surviving husbands would decide whether our organs could be used for transplant. Should, alas, those same husbands not survive us, the decision would fall to Margot Brazier's adult daughter, and one of Emma Cave's surviving parents. Authorisation from one parent alone would suffice.

Unlike the Human Tissue Act 1961, section 2 of the 2004 Act expressly addresses cadaver donations from minors. It provides that where a person under eighteen has given advance consent to organ donation at a point in her

---

[82] S 4.
[83] Code of Practice, Code 2, para 107.
[84] S 27(4).
[85] '[A] person is another's partner if the two of them (whether of different sexes or the same sex) live as partners in an enduring family relationship', s 54(8).
[86] See s 27(8).
[87] See s 27(6).

life when she was sufficiently mature and intelligent to make such a decision for herself, her consent authorises cadaver transplantation. The *Gillick competent* minor can determine what happens to her body after her death too. In theory, her parents have no say in the matter. Establishing *Gillick competence* retrospectively will be hard. Overriding grieving parents will be painful. Where a child has expressed no wishes of her own, the decision falls to a person with parental responsibility[88] immediately prior to her death. This will normally be her parents. Again, in theory, the consent of one parent alone will be enough.

Violating the Human Tissue Act 2004

17.10 One of the principal causes of the failure of the Human Tissue Act 1961 was that no provision was made for a criminal penalty or civil redress for breach of the Act.[89] The 2004 Act[90] imposes criminal sanctions for any failure to comply with the Act's rules requiring consent for removal of organs for transplant. Any removal of cadaver organs without appropriate consent is a criminal offence unless the person removing the organs reasonably believes that he acts on the basis of such an appropriate consent. Any false representation that such a consent has been obtained is equally a criminal offence. Both offences carry the possibility of a prison sentence of up to three years. Any prosecution requires the consent of the Director of Public Prosecutions.

Some practical problems: the coroner

17.11 The kinds of death likely to yield organs for transplant may often be the kinds of death likely to involve referral to the coroner, for example a fit, healthy adult suffers massive brain injuries in a road traffic collision. Where there is reason to believe that an inquest may have to be held on a body, or a post-mortem examination may be required by the coroner, it will also be necessary to obtain the consent of the coroner to the removal of any part of the body and so risks delaying the opportunity to remove organs. This may be the case particularly where a coroner regards his duty to act as coroner as being of greater importance than the secondary power which he has to authorise the use of organs before his coroner's duties are complete. In a controversial case in Leicester in 1980, the father of a girl who had died in a road accident had given surgeons permission to use any of her organs, including her heart, which had been removed by surgeons. At a subsequent inquest, the coroner complained that he had not given permission for the heart to be removed since permission had been sought from him only for the removal of a kidney. He

---

[88] Or if there is no such person, if for example, parents and child died together in a road traffic collision, consent must be sought from the nearest qualifying relative, usually a grandparent.

[89] See P D G Skegg, 'Liability for the Unauthorised Removal of Cadavers Transplantation Material' (1974) 14 *Medicine, Science and the Law* 153.

[90] See s 5.

therefore directed that in future written permission would have to be obtained from him and countersigned by a pathologist. This incident highlighted the problem that coroners, acting in pursuance of what they regarded as their legal duties, could adversely restrict the use of organs even where parents or other relatives had consented. It was for such reasons that the Home Secretary issued guidance to coroners, stressing that it was not part of a coroner's function to place obstacles in the way of the development of medical science or to take moral or ethical decisions in this matter, and that the coroners should assist rather than hinder the procedure for organ removal. A coroner should refuse his consent only where there might be later criminal proceedings in which the organ might be required as evidence, or if the organ itself might be the cause or partial cause of death, or where its removal might impede further inquiries.[91] The HTA gives complementary advice to doctors and donor co-ordinators about how to proceed in case of potential organ donation that may properly involve the coroner.[92]

Some practical problems: establishing death

17.12   In chapter 16, we noted that heart-beating donors were not under traditional definitions of death strictly 'dead'. The needs of transplant medicine provided the impetus to reformulate that traditional view of death as the irreversible cessation of heartbeat and respiration. The difficulty in persuading the public that 'brain-stem death' truly constitutes the death of a person has beset organ transplantation for decades. And, as we have seen in 2011, both Jewish and Islamic scholars and leaders voiced the judgment that within their religious laws 'brain-stem death' could not be accepted, the person was only dead when the heart stopped beating.[93] Even among those who rationally accept the concept of brain-stem death, fears have been voiced that doctors might have conflicting interests in that, on the one hand, their duty would be to act in the best interests of the ill or dying patient to keep him alive and yet, on the other, there might be pressures to certify a potential donor's death at the earliest possible moment to enable organs to be removed for the benefit of potential recipients.

In 1975, the British Transplantation Society sought to allay public fears by recommending a Code of Practice for Organ Transplantation Surgery (finally agreed in 1979) to provide safeguards for those who needed reassurance about possible abuses of practice by over-zealous transplant teams.[94] Extensive guid-

---

[91]   HC (65) 1977. And see Home Office, *When Sudden Death Occurs: Coroners and Inquests* (2005), p 2, explaining how family can donate their relatives' tissues and organs for transplantation and stipulating that the coroner's consent is required.

[92]   Code of Practice, Code 2, Appendix B.

[93]   See above **16.2**.

[94]   For an argument that it should be permissible to remove organs before brain-stem death is established, see J Savelescu, 'Death, Us and Our Bodies: Personal Reflections' (2003) 29 *Journal of Medical Ethics* 127.

ance to ensure that adequate steps to confirm a diagnosis of brain-stem death are now to be found in the Code of Practice for the Diagnosis and Confirmation of Death, published by the Academy of Medical Royal Colleges.[95] The Code sets out detailed rules including that before organs are removed from a body for transplant, death should be certified by two doctors, one of whom has been qualified for at least five years; neither of these doctors should be members of a transplantation team and at least one of them should be a consultant.

A market in organs

17.13 As we will see, the thrust of current policy in relation to transplantation (endorsed and expanded by the ODT) is to seek to improve the systems for identifying potential cadaver donors and to use public education to encourage voluntary altruistic donations. Whether that strategy will suffice to make up the shortfall in organs needed for transplant remains to be seen. Those who doubt its efficacy attack a tradition that has long held sway in the UK – the tradition that bodily products should be freely given and not traded.[96] Section 32 of the Human Tissue Act 2004 bans payments for live or cadaver organs, although allowing payment of expenses within conditions prescribed by the HTA.[97] The European Convention on Human Rights and Biomedicine[98] states forcefully:

> The human body and its parts shall not, as such, give rise to financial gain.

In support of maintaining a prohibition of a market in organs are a cluster of arguments. They centre on four questions:

(1) Would financial incentives to sell your own, or your deceased relative's organs, risk endangering the safety of organ transplants? In their anxiety to obtain payment might people conceal medical conditions which could endanger the recipient?[99]

(2) Is there a risk that financial pressure on potential vendors is such that they would give a less than voluntary and informed consent. There is evidence from the developing world that economic duress operates to pressure the poor into selling organs to the rich.

(3) Is it intrinsically wrong that, even if properly informed, poorer people should 'have' to 'earn' part of their living by selling off body parts?

(4) In sum, do markets degrade?[100]

---

[95] Academy of Medical Royal Colleges, *Code of Practice for the Diagnosis and Confirmation of Death* (2008) discussed above at **16.2**.

[96] Radcliffe-Richards *et al*, 'The Case for Allowing Kidney Sales' (1998) 351 *Lancet* 1950.

[97] See Code of Practice, Code 2, paras 42–46.

[98] Art 21.

[99] At the heart of Titmuss's argument in *The Gift Relationship: From Human Blood to Social Policy* (1971) Allen & Unwin.

[100] See M Radin, 'Market – Inalienability' (1987) 100 *Harvard Law Review* 1849; N Duxbury, 'Do Markets Degrade?' [1996] 59 *Modern Law Review* 331.

Those proposing markets do so cautiously. They stress the vulnerability of the person needing the transplant. Her life is at risk. Harris and Erin argue that a regulated market,[101] where the NHS is the only permitted 'purchaser', would ensure (1) the quality of organs 'sold' and (2) rigorously monitor the consent process. Provision would be made to ensure that the vendor was adequately informed and acted freely. Fears of exploitation could be met in a regulated market. As to the distastefulness of the poor becoming organ banks, it is contended that worldwide the rich have benefits denied the poor. Mason and Laurie[102] question whether commercialism and altruism are irreconcilable values. They ask why one poor and needy person is allowed to risk his brain in the boxing ring, when another is barred from selling his kidney. They remind us that illegal markets across the world already exploit the poor. Janet Radcliffe-Richards,[103] leading the advocates for markets, sums up the debate:

> The weakness of the familiar arguments suggests that they are attempts to justify the deep feelings of repugnance which are the real driving force of the prohibition, and feelings of repugnance among the rich and healthy, no matter how strongly felt cannot justify removing the only hope of the destitute and dying. This is why we conclude that the issue should be considered again, with scrupulous impartiality.

For the most part, advocates for markets focus on living vendors. But why not allow payments for cadaver organs? The risk of harming the donor's health is nil. 'Donors' might see the promise of an organ for payment as an alternative, or a supplement, to life insurance. Relatives auctioning off Grandma's kidneys might be distasteful, unless your child was dying for want of a kidney. Mason and Laurie[104] find '. . . payment for organs of the dead far less easy to justify than payment to a living donor'. But they somewhat reluctantly suggest that this may come to pass. The justification for banning payments needs more careful thought. The 'safety' arguments advanced by Titmuss[105] have proved fallible in the context of blood donation.[106]

Other inducements[107]

17.14   In debating the ethics of payments for organs, other forms of inducement to donate need to be considered. Is there an issue about any form of inducement or incentive to donate or is it simply money that is seen as 'evil'? In

---

[101] See C Erin and J Harris, 'An Ethical Market in Human Organs' (2003) 29 *Journal of Medical Ethics* 137.

[102] *Mason and McCall Smith*, pp 544–546.

[103] Radcliffe-Richards *et al* (1998) 351 *Lancet* 1950.

[104] *Mason and McCall Smith*, pp 558–559.

[105] R M Titmuss, *The Gift Relationship: From Human Blood to Social Policy* (1971) Allen & Unwin.

[106] See A-M Farrell, 'Is the Gift Still Good? Examining the Politics and Regulation of Blood Safety in the European Union' (2006) 14 *Medical Law Review* 155.

[107] See M Brazier and J Harris, 'Does Ethical Controversy Cost Lives?' in Farrell, Price and Quigley, *Organ Shortage: Ethics, Law and Pragmatism* (2011) CUP, pp 15–34.

permitting 'paired' and 'pooled' donations, inducements are sanctioned. The potential 'reward' of a kidney for your husband or child may be a much more powerful inducement than money. What of the promise of priority for registered donors or families who have agreed to donation should they later require an organ? Such a scheme is now embodied in Israeli law. Registered donors of at least three years' standing are granted priority should they themselves need an organ transplant. A similar priority is given to close relatives of registered and deceased donors.[108] Then, if non-monetary inducements are considered acceptable, we return to the issues of cash payments and must consider if a moderate financial 'reward' short of a sale might be considered. In many countries the state will at least meet the funeral expenses of the deceased donor.

Conditional donations

17.15 Should the ban on conditional donation, whereby families seek to direct to whom a cadaver organ might go or to place some restrictions on who may benefit from a cadaver donation, be revisited? The ban arose when a family sought to restrict the use of relatives' organs to white recipients only. Such an attempt to restrict donation to persons of one's own racial group, or religious persuasion, appears fairly odious at first sight, and after an investigation the Department of Health ruled out acceptance of conditional donations.[109] But should any form of conditional directed donation be banned? We allow living donors to direct to whom their gift should be donated. Consider this example. A young man dies in a road accident. His twin sister has end-stage renal failure. His parents are prepared to donate all his organs if one of his kidneys is made available to his sister. In 2008, something not dissimilar occurred. A young woman, Laura Ashworth, died suddenly after an acute asthma attack. Before her death she had discussed donating a kidney to her mother but had not taken any formal steps to become a living donor. The family asked that one of her kidneys be given to Laura's mother, but that wish was overruled and both kidneys went to strangers. The HTA vigorously rejected ensuing criticism.[110]

Xenotransplantation

17.16 A once much-vaunted development in the field of organ transplantation involves the use of non-human animals. Non-human animal to human transplant attempts are not new. Early efforts resulted in disastrous rejection episodes. Scientists responded by seeking to develop procedures to modify the

---

[108] See J Lavee, T Ashkenazi, G Gurman, D Steinberg, 'A New Law for the Allocation of Donor Organs in Israel' (2010) 375 *Lancet* 1131–33 and M Quigley, 'Incentivising Organ Donation' in Farrell, Price and Quigley, *Organ Shortage: Ethics, Law and Pragmatism* (2011) CUP, pp 89–103.

[109] See DH, *An Investigation into Conditional Organ Donation* (2000).

[110] HTA, Press release, 12 April 12 2008.

genetic make-up of pigs to provide tailor-made organs suitable to transplant into humans. The technical progress with xenotransplantation has been slow. The range of problems associated with it is vast.[111] Is it right to use non-human animals in this way?[112] What about infection risks? How will the first human volunteers be recruited?[113] The UK government initially responded cautiously, setting up an interim regulatory body, the United Kingdom Xeno-transplantation Interim Regulation Authority (UKXIRA).[114] For those that are satisfied that breeding animals for transplant is ethical, the major problem becomes the risk to humans. Zoonoses are diseases that cross the species bar-rier, as it would appear swine flu has done. Genetically engineered pigs may carry viruses harmless to pigs, but lethal to humans. In the light of this risk, it is argued, xenograft recipients would have to consent to lifelong monitoring, sterilisation and abstention from unprotected sexual intercourse. How would such draconian rules be policed? Should recipients be allowed to create risks for us all?[115] Yet in 2006 the government announced its decision to abolish UKXIRA, and UKXIRA ceased to exist from 12 December 2006, issuing new guidance stating that the Medical and Healthcare Products Regulatory Author-ity (MHRA) and research ethics committees are now suitably equipped to make any necessary decisions about clinical trials of xenografts in humans.[116]

Liability for mishaps[117]

17.17 A number of questions about potential liability arise if organ trans-plantation goes awry. In February 2011 a living donor whose life was wrecked when the operation to remove his kidney was botched was awarded £6.75m in damages. Massive blood loss destroyed his remaining kidney and the donor had himself to receive a kidney from his sister.[118] A failed transplant

---

[111] See M Fox and J McHale, 'Xenotransplantation: The Ethical and Legal Ramifica-tions' (1998) 6 *Medical Law Review* 42; Nuffield Council on Bioethics, *Animal to Human Transplants* (1996).

[112] See W Cartwright, 'The Pig, the Transplant Surgeon and the Nuffield Council' (1996) 4 *Medical Law Review* 250.

[113] See S Fovargue, 'Oh Pick Me, Pick Me – Selecting Participants for Xenotransplant Clinical Trials' (2007) 15 *Medical Law Review* 176.

[114] See HSC 1998/126 and 'Animal Tissue into Humans', Report of the Advisory Group on the Ethics of Xenotransplantation (1996); the Government Response to 'Animal Tissue into Humans' (1997).

[115] See S Fovargue, 'Consenting to Bio-Risk: Xenotransplantation and the Law' (2005) 25 *Legal Studies* 405.

[116] See DH, *Xenotransplantation Guidance* (2006). As to the efficacy of the MHRA and RECs, see above, ch 15. And see L Williamson, M Fox and S Mclean, 'The Regula-tion of Xenotransplantation after UKXIRA: Legal and Ethical Issues' (2007) 34 *Journal of Law and Society* 441.

[117] In *Urbanski v Patel* (1978) 84 DLR (3d) 850, the donor claimed that the defendant's negligence in removing his daughter's only kidney caused injury (the loss of his kid-ney) to him.

[118] (2011) *Times,* 15 February, p 16.

will not of itself give rise to any legal claim by the recipient. The renal surgeon does not guarantee success any more than any other medical practitioner. But what if, for example, donated blood or kidneys prove to be infected, perhaps with HIV? Might the donor, or the transplant team, be liable in tort? It would seem unchallengeable that donors owe a duty of care to recipients which is breached by a donor knowingly donating organs or tissue when he is aware that he is infected by, say, hepatitis or HIV.[119] The recipient's problem may be tracing the donor. Public policy grounds for protecting the anonymity of donors may be found to outweigh the recipient's individual right of action.[120]

Realistically any claim in respect of contaminated body products will be brought against the hospital supplying those products. Actions in negligence against the Department of Health by haemophiliacs who contracted HIV from contaminated Factor 8 were settled out of court.[121] The Pearson Commission recommended that strict liability should be imposed on authorities responsible for the supply of human blood and organs. It is now clear that the Consumer Protection Act 1987, imposing strict liability for defective products, includes human tissue in its definition of a product.[122]

Foetal tissue and neonatal transplants

17.18 The potential for the use of foetal tissue for transplantation initially aroused much ethical debate. Foetal brain cells can be taken from aborted foetuses and transplanted into the brains of patients with Parkinson's disease, and perhaps other neurodegenerative conditions, in the hope of improving the recipient's condition. Currently, further trials of such foetal transplants are on hold and many doctors see stem cell therapies as a much better potential line of treatment.[123] In 1989, a committee chaired by the Rev. Dr Polkinghorne reported and recommended a Code of Practice for the use of foetuses and foetal material in research and treatment.[124] Many of the fears about the use of foetal tissue focus on concern that women with relatives suffering from Parkinson's disease might deliberately become pregnant, intending to abort the foetus to provide the needed brain cells. The law is relatively simple. Any abortion must conform to the provisions of the 1967 Act. The Polkinghorne Code of Practice mandated that any question of the use of foetal tissue must be independent of decisions relating to the management of the pregnancy. The only

---

[119] And might be criminally liable for causing grievous bodily harm? See *R v Dica* [2004] 3 A11 ER 593, CA.

[120] A Scottish court so found in relation to a claim against a blood donor; see *AB v Scottish Blood Transfusion Service* [1990] SL 203.

[121] See above at **10.1**.

[122] See *A v The National Blood Authority* [2001] Lloyd's Med Rep 187 discussed above at **10.6**.

[123] See *Mason and McCall Smith*, pp 563–564.

[124] Review of the Guidance on the Research Use of Fetuses and Fetal Material, Cm 762 (1989) HMSO.

remaining question was whether the woman's consent was needed before doctors may make use of the aborted foetus. The Polkinghorne Code of Practice required consent in the sense that no foetal tissue could be put to any use without the woman's agreement, but subject to a principle of 'separation', meaning that the woman had no claim to know or direct what uses the foetal tissue was put to. So she could not for example specify that the tissue be used to treat her father suffering from Parkinson's, or that it be used for transplant rather than other research. Foetal tissue is now governed by the Human Tissue Act 2004 and the HTA[125] has issued guidance that makes it clear that foetal tissue is to be treated as the mother's tissue and that, as with any other human tissue, her informed consent is needed for any use of tissue that she elects to donate and she must be told of the proposed purposes to which the tissue will be put.

A rather different question arises in relation to anencephalic neonates. Could a baby born without a brain be used as a donor of organs for a baby born with a defective heart? As we have seen, the usual criteria for brain-stem death are not applicable to newborn babies.[126] Nonetheless the removal of organs for donation (with parental consent) was endorsed in a report from the medical Royal Colleges in 1998 when 'two doctors, who are not members of the transplant team, agree that spontaneous respiration has ceased'.[127]

Transplantation: the future

17.19 Developments in transplant medicine create the potential for transplant of an ever-greater range of organs. Since the publication of the last edition of this work, face and limb transplants have become more common. Face transplants have excited popular attention but it is doubtful that face transplants pose any new ethical or legal questions.[128] Controversy about such transplants may, however, re-kindle more general concerns about transplant medicine. And the major challenge for transplant medicine remains the need for an adequate supply of suitable organs. The UK's poor record for donation rates prompted the government to set up the Organ Donation Taskforce (ODT). The Taskforce delivered its first report in 2008,[129] setting a target of a 50 per cent increase in cadaver donation rates and making fourteen highly practical recommendations focusing on donor-identification and referral, donor co-ordination and organ-retrieval arrangements. We note just some of them here. Legal and ethical issues that might constitute obstacles to donation

---

[125] Code of Practice, Code 1, paras 157–161.
[126] See Academy of Medical Royal Colleges, *A Code of Practice for the Diagnosis and Confirmation of Death*, Appendix 4.
[127] Report of the Working Party of the Conference of Medical Royal Colleges and their Faculties in the United Kingdom on Organ Transplantation in Neonates (1988), discussed in *Mason and McCall Smith*, pp 560–563.
[128] See R S Hartman, 'Face Values: Challenges of Transplant Technology' (2005) 31 *American Journal of Law and Medicine* 7.
[129] ODT Report 1.

should be addressed by a UK-wide Donation Ethics group; systems for identifying and notifying potential donors needed radical improvement; donor co-ordination services should be overhauled. All health professionals likely to be involved in the treatment of potential donors should receive mandatory training in the principles of donation. The central message of this first report is summed up in Recommendation 4 that all parts of the NHS must 'embrace organ donation as a usual, not an unusual event'. Recommendation 12 proposed that ways should be sought to recognise the gift made by organ donors, but the report did not touch on radical reforms such as a market in organs or presumed consent. It was the latter to which the government asked the taskforce to return and towards the end of 2008 the ODT issued its second report: *The potential impact of an opt out system for organ donation in the UK.*[130] The ODT came to a clear consensus that such a system should not be introduced in the UK at present. They were not satisfied that such a change would result in a sufficient increase in the number of donors to justify the human and financial costs of the change. And they feared that a change in the law might even have a negative impact on donation, in particular eroding the trust between clinicians and families.[131] The debate will go on.[132]

---

[130] ODT Report 2.

[131] See B Farsides, 'Negotiating Change: Organ Donation in the United Kingdom' in Farrell, Price and Quigley (eds), *Organ Shortage; Ethics, Law and Pragmatism* (2011) CUP, pp 214–226.

[132] See D Price, 'Promoting Organ Donation: The Challenges for the Future' in Farrell, Price and Quigley (eds), *Organ Shortage: Ethics, Law and Pragmatism* (2011) CUP, pp 245–268.

Chapter 18

THE HUMAN BODY
AND ITS PARTS

18.1 We take our bodies for granted most of the time. The purpose of our organs and tissue is to sustain us, the people who live in those bodies. We refer without reflection to 'our' hands, 'our' hearts. Whether that language of ownership is reflected in the law may be doubted, although the decision of the Court of Appeal in *Yearworth v North Bristol NHS Trust*[1] may usher in a new era in debates on owning at least some parts of ourselves. What is beyond doubt is that our human body parts have value to others.[2] 'My' kidney may save 'your' life. That kidney could become 'yours' while I remain alive. 'My' heart could also save your 'life', but only when my 'life' has ended. Once again, in modern times, it was the development of transplantation that highlighted the usefulness of human body parts, taken from both the living and the dead. However, doctors and scientists have been learning from the bodies, and body parts, of the dead for centuries. Medicine has developed from the knowledge gathered from the dissection of corpses. Dissection, however good its ends, has a murky history.[3] Bodies were stolen in the seventeenth and eighteenth centuries. The Anatomy Act 1832 conscripted the bodies of the poor to help train medical students in anatomy and provide material for early medical research. In the twentieth century, the public knew little about practices whereby doctors retained organs and tissue for both research and education. Post-mortem examinations were rarely discussed. Only when the controversy surrounding organ retention erupted at the end of that century was the public gaze fixed on the uses of bodies and their parts. That controversy may have obscured the fact that donation of tissue for research and education, and donation of bodies to train doctors has an even greater role in saving lives and preserving health than the better known practice of organ transplantation.

---

[1] [2009] EWCA Civ 37. See below at **18.9**.
[2] See M Brazier, 'Human(s) (as) Medicine(s)' in S A M McLean (ed), *Do No Harm* (2006) Ashgate, p 187.
[3] See R Richardson, *Death, Dissection and the Destitute* (2nd edn, 2000) Chicago Press.

In this chapter,[4] we examine how (outwith the context of transplantation) English law regulates the removal, retention and uses of human body parts and we consider how far (if at all) we own our own bodies. We revisit those parts of the Human Tissue Act 2004 not examined in the previous chapter. As has been the case with many other chapters, the law is in a state of flux. We noted in the previous chapter that the government has proposed that the Human Tissue Authority (HTA) should cease to exist as an independent public body and its functions should be divided up and shared among other organisations, notably the Care Quality Commission (CQC) and a new research regulator,[5] possibly the Health Research Agency proposed by the Academy of Medical Sciences.[6] The Academy also proposes some fairly minor amendments to the Human Tissue Act 2004 and others may see the opportunity to seek to dilute the substantive provisions of the Act as it relates to uses of human tissue other than transplantation. Finally the operation of the coronial system is a key factor in the regulation of the use of bodies and body parts post mortem. The Coroners and Justice Act 2009 was enacted to reform both the substantive law on the investigation of deaths in England and Wales and to reform the operation of the coroners' service, a central part of the latter being the creation of the office of Chief Coroner. The government at one stage sought to add the Chief Coroner to the list of posts to be abolished, but the House of Lords has currently blocked that proposal.[7] However, at the time of writing, most of the sections of the Coroners and Justice Act that relate to coroners have not been brought into force, including the provisions relating to the post of Chief Coroner.

Removal of body parts from the dead

18.2 It was organ retention from the bodies of the dead that resulted in the enactment of the Human Tissue Act 2004. For this reason we reverse the natural order, and consider first the questions relating to the use of corpses before addressing retention of organs and tissue from the living. In the course of the Inquiry[8] established in 1998 to investigate the paediatric cardiac service at Bristol Royal Infirmary, evidence emerged of a widespread practice of organ and tissue retention. Over a long period of time, organs and tissue had been taken at, or after, post-mortem examinations from children's bodies and used '. . . for a variety of purposes, including audit, medical education and research, or had simply been stored'. The Bristol Inquiry Team, led by Professor Ian

---

[4] For this chapter too, see D Price, *Human Tissue in Transplantation and Research* (2009) CUP.

[5] DH, *Liberating the NHS: Report of the Arms-Length Bodies Review* (2010).

[6] Academy of Medical Sciences, *A New Pathway for the Regulation and Governance of Health Research* (2011).

[7] See C Fairburn, *Abolition of the Office of Chief Coroner* (2011) House of Commons Library, accessible at http://www.parliament.uk/.

[8] *Learning from Bristol*: The Report of the Public Inquiry into Children's Heart Surgery at the Bristol Royal Infirmary 1984–1995, Cm 5207 (1) (2001).

Kennedy, issued an Interim Report, *Removal and Retention of Human Material*,[9] in May 2000. The Report noted that this had become an '... issue of great and grave concern', generating an outcry not confined to the Bristol parents. Worse was to follow. Almost in passing, one of the witnesses to the Bristol Inquiry, Professor R H Anderson, in explaining the benefits of retaining hearts for educational purposes, noted the existence of many collections of children's hearts elsewhere. The largest collection, he commented, was at the Royal Liverpool Children's Hospital (Alder Hey). His evidence prompted the Department of Health to set up an Independent Confidential Inquiry under section 2 of the National Health Service Act 1977 chaired by Michael Redfern QC. The Inquiry was instructed to investigate the removal and disposal of human organs and tissue following post-mortem examinations at Alder Hey.

The Redfern Report[10] published in January 2001 proved to be political dynamite. It revealed longstanding practices of removing and retaining children's organs without the consent or even knowledge of their grieving parents. In some cases, infants were literally stripped of all their organs and what was returned to their families was an 'empty shell'. In a horrifying number of cases, organs and tissue retained were simply stored. They were put to no good use. In some instances, the whole of a foetus or still-born infant was kept and stored in pots. The Report is 535 pages long. It addresses not just the original wrong of retaining organs, but subsequent mishandling of organ return and a range of other appalling practices and mismanagement. In this chapter, we focus on the legal issues arising out of organ retention.

Simultaneously with the publication of the Redfern Report, the Chief Medical Officer published a census carried out to ascertain the extent of organ retention since 1970 across the NHS in England and Wales.[11] What became apparent was that practices whereby pathologists simply took and retained human material after post-mortem examination were routine. The extent to which the deceased's family was involved at all in such decisions varied radically. What was clear was that adequate and free consent was rarely obtained, or even thought necessary. Nor was this a practice limited to children. Many families were to learn about organs stripped from adult relatives.[12]

---

9   The Inquiry into the Management of Care of Children Receiving Complex Heart Surgery at the Bristol Royal Infirmary Interim Report, *Removal and Retention of Human Material* (available at www.bristol-inquiry.org.uk), hereafter Bristol Interim Report.

10 *The Royal Liverpool Children's Inquiry Report* (2001) HC 12-11 (hereafter the Redfern Report). Michael Redfern QC later completed a further inquiry on the retention of tissue from workers in the nuclear industry; see *The Redfern Inquiry into Human Tissue Analysis in UK Nuclear Facilities* (2010) HC 571-1.

11 DH, *Report of a Census of Organs and Tissue Retained by Pathology Services in England* (2001).

12 See, in particular, DH, *The Investigation of Events that Followed the Death of Cyril Mark Isaacs* (2003). The Bristol Interim Report, the Alder Hey Report and the Chief Medical Officer all made extensive recommendations about how the NHS should seek to manage and resolve the process of informing families about organ retention

The value of taking and retaining organs after post-mortem examination in certain cases should not be doubted. Ascertaining the cause of death is self-evidently important. And often, especially with infants, tests on organs and tissue may have crucial value to the child's family. Investigations which reveal genetic disease may be the key to helping that family have further healthy children. In the wider public interest, medical research is dependent on access to human organs and tissue. Medical education requires such material. One simple example illustrates the educational use of human organs. If a child dies tragically and is found to have a grossly abnormal heart, retaining that heart so that paediatric surgeons can examine it before attempting to operate on and save the life of a child with a similar abnormality makes sense. It can only be ethical to do so with the family's consent. For the devout Jew or Muslim, it is a religious imperative to bury the body intact. For other families, the pain of not laying their relative to rest complete is overwhelming. However, for many families involved in the organ retention controversy, what motivated their anger was the loss of control over their relative's burial or cremation. Many relatives said publicly that had they been consulted they would have agreed to doctors retaining the organs of the dead child or other relatives. They would have been content to 'gift' some parts of the body to achieve good ends, ends fully explained to them. What they abominated was the lack of respect shown to them and their relative. They felt that someone whom they loved dearly had been treated as a mere convenience, treated with contempt.[13]

Post-mortem examinations

18.3　Before looking at the law relating to retention of dead bodies, organs and tissue, we need to say a little about post-mortem examinations, sometimes referred to as autopsies. A post-mortem examination is conducted by a pathologist to investigate (inter alia) the cause of a death, and to understand more fully the nature of the patient's disease, including an evaluation of any medical or surgical treatment given to him. Such examinations are a key tool of modern scientific medicine. One distinguished doctor and philosopher has said: 'Of all the clinical disciplines, pathology is the one that most directly reflects the demystification of the human body that has made scientific medicine so effect-

and organ return, about support for families and how to resolve past controversies as well as how the law should be reformed. The Secretary of State established a special health authority, the NHS Retained Organs Commission, to manage the process by which NHS trusts provided information to families about organ retention, oversee the process of organ return, act as an advocate for families and develop a new regulatory framework for organ and tissue retention.

13　For diametrically opposed views about the ethics of organ retention, see J Harris, 'Law and Regulation of Retained Organs: the Ethical Issues' (2002) 22 *Legal Studies* 527 and M Brazier, 'Retained Organs: Ethics and Humanity' (2002) 22 *Legal Studies* 550. And see S McGuiness and M Brazier, 'Respecting the Living Means Respecting the Dead Too?' (2008) 28 *Oxford Journal of Legal Studies* 297.

ive and so humane'.[14] To the layperson, what is done to the body in a full post-mortem examination may seem grisly. The body is opened and organs removed, weighed and sometimes dissected. In some cases, organs must be retained for a period of time to be treated before they can be fully examined, or organs and tissue may be sent away for tests elsewhere. Some religious faiths, including Orthodox Judaism and Islam, mandate the swift burial of the intact body. Post-mortem examinations (save in exceptional circumstances)[15] thus offend those faiths.[16]

Post-mortem examinations in this country can either be compulsory on the orders of the coroner, or voluntary, conducted with the consent of the deceased or his family. This latter form of post-mortem examination, we shall refer to as a hospital autopsy.

Post-mortem examinations must be distinguished from anatomical examinations. Anatomical examinations involve what is more commonly known as dissection. People donate their whole bodies to medical schools to assist in medical education, primarily to educate students in human anatomy and train them in dissection.

The law before 2004: complex and obscure[17]

18.4 Doctors, especially pathologists, endured odium in the wake of revelations in the Bristol Interim and Redfern Reports. Some of the blame lay with the unsatisfactory state of the law prior to the Human Tissue Act 2004. The Bristol Interim Report said simply but tellingly:[18]

> ... we have no doubt that the complexity and obscurity of the current law will be manifest to all. Equally we have no doubt that there will be general agreement that this state of affairs is regrettable and in need of attention.

Prior to the 2004 Act, a complicated mixture of ancient common law principles and statutes governed the retention and use of body parts taken from the dead. The common law asserted that there was 'no property in a corpse'.[19] This principle remains untouched by the 2004 Act. When a family member

---

[14] See R Tallis, *Hippocratic Oaths: Medicine and Its Discontents* (2004) Atlantic Books, p 195.

[15] See, for example, M Lamm, *The Jewish Way in Death and Mourning* (1998) Jonathan David, p 100; A Sheikh and A R Gartrad, *Caring for Muslim Patients* (2000) Radcliffe Medical Press, p 107.

[16] One option may be to carry out a limited post-mortem, so restricting the intrusion on the body: see generally *Guidelines on Autopsy Practice* (2005) Royal College of Pathologists.

[17] See D Price, 'From Cosmos and Damian to Van Velzen: The Human Tissue Saga Continues' (2003) 11 *Medical Law Review* 1.

[18] At p 20.

[19] *Doodeward v Spence* (1908) 6 CLR 906. And see below at **18.9**.

dies, his family have no claim by which they can assert 'this is now our body and we have unfettered rights to dispose of it or its parts'. However, the executors or administrators of the deceased's estate are subject, ultimately, to a common law duty to dispose of the body decently. This duty confers on them a right to possession of the body to fulfil that duty of decent disposal of the body.[20] Several Acts of Parliament touched on the lawful use of dead bodies. The three key statutes were the Anatomy Act 1984, the Human Tissue Act 1961 and the Coroners Act 1988.

The Anatomy Act 1984 enabled people to donate their bodies or their parts for use for anatomical examination. The details of the 1984 Act were in some ways as fuzzy as was the case with the Human Tissue Act 1961. The framework for the use of donated bodies was, however, closely regulated, and subject to the supervision of HM Inspector of Anatomy. Violation of the Anatomy Act resulted in criminal liability. The Anatomy Act worked well, within a culture of respect for the donors of the bodies given to medical schools. However, it was that vast majority of cases not regulated by the Anatomy Act which provoked the controversy around organ retention. First, a distinction must be made between removal of organs and tissue after a hospital autopsy, and removal of body parts subsequent to a coroner's post-mortem examination. The Human Tissue Act 1961 governed removal and retention of organs after a hospital autopsy. It provided that where no coroner's inquiry was likely, the person lawfully in possession of the body (the hospital) could authorise an autopsy where, after:[21]

> ... such reasonable enquiry as may be practicable, there is no reason to believe:
> (a) that the deceased had expressed an objection to his body being so used after his death ... or (b) that the surviving spouse or any surviving relative objects to his body being so dealt with.

Under the 1961 Act, a person was not empowered to authorise an autopsy on himself in advance of his death. If body parts were to be retained after completion of the autopsy, a further enquiry was supposed to establish that there was no objection to retention and use of those parts. 'Consent' to an autopsy should not have been judged to presume consent (or no objection) to organ retention.

In relation to transplants, doctors were reluctant to exercise the powers granted by the Human Tissue Act 1961. They sought positive and explicit consent from families before removing organs for transplant, even if the deceased carried a donor card. In the context of organ retention, the opposite ethos seems to have prevailed. The 1961 Act was obscure. It did not require explicit consent. Rather, it set up a 'no objection' rule. Put crudely, hospitals thought that they could take organs and tissue for purposes of education and research

---

[20] *Williams v Williams* (1882) 20 Ch D 659.
[21] See ss 2(2) and 1(2) and see P D G Skegg, 'The Use of Corpses for Medical Education and Research: The Legal Requirements' (1991) 31 *Medicine, Science and the Law* 345.

if no family member voiced dissent. The Bristol Interim Report suggests that even where families were asked their views and expressed no objection, 'agreement' both to hospital autopsies and subsequent removal of body parts was often given with little understanding of what was entailed. It might be an 'agreement' given at a time of great personal trauma, for example, shortly after the death of a child. In some cases, families, knowing nothing of the distinction between hospital autopsies and coroners' post-mortem examinations, did not realise that they had a right to object. The use of the word 'tissue' confused people. Understandably, lay people assumed that in agreeing to the removal of tissue, they agreed to doctors taking small specimens from organs, not whole organs. The Redfern Report revealed a bleaker picture. Organs had been taken and stored without even any pretence of seeking the family's views. The flaws in the Human Tissue Act 1961 became patent. Even if it could be shown to have been flouted, the lack of sanctions punishing violation of the Act rendered it toothless.

The position in relation to coroners' post-mortem examinations was no better. The overwhelming majority of post-mortems were and are performed on the orders of the coroner. Put briefly, under the Coroners Act 1988 (which remains in force at the time of writing),[22] a coroner may order a post-mortem if he is informed that the body of the deceased is lying within his district and there is reasonable cause to suspect that the deceased:[23]

(a)   died a violent or unnatural death;
(b)   has died a sudden death of which the cause is unknown; or
(c)   has died in prison or such a place or in such circumstances as to require an inquest under any other Act.

Section 1 of the Coroners and Justice Act 2009 will, when in force, make fairly minor alterations to the jurisdiction of the coroner. Requirement (b) above will remove the proviso that death must be sudden and (c) will read that 'the deceased died while in custody or otherwise in state detention'. Regulations[24] made under the Coroners' Act 1988 elaborated on the rules governing which deaths must be reported to the coroner, placing an emphasis on reporting surgical deaths or deaths where some medical negligence may have occurred, and similar Regulations will complement the 2009 Act if and when it is brought into force. A pathologist carrying out a coroner's post-mortem examination acts under the coroner's authority. Rule 9 of the Coroner's Rules (as it was formulated until 2005 and so in force at the time of the organ retention controversy) placed a duty on the pathologist to remove and preserve 'materials' which in his opinion bore on the cause of death. If a baby died in the course of cardiac surgery, the pathologist might lawfully remove and retain his heart until it was possible to ascertain why the infant died. However, there was

---

[22]   For a much fuller account, see the Bristol Interim Report, Annex B 'Law and Guidelines'.
[23]   Coroners Act 1988, s 8(1).
[24]   SI 1987/ 2088, reg 41(e).

no power to retain organs for research or teaching purposes. Once the cause of death was established, neither the coroner nor the pathologist had any further legal power to retain body parts. Such 'material' should have been disposed of, unless the relatives of the deceased authorised retention for research or teaching purposes. In practice, coroners simply allowed pathologists to do what they wished with human material no longer required for the purposes of verifying cause of death. Pathologists, in ignorance of the law in many cases, retained organs and tissue over long periods of time and for a multiplicity of purposes. By 2001, NHS hospitals were in possession of literally tens of thousands of organs and vast collections of blocks and tissue slides. Leading teaching hospitals and medical museums such as the Royal College of Surgeons had extensive archival material of body parts, some including collections long predating the NHS.

The Human Tissue Act 2004: the dead[25]

18.5 The Human Tissue Act 2004 came into force in September 2006 and governs the removal, retention and use of body parts taken from the dead, except where body parts are removed and retained solely for the purpose of investigating a death under the authority of the coroner. The Act also governs the performance of hospital autopsies. The Anatomy Act 1984 and the Human Tissue Act 1961 are wholly repealed. The Act, as we have seen, makes 'appropriate' consent the fundamental principle governing retention and use of whole bodies and body parts. The Act also introduces extensive regulation of hospital autopsies and retention and use of both bodies and what is 'relevant material'. It is tortuous to read. It does not apply in Scotland.[26] The scope of the Act will surprise many for it covers much more than organs such as hearts or kidneys and at present encompasses nearly all human bodily products. Defining organs and tissue and attaining a common understanding of what those words meant had been a major source of controversy in the debates surrounding organ retention. Section 53 defines 'relevant material' as 'material, other than gametes, which consists of or includes human cells', save that embryos outside the human body are excluded,[27] as are hair and nails from living subjects. But blood and urine are within the Act. The Academy of Medical Sciences has proposed that the definition be amended to exclude plasma, serum, urine, faeces and saliva.[28]

---

[25] See D Price, 'The Human Tissue Act 2004' (2005) 68 *Modern Law Review* 798; K Liddell, A Hall, 'Beyond Bristol and Alder Hey: The Future Regulation of Human Tissue' (2005) 13 *Medical Law Review* 170.

[26] See the Human Tissue (Scotland) Act 2006.

[27] Regulated by the Human Fertilisation and Embryology Act 1990; see above chs 12 and 13.

[28] Academy of Medical Sciences, *A New Pathway for the Regulation and Governance of Health Research*, Rec 11.

Let us start with the circumstances in which it is lawful to conduct a post-mortem examination. All post-mortem examinations must now be performed in premises licensed by the HTA. The Human Tissue Act 2004 does not govern when a post-mortem examination can be ordered by the coroner. So if a person dies in hospital and there is suspicion that her death may be as a result of some crime or medical malpractice, the coroner will be informed. If the coroner orders a post-mortem examination, the family (at present) have no formal right to object. Section 40 of the Coroners and Justice Act 2009 provides for an appeal to the Chief Coroner. We wait to see if and how these provisions will be brought into force'. The new Act is to be supported by a Charter for Bereaved People to assist families coping with the trauma of the investigation into a relative's death but while so much of the Act is not in force the Charter also remains in limbo.

Beyond the jurisdiction of the coroner, there are many other circumstances when doctors might want to conduct a post-mortem examination, or carry out a hospital autopsy. There may be uncertainty about the exact cause of death. There may be a wish to learn more about why treatment failed and the underlying disease or injury. Doctors (and families) may want to explore whether any genetic factors are implicated in the deceased patient's disease. Any such hospital autopsy will be lawful only if[29] the deceased himself gave appropriate consent to the autopsy in advance of his death, or such consent is given by his nominated representative,[30] or failing any advance consent by the deceased or authorisation by his nominated representative, appropriate consent is obtained from a person who stood in a qualifying relationship to the deceased.[31] Whatever the purpose of the hospital autopsy, be it to determine the cause of death, investigate the effect of treatment on him, or examine genetic factors, what is done can only be done with consent.[32]

Should doctors wish to retain body parts after the hospital autopsy, explicit consent to both the retention, and the projected use of those parts, must be obtained additionally, and separately, from any consent to the autopsy.[33] Imagine that knowing she is dying from ovarian cancer, a woman consents in advance to an autopsy, especially in order to assess any genetic risk to her daughters. In the course of the autopsy, pathologists identify further tumours in her kidneys and liver. They want to retain those organs for further investigation and research. For such retention and use to be lawful, appropriate consent will have to be obtained from the woman's husband or partner, if she had one, or from one of her daughters. Retention of body parts from the dead

---

[29] Human Tissue Act 2004, ss 1, 3, and Sch 1, paras 2 and 3.
[30] Human Tissue Act 2004, s 4.
[31] For discussion of who constitutes such a person, see above at **17.9**.
[32] The bare rules of the Human Tissue Act 2004 are elaborated in this context by two Codes of Practice: HTA, Code of Practice: Consent, Code 1 (2009) (hereafter Code of Practice, Code 1) and HTA, Code of Practice: Post Mortem Examination, Code 3 (2009) (hereafter Code of Practice, Code 3).
[33] See the Human Tissue Act 2004, s 1 and Sch 1.

must be authorised by appropriate consent, be the purpose of retention, research, audit, education, performance assessment, public health monitoring or surveillance.[34]

Albeit no consent is required when the coroner orders a post-mortem examination, once that examination is complete, should a pathologist wish to retain body parts removed in the course of that investigation, appropriate consent must be sought to make such retention and any projected use of those parts lawful. If our hypothetical patient with ovarian cancer died unexpectedly on the operating table, the coroner may well order a post-mortem. Should the examination establish that her death was in no sense caused by any error or lack of care, but pathologists still wish to retain her organs, consent must be sought for the retention and use of those organs even though it was not required for the post-mortem examination itself. Amendments to the Coroner's Rules[35] now require that a coroner ordering a post-mortem examination and notified about retention of organs and tissue must inform the deceased's family (inter alia) that organs and tissue will be retained, about the options once examination of retained material is complete and (if the relatives wish the material to be returned to them) about what arrangements may need to be made.[36]

Somewhat surprisingly, the Human Tissue Act 2004 prescribes no formalities for consent to a hospital autopsy, or to retention and use of organs after post-mortem examination. There is no statutory rule requiring that consent must be given in writing. Greater formality is required for two particular uses of dead bodies, and their parts. A person who wishes to donate his body for anatomical examination or for public display must (normally) do so in writing and in the presence of at least one witness.[37] Moreover *only* the individual himself can donate his body to anatomical examination[38] or public display.[39] Should the authors of this book die in advance of our respective husbands having expressed no instruction about the use of our corpses, those husbands could authorise a hospital autopsy and donate our organs and tissue for medical research or education. Only we can donate our whole bodies to the local medical school or gain a strange sort of immortality in exhibitions such as *Bodyworlds*, where plastinated human bodies are on display as public 'entertainment'.

Section 2 of the Human Tissue Act 2004 makes express provision in relation to children and young people who die before reaching the age of maturity at eighteen.

---

[34] See also HTA, Code of Practice: Disposal of Human Tissue, Code 5 (2009).
[35] Coroners (Amendment) Rules 2005, SI 2005/420. When the 2009 Act is brought into force, new regulations will be forthcoming.
[36] And see HTA, Code of Practice, Code 3, paras 27–40.
[37] See ss 3(4) and (5).
[38] For further information about anatomical examination, see HTA, Code of Practice: Anatomical Examination, Code 4 (2009) (hereafter Code of Practice, Code 4).
[39] HTA, Code of Practice, Public Display, Code 7 (2009) (hereafter Code of Practice, Code 7).

If a young person was sufficiently mature and intelligent to make an advance direction about the conduct of an autopsy or retention of body parts, her advance direction authorises implementation of her wishes. A *Gillick competent* minor can in theory determine what happens to her body after death.[40] Establishing *Gillick competence* retrospectively after death will not be easy. In relation to younger children, normally his parents will be the designated decision-makers. Autopsy and organ retention are lawful only on the basis of appropriate consent from a person with parental responsibility[41] for the dead child. Consent from one parent alone will suffice to make the relevant activity lawful. Overriding an objecting bereaved parent will pose ethical and practical difficulties. Consider this dilemma. A child dies of cancer at the age of four. His Orthodox Jewish father objects to any retention of his organs. His mother desperately wants to know if his disease has any genetic implications for her other children, and so wants his organs retained and samples tested.

The Human Tissue Act 2004: the living

18.6   The Human Tissue Act 2004 was enacted in the wake of controversy about the (mis)use of the bodies of the dead. The Act, however, also regulates the retention and use of 'relevant material' from living patients. So if a patient undergoes surgery to remove a diseased organ, the Act regulates the conditions in which doctors may retain that organ for teaching or research purposes. And the wide definition given to 'material'[42] within the Act, means that not only retention of whole organs is regulated, but also the retention of any specimen including cells, however small that may be. The Academy of Medical Sciences has, as we have seen, sought to amend and restrict the definition of relevant material and pointedly notes that the Scottish legislation is confined to post-mortem tissue.[43] The original Human Tissue Bill imposed almost the same regime of requirements for explicit consent in relation to such surgical or surplus tissue from living patients, as for body parts removed and retained from the dead. The Bill caused an outcry with senior scientists claiming that such burdensome rules would paralyse medicine.[44] Hence, as we shall see, a modified set of rules now govern retention of surgical or surplus tissue from living patients.[45] Many doctors still regard the regulations as unreasonably onerous.

---

[40]   See s 2(3). Only such a *Gillick competent* minor can authorise donation of her body for anatomical examination or public display. Parents cannot donate their children's bodies for such purposes.

[41]   See ss 1, 2 and Sch 1. Where there is not such person, the nearest person in a qualifying relationship to the dead child is the designated decision-maker.

[42]   See s 53 above at **18.5**.

[43]   Academy of Medical Sciences, A New Pathway for the Regulation and Governance of Health Research, p 72.

[44]   See P Furness and R Sullivan, 'The Human Tissue Bill' (2004) 328 *BMJ* 533.

[45]   See Liddell and Hall (2005) 13 *Medical Law Review* 170.

The Human Tissue Act 2004 does not regulate the initial removal of body parts from the living. That continues to be governed by the common law. Any surgery is normally unlawful and a criminal assault unless properly authorised by the patient's consent. A hysterectomy on a mentally competent woman self-evidently requires her consent. But what if doctors want to retain her diseased uterus, either to help train medical students or to pursue research[46] into the kind of cancer that necessitated the surgery? Must doctors seek the woman's explicit consent to retain her uterus, or even any specimens of diseased tissue? It depends on their purpose.[47] If retention is intended for the purposes of audit, education or training, performance assessment, public health monitoring or quality assurance, her consent may be presumed.[48]

Retention to acquire genetic or other information relevant to others will normally require an explicit consent.[49] Retention for research will require such a consent if the identity of the patient will be ascertainable. The Act empowered the Secretary of State to make regulations allowing retention of material from the living for research, without an explicit consent, where the research has been ethically approved by an accredited research ethics committee and the 'source' of the material has been anonymised.[50] Research on surgical or surplus tissue taken from us must be explicitly authorised by us if researchers will be able to discover that the source is Brazier or Cave. Very often, researchers will require this information to be able to, for example, access our medical records. Only research, approved by a Research Ethics Committee, where that link is *not* necessary, and has not been broken, will not require our explicit consent.[51]

The final version of the Human Tissue Act 2004 operates on the assumption that more people have little concern about what happens to 'bits of their body' removed at surgery. They would be indifferent to whether such 'bits' were incinerated or put to some good use. Two caveats should be stated.

(1) Some religious faiths attach an almost equal value to parts separated from the living body as from the dead. When an Orthodox Jew has to have a limb amputated, he will make arrangements for that limb to be stored and ultimately interred with him.

---

[46] And see HTA, Code of Practice: Research, Code 9 (2009).

[47] See generally HTA, Code of Practice, Code 5.

[48] See s 1(d) and (f) and Sch 1.

[49] However, see s 7, which provides that the HTA can in exceptional circumstances, where the original donor of the material cannot be traced, dispense with the need for consent.

[50] See ss 1(7), 1(8) and 1(9); see also the Human Tissue Act 2004 (Ethical Approval, Exceptions from Licensing and Supply of Information About Transplants Regulations) 2006, SI 2006/1260.

[51] S 6 empowers the Secretary of State to make regulations relating to 'deemed consent' by persons who lack the requisite mental capacity to consent on their own behalf. See the Human Tissue Act 2004 (Persons Who Lack Capacity to Consent and Transplants) Regulations 2006, SI 2006/1659, regs 3 and 8.

(2) Surplus tissue is not necessarily mere 'waste'. It can be the source of crucial and sensitive genetic information. It can be the source of medical advances of commercial value.

'Appropriate consent'

18.7 We have so far indicated when an explicit consent is required by the Human Tissue Act 2004. The Act refers to 'appropriate consent'. Just what those two words may mean is crucial to how the Act will operate in practice. The HTA was expressly required by the Act to address what constitutes consent and has done so in a number of Codes of Practice (revised in 2009) including a general Code on *Consent*,[52] and more specific Codes relating to post-mortem examinations,[53] anatomical examination,[54] removal, retention and storage of tissue,[55] and public display.[56] In Code 1 on *Consent*, the HTA stresses that health professionals seeking consent '... should tailor the information they provide to each specific situation as some people may insist on in-depth information, whereas others would prefer to consent having only the basics of the procedure explained to them'.[57] While written consent is only mandatory for consent to anatomical examination or public display, written consent should be obtained wherever possible for any donation of tissue postmortem.[58] A valid consent must be given voluntarily and on the basis of sufficient information. What degree of information is sufficient is difficult. Some families asked to consent to a hospital autopsy and organ retention may not want comprehensive and graphic descriptions of what will be done to their newly dead relative.[59] Some living patients will be happy simply to 'give away' excess tissue or diseased organs uninterested in its fate. Doctors should not, however, assume either that acute distress in the first case or indifference in the second, justifies failing to *offer* information. A number of families brought claims against hospitals retaining organs without consent. In *AB v Leeds Teaching Hospital NHS Trust*,[60] the judge stressed that (even under the old Human Tissue Act 1961) families were '... entitled to have their wishes in respect of their deceased (relative's) body respected and complied with ... those wishes cannot be complied with unless it is explained to the (relative) what is involved'. He rejected any blanket view that information would have been distressing to all relatives, saying: 'In so far as it involved the exercise of a

---

[52] Code of Practice, Code 1.
[53] Code of Practice, Code 3.
[54] Code of Practice, Code 4.
[55] Code of Practice, Code 5.
[56] Code of Practice, Code 7.
[57] Code of Practice, Code 1, para 98.
[58] Code of Practice, Code 1, para 102.
[59] See D Knowles, 'Parental Consent to the Post Mortem Removal and Retention of Organs' (2001) 18 *Journal of Applied Philosophy* 215.
[60] [2004] EWHC 644.

therapeutic privilege it was one which does not appear to have been exercised on a case by case basis'.

We would suggest that both the 1961 and the 2004 Act require that doctors offer to disclose to the person giving consent all the information that any reasonable lay person would need to make a sensible choice about whether or not to give the requested consent.[61] Especially in the context of sudden bereavement, time and support for the decision-maker will be crucial. Information must neither be withheld nor forced on the unwilling recipient. Evidence of compliance with HTA Codes of Practice will weigh strongly with the courts.

In the context of retention for research, one particularly thorny question surfaced. Must consent be specific to every research use of the relevant material? Or will a general consent suffice? If a woman agrees to consent to retention of her diseased uterus for research into one form of cancer therapy and in the course of that research other more promising lines of research emerge, must she be contacted to give specific consent to this further research? The HTA seems to endorse the applicability of a seeking a *general* consent, for multiple purposes.[62] Donors may be asked to make an unconditional gift of their tissue (or that of their deceased relative). The key factor will be to establish what kind of consent was sought and given. Did the patient or relative consent only to the use of the relevant material for Project X, alone, or Project X plus any related research or teaching activities, or did they consent to surrender all control of that material, and 'gift' the body parts in question to the hospital or university?

Regulation

18.8 We have focused in this chapter on the legal requirements for consent to removal, retention and use of body parts. The Human Tissue Act 2004 also imposes substantial regulatory requirements on such activities. We touch on these only briefly. As we saw in relation to transplantation, the HTA at present plays a major role in regulation, a role that may move to the CQC. Its mandate to prepare Codes of Practice means that the HTA profoundly influences how the Act works in practice.[63] More directly, a number of activities now require a licence from the HTA.[64] These include carrying out anatomical examinations and storing anatomical specimens. Medical schools will now have to be licensed by the HTA to carry out and train students in dissection.[65] Post-mortem examinations must be carried out in licensed premises.

---

[61] Modelled on Lord Woolf's definition of informed consent in *Pearce v United Bristol Healthcare NHS Trust* (1999) 48 BMLR 11 (discussed above at **5.7**).

[62] See Code of Practice, Code 1, paras 105–107.

[63] See ss 26 and 27.

[64] See s 16.

[65] Continuing the regulatory regime previously imposed by the Anatomy Act 1984; and see ss 16(2)(a), 17 and 18.

Storage of any body or part of a body for any of the purposes covered by the Act must be licensed, as must the use of bodies and their parts for public display. Pathology museums and archives of tissue will also need to be licensed in respect of acquisitions after the Act came into force. It remains lawful to retain existing holdings (even where there is no evidence of consent).[66] The HTA nonetheless advises that if the views of the deceased person or their relatives are known, those views '. . . must be respected',[67] and it gives extensive advice on the respectful disposal of existing holdings.[68]

The 2004 Act, unlike its predecessor, the Human Tissue Act 1961, has teeth. Proceeding without appropriate consent where consent is required is a criminal offence unless the person reasonably believed that he acted on the basis of an appropriate consent.[69] In the context of consent to the removal and retention of body parts from the dead, a practical question besets obtaining consent. If, for example, a child dies of leukaemia, it is usually the treating clinicians who will approach the family to seek consent to an autopsy and subsequent retention of material. But it is the pathologist who will carry out the autopsy and retain any material. Pathologists will need to ensure that they have a reasonable basis for a belief in consent and that, in most cases, will mean evidence in writing of consent. To ensure doctors charged with seeking consent do their part, it is also a criminal offence to represent falsely to another that appropriate consent has been obtained.[70] Carrying out unlicensed activities where such a licence is required equally engages criminal liability.[71]

Ownership of body parts[72]

18.9   The vexed question of whether we own our bodies is only fleetingly addressed in the Human Tissue Act 2004. We noted earlier the ancient common law assumption that there is no property in a corpse. That statement must be qualified. Consider the Egyptian mummies held in the British Museum. Do they belong to the British Museum? Or might we lawfully help ourselves to one or two? *R v Kelly*[73] confirmed that, once a body or body parts had been changed in nature by work done on them, such parts become capable of being

---

[66] See s 9. And the licensing requirement does not apply to bodies of people who died before the Act came into force and are at least 100 years old (ie archaeologists are exempt).

[67] Code of Practice, Code 5, para 45.

[68] Code of Practice, Code 5, Appendix A.

[69] See s 5(1).

[70] See s 5(2).

[71] See s 25.

[72] See J W Harris, 'Who Owns My Body?' (1996) 16 *Oxford Journal of Legal Studies* 55. Mason and Laurie devote a whole chapter to 'The Body as Property', see J K Mason and G T Laurie, *Mason and McCall Smith's Law and Medical Ethics* (8th edn, 2010) OUP (hereafter *Mason and McCall Smith*), ch 14; and see Price, *Human Tissue in Transplantation and Research* (2009), ch 8.

[73] [1998] 3 All ER 741.

property. A technician was accused of stealing body parts from the Royal College of Surgeons and selling them to an artist who wished to use the parts as moulds for his sculptures. Both were charged with theft. Their defence was the College did not own the parts and so they could not steal them. Upholding the convictions, the Court of Appeal found that body parts became capable of being property for the purposes of the Theft Act 1968 because they had '... acquired different attributes by virtue of the application of skills, such as dissection or preservation technology, for exhibition or teaching purposes'. The notion of 'property', however, is complex in this context. The Court of Appeal in *Kelly* did not find that the Royal College of Surgeons *owned* the stolen body parts. A right to lawful possession of property is all that is required for that property to be stolen from you. The English Court of Appeal concurred with their Australian brethren in *Doodeward v Spence*;[74] in that case Griffith CJ spoke of a body and its parts becoming the subject of property. He said:

> ... when a person has by the lawful exercise of work or skills so dealt with a human body or part of a human body that it has acquired some attributes differentiating it from a mere corpse awaiting burial he requires a right to retain possession of it, at least as against any person not entitled to have delivered to him for the purpose of burial.

Does it follow from *Kelly* that whenever organs or tissue have been retained and, for example, have been preserved in formalin or put in blocks, the hospital in possession of the specimen can assert a property right to it? *Dobson v North Tyneside Health Authority*[75] appears to undermine such an argument. The family of a woman who had died of a brain tumour brought a claim in clinical negligence against the health authority alleging failure to diagnose her condition sufficiently swiftly to offer her effective treatment. To succeed in their claim, they needed to ensure that their expert witnesses could examine samples of the brain. The brain had been removed at a coroner's post-mortem, preserved in paraffin, and later disposed of. The family sued the hospital for conversion, alleging unlawful disposal of the brain. They argued that on completion of the coroner's investigation the family were entitled to the return of the brain. They enjoyed either ownership or, at least, a right of possession of the deceased's brain. The Court of Appeal dismissed their claim. Fixing the brain in paraffin was not a sufficient exercise of skill or labour to give that brain any different attributes to the organ initially removed from the body in the course of post-mortem. There was: [76]

> ... nothing ... to suggest that the actual preservation of the brain after the post-mortem was on a par with stuffing or embalming a corpse or preserving an anatomical or pathological specimen for collection or with preserving a human freak such as a double-headed foetus that had some value for exhibition purposes.

Identifying exactly what must be done to transform an organ taken from a body into property is difficult and somewhat artificial, and we must ask if

---

[74] (1908) 6 CLR 406 at 413–44.
[75] [1996] 4 All ER 479.
[76] [1996] 4 All ER 479 (per Peter Gibson LJ).

Dobson may be a decision soon to be consigned to legal history. Nonetheless the 'no property rule' received further support in *AB v Leeds Hospital NHS Trust*.[77] Parents whose deceased children had been subject to post-mortem examinations and organ retention without their consent brought claims for psychiatric injury to themselves and wrongful interference with the bodies of the children. Gage J, rejecting the latter claim, reasserted the rule of 'no property in a corpse'. He also confirmed that, nonetheless, separated parts of the body subjected to the application of work and skill might become property – the property of he who expended that work and skill. So, pathologists who dissected and fixed organs from the body and transformed them into blocks and slides could acquire ownership of that 'property'. The skill and labour rule creates the odd paradox whereby our bodies and their parts are not our property (or at least do not form part of our estate) but put '. . . to the uses of medicine, their body parts become, as if by magic, property, but property owned by persons unknown for purposes unforeseen by the deceased'.[78]

However, in *R v Kelly*[79] Rose LJ had suggested obiter that the common law could develop to recognise a body part as property, even without the acquisition of different attributes, if it had acquired '. . . a use or significance beyond . . . mere existence'. He even indicated that in such a case outright ownership may be recognised. The Court of Appeal in *Yearworth v North Bristol NHS Trust*[80] took a small further step towards recognising property in separated body parts. Claims were brought by five men and the widow of a sixth in respect of the alleged negligence of the defendant trust in allowing their stored sperm to perish when the temperature in the storage tanks dropped and no attempt was made to ensure the sperm remained safely frozen. All the men had stored sperm for future use before undergoing chemotherapy for cancer. The men's claim that the loss of their sperm constituted personal injury failed. The appeal court allowed their claims for damage to their property, stating that 'developments in medical science now require a re-analysis of the common law's treatment of and approach to the issue of ownership of parts or products of a living body'.[81] The Court acknowledged that they could have used the 'skill and labour' notion to find that the complex process of storing sperm in liquid nitrogen was enough to transform the sperm to property.[82] But Lord Judge CJ was clear that the Court of Appeal was scornful of that principle, saying that its 'ancestry did not commend it as a solid foundation'.[83] Their Lordships preferred to derive their findings from Rose LJ's dictum in *Kelly*. The men had for the purposes of a claim in negligence, 'ownership of the sperm which they ejaculated'. They alone had generated and ejaculated the sperm and done so solely to ensure that it could later be used for their benefit. The storage of the

[77] [2004] EWHC 644.
[78] See Brazier (2002) 22 *Legal Studies* 550, p 563.
[79] [1998] 3 All ER 741 at 750.
[80] [2009] EWCA Civ 37.
[81] [2009] EWCA 37, para 45(a).
[82] [2009] EWCA 37, para 45(c).
[83] [2009] EWCA 37, para 45(d).

sperm was governed by the Human Fertilisation and Embryology Act 1990. The 1990 Act restricted how the men could use the sperm, but entrenched the ability of the men to ensure that 'their' sperm was not used contrary to their direction; their 'negative control over its use remains absolute'. Furthermore, as the Authority could not continue to store the sperm without the continuing consent of the men, the Act recognised a fundamental feature of ownership in that the men and they only could require destruction of the sperm at any time. Analysis of the rights relating to the use and storage of the men's sperm led the Court to conclude that no individual or authority had any *rights* in relation to the sperm.

Yearworth could be seen as a narrow judgment[84] heavily dependent on the context of the claim relating to storage of gametes under the Human Fertilisation and Embryology Act 1990. It is hedged around by qualifications as will have been noted. The judgment of ownership was for the purposes of a claim in negligence and relates to property in products of the living body. But Lord Judge is clear that the old rules must be revisited and the law must keep up with modern science. Another feature of *Yearworth* is this. The restrictions on use of the sperm imposed by the Human Fertilisation and Embryology Act did not undermine the men's ownership claims. It thus does not follow that by allowing ownership you open the door to wholesale commodification. Policy-based restrictions on sale and use are not incompatible with ownership.

As we have seen, section 32 of the Human Tissue Act 2004 prohibits commercial dealings in body parts for transplant purposes, but the Act exempts from this prohibition 'material which is the subject of property because of an application of human skill'.[85] The Bill had originally sought to ban commercial dealings in body parts for any purposes. Such a broad rule would have been unworkable as human tissue is fundamental material in medical research and trade among laboratories is well established. What seems to be objectionable is not for university A to sell human material excess to its requirements to company B but for the human originator of that material to receive any recompense or property rights in his or her body.

The fundamental question of whether we should own our bodies would constitute a book of its own. We might ask – does it matter? The Human Tissue Act 2004 grants us and our families fairly extensive control of what may be done with our bodies and their component parts. A number of reasons suggest that it might matter. Common law dicta that there was no property in a corpse did not derive from any belief that such bodies were without value. Quite the contrary – the dead should not be seen '. . . as other inanimate objects, but were to be treated quite differently, even reverently'.[86] Our bodies were too valuable to be 'things', to be mere property. Would classifying bodies as property devalue them or endorse that value?

---

[84] But see also the latter part of the judgment relating to bailment.
[85] See s 32(9)(c).
[86] See P Matthews, 'The Man of Property' (1995) 3 *Medical Law Review* 237 at 254.

There is no avoiding the evidence that in the modern world bodies have certain sorts of tangible value. Sometimes this value is crudely commercial. Consider the famous case of Mr Moore.[87] Cell lines developed from his excised and diseased spleen made his doctor $15m and much greater profits for the drug company who bought the potential cell line. Yet Mr Moore was held to have no ownership rights in the body part removed. Another value secreted in our body parts is our genetic information. What may seem to be redundant surplus tissue carries within it information about the whole of our health and much about ourselves. We may prefer to retain control of that information.

Until recently, proponents of property models and bodies tended to be motivated by a belief in markets in human tissue. We should own our bodies so we can sell them. The debate is much more sophisticated now. Mason and Laurie[88] have made a powerful case for a modified property model.[89] Finally, we have not touched on the vexed question of intellectual property and refer you again to Mason and Laurie.[90]

---

[87] *Moore v Regents of the University of California* 793 P 2d 479 (Cal 1950).

[88] J K Mason and G T Laurie, 'Consent or Property: Dealing with the Body and its Parts in the Shadow of Bristol and Alder Hey' (2001) 64 *Modern Law Review* 710.

[89] And see L Skene, 'Property Rights in Human Bodies, Body Parts and Tissue: Regulatory Contexts and Proposals for New Laws' (2002) 22 *Legal Studies* 102.

[90] *Mason and McCall Smith*, pp 466–474.

Chapter 19

THE END OF LIFE[1]

19.1 Society has never been comfortable with issues surrounding the process of dying; and as healthcare staff are involved with the dying, they inevitably become involved in ethical as well as medical dilemmas. For the last year or so, the heat of the debate has focused on when the law should permit some sort of assistance for those who help a terminally ill relative or friend end her life, in particular when families have travelled with a relative to the Dignitas clinic in Switzerland where assisted dying is not unlawful. But this is just one of a host of difficult dilemmas. These include whether efforts should always be made to keep a dying person alive in spite of the additional suffering incurred by that person and the cost in terms of human dignity; and when, if ever, attempts may be made to hasten death when there is excessive suffering and when the cause is hopeless.

The practice, of what some regard as 'striving officiously to keep alive' has been facilitated by the increase in high-technology equipment, much of it capable of being used to postpone inevitable death for a time. The benefits of such equipment may often be great; yet there is a cost, both in human and economic terms. Further treatment may sometimes be said to be futile. A vast literature has developed around the concept of medical futility.[2] The very word generates controversy. Mason and Laurie[3] prefer to talk of non-productive treatment, treatment which cannot offer even a minimal likelihood of benefit to the patient. Part of the difficulty in this debate is the problem of separating human and economic considerations. Refusing to order doctors to continue to ventilate a severely injured infant, Balcombe LJ said openly;[4]

---

[1] See Special Issue, 'Legal Challenges and New Horizons for Medicalised Death and Dying' (2010) 18(4) *Medical Law Review*.

[2] J K Mason and G T Laurie, *Mason and McCall Smith's Law and Medical Ethics* (8th edn, 2010) OUP (hereafter *Mason and McCall Smith*), ch 15.

[3] *Mason and McCall Smith*, p 477.

[4] *Re J (A Minor) (Wardship: Medical Treatment)* [1992] 4 All ER 614 at 625, CA. And see GMC, *Treatment and Care Towards the End of Life: Good Practice in Decision Making* (2010), paras 38 and 39.

> ... [A]n order which may have the effect of compelling a doctor or health authority to make available scarce resources and to a particular child ... might require the health authority to put J on a ventilator in an intensive-care unit, and thereby possibly deny the benefit of those limited resources to a child who was much more likely than J to benefit from them.

Language invoking medical futility could be seen as disguising rationing decisions, or even covert euthanasia. Whatever the economic considerations, few would deny the personal cost to the patient and to those close to the patient in terms of human dignity. Do the 'rights' of patients include the right to die with dignity? If so, does that 'right' extend to being 'helped to die'? In preserving and sustaining the life of a patient with a hopeless prognosis, is it in the interests of the patient, the family, or the doctor, to prolong his suffering? Unlimited access to technology may sometimes be as cruel as the illness itself. Doctors concerned with terminally ill patients must make professional and human decisions to give up treatment which may be merely sustaining the function of the organs, and turn to appropriate care at the terminal stage.

In 1993, the tragic case of Tony Bland thrust this question into the public domain.[5] Did the law demand that a young man grievously injured in the horrific disaster at Hillsborough Football Stadium should continue to be kept alive by artificial means? The Law Lords concluded that it did not. The *Bland* judgment rekindled debates on euthanasia, albeit their Lordships and many commentators[6] vehemently rejected suggestions that the decision to allow Tony Bland to die was in any sense sanctioning euthanasia.[7]

The Mental Capacity Act 2005 came into force in 2007. The Act sets down principles by which the social and medical care of persons lacking the mental capacity to make their own decisions should be conducted. A Code of Practice provides guidance on the interpretation of the Act. We examined the wider effects of the Act in chapter 6. In this chapter, we will consider the implications of the Act for end-of-life decisions relating to adults lacking capacity.

Tony Bland lacked the capacity to make his own decisions. But what of patients who retain capacity? Since *Bland*, the courts have been deluged with cases seeking clearer definition of an individual's right to determine the manner of her death, or life. The Human Rights Act 1998 focused attention on what exactly is entailed in the right to life embodied in Article 2. Does the prohibition on inhuman and degrading treatment in Article 3 assist those dying in distress? Does a right to privacy in Article 8 encompass autonomy in decisions on the end of life? The case law remains confused and confusing.

---

[5] *Airedale NHS Trust v Bland* [1993] 1 All ER 821, HL.
[6] *Mason and McCall Smith*, p 506.
[7] See, in particular, *Airedale NHS Trust v Bland* [1993] 1 All ER 821 at 856, CA, per Hoffmann LJ.

In 2002, the President of the Family Division endorsed a tetraplegic patient's right to demand that doctors switch off the ventilator keeping her alive,[8] but when Dianne Pretty argued that she had a right to assisted suicide, the House of Lords found against her.[9] Doctors cannot be forced to administer treatment which they believe to be clinically unnecessary, futile or inappropriate. Does this include artificial nutrition and hydration (ANH)? The Court of Appeal held that it does.[10] An appeal to the European Court of Human Rights was ruled inadmissible.[11] In 2009 Debbie Purdy[12] enjoyed partial success when she approached her battle for a right to assisted suicide from a different angle, claiming that the Director for Public Prosecutions[13] (DPP) was required to clarify guidance on the circumstances when a prosecution would be brought under the Suicide Act 1961 in order to comply with Mrs Purdy's rights under Article 8. In February 2010 the DPP issued new guidance identifying more clearly when prosecution would be deemed in the public interest and controversially placing emphasis on the motive of the suspect.[14]

Nor are the courts the only forum for debates on the end of life. In 2006, Lord Joffe's third attempt to enshrine a right to assisted suicide in law was defeated in the House of Lords by a vote of 148 to 100. Two weeks before the House of Lords decision in *Purdy*, Lord Falconer withdrew a proposed amendment to the Coroners and Justice Bill. The 2009 Act amended the Suicide Act 1961 to reframe the offence of assisted suicide. Lord Falconer had sought to grant statutory protection to those who travel abroad with terminally ill relatives or friends to seek assisted dying. And in December 2010 Margo MacDonald's End of Life Assistance (Scotland) Bill 2010 was defeated in the Scottish Parliament.[15]

Opponents argue for the sanctity of life and for better palliative care.[16] The Department of Health includes end-of-life care as one of eight high-level priorities.[17] Proposals for reform include an improved funding model for

---

[8] *B v An NHS Trust* [2002] EWHC 425.

[9] *R (Pretty) v DPP* [2002] 1 All ER 1, HL. Mrs Pretty's appeal to the European Court of Human Rights also failed: *Pretty v UK* (2002) 35 EHHR 1.

[10] *R (On the application of Burke) v GMC* [2005] EWCA Civ 1003.

[11] *Burke v UK* [2006] App 19807/06.

[12] *R (on the application of Purdy) v DPP* [2009] UKHL 45.

[13] Prosecution requires the consent of the DPP: Suicide Act 1961, s 2(4).

[14] DPP, *Code for Crown Prosecutors and the Policy for Prosecutors in respect of Cases of Encouraging or Assisting Suicide* (2010).

[15] 15 SP Bill 38. The Bill is discussed in G Laurie, J K Mason, 'Assistance in Dying or Euthanasia? Comments on the End of Life Assistance (Scotland) Bill' (2010) 14 *Edinburgh Law Review* 493. In November 2010 the Holyrood Committee recommended that there was no case for changing the law and MSPs rejected the Bill in December 2010.

[16] See NICE, *Improving Supportive and Palliative Care for Adults with Cancer – A Manual* (2004).

[17] DH, *End of Life Care Strategy* (2008).

hospices from 2011,[18] and the extension of 'payment by results' – a national tariff of fixed prices – to end-of-life care from 2012. It is hoped that this will increase patient choice by enabling different aspects of treatment to be provided by different service providers, including commercial or voluntary providers.

The *Concise Oxford Dictionary* defines euthanasia as 'gentle and easy death; bringing about of this, especially in case of incurable and painful disease'. It is a term much used, and misused. It may be popularly invoked to include conduct characterised as 'mercy killing', when somebody, usually a relative, deliberately and specifically performs some act, such as administering a drug, to accelerate death and terminate suffering. Prosecutions for mercy killing, while rare, are sometimes reported, and the courts tend to deal with such cases with compassion. Mercy killing, where doctors are not usually directly involved, may also be termed active euthanasia. This can be contrasted with 'passive euthanasia', which might describe, for example, withholding of life-support treatment. The terminology of the debate is complex and confusing.[19] Active euthanasia involves an act done deliberately, designed to shorten life by however short a span. *Active* euthanasia may involve *voluntary* euthanasia where the act done, the killing of the patient, is done at her specific request. *Non-voluntary* euthanasia may be the term used to refer to ending the life of someone who cannot express a view on the prolongation of her life at the relevant time. A proxy speaks on her behalf and what is done is done at least purportedly for the patient's own good. *Involuntary* euthanasia involves killing a person without her own or any proxy authority. The patient's life may be ended for what others perceive as her good, or could be terminated because of the burden her continued life places on society. *Passive* euthanasia can itself be voluntary, non-voluntary or involuntary. As we shall see, any boundary between passive and active euthanasia is less clear than it might at first be thought to be.[20]

In 2009 a postal survey of medical practitioners' end-of-life decisions revealed that 0.21 per cent of deaths were attributable to voluntary euthanasia; 21 per cent to non-treatment decisions; 17.1 per cent to 'double effect' measures; 16.5 per cent to continuous deep sedation (CDS) and 0.0 to physician-assisted suicide.[21] Now we must explore the legality of this range of decisions.

---

[18] Though there are fears that budget cuts threaten to dilute current levels of commitment. See National Council for Palliative Care, *Response to Equity and Excellence: Liberating the NHS – Overarching Statement* (October 2010).

[19] See *Mason and McCall Smith*, pp 566–567; but see also E Jackson, *Medical Law: Text, Cases and Materials* (2nd edn, 2010) OUP, pp 858–859.

[20] See D Shaw, 'The Body as Unwarranted Life Support' (2007) 33 *Journal of Medical Ethics* 519, arguing that if a competent person wishes to die this is 'unwarranted life support' which arguably can be ended in the same way that a competent person can refuse medical life support. Also see J Busch, 'Life Support and Euthanasia: A Perspective on Shaw's New Perspective' (2010) *Journal of Medical Ethics*, published online.

[21] C Seale, 'End of Life Decisions in the UK Involving Medical Practitioners' 23 (2009) *Palliative Medicine* 198.

Murder, suicide and assisting suicide

19.2 Deliberately taking the life of another person, whether that person is dying or not, constitutes the crime of murder. Accordingly, any doctor who, no matter how compassionately, practises voluntary euthanasia or mercy killing can be charged with murder, if the facts can be clearly established. As Lord Mustill puts it:[22]

> ... 'mercy killing' by active means is murder ... that the doctor's motives are kindly will for some, although not for all, transform the moral quality of his act, but this makes no difference in law.

A doctor convicted of murder faces a mandatory life sentence in prison. Dr Cox was, in a sense, lucky.[23] He injected his patient Mrs Lilian Boyes with potassium chloride. Mrs Boyes suffered unbearable pain from rheumatoid arthritis and begged Dr Cox to end her suffering. Potassium chloride stops the heart. It kills and has no therapeutic or painkilling properties. Before Dr Cox's action came to the attention of the police, Mrs Boyes was cremated. It could not therefore be proved beyond reasonable doubt that the injection administered by Dr Cox killed her. Dr Cox was convicted only of attempted murder. The judge imposed a suspended sentence, and the General Medical Council (GMC) allowed him to continue to practise subject to certain conditions. Had the link between his action and Mrs Boyes's death been clearly established, no such merciful course would have been open to the judge.[24] This applies equally to family members and loved ones.

At present, judicial sympathy for a perpetrator of 'mercy killing' is limited by the extent of their sentencing discretion.[25] This was demonstrated in two recent cases. In 2010 Francis Inglis killed her twenty-two-year-old son, Tom, with a lethal injection of heroin.[26] Tom was in a coma following an accident, but doctors felt there were chances of improvement. Inglis had previously attempted to administer a lethal injection to Tom and been released on bail and banned from seeing him. She entered the hospital under false pretences, injected him with heroin and barricaded herself into the room. Inglis contended that she acted out of compassion and love, but was sentenced to a

---

[22] *Airedale NHS Trust v Bland* [1993] 1 All ER 821 at 850, HL.

[23] *R v Cox* (1992) 12 BMLR 38. See E Jackson, 'Whose Death Is It Anyway? Euthanasia and the Medical Profession' (2004) 57 *Current Legal Problems* 415.

[24] Though the judge might reduce the sentence. See, for example, R Ford, 'Life May Mean Just 3 years for Mercy Killing Husband' (2007) *The Times*, 25 May, involving the case of Frank Lund who was found guilty of murder, having suffocated his wife, who suffered a chronic bowel condition, on her request.

[25] A Green Paper proposes greater sentencing discretion: Ministry of Justice, *Breaking the Cycle*, Cm7972 (December 2010).

[26] Unreported. See S Burns, 'Showing Mercy' (2010) 154(1) *Solicitor's Journal* 6 at 8, also commenting on *R v Gilderdale* (2010), unreported, 25 January (Crown Ct (Lewes)). Kay Gilderdale helped her thirty-one-year-old daughter, who suffered from ME, to die. Gilderdale admitted assisting suicide (for which she received a conditional discharge) and was acquitted of attempted murder.

minimum of nine years' imprisonment. The verdict was much criticised.[27] On appeal the sentence was reduced to five years:[28]

> [T]he law of murder does not distinguish between murder committed for malevolent reasons and murder motivated by familial love. Subject to well established partial defences, like provocation or diminished responsibility, mercy killing is murder.[29]

In January 2011 the Court of Appeal allowed an appeal against sentence by seventy-three-year-old George Webb. Mr Webb was sentenced to two years' imprisonment in 2010 when he was found guilty of manslaughter on grounds of diminished responsibility, having suffocated his seventy-five-year-old wife during her suicide attempt.[30] Substituting a twelve-month suspended sentence, Lord Judge said:

> We recognise, as the judge was at pains to underline, that this is not a case of assisted suicide. It is a case of manslaughter. The facts that we have narrated make that clear. Nevertheless, it seems to us that there are features of this case which bring it close to an assisted suicide.[31]

In 2010 Tony Nicklinson, who suffers from 'locked-in syndrome' and is unable to move, launched a legal bid to allow his wife to kill him. He cannot commit suicide, does not want to suffer withdrawal of nutrition or hydration and wants to die in his own home rather than travelling abroad to an assisted-suicide clinic. His argument is not that Article 8 requires voluntary euthanasia to be legalised, but that the current law on murder, which imposes a life sentence on anyone found guilty of murder, irrespective of whether or not the killing was consensual, disproportionately affects his Article 8 rights.[32] Until the law is changed, or the DPP revises his guidelines to extend beyond assisted suicide,[33] active euthanasia, whatever the circumstances, equals murder in English law.[34]

[27] L Bannerman, 'Jury Heckled over Murder Verdict for Mother Francis Inglis who "Acted out of Love"' (2010) *The Times,* 21 January.

[28] *R v Inglis* [2010] EWCA Crim 2637.

[29] Per Judge LCJ at 37.

[30] See 'Pensioner Cleared of Murdering Wife in Mercy Killing' (2010) *Guardian,* 9 December.

[31] *R v Webb* [2011] EWCA Crim 152 at 19–20.

[32] S Chahal, 'Tony Nicklinson's Case: Submission to Commission on Assisted Dying' (December 2010), para 7. See also T Nicklinson, 'A Scheme for Assisted Death: Submission to Commission on Assisted Dying' (December 2010).

[33] DPP, *Code for Crown Prosecutors and the Policy for Prosecutors in respect of Cases of Encouraging or Assisting Suicide* (2010), para 33: 'It is murder or manslaughter for a person to do an act that ends the life of another, even if he or she does so on the basis that he or she is simply complying with the wishes of the other person concerned.'

[34] See E Jackson, *Medical Law: Text, Cases and Materials* (2nd edn, 2010) OUP, pp 859–861.

Double effect

19.3   The only exception to that rule was spelt out by Devlin J in the case *R v Adams*[35] in 1957. Dr Adams was charged with the murder of an eighty-one-year-old patient who had suffered a stroke; it was alleged that he had prescribed and administered such large quantities of drugs, especially heroin and morphine, that he must have known that the drugs would kill her. In his summing-up to the jury, Devlin J first stated:

> . . . it does not matter whether her death was inevitable and her days were numbered. If her life was cut short by weeks or months it was just as much murder as if it was cut short by years. There has been much discussion as to when doctors might be justified in administering drugs which would shorten life. Cases of severe pain were suggested and also cases of helpless misery. The law knows no special defence in this category . . .

However, he went on to say:

> . . . but that does not mean that a doctor who was aiding the sick and dying had to calculate in minutes, or even hours, perhaps, not in days or weeks, the effect on a patient's life of the medicines which he would administer. If the first purpose of medicine – the restoration of health – could no longer be achieved, there was still much for the doctor to do and he was entitled to do all that was proper and necessary to relieve pain and suffering even if the measures he took might incidentally shorten life by hours or perhaps even longer. The doctor who decided whether or not to administer the drug could not do his job, if he were thinking in terms of hours or months of life. Dr Adams's defence was that the treatment was designed to promote comfort, and if it was the right and proper treatment, the fact that it shortened life did not convict him of murder.

Devlin J introduced into English law a version of the 'double-effect' principle, whereby if one act has two inevitable consequences, one good and one evil, the act may be morally acceptable in certain circumstances. His ruling is endorsed in *Bland*.[36] It is not crystal clear in its meaning. In one passage, Devlin J referred to the incidental shortening of life by hours and, in another passage, he referred to the shortening of life by hours or months. It must be a matter of judgment in each case.[37] Clearly he was dealing with terminally ill patients where, in order to alleviate pain, it is permissible to disregard the fact that the treatment involved may accelerate the patient's death.

---

[35]   *R v Adams* [1957] Crim LR773.

[36]   *Airedale NHS Trust v Bland* [1993] 1 All ER 821 at 868, HL. But consider the impact of *R v Woollin* [1999] AC 82, HL (jury may infer intent to kill even if causing death is not the accused's primary purpose); see E Jackson, *Medical Law: Text, Cases and Materials* (2nd edn, 2010) OUP, p 923.

[37]   See, for example, the investigation surrounding forty-three cases of patient deaths under GP Howard Martin. In 2005 Martin was cleared of murdering three patients by injecting them with morphine. See 'Morphine Doctor Cleared of Murder' (2005) *The Times*, 14 December. Further investigation followed and Dr Martin was struck off by the GMC in 2010 on the basis that he had hastened the death of eighteen patients.

19.4 *The End of Life*

In recent years there is evidence of increased use of continuous deep sedation (CDS) – medically induced unconsciousness at the end of life – as a form of palliative care. One study claims that it is used in around 18 per cent of medically attended deaths in the UK.[38] Use of CDS is inconsistent and poorly documented. Clive Seale's postal survey indicates that it is used more prolifically by non-religious doctors.[39] Mason and Laurie recognise that CDS might be accompanied by removal of artificial life support, which might hasten death. They warn that 'while terminal sedation could be used in the normal process of good medical practice, it is equally likely to represent an instance of euthanasia hiding under emollient terminology'.[40]

The application of laws relating to murder and suicide are central to an understanding of law controlling treatment of the dying. It will be appropriate to consider first the case of the 'competent' patient, that is a person with full legal and mental capacity, who is aware of what is happening and who may wish to make decisions himself about his quality of life: the way he will be treated and how he will continue to live or die. Second, the case of the adult 'incapacitated' patient will be considered: unconscious patients or persons who do not have the mental or physical capacity to make their own wishes known at the relevant times.[41]

Competent patients: is there a 'right' to die?

19.4 Does a patient have a 'right' to die? The answer will depend on the circumstances in which she seeks to exercise such a 'right'. The Court of Appeal in *Re T*[42] made it clear that an adult patient with mental capacity enjoys an absolute right to refuse further treatment even where refusing treatment means certain death. The patient who is terminally ill, or who, even if not terminally ill, suffers from intractable pain or unbearable disability, can refuse further treatment. The only caveat is that the evidence that her refusal of treatment was free and informed must be unequivocal. Her reasons to refuse treatment are not material. A patient dying of cancer has the right to say 'no more', however strongly her doctor may argue that more chemotherapy would offer her some additional months of life. A person paralysed by multiple sclerosis can refuse to be ventilated. A patient whose condition is no longer bearable to her can take her own life if she has access to the means to do so, and is still

---

[38] C Seale, 'Continuous Deep Sedation in Medical Practice: A Descriptive Study' (2010) 29(1) *Journal of Pain and Symptom Management* 44.

[39] C Seale, 'The Role of Doctors' Religious Faith and Ethnicity in Taking Ethically Controversial Decisions During End-of-Life Care' (2010) *Journal of Medical Ethics*, published online.

[40] *Mason and McCall Smith*, p 580. And see A Brimelow, 'The Alternative to Euthanasia', *BBC News* (website) 12 August 2009.

[41] It should be noted, of course, that it may not always be an easy issue to determine whether a person is clinically or legally competent: see above, ch 6. Children and infants are considered in ch 14.

[42] *Re T (Adult: Refusal of Treatment)* [1992] 4 All ER 465, CA; discussed at **5.2**.

independently capable of such action. There is a right to prevent others forcing you to live.

The first major difficulty is this · ˉ patient who wishes to die may already be receiving life-sustaining treatment. She is hooked up to a ventilator or receiving artificial nutrition via a naso-gastric tube or intravenous drip. She wants her life support withdrawn and to be permitted to die. Intrinsically her position seems indistinguishable from the patient who refuses further chemotherapy, or instructs her doctors not to ventilate her. However, someone will have to intervene in this scenario to switch off the ventilator or remove the feeding tube. Will a doctor who does the relevant act risk prosecution for murder or assisting suicide?

The decision in *Airedale NHS Trust v Bland*[43] made it clear that if a doctor disconnects a patient from life support at her specific request, that act does not constitute either murder or assisting suicide. *Bland* exposes the fragility of distinctions made between active and passive euthanasia.[44] Three principles emerge from *Bland*:

(1) Treatment involving any invasive procedure constitutes a battery, unless authorised by the patient, or if he is unable to authorise his own treatment, it is justified by other lawful authority.

(2) Continuing invasive treatment, once justification for that treatment is withdrawn, becomes a battery and therefore unlawful.

(3) ANH constitutes treatment as much as drug therapy or ventilation. If a patient instructs doctors to switch off a ventilator or withdraw a naso-gastric tube, failure to act on those instructions renders continuing treatment unlawful.

In *B v An NHS Trust*,[45] Ms B suffered a haemorrhage in the spinal column in her neck. Her condition deteriorated rapidly. Within two years she was paralysed from the neck down and could breathe only supported by a ventilator. Doctors told her that she was unlikely to recover. Rehabilitation programmes to allow her to live outside hospital on the ventilator were proposed to her. Ms B was adamant that she did not want to survive in such a condition. She instructed doctors to switch off the ventilator. The doctors treating her refused, citing conscientious objections to such a course of action and challenging Ms B's mental capacity to refuse further treatment. Butler-Sloss P held that Ms B retained mental capacity.[46] That being the case, continuing to ventilate

---

[43] [1993] 1 All ER 821, HL; and see *Nancy B v Hôtel Dieu de Quebec* (1992) 86 DLR (4th) 385 (Canada); *Auckland Area Health Board v A-S* [1993] 1 NZLR 235 (New Zealand); *Bouvia v Superior Court* (1986) 225 Cal Reptr 297.

[44] But see A McGee, 'Finding a Way Through the Ethical and Legal Maze: Withdrawal of Medical Treatment and Euthanasia' (2005) 13 *Medical Law Review* 357 and J Keown, 'A Futile Defence of Bland: A Reply to Andrew McGee' (2005) 13 *Medical Law Review* 393.

[45] [2002] EWHC 429.

[46] Discussed more fully above at **6.4**.

her against her will was unlawful. She was entitled to demand that the ventilator be switched off, though not to require an individual clinician to act contrary to his conscience. Yet there can be no doubt that switching off a ventilator or removing a naso-gastric tube is an act hastening death. The Law Lords in *Bland* skirt around the logical implications of their findings. Lord Browne-Wilkinson is honest in his appreciation of the dilemma. He says:

> Mr Munby QC ... submits that the removal of the naso-gastric tube necessary to provide artificial feeding and the discontinuation of the existing regime of artificial feeding constitute positive acts of commission. I do not accept this. Apart from the act of removing the naso-gastric tube, the mere failure to continue to do what you have previously done is not, in any ordinary sense to do anything positive; on the contrary it is by definition an omission to do what you have previously done.
>
> The positive act of removing the naso-gastric tube presents more difficulty. It is undoubtedly a positive act, similar to switching off a ventilator in the case of a patient whose life is being sustained by artificial ventilation. But in my judgment in neither case should the act be classified as positive, since to do so would be to introduce intolerable fine distinctions. If instead of removing the naso-gastric tube, it was left in place but no further nutrients were provided for the tube to convey to the patients' stomach, that would not be a positive act ... if the switching off of a ventilator were to be classified as a positive act, exactly the same result can be achieved by installing a time-clock which requires to be reset every 12 hours; the failure to reset the machine could not be classified as a positive act. In my judgment, essentially what is being done is to omit to feed or ventilate; the removal of the naso-gastric tube or the switching off a ventilator are merely incidents of that omission.[47]

Eliding acts and omissions enable the Law Lords to achieve the desired result. Consider its implications. James is sustained by a ventilator. He asks his wife, Claire, to switch it off because his doctor refuses to do so. James rejects advice to seek a declaration from the courts to overturn his doctors' advice. Reluctantly, Claire pulls the switch and James dies. Is Claire exempt from a charge of murder, or is a *Bland* defence exclusive to doctors? In the light of *B v An NHS Trust,* could Claire argue thus? Continuing to ventilate James against his will constitutes the tort of battery and the crime of assault. When Claire switched off the ventilator, all she did was use reasonable measures to prevent a crime. Then there is the most awkward question of all. What of the patient whose illness renders their life intolerable, but who is not reliant on treatment or life support to survive? Their condition is such that they cannot take their own life.

Assisted dying

19.5 Since the Suicide Act 1961, it is no longer a criminal offence to commit, or attempt to commit, suicide. However, section 2 of the Act, as amended in 2009[48] provides that:

---

[47] [1993] 1 All ER 821 at 881.

[48] S 59 of the Coroners and Justice Act 2009 reframes the offence, modernising the wording and combining the offence of assisting in a suicide and the offence of

> A person (D) commits an offence if (a) D does an act capable of encouraging or assisting the suicide or attempted suicide of another person, and (b) D's act was intended to encourage or assist suicide or an attempt at suicide.

It is a crime that may be committed for diverse reasons, ranging from the avaricious to the compassionate. In *R v McShane*,[49] a daughter was found guilty of trying to persuade her eighty-nine-year-old mother in a nursing home to kill herself so that she could inherit her estate. A secret camera installed by the police showed the daughter handing her mother drugs concealed in a packet of sweets, and pinning a note on her dress saying 'Don't bungle it'.

Clear evidence of aiding and abetting a particular act of suicide is necessary before a prosecution can be successful. In *A-G v Able*,[50] the court was asked to declare that it was an offence for the Voluntary Euthanasia Society to sell a booklet to its members aged twenty-five and over, setting out in some detail various ways in which individuals could commit suicide. The Society neither advocated nor deplored suicide; it had a neutral stance and regarded such decisions as matters of personal belief and judgment.[51] Evidence in the case suggested that over a period of eighteen months after the first distribution of the booklet, there were fifteen cases of suicides linked to the booklet, and nineteen suicides where documents were found which showed that the deceased was a member of, or had corresponded with, the Society. The court concluded that in most cases the supply of the booklet would not constitute an offence. Normally, a member requesting the booklet would not make clear his intentions, and the booklet would be supplied without any knowledge by the supplier of whether it was required for general information, research, or because suicide was contemplated. To establish an offence, it would have to be proved that the Society distributed the booklet to a person who, at the time of the distribution, was known to be contemplating suicide, with the intention of assisting and encouraging that person to commit suicide by means of the booklet's contents, and, further, that that person was in fact assisted and encouraged by the booklet to commit or attempt to commit suicide.

So too the doctor who knowingly provides someone with sufficient tablets with which to end a life, and advises how best to take them, risks prosecution. In 2010 the CPS decided not to charge Dr Wilson, a member of pro-euthanasia group Friends At The End (Fate), for advising a multiple sclerosis sufferer, Caroline Loder, how to commit suicide. Dr Wilson did not meet Loder, and nor did she encourage her suicide. However, the offence encompasses both encouragement and assistance. In a press statement, the CPS said that there was 'sufficient evidence to lead to a realistic prospect of conviction' but because

attempting to assist in a suicide into one single offence. The scope of the law is unchanged.

49 (1977) 66 Cr App R 97.
50 [1984] QB 795.
51 Compare with the US case where, at the time of writing, William Melchert-Dinkel has pleaded not guilty to charges of aiding suicide, having allegedly encouraged people (including a Briton) he 'met' in internet chat-rooms to commit suicide.

Dr Wilson's input was minimal, it was not in the public interest to prosecute.[52]

The well-informed and able may kill themselves. The patient dying of degenerative disease, or in the terminal throes of cancer, may need help to do so. If Jane can breathe only with the aid of a ventilator, she can require her doctor to switch off the ventilator. If Jane is slowly choking to death with motor neurone disease, but can still swallow enough lethal sleeping tablets, Jane can end her misery. If Jane is so weakened by the disease that she cannot reach for the tablets or swallow, she must endure her suffering.

An increasing number of commentators now advance the case for legalising physician-assisted dying.[53] But what does this mean? The Oregon Death with Dignity Act 1994 and the Washington State Death with Dignity Act 2009[54] allow doctors to comply with a patient's request for medication to end their life. But this does not meet the truly hard cases where the patient, even if supplied with medication, cannot take the dose independently. As we shall see, recent attempts to introduce legislation legalising physician-assisted dying in England and Wales have so far proved unsuccessful.

The patient who cannot commit suicide

19.6   Does the patient who cannot, or does not wish to, administer the means of suicide himself, have a right to assistance? Articles 2, 3, 8, 9 and 14 of the European Convention on Human Rights have been employed, to date unsuccessfully, in defence of such a right.

This matter first came before the UK courts in the sad case of Dianne Pretty. Mrs Pretty was dying of motor neurone disease. Gradually she had lost all ability to use her muscles. She could barely speak and could not swallow. She was fed by a tube. Mrs Pretty sought an assurance from the Director of Public Prosecutions that no charge would be brought against her husband should he help her to die at a time of her choice. The DPP refused to give any such assurance. Mrs Pretty brought an application for judicial review. She argued that the DPP acted unlawfully. He failed to pay due regard to Mrs Pretty's fundamental human rights. Her application failed before the Divisional Court,[55] as did her subsequent appeal to the House of Lords.[56] She took her case to the

---

[52]   CPS, Press Statement: 'No Charges Following Death of Caroline Loder' (16 August 2010).

[53]   Notably and eloquently, D W Meyers and J K Mason, 'Physician Assisted Suicide: A Second View from Mid-Atlantic' (1999) 29 *Anglo-American Law Review* 39.

[54]   Discussed below at **19.19**. And see I Kennedy and A Grubb, *Medical Law* (2000) Butterworths, p 1950.

[55]   [2001] All ER (D) 251.

[56]   [2002] 1 All ER 1, HL.

European Court of Human Rights at Strasbourg, but lost again.[57] The Law Lords held that the decision not to promise immunity to Mr Pretty should he help his wife to die was not, in the circumstances, amenable to judicial review.[58]

What human rights arguments did Mrs Pretty raise? It was put to the judges that Article 2, endorsing the right to life, carried with it the corollary of a right to die at a time and in a manner of one's own choosing. The Law Lords were unimpressed. They could read nothing into Article 2 to confer a right to be helped to die. Lord Bingham regarded Article 2 as embodying the traditional doctrine of sanctity of life. He put it thus:[59]

> Whatever the benefits which, in the view of many, attach to voluntary euthanasia, physician-assisted suicide and suicide without the intervention of a physician, these are not benefits which derive protection from an Article framed to protect the sanctity of life.

Nor did an argument based on Article 3 prohibiting inhuman or degrading treatment find any greater favour. Dignity in sickness and dying should be protected. Nothing in Article 3 conferred a positive obligation to help an individual end her life.[60] The Divisional Court declared:

> ... far from having the effect contended for by Mr Havers, Article 2 and 3 between them are aimed at the protection and preservation of life and the dignity of life, because of its fundamental value, not only to the individual but also to the community as a whole. It is to stand the whole purpose of these Articles on its head to say that they are aimed at protecting a person's right to procure their own death.

In the Lords, Lord Bingham[61] doubted whether any positive obligation to prevent citizens being subjected to degrading treatment could translate into a duty to ensure a person could seek help to die. Lord Steyn was clear that: '... Article 3 was not engaged'. It was:[62]

> ... singularly inapt to convey the idea that the state must guarantee to individuals a right to die with the deliberate assistance of third parties. So radical a step, infringing the sanctity of life principle, would have required far more explicit wording.

Lord Hope[63] was not convinced that Mrs Pretty's condition met the minimum level of severity required in Article 3. Since she could not be compelled to

---

[57] *Pretty v UK* (2002) 35 EHHR 1.
[58] Although at least some of their Lordships left open the question of whether on different facts such an application might succeed.
[59] [2002] 1 All ER 1 at 7, HL. The ECtHR concurred that Art 2 'could not be interpreted as involving a negative aspect'.
[60] But see the persuasive arguments of J Coggon, 'Could the Right to Die with Dignity Represent a New Right to Die in English Law?' (2006) 12 *Medical Law Review* 219.
[61] [2001] EWHC Admin 788 at para 51.
[62] [2002] 1 All ER 1 at 11–12, HL.
[63] At 37.

accept treatment and, in his view, palliative treatment was available, Lord Hope doubted that her state was degrading.[64]

Arguments centred on Article 8, the right to respect for private and family life, fared a little better. The Divisional Court conceded that Article 8 could extend to embrace a right to bodily integrity, including a right to refuse life-saving treatment. They were even prepared to assume Article 8(1) could extend to a right to be allowed to take one's own life. In some of their speeches, the Law Lords suggest Article 8 does not even go that far. Lord Steyn puts it bluntly:[65]

> ... Article 8 prohibits interference with the way in which an individual leads his life and it does not relate to the manner in which he wishes to die.

The European Court of Human Rights, on the other hand, was 'not prepared to exclude that this constitutes an interference with [Dianne Pretty's] right to respect for private life as guaranteed under Article 8(1) of the Convention'.[66] However, the European Court and House of Lords concurred with the Divisional Court that even if some sort of right to choose one's manner of dying can be inferred from Articles 8(1), Article 8(2), placing restrictions on privacy rights, justifies the state in criminalising assisted dying. The need to afford protection for vulnerable people, especially the elderly, justifies the provisions of the Suicide Act 1961 as they stand. Lord Bingham says:[67]

> It is not hard to imagine that an elderly person, in the absence of any pressure, might opt for a premature end to life if that were available, not from a desire to die or a willingness to stop living, but from a desire to stop being a burden to others.

Arguments grounded on Article 9 and 14 of the Convention also failed. Two policy questions perhaps influenced the judges in the Divisional Court and the Lords? First, note that Mrs Pretty did not seek physician-assisted suicide, but her husband's help to die. The Divisional Court noted:[68]

> We are not being asked to approve physician assisted suicide in carefully defined circumstances with carefully defined safeguards. We are being asked to allow a family member to help a loved one die, in circumstances of which we know nothing, in a way of which we know nothing, and with no continuing scrutiny by any outside person.

Second, the Law Lords were much exercised by the European scope of the Convention. Lord Steyn made this point:[69]

> The fact is that among the 41 member states ... there are deep cultural and religious differences in regard to euthanasia and assisted suicide. The legalisation of

---

[64] At 37.
[65] At 29.
[66] (2002) 35 EHRR 1.
[67] (2002) 35 EHRR 1 at 18. A view endorsed by the ECtHR.
[68] [2001] EWHC Admin 788 at para 60. See also [2002] 1 All ER 1 at 21, per Lord Bingham.
[69] At 27.

euthanasia and assisted suicide as adopted in the Netherlands would be unacceptable in predominantly Roman Catholic countries in Europe. The idea that the European Convention requires states to render lawful euthanasia and assisted suicide (as opposed to allowing democratically elected legislatures to adopt measures to that effect) must therefore be approached with caution.

Debbie Purdy tried a different approach. She was diagnosed with multiple sclerosis in 1995, after which her condition deteriorated. Like Dianne Pretty she was concerned that she would need the support of her husband to travel abroad to an assisted-suicide clinic, in which case he might be prosecuted under section 2(1) of the Suicide Act 1961. Her argument was that the lack of specific guidance on assisted suicide in the Code for Crown Prosecutors breached her right under Article 8 of the European Convention on Human Rights. That lack of clarity prevented her from identifying the facts and circumstances relevant to any future prosecution. The House of Lords, in their final decision before moving to the Supreme Court, overruled the Court of Appeal decision. The House of Lords did not rule whether or not it was lawful to assist another in their suicide by travelling abroad to a suicide clinic, but it did require the DPP to clarify his guidance.[70]

R (on the application of Purdy) v DPP[71] has connotations for public law[72] but is also significant in its application of Article 8. Purdy argued that the Article was engaged, as was indicated in the European Court of Human Rights decision in *Pretty*. But the lower courts were bound by the House of Lords decision, concluding: 'it is their Lordships who, if they think it appropriate, must release the knot'.[73] The House of Lords acknowledged not only that Article 8(1) was engaged, but that the level of discretion exercised by the DPP was not justified under Article 8(2).[74] The last (judicial) word on physician-assisted suicide may still be to come. Hopes that Parliament will take this burden from judges and prosecutors have so far proved unfounded.

Death tourism

19.7 With the development of the freedom of movement in Europe, some patients have travelled abroad to take advantage of laws permissive of assisted dying in a practice labelled 'death tourism'. In Switzerland, assisted dying is not illegal provided it is not motivated by self-serving ends. The practice of assisting dying is not limited to doctors and the suicide organisations in Switzerland

---

[70] For commentary, see N Cartwright, '48 Years On: Is the Suicide Act Fit for Purpose?' 17 (2009) *Medical Law Review* 467.

[71] [2009] UKHL 45.

[72] R Daw, A Solomon, 'Assisted Suicide and Identifying the Public Interest in the Decision to Prosecute' (2010) *Criminal Law Review* 737.

[73] *R (on the application of Purdy) v DPP* [2009] EWCA Civ 92 at 54.

[74] [2009] UKHL 45: 'Our decision is simply that the Article 8 rights of Ms Purdy entitle her to be provided with guidance from the director as to how he proposes to exercise his discretion under s 2(4) of the 1961 Act . . .' per Lord Neuberger at 106.

are some of the few in the world willing to accept foreign patients.[75] The English courts are powerless to intervene unless someone 'does an act capable of encouraging or assisting the suicide or attempted suicide of another person'. Many applicants are too ill to make all the arrangements themselves and are helped by a doctor or loved one.

In *Re Z (An Adult: Capacity)*,[76] Mr Z informed his local authority that he and his wife, Mrs Z, would travel to Switzerland where arrangements had been made for her to end her life at the Zurich-based assisted-suicide clinic, Dignitas. Could the court prevent him from assisting his wife? The judge satisfied himself that Mrs Z remained competent and was not subject to any undue influence. The decision to travel to Switzerland was hers. Any question of her husband's criminal liability was a matter for the DPP who had not authorised any prosecution:[77]

> [A]lthough an act may be criminal, it is not always in the public interest to prosecute in respect of it.

Hirst argues that no offence is committed in these circumstances on the basis that, unless statute provides otherwise, the criminal law has no application outside this country.[78] Nor, Hirst argues, would initial preparations in this country necessarily lead to a prosecution, because, arguably,[79] assisted suicide is criminal only when the assisted suicide or attempted assisted suicide actually occurs. These arguments were considered in *Purdy* but not resolved as they were not central to the case.[80] Consequently, rather than relying on jurisdictional arguments, those travelling abroad to assist a loved one in his suicide should pay heed to the DPP's guidelines about prosecution.[81]

The DPP's *Policy for Prosecutors*

19.8 Following a public consultation exercise, the DPP issued a *Code for Crown Prosecutors and the Policy for Prosecutors in respect of Cases of Encouraging or Assisting Suicide*, in February 2010. The Code shifts emphasis

---

[75] Since the Swiss clinic, Dignitas, was set up in 1998, there have reportedly been 1,041 assisted suicides, including more than 30 assisted suicides of Britons in 2009. See M Beckford, 'Record Number of Britons Ended their Lives at Dignitas Last Year' (2010) *The Telegraph,* 22 February.

[76] [2004] EWHC 2817 (Fam). See P De Cruz, 'The Terminally Ill Adult Seeking Assisted Suicide Abroad' (2005) 13 *Medical Law Review* 257.

[77] *Re Z (An Adult: Capacity)* ibid, per Hedley J at para 14.

[78] M Hirst, 'Suicide in Switzerland – Complicity in England?' (2009) *Criminal Law Review* 335.

[79] There is some doubt following *Smith (Wallace Duncan) (No 4)* [2004] EWCA Crim 631.

[80] [2009] UKHL 45 at 94.

[81] M Hirst, 'Assisted Suicide after Purdy: The Unresolved Issue' (2009) *Criminal Law Review* 872.

from the characteristics of the victim, to the motives of the suspect.[82] It encompasses not only those travelling abroad for assisted dying, but also those who assist or attempt to assist dying in England and Wales.[83] It imposes a two-stage test. For the evidential stage to be satisfied, the prosecution must prove that the victim attempted to commit suicide and the suspect has done an act capable of encouraging or assisting the suicide or attempted suicide of another person. At the public-interest stage each case is considered on its merits. The Code lists sixteen factors in favour of prosecution (for example where the victim is under eighteen; the suspect was not motivated purely by compassion; or the suspect acted in his capacity as a healthcare professional[84]) and six against. Factors against prosecution include:

- the victim had reached a voluntary, clear, settled and informed decision to commit suicide;
- the suspect was wholly motivated by compassion;
- the actions of the suspect, although sufficient to come within the definition of the offence, were of only minor encouragement or assistance;
- the suspect had sought to dissuade the victim from taking the course of action which resulted in his or her suicide;
- the actions of the suspect may be characterised as reluctant encouragement or assistance in the face of a determined wish on the part of the victim to commit suicide;
- the suspect reported the victim's suicide to the police and fully assisted them in their enquiries into the circumstances of the suicide or the attempt and his or her part in providing encouragement or assistance.[85]

To date, the guidelines have resulted in a permissive approach. The CPS had the required evidence to prosecute Michael Bateman who helped his wife to commit suicide. She was in chronic pain and had a settled wish to die. Bateman put a plastic bag over her head and assembled helium gas apparatus, but Mrs Bateman tightened the bag and turned on the helium.[86] The CPS decided that prosecution was not in the public interest.[87] Similarly, there was sufficient evidence to prosecute Dr Michael Irwin, but again, the CPS decided it would not

---

[82] But will it adequately safeguard the 'victim'? See A Mullock, 'Overlooking the Criminally Compassionate: What are the Implications of Prosecutorial Policy on Encouraging or Assisting Suicide?' (2010) 18(4) *Medical Law Review* 442.

[83] P Lewis argues that this makes the informal changes brought in by the Code more significant than was originally thought would be the case: 'Informal Legal Change on Assisted Suicide: The Policy for Prosecutors' (2010) *Legal Studies (Online)*, 13 October.

[84] Regarding the latter factor, see below at **19.19**.

[85] DPP, *Code for Crown Prosecutors and the Policy for Prosecutors in respect of Cases of Encouraging or Assisting Suicide* (2010), para 45.

[86] Compare with the 2006 case of David March who was given a nine-month prison sentence suspended for twelve months when, with the consent of his wife who suffered from multiple sclerosis, he tied up a plastic bag which she had placed over her head to commit suicide.

[87] CPS, *Assisted Suicide Charge Not in the Public Interest* (24 May 2010).

be in the public interest to do so.[88] Dr Irwin accompanied Raymond Cutkelvin to the Dignitas clinic in 2007 and paid part of the associated costs. Mr Cutkelvin's plans were made in advance of meeting Dr Irwin, who was seventy-nine when the DPP made his decision. The DPP accepted that it was unlikely that a court would have imposed a penalty on him.

The DPP's permissive approach to assisted dying has not received universal acclamation. Laing questions the constitutionality of the DPP's Code, suggesting that the lenient approach it endorses will gradually alter criminal law without recourse to Parliament.[89] On the other hand, some campaigners argue that the reformed Code is not permissive enough.[90] In late 2010 Lord Falconer launched a commission, funded in part by Sir Terry Pratchett, and supported by the think-tank Demos,[91] asking whether and, if so, how to support people assisting a loved one to die. It is expected to report in late 2011. At the time of writing, the Commission has been subjected to criticisms that it lacks transparency, independence and impartiality. In 2009 Lord Falconer withdrew his amendment to the Coroners and Justice Bill in part as a result of the change in prosecution policy. He had hoped to remove the threat of prosecution when people travel with loved ones to assisted-suicide clinics. The former Lord Chancellor has made his views on the subject clear, but does this necessarily detract from the Commission's aim to resolve the public policy issue of the legal and ethical status of assisted dying?

The unconscious patient

19.9 What of the fate of the patient whose illness or injury has rendered him unconscious and unlikely ever to regain consciousness? What test should be employed to determine the appropriate course of action? Two tests were examined in chapter 6; the substituted-judgment test and the best-interests test, and we have seen that in England the Mental Capacity Act 2005 has given statutory force to the best-interests test. The substituted-judgment test was employed in the seminal American case of Karen Quinlan,[92] a young woman

---

[88] CPS, *The Suicide of Mr Raymond Cutkelvin – Decision on Prosecution* (25 June 2010).

[89] J Laing, 'On the Wrong Track' (2010) 154(2) *Solicitor's Journal* 8. The lack of prosecutions predates the DPP's Code and indicates that this phenomenon had been going on for some time. See, for example, A Mullock, 'Prosecutors Making (Bad) Law?' (2009) 17(2) *Medical Law Review* 290, on the DPP's decision regarding the death of Daniel James.

[90] For example, Sir Terry Pratchett has argued that tribunals should be set up to look into cases prospectively. See T Pratchett, 'My Case for a Euthanasia Tribunal' (2010) *Guardian,* 2 February, which contains an edited version of his Richard Dimbleby lecture.

[91] *Commission on Assisted Dying*, launched 30 November 2010, accessible at http://commissiononassisteddying.co.uk.

[92] *In re Quinlan* (1976) 355 A 2d 647. And see *Cruzan v Director Missouri Department of Health* (1990) 110 S Ct 2841 (USA Supreme Court).

who, suddenly stricken with illness, lay in a coma attached to a life-support machine. Although she was not brain-stem dead, her doctors were satisfied that there was no hope that she would ever recover a cognitive state: she was characterised as being in a 'chronic, persistent, vegetative condition', kept alive only with the assistance of a ventilator. Karen's parents decided that it would be best for her to be removed from the life-support machine. Accordingly, her father applied to the court to be appointed her guardian and claimed that, as guardian, he would be entitled to authorise the discontinuance of all 'extraordinary' medical procedures sustaining Karen Quinlan's life. The Supreme Court of New Jersey upheld the father's claim. First, had Karen Quinlan been conscious and lucid, she would have had a right, just like Ms B, to decide to discontinue life-support treatment in circumstances where it was simply prolonging for a short period a terminal condition. She was not conscious or lucid. Second, because of her condition, her father was appointed guardian and the question then arose whether he could make a decision of that kind on her behalf. He was entitled to go to the court to seek assistance; and the court was prepared to 'don the mental mantle of Karen Quinlan' to make a decision for her which she would have made had she been able to do so. Thus, by applying a 'substituted-judgment' test, the court decided that if, upon the concurrence of the guardian and the family of the patient, the attending physicians should conclude that there was no reasonable possibility of her ever emerging from her comatose condition to a cognitive state and that the life-support apparatus should be discontinued, they should consult with the Hospital Ethics Committee and, if that body agreed, the life-support system might be withdrawn, without any civil or criminal liability on the part of any participant. Following that judgment, a Hospital Ethics Committee was convened and the decision was taken to remove the life-support system machine. It is an interesting reflection on the fallibility of human judgment that withdrawal of the life-support system did not lead to a swift death, and Karen Quinlan survived for ten long years after falling into the coma.

Quinlan illustrates the substituted-judgment test working smoothly, but where relatives disagree as to the appropriate course of action, the substituted-judgment test can result in acrimonious legal action. Another American example involves the tragic case of Terri Schiavo, who had been in a PVS for five years when her husband filed a petition for the removal of her feeding and hydration tubes. He argued that Mrs Schiavo would not have wanted to continue living in these circumstances. Her Roman Catholic parents vehemently disagreed. Over the following four years, Schiavo's tubes were withdrawn twice, but legal challenges resulted in them being reinserted soon afterwards. They were removed for a third time in 2005 and Terri Schiavo died thirteen days later.[93] Difficult decisions remain difficult whether the legal test is best interests or substituted judgment.[94]

---

[93] See K Goodman (ed), *The Case of Terri Schiavo: Ethics, Politics and Death in the 21st Century* (2009) OUP (USA).

[94] For another controversial case, see S Moratti, 'The *Englaro* Case: Withdrawal of

English law has rejected a test whereby the next-of-kin should automatically enjoy proxy powers of consent. Instead, both the case law and the Mental Capacity Act 2005 embrace a modified best-interests test. The Mental Capacity Act introduces important changes in practice. There is a Court of Protection which can appoint a 'deputy' to act for the patient. Alternatively the patient himself can, whilst competent, appoint a donee of a Lasting Power of Attorney (LPA) to make certain decisions on his behalf if, or when, he loses capacity to make them himself. He may also make an advance directive refusing treatment.[95] Decisions of the LPA and the relevance and applicability of advance directives are subject to stringent controls.[96] The best-interests test survives the reform, and earlier case law remains relevant. As we shall see, the best-interests test involves a careful balancing of the sanctity of life, the quality of life and the individual's rights and interests in dignity and autonomy.[97]

Bland: crossing the Rubicon?[98]

19.10   At seventeen, Anthony Bland suffered crush injuries at Hillsborough Football Stadium. He suffered catastrophic and irreversible damage to his brain. The condition from which he suffered is known as a persistent vegetative state (PVS).[99] He had lost all cortical (higher brain) function, but his brain stem continued to function. PVS patients continue to breathe independently and their digestion continues to function. Tony Bland was incapable of voluntary movement and could feel no pain. He could not see or hear, taste or smell.[100] He remained alive, fed through a tube. All his excretory functions were managed mechanically. Doctors were agreed that there was no hope of recovery of any sort. In this condition, the young man existed for two years

Treatment from a Patient in a Permanent Vegetative State in Italy' (2010) 19 *Cambridge Quarterly of Healthcare Ethics* 372.

[95]   The Royal College of Physicians sets out clinical guidance: RCP, *Advance Care Planning: National Guideline* (2009).

[96]   See below at **19.14**.

[97]   The law is supplemented with professional guidance. The BMA produced *Withholding and Withdrawing Life-Prolonging Medical Treatment: Guidance for Decision Making* in 2007, and the GMC issued *Treatment and Care Towards the End of Life: Good Practice in Decision Making* (2010).

[98]   *Airedale NHS Trust v Bland* [1993] 1 **All** ER 821, HL

[99]   On which, see B Jennett, *The Vegetative State: Medical Facts, Ethical and Legal Dilemmas* (2002), CUP. According to NHS Choices (available at www.nhs.uk), 'The term "vegetative state" describes a person who is conscious but has no sense of awareness.' A person in a vegetative state for one month is said to be in a 'persistent vegetative state'. A person in a persistent vegetative state for more than a year is said to be in a 'permanent vegetative state'. We refer to the *persistent* vegetative state, indicating that the condition is continuing. Permanency is a prediction that is ultimately uncertain. See BMA, *Treatment Decisions for Patients in Persistent Vegetative State* (2006); RCP, *The Vegetative State: Guidance on Diagnosis and Management* (2003).

[100]   This incontrovertible physical evidence and irreparable damage to the brain distinguishes *Bland* from some subsequent cases.

until, with the concurrence of his family, the hospital applied for a declaration that they might lawfully discontinue ANH. The House of Lords unanimously granted that declaration.

We have seen[101] how their Lordships managed to find that withdrawing the naso-gastric tube was not an act hastening death such as to expose doctors to liability for murder. Tony Bland, however, could not instruct his doctors to cease treatment. Unlike in the Karen Quinlan case in the USA, his family could not seek to be appointed as guardians of their adult son. The Law Lords fell back on *F v West Berkshire Health Authority*.[102] When a patient was incapable of deciding whether to continue treatment for himself, what could lawfully be done to him depended on what constituted treatment in his best interests and in conformity to responsible medical practice. For Lords Goff, Keith and Lowry, the evidence of medical opinion and professional guidelines on diagnosis and confirmation of PVS assisted them to conclude that, as Tony Bland received no benefit from treatment, it was not in his best interests to continue naso-gastric feeding. They reasoned: the regime of artificial feeding constitutes treatment; an overwhelming body of medical opinion supported withdrawing ANH from patients confirmed in PVS.[103] Therefore withdrawing 'treatment' was lawful.

Lord Mustill acknowledged[104] the complexity of best interests in this context. Tony Bland was not suffering; he felt no pain.

> By ending his life the doctors will not relieve him of a burden become intolerable, for others carry the burden and he has none. What other considerations could make it better for him to die now rather than later? None that we can measure, for of death we know nothing. The distressing truth which must not be shirked, is that the proposed conduct is not in the best interests of Anthony Bland, for he has no best interests of any kind.

Lord Mustill turned traditional analyses of best interests on their heads. He looked at the justification for what was being done to Tony Bland's body: the tubes feeding him; the tubes excreting his waste. Absent evidence that such invasive treatments were necessary to promote his best interests, they were themselves unlawful, a trespass on the youth's unconscious body. Thus treatment not in his interests could and must be withdrawn. *Bland* is an exceptional, difficult case. No one could fail to sympathise with a family whose child was breathing, but effectively a 'living corpse'. Yet where does *Bland* lead?[105] Can something as basic as feeding be withheld to bring about death? Would this

---

[101] Above at **19.1**.

[102] [1989] 2 All ER 545, discussed fully above at **6.6**.

[103] The Royal College of Physicians offers clinical guidance: RCP, *Oral Feeding Difficulties and Dilemmas* (2010).

[104] [1993] 1 All ER 821 at 894, HL.

[105] For critical appraisal of *Bland*, see J M Finnis, 'Bland: Crossing the Rubicon?' (1993) 109 *Law Quarterly Review* 329; J Keown, 'Restoring Moral and Intellectual Shape to the Law after *Bland*' (1997) 113 *Law Quarterly Review* 481.

mean staff caring for a patient in advanced stages of dementia who could swallow, but did not demand food, could stop spoon-feeding?

The Law Lords saw the dangers of their decision. They advised that before treatment was discontinued, a declaration should be sought from the courts. They warned that their ruling covered only patients in PVS. They sought to restrain any slide down slippery slopes. Withdrawal of ANH required evidence that:

(1)   every effort should have been made to provide rehabilitation for at least six months;

(2)   diagnosis of irreversible PVS should not be considered confirmed until at least twelve months after the injury;

(3)   diagnosis should be agreed by two independent doctors; and

(4)   generally the views of the patient's immediate family will be given great weight.[106]

Bland is a limited and cautious decision. Even on its own facts it provokes numerous questions. The experts who gave evidence in *Bland* expressed total confidence in medical ability to judge that a patient was irreversibly in PVS. Others are more dubious, concerned that diagnosis may be mistaken and arguing that in some cases, intensive treatment can result in limited recovery. In 2010, new sophisticated scans revealed that Rom Houben, who was thought to have been in PVS for twenty-three years, was in fact suffering from 'locked-in syndrome' (or 'unresponsive wakefulness syndrome' as his doctors have named it[107]). He now enjoys limited communication via a computer.

The *legerdemain* by which their Lordships classified removal of a feeding tube as an omission not an act, provokes charges of covert legalisation of euthanasia.[108] Lord Mustill[109] recognised that it is difficult to find any moral difference between inaction resulting in a slow death and action resulting in a swift one. Can the legal distinction be maintained?[110] If it is a matter of policy rather than legal principle, then should the mantra of sanctity of life be swapped for that of quality of life and euthanasia legalised?[111] If Tony Bland's life was sacred, for itself, not its quality, how can withholding basic food and water be acceptable?

---

[106] And see BMA, *Withholding and Withdrawing Life-Prolonging Medical Treatment: Guidance for Decision-Making* (2nd edn, 2001, updated 2005); *Guidelines on Treatment of Patients in Persistent Vegetative State* (2006).

[107] S Laureys *et al*, 'Unresponsive Wakefulness Syndrome: A New Name for the Vegetative State or Appalic Syndrome' (2010) 8 *BMC Medicine* 68. For legal analysis, see S Burns, 'Life . . . But Not as we Know it' (2010) 160 *NLJ* 121.

[108] See the incisive arguments of Finnis (1993) 109 *Law Quarterly Review* 329 and Keown (1997) 113 *Law Quarterly Review* 481.

[109] [1993] AC 789 at para 885, HL.

[110] See L Doyal, 'Dignity in Dying Should Include the Legalization of Non-Voluntary Euthanasia' (2006) 1(2) *Clinical Ethics* 65.

[111] See P Singer, *Rethinking Life and Death* (1994) OUP, p 75.

After *Bland*: PVS to 'near-PVS'

19.11 *Bland* has led to radical change in the law governing the ending of life. The carefully constituted limitations built into *Bland* to keep that decision within bounds were eroded step by step. In *Frenchay Healthcare NHS Trust v S*,[112] the patient was said to have been in PVS for two and a half years following a drug overdose. His feeding tube was accidentally disconnected. The hospital immediately sought a declaration that it could lawfully refrain from re-inserting the tube. The Court of Appeal granted the declaration in haste and without any independent medical opinion confirming that S was irreversibly in PVS. The court recognised that the evidence as to S's condition was neither as unanimous nor as emphatic as in *Bland*. The judges found that in the emergency which had arisen because of the disconnection of the tube, there was no benefit conferred on S by re-inserting the tube. Indeed, following Lord Browne-Wilkinson's reasoning in *Bland*, it might be construed as an assault on S to do so. In these circumstances, the further inquiry necessary to take an independent medical opinion could be dispensed with. A fortuitous event affected the criteria set out in *Bland* to protect patients. On the facts of S, some doubt exists whether S was truly in PVS. There was evidence of restlessness and distress for which S was receiving medication.[113] Condition 3, set by Lord Goff in *Bland*, independent evidence confirming PVS, survived barely a year.

Subsequent decisions eroded the *Bland* limitations yet further. In *Re D*,[114] the patient had suffered serious brain-damage after a road accident. As in *Frenchay,* her feeding tube became disconnected. Stephen Brown P accepted evidence that D's condition did not fully conform to guidelines for diagnosis of PVS laid down by the Royal College of Physicians (RCP). He was satisfied that there was 'no evidence of any meaningful life whatsoever' and held that it was lawful to refrain from re-inserting the tube. In *Re H*[115] a forty-three-year-old woman had suffered brain injuries in a car crash. She retained some rudimentary awareness and like D, did not fit squarely within the RCP definition of PVS. The President of the Family Division approved cessation of artificial feeding. He was: '. . . satisfied that it is in the best interests of this patient that the life sustaining treatment currently being artificially administered should be brought to a conclusion'.[116]

After *Bland*: beyond PVS?

19.12 Another lesson which may be drawn from post-*Bland* cases on PVS, or near-PVS, is that PVS cases are no longer 'special'. Nor is withdrawal of

---

[112] [1994] 2 All ER 403.
[113] See J Stone, 'Withholding of Life-Sustaining Treatment' (1995) *New Law Journal* 354.
[114] *Re D (Medical Treatment)* [1998] FLR 411.
[115] *Re H (A Patient)* [1998] 2 FLR 36.
[116] [1998] 2 FLR 36 at 41.

feeding seen as much more of a dilemma than withdrawal of any other form of treatment, such as dialysis.[117] The *Practice Note*[118] setting out procedures to obtain court sanction to withdraw treatment from an adult lacking mental capacity embraces PVS within a wider range of medical and welfare disputes leading to litigation. Each case turns on the best interests of the patient. Best interests is a phrase easy to utter and difficult to interpret. It inevitably involves judgments of quality of life. In *Re D*,[119] a patient who had been hospitalised for much of his life with serious psychiatric illness developed renal failure and required dialysis. D lacked mental capacity to consent to treatment and often would not be co-operative in dialysis treatment. To continue dialysis he might have to be anaesthetised on each occasion. The judge ruled that it was not in the patient's interest to impose dialysis on him where in the doctors' opinion 'it is not reasonably practicable to do so'.

In *W Healthcare NHS Trust v H and Another*,[120] the feeding tube of a fifty-nine-year-old multiple sclerosis sufferer, KH, fell out. KH was conscious, but lacked the capacity to make her own decisions. She recognised nobody, had difficulty swallowing and had required a feeding tube for the past five years. The family opposed the carers' wish to replace the tube. In the absence of a valid advance directive, the court held that it was in KH's best interests for the tube to be reinserted: death by starvation would be even less dignified than the death she would face if the feeding tube was reinserted.[121] Whether judges like it or not, the effect of the long series of judicial decisions relating to withdrawal of treatment is that judges are making life or death decisions.[122]

A right to artificial nutrition and hydration (ANH)?

19.13 The entry into force of the Human Rights Act 1998 raised questions about the legality of the reasoning in *Bland* and the cases which followed *Bland*. Were decisions to cease feeding, especially to withdraw ANH, lawful? Or did they contravene Article 2 of the Human Rights Convention protecting the right to life? In *NHS Trust A v M*,[123] the President of the Family Division ruled that in the circumstances of cases such as *Bland*, where a recovery allowing the patient to enjoy any sort of cognitive abilities was nigh on impossible, nothing in Article 2 required measures to ensure prolongation of survival.

---

[117] For example, *Re D (Medical Treatment: Mentally Disabled Patient)* [1998] 2 FLR 22.

[118] *Practice Note (Official Solicitor: Declaratory Proceedings: Medical and Welfare Decisions for Adults who Lack Capacity)* [2001] 2 FLR 569.

[119] *Re D (Medical Treatment)* [1998] FLR 411.

[120] [2004] EWCA Civ 1324.

[121] [2004] EWCA Civ 1324 per Brooke LJ at paras 22 and 27.

[122] A series of cases involving the withdrawal of treatment from children is examined above in ch 14, **14.6–14.12**.

[123] [2001] 1 All ER 801 and see E Wicks, 'The Right to Refuse Medical Treatment Under the European Convention on Human Rights' (2001) 9 *Medical Law Review* 17.

The GMC produced guidance in 2002 indicating that, where a patient's disease is severe and the prognosis poor, ANH will not always be appropriate, even if death is not imminent.[124] This prompted Leslie Burke, who suffers from a degenerative neurological condition, cerebellar ataxia, to fight for the right to ANH in the event that he is unable to voice his wishes. His condition gradually reduces his coordination while his mental faculties are unimpaired. He will lose the abilities to walk, hear, see and swallow. He could make an advance directive, but his worry is that, after a significant deterioration, the GMC guidance would sanction the discontinuation of ANH in spite of it, and that he would be aware of great pain and suffering caused by malnutrition and dehydration. His argument is that, in his personal view, knowing as he does the likely progression of his disease, ANH will never be futile.

Mr Burke argued that the GMC guidance offended his human rights in four ways. First, the right to life in Article 2(1) contains both a negative obligation not to unlawfully take life and a positive obligation to protect it. The guidance failed to adequately protect his life. Second, by failing to protect him from death by malnutrition and dehydration, it offended Article 3 which protects him from inhuman and degrading treatment. Third, by failing to give his advance directive legal force, the guidance offended Article 8 which protects his right to a private and family life. Finally, it discriminated against those incapable of making a competent decision and therefore offended Article 14. At first instance, it was held that the GMC guidance was incompatible with Articles 3 and 8 of the Human Rights Act 1998.[125] Munby J's decision was controversial because it suggested a positive right to demand treatment that was not, in the doctors' views, in his medical best interests.[126] Could the principle be extended beyond the provision of ANH, to other forms of treatment? The GMC feared that it might and took the case to the Court of Appeal where Munby J's decision was overturned.[127] Mr Burke's concerns, the Court held, were already addressed by the law. Where a competent patient indicates his wish to be kept alive through ANH, a doctor who deliberately brings that life to an end by removing ANH may be guilty of murder. Mr Burke was more concerned about what should happen in the event that he loses capacity. The

---

[124] GMC, *Withholding and Withdrawing Life-Prolonging Treatments: Good Practice in Decision-Making* (2002). Para 16 provides: '. . . Doctors must take account of patients' preferences when providing treatment. However, where a patient wishes to have a treatment that – in the doctor's considered view – is not clinically indicated, there is no ethical or legal obligation on the doctor to provide it . . .' The 2002 guidelines were replaced by GMC, *Treatment and Care Towards the End of Life: Good Practice in Decision Making* (2010).

[125] *R (On the application of Burke) v GMC* [2004] EWHC 1879 (Admin).

[126] See R Gillon, 'Why the GMC is Right to Appeal Over Life-prolonging Treatment' (2004) 329 *BMJ* 810. In support of the High Court judgment, see H Biggs, 'In Whose Best Interests: Who Knows?' (2006) 1(2) *Clinical Ethics* 90; D Gurnham, 'Losing the Wood for the Trees: Burke and the Court of Appeal' (2006) 14 *Medical Law Review* 253. Also see J Coggon (2006) 12 *Medical Law Review* 219, who argues that a right to die with dignity cannot exist if a right to die does not.

[127] *R (on the application of Burke) v GMC* [2005] EWCA Civ 1003.

Court is clear. Doctors cannot be forced to administer treatment which they believe to be clinically unnecessary, futile or inappropriate. There is no discrimination, as the law applies equally to both a competent patient demanding treatment and an incompetent patient whose demands are expressed through an advance directive. Doctors are guided by the indistinct and complex concepts of futility and best interests. The Court of Appeal decision (on the facts of this case) is a setback to patient autonomy and a victory for medical paternalism.

In 2006, Leslie Burke lodged an appeal with the European Court of Human Rights. His application was ruled inadmissible.[128] There was no imminent risk that ANH would be withdrawn in circumstances that would lead to death by malnutrition and dehydration. In many ways, Mr Burke made his case too early: the emphasis on 'imminent' risk and the court's view that no issue arose under Articles 2, 3 and 8 on the basis that 'the applicant cannot pre-determine the administration of specific treatment in future unknown circumstances'[129] must come as a blow given that, by the time the issues are 'imminent', Mr. Burke is unlikely to be competent to bring the proceedings himself. Nevertheless, the Court affirms the position taken in the Court of Appeal that the GMC guidelines do not have legal status and make no recommendations contrary to the law. Nor is there any discrimination within the meaning of Article 14: neither competent nor incompetent patients can require a doctor to provide treatment that he does not believe is clinically justified.

As we shall see, section 4(5) of the Mental Capacity Act 2005 offers further guidance. It provides that decisions relating to life-sustaining treatment must not be motivated by a desire to bring about the patient's death. Does this mean that there is a positive obligation on doctors to provide life-sustaining treatment? This is unlikely. The Code of Practice provides that:[130]

> Where a person has made a written statement in advance that requests particular medical treatments, such as artificial nutrition and hydration (ANH), these requests should be taken into account by the treating doctor in the same way as requests made by a patient who has the capacity to make such decisions. Like anyone else involved in making this decision, the doctor must weigh written statements alongside all other relevant factors to decide whether it is in the best interests of the patient to provide or continue life-sustaining treatment.

This guidance is reiterated in more recent guidance from the Department of Health.[131] Mr Burke's remaining options are to make an advance directive refusing treatment, or to appoint an LPA.

---

[128] *Burke v UK* [2006] App 19807/06.
[129] [2006] App 19807/06, per Casadevall J.
[130] Department for Constitutional Affairs, Mental Capacity Act 2005, Code of Practice, para 5.34.
[131] DH, *Reference Guide to Consent for Examination or Treatment* (2nd edn, 2009), ch 4, para 14.

The Mental Capacity Act 2005[132]

19.14   The Mental Capacity Act 2005 governs decision-making on behalf of adults who temporarily or permanently lack mental capacity. It endorses the modified best-interests test employed by the case law, but introduces a number of important practical changes. A Court of Protection, established by section 45 of the Act, is pivotal to the regime. The powers of the Court of Protection extend only to grant declarations relating to the patient's capacity to determine her own treatment and the lawfulness of decisions taken on her behalf. The court may also appoint a 'deputy' to make welfare and treatment decisions on behalf of the patient lacking capacity.[133]

How does the Act affect end-of-life decisions? As we have seen, the test of lawfulness remains the best interests of the patient. But an element of substituted judgment is incorporated into the statutory checklist for best interests. Decision-makers must give due consideration to the patient's previous wishes, beliefs and values.[134] So Mr Burke's wish to prolong his life would have to be taken into account even after the Act. Particular attention must be paid to any written statement made by the patient when he had capacity.[135] But though an advance directive purporting to *demand* treatment may be persuasive, it is not binding.[136] Many patients in Mr Burke's condition might prefer to ensure that life-sustaining treatment was not prolonged. We saw in chapter 6 that advance decisions to *refuse* treatment are not valid if:[137]

- the treatment in question 'is not the treatment specified in the advance decision'; or
- 'any circumstances specified in the advance decision are absent' or
- 'there are reasonable grounds for believing that circumstances exist which [the patient] did not anticipate at the time of his advance decision and which would have affected his decision had he anticipated them'.

In addition, where the advance decision to refuse treatment relates to life-sustaining treatment, special conditions apply. It must incorporate a statement that the decision stands, even if life is at risk. It must be in writing, signed, witnessed and verified by the author.[138] If so, it is as binding as a statement refusing life-sustaining treatment made by a competent patient such as Ms B. Yet there is no requirement that

---

[132] See also above ch 6.

[133] Mental Capacity Act 2005, s 16. The deputies' powers are limited in s 20. S 20(5) provides: 'A deputy may not refuse consent to the carrying out or continuation of life-sustaining treatment in relation to P.'

[134] Mental Capacity Act 2005, s 4(6)(b).

[135] Mental Capacity Act 2005, s 4(6)(a) and see ss 24–26 on advance decisions to refuse treatment.

[136] This was also the case in common law: *R (on the application of Burke) v GMC* [2005] EWCA Civ 1003, CA at para 35.

[137] S 25(1).

[138] See ss 25(5)–(6).

the patient discuss the content or implications of the statement with a health professional or that they be fully informed.

Alternatively, a competent patient may appoint a proxy to act for her via an LPA and make decisions on her behalf in the event that she loses capacity.[139] Again, special conditions apply if the LPA is to make decisions regarding life-sustaining treatment. The LPA may only make such decisions if the donor of the LPA expressly enabled him to do so.[140] Even then, the decision of an LPA is subject to the conditions of the Act. If the LPA and the doctors or carers disagree about what is in the best interests of the patient, the court will usually be called upon to make a decision or declaration.[141] As we shall see, the court as 'decision-maker' will be guided, but not bound by the views of the LPA.

Whoever is making the crucial decision, doctors, any attorney, or the Court, section 4(5) of the Mental Capacity Act 2005 contains special considerations relating to life-sustaining treatment, which is defined as 'treatment which in the view of a person providing health care for the person concerned is necessary to sustain life':[142]

> Where the determination relates to life-sustaining treatment [the person making the decision] must not, in considering whether the treatment is in the best interests of the person concerned, be motivated by a desire to bring about his death.

This peculiar statement was framed to appease those who feared that the Mental Capacity Act 2005 would sanction covert euthanasia. It forbids the decision-maker from being 'motivated by a desire to bring about the person's death'.[143] We are at a loss to define 'desire' in this context. The Code of Practice states:[144]

> ... there will be a limited number of cases where treatment is futile, overly burdensome to the patient or where there is no prospect of recovery. In circumstances such as these, it may be that an assessment of best interests leads to the conclusion that it would be in the best interests of the patient to withdraw or withhold life-sustaining treatment, even if this may result in the person's death ...

The Code recognises that those making the treatment decision might wish the patient dead (either to ease his suffering or for other reasons) but insists that this is not the motivation for the discontinuation of treatment.

---

[139] LPAs are governed by ss 9–14.
[140] See s 11(8)(a).
[141] See, for example, *Re AVS v An NHS Trust* [2010] EWHC 2746 (COP), discussed below at **19.16**.
[142] S 4(10).
[143] Mental Capacity Act 2005 Code of Practice, para 5.29.
[144] Mental Capacity Act 2005 Code of Practice, para 5.31. And see J Coggon, 'Ignoring the Moral and Intellectual Shape of the Law after *Bland*: the Unintended Side-effect of a Sorry Compromise' (2007) 27 *Legal Studies* 110.

The role of the courts

19.15 It is good practice to seek prior judicial sanction in cases of dispute or uncertainty as to the patient's capacity or his best interests, but is there a legal requirement to do so? We saw in chapter 6 that there is not. In *Burke*, Lord Phillips MR stated:[145]

> Good practice may require medical practitioners to seek such a declaration where the legality of proposed treatment is in doubt. This is not, however, something that they are required to do as a matter of law.

Nor does the Mental Capacity Act 2005 mandate resort to the court. The Code of Practice advises that a declaration should be sought in certain circumstances, including any proposal to withdraw artificial nutrition or hydration.[146] The Act maintains that transgression of the Code by certain individuals (including healthcare professionals) will be 'taken into account in proceedings in any court or tribunal'.[147] Most controversial cases therefore appear before the Court of Protection. However, as we noted in chapter 6, where there is consensus regarding a course of action, there may be no one to enforce recourse to the court. The patient will lack an advocate.

Where there is disagreement as to the proposed course of action and an application to the Court of Protection is made, how do the courts determine what is in the patients' best interests? What weight is given to the views of carers and family members?

Where carers disagree

19.16 In *Bland*, *Frenchay*, *D* and *H*, the patient's family supported the doctors' judgment to cease treatment. The Mental Capacity Act 2005 gives statutory force to a process of consultation with all those concerned with the patient's care – formalising the less clear requirements of consultation of the common law. Under the Act, any decision-maker must take into consideration the past and present wishes and feelings of the patient[148] and, where appropriate and practicable, the views of carers, family, LPAs and court-appointed deputies when determining best interests.[149] But what happens when these views conflict?

Pre-Mental Capacity Act 2005 case law gives some guidance. In *Re G*,[150] G suffered serious injuries while riding his motorcycle. In the course of attempts to resuscitate him, he suffered a heart attack which resulted in the interruption

---

[145] [2005] EWCA Civ 1003, at para 80.
[146] For fuller advice, see Mental Capacity Act 2005, Code of Practice, ch 8.
[147] Ss 42(4) and 42(5).
[148] Ss 4(6)(a) and 4(6)(b).
[149] S 4(7).
[150] *Re G (Persistent Vegetative State)* [1995] 2 FCR 46.

of blood flow to his brain. He was diagnosed as being in PVS, a state in which he had lain for nearly two years at the time of the application to court to withdraw feeding. G's wife and mother remained devoted to him and visited regularly. G's wife somewhat reluctantly supported the application to withdraw feeding from G. His mother opposed the application. Stephen Brown P said that he was satisfied that doctors had taken into account all the views of G's family. The mother's views could not prevail against what was considered to be the best interests of the patient. It might be argued that the wife's judgment should be preferred. This is not the basis of the finding in *Re G*. The judge seems to give relatively little weight to any relative's views. He says:[151]

> It would indeed be an appalling burden to place upon any relative to transfer as it were the responsibility for making a decision in a case of this nature to that relative. In this case, the responsibility must ultimately remain with the doctors in charge of the case, albeit taking fully into account views of relatives.

In *An NHS Trust v A*,[152] there was disagreement between the NHS trust and the family, and also between medical experts. An eighty-six-year-old man suffered a heart attack and was brought into intensive care. His heart, lungs and kidneys were artificially supported and he was given artificial nutrition. A was sentient and made attempts to remove the tubes. Given the remote likelihood of any meaningful recovery, it was proposed that he should be given palliative care only. The family disagreed and their expert medical witness stated that A might have a 20 per cent chance of recovery. At first instance, it was held that A lacked capacity to decide and that it was not in his best interests to continue treatment that would not improve his condition. A's son appealed, arguing that the judge had not taken into consideration the family's views and in particular, their religious beliefs. Further, it was argued that, applying *Bolam v City & Hackney Health Authority*,[153] if a responsible body of medical opinion did not support the view that withdrawal of treatment was in A's best interests, then the court had no authority to hold to the contrary. The appeal was dismissed. The court, and not the doctors, are responsible for deciding what was in A's best interests, which go wider than medical interests alone. The judge at first instance had taken into account the religious and other views of the family. The views were 'material' but not 'governing factors' in determining the patient's best interests.[154]

In *An NHS Trust v J*,[155] the court once again had to declare whether withdrawal of ANH was in the best interests of a patient in circumstances where

151 [1995] 2 FCR 46 at 51.
152 [2005] EWCA Civ 1145.
153 [1957] 2 All ER 118, discussed fully in ch 7.
154 [2005] EWCA Civ 1145 at para 59, per Waller LJ.
155 [2006] All ER (D) 290 (Nov). Discussed in P Lewis, 'Withdrawal of Treatment from a Patient in a Permanent Vegetative State: Judicial Involvement and Innovative "Treatment"' (2007) 15 *Medical Law Review* 392 and L Skene *et al*, 'Neuroimaging and the Withdrawal of Life Sustaining Treatment from Patients in Persistent Vegetative State' (2009) 17(2) *Medical Law Review* 245.

the doctors and family disagreed, but here the family proposed the immediate withdrawal of treatment. The Official Solicitor, an officer appointed by the court when no other person is either suitable or willing to act, proposed a delay. J suffered a subarachnoid and interventricular brain haemorrhage whilst on holiday in 2003. She was without oxygen for around twelve minutes which experts agreed was likely to cause profound and permanent brain damage. J was in PVS for three years whereupon the NHS trust sought a declaration from the Court that J lacked capacity, and that it was not in her best interests to continue ANH. J's husband, mother and two daughters supported the application. Sir Mark Potter P would have granted the application,[156] but the Official Solicitor opposed the immediate grant of the declarations on the basis of two research articles indicating the potential of the insomnia drug Zolpidem to enhance the neural responses of patients in PVS. The expert witness doubted the drug would work on account of J's age and the nature of her brain injury, but saw no harm in trying. Zolpidem is not harmful and any effect on neural activity is immediate; no response within forty-five minutes would indicate that the drug had not worked. The family, however, opposed it. They were concerned that J would not have wanted her life prolonged in this way, and that the experimental use of the drug might induce a sense of awareness that would be distressing for both J and her family. Even if the drug worked, J would have no meaningful quality of life. Sir Mark Potter was much impressed by the expert medical evidence. He declared that J lacked capacity to make a decision and that a three-day course of Zolpidem was in her best interests. He did so with a view to a return to court if the drug failed to have an effect, in which case there is no reason why the removal of ANH would not be declared lawful.

The views of family, it seems, had little weight. Does the Mental Capacity Act 2005 make a difference? The relevance and weight of the various considerations going to best interests is dependent upon who is the decision-maker. What if the patient has appointed a proxy, an LPA? We have seen that the powers of LPAs do extend in some circumstances to decisions about life-sustaining treatment. Does this herald a new era of substituted judgment – the proxy will be more likely to make the decision that she believes the donor would have wanted? Three factors limit the powers of the new attorney. First, such a proxy can only make decisions concerning the continuation of life-sustaining treatment if expressly authorised to do so by the patient. Second, she must act in the best interests of the patient, which include the duty to consult other interested parties and the requirement that she must not be motivated by a desire to bring about the patient's death. Where her views conflict with the doctors', the Code of Practice recommends that life-sustaining treatment is continued until clarification is obtained from the court.[157] In *Re AVS v An NHS Trust*[158] a hospital argued that treatment of a patient suffering from Creutzfeldt-Jacob Disease with Pentosan Polysulphate was no longer in his

---

[156] [2006] All ER (D) 290 (Nov) at para 31.
[157] Mental Capacity Act 2005, Code of Practice, para 5.33.
[158] [2010] EWHC 2746 (COP). A directions appointment case.

best interests. The LPA, the patient's brother, disagreed. His relationship with the hospital broke down and Sir Nicholas Wall P concluded that the LPA lacked objectivity. The Official Solicitor was called in to give a 'dispassionate assessment', which leads us to the final restriction. Where the outcome of a decision is very serious, as in the proposed withdrawal of ANH,[159] for example, it is still good practice to bring each case before the court. Where the court is the decision-maker, it must merely 'take into account, if it is practicable and appropriate to consult them',[160] the views of (inter alia) the attorney. Despite the extended powers of LPAs and the statutory recognition of advance directives, best interests rather than substituted judgments remain the dominant test.

DNAR orders[161]

19.17 DNAR (do not attempt resuscitation) orders are not expressly referred to in the Mental Capacity Act 2005. What is in issue is not withdrawing treatment, but whether or not the patient should be given cardio-pulmonary resuscitation (CPE) if he suffers a cardiac arrest. Whose decision should determine whether or not a DNAR order is made? In some cases, the patient can be consulted. Where she lacks capacity, an advance refusal of treatment may be effective, or where the donor expressly authorises it, the LPA may 'authorise the giving or refusing of consent to the carrying out or continuation of life-sustaining treatment'.[162] In other cases, guidelines on DNAR orders make it clear that decision-making is not an exclusively medical role. The patient's wishes, if known, must be respected.

Guidelines developed jointly between the British Medical Association, the Resuscitation Council (UK) and the Royal College of Nursing encourage advance care-planning, but point out that decisions must be made on an individual basis; not simply on the basis of the person's age or condition.[163] Decisions should be made on the basis of appropriate consultation with other staff and the patient's family. Once a DNAR order is in place, the guidelines state that 'A DNAR decision does not override clinical judgement in the unlikely event of a reversible cause of the patient's respiratory or cardiac arrest that does not match the circumstances envisaged'.[164] Where a DNAR order has not been made and the wishes of the patient are unknown, CPR should

---

[159] Mental Capacity Act 2005, Code of Practice, para 6.18.

[160] S 4(7).

[161] See also discussion of *Re Wyatt* [2004] EWHC 2247, [2005] EWHC 693, [2005] EWHC 1181, [2005] EWHC 2902 and *Re B (A Minor)* [2008] EWHC 1996 (Fam), below at **14.11**.

[162] S 11(8)(a).

[163] See BMA/RC(UK)/RCN, *Decisions Relating to Cardio-Pulmonary Resuscitation* (2007), p 7.

[164] BMA/RC(UK)/RCN, *Decisions Relating to Cardio-Pulmonary Resuscitation* (2007), p 3.

generally be attempted if cardiac or pulmonary arrest occurs, though there may be cases where this is not appropriate, for example, if the patient is in the final stages of terminal illness and has not requested CPR.

Fears about DNAR decisions focus on *who* makes the decision about life or death, whether such decisions may be made arbitrarily or in a discriminatory fashion, and whether the patient will be treated well once a DNAR order is in place.[165] DNAR orders are made more often in relation to elderly patients. That of itself may not be surprising. It is the quality of decision-making which counts and how prospects of successful resuscitation and future quality of life are assessed. A greater number of very elderly patients who are also gravely ill may be more unlikely to recover than their grandchildren in their twenties and thirties. Disturbingly, Mason and Laurie note that the relevance of the age factor often depends on the age of the physician making the decision.[166] Junior doctors in particular require training to understand the needs of their elderly patients. The criteria governing the assessment of the patient and the weight given to his or her family's wishes should not vary with age.

The validity of DNAR orders came before the English courts in *Re R (Adult: Medical Treatment)*.[167] R was twenty-three. He was born with a severe malformation of the brain. He developed epilepsy in infancy. He suffered from multiple disabilities and had no real means of communicating with others. He had severe and debilitating intestinal troubles, including ulcers 'all the way through his guts'. His only real response to others seems to have been to being cuddled. He appeared to experience quite acute pain. He was not in PVS or anything akin to 'near-PVS'. Since he was nineteen, he had lived in a nursing home, attending a day-centre and going home to his devoted family most weekends. In the year before the court proceedings, R had been hospitalised five times. His doctors, with the full agreement of R's parents, issued a DNAR order. Should R suffer from a life-threatening condition involving a cardiac arrest he should not be resuscitated. Staff at R's day-centre were concerned about the use of DNAR orders in R's case, and made an application for judicial review of the order. The NHS trust responsible for R's care sought a declaration both to declare the DNAR order lawful and to support a wider non-treatment policy, including withdrawing nutrition and hydration. This part of the trust's application was later withdrawn. Sir Stephen Brown P upheld the DNAR order. He was persuaded that the evidence established that in cases such as R, CPR was unlikely to succeed. Indeed, the very process might do R further injury. R had never been able to articulate his wishes. Nonetheless, the

---

[165] See R Dobson, 'Stroke Patients with "Do Not Resuscitate" Orders are Treated Worse Than Those Without' (2005) 331 *BMJ* 926; T Shakespeare, B Vernon, 'Disability Rights and Resuscitation: Do Not Attempt Reconciliation' in L Clements and J Read (eds), *Disabled People and the Right to Life: The Protection and Violation of Disabled People's Most Basic Human Right* (2007) Routledge Cavendish, ch 5; D Rose, 'Nurses to Decide if Patients are Revived' (2007) *Times*, 27 October.

[166] *Mason and McCall Smith*, p 578.

[167] (1996) 31 BMLR 127.

judge concluded that it was permissible to consider the patient's quality of life in assessing his best interests. DNAR orders do not involve measures to terminate life or accelerate death. Where continued existence involved a life 'so afflicted as to be intolerable',[168] policies designed to limit lifesaving intervention could be approved. In the absence of consent from the patient, the decision to institute a DNAR order should usually be made by the physicians, family and carers. Recourse to the courts is rare indeed and should be reserved for cases of serious disagreement.

The euthanasia debate[169]

19.18 English law is imprecise and uncertain. Doctors cannot always be given clear advice about the legality of various procedures. Is this fair to the medical profession? Is it right that some doctors, even acting with the best of motives, may under a screen of silence do things which they believe may be unlawful? There is some evidence that doctors practise covert euthanasia.[170] If what is taking place in medical practice is acceptable to society, it is argued that the law should be changed to set out clearly the parameters within which they should be acting. If society disapproves of certain procedures, how can they be controlled? Is it right, again, for the law to be left obscure, yet when clear evidence of euthanasia occurs prosecutors may elect not to enforce the law? On the other hand, there are those who oppose legislation on the grounds that the current fudge allows for maximum flexibility for a caring medical profession.

Once any proposal to clarify the current fudge surfaces, opinions polarise sharply.[171] Pro-life campaigners sought unsuccessfully to reverse the decision in *Bland*[172] and to encourage police and prosecutors to pursue vigorously any evidence of covert euthanasia. Supporters of voluntary euthanasia argue their contrary case with equal passion. As Kennedy and Grubb note, '. . . whenever the topic of voluntary euthanasia is broached, rational argument becomes an early casualty'.[173]

---

[168] See *Re J (A Minor) (Wardship: Medical Treatment)* [1990] 3 All ER 930, CA.

[169] See generally, J Keown (ed), *Euthanasia Examined: Ethical, Legal and Clinical Perspectives* (1995) CUP; M Otlowski, *Voluntary Euthanasia and the Common Law* (1997), Clarendon Press.

[170] See R S Magnusson, 'Above Ground, Below Ground' (2004) 30 *Journal of Medical Ethics* 441; S Ost, *An Analytical Study of the Legal, Moral and Ethical Aspects of the Living Phenomenon of Euthanasia* (2003) Edwin Mellen Press; J Keown, *Euthanasia, Ethics and Public Policy* (2002) CUP.

[171] See, most recently, HL Deb, 3 February 2010, vol 717, cGC69SD.

[172] In the Medical Treatment (Prevention of Euthanasia) Bill discussed in J Keown, 'Dehydrating Bodies: the *Bland* Case, the Winterton Bill' in A Bainham, S D Sclater, M Richards (eds), *Body Lore and Laws* (2002) Hart Publishing, at 245.

[173] Kennedy and Grubb, *Medical Law: Text and Materials* (2000) Butterworths, p 1997.

The case for voluntary euthanasia is deceptively simple. It rests on the principle of autonomy. The individual is the '... final determinant of his or her destiny'.[174] We enjoy the right to control our death just as we enjoy the right to control our lives. Moreover, dignity and welfare, it is contended, impel us to allow the individual the right to end an intolerable life. A compassionate society should not force people dying, or living, with pain and disability, to continue to live. The patient in the terminal stages of motor neurone disease should not be compelled to suffer all the consequences of a drawn-out death. Human rights are invoked in support of the pro-euthanasia case. Article 3 prohibits inhuman and degrading treatment. Does the absence of a euthanasia option in effect impose such degrading treatment? Article 8 protects our private and family lives. Do laws preventing my doctor, or indeed my husband, from helping me to end an intolerable life violate my privacy? We have seen that the House of Lords decision in *Purdy* may herald renewed interest in the relevance of Article 8.

Those opposed to legislation permitting voluntary euthanasia advance several objections. For many, though not all, opponents of euthanasia, central to their opposition to euthanasia is their commitment to the doctrine of sanctity of life.[175] But other concerns are voiced. Just how voluntary would such euthanasia be? Would the introduction of such laws result in a change of attitude by society towards the sanctity of life generally, towards the elderly, infirm and the mortally sick? Would the existence of such laws impose pressures upon elderly and terminally ill patients to seek euthanasia, rather than remain a burden on relatives or on society? Would the existence of such legislation provide opportunities for fraud and abuse, and undermine the relationship of trust between doctor and patient? How easy would it be to apply such a law?

Let us examine what kind of form legislation might take. It seems increasingly likely that any reform would centre on human rights rather than the criminal law.[176] Two rather different sorts of laws might be envisaged – both of which have models in other jurisdictions. Legislation could sanction physician-assisted dying (as is the case in the States of Oregon and Washington, USA) or could allow voluntary active euthanasia (as is the case in the Netherlands and Belgium[177]).

Physician-assisted suicide (PAS)[178]

19.19   The Oregon Death with Dignity Act 1994 came into force in 1997. It applies only to adults who have been diagnosed as terminally ill. A prescription

---

[174] See M Otlowski, *Voluntary Euthanasia and the Common Law*, p 189.
[175] See L Gormally (ed), *Euthanasia, Clinical Practice and the Law* (1994) The Linacre Centre. And see **3.10–3.13** above.
[176] *Mason and McCall Smith*, p 590.
[177] See P Lewis, 'Euthanasia in Belgium Five Years After Legalisation' (2009) 16 *European Journal of Health Law* 125.
[178] For comparative assessments of euthanasia and assisted suicide, see P Lewis, *Assisted*

for oral medication is the only assistance sanctioned. Direct assistance with suicide is prohibited.[179] The Washington State Death with Dignity Act 2009 allows terminally ill adults with less than six months to live to ask their doctors for a life-ending prescription.[180]

Lord Joffe's Patient (Assisted Dying) Bill 2003 was modelled on the Oregon Act, but incorporated voluntary euthanasia for those physically incapable of taking the final steps to end their life. It did not progress beyond a Second Reading. His ill-fated Assisted Dying for the Terminally Ill Bill 2004 ran out of time. It was more restrictive than the 2003 Bill, applying only to terminally ill patients and including a requirement for a discussion of the option of palliative care. The Select Committee on the Assisted Dying for the Terminally Ill Bill reported in April 2005.[181] Nine recommendations were made for any future bills, including (inter alia):[182]

- a clearer delineation between euthanasia and physician-assisted suicide;
- a statement of the actions which a doctor may or may not take in providing assisted suicide or administering voluntary euthanasia;
- a clinical definition of terminal illness (if terminal illness is a qualifying condition);
- a definition of mental competence so as to differentiate between applicants lacking mental capacity and those suffering a mental disorder.

Lord Joffe accepted four of the nine recommendations when introducing his third Bill in 2005. It was outvoted in the House of Lords by 148 to 100.[183] Physician-assisted suicide remains unlawful. In fact, the DPP's Code distinguishes between suicide assisted by loved ones and by doctors. One factor in *favour* of prosecution is:

> The suspect was acting in his or her capacity as a medical doctor, nurse, other healthcare professional, . . . and the victim was in his or her care.[184]

Dying and Legal Change (2007) OUP, and Griffiths, Weyers & Adams, *Euthanasia and the Law in Europe: With Special Reference to the Netherlands and Belgium* (2008) Hart.

[179] Upheld by the US Supreme Court in *Gonzales v Oregon* (04-623) 546 US 243 (2006). See http://www.oregon.gov/DHS/ph/pas/docs/year13.pdf?ga=t for the 2010 annual report on the operation of the Act. Of the ninety-six prescriptions for lethal medication written in 2010, over 70 per cent of patients were aged seventy or over; 68.5 per cent had cancer; and 92.6 per cent were enrolled in palliative care.

[180] A Bill (SB 167) to allow the prescription of lethal medication in Montana was defeated in February 2011. Another Bill (SB 116) proposed to reverse the controversial 5:2 decision in *Baxter v Montana* No. DA 09-0051 (Montana Supreme Court, 2009), that a competent terminally ill patient's rights to privacy and dignity protect their right to die. The Bill was defeated in February 2011.

[181] HL Paper 86.

[182] HL Paper 86, para 269(c).

[183] See J Keown, 'Physician-Assisted Suicide: Lord Joffe's Slippery Bill' (2007) 15(1) *Medical Law Review* 126.

[184] DPP, *Code for Crown Prosecutors and the Policy for Prosecutors in respect of Cases of Encouraging or Assisting Suicide* (2010), para 43.14. See above **19.8**. In 2010 the

What of those people who do not have friends or family willing or able to assist them? Should patients be able to turn to their doctor for help? On the other hand, to have adopted a permissive approach to physician-assisted suicide might have been hailed a radical (and unconstitutional) change in law. Doctors are primarily concerned with preserving life. Though in 2005, the British Medical Association changed its policy on assisted dying from one of opposition to one of neutrality,[185] the Royal College of General Practitioners and the RCP maintained their opposition to both physician-assisted suicide and voluntary euthanasia, and, in a spectacular U-turn, the BMA reverted to opposition in 2006.[186] Not all doctors support this approach. In 2010 a body of medical professionals dedicated to changing the law on the right to die launched Healthcare Professionals for Change.[187] In 2010 Lord Joffe suggested an alternative solution which would 'take doctors out of the investigative and decision-making process'.[188] Instead, a legal body (whether the High Court, Court of Protection or a special tribunal) would investigate a case where a person requests the right to assisted suicide, apply specially formulated guidelines and decide whether or not to administer a prescription of life-ending medication to the person. Taking doctors 'out of the loop' moves away from arguments based on dignity and caring and towards a strong autonomy-based approach. Is 'choice' an adequate safeguard? If the reason for wanting to die is altruistic this does not necessarily render the decision any less autonomous. But will the public back a measure that allows free choice even if that choice results from a wish to no longer burden family?

Active euthanasia

19.20 Meyers and Mason[189] envisaged the doctor 'providing or *administering* a lethal dose of medication'. But surely a lethal injection performed by the doctor must be killing, not simply assisting suicide? Do we have to resort to complex mechanical devices whereby the doctor sets up a machine to inject the patient with her lethal dose and somehow (maybe via a computer) she triggers the mechanism delivering the injection? The line between assisted dying and killing becomes as fragile as the artificiality of the current law. In *Pretty*, Lord Bingham[190] exposed the dilemma.

BMA released guidance advising doctors how to handle patients who make requests relating to assisted suicide: BMA, *Responding to Patient Requests Relating to Assisted Suicide: Guidance for Doctors in England, Wales and Northern Ireland* (2010).

[185] Available at: http://www.bma.org.uk/ap.nsf/Content/AssistedDyingDebate.

[186] N Hawkes, 'Doctors Reject Making Euthanasia Legal' (2006) *The Times,* 29 June; BMA, *End-of-Life Decisions* (2006), p 4; BMA, *End-of-Life Decisions: View of the BMA* (2009).

[187] See http://www.healthcareprofessionalsforchange.org.uk/.

[188] J Joffe, 'A New Proposal for Assisted Suicide' (2010) *Guardian,* 28 July.

[189] (1999) 29 *Anglo-American Law Review* 39.

[190] *R (on the application of Pretty) v DPP* [2002] 1 All ER 1 at 6–7, HL.

If Article 2 does confer a right of self-determination in relation to life and death, and if a person were so gravely disabled as to be unable to perform any act whatsoever to cause his or her own death, it would necessarily follow in logic that such a person would have a right to be killed at the hands of a third party . . .

In the Netherlands, an informal agreement between the prosecution authorities and the medical profession allowed active euthanasia for several years. The *Postma*[191] case was the first in a series of rulings easing restrictions on euthanasia. Dr Postma gave his disabled mother, who had previously attempted suicide and no longer wanted to live, a fatal dose of morphine. The court imposed a suspended sentence of one-week imprisonment and indicated that euthanasia might be acceptable provided that the patient was incurably ill, was suffering unbearably, had requested assisted suicide, and that the act was performed by the patient's own doctor or in consultation with her. Nine years later, the prosecution authorities agreed not to prosecute any doctor who ended his patient's life within the parameters set by agreed guidelines.[192] The patient must have freely requested 'help in dying' and the physician must assure himself that that request is truly voluntary and well considered. The patient and his doctor must be satisfied that there are no other means of relieving the patient's suffering or other incurable condition. A second doctor must be consulted. It is estimated that thousands of patients each year have opted for active euthanasia in the Netherlands, perhaps 2.7 per cent of all reported deaths.[193] Nonetheless, until 2000, euthanasia remained formally unlawful in the Netherlands. Legislation to give legal effect to the earlier informal arrangements came into force in 2002.[194] Controversially, individuals can make advance requests for euthanasia and children over twelve may request it, though until they are sixteen, parental assent is required.[195]

The impact of Dutch practice and their new laws is much debated. Opponents argue[196] (inter alia) that: (1) the incidence of active euthanasia is under-reported; (2) there is evidence of termination of life without an explicit request from the patient (in perhaps as many as one in five cases; (3) withdrawal of treatment with minimal safeguards is common; (4) depressed and mentally disturbed patients are helped to die. The nub of the case is that what is supposed to be a limited provision to allow free and informed choices by

---

[191] *Nederlandse Jurisprudentie* 1973, No 183, District Court of Leeuwarden, 21 February 1973.

[192] *Wertheim, Nederlandse Jurisprudentie* 1982, No 63, Rotterdam Criminal Court.

[193] See *Mason and McCall Smith*, p 602.

[194] Termination of Life on Request and Assisted Suicide (Review Procedures) Act 2000. Discussed in J de Haan, 'The New Dutch Law on Euthanasia' (2002) 10 *Medical Law Review* 57.

[195] Discussed by E Jackson, *Medical Law: Text, Cases and Materials* (2nd edn, 2010) OUP, p 912.

[196] See J Keown, 'The Law and Practice of Euthanasia in the Netherlands' (1992) 108 *Law Quarterly Review* 51; H Jochenson and J Keown, 'Voluntary Euthanasia under Control? Further Empirical Evidence from the Netherlands' (1999) 25 *Journal of Medical Ethics* 16.

competent patients to end their lives has become a convenient means of disposing of the elderly and grievously sick.[197] Supporters[198] equally passionately refute these allegations. Dispassionate analysis of how voluntary euthanasia 'works' in the Netherlands is hard to find.

The first Euthanasia Bill in this country was introduced into Parliament in 1936. The Bill was quickly rejected. Another Voluntary Euthanasia Bill, introduced in 1969, was designed to allow a patient or prospective patient to sign in advance a declaration requesting the administration of euthanasia if he was believed to be suffering from a fatal illness or was incapable of rational existence. Again, the Bill failed. The *coup de grâce* was applied with the following comment:

> Such a Bill is medically unnecessary, psychologically dangerous and ethically wrong. Unnecessary, because legal rigidity should not be substituted for medical discretion. Dangerous, because this Bill would diminish the respect for life, blurring the line between crime and medicine. Ethically wrong, because it infringes on the absolute value of life.

Subsequent Bills in the mid-1970s were more modest and attempted to avoid being seen as attempts to legalise euthanasia or 'mercy killing'. In the wake of the decision in *Bland*, the House of Lords set up a Select Committee on Medical Ethics[199] to investigate legal, ethical and social issues surrounding treatment decisions at the end of life. The Committee endorsed the judges' ruling in *Bland*, commended, but refused to endorse, legislation to give effect to advance directives, and in total delivered a Report of almost amazing banality. Their recommendations in effect were no change and leave such difficult questions to the doctors. The Report came out firmly against legalising voluntary euthanasia. Their Lordships considered that argument based on autonomy and the right to choose to die constituted '. . . insufficient reason to weaken society's prohibition on intentional killing'. It was not, in their view, possible to set secure limits in voluntary euthanasia, and vulnerable people might be pressured into requesting early death. Moreover, there was good evidence that palliative care could relieve pain and distress in the majority of cases. The debate intensifies. It does not seem to move on.

---

[197] And see L Clements and J Read (eds), *Disabled People and the Right to Life: The Protection and Violation of Disabled People's Most Basic Human Right* (2007), Routledge Cavendish.

[198] J M Van Delden, 'Slippery Slopes in Flat Countries – a Response' (1999) 25 *Journal of Medical Ethics* 22.

[199] Report of the Select Committee on Medical Ethics, 1993–4, HL-21.

INDEX

Index

Index

Index

Index

Index

Index

Index

Index

Index

Index

Index